TRADE REFORM AND REGIONAL INTEGRATION IN AFRICA

Trade Reform and Regional Integration in Africa

Editors

Zubair Iqbal
Mohsin S. Khan

Papers presented at the
IMF African Economic Research Consortium Seminar
on Trade Reform and Regional Integration in Africa
December 1–3, 1997

IMF Institute
International Monetary Fund
Washington, D.C.

Production: IMF Graphics Section
Cover design: Massoud Etemadi
Typesetting: Joseph A. Kumar

Library of Congress Cataloging-in-Publication Data

Trade reform and regional integration in Africa / editors, Zubair Iqbal, Mohsin S. Khan.
p. cm.
"Papers presented at the IMF and African Economic Research Consortium seminar on Trade reform and regional integration in Africa, December 1997."
Includes bibliographical references.
ISBN 1-55775-769-0
1. Africa, Sub-Saharan—Commercial policy—Congresses. 2. Africa, Sub-Saharan—Economic conditions—Regional disparities—Congresses. 3. Africa, Sub-Saharan—Economic integration—Congresses. 4. Africa, Sub-Saharan—Foreign economic relations—Congresses. I. Iqbal, Zubair. II. Khan, Mohsin S. III. International Monetary Fund. IV. African Economic Research Consortium.
HF1611.T734 1998 98-11659
382'.3'0967—dc21 CIP

Price: $22.00

Address orders to:
International Monetary Fund, Publication Services
700 19th Street, N.W., Washington D.C. 20431, U.S.A.
Telephone: (202) 623-7430
Telefax: (202) 623-7201
E-mail: publications@imf.org
Internet: http://www.imf.org

Preface

In recent years, economic performance in most of sub-Saharan Africa has improved. Growth has picked up, resulting in an increase in per capita output in a number of countries, inflation has decelerated markedly, and the fiscal and external deficits have been reduced. In large part, the economic recovery can be attributed to improved macroeconomic and structural policies rather than to favorable external developments, such as terms of trade gains. Indeed, these favorable developments have been achieved at a time when official development assistance has been declining. Key structural reforms have been implemented in many African countries, including curtailing of price controls, dismantling of some inefficient public monopolies, privatization, elimination of nontariff barriers in most countries, and a reduction in import duties in many. At the same time, exchange rates have been largely freed and unified, restrictions on current transactions liberalized, and important progress has been made toward market-determined interest rates in most countries.

The economic situation remains difficult. But sub-Saharan Africa may have reached a turning point. The incipient improvements need to be nursed assiduously if the recent gains are to be translated into sustained growth.

Experience and research demonstrate that trade liberalization is a critical element in a growth strategy. As part of the effort to address trade issues in Africa, the IMF, in collaboration with the African Economic Research Consortium (AERC), conducted a seminar on Trade Reform and Regional Integration in Africa in Washington in early December 1997. The event provided an important opportunity to government officials, academics, and representatives from multilateral and regional agencies to exchange views on the complex issues relating to trade reform and regionalism in Africa. This volume brings together papers presented during the seminar. They cover a range of important issues, including the role of trade liberalization in promoting sustained growth, interdependence of trade and macroeconomic policies, impediments to effective trade reforms, and steps needed to accelerate trade reform in Africa. The role that regional interaction can play in supporting trade reform is also covered extensively.

What emerges from these papers, and the ensuing seminar discussions, is a clear consensus that trade liberalization is essential if African countries are to take advantage of globalization. Combining forces with similarly placed African countries through the formation of appropriate regional trading arrangements can lead to faster liberalization and can reduce vulnerability to external shocks.

STANLEY FISCHER
First Deputy Managing Director
International Monetary Fund

Acknowledgment

We are grateful to the following for their advice and support: Michael Mussa, Economic Counselor and Director, Research Department, IMF; Evangelos Calamitsis, Director, African Department, IMF; Pierre Dhonte, Deputy Director, Middle Eastern Department, IMF; and Benno Ndulu, Executive Director, African Economic Research Consortium. Thanks are also due to Alfred F. Imhoff for providing valuable editorial help; to Juanita Roushdy, External Relations Department, for editorial guidance; to Arturo Rios and Rosa Vera-Bunge, IMF Institute, for research assistance; and especially to Susan E. Jones, IMF Institute, for preparing the manuscript speedily and efficiently. We would also like to express our gratitude to many other staff members of the IMF Institute who helped in organizing the joint AERC-IMF seminar where papers contained in this volume were presented.

ZUBAIR IQBAL
MOHSIN S. KHAN

List of Abbreviations

Several African regional organizations have abbreviations based on their proper French names; however, the commonly used English translations of the names are given here.

AEC	African Economic Community
AERC	African Economic Research Consortium
BEAC	Central African Monetary Union
CFA	Communauté francophone d'Afrique
CBI	Cross-Border Initiative
CEAO	Central African Economic Community
COMESA	Common Market for Eastern and Southern Africa
ECA	Economic Commission for Africa
ECCAS	Economic Community of Central African States
ECOWAS	Economic Community of West African States
EFF	Extended Fund Facility
ESAF	Enhanced Structural Adjustment Facility
EU	European Union
FDI	Foreign direct investment
FTA	Free trade area
GATT	General Agreement on Tariffs and Trade
IMF	International Monetary Fund
MFA	Multifiber Arrangement
NAFTA	North American Free Trade Agreement
NTBs	Nontariff barriers
OAU	Organization of African Unity
OECD	Organization for Economic Cooperation and Development
PTA	Preferential trade area
QRs	Quantitative restrictions
SACU	Southern African Customs Union
SADC	Southern African Development Community
SADCC	Southern African Development Coordination Conference
SAF	Structural Adjustment Facility
SAP	Structural Adjustment Program
UEMOA	West African Economic and Monetary Union

UDEAC	Central African Economic and Customs Union
UNCTAD	United Nations Conference on Trade and Development
VAT	Value-added tax
WTO	World Trade Organization

Contents

The following symbols have been used in this book:

. . . to indicate that data are not available;

– between years or months (e.g., 1995–96 or January–June) to indicate the years or months covered, including the beginning and ending years or months; and

/ between years (e.g., 1996/97) to indicate a fiscal (financial) year.

"Billion" means a thousand million.

Dollars are U.S. dollars.

Minor discrepancies between constituent figures and totals are due to rounding.

Opening Address 1

Alassane D. Ouattara

It is a great pleasure for me to welcome you all to this seminar on Trade Reforms and Regional Integration in Africa, sponsored jointly by the International Monetary Fund and the African Economic Research Consortium (AERC).

The topic of the seminar is central to today's African development paradigm. That so many ministers, senior officials from member countries and multilateral institutions, and academics have taken time from their busy schedules to attend this seminar obviously attests to the importance that issues related to trade reforms and regional integration have for Africa both now and in the future.

As you are all aware, trade liberalization has long been of major interest to the IMF. We see trade liberalization as an engine of growth, one that must be an integral part of comprehensive adjustment and reform programs. We are therefore encouraged to note Africa's progress in this area during the past decade, but we are also well aware that much more needs to be done. This is why we welcome the greater degree of interest in trade reforms, which has come about partly at the initiative of the Group of Seven countries, and partly as a result of the general trend toward market-friendly approaches across Africa. There is no question that opening up further their economies will enable African countries to take advantage fully of the globalization process.

We will also be discussing regional arrangements in the seminar, and here too there is a considerable interest for several reasons. First, regional cooperation is increasing. I have in mind the increased coordination within the West African Economic and Monetary Union, for example, and the implementation of the Cross-Border Initiative. Second, the prospective renewal of the Lomé Convention provides a powerful incentive to consider the role of regional arrangements. Third, regional arrangements can provide the impetus for trade liberalization, as well as mutual support to their members in their reform efforts, and can assist African economies to face the challenges of a globalized environment.

Of course, the beneficial effects of trade liberalization and regional integration presuppose the continued implementation of accelerated structural reforms within the framework of macroeconomic stability.

Africa has already made important progress in this regard, which has led to a reduction in inflation, a decline in internal and external imbalances, and a pick up in per capita growth in many countries.

We are particularly pleased to have the AERC as the cosponsor of this seminar. I am sure Benno Ndulu, executive director of the AERC, will tell you more about what the AERC is doing. Let me just say that I think it is the premier organization supporting policy-oriented research in sub-Saharan Africa. Its success has made it a model that is being emulated in other parts of the developing world. The quantity and quality of macroeconomic research in Africa have risen markedly as a direct result of the AERC. We will see some of the best of this research in the papers being presented here by AERC-affiliated economists.

The IMF has had a long association with the AERC. Mohsin Khan was involved in the discussions among donors, foundations, policymakers, and researchers in Africa in the late 1980s that led to the creation of the AERC. Since the formal establishment of the AERC in 1989, we have had IMF staff participate regularly as resource persons in the semiannual AERC workshops. The IMF has also had an arrangement with the AERC by which a number of AERC-supported researchers visit us for short periods of time. This program—known as the IMF-AERC Visiting Scholars Program—provides opportunities for AERC researchers to work and interact with IMF staff. Since May 1994, when the program was initiated, some 40 African researchers—and many of them at this seminar—have visited the IMF Headquarters. We believe this program has been a major success, and we certainly intend to continue with it. More generally, the IMF will try to provide the AERC with the necessary support to help further its mission to create a broadly based community of economic scholars and a culture of economic scholarship in Africa. Everyone—the governments in the region, multilateral institutions, donor countries, and the economics profession—stands to gain if the AERC achieves its goals.

Coming back to the seminar we have organized, I believe that there are several critical questions that need to be addressed. These include:

- What is the analytical basis for the proposals for trade reforms and regional arrangements?
- How can regional trade arrangements help facilitate progress toward nondiscriminatory, multilateral liberalization?
- What have African countries achieved in these areas to date?
- What remains to do, and how best can it be done?

I hope the arguments we will hear in the seminar will help us identify the directions that policymakers like you, as well as the IMF and other multilateral agencies, need to take. In conclusion, I trust you will find the seminar both interesting and productive. And I want to thank all of you for making the effort to attend. I hope that soon we will be discussing the liberalization of capital movements in Africa as countries accept the proposed amendment to the IMF Articles of Agreement. Then Africa will reap the full benefits of the globalization of international goods and financial markets.

Trade Reforms and Regional Integration—An Overview 2

Zubair Iqbal and Mohsin S. Khan

During the past few years, economic performance in sub-Saharan Africa has improved significantly. Growth of real GDP has picked up, inflation has moderated, and fiscal and external current account imbalances have contracted. The external debt situation started to improve, access to international capital markets was restored for some African countries, and the HIPC Debt Initiative was put into effect to address the excessive debt burden faced by a number of the countries in the region. These improvements in economic performance appear to have resulted mainly from strengthened policies rather than from favorable external developments such as terms of trade gains or increases in foreign economic assistance.[1] Nor did Africa benefit from better weather conditions, which were basically unchanged in the 1990s. In conjunction with macroeconomic stabilization, there have been concerted structural reforms in many African countries, including domestic price decontrols, public sector reforms and privatization, progress toward the introduction of market-based interest rates, rationalization of exchange rate and payments policies, and trade liberalization initiatives.

Although a clear break with the past is discernable, the overall economic outlook for sub-Saharan Africa remains difficult. Domestic saving and capital formation continue to be low relative to other developing regions. Only a few countries have been able to attract substantial private foreign capital, while official flows have declined. Moreover, output remains concentrated in a few primary products that are highly sensitive to weather conditions and terms of trade developments. In the period ahead, sub-Saharan Africa will encounter several challenges that will, unless addressed urgently and comprehensively, militate against sustaining the recent economic turnaround. More specifically, it will be necessary to raise investment rates and strengthen the economic environment by pursuing appropriate macroeconomic and structural policies and establishing an appropriate

[1]S. Fischer, E. Hernandez-Cáta, and M. Khan, "Africa: Is This the Turning Point?" (paper presented at the American Economic Association Meeting, Chicago, May 1998).

institutional framework to raise productivity in a sustainable fashion so that Africa can effectively participate in, and benefit from, the ongoing globalization. An important element of such transformation will be the liberalization of the generally restrictive trade regimes in sub-Saharan African countries.

To discuss the role of trade liberalization in the African context, the IMF, in collaboration with the African Economic Research Consortium (AERC), held from December 1 to 3, 1997, a seminar on Trade Reforms and Regional Integration for high-level officials from selected African countries, regional and multilateral organizations, and academics. This volume consists of papers presented at the seminar. They have been grouped into two broad areas, covering: (1) trade liberalization, including its role in promoting sustained growth, interdependence of trade and macroeconomic policies, impediments to effective trade reforms, and steps needed to speed up trade policy reform in Africa to accelerate the integration of African countries into the world economy; and (2) experience with regional integration in Africa and the role that regional trade arrangements can play in facilitating trade reform. This chapter summarizes the thrust of discussions and highlights the broad conclusions reached at the seminar.

Trade Reform, Macroeconomic Adjustment, and Growth

Part I of the book consists of 10 papers analyzing the linkage between trade reform, macroeconomic adjustment, and growth and its application to sub-Saharan Africa. In his paper, "Trade Liberalization," Mussa emphasizes that distorted trade regimes operate as impediments to both macroeconomic reform and structural adjustment. Trade reform can contribute importantly to improving the efficiency of resource allocation, reducing the anti-export bias of the economy and exposing it to competition, promoting realistic exchange rates and balance of payments adjustment, spurring investment, and diversifying the economy, thereby promoting growth. However, trade reform in turn cannot function as an agent of growth in the absence of complementary prudent macroeconomic and structural policies. In fact, Mussa contends that reversals of trade liberalization were more commonly associated with poor macroeconomic policies than with any other factor, including power of protectionist interests. Inappropriate fiscal, monetary, and exchange rate policies constrain the ability of economic agents to compete abroad and thus intensify protectionist pressures. To be effective, trade liberalization must be bold and sustained, with the consistency and credibility of the reform being more important than the size of the reduction in trade barriers. Moreover, trade reforms should be appropriately sequenced in concert with macroeconomic policy reform. At the outset, quantitative restrictions (QRs) should be converted into tariffs, followed by a reduction in the range of tariffs to simplify the tariff structure, broadening of the tax base, and lowering of the average level of tariffs. Experience suggests that major trade reforms are easier to initiate and sustain when accompanied by an improvement of the fiscal position and a real exchange depreciation to avoid adverse balance of payments effects. Ideally, adjustment programs should integrate trade policy with fiscal and exchange policies while adhering to a medium-term trade reform strategy with clearly established short- and medium-term goals.

Although progress has been made, trade regimes of countries in sub-Saharan Africa remain more restrictive than other regions. Therefore, early and durable trade reform would be helpful in sustaining growth. Mussa proposes a five-year, two-stage approach to trade reform supported by appropriate macroeconomic policies for African countries. In the first stage, QRs will be removed; in the second stage, tariff rates and bands could be reduced. Given the narrow industrial base, supply responses will be somewhat more sluggish than in other regions, but pressures to protect "infant industries" should be resisted. Moreover, the fiscal impact of trade liberalization may be negative, requiring a careful consideration of the manner and speed of reforms. Additional macroeconomic actions might be needed to minimize possible short-run adverse effects on the external and fiscal positions. In the context of regional integration, Mussa argues for larger countries in the arrangement to undertake a more ambitious trade reform program in order to bring along the entire region.

Sharer, in his paper, "Trade Liberalization in Sub-Saharan Africa," reviews the role of trade reforms in IMF-supported adjustment programs in 14 countries of sub-Saharan Africa and compares their performance with that of 14 countries in Asia, Eastern Europe, the Middle East, and the Western Hemisphere. Although there was a marked reduction in the restrictiveness of trade regimes in sub-Saharan Africa, the paper concludes that the appropriate degree and pace of trade reform depend crucially on country-specific circumstances. Progress toward an open trade regime is affected, inter alia, by the initial degree of restrictiveness of the trade system, the country's administrative capacity, and the real or perceived short-term adjustment costs. The experience of the "best practices" countries shows that trade reform should be viewed as a medium- to long-term process, hence the importance of well-specified and comprehensive medium-term program targets for trade reforms. The paper points out that fiscal considerations were the main factor having influenced trade reform objectives, even though there was no direct relationship between the strength of trade reforms, achievements, and countries' initial fiscal circumstances.

Ebrill and Stotsky, in their paper, "The Revenue Implications of Trade Liberalization," argue that the revenue effects of trade reform depend upon a number of factors, including the nature of existing barriers to trade, the sequencing of reforms, the extent to which improvements are made in tax structure and tax and customs administrations, supporting macroeconomic policies, and other economic adjustments. Reforms that would be expected to have a positive revenue effect include the tariffication of QRs, the reduction or elimination of exemptions, reduced incentives for smuggling through lower tariff rates, and increased minimum tariff rates. In addition, increased customs revenues could be the consequence of improved customs administration as well as increased imports, which could be the outcome of devaluation, higher growth, and generalized liberalization. The authors emphasize that theoretical predictions are ambiguous, while empirical evidence also suggests that a variety of outcomes is possible. Therefore, reforms need to be crafted to avoid negative revenue effects. The negative fiscal impact could be minimized by a proper sequencing of reforms and a concurrent broadening of the domestic revenue base. Therefore, the possible negative revenue effects should not be used as a justification for slowing down or postponing trade liberalization. Ebrill and Stotsky note that, even though the process of reducing reliance on trade taxes has been slow in many African countries, over the long run the share of trade taxes in total government revenues is likely to decline. It is important that sub-Saharan African countries follow the "best practices" in the tax and tariff systems, which generally conform to the results of optimal tax theory; that is, they cause a minimum of distortions in the allocation of resources, are equitable, and are relatively easy to administer. Such an approach implies a minimal dependence on taxes on international trade.

Analyzing factors militating against actual and potential gains from globalization for Africa, Collier in his paper, "Globalization: Implications for Africa," places much of the blame on the present policy environment. Although inadequate trade and exchange rate policies continue to be central, their negative effects on Africa's ability to benefit from a more open world economy may have been compounded by domestic policies that have increased the "transactions costs" of doing business in Africa and have added to perceived political risks for investment. In particular, transactions costs are high because of high transport costs, difficulties in contract enforcement, ineffective judicial infrastructure, the high cost of information, and the poor quality of ancillary public services. The high transactions costs have had negative implications for comparative advantage and may have discouraged inflows of portfolio capital and encouraged capital flight. They have also weakened the transition from primary to manufacturing and financial services, which are transactions-intensive activities. African firms face more risks and yet make the least use of risk management financial instruments. In addition, the high political risk derives from the credibility problem, that is, the fear of policy reversal, especially with regard to macroeconomic policy, investor rights, and trade policies. Maintenance of good policies in these areas during a period of time will overcome the credibility problem. In this context, Collier recommends that "agencies of restraint,"which force governments to be "locked in" to policy reforms either by building penalties against policy slippages or by shedding authority, should be created to reduce political risks. These agencies of restraint include not only donor conditionality but also, and more important, domestic agencies such as independent central banks, cash budget, capital account convertibility, public insurance agencies, credit syndications, and investment charters.

In his paper, "Why Is Trade Reform So Difficult in Africa?" Rodrik argues that although there is a broad consensus on what constitutes a reasonable strategy of trade liberalization for Africa, it has been difficult for a number of reasons to implement the strategy. In particular, distributional issues, especially the likely adverse effects on groups with vested interests, have tended to discourage trade reform. Moreover, incomplete information about the losses and gains of policy reform has tended to generate political inertia and resistance to change. Other elements that supplement distribution issues in explaining the pervasive feature of resistance to trade reform include the institutional weaknesses of African countries that highlight the dynamic inconsistency of policymaking across Africa and amplify the lack of credible commitment to policies. Meaningful trade reform will require mechanisms to deal with redistributive conflict, such as those undertaken in Mauritius through the establishment of export zones. At the same time, the credibility of commitments to policies should be increased through the strengthening of agencies of restraint. Therefore, advocacy of reform has to be complemented with a clearer understanding of the real political challenges that have to be encountered through appropriate political action. Rodrik concludes that there is no substitute for creative political leadership in identifying and exploiting the opportunities that difficult times present. Therefore, technical advice should be supplemented with help on political strategies.

Reflecting inward-looking trade policies and narrowly defined product structures, the African economies have become increasingly less visible in global trade flows and have had little involvement in the various rounds of global trade liberalization. In this regard, Wang and Winters, in their paper, "Africa's Role in Multilateral Trade Negotiations: Past and Future," reaffirm the view that African economies need to open up to world trade by participating more actively in multilateral trade negotiations, which would help stimulate their growth. Under the Uruguay Round, these economies undertook rather little liberalization and in return received fewer benefits than other developing regions. However, they still emerged from it facing fewer or lower trade barriers than others. In the period ahead, they should play a more active role in multilateral trade negotiations, which will require improvements in domestic resource allocation and enhanced efficiency so that they could offer suitable reciprocal concessions in return for liberalization of access to their exports. This policy stance would benefit from accelerating the unilateral trade reforms. The authors argue that preferences are not a constructive way of pursuing long-run integration with the global economy. Instead, African countries should use their negotiating rights to achieve unfettered access to markets on a sound most-favored-nation (MFN) basis. Presently they stand at risk of not being sufficiently involved in the negotiations to liberalize telecommunications and financial services in which they have high stakes.

In their paper, "Trade and Growth in Sub-Saharan Africa," Ndulu and Ndung'u demonstrate empirically that trade openness, higher investment, and appropriate macroeconomic policies have a positive effect on real income growth. Openness to trade and international finance facilitate the effectiveness of investment and macroeconomic conditions that are conducive to growth. They distinguish three channels of how trade influences growth: (1) the efficiency-enhancing advantages of a more open trade regime; (2) improved incentives for production of exportables and reduction of the high transactions costs associated with import barriers; and (3) reduction in explicit and implicit barriers to export or outward orientation of production. The increase in the share of exports—a proxy for openness—was found to be positively related to growth. Also, the authors find that strong growth has in turn had an influence on trade performance that facilitates the "virtuous cycle" of liberalization and growth. On the basis of these results, they argue that Africa's marginalization in world trade will be ended only if conditions are created for improved growth. Therefore, trade-enhancing policies matter because they enhance the effectiveness of macroeconomic policies and thus growth. However, the authors stress that the excessive external debt burden of many countries in sub-Saharan Africa—which crowds out domestic expenditures on building productive capacity and infrastructure—has tended to inhibit trade liberalization. Moreover, the underdeveloped state of human capital would make it difficult to absorb technology following the opening up of trade and capital flows, which is essential to benefit from liberalization. Moreover, binding commitments to a more open economy are critical.

Building upon the theme of trade liberalization and growth, Soludo, in his paper, "Africa: Industrialization Strategy in the Context of Globalization," stresses that unlike in the past, when interventionist regimes could spur export-led growth, African economies would need to industrialize without the benefits of preferential and differential treatment or protective and interventionist trade regimes. Tracing the history of attempts at industrialization in Africa, Soludo notes that the import-substituting industrialization (ISI) strategy failed because of excessive protection and the absence of performance-based criteria for incentives. The subsequent liberalization towards a "neutral" trade regime could not be sustained, owing to its perceived incompatibility with the goals of balance of payments and fiscal viability. Thus, inadequate policies combined with the poor infrastructure, limited domestic markets, and poor institutional capacity to manage the economy caused industrial stagnation and persistence of low competitiveness. Soludo, therefore, calls for a shift in the industrialization strategy for Africa to be in consonance with the ongoing globalization. The private sector and private investment would serve as pillars of such a strategy. These should be supported by appropriate trade policy along with an outward orientation in conjunction with a competitive exchange rate. Export promotion should be associated with import liberalization in a sequential fashion. Soludo would expect regional integration to play an important role in this strategy, not only by providing an expanded regional market, but also by strengthening the bargaining power of African countries. Finally, this strategy would call for open global markets for African exports and support in developing the needed infrastructure in African countries.

Regional Integration in Africa

Successful regional integration, specifically one that has a net trade-creating effect, entails a number of restrictive preconditions, many of which are presently lacking in sub-Saharan Africa. Moreover, effective regional integration presupposes effective multilateral trade reform and a focus on promoting progress to multilateralism. Part II of the book consists of papers on regional integration as a vehicle for trade liberalization, prerequisites for regional trading arrangements to facilitate globalization, experience with regional integration in Africa, and the future outlook in the context of trade reform.

Hufbauer and Kotschwar, in their paper, "Regional Integration: Lessons from Asia and the Western Hemisphere," describe the preconditions for efficient regional integration arrangements that can serve as a means to further developing countries' economic liberalization programs and to facilitate their integration into the global economy. They argue that, if effected in a manner that reduces barriers and liberalizes trade among members, such arrangements can also serve as a mechanism to "lock in" domestically implemented liberalization measures. The authors identify 12 steps for successful regional integration. In particular, they emphasize that regional trading initiatives should be seen as an extension of domestic reform, which in turn should be anchored in macroeconomic stability. Countries should either be adjacent or should have a high volume of trade with each other and should have unambiguous commitment to regional integration. It is important to keep the approach simple, and the starting point for integration should be the elimination of tariffs and quotas so that basic liberalization can be effected, leaving the more complex issues to be tackled in due course. The success of an arrangement also depends critically on the commitment of the large countries of the region, which should not only lead but also take care of the smaller economies. Moreover, a piecemeal approach along sectoral lines should be avoided and a level of integration that is easier to manage should be chosen. Finally, Hufbauer and Kotschwar stress that the private sector should be actively involved in the decision-making process of regional integration.

In his paper, "Trade Policy and Regional Integration in Sub-Saharan Africa," Oyejide explores the scope that exists for the regional integration schemes in sub-Saharan Africa to serve as vehicles for more effective trade policy, which could help circumvent the constraints imposed by small domestic markets and promote industrialization. His assessment is that, owing to a number of constraints, the membership of a regional integration arrangement has been the least significant stimulus for trade liberalization. Instead, effective trade liberalization has been largely initiated and stimulated by structural adjustment programs supported by the IMF and the World Bank. The author nonetheless emphasizes that given the implications of size, scale effects, and spillover effects, trade policy in sub-Saharan Africa should feature a regional approach because apart from providing a larger market, regional integration could facilitate policy harmonization and act as an "agency of restraint," provide credibility to regional security, and ensure the coordination of negotiating positions, which could enhance bargaining power.

François and Subramanian, in their paper, "Beyond Trade: Regional Arrangements as a Window on Globalization," discuss how regional integration in Africa can facilitate orderly progress toward globalization. They argue that regional arrangements can be an important practical vehicle for helping African countries integrate themselves into the world economy, provided appropriate regional integration strategies are implemented. Such strategies should encompass not only effective trade liberalization but also ensure macroeconomic stability, structural reforms, and policy credibility. Thus, government intervention should be in support of, rather than a substitute for, private sector activity. The regional approach, which would facilitate globalization, would require nurturing domestic and regional institutions, promote the transmission of regional "demonstration effects," and facilitate effective regional infrastructure networks. Equally important, the authors contend, is to avoid a plethora of overlapping, even conflicting regional initiatives, and overbureaucratization. There is also a need to address the lack of political will to make tough decisions on resource allocation and income distribution.

The paper by Elbadawi and Mwega, "Regional Integration, Trade, and Foreign Direct Investment in Sub-Saharan Africa," traces the possible beneficial effect of regional integration on foreign direct investment (FDI) in the region by providing an expanded market and policy credibility. FDI is assumed to be influenced by variables such as basic "fundamentals," including profitability of FDI, the state of macroeconomic policy as proxied by the real exchange rate and the fiscal deficit, public sector investment, external shocks such as terms of trade developments and the external debt burden, and risks associated with the sociopolitical environment such as the quality of institutions. These factors are then tested empirically using panel data regressions of a behavioral model of FDI that also accounts for the effects of regional integration schemes. The paper concludes that regional integration schemes in sub-Saharan Africa have, by and large, had little impact, not only on intraregional trade but also on FDI.

The next four papers focus on forces spurring the growth of regional integration in sub-Saharan Africa and their effectiveness in promoting growth and progress toward globalization. Aryeetey, in his paper, "Sub-Saharan African Experiences with Regional Integration," presents an overview of factors underlying the proliferation of regional arrangements, considers experience with such institutions, and sheds light on what can and should be achieved with regional integration in the period ahead. He argues that regional integration has been driven by the quest for industrialization and for the benefits of the dynamic efficiency gains. In the event, there has been some improvement in intraregional trade flows, but very little progress has been made toward integrated infrastructural development despite potential for very high benefits. Aryeetey cites a variety of reasons for the limited success of regional integration in Africa. These include multiple objectives, absence of strong supranational institutions, difficulties in implementing harmonization provisions, lack of political commitment, and inequalities in the distribution of gains from integration. For the period ahead, he stresses that there should be less focus on the mode of integration and more emphasis on how to effectively use the available institutional structure to attract investments and thus accelerate growth in the region. There was a greater need for regional collaboration on private capital flows, infrastructural development, industrial policy, effective compensation mechanisms, and cooperation in international negotiations.

The other three papers—by Hartzenberg and Maasdorp, "Regional Integration Arrangements in Southern Africa: SADC and SACU"; Kasekende and Abuka, "Regional Trade Arrangements: The COMESA Experience"; and Jebuni, "The Role of ECOWAS in Trade Liberalization"—evaluate the experience of specific regional arrangements in sub-Saharan Africa. The mixed results of these arrangements are attributable to a number of factors that have also been cited by Aryeetey, including the proliferation of such arrangements, potentially conflicting objectives, generally weak commitment of members to the integration schemes' objectives, and limited administrative resources. Moreover, the absence of an active private sector to take advantage of the expanded regional markets also appears to have been a factor. However, Hartzenberg and Maasdorp note that the Southern Africa Customs Union (SACU) has been an exception; its success lay largely in national liberalization and adjustment, the dominant role of the private sector in benefiting from liberalized intraregional trade, and the low "transactions costs" on account of an effective physical and institutional infrastructure.

Concluding Remarks

In broad terms, seven conclusions emerged from the discussions during the seminar. First, despite considerable progress in trade liberalization, the trade systems of many sub-Saharan African countries remain quite restrictive and could benefit from further reforms. To be effective, trade liberalization should be bold and sustained and complemented by prudent macroeconomic policies and structural reforms. Consistency and credibility of the reform program are more important than simply the size of reduction in trade restrictions. Reform measures should be appropriately sequenced. At the outset, QRs should be converted into tariffs, followed by a reduction in the range of tariffs to simplify the tariff structure, broadening of the tax base, and lowering of the average level of tariffs.

Second, macroeconomic stability is critical to the success of trade liberalization. Much of the successful trade liberalization in Africa has been initiated and spurred by the implementation of comprehensive adjustment programs on a unilateral basis. Inappropriate fiscal, monetary, and exchange rate policies could constrain the ability of economic agents to compete abroad and thus intensify protectionist pressures domestically. Tighter domestic demand management and appropriate exchange rate adjustments to ensure the desired real depreciation may be needed to protect against the short-run adverse balance of payments effects of liberalization. The possible negative fiscal impact of trade liberalization could be minimized by a proper sequencing of reforms and a concurrent broadening of the domestic revenue base. The removal of exchange and other controls, along with tariff reforms, can be an effective mechanism to ensure a positive fiscal effect.

Third, trade liberalization in sub-Saharan Africa has been constrained, in part, by structural distortions that have raised transactions costs for economic agents and impeded effective resource allocation and globalization. Such distortions have not only kept African exports narrowly focused on raw materials, but have also encouraged capital outflows. The high transactions costs, reflecting inadequate transport, information, and communications infrastructure, weak contract enforcement, and ineffective judicial infrastructure also appear to have impeded industrial growth and encouraged protectionist policies. Structural reforms, therefore, must accompany liberalization. These reforms should address the underdeveloped financial sector, inappropriate relative prices, labor market rigidities, inconsistent domestic incentives policies, and capital market controls, so that an efficient private sector could develop. Reforms should be locked in and institutions should develop to act as instruments of restraint against policy slippages.

Fourth, the modified approach toward regionalism should be focused on reducing transactions costs and strengthening agencies of restraint. The IMF and the World Bank could promote trade-liberalizing strategies as part of their overall programs of structural adjustment that would facilitate a positive approach to regional cooperation.

Fifth, given the limited room for intraregional trade, integration schemes should be considered as a step toward globalization. Properly crafted regional integration schemes can play an important role in facilitating Africa's orderly transition to a relatively free multilateral trade environment. However, a number of preconditions will have to be created before regional integration can have a net trade-creating effect. To be effective, regional arrangements should be recast to focus on a few mutually complimentary objectives supported by steps to allow the beneficial resource allocation aspects of trade liberalization to take hold. Moreover, the private sector should be encouraged to take advantage of the expanded regional markets.

Sixth, Africa should more actively participate in multilateral trade negotiations to ensure long-term gains from the opening up of global markets.

Seventh, the politically difficult efforts at trade reform being made in Africa should be reciprocated by bold measures by industrial countries to ease access of African exports to their economies.

Part I

Trade Reform, Macroeconomic Adjustment, and Growth

Trade Liberalization 3

Michael Mussa

The Road to Uruguay

Before Uruguay: Growing Liberalization

During the 1960s and the 1970s, industrial countries increasingly adopted trade liberalization. The General Agreement on Tariffs and Trade (GATT) provided them with a framework for a more coordinated multilateral liberalization of trade; successive GATT rounds of negotiations reduced tariffs and QRs among them. From the first round of multilateral talks to the close of the Tokyo Round in 1979, the average tariff on manufacturing in the major industrial countries was reduced from 40 percent to between 6 and 8 percent. In contrast, many developing countries, in their efforts to modernize, pursued inward-looking strategies, adopting "infant industry" support of nascent industries, and "import substitution" for the development of domestic industry. As part of this inward-looking strategy, tariffs, quota, and exchange and payments restrictions in many developing countries were increased.

Meanwhile, theoretical and empirical evidence mounted on the costs of protection to develop intellectual support for trade liberalization. The costs of import substitution as well as the benefits of outward-oriented development strategies, emphasizing development of competitive export sectors, was demonstrated by the success of the fast-growing countries of the Pacific Rim, which became increasingly visible by the early 1980s. Rapid growth in output and trade and efficient industrialization came to be associated with these outward-oriented policies. The gains from outward-looking strategies were clearly determined to outweigh the costs of protection. During the 1980s, the weight of this evidence began to be felt on policy in many other developing countries. The process of unilateral liberalization of trade regimes was begun in many of them in the context of comprehensive adjustment programs, often supported by the IMF and the World Bank.

World trade has expanded rapidly during the past three decades in response to this increasing acceptance of openness by countries, as well as decreasing transport and information costs; growth in world trade has far exceeded that in world production. The composition of trade has also changed substantially as developing countries have begun to exploit opportunities for technological improvement. The volume of intra-industry trade also expanded rapidly, allowing various stages of manufacturing to be located in different countries. This "slicing of the value-added chain" opened up many new opportunities for all countries as more flexible criteria for the location of industry were made possible by advancing technology.

There were, however, some developments that raised concerns about the forward momentum for further liberalization of the world trading system:

- First, negotiations for the Uruguay Round (1986–93) were protracted, with their successful conclusions sometimes in doubt.
- Second, regionalism, which had not been in vogue since the 1960s, reemerged. While frustration with the multilateral process was a factor, the political and economic imperatives of the regional partners were an additional motive. Fears of the emergence of warring trade blocs added to prevailing uncertainties, but no serious regional conflicts occurred.
- Third, protectionist pressures and trade frictions escalated in some areas as growth slowed and unemployment increased in major trading nations. Delays in concluding the Uruguay Round, and new competitive challenges emanating from globalization and the dynamic trade performance of some developing and transition economies, increased the demand for protection and retaliatory trade measures. Resort to bilateral and unilateral approaches to trade disputes intensified at the same time as disputes brought to the GATT also increased. Notwithstanding increasing trade frictions and a number of specific actions, however, resort to nontariff measures did not increase on balance in industrial countries. Nonetheless, subsidies remained high, voluntary export restraints (VER) continued, and increasing attention was given to the efficacy of setting import targets (i.e., "voluntary import expansions"or VIEs). Increased use of trade remedy laws, especially antidumping ones, as an instrument of protection was also seen, and it spread to developing countries even while they liberalized their trade in other respects.
- Fourth, as a more dynamic notion of comparative advantage emerged from growing and more flexible arrangements for trade, trade policy was interpreted more widely to include broader policy objectives—for example, competition policy and better environment and labor standards. These issues began to receive at-

tention in national and international forums and were viewed as a possible backdoor means for protectionism.

The Uruguay Round

The successful conclusion of the Uruguay Round toward the end of 1993 helped to restore the credibility of the multilateral trading system, as well as significantly increase the scope and breadth of coverage of the issues by the multinational trade negotiations. Significant progress was made in three major areas:

- Significant market liberalization was achieved, which according to preliminary estimates is expected to add approximately 1 percent to world real GDP and 12 percent to world trade upon full implementation of the agreement,
- Rules and institutional structures were strengthened, particularly with the creation of the World Trade Organization (WTO), designed for better adjudication of disputes and more efficient surveillance over trade as well as unilateral and bilateral approaches outside the multilateral system,
- New areas (e.g., agreements on services and trade-related intellectual property rights, or TRIPs, and the traditional "sensitive" sectors, agriculture, textiles, and clothing) were integrated into the multilateral trading system.

The last element may well be the most remarkable achievement, given the history of the Multifiber Arrangement (MFA), failure of past attempts to bring agriculture under multilateral disciplines, and the North-South differences over TRIPs and services.

As can be expected, there remain several areas of concern that will hopefully be ironed out in the course of implementation. For example, transition periods to liberalization of key sectors such as textiles may be too long; liberalization of agriculture may not be sufficient, or it may result in higher food prices; and the inclusion of TRIPs may make essentials like drugs more expensive for the poor countries. Implementation of the agreement may also involve transitional costs in specific areas for some countries and benefits for others. It is expected that the round will in general be beneficial for all countries and that, where adjustments are required, the implementation period will be fairly long to allow a gradual transition. Two important types of transition costs have been identified for some developing countries: those arising from the erosion of preference margins and from the possibility of higher costs of food imports. Preliminary analyses suggest that the erosion of preferences is likely to be small for most African and Caribbean countries but could be more significant for some North

African countries. Moreover, as tariffs come down in successive rounds, and the world economy gets increasingly integrated, reliance on preferences as a basis for long-term export growth is not a viable strategy. Regarding food imports, the direct impact of possible higher prices is likely to be felt by those relying most heavily on commercial food imports and will depend on the extent of the rise in food prices. Conversely, the long-term trend for real food prices has been distinctly downward, and there is no reason to expect that this trend is about to end.

Beyond the Uruguay Round

The process of liberalization at the country level and for globalization at the international level will continue in the coming years. However, difficulties still lie ahead. While empirical as well as theoretical analyses show that openness is a strong determinant of economic success, the process of liberalization often leads to domestic opposition as the abolition of trade barriers imposes costs on those who benefited from protection. Given the political economy of trade liberalization in individual countries, it is easy to see that several themes and issues will dominate the debate in this area for some time to come.

Regional Trade Arrangements

Regional arrangements gained momentum as multilateral negotiations through the Uruguay Round became protracted. There are now at least 67 preferential regional trade agreements (RTAs). The most important RTAs are the EU, NAFTA, and the Asia Pacific Economic Cooperation forum (APEC).

All of us recognize that regional arrangements are second best and that multilateral liberalization is the preferred approach for the globalization of trade. Regionalism raises fears of trading blocs that potentially could eliminate access by outsiders. Moreover, gravitation toward large regional blocs may lead to an increased apprehension of retaliation and trade conflicts.

On balance, however, recent regionalization has not inhibited the growth of world trade or global integration. In general, there has been no increase in protectionism on the part of the major RTAs; the development of RTAs has proceeded alongside an expansion of trade with nonmembers.

Thus, regionalism is not inimical to global liberalization. Indeed, RTAs can often supplement the process of globalization. Neighboring countries may find that agreements between them are easier to achieve than those with all countries in the world, thus allowing a faster pace of liberalization in a regional context than in a global context. Regional groupings may also be more ambitious toward opening out than countries that rely only on a unilateral approach. However, we need to continuously monitor how regionalism develops, so that trade-creating aspects of RTAs are emphasized. At a minimum, we should expect that RTAs cover substantively all trade and not increase restrictions on third countries. We should also expect that RTAs have transparent and liberal rules of origin and accession provisions for potential new members.

Political Economy: Special Interests and Jobs

Why does protectionism enjoy broad support even in those countries, such as the United States, that have championed the cause of liberalism? There are two answers to this difficult question. First, in the practical determination of trade policy through the political process, the special interests of highly organized groups that correctly perceive the benefits to themselves from protectionist measures often operate more effectively than the relatively diffuse general interests that are comprehended in the economist's concept of social welfare. As I sometimes like to put it, "In Washington, the truth is just another special interest, and one that is not particularly well financed." Without going into the political economy of trade, a subject that is the subject of intense and rigorous analysis, I would only like to point out that economists who are involved in the determination of trade policy—hopefully on the side of the angels—should prepare themselves to use valid and effective arguments to counter those of the special interests.

Second, from the broad support often seen for protectionist policies, it is clear that such support does not come only from those who have a vested interest in such policies. Rather, it is based on a widespread and deep-seated feeling that opportunities for employing domestic resources to meet domestic needs should somehow be protected from foreign competition. Simply put, the issue is "jobs, jobs, jobs." The commonsense perception is that if foreigners are allowed to supplant domestic producers of some product, then the domestic resources used in such production will become unemployed; or, more succinctly, "jobs will be lost." These special interests fail to perceive that openness of trade, through a reallocation of resources, will result in job displacement from specific sectors only. In the aggregate, jobs can be expected to increase as a result of more openness as the efficiency gains from the increased trade take root. Those who are displaced will be able to find opportunities elsewhere.

In actual fact, the fixed-number-of-jobs fallacy often results in the adoption of trade-restricting policies that likely constrain economic growth, and hence employment. The arguments are based on the natural sympathy that everyone has for those who might lose their jobs because of foreign competition—a sympathy that is reinforced by the reality of prolonged periods of unemployment as a result of some sectoral shifts following a withdrawal of protection. The practical question for economists and policymakers, then, is, "How do we minimize the transition costs that arise from moving toward free trade?" It should be recognized that these costs occur only in the short run and can be (and have been) dealt with through appropriately designed social safety nets.

Fair-Trade Versus Free-Trade: Level Playing Field

With globalization and improved technology, production centers move easily to exploit cost advantages. Producers have, therefore, become very sensitive to the possibility of "unfair" advantage by foreign competition and raised the "level playing field"argument or the "fair trade before free trade" argument to demand partial (or total) harmonization of domestic policies.

It is not surprising that attention is focused on newer issues affecting market access now that traditional trade barriers have come down. In some cases, even though tariff reductions have taken place and QRs have been eliminated, market access appears to be limited to foreign competition. This naturally raises questions, such as "Can domestic, as opposed to border measures, be used for impeding trade?" "Is competition policy being enforced properly?" or "Is it effectively favoring domestic industries over foreign production?" Domestic policies toward foreign investment also influence market access. Hence, trade-related investment policies and the need for new multilateral rules on investment (particularly FDI) are also issues for the new trade agenda.

However, competition policy issues and its instruments need better definition and analysis before multilateral approaches can be formulated to tackle emerging trade frictions in this area. There is also a danger of trade policy being overloaded with objectives. For example, trade restrictions are being suggested to counter "eco-" or "social" dumping. The links between trade policy and environmental and labor policies are likely to get further attention in the future. Environmental and labor objectives are undoubtedly important and should be advanced without reliance on trade sanctions as an enforcement mechanism. More generally, there is no presumption that harmonization of all domestic policies and business practices is necessary for trade to be mutually beneficial—if it were, should we also demand the harmonization of climate?

Liberalization: What Can We Learn?

While major progress in liberalizing exchange and trade regimes has been made in recent years, it is important to note that some countries, especially the low-income ones, remain more restrictive compared with other regions of the world. However, it is encouraging that this restrictive stance of the poor countries is being perceived by most stakeholders as a major impediment to accelerating growth. Indeed, recent initiatives for sub-Saharan Africa have identified trade liberalization as a key reform area.

The promotion of open trade regimes is also considered an important element in the IMF's work, both in terms of surveillance and program design, because distorted trade regimes operate as impediments to both macroeconomic reform and structural adjustment. Trade reform can contribute importantly to improving the efficiency of resource allocation, reducing the anti-export bias of the economy, exposing it to competition, promoting realistic exchange rates and balance of payments adjustment, spurring investment (including FDI), and diversifying the economy.

Given the underlying political and economic interests, trade reform remains a complex process, with each attempt at liberalization being confronted by differing circumstances. Nevertheless, several common themes emerge from the experience of liberalization in the past two decades. From these, we can derive valuable lessons for the countries of Africa in the design of their own liberalization experiences.

Complementary reform: Trade liberalization cannot function as an engine of growth in the absence of complementary actions in other macroeconomic and structural areas. While trade reforms continue to be narrowly defined to cover (import and export) tariffs and nontariff barriers (NTBs), policies such as exchange restrictions and the exchange rate, price controls, and state trading monopolies are closely related to trade reform and have direct significant effects on trade flows. The effectiveness of trade reform is enhanced when it is accompanied or preceded by reforms in the exchange system, price controls, and the privatization of state trading. Experience suggests that the most successful trade reforms have been part of comprehensive adjustment packages.

Bold and comprehensive strategies: Trade liberalization programs that started boldly and were followed through with vigor proved more durable than ones that took a more hesitant approach. The main elements of such a program are sharp reductions in tariffs and elimination of QRs in the context of a broader structural reform and stabilization package. If such efforts are sustained for 6 or more years, the liberalization effort is likely to be sustained. For the credibility of the reform process, it has also been found to be useful to preannounce the phased medium-term reform to provide economic agents with the signals and the time to adjust to the new structure.

Prudent macroeconomic policies: Successful reformers have shown themselves to be more fiscally prudent than others. Reversals of liberalization were more commonly associated with poor macroeconomic policies than with any other factor, including the power of vested interests and increased short-run unemployment. The perceived potential, adverse short-term impact of liberalization on the external and fiscal positions can be minimized. The balance of payments effects can be kept manageable, as long as domestic demand policies are properly managed, and the trade liberalization is appropriately phased and accompanied, as necessary, by an exchange rate adjustment. In general, with the adoption of flexible exchange rate policies in many African countries, the balance of payments argument for postponing trade reform is no longer credible, except perhaps for very short periods in particular cases of precarious reserve levels.

Sequencing and design issues: Credible and comprehensive trade reform can be out *pari passu* with macroeconomic stabilization. There is no compelling reason to wait for the completion of macroeconomic stabilization to initiate major trade reforms. Indeed, such an approach risks undue delays in commencing trade liberalization. However, such a delay may not be inappropriate if the inflation and reserve situations are so severe as to require immediate and major contractions in domestic demand, and these measures are expected to stabilize the position in the near term (1 year). If the achievement of macroeconomic stabilization is expected to occur gradually (say, over 2 to 5 years), it is prudent to integrate concomitant trade liberalization into the overall adjustment package.

QRs should be eliminated as a matter of priority because they are less transparent and more restrictive than tariffs. (QRs include prohibitions, quotas, licensing, and so forth.) It is preferable to phase out QRs (excluding those for security and health reasons) during a 2- to 3-year period at the beginning of the trade reform. The QRs should be replaced by tariffs; if necessary, these could be temporarily higher than normal maximum tariffs but should not exceed their tariff equivalents; they should be phased down to the normal maximum tariff within 2 to 3 years.

Measures for transparency and for reducing anomalies in the tariff structure should be implemented early in a program. For example, many sub-Saharan African countries resort to statutory and discretionary exemptions and have multiple duties and charges on imports over and above the basic tariff. Exemptions should be strictly limited to normal obligations under international conventions (for example, embassies), and eliminated for the rest, including parastatals, state trading enterprises, donors, and nongovernmental organizations. Once this is accomplished, it is easier to design a meaningful tariff reform that can aim at simplifying the structure to a few rates (3 to 5, including 0), and then reduce the level and dispersion of tariffs by reducing maximum and average tariffs.

Maintaining competitive exchange rates: The experience of successful reformers suggests that major trade reforms are easier to initiate and sustain when accompanied by a real exchange depreciation and an improvement of the fiscal position. This is particularly true if the initial level of protection is high and widespread and the reform period is concentrated over a few years, because the high level of protection itself artificially raises the value of the currency (compared with the equilibrium level in the absence of the restrictions). However, in some cases when temporary upsurges in capital inflows generate an appreciation of the exchange rate, trade liberalization is difficult to sell domestically and may also face a balance of payments constraint, unless the external reserve position is strong. The experience with sequencing thus indicates that programs could face risks if capital-market liberalization preceded trade liberalization, especially if it resulted in a surge of imports.

Costs of adjustment may not be large: Regarding output effects, a World Bank multicountry study suggests that short-term costs were surprisingly small. In particular, reallocation of resources to more efficient patterns suggested that overall output and employment were not very adversely affected and that the reallocation of labor was achieved largely within sectors, causing less disruption than might have been feared. Indeed, the short-term effect of liberalization on overall national output in Latin American countries was strongly positive, and on employment it was, at worst, neutral.

Trade Reform in Africa

Trade liberalization is now widely accepted in sub-Saharan Africa. Many countries have eliminated QRs and reduced maximum tariffs from triple-digit levels to the range of 20–40 percent. How much further should they go, and during what period? Although theory suggests that a small economy cannot influence world prices, and that the optimal tariff is zero, practical and political considerations make this level impractical. We can, therefore, assume that tariff rates will be positive for purposes of domestic protection and to generate fiscal revenues. There is no magic formula to determine the appropriate level of tariffs pertinent to the implementation of a medium-term growth strategy in sub-Saharan Africa, and ultimately the particular circumstances of each country will determine the extent and pace of reform. As a general rule, countries could consider a two-stage approach to trade reform. The first stage would be implemented on an accelerated basis, and the second stage in the medium term. The first stage would aim to remove all QRs (except for security and health) and to bring down tariffs to a range of 0–30 percent, with an average tariff of not more than 15 percent, within a period of less than 2 years. Some sub-Saharan African countries have already reached this stage, and a number of others are close to it. These countries can proceed to the second stage, which would cover a 3-year period where tariffs are further reduced to a range of 0–15 percent, with an average tariff of 10 percent or less. Tariffs on some luxury imports for which domestic production is infeasible may be at a somewhat higher level for revenue purposes and for tax equity in the absence of a capacity to effectively enforce other progressive taxes. The above two-stage approach provides for a 5-year period to implement tax reforms that would substitute domestic revenue mobilization for trade taxes. This would constitute an ambitious but feasible reform program that would enable Africa to compete on equal or better terms (ceteris paribus) with the successful reformers in Latin America and Southeast Asia.

While liberal trade policies contribute to the improvement of efficiency, promote export growth, and enhance an economy's adaptability, they have to be supported by an appropriate macroeconomic policy stance. Inappropriate fiscal, monetary, and exchange rate policies can constrain the ability of economic agents to compete abroad and also generate protectionist pressures. Exchange and trade restrictions restrain trade, and hence negate trade liberalization. Trade policy, in turn, can affect macroeconomic performance through its impact on fiscal balances (e.g., the revenue effects of tariff reforms), on the balance of payments (e.g., in the short term through incentives to export and import), and on the exchange rate (e.g., heavy reliance on trade restrictions can amount to overvalued—effective—exchange rates).

In African countries where the industrial base is narrow and highly dependent on protection, the contraction of output in the protected industries may not be as rapidly offset by the development of export industries. However, this is more a question of the length of the lags rather than the nature of the response. Also, there may well be instances where domestic industries with high effective protection on final products have negative value added for the economy. Output losses for such industries are immediately beneficial for the economy as a whole.

Supply responses in sub-Saharan Africa may be more sluggish than in other regions because of the existence of more bottlenecks in complementary areas, such as poor infrastructure, power and telecommunication facilities, and lack of marketing information. This, again, points to the need to integrate reforms into comprehensive structural adjustment packages that include measures to ease supply bottlenecks.

The experience with special protection for infant industries in Africa (and most other regions) has been generally poor. In the few cases where such a policy has been "successful," it has entailed large costs and has been accompanied by circumstances that do not prevail or cannot be replicated in Africa (e.g., a very high rate of domestic savings, skilled administrative capacity, and macroeconomic stability). African governments should be discouraged from diverting scarce resources to dubious infant industry development, which often is a pretext for the support of particular vested interests.

Fiscal Policy and Trade Liberalization

The relationship between tariff reforms and fiscal revenues is problematic. Sub-Saharan Africa depends on trade taxes for fiscal revenues to a greater extent than most other regions. Finding domestic sources of revenue to reduce reliance of trade taxes has been an important cause of delays in initiating, following through, or completing major trade reforms. Often the difficulties have been compounded by poor tax administration capacity. In some cases, the fiscal argument has been exaggerated or used as a pretext to delay trade reform. Indeed, a well-designed tariff reform may actually improve the import tax collection rate at the same time as statutory tariff levels come down, particularly if the original high tariffs have lead to widespread exemptions, smuggling, tax evasion, misclassification, and corruption. The incentive for these activities is reduced with the reduction in tariffs.

Nonetheless, the fiscal impact of trade liberalization may be negative, requiring a careful consideration of the manner and speed of implementing trade reforms. Alternative sources to domestic revenue, such as the value-added tax (VAT), need to be designed and implemented. Taxation of primary commodity exports may be an important source of revenue, while the collection of income taxation in rural areas and on small farmers scattered over a wide area may be difficult. Notwithstanding these difficulties, the design and implementation of tariff and fiscal reform should be well coordinated and synchronized to manage these difficulties over the medium term. The aim should be to broaden the effective tax base and, if the sources of revenue are limited, to emphasize better expenditure control. Waiting for the "right" time vis-à-vis the fiscal situation may inordinately delay the initiation of trade reform.

Regional Integration in Africa

Regional integration movements, which are being developed in Africa, should be encouraged to the extent that they are consistent with multilateral liberalization and carry economic benefits for the concerned country, its neighbors, and its trading partners. Trade reform in the regional context in sub-Saharan Africa should bear two considerations in mind. First, countries in a proposed regional grouping should incorporate specific trade liberalization measures to ensure, broadly, the same scope and timing of trade reforms. This has been missing, for example, in the programs for Cross-Border Initiative (CBI) participants, probably because the individual economic circumstances are different, even with the intention to harmonize tariffs on a given timetable. Second, while it is theoretically desirable to aim for a common or harmonized tariff for a given product at the level of the lowest tariff among the participants within a regional grouping, in practice this is difficult to implement. Indeed, in some cases, joining a regional arrangement may have the effect of raising tariffs to the regional standard, thereby reducing welfare in the country concerned. In such cases, the strategy should be to persuade the bigger economies in the regional arrangement to undertake an ambitious trade reform program, in the expectation that this route would carry the whole group forward more rapidly.

The Role of the IMF

IMF surveillance and programs have as their objectives the attainment of sustainable growth and the balanced expansion of trade. In this context, the linkages between macroeconomic and structural policies and trade policy developments have an important bearing on the IMF's work. Maintaining open markets is especially important for the success of adjustment efforts of members undertaking IMF-supported programs. Further attention is likely to be given to strengthening the analysis of the effects of trade measures and of the links between trade policy and other macroeconomic and structural policies, including assessment of the impact of protection on domestic adjustment. Some of this analysis may also be conducted at the regional level if required.

Similarly, problems of developing countries and economies in transition with access to markets will also receive attention. The recent increased emphasis on structural issues, the trade policy content of IMF-supported programs, has significantly increased. A review of design issues highlights the importance of integrating trade policy with other program policies—particularly fiscal and exchange rate—and adhering to a medium-term trade reform strategy with clearly established short- and medium-term goals.

The IMF's work on trade reform complements that of the WTO. The major focus of the WTO is the implementation of multilateral rules and disciplines on trade in goods and services, the settlement of disputes, and the conduct of multilateral trade negotiations. The policy advice of the IMF and the World Bank is consistent with the general rules of the WTO and with the individual country's specific commitments and legal obligations in the WTO. The IMF will need to monitor carefully members' adjustment to the Uruguay Round agreement, including its impact on their balance of payments, and help countries manage an orderly transition. The IMF and the World Bank stand ready to use their existing facilities where appropriate to address external financing and policy adjustment needs arising from implementation of the Uruguay Round.

Trade Liberalization in Sub-Saharan Africa 4

Robert Sharer

This chapter assesses the role of trade reform in IMF-supported, medium-term adjustment programs in sub-Saharan Africa, by reviewing multiyear arrangements with countries in that region during the 1990s. The chapter also provides an analytical framework for trade liberalization and introduces an index that classifies the relative aggregate restrictiveness of trade regimes. The review of sub-Saharan African countries assesses the initial degree of restrictiveness of each country's trade regime, the targeted trade liberalization objectives in each program, and the degree of trade restrictiveness at the end of the program. The trade liberalization efforts in sub-Saharan African countries are compared with those of other regions that had IMF-supported medium-term programs during the same period. The chapter is in large part based on a recently completed comprehensive study of trade liberalization in IMF-supported programs. The study also discusses the main factors affecting trade policy targets, including in particular the impact of fiscal considerations.

The study finds that the majority of sub-Saharan African countries reviewed had relatively restrictive trade regimes at the outset of their programs. Thus there was a clear need for trade liberalization. More than 70 percent of programs with sub-Saharan African countries reviewed targeted a quantifiable reduction in restrictiveness, as measured by the index of aggregate trade restrictiveness used in the study. The remaining 30 percent of countries, however, did not target changes in trade restrictiveness sufficient to change their index classification, despite the fact that some of the countries started out with highly restrictive trade regimes. Programs generally achieved their targeted trade reform objectives, thus contributing to a marked movement toward less restrictive regimes. The strength of conditionality was related to the importance of the measure for the program, and it appears to have facilitated implementation. However, more liberalization should probably have been targeted in a significant number of programs, particularly in countries with initially restrictive regimes.

The issue of ambitiousness is discussed. Key factors that may be relevant in determining the appropriate pace of liberalization include the initial degree of trade restrictiveness, the country's administrative capacity, and the short-term adjustment costs. The experiences of some "good practice" countries outside sub-Saharan Africa that have achieved open trade regimes within 7–10 years is also instructive. Although there were no clear-cut examples of sub-Saharan African countries that have implemented the same degree of trade liberalization on a sustained basis, as in these "good practice" cases, some countries in the region are making significant reform efforts on an ongoing basis, and have experienced a marked improvement in their economic performance. Two such cases are illustrated as additional comparators.

Fiscal policy concerns were often cited as an important factor limiting the extent of trade reform targeted. However, the review found no direct relationship between the strength of trade reform objectives and achievements, and the countries' initial fiscal circumstances. This is consistent with available information, albeit limited, which indicates that the design of the successful trade reform programs was done in a way to counter fiscal or other concerns raised at the outset. This included focusing initially on the removal of nontariff barriers (NTBs), with potentially revenue-reducing tariff reform left to a later stage, and by introducing more broadly based taxes and targeting a reduction in exemptions.

The available information indicates that a significant factor for successful liberalization in the countries studied was the authorities' commitment to expeditious implementation of trade reform and (generally) to the adoption of liberal, market-oriented policies, as well as the authorities' ownership of the program. This manifested itself in trade reform being viewed as a key medium-term objective with preannounced targets, which was found to be important in program implementation.

The chapter is organized as follows. The first section briefly provides an analytical framework on the importance of trade reform and its main elements. The second section reviews trade reform in IMF-supported programs in sub-Saharan Africa. The third section discusses program ambitiousness. The fourth section describes factors influencing the implementation of trade reform, particularly fiscal considerations, and the fifth section summarizes the findings and concludes the chapter. The index of aggregate trade restrictiveness noted above is described below, and in a methodological appendix.

Analytical Framework and Elements of Trade Reform

Economic Rationale

The economic rationale for trade liberalization is based on improved efficiency of resource allocation and enhanced growth prospects. An open trade regime expands trade and investment options and allows countries to specialize in and export those products for which they have a comparative advantage. Trade barriers on imports result in higher prices and cause inefficiency as consumers shift to higher-cost domestic substitutes or forgo consumption of products they would otherwise prefer. Import barriers also give rise to an anti-export bias through higher costs to exporters, the impact on the exchange rate (which tends to be more appreciated) and because import-competing industries tend to bid workers and capital away from would-be exporters or other potentially more efficient economic activities.

As with other economic distortions, trade policy distortions shift an economy to a less efficient mix of investment, production, and consumption. They create incentives to produce and invest in goods for which the economy's rate of return is below the rate of return for the individual enterprise. These distortions depress real economic growth, and their removal therefore enhances growth prospects.[1] The empirical literature on trade and growth confirms the theoretical case for open trade policies, as do new developments in the theory of economic growth such as endogenous growth theory, which has highlighted dynamic gains from trade liberalization. These recent studies and findings provide further credibility and confirmation that trade openness tends to be associated with higher rates of economic growth.[2]

In general, the beneficial effects of trade reform are best realized in an appropriate macroeconomic environment supported by other structural reform policies to improve the efficiency of resource allocation. In particular, there are strong and mutually supporting links between trade reform, an appropriate level for the real exchange rate, and a liberal exchange system, because exchange and trade restrictions often act as substitutes and the benefits of liberalizing one may not be fully realized without liberalizing the other. In one direction, an open trade regime is needed so that international price signals promote efficient resource allocation for a country with an appropriate real exchange rate and a liberal exchange regime. In the other direction, an appropriate exchange rate and a liberal exchange regime are needed so that the tradable sector can exploit its comparative advantage and maintain the momentum of trade liberalization efforts and macroeconomic stabi-

[1]Indeed, it is even possible in a distorted trade regime that new investment or increases in other factor supplies can reduce national income—so-called immiserizing growth. See Bhagwati and Srinivasan (1983) and Brecher and Diaz-Alejandro (1977) for further elaboration

[2]The general results and summaries of the literature have been included in *World Economic Outlook* (IMF, 1993), *The East Asian Miracle* (World Bank, 1993), and *International Trade Policies: The Uruguay Round and Beyond* (IMF, 1994). Recent studies and findings include Barro and Sala-i-Martin (1995); Sachs and Warner (1995); and Frankel, Romer, and Cyrus (1996).

lization. In particular, if the exchange rate is overvalued, then a real depreciation may be an important complement to trade liberalization.[3]

Elements of Liberalization

The main goal of trade reform should be to improve economic efficiency by creating a transparent and neutral system of incentives that eliminates anti-export bias, direct impediments to trade, and economic distortions caused by the trade regime. This would involve removing export barriers and quantitative restrictions (QRs) and other NTBs[4] on imports, reducing tariff dispersion through introducing low and relatively uniform tariffs administered in a transparent and evenhanded manner, and establishing neutral treatment of imports and domestic goods under domestic economic policies. Trade reform is often sequenced so that initial action on import barriers focuses on QRs and other NTBs,[5] which tend to be the most distortionary trade restrictions. Measures to reform import tariffs include reductions in the maximum and higher tariffs and in the number of tariff bands; conversion of specific tariffs into ad valorem rates; consolidation of other import taxes or charges into a single rate; and reduction or elimination of tariff exemptions for individuals, organizations, or groups. Trade reform may also include other measures to ensure equal treatment of domestic and imported goods, and it implies an absence of controls on domestic trade, such as price or marketing controls.

Trade Reform, Political Economy, and Governance

Usually, the most important impediments to trade reform are political economy factors.[6] In some cases, this may be a response to the adjustment costs and disruption associated with any policy changes that lead to changes in resource allocation. In the case of trade reform, the

[3]Exchange rate policies are linked in important ways to trade policy but generally fall outside the scope of trade liberalization, narrowly defined, and hence are generally excluded from the study, except where such restrictions act as binding trade restrictions.

[4]NTBs here are defined as measures that restrict trade either by limiting quantities that may be traded or by inserting administrative discretion in the export/import process that acts as a barrier to trade. Such NTBs include quantitative restrictions, quotas, bans, restrictive licensing requirements, restrictive foreign exchange practices, state trading monopolies, restrictive technical and phytosanitary standards, and restrictive customs procedures.

[5]Often, import quantitative restrictions are replaced by tariffs.

[6]See, for example, Baldwin (1985), Bhagwati (1982), Krueger (1974, 1993), Leidy (1995), Magee, Brock, and Young (1989), Rodrik (1995), and Williamson (1994). While critically important to the design, pace, and implementation of reform, the political economy of trade liberalization is beyond the scope of this chapter.

most concentrated group of losers are usually readily identifiable producers facing the loss of existing sources of income, while beneficiaries are widely dispersed among consumers and potential exporters that may be difficult to identify. However, beyond adjustment costs, the often highly focused economic impact of trade policy makes it a particularly attractive target of rent-seeking behavior and lobbying, in many cases, by small well-organized groups, while the costs associated with restrictive trade policies are widely dispersed throughout the economy and are not transparent. These political economy factors, together with the government's commitment to liberal, market-oriented reforms, "ownership" of the program, and garnering political support, are likely to be the most critical factors in effective trade reform. Other related factors that can constrain trade reform include lack of an adequate social safety net, supply constraints for countries with undiversified economies or inadequate physical infrastructure, and concerns about the effects of trade reform on unemployment and the impact of openness on consumption patterns and income distribution.

Trade liberalization has important beneficial effects on the quality of governance. Because of their highly disaggregated nature, trade policies are particularly suited to the redirection of resources by the government to narrow interest groups, while those adversely affected by trade policy are often affected indirectly and may not be aware of the effect. Liberalization and simplification can reduce this adverse impact and improve the ability of those affected by the policy to detect and understand the impact of the remaining trade policy instruments. Even beyond legal but inefficient and nontransparent rent-seeking, complex and discretionary trade policy regimes create opportunities for corruption, particularly in the case of discretionary licensing and tariff exemptions.

The elimination of discretionary licensing and regulatory requirements and ad hoc tariff exemptions improves transparency and the quality of governance. As these policies generate private windfalls rather than government revenue, their elimination reduces rent-seeking activities on the part of firms. On the part of the government, a nondiscriminatory, and therefore more predictable, licensing and tariff exemptions system improves the quality of governance by reducing incentives for corruption, and also economizes on scarce administrative resources. Another element of trade liberalization that has the added benefit of improved governance is the adoption of a relatively low and uniform tariff rate. In addition to the gains from administrative simplicity and transparency, and the economic efficiency benefits of reducing effective protection levels,[7] a uniform tariff rate regime is also preferred on political economy grounds. If a government can establish a credible commitment to a reasonably low and uniform tariff, firms are less likely to lobby for increased tariff protection, thereby sharply reducing rent-seeking costs.

Review and Assessment of IMF-Supported Programs

The review covers 14 programs in 13 sub-Saharan African countries supported by 16 arrangements under the Extended Fund Facility (EFF), Structural Adjustment Facility (SAF), and Enhanced Structural Adjustment Facility (ESAF)[8], which were initiated and concluded between January 1990 and June 1996 (see Table 1).[9] The review provides a snapshot of trade reform in each program and does not consider directly trade reform before, or following, the programs under review. This section discusses the underlying methodology and assesses the restrictiveness of sub-Saharan African countries' trade regimes at the start of the program, the targeted change in restrictiveness envisaged, and the overall restrictiveness at the end of the program. The ambitiousness of trade reform in these programs is then considered, and factors that influenced implementation of trade reform in the programs are also discussed.

Quantification of Overall Policy

Measurement of trade liberalization in the countries reviewed was based on the index of aggregate trade policy restrictiveness noted above. The index, which is described in more detail in the appendix, consists of a 10-point scale that combines measurements of the restrictiveness of tariffs and NTBs.[10] It measures the overall restrictiveness of a country's trade system relative to protection levels in all IMF mem-

[7]A common feature of many tariff regimes is that lower tariff rates apply to imported inputs and higher ones to final products. Tariff escalation, therefore, is a common cause for high levels of effective protection in some industries, especially when local producers depend to a large extent on imported inputs.

[8]The review was limited to multiyear arrangements under these facilities due to their focus on medium-term structural adjustment policies, including trade reform.

[9]Two arrangements were approved for Burkina Faso: an SAF arrangement in 1991 and an ESAF in 1993. The policy programs supported by these arrangements were distinct and separate. Three arrangements were approved for Zimbabwe, but these arrangements were supported by one policy program.

[10]Changes in tariff dispersion, maximum tariffs, exemptions, export taxes, and improvements in customs administration were not explicitly incorporated into the overall index due to the complexity of aggregating additional dimensions of trade policy and the difficulties of obtaining comparable cross-country data on these variables. However, the inclusion of average tariffs in the index implicitly also captures, at least to some extent, these other measures of restrictiveness.

Table 1. Arrangements Included in the Review of IMF-Supported Programs in Sub-Saharan Africa[1]

Country	Extended Fund Facility	Structural Adjustment Facility	Enhanced Structural Adjustment Facility
Benin			1/25/93
Burkina Faso		3/13/91	3/31/93
Comoros		6/21/91	
Equatorial Guinea			2/3/93
Ethiopia		10/28/92	
Lesotho			5/22/91
Mali			8/28/92
Mauritania			12/9/92
Mozambique			6/1/90
Sierra Leone[1]			4/3/92
Tanzania			7/29/91
Zambia[1]			7/17/92
Zimbabwe	1/24/92 9/11/92		9/11/92

Source: IMF data.

Note: Includes multiyear programs (at least two years) approved after January 1, 1990 that expired at the latest by June 30, 1996. The ESAF arrangements with Burundi and Rwanda, both of which began in 1991, are excluded.

[1]Rights Accumulation Program (RAP).

ber countries. The restrictiveness of the import tariff regime was based on the average unweighted statutory tariff rate, classified into five categories, from open to restrictive, based on the distribution of tariff rates of all IMF member countries. NTBs were classified into three categories based on coverage and restrictiveness, including both import/export QRs, bans, restrictive licensing, state trading monopolies, restrictive foreign exchange practices which act as binding trade restrictions, and other NTBs.[11] A rating of 1 on the index represents the most open trade regime, and 10 the most restrictive.[12] The index gives relatively more weight to NTBs since, as noted above, they generally result in larger economic distortions and less transparent policy regimes than high tariff rates.

[11]Other NTBs include safeguard actions, antidumping/countervailing duties, reference prices, quality controls, and indicative export prices.

[12]In principle, the index could understate the degree of liberalization targeted in the most restrictive trade regimes, when significant changes are introduced but are insufficient to move the country below the highly restrictive category. However, an examination of the data shows this rarely occurred in the programs reviewed and did not affect the results of the study.

Aggregation of different types of trade restrictions is not without challenges. Ideally, assessment of the overall restrictiveness of the trade regime should capture the distortions in relative prices and resource allocation due to the trade regime. In practice, construction of such measures requires very substantial amounts of information and analysis. Previous studies have: (1) presented tariff and NTB measures separately without attempting to form an overall index of restrictiveness; (2) developed very simple binary indicators of openness; or (3) conducted massive case studies to develop quantitative summary measures, such as effective rates of protection and effective exchange rates for exports and imports. The index used in this chapter is based on an intermediate approach that goes further than the first two categories toward providing comprehensive, objective measures of the overall stance of countries' trade regimes, while avoiding the impractical resource costs and data requirements of the third method.

Summary of Results

The review found that at the outset of their IMF-supported programs, virtually all sub-Saharan countries reviewed had restrictive trade regimes relative to the spectrum of IMF member countries. Accordingly, most of the programs aimed for a significant reduction in restrictiveness during the period of the program. Most of the sub-Saharan countries were successful in implementing significant trade reform, and thus the countries, as a group, made substantial progress toward more open trade regimes. Trade restrictiveness in the group of regions other than sub-Saharan Africa was less severe than in sub-Saharan Africa at the outset of their programs, although this overall picture conceals significant regional differences. As with sub-Saharan Africa, most of these countries targeted a marked reduction in trade restrictiveness, and for the most part were successful in achieving it.

Initial Conditions

Before the beginning of the IMF-supported programs, most sub-Saharan African countries reviewed had relatively restrictive trade regimes (see Figure 1 and Table 2).[13] About 70 percent of these countries could be characterized as having had a relatively restrictive

[13]It should be noted that analysis of the initial conditions of the trade system refers to the state of the trade policy regime before implementation of any action related to the program (including prior actions).

Figure 1. Distribution of Overall Restrictiveness, Initial Conditions

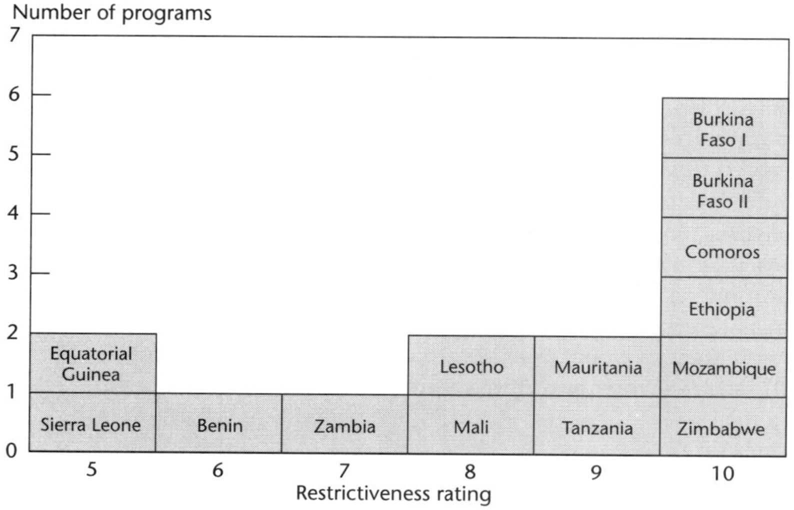

Source: IMF staff estimates.

trade regime, classified as 8–10 on the index.[14] Indeed more than half of the countries classified as restrictive, or some 40 percent of the total sub-Saharan African sample, had a rating of 10 on the index, indicating highly restrictive trade regimes. The remaining 30 percent had moderately restrictive trade regimes; none of the sub-Saharan African countries reviewed was classified as having an open trade regime.

The above profile of overall trade restrictiveness reflected both high average tariffs and extensive NTBs. For example, 8 out of the 14 programs with sub-Saharan African countries had the highest average tariff classification, and none of the remaining countries had average tariffs below the middle classification of all IMF members (see Table 3). Similarly, NTBs were widespread, and, again, 8 of the programs reviewed were in the highest NTB categorization. However, in contrast to tariffs, 2 of the countries were at the other end of the spectrum with virtually no NTB restrictions (see Table 4). In addition to the many cases

[14]For purposes of analysis, countries with index classifications of 8–10 can be considered restrictive; of 5–7, moderate; and of 1–4, open.

Table 2. Initial Overall Rating and Targeted Change in Restrictiveness Rating

Region and Country	Initial Overall Rating	Targeted Overall Rating	Final Overall Rating	Targeted Overall Change	Actual Overall Change
Sub-Saharan Africa	8.4	6.2	6.5	–2.1	–1.9
Burkina Faso I (1991)	10	10	10	0	0
Burkina Faso II (1993)	10	7	7	–3	–3
Comoros (1991)	10	8	8	–2	–2
Ethiopia (1992)	10	8	8	–2	–2
Mozambique (1990)	10	6	6	–4	–4
Zimbabwe (1992)	10	6	8	–4	–2
Mauritania (1992)	9	9	9	0	0
Tanzania (1991)	9	5	5	–4	–4
Lesotho (1991)	8	8	8	0	0
Mali (1992)	8	5	5	–3	–3
Zambia (1992)	7	4	4	–3	–3
Benin (1993)	6	3	6	–3	0
Equatorial Guinea (1993)	5	3	3	–2	–2
Sierra Leone (1992)	5	5	4	0	–1
Other regions[1]	7.4	5.7	5.8	–1.7	–1.6
Asia	7.0	4.8	4.8	–2.2	–2.2
Eastern Europe	9.5	7.5	6.5	–2.0	–3.0
Middle East	10.0	9.0	9.0	–1.0	–1.0
Western Hemisphere	6.0	4.6	5.2	–1.4	–0.8

Source: IMF staff estimates.

Note: The methodology of combining NTB coverage and average import tariffs into an overall index of trade restrictiveness is described in the appendix. Each program's approval date is indicated in parentheses.

[1]The Asia region consists of Bangladesh, Mongolia, Nepal, Philippines, and Sri Lanka. Eastern Europe consists of Hungary and Poland. Middle East consists of Egypt and Jordan. The Western Hemisphere consists of Argentina, Guyana, Jamaica, Panama, and Peru.

of quantitative restrictions on imports and exports (in the forms of quotas, bans, or restrictive licensing), state trading monopolies, usually covering commodities described as vital to the national interest, played a significant role in many sub-Saharan African countries reviewed.

By way of contrast, the 14 non-sub-Saharan African countries covered in the review[15] had, on average, somewhat less restrictive trade

[15]An attempt was also made to compare trade reform during 1990–96 in sub-Saharan African countries covered in the review with other sub-Saharan African countries that did not have such programs. However, the small sample size of the latter, and data difficulties on trade regimes in the early part of the 1990s, made such a comparison problematic. Nonetheless, when the level of trade restrictiveness at the end of the period was examined, the available data indicated that sub-Saharan African countries that had IMF-supported programs had, on average, significantly more liberal trade regimes than sub-Saharan African countries in the region that had not pursued IMF-supported programs, thus confirming the broad degree of success of most countries in achieving a marked reduction in trade restrictiveness.

Table 3. Initial Tariff Rating and Targeted Change in Restrictiveness Rating

Region and Country	Initial Tariff Rating	Targeted Tariff Rating	Final Tariff Rating	Targeted Tariff Change	Actual Tariff Change
Sub-Saharan Africa	4.4	3.9	3.9	–0.5	–0.4
Comoros (1991)	5	5	5	0	0
Equatorial Guinea (1993)	5	3	3	–2	–2
Ethiopia (1992)	5	5	5	0	0
Lesotho (1991)	5	5	5	0	0
Mali (1992)	5	5	5	0	0
Mozambique (1990)	5	3	3	–2	–2
Sierra Leone (1992)	5	5	4	0	–1
Zimbabwe (1992)	5	3	5	–2	0
Burkina Faso I (1991)	4	4	4	0	0
Burkina Faso II (1993)	4	4	4	0	0
Zambia (1992)	4	4	4	0	0
Benin (1993)	3	3	3	0	0
Mauritania (1992)	3	3	3	0	0
Tanzania (1991)	3	2	2	–1	–1
Other regions[1]	4.0	3.4	3.5	–0.6	–0.5
Asia	4.2	3.6	3.6	–0.6	–0.6
Eastern Europe	3.5	3.0	3.5	–0.5	0.0
Middle East	5.0	5.0	5.0	0.0	0.0
Western Hemisphere	3.6	2.8	2.8	–0.8	–0.8

Source: IMF staff estimates.

Note: Each program's approval date is indicated in parentheses.

[1]The Asia region consists of Bangladesh, Mongolia, Nepal, Philippines, and Sri Lanka. Eastern Europe consists of Hungary and Poland. Middle East consists of Egypt and Jordan. The Western Hemisphere consists of Argentina, Guyana, Jamaica, Panama, and Peru.

regimes at the outset of their programs.[16] About 60 percent of these countries' trade regimes were classified as restrictive, with the remainder divided equally between those with moderate and with open trade regimes. However, the average initial rating for non-sub-Saharan African countries masked a wide dispersion among the four other regions (Asia, Eastern Europe, Middle East, and Western Hemisphere). It is difficult to draw any firm conclusions on the restrictiveness of each region, since the sample size for each is so small. Nevertheless, on average, Asia and the Western Hemisphere countries had less restric-

[16]As shown in Table 2, the initial average overall rating for non-sub-Saharan African countries was 7.4 on the index, compared with 8.4 for the sub-Saharan African countries.

Table 4. Initial Nontariff Barrier Rating and Targeted Change in Restrictiveness Rating

Region and Country	Initial Tariff Rating	Targeted Tariff Rating	Final Tariff Rating	Targeted Tariff Change	Actual Tariff Change
Sub-Saharan Africa	2.4	1.8	1.9	–0.6	–0.6
Burkina Faso I (1991)	3	3	3	0	0
Burkina Faso II (1993)	3	2	2	–1	–1
Comoros (1991)	3	2	2	–1	–1
Ethiopia (1992)	3	2	2	–1	–1
Mauritania (1992)	3	3	3	0	0
Mozambique (1990)	3	2	2	–1	–1
Tanzania (1991)	3	2	2	–1	–1
Zimbabwe (1992)	3	2	2	–1	–1
Benin (1993)	2	1	2	–1	0
Lesotho (1991)	2	2	2	0	0
Mali (1992)	2	1	1	–1	–1
Zambia (1992)	2	1	1	–1	–1
Equatorial Guinea (1993)	1	1	1	0	0
Sierra Leone (1992)	1	1	1	0	0
Other regions[1]	2.2	1.8	1.8	–0.4	–0.4
Asia	2.0	1.4	1.4	–0.6	–0.6
Eastern Europe	3.0	2.5	2.0	–0.5	–1.0
Middle East	3.0	2.5	2.5	–0.5	–0.5
Western Hemisphere	1.8	1.6	1.8	–0.2	0.0

Source: IMF staff estimates.

Note: Each program's approval date is indicated in parentheses.

[1]The Asia region consists of Bangladesh, Mongolia, Nepal, Philippines, and Sri Lanka. Eastern Europe consists of Hungary and Poland. Middle East consists of Egypt and Jordan. The Western Hemisphere consists of Argentina, Guyana, Jamaica, Panama , and Peru.

tive trade regimes than sub-Saharan African countries, while Eastern Europe and the Middle East had more restrictive trade regimes.

Trade Reform Objectives

IMF-supported programs aimed for a marked movement toward open trade regimes, represented by a significant move along the index.[17] The average targeted improvement in restrictiveness for the sub-Saha-

[17]In assessing the program objective for trade liberalization, all measures targeted during the program were taken into account, including prior actions as well as measures specified after approval of the arrangement; for example, as part of the second- or third-year programs.

Figure 2. Targeted Change in Overall Restrictiveness

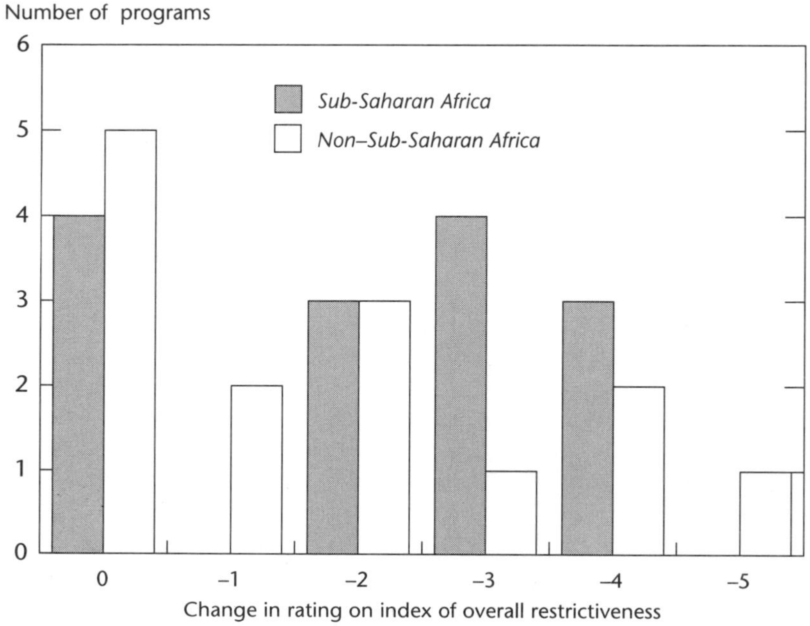

Source: IMF staff estimates.

ran African group ranged from 0 to 4 points (see Figure 2), with an average of 2.1 points on the index. Seven countries targeted an improvement of 3 or more points, including three that targeted improvement in trade liberalization equivalent to a 4-point movement on the index. Conversely, three of the programs reviewed did not target a reduction in trade restrictiveness large enough to register on the 10-point scale.

Programs for non-sub-Saharan African countries targeted a somewhat smaller improvement in their trade restrictiveness, averaging about 1.7 on the index, which may to some extent reflect the somewhat lower initial degree of trade restrictiveness of these countries. As with the sub-Saharan African countries, the extent of trade liberalization targeted varied widely, both by country and by region; the Asian and Eastern European countries targeted a markedly greater reduction in trade restrictiveness than Middle East and Western Hemisphere countries. However, it should be noted that the latter group of countries had the most open trade regimes at the initiation of their programs.

Most of the programs in sub-Saharan African countries targeted some reduction in NTBs sufficient to lower the classification of restrictiveness. Indeed, there were at least twice as many countries that targeted a quantifiable reduction in NTBs (nine countries) as those that targeted a reduction in tariffs (four countries). This result suggests that the sequencing of trade reform has generally followed the recommended practice of first targeting NTBs, followed (or accompanied) by a reduction in tariff protection. Each of the seven programs with countries that had an initial restrictive classification, and that targeted a quantifiable change in restrictiveness, targeted a reduction in NTB classification; only three of these countries also targeted tariff reduction. None of the countries under review that had relatively restrictive trade regimes targeted tariff reform alone. Indeed, for all the sub-Saharan African programs, only Equatorial Guinea, which initially had a moderately open trade regime, targeted a reduction in restrictiveness by reducing tariffs alone. In a similar vein, the sequencing of trade reforms in other regions focused more extensively on removing NTBs. In this context, all four other regions targeted a quantifiable reduction in NTBs, while only three of these regions targeted a quantifiable reduction in tariff protection.

End-of-Program Outturns and Monitoring

The sub-Saharan African countries covered by the review achieved a high degree of success in achieving the trade liberalization objectives included in the programs. In fact, the targeted degree of trade reform was met or exceeded in about 86 percent of IMF-supported programs in the region (see Figure 3). However, it should be noted that these results include the programs that did not target any change in restrictiveness. This favorable implementation record was equally true for targeted import tariff and NTB liberalization. Reflecting the favorable implementation record, sub-Saharan African countries made significant progress toward open trade regimes by the time the programs were concluded. As noted above, countries with a trade regime classified in the 8–10 range on the index are considered restrictive. The number of countries in the region in this category declined by almost half, to 40 percent of programs reviewed, compared with 70 percent initially; moreover, 20 percent of the countries moved to being classified as having an open trade regime, whereas there were none initially (see Figure 4). For those countries that achieved a quantifiable reduction in restrictiveness, the extent of trade liberalization was evenly divided between countries that improved their rating by 1–2 points and those that improved by 3–4 points.

The performance of the countries outside the region in achieving the targeted objectives was equally impressive. In fact, 90 percent of these

Figure 3. Sub-Saharan Africa: Overall Trade Liberalization, Final Outcome Versus Program Objectives

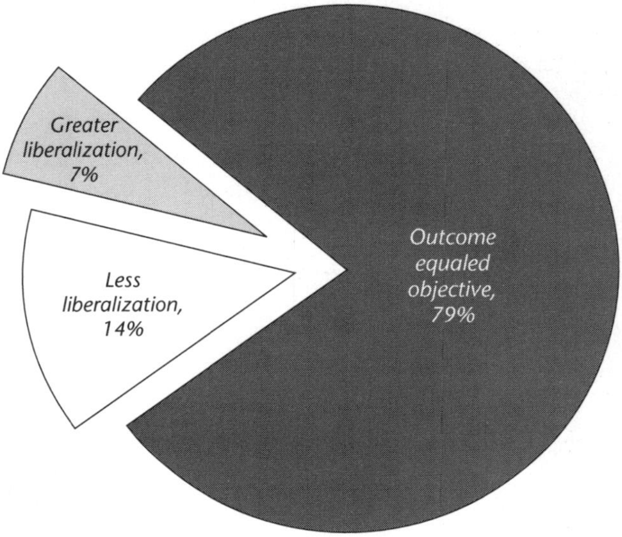

Source: IMF staff estimates.
Note: Includes cases where there was no targeted change in the restrictiveness rating.

programs achieved the targeted trade liberalization. For the group as a whole, the overall restrictive rating fell by 1.6 points, slightly less than the average reduction of 1.9 points for sub-Saharan African countries, reflecting the latters' somewhat more ambitious objectives.

In line with program design, the actual reduction in the overall restrictiveness of trade regimes in sub-Saharan Africa was due primarily to reductions in NTBs. As a result, by the end of the program period only one country still retained the most restrictive categorization of NTBs, compared with seven countries at the outset.[18] With regard to reduction in tariff protection, all the programs except one achieved the targeted reduction, and in one case tariff protection was reduced by more than had been anticipated in the program. In addition, although not directly reflected in the index, progress was made in reducing maximum

[18]Burkina Faso's first program also did not include a quantifiable reduction in NTBs. However, its second program targeted a reduction of 2 points on the index. Mauritania did not target NTB liberalization sufficient to lower the restrictiveness classification.

Figure 4. Initial, Targeted, and Final Overall Distribution of Trade Restrictiveness Index in Sub-Saharan Africa

(Number of programs)

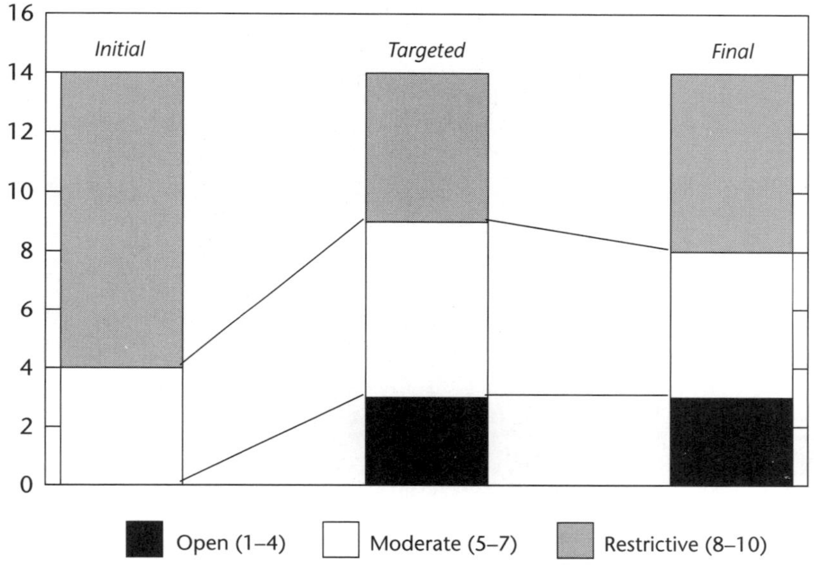

Source: IMF staff estimates.

tariffs, and available information also indicates that there was some progress in curtailing exemptions, hence reducing tariff dispersion. Indeed, about half the sub-Saharan African countries reviewed managed to reduced their maximum tariff rate, mostly by significant amounts.

To an extent, the success in attaining program targets reflects appropriate use of binding monitoring, namely prior actions, performance criteria, structural benchmarks, and reviews. Conditionality of at least one trade liberalization measure was used in all except two of the programs, and these measures were implemented on time in virtually all cases (see Figure 5). Of the measures not subject to such monitoring, about half experienced problems with delayed implementation.

Program Ambitiousness

General Principles

The objective of medium-term structural adjustment programs should be to move toward an open trade system characterized by the absence of quantitative restrictions and other NTBs (except for health

Figure 5. Monitoring Instruments Used in IMF-Supported Programs

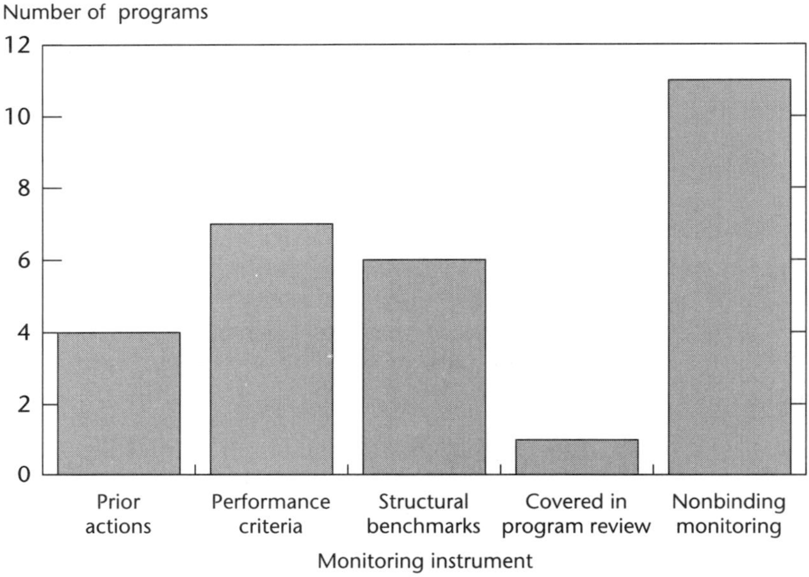

Source: IMF staff estimates.
Note: Multiple instruments may have been used in a program.

and security reasons) and low, relatively uniform tariff protection, applied in a transparent and evenhanded manner. Indeed, movement from restrictive to open categories, as measured by the index, means the progressive elimination of NTBs for purposes of controlling trade, and reducing tariff protection to low levels by comparison with all IMF member countries. However, the speed with which this objective should be accomplished is an inherently difficult issue. In principle, such movement should be undertaken as rapidly as possible, but in practice judgments need to be made on a case-by-case basis, taking account of the particular circumstances of the country concerned. This section sets forth some general observations and factors that may be considered in making such judgments.

Clearly, a major element determining the pace at which reform should be pursued is the country's initial conditions. Trade regimes that are more restrictive at the outset incur higher costs from trade distortions and hence need stronger trade liberalization efforts. Economic principles would seem to indicate that, in sequencing trade reform, one should first target the most distortionary aspects of the trade regime, namely NTBs, in tandem with other reforms. Such a strategy would not only reap the benefits of reduced distortions, but the tariffication of NTBs would almost invariably increase revenue, as discussed below. The pace of reform may also depend on factors such as overall macroeconomic conditions, the need to coordinate with other structural reforms (including, for example, price liberalization and privatization), the extent of real or perceived short-term adjustment costs (and the readiness of social safety nets to address these costs), and the government's commitment to liberalization policies (and the extent of political resistance to liberalization).

The experience of "good practice" countries that have achieved markedly improved trade and economic growth performance through the adoption of liberal, outward-looking policies is also instructive in determining the appropriate pace of trade liberalization. The review looked at the experience of four such countries (Chile, Colombia, New Zealand, and Singapore[19]) that made steady and sustained progress in trade liberalization by virtually eliminating all NTBs and reducing or maintaining relatively low tariff rates, thereby moving from restrictive to open trade regimes (as measured by the index), during a period of about 7 to 10 years from 1984 to 1996.[20] Their trade regimes have been classified according to the 10-point scale, and Figure 6 illustrates how they have opened their trade regimes during this period. Although these countries are more developed than the countries covered by this review, their experience, nevertheless, clearly supports the fact that sustained trade reform may contribute significantly to strengthening a country's economic performance (see Box 1).

During the period, these economies experienced strong economic activity, with exports and GDP growing by an average rate of 13 percent and 5 percent, respectively. Their experience also confirms that far-reaching trade reform is a medium- to long-term process, thus underscoring the need for specific, monitorable medium-term trade targets to be included in the initial objectives of programs.

Until recently, few, if any, African countries had trade regimes as liberal as these good practice countries. However, several African coun-

[19]Although Chile's average tariff sets it just above the level needed for a rating of 1 under the 10-point classification, the uniform tariff is likely much less distortionary than some other tariff regimes with an average tariff several percentage points below Chile's.

[20]Background sources for information on tariffs and nontariff barriers were *Survey of Impediments to Trade and Investment in the APEC Region* (PECC, 1995); *Trade Policy Review of New Zealand* (GATT, 1990); *Trade Policy Review of Chile* (GATT, 1991); *Trade Policy Review of Colombia* (WTO, 1996a); *Trade Policy Review of New Zealand* (WTO, 1996b); *Trade Policy Review of Singapore* (WTO, 1996d); and various GATT/WTO Trade Policy Reviews.

Figure 6. Trade Policies in Selected "Good Practice" Countries

(Restrictiveness rating)

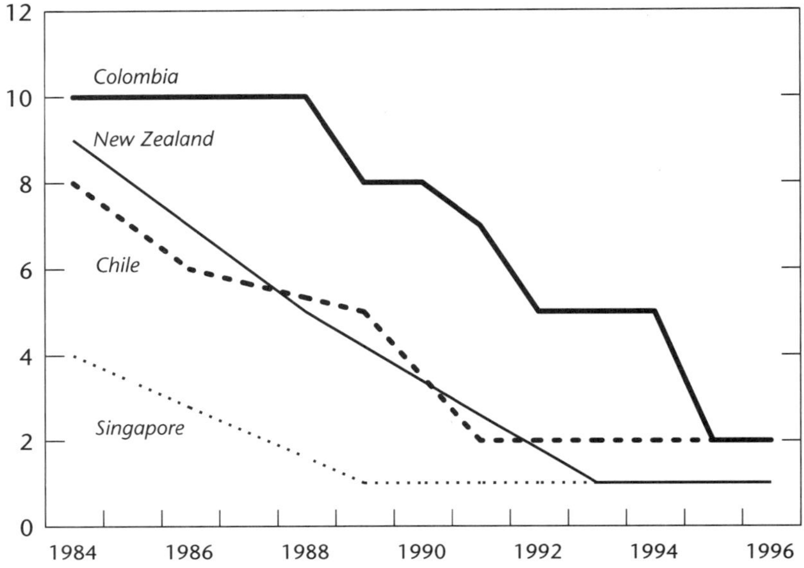

Source: IMF staff estimates.

tries have undertaken ambitious trade reforms in recent years and are approaching the levels of openness in the good practice countries. As noted above, Ghana and Uganda are two illustrative cases in sub-Saharan Africa where considerable trade reform has already taken place, and where more liberalization is expected over the medium term. This would result in these countries achieving levels of openness similar to the good practice countries (see Figure 7). The beneficial effects of structural reforms, including trade reforms, are already evident in these countries. During the period, Ghana and Uganda experienced strong economic activity, with GDP growing at an average rate of 4 and 7 percent, and exports increasing by an average of 10 and 24 percent, respectively.

Assessing the Programs Reviewed

Given the above considerations, it is difficult to translate the range of the trade liberalization objectives of the IMF-supported programs in sub-Saharan Africa into a general assessment of the ambitiousness of

Box 1. Trade Policies in Selected "Good Practice" Countries and in Selected Sub-Saharan African Countries

This box provides some benchmarks for trade reform in Chile, Colombia, New Zealand, and Singapore, which are known to have open or "good practice" trade policies. Their progress in liberalizing their trade regimes during the past decade is illustrated in Figure 6. The box also looks at two examples of sub-Saharan countries, Ghana and Uganda, which have progressively liberalized their trade regimes in the context of broad reform efforts, and which are beginning to show favorable results from these reforms (see Figure 7 below).

During the 1980s, Chile virtually eliminated NTBs, and progressively reduced tariffs to a uniform rate of 11 percent. The share of imports facing NTBs during the period 1991–93 was just 0.1 percent. When it started reforms in 1984, more than 80 percent of Colombia's imports required permits, while imports of some 800 products were prohibited and tariffs averaged near 60 percent. During the next decade, NTBs were virtually eliminated, and the average tariff was reduced to under 12 percent. In Singapore, the proportion of tariff lines covered by NTBs was reduced to 1 percent in the late 1980s and to less than 0.5 percent in the early 1990s; tariffs have averaged less than 1 percent since 1980. Finally, in New Zealand, tariffs averaged 16 percent in 1984, and most imports were subject to restrictive import licensing. By 1993, NTBs applied to less than 0.5 percent of imports, and tariffs had been cut to 8.5 percent and fell further to 6.2 percent in fiscal 1996/97.

In 1985, Ghana and Uganda had highly restrictive trade regimes with high tariffs, pervasive NTBs, and distorted exchange regimes. On the index of trade restrictiveness, Ghana and Uganda were rated 10 and 9, respectively. However, beginning in the mid-1980s through the early 1990s, these countries embarked on ambitious trade policy reforms, which generally focused initially on removing the more distortive nontariff barriers. As a result, both Ghana and Uganda now have only a few nontariff import barriers remaining, and these may also be removed during the next few years. Reflecting the marked opening of these economies to external competition, both countries' rating on the restrictiveness index fell to a category 5 by 1996, and it is expected that by the year 2000, these countries are projected to reduce further their trade restrictiveness to a rating of 3 or lower on the index.

the targeted trade reform. However, a quantifiable change in restrictiveness, involving a move of 3–4 points on the index, which should be considered far-reaching and extensive by any standards, was targeted in half of the countries, and most of these countries achieved their tar-

Figure 7. Trade Policies in Two "Good Practice" Sub-Saharan African Countries

(Restrictiveness rating)

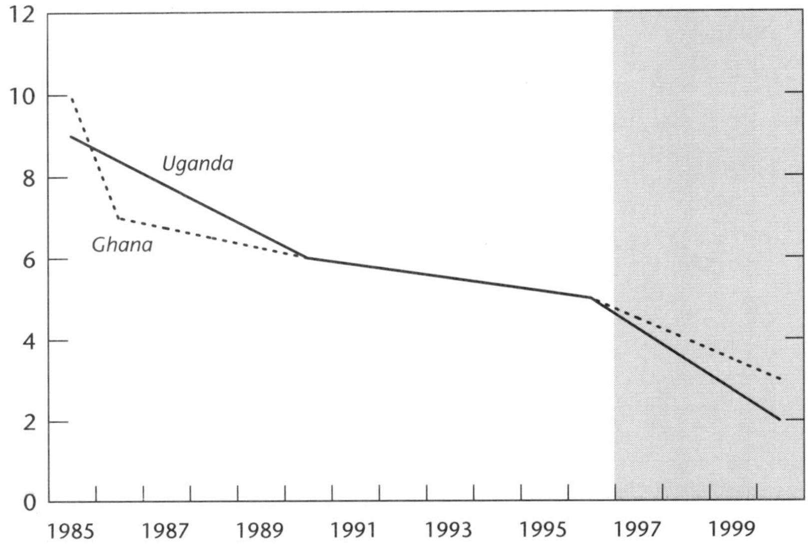

Source: IMF staff estimates.
Note: Shaded area indicates IMF staff projections.

gets. At the other end of the scale, more than a quarter of the programs did not target any quantifiable change in restrictiveness, and most of these were for countries with restrictive trade regimes. As would be expected, the programs in sub-Saharan African countries with initially restrictive regimes targeted a slightly larger move on the index than countries classified as having moderately restrictive trade regimes (see Table 5). This may reflect the fact that countries with highly restrictive trade regimes are those that have most strongly resisted liberalization. This latter point was in contrast to the pattern for non-sub-Saharan African countries, where countries that initially had less restrictive regimes, targeted a much larger improvement in restrictiveness than those that had restrictive regimes. However, in line with the experience in sub-Saharan Africa, a significant percentage of the non-sub-Saharan African programs did not target any quantifiable change in trade restrictiveness, and this was equally true for countries with restrictive regimes as for those with moderately restrictive regimes.

On balance, the findings of the review indicate that, notwithstanding the difficulties of judging the ambitiousness of trade reform efforts,

Table 5. Ambitiousness of Programs Reviewed

Initial Classification	Number of Programs	Average Targeted Change in Index	Programs That Targeted No Change in Overall Restrictiveness
Sub-Saharan Africa			
Restrictive	10	2.2	3 (30 percent)
Moderate	4	2.0	1 (25 percent)
Other regions			
Restrictive	8	1.8	2 (25 percent)
Moderate	3	3.0	1 (33 percent)

Source: IMF staff estimates.

a substantial number of programs in sub-Saharan African countries targeted and achieved extensive trade reform. However, more liberalization of the trade system should probably have been targeted in a significant number of IMF-supported programs, and particularly in those countries with initially restrictive regimes. These results are broadly similar to those of the comparator group of countries outside the region.

Factors in Implementing Trade Reform

The review attempted to identify the prevalence of a number of factors that might be expected to hinder or promote trade reform. These focused primarily on balance of payments and fiscal considerations. Other factors that were considered included the impact of the World Trade Organization (WTO) and regional trading arrangements (RTAs). Of the 13 sub-Saharan African countries under review, 10 are WTO members. The other three countries (Comoros, Equatorial Guinea, and Ethiopia) were not engaged in accession negotiations. The implementation of multilateral commitments under the WTO did not appear to have had an impact on trade liberalization in the sub-Saharan African countries. Regarding participation in RTAs, there is some evidence that it may have promoted trade liberalization in some countries (e.g., Zambia's participation in the Cross-Border Initiative appears to have influenced its trade policy). Equally important, however, was the authorities' commitment to trade reform.

As noted above, meaningful and sustainable trade reform needs to be developed as part of a coherent package of structural and macroeconomic policy reforms. Fiscal and balance of payments positions are central elements of the macroeconomic framework, and appropriate exchange rate policies are an integral part of IMF-supported programs. Balance of payments concerns may influence the extent and pace of trade liberalization, particularly if appropriate exchange rate policies are not adopted and if existing restrictions are thought to be needed to manage the balance of payments position to preserve macroeconomic stability. However, while balance of payments considerations are central to the policy objectives of IMF-supported programs, balance of payments difficulties were rarely cited explicitly as a factor that hindered trade reform commitments or implementation. Fiscal policy considerations and concerns, however, were pervasive. The remainder of this section sets out the fiscal policy aspects of trade reform in general, and the extent to which these considerations affected the design and implementation of trade policy in the programs reviewed.

Fiscal Policy Aspects

Fiscal policy concerns are frequently cited as a reason for delaying trade reform. In practice, however, the fiscal impact of liberalizing the trade system could be positive, negative, or neutral, depending on the reforms introduced and the specific circumstances of the country concerned.[21] Although lowering the average tariff in a system with already low or moderate tariff rates will, other things being equal, generally reduce revenue,[22] at least in the short term, the fiscal impact of most other aspects of trade reform is likely to be positive or ambiguous (see Table 6). Tariffication of QRs and other NTBs on imports or exports will improve government finances, possibly significantly, as will the elimination of tariff exemptions (excluding export-duty drawback schemes) and trade-related subsidies. Simplification of the tariff system through a move to more uniform rates or a reduction in the number of rates may also tend to increase fiscal revenue through increased transparency and simplification of tax administration. Even lowering export taxes may, in some circumstances, have a positive impact on

[21]It should be noted that in the context of IMF-supported programs the ratio of trade taxes to GDP may increase during trade reform, because of factors such as exchange rate changes, increases in the ratio of imports to GDP (including the impact of increased donor financing associated with adoption of the medium-term program), and improvements in tax and customs administration.

[22]However, if the average tariff is very high, the impact of a reduction may be ambiguous, because the effect of expanded imports may outweigh the reduced tax rate. Nogués and Gulati (1992) found that, in the case of Chile, reductions in very high tariffs were associated with increases in tariff revenue and found "no evidence that higher tariff protection is associated with higher tariff and tax revenues" in a sample of five Latin American countries.

Table 6. Fiscal Impact of Trade Reform Elements

Trade Reform	Expected Fiscal Impact
Reduce moderate or low average tariff	Negative
Reduce high average tariff	Ambiguous
Lower maximum tariff	Ambiguous
Reduce tariff dispersion	Ambiguous/positive
Replace quantitative restrictions with tariffs and liberalize other nontariff barriers on trade	Positive
Eliminate tariff exemptions	Positive
Eliminate trade-related subsidies	Positive
Eliminate state trading monopolies	Ambiguous/positive
Eliminate export taxes	Ambiguous/negative

Sources: IMF data; World Bank data.

revenue, depending on the extent and speed with which it expands total trade and reduces illegal activity such as smuggling.

The net fiscal impact of trade reform will depend crucially upon the mix of elements in the trade reform package, as well as the countries' initial circumstances. Clearly, the above argues for the early focus of trade reform to be broadly based and to include the likely positive revenue elements.[23] Even if a first-round revenue loss from trade reform is anticipated, a preferred policy response would be to increase revenues from other less distorting, more broadly based taxes, such as value-added taxes (VATs) applied equally to imports and domestic production.[24] Tax administration concerns also favor tariff reform in spite of the low cost of administering trade taxes relative to the revenue; this is true both because many elements of tariff reform simplify tax administration by reducing evasion or eliminating exemptions.

Nevertheless, there are some fiscal arguments for gradualism in trade reform. To the extent that trade taxes account for a significant part of fiscal revenue and that total revenue is low, fiscal considerations may be an important factor in the design and pace of trade reform, particularly regarding lowering average tariffs. A shift to more broadly based tax, such as a VAT, will reduce reliance on trade taxes, but generally requires careful preparation. Further, a country may

[23]Papageorgiou, Michaely, and Choksi (1991), World Bank (1992), and Thomas and others (1991) each examined individual country cases from the 1970s and 1980s and found that trade reform may well be associated with an increase in revenue from import taxes when elimination or tariffication of nontariff barriers is an important focus of the trade reform.

[24]From a trade perspective, a VAT may be preferable to a cascading sales tax, since the latter tends to discriminate in favor of imports and against exports.

have difficulty collecting taxes because of an overly complex tax system, lack of effective sanctions for tax offenders, lack of trained personnel, tax avoidance and evasion, and generally weak administrative capacity (Faria and Yücelik, 1995).

The Impact of Fiscal Concerns

The main focus in examining the role of fiscal factors was on the extent to which fiscal considerations might have inhibited the degree of trade reform targeted and implemented. In this context, the fiscal conditions likely to present the most difficulties would include relatively heavy dependence on trade taxes, relatively low revenues in relation to GDP, and a weak overall fiscal position. On this basis, the review included four indicators to assess initial fiscal conditions: (1) the ratio of trade taxes to total taxes; (2) the ratio of trade tax revenue to GDP; (3) the ratio of tax revenue to GDP; and (4) the targeted change in the ratio of the budget deficit to GDP.

The results for these indicators are summarized in Figure 8. As can be seen, a direct relationship between the initial fiscal conditions and the ambitiousness of trade reform targeted, including for the ratio of trade taxes to total taxes, is not evident for the programs reviewed. The review found that there were only three cases in which the initial fiscal conditions may have been expected to act as a constraint on trade reform. In these cases, countries lacked a VAT and at least two of the three conditions of high dependency on trade taxes—low revenue effort and large targeted reduction in the budget deficit—were satisfied.[25] Despite these adverse initial conditions, two of these programs targeted and implemented trade reform of at least 3 points on the 10-point scale, and the third program targeted and implemented trade reform of 2 points on the index. The evidence available in this review, albeit limited, indicates no direct relationship between fiscal conditions and trade reform objectives and that trade reform should not necessarily be ruled out because of a backdrop of difficult fiscal circumstances. This conclusion is consistent with the observation made earlier that a significantly larger proportion of sub-Saharan African countries targeted a reduction in NTBs, compared with those that tar-

[25]Fiscal conditions are considered as a possible constraint on trade reform if trade taxes were a high proportion of total taxes (more than 30 percent), tax revenue was low (less than 10 percent of GDP), the targeted reduction in the budget deficit during the period of the arrangement was high (more than 4 percent of GDP), or if there was no broadly based consumption tax, such as a VAT. These cutoff levels were based on a review of GFS and World Economic Outlook data for developing countries and IMF programs.

Figure 8. Initial Fiscal Indicators for the Sub-Saharan African Programs Reviewed

(Percent)

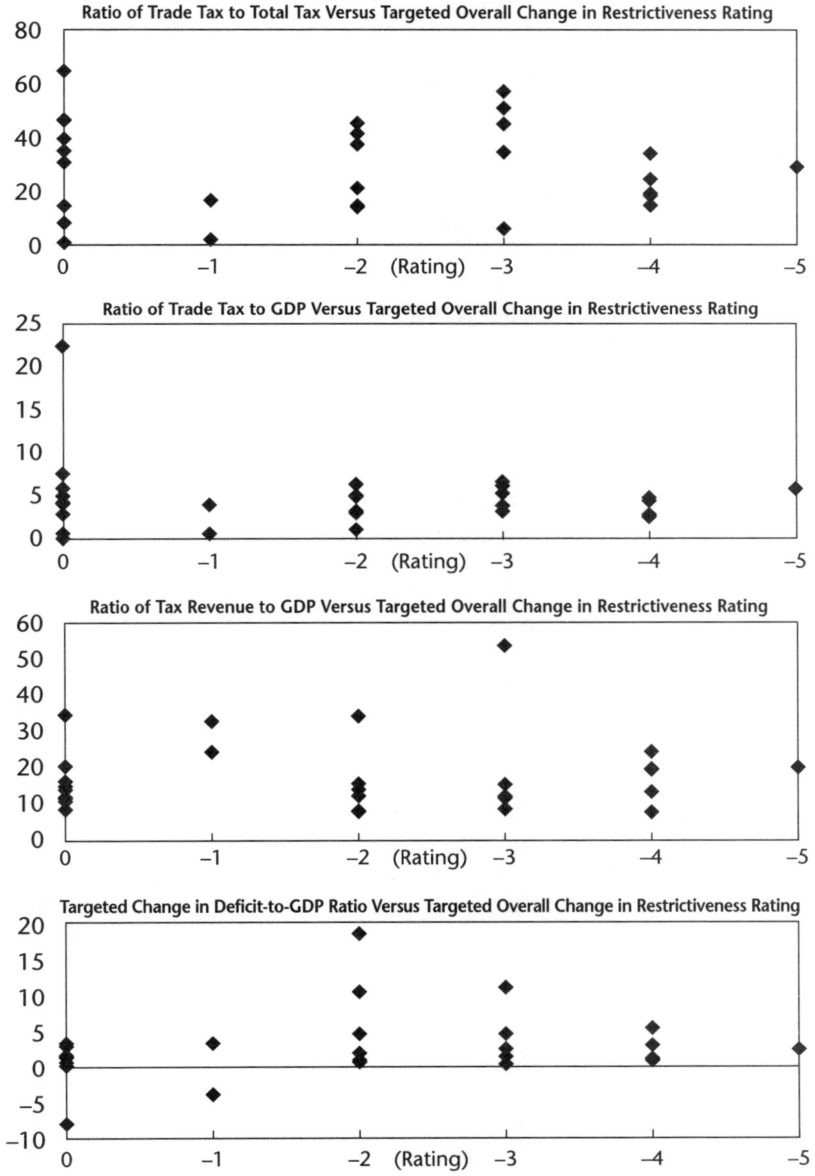

Source: IMF staff estimates.

geted a tariff reduction. Moreover, while it is beyond the scope of this chapter to assess the availability of alternative revenue sources and other fiscal actions, the review indicated that exemptions were noted as a problem in many of the cases, state trading monopolies in a majority of the countries, and as indicated above, NTBs were prevalent throughout.

Nevertheless, the problems posed by introducing trade reform should not be minimized, particularly in cases where that reform is perceived as likely to have negative first-round fiscal implications. Even if alternative revenue sources or expenditure restraint appear to be readily available, action in these areas is likely to pose its own political and economic challenges. Moreover, the consideration of fiscal alternatives will be in the context of program design, which usually involves fiscal pressures in many areas of both revenue and expenditures, including outlays in support of structural reforms other than trade policy. This underlines the importance of introducing broadly based trade reform programs that include, at an early stage, elements such as the tariffication of QRs and other NTBs, reduced exemptions, and trade-related subsidies as well as efforts to broaden the tax base and improve tax administration.

Conclusions

Liberal trade policies complemented by appropriate macroeconomic and other structural policies in IMF-supported adjustment programs have an important impact on allocative efficiency and thereby on economic growth. Trade reform also contributes to improved transparency and good governance by reducing incentives for lobbying for trade protection and opportunities for rent-seeking, and by eliminating administrative discretion. These factors underline the importance of trade reform as a key component of structural adjustment efforts.

The study reported on here found that about 70 percent of those countries in sub-Saharan Africa that were reviewed started IMF-supported programs with relatively restrictive trade regimes, as measured by the index of restrictiveness. The majority of these programs targeted a marked reduction in trade restrictiveness and the targets were, for the most part, achieved. However, a significant number of programs, including for those countries starting with highly restrictive regimes, did not target any quantifiable change in restrictiveness.

The initial position of the sub-Saharan African countries was somewhat more restrictive at the outset of their programs than for the comparator countries outside the region. However, the sub-Saharan African countries targeted somewhat more extensive trade reform, as measured by the index. There were marked differences in the four other regions. As with the sub-Saharan African countries, there was a high degree of success in achieving the targeted trade reforms.

The appropriate degree and pace of trade reform depends crucially on country-specific circumstances. However, a number of factors may be seen as relevant in this regard in moving toward an open trade regime. These include, inter alia, the initial degree of restrictiveness of the trade system, the country's administrative capacity, and the real or perceived short-term adjustment costs. The experience of the good practice countries that achieved open trade regimes within 7–10 years is also instructive, and suggests that trade reform should be viewed as a medium- to long-term process. This highlights the importance of well-specified and comprehensive medium-term program targets for trade reform. Several sub-Saharan African countries have recently made significant progress in trade liberalization in the context of broad structural reform efforts and are expected to achieve levels of openness similar to the good practice countries during the next few years. As a result of this liberalization, together with other structural reforms and an appropriate macroeconomic framework, these countries have already achieved an improvement in their growth, export, and investment performance.

Fiscal considerations were the main factors cited as having influenced trade reform objectives. However, the review found no direct relationship between the strength of trade reform objectives and achievements and countries' initial fiscal circumstances. The initial fiscal impact of trade reform is not necessarily adverse and will depend on country-specific circumstances and the mix of components in the trade reform package. Certain elements of trade reform are likely to strengthen a country's fiscal position, particularly replacing QRs and other NTBs by tariffs, and eliminating customs duty exemptions and trade-related subsidies. This suggests that trade reform should be as broadly based as possible and include these elements in the initial stages of reform. Even where the first-round fiscal effects of trade reform are negative, alternative less distortionary sources of fiscal revenue should be mobilized to the extent feasible.

Methodological Appendix

This appendix presents the methodological basis for the review of trade policy in IMF-supported programs, including the selection of IMF arrangements for review, and the 10-point scale for classifying the restrictiveness of trade regimes. The approach will also be compared with other studies on trade reform in developing countries.

The study reviews programs supported by IMF arrangements to provide a basis for assessing the ambitiousness of trade reform in IMF-supported programs and the implementation record. The trade regime of each country is examined at the outset of the program and its overall trade restrictiveness is assessed, based on a 10-point scale, with a rating of 1 indicating an open trade regime and a rating of 10 indicating a highly restrictive regime, as described below. The index combines the restrictive effects of import tariffs and NTBs.

The ambitiousness of targeted trade reform can be assessed by identifying the trade content of each program and assessing how far along the 10-point scale these measures would have moved the trade regime if fully implemented.

The implementation of trade reform is assessed by evaluating the overall restrictiveness of the regime at the end of the program period, again based on the 10-point scale.

Selection of IMF Arrangements for Review

The review covers all IMF arrangements of two years or more in length, that were approved after 1990 and that ended by June 30, 1996. Arrangements of less than 2 years duration are excluded, because these typically focus on financial stabilization and would be expected to have less emphasis on structural policies, including trade policy reforms. The cutoff point of mid-1996 was selected to ensure the availability of at least one staff report that follows the conclusion of the arrangement to permit a proper assessment of performance under the IMF-supported program. On this basis, 30 arrangements supporting 28 programs for 27 countries were reviewed, of which 16 arrangements supporting 14 programs for 13 sub-Saharan African countries were included. These included arrangements under the EFF, SAF, and ESAF,[26] as well as two Rights Accumulation Programs (RAPs), and four Stand-by Arrangements.

Ten-Point Classification

The overall restrictiveness of trade regimes is assessed based on a 10-point scale, which combines measures of the trade restrictiveness of import tariffs and NTBs. Five ranges are specified for import tariffs, with the lowest range (0–10 percent) being the least restrictive and the

[26]The ESAF arrangements with Burundi and Rwanda, both of which began in 1991, are excluded.

Table 7. Classification Scheme for Overall Trade Restrictiveness

	Nontariff Barriers		
	Open	Moderate	Restrictive
Tariffs			
Open	1	4	7
Relatively open	2	5	8
Moderate	3	6	9
Relatively restrictive	4	7	10
Restrictive	5	8	10

Source: IMF staff estimates.

highest range (25 percent and above) being the most restrictive. Three categories have been specified for NTBs, ranging from open to restrictive. These categories are based on the number of sectors covered by NTBs (whether NTBs are confined to a few sectors of the economy), on the production (whether they cover entire stages of production) on trade coverage of these barriers, and on their restrictiveness.

The five classifications of import tariffs and three classifications of NTBs yield a 15-cell matrix. Within the matrix, the cells were converted to a 10-point scale by assigning a relative ranking, from 1 to 10, representing the overall restrictiveness of the trade regime. The most open import tariff and NTB regimes were assigned the number 1, and the most restrictive tariff and NTB regimes were assigned the number 10.

Overall Trade Restrictiveness Classification

The following matrix (Table 7) illustrates the assignment of tariff and NTB categories on the 10-point scale. This assignment places more weight on restrictiveness of NTBs, which are inherently less transparent and more distortionary than tariffs.

The restrictiveness of the import tariff regime depends on many factors, including the minimum and maximum tariff rates, the number of bands, the allocation of individual items to the bands, existence of "exceptional" rates that lie outside the basic tariff structure, any other duties and charges (such as differential rates of excise or VAT taxes on imports, import surcharges, and statistical fees), and the extent of customs duty exemptions. The amount of information available on the tariff regime varies considerably among the countries. In many cases, there was enough information to compute an average tariff rate but insufficient information to assess the degree of tariff dispersion or the prevalence of discretionary customs duty exemptions (as opposed to statutory zero customs duty rates). In view of

Table 8. Classification Scheme for Tariff Restrictiveness

Restrictiveness	Average Tariff Range (*t*)
Open	$0 \leq t < 10$ percent
Relatively open	$10 \leq t < 15$ percent
Moderate	$15 \leq t < 20$ percent
Relatively restrictive	$20 \leq t < 25$ percent
Restrictive	25 percent or higher

Source: IMF staff estimates.

these limitations, the study adopted a pragmatic approach and utilized the average import tariff rate as a basis for classifying the tariff regime.[27]

The five-category ranking of average import tariffs is shown in Table 8. The five classifications are based on the average tariff rates of all IMF member countries.

Broadly equal numbers of IMF members fell into each of these ranges based on the latest available information on average import tariff rates. Alternative ranges were considered in connection with the results of the review, but did not have any significant impact on the aggregate classifications of restrictiveness.

Countries employ a wide variety of restrictions on imports and exports other than tariffs, including import/export quotas, restrictive licensing, bans, state trading/monopolies, restrictive foreign exchange allocation, and multiple exchange rates. Such measures in effect provide indirect subsidies to import-competing domestic producers in a nontransparent manner. Information on the presence of NTBs and their restrictiveness (as measured for instance by ad valorem equivalents[28])

[27]The preferred approach was to use, where possible, an unweighted average based on statutory tariff rates and including any other duties and charges applicable to imports. An average of statutory tariff rates is preferable to an average based on customs duties collected since the latter reflect (often extensive) exemptions. An unweighted average is preferable to a trade-weighted average since items with high tariffs would likely have small trade weights. Other duties and charges should be included because these have the same restrictive effects as tariffs.

[28]The ad valorem equivalent of an import quota is the rate of ad valorem tariff that would yield the same import quantity as the quota. There are many circumstances in which import quotas and import tariffs are not equivalent, including where market structures are imperfectly competitive or where trading partners may retaliate against increases in tariffs or quotas; see Bhagwati and Srinivasan (1983) for further discussion and references. Notwithstanding these well-known theoretical difficulties, price-equivalents of NTBs are often computed by comparing domestic with world market prices. Quantification of the price-equivalent of an export restriction is often accomplished in a similar manner.

Table 9. Classification Scheme for NTB Restrictiveness

NTB Regime	Classification Criteria
Open	• NTBs are either absent or minor. • Less than 1 percent of production or trade is subject to NTBs.
Moderate	• NTBs are significant, covering at least one important sector of the economy (e.g., agriculture or textiles) but not pervasive (for example, all consumer goods). • Between 1 and 25 percent of production or trade is subject to NTBs.
Restrictive	• Many sectors or entire stages of production (e.g., all consumer goods) are covered by NTBs. • More than 25 percent of production or trade is subject to NTBs.

Source: IMF staff.
Note: NTB denotes nontariff barrier.

may be limited;[29] the review of previous studies on trade reform in developing countries below shows that others have faced similar difficulties. In view of this, three ranges of NTBs[30] have been utilized in this study, as explained in Table 9.

While more trade variables (such as tariff dispersion or customs duty exemptions) could in principle be included in the overall index of trade restrictiveness, by adding dimensions to the 15-cell matrix, data difficulties and added complexity strongly support the approach of omitting these factors from the overall index. In principle, it would also be preferable to assess the effects of trade restrictions on prices and resource allocation, but this is very difficult and time-consuming even for industrial countries; it is infeasible for the countries analyzed in this review.

References

Baldwin, Robert E., 1985, *The Political Economy of U.S. Import Policy* (Cambridge, Massachusetts: MIT Press).

Barro, Robert J., and Xavier Sala-i-Martin, 1995, *Economic Growth* (New York: McGraw-Hill).

Bhagwati, Jagdish, N., 1982, "Directly Unproductive, Profit-Seeking (DUP) Activities," *Journal of Political Economy*, Vol. 90, No. 5, pp. 988–1002.

[29]Trade or production coverage of NTBs measures the presence of NTBs but does not fully capture their restrictiveness.

[30]NTBs include quantitative restrictions, state trade monopolies, restrictive foreign exchange practices that affect the trade regime (e.g., a surrender requirement at a nonmarket exchange rate), quality controls, and customs procedures that act as trade restrictions.

———, and T.N. Srinivasan, 1973, "The General Equilibrium Theory of Effective Protection," *Journal of International Economics,* Vol. 3, pp. 259–81.

———, 1983, *Lectures in International Trade* (Cambridge, Massachusetts: MIT Press).

Brecher, Richard A., and Carlos F. Diaz-Alejandro, 1977, "Tariffs, Foreign Capital, and Immiserizing Growth," *Journal of International Economics,* Vol. 7, pp. 317–22.

Coe, David T., and Elhanan Helpman, 1993, "International R&D Spillovers, "IMF Working Paper 93/84 (Washington: International Monetary Fund).

Dixit, Avinash, 1985, "Tax Policy in Open Economies," in *Handbook of Public Economics,* Vol. 1, ed. by A.J. Auerbach and M. Feldstein (Amsterdam: North-Holland), pp. 313–74.

Faria, Angelo G.A., and M. Zühtü Yücelik, 1995, "The Interrelationship Between Tax Policy and Tax Administration," in *Tax Policy Handbook,* ed. by Parthasarathi Shome (Washington: International Monetary Fund).

Frankel, Jeffrey A., David Romer, and Teresa Cyrus, 1996, "Trade and Growth in East Asian Countries: Cause and Effect?" NBER Working Paper 5732 (Cambridge, Massachusetts: National Bureau of Economic Research).

GATT (General Agreement on Tariffs and Trade), 1990, *Trade Policy Review of New Zealand* (Geneva).

———, 1991, *Trade Policy Review of Chile* (Geneva).

IMF (International Monetary Fund), 1993, *World Economic Outlook, May 1993: A Survey by the Staff of the International Monetary Fund,* World Economic and Financial Surveys (Washington: International Monetary Fund).

———, 1994, *International Trade Policies: The Uruguay Round and Beyond* (Washington: International Monetary Fund).

———, 1997, *World Economic Outlook, May 1997: A Survey by the Staff of the International Monetary Fund,* World Economic and Financial Surveys (Washington: International Monetary Fund).

Kirmani, Naheed, and others, 1994, *International Trade Policies: The Uruguay Round and Beyond,* Vol. 1, *Principal Issues,* and Vol. 2, *Background Papers,* World Economic and Financial Surveys (Washington: International Monetary Fund).

Krueger, Anne O., 1974, "The Political Economy of the Rent-Seeking Society," *American Economic Review,* Vol. 64, pp. 291–303.

———, 1993, *Political Economy of Policy Reform in Developing Countries* (Cambridge, Massachusetts: MIT Press).

Leidy, Michael P., 1995, "The Political Economy of Trade Policy and the Implications for Trade Policy Reform" (unpublished; Washington: International Monetary Fund).

Magee, Stephen P., William A. Brock, and Leslie Young, 1989, *Black Hole Tariffs and Endogenous Policy Theory: Political Economy in General Equilibrium* (Cambridge: Cambridge University Press).

Nogués, Julio, and Sunil Gulati, 1992, *Economic Policies and Performance Under Alternative Trade Regimes: Latin America During the 1980s* (Washington: World Bank).

Papageorgiou, Demitris, Michael Michaely, and Armeane M. Choksi, eds., 1991, *Liberalizing Foreign Trade,* 7 vols. (Cambridge, Massachusetts: Blackwell).

PECC (Pacific Economic Cooperation Council for APEC), 1995, *Survey of Impediments to Trade and Investment in the APEC Region* (Singapore: Pacific Economic Cooperation Council for the Asia Pacific Economic Cooperation Secretariat).

Rajapatirana, Sarath, 1996, "Trade Policies, Macroeconomic Adjustment, and Manufactured Exports: The Latin American Experience," in *Weltwirschaftliches Archiv,* Vol. 132, No. 3, pp. 558–85.

Rodrik, Dani, 1995, "Political Economy of Trade Policy," in *Handbook of International Economics,* Vol. 3, ed. by Gene M. Grossman and Kenneth Rogoff (Amsterdam: North-Holland).

Sachs, Jeffrey D., and Andrew Warner, 1995, "Economic Reform and the Process of Global Integration," *Brookings Papers on Economic Activity: 1* (April), pp. 1–118.

Stotsky, Janet, 1995, "Summary of IMF Tax Policy Advice," in *Tax Policy Handbook,* ed. by Parthasarathi Shome (Washington: International Monetary Fund).

Summers, Robert, and Alan Heston, 1991, "The Penn World Table (Mark 5) and Expanded Set of International Comparisons, 1950–88," *Quarterly Journal of Economics,* Vol. 106, pp. 327–68.

Thomas, Vinod, John Nash, and Associates, 1991, *Best Practices in Trade Policy Reform* (New York: Oxford University Press).

Williamson, John, ed., 1994, *The Political Economy of Policy Reform* (Washington: Institute for International Economics).

World Bank, 1987, *World Development Report 1987* (New York: Oxford University Press).

———, 1991, *World Development Report 1991* (New York: Oxford University Press).

———, 1992, *Trade Policy Reforms Under Adjustment Programs* (Washington: World Bank).

———, 1993, *The East Asian Miracle: Economic Growth and Public Policy* (New York: Oxford University Press).

———, 1997, *World Development Report 1997* (New York: Oxford University Press).

WTO (World Trade Organization), 1996a, *Trade Policy Review of Colombia* (Geneva).

———, 1996b, *Trade Policy Review of New Zealand* (Geneva).

———, 1996c, *Trade Policy Review of the Republic of Korea* (Geneva).

———, 1996d, *Trade Policy Review of Singapore* (Geneva).

The Revenue Implications of Trade Liberalization 5

Liam P. Ebrill and Janet G. Stotsky

Trade liberalization is part of the global trend toward economic integration. In recent decades, many countries have dismantled trade barriers to open their economies to international competition.[1] This trend toward liberalization has promoted economic efficiency, international competitiveness, and an expansion of trade.

Trade liberalization can take many forms, including unilateral liberalization, multilateral liberalization, and liberalization in the context of customs unions and free trade areas. Multilateral and regional trade arrangements are drawing an ever-larger number of countries within their scope (Harmsen and Leidy, 1994). The conclusion of the Uruguay Round in 1994 and the establishment of the World Trade Organization in 1995 provided a forum for advancing multilateral trade arrangements. Regional trade arrangements have also been given new impetus in recent years. Almost every region of the world has witnessed the establishment of a regional trade arrangement. For example, there are several regional trade arrangements in sub-Saharan Africa. These include the Central African Customs and Economic Union (UDEAC), the West African Economic and Monetary Union (UEMOA), and the Cross-Border Initiative (CBI) among countries in eastern and southern Africa. Regional trade arrangements are also forming in the Mediterranean region. The European Union has recently launched a program to create a free trade area with Southern and Eastern Mediterranean Rim countries.[2]

Note: In addition to the authors, Asegedech WoldeMariam contributed all tables and figures, and Reint Gropp contributed the case study on the Philippines and to the main text, Dominique Simard, the case study on Senegal, and M. Zuhtu Yucelik, the case study on Morocco. The authors also acknowledge valuable comments from George Abed, Michael Keen, Stephen O'Connell, colleagues in the IMF's Fiscal Affairs, African, Asian, and Middle Eastern departments, and participants in the Institute Conference. The opinions expressed in this chapter are strictly those of the authors and do not necessarily reflect the official views of the International Monetary Fund.

[1]For an analysis of the economic benefits and costs of trade liberalization, see Krueger (1995).

[2]In North America, the North American Free Trade Area (NAFTA) has linked the United States, Mexico, and Canada; Argentina, Brazil, Paraguay, and Uruguay have formed the Southern Cone Common Market (MERCOSUR); and in East Asia, the ASEAN (Association of Southeast Asian Nations) Free Trade Arrangement (AFTA) was established.

Nevertheless, despite the obvious progress, trade barriers are still pervasive. In some parts of the developing world, in particular, economies remain insulated from the global economy through a variety of nontariff and tariff barriers, even as the philosophy of import substitution continues to lose ground as a basis for economic development. Arguments advanced against trade liberalization include that trade taxes are needed to protect "infant industries," and also to protect domestic producers from "unfair" trading practices of other nations.[3]

In addition, trade liberalization can be stymied by the concern that it will lead to a loss of tax revenues, and hence a worsening of the government's budgetary balance. This consideration can be especially important if the country is already experiencing significant fiscal imbalances, as has been the case with a number of developing countries.[4] Moreover, for many developing countries, taxes on international trade are a large (and sometimes the largest) source of government revenue. This is particularly the case with sub-Saharan African countries (see Table 1 and Figures 1 and 2), where international trade taxes accounted for 5.0 percent of GDP (using an unweighted average over all the countries).[5]

This chapter focuses on the revenue implications of trade liberalization, a topic which has yet to receive much attention.[6] Despite being typically a suboptimal way to raise revenue,[7] trade taxes are often justified on fiscal grounds in addition to providing protection to domestic producers. However, the revenue implications of trade liberalization depend on how trade reforms are implemented. Some trade reforms improve the structure of protection but may not necessarily lower overall nominal tariff rates. For example, if the sequencing of trade reforms initially favors: (1) the tariffication of quantitative restrictions; (2) the reduction or elimination of exemptions; (3) higher compliance and reduced incentives for smuggling through lower tariff rates; and

[3]See Escolano (1995), Subramanian, Ibrahim, and Torres-Castro (1993), and Farhadian-Lorie and Katz (1988).

[4]For example, the group of African countries that entered into SAF or ESAF arrangements with the IMF during the 1980s and 1990s had overall fiscal deficits averaging more than 9 percent of GDP in their respective preprogram years. See Abed and others (1998).

[5]In interpreting these numbers, note that it is not always possible to obtain a clean separation of customs tariffs per se from other indirect taxes, such as excises and sales taxes, that are also collected at customs (e.g., Benin, Burkina Faso, Mali, and Tanzania).

[6]Exceptions include Blejer and Cheasty (1990); Datta-Mitra (1997); Greenaway and Milner (1991); IMF (1997); Mitra (1992); Rajaram (1994); and Tanzi (1991).

[7]While the optimal tax/tariff solution depends on the range of tax instruments available to the government and the structure of the economy, for one benchmark case (that of the small open economy with the full range of commodity taxes available and no other distortions), the solution to the optimal tax problem has no role for tariffs due to the desirability of ensuring production efficiency (for example, Dixit and Norman, 1980).

Table 1. Sub-Saharan African Countries: Elements of Tax Structure, 1995

(As percentage of GDP)

				Taxes on Income, Profits, and Capital Gains			Domestic Taxes on Goods and Services[2]			International Trade Taxes[2]		
					Of which:			Of which:			Of which:	
Country[1]	Total Revenue	Tax Revenue	Other Revenue	Total	Individual	Corporate	Total	General sales, turnover, or VAT	Excises	Total	Import duties	Export duties
Angola	28.30	28.01	0.29	19.55	0.68	18.87	6.43	. . .	5.76	1.38	. . .	. . .
Benin[3,4]	14.40	11.88	2.52	3.88	0.85	2.50	1.85	1.01	0.34	5.82	5.44	0.03
Botswana[5]	36.48	27.00	9.49	7.73	1.43	6.30	1.57	1.47	0.10	5.58	5.58	0.00
Burkina Faso[3,4]	11.88	10.95	0.93	2.55	1.06	1.38	3.68	2.77	0.29	4.47	4.47	0.00
Burundi[3]	18.83	17.81	1.02	3.62	1.62	1.74	7.09	2.75	4.26	6.98	2.98	3.92
Cameroon[3,4,6]	14.33	10.62	3.71	1.43	0.00	1.43	2.82	1.14	1.09	2.75	2.58	0.17
Cape Verde	26.08	19.89	6.20	6.62	1.89	3.35	3.34	. . .	3.34	8.38	8.24	. . .
Central African Republic[3,4]	9.06	8.65	0.40	1.86	0.86	0.76	2.94	0.62	0.30	3.85	3.15	0.70
Chad[3,4]	8.40	7.44	0.96	2.92	1.35	1.57	1.23	0.32	0.38	2.28	1.80	0.27
Comoros[3]	14.22	12.26	1.95	1.74	0.59	1.09	3.47	1.17	2.30	2.47	1.15	0.38
Congo, Republic of [3,4,6]	24.84	12.95	11.89	3.13	1.48	1.64	3.76	2.46	1.29	4.76	4.76	. . .
Côte d'Ivoire[3,4]	21.92	17.83	4.09	4.02	1.37	1.81	7.54	4.50	2.32	6.28	2.75	3.52
Djibouti	28.38	26.76	1.61	10.72	3.60	1.92	8.93	8.93	. . .	5.53	. . .	. . .
Equatorial Guinea [3,4,6]	14.85	9.27	5.58	0.42	. . .	. . .	3.59	2.15	. . .	4.33	1.57	2.76
Eritrea[3]	28.73	15.29	13.45	7.26	1.58	3.95	5.12	5.12	. . .	2.91	2.91	. . .
Ethiopia[3,5]	17.88	12.37	5.51	4.29	0.86	2.57	5.17	3.79	0.26	2.63	2.32	0.31
Gabon[3,6]	29.52	21.41	8.11	3.11	1.38	1.73	2.49	2.08	. . .	5.20	4.47	. . .
Gambia, The[3,5,7]	19.46	17.45	2.02	3.95	1.61	2.14	9.29	4.34	4.94	4.21	4.21	. . .
Ghana[3]	22.31	15.03	7.29	3.63	1.07	2.07	6.65	2.77	3.88	4.75	2.67	2.07
Guinea[3,8]	11.02	10.33	0.69	1.01	0.57	0.29	4.70	1.44	2.37	1.59	1.50	0.02

Guinea-Bissau[3]	12.65	6.91	5.74	1.00	0.26	0.61	2.13	2.07	0.06	3.46	1.31	0.56
Kenya[3,5]	29.18	25.97	3.21	9.64	. . .	. . .	12.09	5.70	6.39	4.25	4.25	. . .
Lesotho[5]	46.47	39.06	7.41	7.62	5.39	2.05	6.10	4.81	. . .	25.06	25.05	0.01
Madagascar[3]	8.52	8.32	0.21	1.24	0.43	0.62	4.30	3.88	0.01	2.62	1.19	0.33
Malawi[3,5]	17.93	15.58	2.36	5.68	2.89	2.79	5.82	5.01	0.75	4.53	3.02	1.43
Mali[3,4]	14.40	10.68	3.72	2.16	1.15	0.88	2.96	2.81	. . .	4.35	4.02	0.12
Mauritania[3]	23.96	17.01	6.96	5.89	2.82	2.79	5.43	3.46	1.80	5.39	3.41	1.98
Mauritius[5]	17.52	15.96	1.56	2.74	1.38	1.36	5.15	. . .	. . .	6.80	6.80	. . .
Mozambique[3]	18.29	16.69	1.60	3.03	1.64	1.39	8.73	5.13	3.60	4.40	3.16	0.00
Namibia[5]	34.32	30.80	3.53	9.42	5.83	3.32	10.94	7.45	2.64	9.82	. . .	0.03
Niger[3,4]	7.23	6.62	0.62	1.93	. . .	. . .	1.29	. . .	. . .	3.12	. . .	. . .
Nigeria[9]	23.00	7.00	16.00	1.40	1.40	. . .	5.60	1.40	2.90	. . .	. . .	. . .
Rwanda[3]	7.05	6.63	0.43	0.82	0.49	0.24	3.02	0.92	1.74	2.75	2.11	0.55
São Tomé and Príncipe[3]	16.54	9.79	6.74	2.33	0.92	1.28	2.85	2.85	. . .	3.98	3.02	0.95
Senegal [1,3,10]	15.07	13.59	1.48	3.09	1.81	0.85	5.05	4.64	0.28	4.81	4.81	. . .
Seychelles[11]	40.01	28.93	11.07	5.29	. . .	. . .	20.33	. . .	1.29	. . .	. . .	. . .
Sierra Leone[3,5]	9.40	9.17	0.23	1.36	0.72	0.64	5.05	2.41	1.90	2.56	4.61	. . .
South Africa[5]	25.66	24.86	0.80	13.67	10.24	3.42	9.61	6.52	1.31	1.26	1.22	. . .
Sudan[5]	8.69	6.87	1.83	2.49	0.17	1.99	1.66	0.24	1.42	2.52	1.43	0.19
Swaziland[5]	33.69	32.76	0.94	9.44	4.04	4.83	5.36	4.16	. . .	17.88	. . .	. .
Tanzania[3,5]	14.95	12.80	2.15	3.74	1.08	1.71	5.44	3.10	2.34	2.04	2.04	. . .
Togo[3,4]	15.05	13.76	1.28	6.23	1.44	0.80	1.72	0.85	0.70	5.61	4.59	. . .
Uganda[3,5]	10.32	9.69	0.63	1.36	. . .	. . .	3.77	2.67	1.10	4.54	3.72	. . .
Zaïre	5.35	4.93	0.42	1.23	0.44	0.39	1.16	0.56	0.41	1.45	1.33	0.13
Zambia[3]	16.92	15.50	1.42	4.90	3.81	1.09	5.46	3.06	2.40	4.63	. . .	. . .
Zimbabwe[5]	28.49	24.30	4.19	12.28	6.76	4.29	5.95	4.60	1.35	5.62	5.62	. . .

Table 1 (*concluded*)

Country[1]	Total Revenue	Tax Revenue	Other Revenue	Taxes on Income, Profits, and Capital Gains: Total	Of which: Individual	Of which: Corporate	Domestic Taxes on Goods and Services[2]: Total	Of which: General sales, turnover, or VAT	Of which: Excises	International Trade Taxes[2]: Total	Of which: Import duties	Of which: Export duties
Unweighted average, all countries	19.60	15.81	3.79	4.64	1.96	2.35	5.19	3.10	1.88	4.99	3.93	0.85
Unweighted average, SPA countries	15.79	12.54	3.25	3.23	1.23	1.46	4.65	2.78	1.81	3.97	3.09	0.88
Unweighted average, CFA franc zone countries	15.46	11.97	3.48	2.82	1.16	1.40	3.15	2.11	0.78	4.43	3.70	0.95

Sources: Country authorities; IMF staff estimates.

[1]Excluding Liberia and Somalia.

[2]For differentiating the taxes we have used Recent Economic Developments (REDs) except we have reclassified any clearly identified indirect taxes on imports from taxes on international trade to domestic taxes on goods and services.

[3]Special program of assistance countries (SPA).

[4]CFA franc zone countries.

[5]Fiscal year.

[6]Including tax revenue from oil.

[7]Data refer to 1994.

[8]Refers to mining sector revenue.

[9]Data exclude royalty and direct profit income from petroleum production.

[10]Fiscal year ending June 30, through 1991/92; calendar year data starting in 1992.

[11]The trade and service tax replaced import duties, excise taxes, and turnover taxes in 1986; however, payment of certain turnover liabilities were deferred through 1991.

Figure 1. Sub-Saharan African Countries: Relationship of Trade Tax Share to Tax Index, 1995

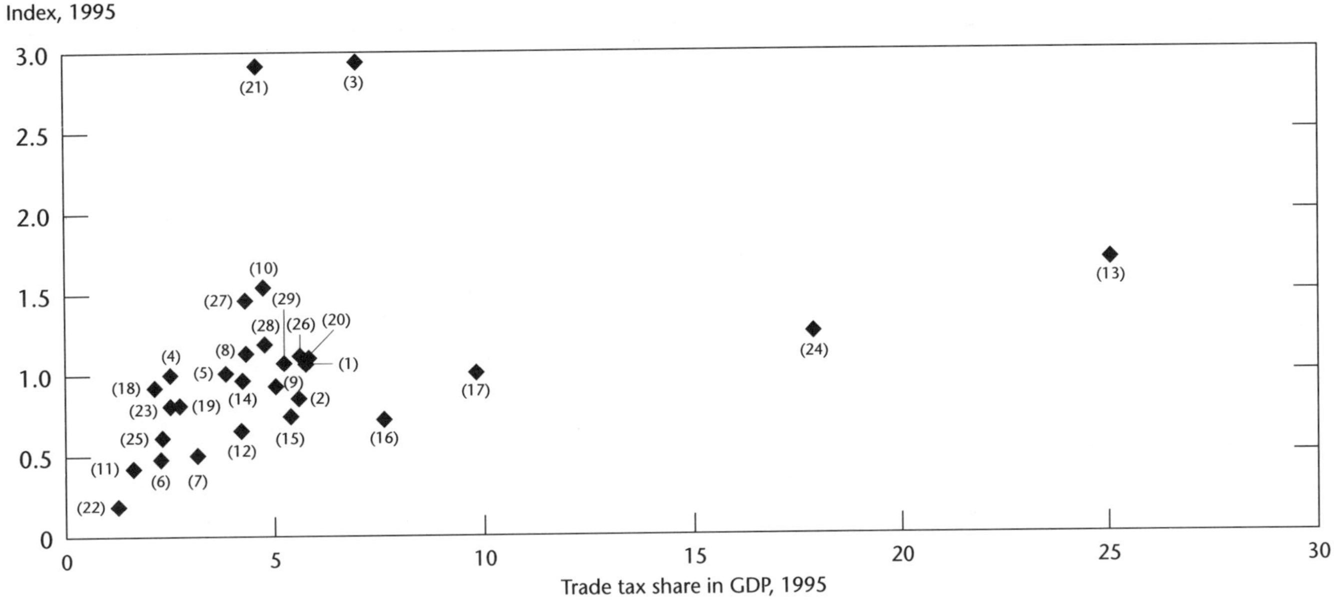

Sources: Data provided by the country authorities; IMF staff calculations.

Key: (1) Benin, (2) Botswana, (3) Burundi, (4) Cameroon, (5) Central African Republic, (6) Chad, (7) Republic of Congo, (8) Equatorial Guinea, (9) Gabon, (10) Ghana, (11) Guinea, (12) Kenya, (13) Lesotho, (14) Mali, (15) Mauritania, (16) Mauritius, (17) Namibia, (18) Niger, (19) Rwanda, (20) Senegal, (21) Sierra Leone, (22) South Africa, (23) Sudan, (24) Swaziland, (25) Tanzania, (26) Togo, (27) Uganda, (28) Zambia, (29) Zimbabwe.

Note: This sample includes sub-Saharan African countries for which complete data were available. Data refer to 1993 for Equatorial Guinea, Gabon, Senegal, and Zambia. Data refer to 1994 for Cameroon, the Republic of Congo, Guinea, and Sierra Leone.

Figure 2. Sub-Saharan African Countries: Change in Trade Tax Indexes, 1990–95

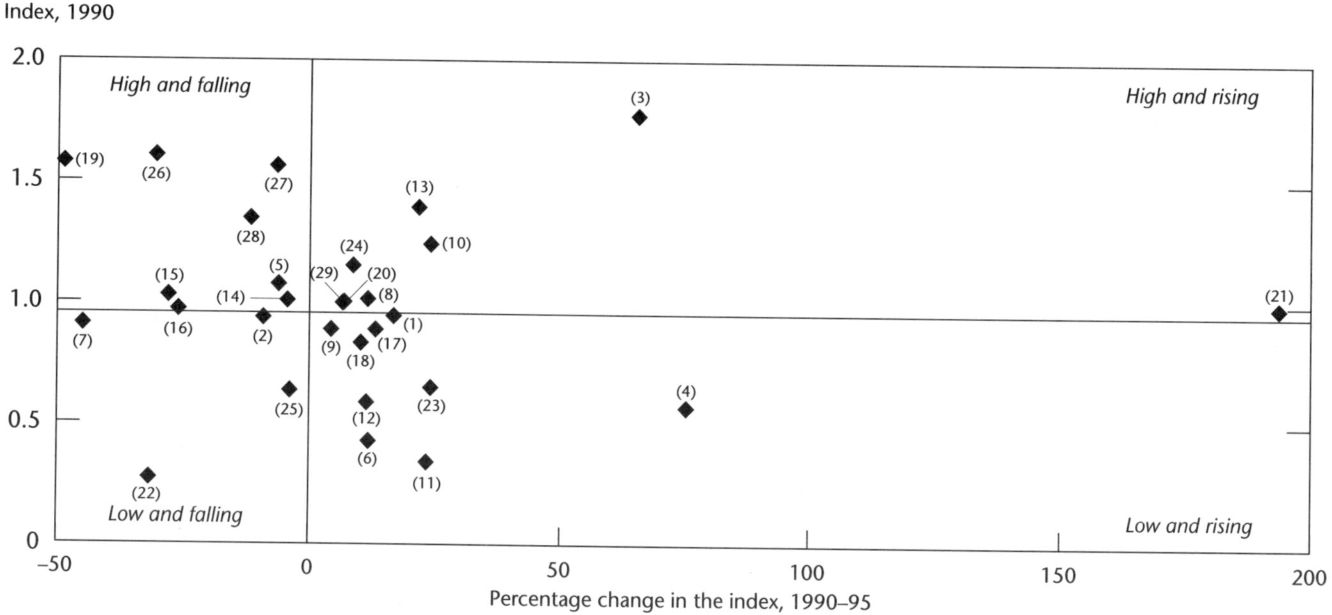

Sources: Data provided by the country authorities; IMF staff calculations.

Key: (1) Benin, (2) Botswana, (3) Burundi, (4) Cameroon, (5) Central African Republic, (6) Chad, (7) Republic of Congo, (8) Equatorial Guinea, (9) Gabon, (10) Ghana, (11) Guinea, (12) Kenya, (13) Lesotho, (14) Mali, (15) Mauritania, (16) Mauritius, (17) Namibia, (18) Niger, (19) Rwanda, (20) Senegal, (21) Sierra Leone, (22) South Africa, (23) Sudan, (24) Swaziland, (25) Tanzania, (26) Togo, (27) Uganda, (28) Zambia, (29) Zimbabwe.

Note: This sample includes sub-Saharan African countries for which complete data were available. Data refer to 1993 for Equatorial Guinea, Gabon, Senegal, and Zambia. Data refer to 1994 for Cameroon, the Republic of Congo, Guinea, and Sierra Leone.

(4) increased minimum tariff rates to reduce tariff dispersion, such reforms could be consistent with an increase in trade revenues. In contrast, if trade reforms entail lowering of nominal tariff rates, then a decrease in trade revenues is more likely; though expansion of the import base as a result of lower tariffs, the often accompanying devaluation of the currency, and faster growth, may buoy trade tax revenues.

The ability to reduce the taxation of international trade while maintaining adequate overall revenue collections also depends on both a well-functioning system of domestic taxation and effective tax and customs administrations. This chapter accordingly also reviews the role played by the domestic tax structure and tax and customs administrations in influencing the pace of trade liberalization and suggests a set of best practices for domestic tax reform, which over time would permit a reduction in a country's reliance on international trade taxes. Nonetheless, even if reforms are implemented expeditiously, significant shifts in the structure of revenues will emerge only over prolonged periods of time. The combination of the level of economic development and associated economic structure will tend to be the preponderant influence on the tax system that typically emerges. Only as domestic productive capacity (and hence the domestic tax base) grows and broadens and administrative capacities improve will a major shift from international trade taxation to domestic taxation occur.

The remainder of the chapter is organized as follows. The second section examines the revenue implications of trade liberalization, drawing on case studies of Malawi, Morocco, the Philippines, and Senegal. The third section examines trends in tax collections on international trade. The fourth section concludes. The appendix presents the case studies.

Revenue Implications of Trade Reform

Economists typically favor a sequencing of trade liberalization reforms, with quantitative restrictions and other nontariff barriers to trade being liberalized first, followed by tariff reform, including a reduction in both the number and dispersion of tariff rates, and an overall reduction in the levels of tariffs. By focusing initially on the removal of nontariff barriers, it may be possible to preserve the revenue yield while at the same time reducing the severe distortions associated with nontariff barriers.[8] In practice, however, there is no specific observed

[8]For example, in addition to not providing revenue to the budget, quotas are associated with wasteful rent-seeking activities that would typically be more significant than the excess burden distortions associated with traditional tariffs.

pattern to liberalization, and some countries have pursued alternative sequences or only chosen to liberalize certain aspects of the trade regime. What are the economic consequences and revenue implications of the disparate elements of trade liberalization?

Reform of Quantitative Restrictions

Reducing quantitative restrictions is typically a high priority of trade liberalization. In their study of countries undergoing World Bank–assisted trade liberalization, Papageorgiou, Choksi, and Michaely (1990) conclude that half of strong liberalizations included significant reductions in quantitative restrictions and that this was a critical ingredient for success, facilitating an overall high success rate. Liberalizations that did not include a significant element of reduction of these restrictions had a much lower rate of success.

Takacs (1990) outlines the different methods of liberalizing import quotas. These include: (1) raising quota ceilings on imports to allow the volume of imports subject to the quota to rise in gradual fashion until the quota is raised to a nonbinding level; (2) converting quotas into equivalent tariffs with the ultimate goal of reducing these tariffs (in theory, the equivalent tariff is set at a rate equal to the percentage difference between the domestic price and the import price under the quantitative restriction, though, in practice, it may be difficult to establish the equivalent tariff); (3) auctioning licenses or permits to import a specific quantity of the item (the number of licenses can then be gradually increased or these licenses can be converted into tariffs); and (4) converting quotas to tariff quotas (i.e., there are two rates of tariffs—a lower rate applied to some volume of imports and a higher, often prohibitive, rate applied to any imports above that volume) and then reducing the tariff rates.

Of course, quantitative restrictions take many forms other than quotas, including bans, restrictive practices for import licenses, state trading monopolies, and so forth. In addition, in many countries, limits on the ability to buy foreign exchange constrain imports (at least through formal markets). These controls often give rise to black markets in the currency, where purchasers pay a significant premium over official exchange rates to obtain controlled foreign exchange. These restrictions have serious efficiency and distributional implications for markets, especially by encouraging rent-seeking activities.

Some of the patterns of quantitative restrictions have been regional. For example, in CFA franc zone countries, these restrictions generally took the form of bans, quotas, import licenses, and state trading monopolies. In non–CFA franc zone sub-Saharan African countries, foreign exchange controls have been especially prevalent. In their review of trade liberalization in Africa, Dean, Desai, and Riedel (1994) note that, in almost all non–CFA franc zone countries, highly overvalued exchange rates (with large black market premiums) and extensive restrictions on the allocation of foreign exchange were the principal trade barriers and that initial reforms emphasized the liberalization of the foreign exchange market.

Although liberalizing quantitative restrictions is generally the first step in trade reform, it is unusual for countries to liberalize all quantitative restrictions at once. Typically, countries liberalize these restrictions over some period of time to minimize disruptions to the domestic economy, which could generate political problems, and to prevent a sudden surge in imports that could lead to balance of payments problems. Often quantitative restrictions are reduced or eliminated first on raw material and intermediate goods and other goods that are not viewed as competing with domestic production, as in reforms in sub-Saharan Africa in the late 1980s and early 1990s. These reforms are then typically extended to final goods, including those competing with domestic production.

The elimination of quantitative restrictions and other nontariff barriers to trade is likely to have a significant effect on trade tax revenues, though the channels will differ, depending on the nature of the restriction and on the manner of the elimination. Taking the example of quotas, even with no change in the level of imports, tariffication of quotas (or auctioning of licenses) would be likely to lead to an increase in revenues as rents are transferred from domestic producers to the government in the form of trade tax revenues. The application of tariffs to imports would also increase the base of other indirect taxes levied on these goods (though there might be offsetting revenue effects of these price increases in the economy and further indirect effects).

The other methods of liberalizing quotas described by Takacs (1990) would increase revenues primarily through an increase in the volume of trade. In the absence of tariffication, the response of trade volumes to the elimination of quantitative restrictions would depend first on the difference between the equilibrium market price and the shadow price at the restricted level. If the restrictions were only partly eliminated or relaxed, then the response would depend on the degree to which the constraints were relaxed. The larger the difference between the equilibrium market price and the shadow price at the restricted level, the greater the likely response of imports. If the restrictions were tariffied rather than just eliminated, then the response would depend on how closely the tariff-inclusive price matched the shadow price at the restricted level. The elimination of foreign exchange controls or the relaxation of restrictive licensing practices could similarly result in dramatic changes in the trade environment, possibly leading to an increase in imports and revenues from imports.

All the case studies provide evidence that a high priority was assigned to attacking quantitative restrictions, at least as a policy objective, though the pace and nature of that reform appears inter alia to have reflected revenue concerns. Both Malawi and Senegal pursued a strategy in the late 1980s and 1990s that stressed bolstering the domestic tax system and moving less rapidly with the outright elimination of quantitative restrictions. Nonetheless, there was progress in reducing such restrictions. Malawi's trade liberalization program in the late 1980s included a program to eliminate foreign exchange rationing. Similarly, Senegal embarked in 1986 on a phased reduction in quantitative restrictions, focusing initially on goods not produced locally. In contrast, the Philippines was notable for a focus on the tariffication of quantitative restriction during the initial phases of its trade liberalization efforts. Finally, in the case of Morocco, reflecting a trade liberalization strategy adopted in 1983, reforms included a gradual elimination of quantitative restrictions on imports and the abolition of import deposit requirements.

The effect of relaxing quantitative restrictions on import volumes and revenues also depends on the flexibility of administrative capabilities. Without adequate reform, customs administrations could be incapable of handling the possible surge in imports and also of adapting their processes to focusing on certifying the value of imports rather than just the validity of licenses to import and volumes of imports, as would be necessary under a system where most trade was limited by quantitative restrictions (Tanzi, 1994). The importance of complementary customs administration reforms is a point that has often gone unnoticed in trade reform programs. Malawi and Morocco both undertook trade liberalization without first improving customs administration. Only recently have both countries made customs administration reform a central component of trade liberalization.

Tariff Reform

In addition to the elimination of quantitative restrictions (or in the absence of quantitative restrictions), the other major element of trade reform is typically the rationalization and reduction of tariff rates. There are several distinct issues to consider.

Characterization of Tariff Structures

Tariff structures are often rather complex and resist easy characterization by summary measures, thereby complicating any analysis of the revenue implications of tariff reductions (Dean, Desai, and Riedel, 1994). Unlike most broadly based domestic taxes, tariff schedules may contain dozens of different rates, ranging from zero to several hundred percent. For imports, the unweighted average of tariff rates is often taken as the simplest measure of the importance of tariffs. A simple average, however, does not accurately gauge the overall importance of trade taxes. For instance, there may be a few very high rates that apply to only a small volume of trade, introducing an upward bias to the average. A weighted average of tariff rates (or the collected tariff rate), where the weights are the shares of imports at each rate in total imports, may be a more suitable alternative measure, but it suffers from the important drawback that imports facing a high tariff are likely to be demanded in reduced quantity, introducing a downward bias to the measure. (This measure offers only an ambiguous measure of liberalization, because in fact it could rise even with a reduction in nominal tariff rates if exemptions were reduced or compliance improved.) Another useful summary indicator of tariff structure is the dispersion of the tariff rates. Some schedules may have rates that show relatively little dispersion around an average value, while others show considerable dispersion. The dispersion is often useful as a supplement to the average rate, because a low average rate could mask large dispersion in rates, and hence large differences in effective protection across goods.

Complicating measurement, in many countries there may be a considerable difference between explicit tariff rates and implicit tariff rates because of institutional features of the trade regime that distort measurement of import value. For example, where foreign exchange controls apply, the official exchange rate may differ from the exchange rate determined in the secondary (or black) market. Tariffs may be applied to import values at the official rate of exchange or at some other exchange rate, depending on the source of the funds used for importation. This may result in implicit tariffs on market values of goods being considerably different from the explicit tariffs applied to the good. In some countries, imported goods are valued at reference prices set by the government. Although these prices are presumably set to reflect market value, often they do not, and this also may create a divergence between implicit and explicit tariffs. Tariff reform may be undertaken at the same time as reform of exchange rates and reference prices, and hence changes in explicit tariffs may be a misleading indicator of changes in implicit tariffs because of changes in the valuation of the base of the tax. In practice, it may be difficult to separate these confounding influences.

Reductions in Tariff Levels

The effect of tariff reductions on revenues depends on the levels and coverage of existing tariffs, and on the extent to which they are reduced. The precise impact on revenues is difficult to predict because it depends on complex economic responses. If import values are unchanged, the immediate effect of a reduction in tariff rates is to lower revenues (if trade taxes are included in the base of domestic taxes on imports, then this reduction in trade taxes is accompanied by a reduction in excise and VAT collections levied on imports, though possibly with some offsetting revenue effects elsewhere in the economy). This potential loss of revenue is often at the root of opposition to reducing tariffs.

However, the value of imports can be expected to change in response to tariff reductions, with the magnitude of that change depending directly on the price elasticity of demand for imports. Since imports include a broad category of goods, it is hard to generalize about the price elasticity of demand. Imports of final consumption goods are likely to be more price elastic than imports of intermediate and raw materials. In many developing countries, imports of consumer goods constitute only about 10–20 percent of total imports. The aggregate elasticity of demand is therefore likely to be low in the short term, so that a reduction in tariffs is likely to lead to a revenue loss. To the extent that low imports of consumer goods reflect the effect of high tariffs, however, the aggregate elasticity of demand could be higher than the existing pattern of imports would suggest.

The response of import values also depends on the price elasticity of supply of import substitutes. The less elastic is this supply, the smaller the reduction in output for a given fall in price and hence the smaller the increase in import values. Therefore, a combination of inelastic price elasticities of demand for imports and supply of import substitutes implies relatively little increase in import values in the short term. Moreover, since price elasticities of demand and supply typically are not constant over the entire range of prices, the starting point for tariff reform is also likely to affect economic responses. For instance, the elasticity of demand is likely to be higher at high tariffs than at low tariffs. Indeed, if protectionist motives dominate the setting of tariff rates, then tariffs may more plausibly be above their revenue-maximizing levels.

Although the potential revenue effects of tariff reductions have been cast in terms of elasticities, the observed responses on any occasion will depend, inter alia, on the macroeconomic environment, and in particular on the supporting macroeconomic policies. This point is underscored by the case studies (discussed below), all of which stressed tariff reductions in their reform programs, though with mixed success, in part due to differing circumstances. Morocco was notable for its success in reducing the collected tariff rate,[9] which declined from 26.3 percent in 1980 to 14.9 percent in 1995—the success in this case owes much to the manner in which improved stabilization policies supported an opening of the economy, resulting in strengthened revenue performance, which allowed the rates to decline. In contrast, Senegal's early trade liberalization efforts in the mid-1980s faltered in the face of weaknesses in macroeconomic management and stagnant trade, and as a consequence tariff reductions were accompanied by serious revenue shortfalls, which subsequently led to a reversal of the tariff cuts. Senegal's second phase, implemented in conjunction with the 1994 devaluation of the CFA franc, was much more successful. Reduced reliance on trade taxes in the Philippines has at times been constrained by the weakness of domestic tax mobilization. The tariffication of quotas has already been noted. In addition, the Philippines imposed a temporary import surcharge in the early 1990s. As a result, the collected tariff rate declined only slightly from 16.7 percent in 1985 to 14.4 percent in 1995. Finally, Malawi imposed a temporary export levy in the same period to address revenue shortfalls that compromised trade liberalization efforts.

Reduction in Tariff Dispersion

As already noted, reducing the dispersion of tariffs is often an objective of tariff reform. There are many different ways in which the dispersion of tariffs could be reduced. If tariff reform reduced the dispersion of the tariffs around an average value by lowering the higher tariffs and increasing the lower tariffs, the revenue effects would depend in part on which goods were affected by these changes. If those goods on which tariff rates were being reduced were relatively price elastic in demand compared with those on which tariff rates were being raised, then reducing the dispersion (leaving the average rate unchanged) could raise revenues. In some cases, a reduction in the dispersion of tariffs could be achieved by increasing the minimum rate,

[9]This is measured as the ratio of import tax collections to import values.

which could imply some overall increase in the average rate (at least temporarily), increasing the chances that the reforms would increase revenues.

Reducing the dispersion of tariff rates could also influence revenues by reducing tax evasion. Taxes that are levied at a uniform rate tend to minimize evasion and administrative difficulties, especially by reducing opportunities for mistakes and misclassification. Reducing the dispersion of tariff rates could also enhance economic efficiency by equalizing protection across goods. However, there would not seem to be any a priori reason to expect that reducing dispersion would necessarily have a large effect on revenues, except where there was a significant increase in the level and/or coverage of the minimum rate.

Related to dispersion, tariff consolidation and simplification are also often goals of trade reform. It is common to find that countries have many overlapping levies on imports, including tariffs, surcharges, fees, and stamp duties. One goal of trade reform is to rationalize and simplify this system, so that the overall charge on imports is transparent. Although simply consolidating many levies into one would not necessarily change revenues, by reducing administrative burdens, it might lead to lower evasion.

Again, the case studies provide numerous examples of the high priority that in practice has been accorded to reducing tariff dispersion and consolidating tariff structures. In the late 1980s, Malawi reduced the range of tariffs from 0–220 percent to 0–45 percent—by August 1997, the maximum tariff rate had been reduced to 35 percent. In its early reform efforts, Morocco considerably simplified and rationalized overly complex tariff schedules—the maximum tariff rate was reduced from 400 percent in 1982 to 60 percent in 1984, and the number of tariff bands was reduced from 47 in 1980 to 6 in 1996. Similarly, Senegal made progress in rationalizing its tariff structure. The Philippines had originally focused on the tariffication of quotas, which tended to militate against a reduction in measured tariff dispersion, but has more recently also successfully lowered tariffs.

Impact of Tariff Reform on Tax Evasion

A reduction in tariff rates may influence compliance with customs and tax laws. The extent of tax evasion is directly related to the potential benefits from evasion, which is reflected in the marginal tax rate on goods subject to tax (Tanzi and Shome, 1993). The lower the tariff, the lower the marginal benefit from tax evasion. Many costs are associated with customs evasion, including the need to find alternative (often more expensive) routes to avoid customs check posts, to package goods to conceal their presence or their true value, and to bribe corrupt officials; the lack of proper invoices for subsequent use of the goods, such as crediting under a VAT; and punishment, if caught. The reduction in the marginal benefit of evasion is likely to lead to a lower level of evasion where marginal benefits are again equal to the marginal cost of evasion. Evasion of customs duties is a pervasive feature of most countries with high tariffs; and revenue losses, as a result of a reduction in tariffs, would be mitigated to the extent that evasion also falls.

Export Taxes

The elimination of export taxes is also a goal of trade liberalization. Nevertheless, in some developing countries they can make up a significant component of trade tax collections. Typically, they are levied on primary commodities where there are relatively few exporters, and they represent an important component of national output. There are several arguments for export taxes. First, they may be a substitute for income taxation, where the domestic tax administration is poor and it is difficult to collect revenues from large producers of exportable commodities. Second, they may tax windfall gains from changes in international prices of commodities. Third, they may reduce supply and increase prices for the commodity. Export taxes are mainly an expedient means of raising revenue, since improvements in the domestic tax system would yield a more desirable tax system.

Export taxes often take the form of explicit tariffs on exports, levied as a combination of a basic tax, tied to a reference price, and a progressively rising rate on price increments. They may also take the form of implicit tariffs. Certain practices may give rise to implicit tariffs. Examples include overvalued exchange rates or a multiple exchange rate system, foreign exchange surrender requirements at overvalued rates, or the use of marketing boards for exports, which do not pay producers market prices. The use of implicit taxes may distort the overall picture of revenues in that they are not recorded under revenue collections, though they certainly influence the ability and willingness to pay other taxes.

Given that export taxes are often substitutes for domestic income taxes, their successful elimination will be more likely if implemented as part of an overall tax reform package to broaden the base for taxes. In Africa, progress in eliminating export taxes has been mixed. A significant achievement of tax reform in Uganda was the elimination of the coffee export tax. In Kenya, the reform package included the elimination of export taxes on commodities and manufactured products. In a few countries, however, export duties were reintroduced or maintained as a proxy for an income tax in hard-to-tax agriculture (e.g., Côte d'Ivoire and Ghana). As regards the case studies, in Malawi, the opportunity to capture windfall gains on the depreciation of the currency and a deteriorating revenue performance led to the imposition of an export levy on certain agricultural exports, though its introduction was accompanied by a plan to phase it out, which took place in 1998. In Morocco, the ad valorem taxes levied on exports were abolished in 1995, leaving only raw phosphate exports subject to a specific tax.

Regional Trade Arrangements

Trade liberalization is frequently undertaken in the context of regional trade arrangements. These arrangements lower tariffs between members but do not lower them for countries outside the arrangement. The trade-creating and trade-diverting implications of such agreements are well known. In that connection, Foroutan (1993, p. 255) argues that revenue considerations in trade liberalization clash with the conditions that minimize the likelihood of trade diversion, and that this concern is of particular importance to sub-Saharan African countries. The conditions for minimizing the likelihood of trade diversion are that the partners have extensive trade links and that they do not raise their trade barriers relative to the rest of the world. But the stronger the trade links between the partners, the greater the likelihood of a revenue loss from trade integration, and any loss is more likely to be met by raising tariffs to the rest of the world. This would enhance the trade diversion effects of integration. As a result, concerns about revenue losses from trade liberalization may make trade-creating trade arrangements less likely and trade-diverting arrangements more likely. So far, sub-Saharan Africa does not appear to have experienced significant benefits from regional trade arrangements, apart from some discipline having been imposed on the underlying trade liberalization strategy.

Taking examples from the case studies, Malawi's trade reform efforts in recent years have been guided by its participation in regional trade initiatives, principally the Cross-Border Initiative. The CBI calls, inter alia, for members to dismantle quantitative restrictions on a reciprocal basis and to establish a common external tariff by 1998. Morocco currently faces the fiscal challenge posed by its recent (February 1996) Association Agreement with the European Union (AAEU) of removing all tariffs on industrial goods imports from the EU during 12 years. To appreciate the scale of the challenge, one estimate (Abed, 1997) is that the revenue losses Morocco will experience as a result of the AAEU could amount to 2–2.6 percent of GDP by the end of the 12-year transition period.[10]

Additional Aspects of Trade Liberalization

There are additional aspects of trade liberalization that clearly bear on the revenue implications of such liberalization but whose revenue implications are hard to quantify.

Tariff Exemptions

The tax base is often eroded by extensive exemptions from tariffs. In a study of several developing countries, Pritchett and Sethi (1994) found that there was only a weak relationship between statutory tariff rates and collected tariff rates (measured as the ratio of import tariff revenue to import values). They argued that as tariff rates rise, importers put more effort in gaining exemptions, so that revenue collections do not increase in proportion to the increase in tariffs (which implies the converse—that reducing very high tariffs does not always lead to a proportionate fall in revenues). As a consequence, eliminating tariff exemptions can contribute to trade reform by broadening the tax base. In addition to their direct impact on revenues, when exemptions become more prevalent, the opportunities of diversion of exempt products to nonexempt uses also grows, further contributing to a lower rate of compliance. Typically, exemptions apply to international organizations, diplomats, expenditures related to aid projects, government, foreign joint ventures, and other favored clients.

Implicit Quotas and Taxes

Modern forms of protection, in the form of voluntary export restraints and antidumping provisions, are essentially like implicit quotas and implicit or explicit taxes. By limiting volumes, voluntary export restraints function as implicit quotas, with the same distorting effects on trade, prices, and revenues (though there is some presumption that the implicit revenue accrues to exporters rather than importers in the case of quotas). These restraints limit the volume of imports and hence tax revenues from imports. Antidumping provisions, which may go into effect when the prices of exported goods are

[10]The range reflects alternative assumptions about how much Morocco substitutes non-EU imports for EU imports.

deemed to be lower than the "market" value of those goods, often take the form of duties levied on the offending goods. These duties would not be different from explicit duties in their effect on revenues. They do, however, create different incentives for producers, in that they can be avoided by upward adjustments in the price of goods. As producers adjust upward the prices of exports to avoid antidumping provisions, tax revenues would diminish. The resulting higher prices could be seen as imposing an implicit tax on consumers, with the revenue accruing to the foreign firms.

Indirect and Interactive Effects

Trade liberalization can interact with the domestic tax system and the macroeconomic environment with implications for the overall budgetary situation.

Import Composition and Economic Growth

Both relaxation of quantitative restrictions and tariff reforms may lead to considerable changes in the composition of imports. If trade reforms diminish the share of import-substituting industries in the economy, then imports of these goods will increase. If these goods are taxed at a higher rate than intermediate goods and other inputs, then this might induce an increase in revenues. If liberalization stimulates a higher share of investment or exports, this may reduce tax bases (since investment and exports are usually more lightly taxed than consumption and imports). In the medium to long term, liberalization should stimulate a higher rate of economic growth, and this should expand all potential tax bases. Investment and exports should lead to higher levels of income, which in turn are linked to higher levels of consumption and imports. But the improvements in productive efficiency of domestic suppliers may lead to lower import volumes than there otherwise would be.

Role of Domestic and International Trade Taxes

Domestic indirect taxes may reinforce protective elements of trade taxes. There are several distinct channels. One is through the differential application of excises and VAT to imports and domestic production. As taxes on domestic consumption (rather than production), excises and VATs should be applied equally to both imports and domestic production. Differential application of VATs to imports and domestic production is rare. Generally, the same rate of tax is applied to the relevant tax base, though in a few cases, surcharges may be added onto the VAT on imports. For instance, in Malawi, until 1992/93, the surtax (a broadly based sales tax) effectively taxed imported goods competing with domestic goods at a higher rate than domestic goods to reinforce the protective effect of import duties. This differential was eliminated that year, in combination with an upward adjustment in import duty rates on imported goods previously carrying the higher effective surtax rate as an offset.

Differential application of excises to imports and to domestic production is more common. Unlike other taxes, excise taxes may frequently be levied on a specific basis, as opposed to an ad valorem basis. One way in which excisable goods are treated in a differential fashion is to apply a different basis for taxation to imports than to domestic production. For instance, in some countries, excises on domestic production are levied on an ad valorem basis and on imports on a specific basis. The opposite may also be found. Or both taxes may be levied on a specific or ad valorem basis but at different effective rates. For instance, in some former Soviet Union countries, excises were levied on domestic production on a tax-inclusive basis, while they were levied on imports on a tax-exclusive basis but at the same ad valorem rate. Since the tax-exclusive rate that would correspond to a tax-inclusive rate is much higher, domestic production was effectively taxed at a much higher rate.

Some countries apply two different schedules of excise rates, levying lower rates on imports than on domestic production. For instance, in some Commonwealth countries, excise taxes apply only to domestic production. In some cases, import duties can be adjusted to compensate for this differential treatment of imports and domestic production, but in practice, this adjustment is unlikely to eliminate the differences completely and is equivalent to reducing the protective element in trade taxes. Some countries levy higher rates on imports than on domestic production for the purpose of adding to protective elements in trade taxes. For example, in Poland, excise tax rates on some items are 5 percent higher on imports than on domestic production. An excise tax levied at a higher rate on imports than on domestic production is economically no different from levying a higher tariff and then equivalent excise taxes (the exact equivalence depends on the rates). Customs duties on goods that are not produced domestically are equivalent to excises and should be explicitly brought under the domestic tax system.

Interactions with Accompanying Policies

Tax and customs administration reform is an essential component of trade liberalization since without improvements in the structure and administration of the tax system, it is not possible to reduce successfully the reliance on international trade taxes. Examples of where reform of customs administration has bolstered revenues include Burkina Faso and Uganda.

Box 1 provides an outline of critical reforms to improve tax structure and administration in low-income countries with special reference to sub-Saharan Africa. In recent years, several African countries have undertaken reform of the tax system. The most successful has been Benin, which has significantly raised its tax share in GDP, though other countries have made substantial progress (Abed and others, 1998). In many countries facing fiscal imbalances, near-term or immediate measures have sometimes been resorted to so as to mobilize revenues until the important structural reforms take effect. For example, an important component of Kenya's fiscal reforms was a package to change the tariff system to lower the average rate of effective protection, reduce the dispersion of rates, phase out export duties, and enhance the transparency of the structure of international trade taxation in general. However, the authorities also planned to introduce a presumptive tax of 5 percent on the value of gross sales of agricultural products to offset the revenue loss from the elimination of the export tax on coffee and tea.

As regards the experience in the case studies, it is instructive that all the countries recognized the importance of broadening the base for taxation as part of an overall package to liberalize their economies. In the late 1980s, Malawi embarked on a program to reform both the tax system and tax and customs administration—and greater success was achieved in attaining the objective of broadening the tax base and lowering marginal tax rates than in bolstering tax and customs administration. Trade liberalization in Morocco, for example, has been accompanied by gradual improvements in both tax structure and tax and customs administration, with the introduction of a VAT in 1986 and more recently a complete overhaul of the tax and customs administrations. In the Philippines, there was considerable progress in reforming both direct and indirect taxation, the latter through the introduction of a VAT; however, there was less progress in bolstering tax administration. Paralleling the experience of other countries, Senegal has been successfully refining its VAT (reducing the number of rates and expanding the base) to bolster revenue mobilization.

Interactions with Macroeconomic Developments

The economic adjustments to trade liberalization may also include significant changes in the macroeconomy as well. Often trade reform

Box 1. Best Practices for Taxes and Tariffs

Theoretical and practical considerations have yielded a set of "best practices" in tax and tariff systems in developing countries (Abed, 1997). "Best" tax systems are those that cause a minimum of distortion in the allocation of resources, are equitable, and are relatively easy to administer.

In practice, comprehensive tax and tariff policy reforms typically include most or all the following key elements:

- The introduction or strengthening of a broadly based consumption tax, notably a VAT, preferably with a single rate and minimal exemptions, and a threshold to exclude the smaller enterprises. Although VATs are often initially applied to manufactures and imports, they are typically subsequently extended to the distribution sector and agricultural inputs. Excise taxes should be levied at ad valorem rates (unless there are particularly severe problems with valuation) and restricted to a limited list of products, principally petroleum products, alcohol, and tobacco and some luxury items. VAT and excises should be applied equally to imports and domestic products.
- Taxes on international trade should play a minimal role. Import tariffs should have a low average rate and a limited dispersion of rates to reduce arbitrary and excessive rates of protection. Exporters should have duties rebated on inputs used for producing exports. Export duties should generally be avoided, though at times these taxes have been defended as expedients for income taxes in hard-to-tax sectors such as agriculture.
- The personal income tax should be characterized by only a few marginal tax brackets and a moderate top marginal rate; limited personal exemptions and deductions; a standard exemption that excludes persons with low incomes; and extensive use of final withholding. The corporate income tax should be levied at one moderate rate. Depreciation allowances should be uniform across sectors. There should be little use of tax incentives.
- The reforms above may be usefully complemented in some countries by the introduction of a simplified tax regime for small businesses and the informal sector.
- Tax and customs administration reforms should modernize systems and procedures. Simplification of the tax and tariff system provides strong support for administrative reforms. Typical reforms stress the reorganization of tax and customs administrations along functional lines; the adoption of effective procedures for a national system of unique taxpayer registration numbers; strengthening audit and enforcement and improved taxpayer services. Computerization is generally a central component of reform along with upgrading the skills of tax and customs officers and providing them with administrative autonomy and pay incentives.

is accompanied by a fall in the real value of the domestic currency. If trade balances initially worsen with tariff reductions, this may lead to depreciation of the currency. In many cases, trade reform is accompanied by an intentional devaluation of the currency, such as in the CFA franc zone countries in 1994. In general, the effect of a fall in value of the currency on trade tax revenues is ambiguous since it has offsetting effects on prices and quantities, and other important effects elsewhere on the budget and in the economy (Tanzi, 1991). From the revenue perspective, the reduction in value of the currency raises the domestic currency value of a given volume of imports. Since taxes are levied on domestic value, this would tend to increase revenues. The fall in the value of the currency also tends to decrease import volumes, hence this would limit any potential expansion of the base. The price elasticity of demand again critically influences the ultimate value of the base and hence revenues. If aggregate demand is inelastic, then depreciation of the currency is likely to increase revenues.

The 1994 devaluation of the CFA franc underscores the importance of the circumstances surrounding a change in the value of a currency for tax revenues. The CFA franc had been at a relatively appreciated level for some time before the devaluation, with a low level of economic activity leading to a compression of imports. Accordingly, when the currency was devalued as part of an overall adjustment package, the result was a sharp increase in imports; this surge had a positive impact on revenues.[11]

Summary and Complementary Evidence

To sum up the conclusions of this section, it is clear that some forms of trade liberalization are more likely to enhance revenues than others. Tariffication of quantitative restrictions or auctioning of licenses to import are sure ways to increase revenues by transferring rents from foreign producers and domestic importers to the government. The removal of quantitative restrictions is also likely to increase revenues simply by increasing volumes of trade, though the extent of increase would depend critically on how binding these restrictions were. The

[11]The CFA franc devaluation was also associated with a series of IMF-supported adjustment programs for the countries involved. As it happened, the increases in the trade values in response to the devaluation were overestimated, in part because the devaluation had been widely anticipated. There is also some evidence of over-importing before and under-importing after the devaluation (Clément and others, 1995).

reform of the tariff structure is more mixed in its likely effects on revenues. Reduction of tariffs is likely to reduce revenues; but to the extent that it is accompanied by measures to reduce exemptions and that it stimulates greater levels of trade, revenues may not fall and could even rise, over some medium-term horizon, especially if the initial level of tariffs is high. Regional trade arrangements and the nonuniformity they create in tariff barriers alter simple notions about the likely economic responses to tariff changes. Reducing the dispersion of tariffs is not likely to have a strong effect on revenues, though this would depend to some extent on whether it is accompanied by an increase in a minimum tariff rate and the elasticities of demand and supply that apply to the different goods on which tariffs are being adjusted. New forms of trade barriers, such as voluntary export restraints and countervailing and antidumping duties, may lead to less reduction in trade barriers than explicit reductions in quantitative restrictions and tariffs might suggest. But at the same time, countervailing and antidumping duties could serve to maintain revenue collections. The ability of domestic markets to adjust to the new trade regime and the ability of the domestic tax and customs administrations to administer the tax system in a changed environment are likely to influence revenue collections and the ability to sustain reforms. The interaction of reforms in the trade system with broader macroeconomic developments is also critical. In their analyses of the revenue implications of trade reform, Blejer and Cheasty (1990) and Tanzi (1991) both conclude that ultimately these are an empirical matter.

In an empirical case-study approach in which they analyze the revenue implications of World Bank-supported structural adjustment loans, Greenaway and Milner (1991) conclude that a range of outcomes is possible, depending upon the initial conditions and the components of the reform package. In a recent study examining the connection between reform of trade taxes and domestic taxes in World Bank programs, Rajaram (1994) examines whether the revenue effects of tariff reform proposals were anticipated and complemented by other tax measures. He finds that in some (but not all) cases, the revenue implications of trade reform and complementary reforms of the domestic tax system were considered. He suggests that there is a need for more systematic integration of revenue and protection objectives in World Bank programs. Mitra (1992) and Datta-Mitra (1997) also conclude that in some countries with World Bank reform programs there was a need for greater emphasis on revenue issues.

Although focused on the broader issue of trade liberalization in general, a recent IMF study of countries undergoing IMF-supported programs (IMF, 1997) also finds a range of fiscal outcomes to trade liberalization. This study concludes that, in some cases, programs could have targeted more extensive trade reform if more attention had been given to supporting fiscal policies and to revenue-neutral trade measures.

Trade Liberalization and Revenue Trends

In analyzing the impact of trade liberalization on revenues, two general observations from the discussion above need to be kept in mind. First, important determinants of the degree of reliance on international trade taxes are the level of economic development and the structure of the economy of the individual countries. Second, it is unclear even how to measure the extent of trade liberalization in an economy because there are various measures of trade liberalization, including the average tariff and the collected tariff rate (Dean, Desai, and Riedel, 1994). The simple correlation between the collected tariff rate and the share of import tariffs in GDP is 0.419, for a sample of 28 sub-Saharan African countries during the 1990–95 period.

Focusing initially on the issue of reviewing trends in trade liberalization, the long-term trend in the collected tariff rate (calculated by dividing revenue from import tariffs by imports) is one potentially useful indicator of whether countries are becoming more open to international trade—in particular, unlike the average tariff, collected tariff rates are straightforward to calculate over a period of time. Collected import tariff rates are given in Tables 2–7.

Overall, the average collected tariff rate has declined from 12.7 percent in 1975 to 9.1 percent in the last available year (Table 2). Turning to a consideration of the regional data (Tables 2–7), there were clear differences in the regional developments. Sub-Saharan African countries made progress in reducing average collected tariff rates between 1975 and the 1990s, though the level of collected tariff rates remained higher in that region than in the other regions. Other regions also reduced their dependence on trade taxes. The fact that, proportionately, the sharpest collective tariff reductions were in the OECD may well in part reflect the relative ease with which those countries have been able to diversify their tax bases by means of the VAT and other taxes.

Turning to a consideration of individual countries, Table 4 reveals that, in sub-Saharan Africa, the tax burden on trade varies widely, as did developments over time. Only 10 of 19 countries[12] reduced their collected tariff rates, though some dramatically. The reduction was greatest in Côte d'Ivoire, Ethiopia, South Africa, and the Democratic

[12]Data on other sub-Saharan African countries were incomplete.

Table 2. Collected Tariffs
(In percent)

Region	1975	1980	1985	1990	Last Available Year[1]
All countries	12.62	11.36	12.27	11.08	9.82
OECD countries[2]	5.81	4.19	3.51	2.88	1.69
Non-OECD countries	15.64	14.27	15.89	14.41	13.07
African countries	19.31	17.36	19.09	18.31	16.34
Asian countries	14.05	12.04	15.63	16.48	13.46
Middle Eastern countries	16.47	14.33	14.07	10.70	11.39
Western Hemisphere countries	12.37	12.67	13.77	11.09	10.20

Sources: IMF, *Government Finance Statistics* and *World Economic Outlook* (May 1997); and OECD, *Revenue Statistics*.

Note: Collected tariffs are defined as import tax revenues divided by imports. OECD is Organization for Economic Cooperation and Development.

[1]Last available year is 1995 for most countries, but when this information is not available the last available year is used.

[2]Excluding Czech Republic, Hungary, Luxembourg, and Poland.

Republic of Congo, all of which reduced collected tariff rates by more than 50 percent.

Table 5 reveals that many of the larger economies in Asia (Indonesia, Republic of Korea, Malaysia, Singapore, and Thailand) all reduced collected tariff rates; the unweighted average largely reflects the lack of liberalization in smaller island economies (such as the Solomon Islands) as well as India and Myanmar. In Middle Eastern countries (Table 6), the reduction in the average collected tariff rate of the region took place in only a few countries, such as Egypt (from 43.2 percent in 1975 to 16.7 percent in the last available year), Syria (from 16.4 percent in 1975 to 9.9 percent in the last available year), Morocco (from 25.4 percent in 1975 to 14.9 percent in the last available year), and Israel (from 4.4 percent in 1980 to 0.6 percent in the last available year). In Western Hemisphere countries, the apparent lack of progress hides the significant liberalization that took place in the region's largest economies, notably Brazil and Argentina in recent years (Table 7).

Tables 8 to 12, which summarize trends in the collection and composition of trade tax revenue during the past 20 years by region, reveal much of the same trends as observed with the collected tariff rates, suggesting that trade liberalization has on average resulted in a decline in trade tax revenues. In particular, Table 8 indicates that, as a percentage of GDP, trade taxes have diminished in importance over the past 20 years; they have declined from 4.2 percent of GDP in 1975 to 3.3 percent of GDP most recently. All regions witnessed declines in

Table 3. Collected Tariffs in Countries Belonging to the OECD
(In percent)

Country[1]	1975	1980	1985	1990	Last Available Year[2]
Australia	11.2	59.60	9.32	6.65	3.98
Austria	3.75	1.55	1.48	1.46	0.41
Belgium	1.47	1.33	1.06	1.02	0.99
Canada	5.54	4.45	3.68	2.86	1.41
Denmark	1.54	1.01	0.92	0.96	0.82
Finland	3.17	1.90	0.98	1.42	1.01
France	1.58	1.24	0.99	0.92	0.77
Germany	2.43	1.88	1.36	1.44	1.15
Greece	2.83	5.43	4.74	1.40	0.95
Iceland	19.97	17.24	13.28	10.48	1.68
Ireland	1.02	0.90	1.09	0.94	0.97
Italy	0.42	0.67	1.13	1.11	0.84
Japan	3.35	2.72	2.61	2.99	3.65
Mexico	15.27	10.52	9.06	7.56	3.20
Netherlands	1.79	1.48	1.19	1.41	1.52
New Zealand	4.01	4.35	4.74	3.62	4.25
Norway	1.35	0.86	0.77	0.76	1.29
Portugal	4.74	4.99	3.44	3.11	0.87
Spain	5.21	4.03	4.36	4.00	0.99
Sweden	2.41	1.71	2.51	2.59	0.96
Switzerland	2.98	1.54	1.22	1.19	1.21
Turkey	36.12	15.60	8.65	6.40	3.63
United Kingdom	2.38	2.46	1.76	1.52	1.49
United States	4.80	3.18	3.82	3.34	2.59
Unweighted average	5.81	4.19	3.51	2.88	1.69

Sources: IMF, *Government Finance Statistics* and *World Economic Outlook* (May 1997); and OECD, *Revenue Statistics.*

Note: Collected tariffs are defined as import tax revenues divided by imports. OECD is Organization for Economic Cooperation and Development.

[1]Excluding Czech Republic, Hungary, Luxembourg, and Poland.

[2]Last available year is 1995 for most countries, but when this information is not available the last available year is used.

the ratio of trade tax revenue to GDP. However, the timing of the decline in trade taxes as a percentage of GDP varies markedly across regions. OECD countries appear to have reduced their reliance on trade taxes gradually over the past 20 years. Asian and Western Hemisphere non-OECD countries began their reform process much later, so that the reduction in trade taxes as a percentage of GDP only began in the 1990s. Conversely, in the Middle East, the reform process began earlier, but appears to have slowed in recent years. Despite the reduction of taxes on trade from 6.7 percent of GDP to 5.6 percent of GDP, trade

Table 4. Collected Tariffs in Selected African Countries[1]
(In percent)

Country	1975	1980	1985	1990	Last Available Year[1]
Botswana	18.81	23.25	18.46	15.44	19.07
Burundi[2]	24.75	20.46	18.23	. . .	14.90
Cameroon	22.11	22.43	25.91	19.77	19.03
Côte d'Ivoire	. . .	28.07	31.96	22.73	11.73
Ethiopia	34.76	18.98	17.44	21.37	13.97
Gabon[2]	21.63	31.74	24.90	24.68	24.69
Gambia, The	17.18	21.47	26.79	16.05	14.55
Ghana	18.56	14.45	18.06	16.06	11.18
Kenya	14.95	11.78	15.83	14.25	14.28
Lesotho	27.59	. . .	22.05	18.35	29.00
Malawi[2]	5.32	11.48	15.07	12.16	10.89
Mauritius	11.12	16.71	22.86	19.22	14.54
Rwanda	25.34	19.92	. . .	24.70	27.30
Senegal[2]	18.17	15.73	15.40	24.63	19.22
Sierra Leone	19.98	18.78	17.18	13.01	22.86
South Africa	4.02	3.08	3.88	6.21	1.04
Zaïre[2]	38.65	22.08	18.18	22.89	8.73
Zambia	5.34	7.43	8.93	12.19	11.39
Zimbabwe	. . .	4.57	22.45	25.80	22.19
Unweighted average	19.31	17.36	19.09	18.31	16.34

Sources: IMF, *Government Finance Statistics* and *World Economic Outlook* (May 1997).
Note: Collected tariffs are defined as import tax revenues divided by imports.
[1]Last available year is 1995 for most countries, but when this information is not available the last available year is used.
[2]Data from country authorities; and IMF staff estimates.

taxes in sub-Saharan Africa are still higher than in other developing countries. Table 10 shows marked divergences in the reliance on international trade taxes across the individual countries of Africa.

Turning to a consideration of the importance of international trade taxes to overall revenue collections (Table 9), the share of import duties in tax revenue for non-OECD countries has diminished only a little during the past 20 years. Whereas OECD countries more than halved the share of import duties in tax revenue (from 3.4 percent in 1975 to 1.0 percent most recently), non-OECD countries reduced their share only from 25.5 to 22.7 percent of tax revenue, and therefore have only marginally diminished the importance of import taxes in overall revenue. Regionally, of the non-OECD countries, only Asian and African countries reduced their reliance on import duties, as measured in percentage of tax revenue. Note that this stands in contrast to the conclu-

Table 5. Collected Tariffs in Selected Asian Countries
(In percent)

Country	1975	1980	1985	1990	Last Available Year[1]
Botswana		23.25	18.46	15.44	19.07
Fiji	15.82	13.47	20.96	16.14	12.61
India	29.77	25.72	48.19	48.21	25.54
Indonesia	8.72	6.88	4.53	5.83	5.01
Korea, Republic of	6.25	7.73	8.58	7.99	4.70
Malaysia	11.01	9.00	8.77	4.86	4.02
Myanmar	27.58	20.24	25.22	36.34	42.90
Nepal	17.11	15.72	14.43	14.14	9.16
Papua New Guinea	6.82	6.49	11.98	17.13	18.40
Philippines[2]	20.88	17.24	16.70	15.47	14.39
Singapore	1.37	0.92	0.73	0.00	0.26
Solomon Islands	14.05	11.26	14.75	21.58	21.58
Sri Lanka	9.62	10.65	14.39	15.60	9.02
Thailand	13.68	11.16	13.99	10.96	7.35
Unweighted average	14.05	12.04	15.63	16.48	13.46

Sources: IMF, *Government Finance Statistics* and *World Economic Outlook* (May 1997).
Note: Collected tariffs are defined as import tax revenues divided by imports.
[1]Last available year is 1995 for most countries, but when this information is not available the last available year is used.
[2]Data from country authorities and IMF staff estimates.

sions reached from examining Table 8, which indicates that both of these regions increased import taxes as a percentage of GDP. This implies that, in these regions, overall tax revenues rose considerably as a share of GDP, which permitted a decline in the relative importance of tariff revenue. Reliance on import taxes remained virtually unchanged in all other non-OECD regions. Table 11 again indicates the differences across sub-Saharan African countries. All regions have made progress in the reduction of export duties.

In most countries, domestic indirect taxes collected upon imports are another important source of revenues (though the ultimate incidence is thought to be shifted forward to the consumer). Customs administrations typically collect trade taxes and any domestic indirect taxes on imports (VAT and excises) at the border. Trade taxes are levied on import values, while domestic indirect taxes are generally levied on a tax base inclusive of customs duties. Excise duties on imports are usually collected on a tax base inclusive of customs duties and then broadly based indirect taxes, such as the VAT, are stacked on top of trade taxes and excises.

Table 6. Collected Tariffs in Selected Middle Eastern Countries
(In percent)

Country	1975	1980	1985	1990	Last Available Year[1]
Bahrain	2.26	2.24	3.53	2.61	3.61
Egypt	43.24	25.84	28.57	9.58	16.72
Iran	9.49	20.93	11.23	6.49	12.28
Israel	. . .	4.43	4.96	1.58	0.63
Jordan	11.94	16.47	14.05	9.51	12.31
Kuwait	. . .	2.98	3.77	5.43	3.52
Morocco[2]	25.38	26.32	15.37	19.08	14.92
Oman	0.12	1.32	3.68	3.36	3.07
Pakistan	19.54	24.61	25.53	31.65	28.73
Syria	16.40	11.56	. . .	8.43	9.93
Tunisia	19.84	20.91	29.97	19.98	19.62
Unweighted average	16.47	14.33	14.07	10.70	11.39

Sources: IMF, *Government Finance Statistics* and *World Economic Outlook* (May 1997).
Note: Collected tariffs are defined as import tax revenues divided by imports.
[1]Last available year is 1995 for most countries, but when this information is not available the last available year is used.
[2]Data from country authorities and IMF staff estimates.

There are several reasons that it is useful to assess a country's overall dependence on tax collections on imports, when evaluating the impact of trade liberalization on revenues. First, overall collections on imports more accurately reflect the immediate vulnerability of a country's revenue collections to shifts in foreign trade.[13] Second, the interaction between trade taxes and domestic indirect taxes on imports may be important in the design of trade and tax reforms where eliminating protection is one objective. Unfortunately, the lack of data availability does not allow a comprehensive analysis of this question. Hence only a number of illustrative examples are given in Table 13. The small sample for which domestic taxes on imports could be precisely identified shows that their importance might be substantial. In several sub-Saharan African countries, domestic taxes on imports were significant. These countries not only have to gauge the revenue effect of trade liberalization with respect to import tariffs, but also with respect to domestic taxes on trade.

[13]For example, whereas the revenue effect of a reduction in import tariffs on revenue from import duties is ambiguous, for domestic taxes on imports it is unambiguously positive, as long as some positive import elasticity exists.

Table 7. Collected Tariffs in Selected Non-OECD Western Hemisphere Countries
(In percent)

Country	1975	1980	1985	1990	Last Available Year[1]
Argentina[2]	5.70	22.61	16.18	10.40	9.74
Bahamas	26.21	26.12	30.80	28.67	29.06
Bolivia	. . .	12.34	7.85	4.75	5.01
Brazil	. . .	16.42	6.59	10.53	7.88
Chile	17.33	7.29	16.69	10.37	10.56
Colombia	12.26	10.37	14.82	18.54	9.06
Costa Rica	5.96	6.96	10.64	10.29	8.26
Dominican Republic[3]	22.22	15.56	14.58	10.60	12.80
Ecuador	14.93	16.35	24.26	13.14	8.27
El Salvador	8.49	4.35	4.25	4.69	5.88
Guatemala	9.13	7.60	11.89	7.03	8.42
Nicaragua	7.15	8.14	6.44	8.61	13.45
Panama	5.93	6.26	10.90	11.38	9.59
Paraguay	10.51	9.44	5.14	5.88	7.95
Peru	22.57	17.11	28.18	11.01	11.77
Uruguay	8.02	17.18	13.50	12.72	6.07
Venezuela	9.22	11.36	11.44	9.99	9.65
Unweighted average	12.37	12.67	13.77	11.09	10.20

Sources: IMF, *Government Finance Statistics* and *World Economic Outlook* (May 1997).

Note: OECD is Organization for Economic Cooperation and Development. Collected tariffs are defined as import tax revenues divided by imports.

[1]Last available year is 1995 for most countries, but when this information is not available the last available year is used.

[2]Data from country authorities and IMF staff estimates.

As can be seen from the appendix, the case studies afford useful examples of how the interaction between the many dimensions of trade liberalization and the economic circumstances of individual countries played out. We consider each country in turn.

Malawi

Trade liberalization and economic reform in general went through phases. During the late 1980s, complementary tax reforms were revenue enhancing, the liberalization of foreign exchange restrictions resulted in a modest increase in the GDP share of imports, and the collected import tariff rates remained broadly constant. This would appear to be an example where the combination of focusing initially on reductions in quantitative restrictions and tariff dispersion and the favorable impact of liberalizing the foreign exchange market resulted

Table 8. Taxes on International Trade
(As percentage of GDP)

Tax	1975	1980	1985	1990	Last Available Year[1]
Trade taxes					
All countries	4.23	4.19	4.28	3.38	3.25
OECD countries	1.20	0.91	0.77	0.60	0.37
Non-OECD countries	5.30	5.21	5.36	4.40	4.29
African countries	6.67	6.22	6.50	5.31	5.57
Asian countries	3.80	4.83	5.26	4.36	3.79
Middle Eastern countries	5.01	4.32	4.16	3.49	3.58
Western Hemisphere countries	4.28	4.52	4.49	4.01	3.70
Import duties					
All countries	3.25	3.38	3.50	3.09	2.99
OECD countries	1.11	0.87	0.75	0.58	0.37
Non-OECD countries	4.00	4.17	4.35	4.06	3.94
African countries	4.98	5.01	5.30	5.00	5.00
Asian countries	2.78	3.14	3.78	3.87	3.35
Middle Eastern countries	4.34	4.18	3.95	3.28	3.47
Western Hemisphere countries	3.08	3.67	3.70	3.70	3.51
Export duties					
All countries	0.86	0.70	0.51	0.22	0.17
OECD countries	0.07	0.02	0.01	—	—
Non-OECD countries	1.14	0.91	0.66	0.30	0.23
African countries	1.61	1.14	1.04	0.31	0.33
Asian countries	0.71	1.25	0.71	0.49	0.43
Middle Eastern countries	0.56	0.09	0.05	0.04	0.05
Western Hemisphere countries	1.00	0.78	0.40	0.31	0.07

Sources: IMF, *Government Finance Statistics* and *World Economic Outlook* (May 1997); and OECD, *Revenue Statistics.*

Note: "OECD" is Organization for Economic Cooperation and Development.

[1]Last available year is 1995 for most countries, but when this information is not available the last available year is used.

in both strengthened revenue mobilization and a more liberalized trade regime. The more recent phase of reform provides an example of how difficult it is accurately to gauge trade liberalization. Despite reductions in tariff rates in the mid-1990s, the measured collected import tariff rate rose, likely reflecting a combination of improvements in tax and customs administration and some compositional shift in import demand toward finished goods with higher tariffs.

Morocco

With reform of its domestic tax system taking place alongside its program of trade liberalization, Morocco, during its initial reform

Table 9. Taxes on International Trade
(As percentage of tax revenue)

Tax	1975	1980	1985	1990	Last Available Year[1]
Trade taxes					
All countries	26.08	25.77	24.62	21.65	19.79
OECD countries	3.74	2.78	2.21	1.70	1.01
Non-OECD countries	33.63	33.03	31.51	28.79	26.32
African countries	41.23	36.65	35.91	32.92	32.69
Asian countries	29.59	33.73	33.25	27.46	24.17
Middle Eastern countries	29.39	31.80	30.39	28.98	26.88
Western Hemisphere countries	26.89	27.76	24.88	25.35	20.71
Import duties					
All countries	19.87	19.94	19.30	18.35	17.04
OECD countries	3.42	2.65	2.15	1.67	1.01
Non-OECD countries	25.51	25.47	24.64	24.61	22.69
African countries	30.87	28.33	27.31	26.75	26.17
Asian countries	23.06	21.96	23.67	21.95	19.09
Middle Eastern countries	25.35	30.81	29.18	27.07	26.31
Western Hemisphere countries	19.15	21.02	19.84	22.95	19.61
Export duties					
All countries	5.12	4.91	3.64	1.98	1.45
OECD countries	0.29	0.07	0.02	0.01	0.00
Non-OECD countries	6.78	6.46	4.77	2.70	1.97
African countries	9.34	8.92	8.50	4.82	4.10
Asian countries	4.63	6.60	3.70	2.10	2.04
Middle Eastern countries	3.14	0.61	0.30	0.19	0.28
Western Hemisphere countries	6.50	6.00	2.87	2.28	0.41

Sources: IMF, *Government Finance Statistics* and *World Economic Outlook* (May 1997); and OECD, *Revenue Statistics.*

Note: "OECD" is Organization for Economic Cooperation and Development.

[1]Last available year is 1995 for most countries, but when this information is not available the last available year is used.

phase in the 1980s was able to maintain a relatively stable ratio of tax revenue to GDP even as the collected import tariff rate and taxes from international trade declined. In more recent years, the sharp decline in the collected import tariff rate was largely offset by the surge in imports in response to liberalization and sounder policies.

The Philippines

The interesting phase of reform in the Philippines is that which occurred after 1986 against the background of a weak overall revenue

Table 10. International Trade Taxes in African Countries
(As percentage of GDP)

Country	1975	1980	1985	1990	Last Available Year[1]
Benin	...	...	...	...	...
Botswana	11.47	13.29	8.19	6.61	5.85
Burkina Faso	5.54	6.81	5.24	...	...
Burundi[2]	3.52	5.45	5.15	...	4.17
Cameroon	6.84	6.53	3.45	2.23	3.58
Central African Republic	...	...	...	...	...
Chad	4.57	...	...	2.31	11.32
Congo	5.57	4.57	...	...	...
Côte d'Ivoire	...	9.79	9.22	6.98	6.98
Djibouti	...	1.22	1.67	...	...
Ethiopia	3.72	6.68	4.52	2.53	2.50
Gabon[2]	8.01	6.99	6.72	3.89	5.04
Gambia, The	9.32	15.18	11.11	8.79	8.79
Ghana	8.04	3.04	4.61	4.57	4.48
Guinea	...	...	...	...	...
Kenya	3.53	4.16	3.82	3.84	3.94
Lesotho	14.16	...	29.31	22.01	32.28
Liberia	5.54	7.42	5.47	...	...
Madagascar[2]	...	4.52	3.93	3.78	3.39
Malawi[2]	2.81	4.09	4.61	3.05	4.53
Mali	3.71	2.23	3.39	...	...
Mauritania	5.52	...	9.36	...	...
Mauritius[2]	9.30	10.44	12.12	11.35	6.74
Niger	...	5.25	...	...	...
Nigeria	3.14	...	1.45	...	...
Rwanda	4.43	5.42	...	3.07	4.08
Senegal[2]	6.91	5.21	4.45	5.03	4.81
Sierra Leone	6.67	8.14	2.31	2.30	3.67
Somalia	5.49	...	...	...	...
South Africa	1.18	0.79	0.78	0.98	0.45
Sudan	6.88	4.72	...	...	...
Swaziland	26.02	23.75	18.38	...	...
Tanzania	3.82	3.05	1.29	...	...
Togo	...	9.79	9.23	...	...
Uganda	4.36	1.28	4.56	...	...
Zaïre[2]	10.95	3.65	4.43	3.64	1.45
Zambia	2.41	2.08	4.93	3.59	3.06
Zimbabwe	...	1.06	4.71	5.91	5.88
Unweighted average	6.67	6.22	6.50	5.31	5.57

Source: IMF, *Government Finance Statistics.*

[1]Last available year is 1995 for most countries, but when this information is not available the last available year is used.

[2]Data from country authorities and IMF staff estimates.

Table 11. Import Duties in African Countries
(As percentage of GDP)

Country	1975	1980	1985	1990	Last Available Year[1]
Benin	. . .	. . .	. . .	. . .	. . .
Botswana	11.21	13.22	8.16	6.60	5.85
Burkina Faso	5.01	5.94	4.53	. . .	. . .
Burundi[2]	2.97	3.74	2.37	. . .	2.51
Cameroon	4.96	4.81	2.88	2.04	2.56
Central African Republic	. . .	. . .	. . .	. . .	. . .
Chad	3.88	. . .	. . .	. . .	—
Congo	5.43	4.46	. . .	. . .	. . .
Côte d'Ivoire	. . .	7.41	6.38	6.17	6.17
Djibouti	. . .	1.17	1.63	. . .	. . .
Ethiopia	2.90	2.76	2.78	2.19	2.30
Gabon[2]	7.21	6.14	6.07	3.34	4.47
Gambia, The	7.26	12.56	10.42	8.76	8.76
Ghana	2.63	0.84	1.92	3.11	3.37
Guinea	. . .	. . .	. . .	. . .	. . .
Kenya	3.53	3.89	3.28	3.83	3.94
Lesotho	14.04	. . .	29.26	21.95	32.27
Liberia	5.35	7.20	5.40	. . .	. . .
Madagascar[2]	. . .	4.12	0.86	0.84	1.19
Malawi[2]	2.81	4.09	3.70	3.05	3.02
Mali	2.93	1.73	1.69	. . .	. . .
Mauritania	5.06	. . .	5.88	. . .	. . .
Mauritius[2]	5.50	7.50	9.48	10.21	6.74
Niger	. . .	4.54	. . .	. . .	. . .
Nigeria	3.14	. . .	1.43	. . .	. . .
Rwanda	3.05	2.98	. . .	2.17	3.22
Senegal[1]	6.02	4.98	4.42	5.03	4.81
Sierra Leone	5.24	6.01	2.18	2.25	3.62
Somalia	5.13	. . .	. . .	. . .	. . .
South Africa	1.11	0.72	0.73	0.98	0.18
Sudan	4.81	4.53	. . .	. . .	. . .
Swaziland	11.20	20.58	18.37	. . .	. . .
Tanzania	2.64	1.94	1.27	. . .	. . .
Togo	. . .	7.05	7.45	. . .	. . .
Uganda	1.21	0.28	0.58	. . .	. . .
Zaïre[1]	5.89	1.94	3.17	3.26	1.33
Zambia	2.32	2.07	2.86	3.53	3.06
Zimbabwe	. . .	1.06	4.57	5.73	5.72
Unweighted average	4.98	5.01	5.30	5.00	5.00

Source: IMF, *Government Finance Statistics.*

[1]Last available year is 1995 for most countries, but when this information is not available the last available year is used.

[2]Data from country authorities and IMF staff estimates.

Table 12. Export Duties in African Countries
(As percentage of GDP)

Country	1975	1980	1985	1990	Last Available Year[1]
Benin	. . .	. . .	. . .	. . .	. . .
Botswana	0.26	0.06	0.03	0.01	—
Burkina Faso	0.32	0.45	0.30	0.11	. . .
Burundi[2]	0.54	1.70	2.77	. . .	1.60
Cameroon	1.86	1.66	0.52	0.19	1.02
Central African Republic	. . . .	. . .	. . .	. . .	. .
Chad	0.69	. . .	. . .	. . .	—
Congo	0.14	0.07	. . .	. . .	. . .
Côte d'Ivoire	. . .	2.37	2.84	0.81	0.81
Djibouti	. . .	—	0.03	. . .	. . .
Ethiopia	0.81	3.92	1.74	0.34	0.19
Gabon[2]	0.64	0.85	0.65	0.23	0.88
Gambia, The	2.05	2.53	0.69	0.04	0.04
Ghana	5.41	2.16	2.67	1.34	0.91
Guinea	. . .	. . .	. . .	. . .	. . .
Kenya	—	0.27	0.54	0.01	—
Lesotho	0.12	. . .	0.05	0.06	0.02
Liberia	0.10	0.16	0.06	. . .	. . .
Madagascar[2]	. . .0	0.41	1.48	0.80	0.33
Malawi[2]	—	—	0.94	—	—
Mali	0.77	0.43	1.65	. . .	. . .
Mauritania	0.17	. . .	3.48	. . .	. . .
Mauritius[2]	3.80	3.30	2.23	1.07	—
Niger	. . .	0.59	. . .	. . .	. . .
Nigeria	—	. . .	0.02	. . .	. . .
Rwanda	1.38	2.44	. . .	0.78	0.59
Senegal[2]	0.89	0.23	0.02	. . .	. . .
Sierra Leone	1.43	2.09	0.13	0.02	—
Somalia	0.36	. . .	. . .	. . .	. . .
South Africa	0.07	0.04	0.05	—	—
Sudan	0.58	0.20	. . .	. . .	. . .
Swaziland	14.82	3.17	—	. . .	. . .
Tanzania	1.18	1.10	0.01	. . .	. . .
Togo	. . .	1.39	0.28	. . .	. . .
Uganda	3.13	0.98	3.88	. . .	. . .
Zaïre[2]	5.01	1.71	1.26	0.38	0.13
Zambia	—	—	1.83	—	—
Zimbabwe	. . .	—	—	—	—
Unweighted average	1.61	1.14	1.04	0.31	0.33

Source: IMF, *Government Finance Statistics.*

[1]Last available year is 1995 for most countries, but when this information is not available the last available year is used.

[2]Data from country authorities and IMF staff estimates.

Table 13. Tax Revenue and Taxes on International Trade

Tax or Revenue	1986	1987	1988	1989	1990	1991	1992	1993	1994	1995
Tax revenue				*(As percentage of GDP)*						
Côte d'Ivoire	20.35	21.50	20.43	18.09	17.56	16.89	16.93	14.78	16.41	17.84
Ghana	12.20	12.70	12.40	12.30	10.80	12.40	10.00	12.90	16.90	15.00
Madagascar	9.32	10.96	10.49	8.84	9.43	6.85	8.66	8.16	7.69	8.32
Mali	11.90	9.60	8.50	9.80	9.80	12.10	10.40	11.10	10.00	10.70
Nepal	7.40	8.40	8.10	7.04	6.80	6.60	6.90	7.70	8.90	8.66
Niger	9.00	8.04	8.13	8.17	7.90	7.00	6.70	6.60	5.40	6.61
Total taxes on international trade[1]				*(As percentage of GDP)*						
Côte d'Ivoire	7.30	7.22	7.01	6.84	5.70	5.78	4.96	4.48	4.69	5.09
Ghana	2.78	2.38	2.43	3.18	3.23	3.22	3.01	3.55	4.35	4.52
Madagascar	2.90	3.73	4.56	3.86	4.73	3.07	3.98	3.96	3.50	4.31
Mali	4.47	3.59	3.13	3.66	3.71	6.26	5.55	6.12	5.22	5.77
Nepal	2.40	3.05	2.86	2.56	2.46	2.17	2.21	2.42	3.01	2.87
Niger	3.30	2.70	2.73	2.67	3.01	2.35	2.09	2.23	1.95	2.62
Domestic taxes on international trade				*(As percentage of GDP)*						
Côte d'Ivoire	3.13	3.01	2.76	2.66	2.11	1.96	2.00	1.92	2.10	2.25
Ghana	0.46	0.62	0.91	1.31	1.37	1.36	1.18	1.38	1.75	1.85
Madagascar	1.01	1.29	1.64	1.48	1.88	1.27	1.35	1.31	1.58	2.04
Mali	2.01	1.37	1.30	1.58	1.78	1.63	1.43	1.52	1.29	1.69
Nepal	0.23	0.18	0.12	—	0.18	0.30	0.36	0.23	0.38	0.36
Niger	1.85	1.40	1.39	1.35	1.49	1.11	1.00	1.04	0.90	0.98
Customs duties				*(As percentage of GDP)*						
Côte d'Ivoire	4.17	4.21	4.25	4.18	3.59	3.82	2.95	2.55	2.59	2.84
Ghana	2.33	1.77	1.52	1.88	1.86	1.87	1.83	2.17	2.60	2.67
Madagascar	1.90	2.44	2.92	2.38	2.85	1.79	2.62	2.66	1.93	2.27
Mali	2.46	2.22	1.83	2.08	1.93	4.63	4.11	4.60	3.93	4.09
Nepal	2.17	2.88	2.75	2.56	2.29	1.87	1.85	2.18	2.63	2.51
Niger	1.46	1.30	1.34	1.32	1.52	1.24	1.09	1.19	1.05	1.63
Domestic taxes on international trade			*(As percentage of international trade taxes)*							
Côte d'Ivoire	42.91	41.64	39.35	38.86	36.98	33.96	40.40	42.99	44.74	44.21
Ghana	16.35	25.88	37.37	41.03	42.37	42.05	39.11	38.94	40.28	40.88
Madagascar	34.69	34.51	35.93	38.36	39.80	41.47	33.99	32.98	45.03	47.38
Mali	44.92	38.21	41.62	43.10	48.00	26.00	25.84	24.89	24.77	29.25
Nepal	9.70	5.75	4.13	—	7.15	13.81	16.47	9.55	12.55	12.56
Niger	55.92	51.94	50.81	50.52	49.59	47.34	47.83	46.79	46.31	37.54
Customs duties			*(As percentage of international trade taxes)*							
Côte d'Ivoire	57.09	58.36	60.65	61.14	63.02	66.04	59.60	57.01	55.26	55.79
Ghana	83.65	74.12	62.63	58.97	57.63	57.95	60.89	61.06	59.72	59.12
Madagascar	65.31	65.49	64.07	61.64	60.20	58.53	66.01	67.02	54.97	52.62
Mali	55.08	61.79	58.38	56.90	52.00	74.00	74.16	75.11	75.23	70.75
Nepal	90.30	94.25	95.87	100.00	92.85	86.19	83.53	90.45	87.45	87.44
Niger	44.08	48.06	49.19	49.48	50.41	52.66	52.17	53.21	53.69	62.46

Sources: Country authorities; and IMF staff estimates.

[1]The classification is based on domestic taxes on international trade plus customs duties, and excluding exports.

performance (about 10 percent of GNP). The exigencies of budgetary pressures implied that trade reform focused on the elimination of quantitative restrictions, reductions in tariff dispersion, while at the same time bolstering revenues inter alia by introducing a surcharge on non-oil imports. Considering 1994–96, 1 percentage point of the increase in trade tax revenue of 2.4 percentage points of GDP could be credited to the import surcharge, with the balance being due to increased imports and the tariffication of quotas. Again, though, the conflicting trends complicate the measurement of trade liberalization.

Senegal

Senegal provides an example of how difficult it can be to pursue trade liberalization in the absence of essential supporting macroeconomic and structural policies. From 1982/83 to 1988/89, taxes on imports declined from about 5.9 to 3.7 percent of GDP even though the collected tariff rate increased. This largely reflected import compression in the face of an overly appreciated exchange rate that hurt economic activity, a problem that was alleviated with the 1994 devaluation of the CFA franc. Since 1994, import taxes have increased, with the revenue implications of significant tariff reductions and simplification being more than counterbalanced by higher import levels and temporary tariff surcharges to ease the adjustment precipitated by the elimination of import licenses (an action that is analogous to tariffication of a quantitative restriction).

Conclusions

Trade liberalization takes different forms, though it typically emphasizes the elimination of quantitative restrictions and the reduction in the level and dispersion of tariffs. The revenue implications of trade liberalization depend on the nature of existing barriers to trade, the sequencing of reform, the extent to which improvements are made in tax structure and tax and customs administrations, supporting macroeconomic policies, and other economic adjustments. The theoretical predictions are ambiguous, while the empirical evidence, based on several case studies, also suggests that a variety of outcomes is possible. The aggregate data suggest that trade liberalization has been associated with some reduction in reliance on international trade taxes for budgetary revenues.

The experience of Africa, which is highlighted in this chapter, suggests that many African countries have progressed in liberalizing trade, at least when measured by examining indicators such as the elimination of quantitative restrictions and reducing maximum tariffs. They have made less progress in reducing the reliance on trade taxes or in reducing the collected tariff rate. Generalizing broadly, it is clear that in East Africa considerable progress with trade liberalization has been made, starting in the late 1980s, while in the CFA franc zone, considerable progress has been made recently, following the devaluation of the CFA franc in 1994. The CFA franc zone is also notable for the fact that trade tax revenues increased despite tariff reductions because the devaluation resulted in a sharp rise in imports, when measured in domestic currency terms.

Turning to the case studies, all the countries made progress in trade liberalization in recent decades, though not without some hesitation and reversals in each case. Although quantitative restrictions varied across the countries, they all made significant progress in removing them. In the Philippines, the tariffication of quantitative restrictions appears to have strengthened revenues; in Morocco, increased trade resulting from trade liberalization most likely also strengthened revenues. All the countries also made progress in reducing nominal tariffs, though the impact on the revenue from trade taxes was less pronounced. Only Morocco appears to have significantly reduced its reliance on trade taxes. All these countries made at least some effort to improve the structure of the domestic tax system, and also, more recently, tried to improve tax and customs administration. Nevertheless, considerable progress remains to be made, particularly in improving administration. These examples illustrate that trade liberalization need not necessarily lead to fiscal imbalances, though successful reform requires a confluence of sound policies.

Appendix: Country Case Studies

Malawi

In the 1980s, economic growth in Malawi was constrained by a combination of poor macroeconomic management, a series of external shocks, and protectionist trade policies. However, in the late 1980s, Malawi embarked on a program of macroeconomic adjustment and structural policy reforms with the assistance of the International Monetary Fund, the World Bank, and other donors. The program included a focus on trade liberalization, which has continued to the present. Following elections in May 1994, the new government also committed itself to trade reform. The economy has performed well in the past few years with high rates of economic growth and an expansion in international trade.

Trade and Tax Reforms

Initial Conditions

In common with other countries in East Africa, taxes on international trade have traditionally comprised a significant part of Malawi's revenue collections, with trade policy being used to contain external imbalances and to protect domestic industries. Throughout the 1980s, Malawi maintained tight administrative controls on the exchange and trade system in addition to high tariffs. Controls included surrender requirements for foreign exchange and mandatory licensing of exports and imports. The result was a flourishing black market for the Malawian kwacha. The tariff schedule was characterized by extensive tax exemptions and escalating tariff rates by stage of production that resulted in high effective rates of protection.

In addition, elements of Malawi's domestic indirect tax system at that time reinforced protectionism. The broadly based sales tax was structured in such a way that: (1) higher tax rates were levied upon some imported goods than upon the same goods produced domestically; and (2) the tax was suspended for some domestic goods, resulting in protection that may in some cases have exceeded the nominal protection through the tariff system.

Trade Policy Actions

Malawi embarked on trade liberalization in the late 1980s in the context of IMF-supported adjustment programs. Important elements included:

- A program to eliminate foreign exchange rationing by loosening exchange controls, initially on raw materials and industrial spare parts and later on intermediate and capital goods, with the eventual intention of loosening controls on most goods.
- The tariff schedule was unified, with the range of tariffs being reduced from 0–220 percent to 0–45 percent.
- The export regime was also liberalized through revisions to the duty drawback and industrial rebate schemes to improve rebating procedures for producers.
- At the same time, and to support the reform efforts, the currency was devalued by 15 percent against the basket of currencies to which it was pegged.

As a result of these and related efforts, Malawi made considerable progress during the period 1988–91 in liberalizing its trade regime. By 1991, almost all products could be imported without foreign exchange approval. Certain goods were still subject to controls, including several agricultural commodities, used clothing, and matches, and some goods were controlled for health, security, and environmental reasons. The ban on used clothing assisted the domestic textiles industry, dominated by one large firm. These reforms led to reduced government intervention in major exports, better linkage of producer prices to world market prices, and an improvement in exchange rate policy.

The process of reform has continued in more recent years. In particular:

- The remaining licensing on imports and exports has been removed.
- There has been additional progress in tariff reform, albeit at a slow pace. The number of tariff bands was reduced to no more than six rates including zero in 1995; the maximum tariff rate was lowered from 45 to 40 percent in April 1996, and to 35 percent in August 1997; as a result, the weighted average tariff declined from about 21 percent in 1989, to 18 percent in 1995, to less than 15 percent in 1997.
- The remaining restrictions on current account transactions have been lifted, and Malawi accepted Article VIII of the IMF's Articles of Agreement in December 1995.

In the face of widening fiscal gaps, in 1995, the government imposed a temporary export levy of 10 percent on key agricultural exports, namely, tobacco, tea, and sugar. The levy was reduced to 8 percent in 1996, to 4 percent in 1997, but was extended to coffee exports in 1997, and then eliminated in 1998.

Complementary Policy Actions

In addition to liberalizing its trade regime in the late 1980s, Malawi also began a comprehensive reform of the tax system and tax and customs administration. The goals were to reduce marginal tax rates, broaden the tax bases, and eliminate protectionist elements in the domestic tax system.

The reform program was successful. In 1987/88, the surcharge on the sales tax rate for imports was eliminated and was replaced by an adjusted (higher) standard sales tax rate. In 1988/89, an import levy was incorporated into the regular duty rates. Moreover, the sales tax was converted into a credit-based VAT, though, as with the sales tax, the VAT did not extend to services or the retail sector.

Subsequent measures included the phased reduction of the standard corporate tax rate and the standard VAT rate to internationally comparable levels. In 1992/93, the higher surtax rate on imported goods competing with domestic goods and all surtax suspensions were eliminated. Import duty rates for goods previously carrying the higher surtax rate were adjusted upward to limit the loss in protection to domestic producers, with the understanding that these rates would be brought down over time. In 1993/94, the base of excise taxes was expanded to cover imports. These measures virtually eliminated the last remaining differences in the treatment of domestic producers and importers in the domestic tax system.

There was less progress in improving tax and customs administration, reflecting both the extent of the underlying problems with both those administrations. In January 1993, the authorities contracted with Société Générale de Survéillance to operate preshipment inspection. However, the use of preshipment inspection resulted in limited benefits, in part, because the officials were poorly trained in using the results of preshipment inspection to reduce customs evasion.

Revenue Implications of Trade and Tax Reforms

Malawi has traditionally maintained a strong tax effort, with a substantial portion of revenues derived from taxes on international trade (see Tables 14 and 15, and Figures 3 and 4). In 1987/88, at the beginning of the reform program, tax revenues were 15.1 percent of GDP. Taxes on international trade were 19.2 percent of total tax revenues, with a collected import tariff rate of 13.4 percent (despite high nominal tariff rates). During this period, tax reforms were revenue enhancing, and as a consequence tax revenues rose to 18.5 percent of GDP in 1989/90. Liberalization of foreign exchange restrictions led to a small increase in the share of imports in GDP (from 21.5 percent in 1987/88 to 24.5 percent in 1989/90) which served to maintain the share of trade taxes in total tax revenues. The collected import tariff rate remained steady in the absence of any significant reduction in tariffs or shift in the composition of imports.

In the next phase of tax reform, reductions in marginal tax rates and rationalization of the tax system, which were not accompanied by a corresponding expansion in tax bases and a strengthening of tax administration, led to a weakening of tax revenues. The ratio of tax revenue to GDP fell steadily to 14.6 percent in 1993/94. The expansion in imports as a share of GDP in this period buoyed trade taxes, which rose slightly as a share of total tax revenues, even though the collected import tariff rate fell toward the end of this period. This decline in the collected import tariff rate appears to have reflected the effect of both trade reforms (including those under in-

Table 14. Summary Measures of Economic Performance and Revenue Trends for Malawi

Measure	1985/86	1986/87	1987/88	1988/89	1989/90	1990/91	1991/92	1992/93	1993/94	1994/95	1995/96	1996/97
GDP (at current market prices, in millions of Malawi kwacha)	2,010.20	2,332.50	2,992.20	3,660.50	4,558.60	5,338.50	6,252.60	7,255.20	9,648.10	13,867.50	24,743.10	34,912.80
Exchange rates (in national currency per U.S. dollar)	1.72	1.86	2.21	2.56	2.76	2.73	2.80	3.60	4.40	8.74	15.28	15.29
Value of trade = value of imports + exports (in billions of U.S. dollars)	0.54	0.51	0.57	0.66	0.67	0.90	1.09	1.11	0.96	0.93	0.96	1.10
(In millions of Malawi kwacha)	922.55	940.21	1,258.37	1,700.53	1,859.29	2,462.00	3,058.53	3,999.06	4,213.04	8,103.92	14,678.19	16,887.79
(As percentage of GDP)	45.89	40.31	42.06	46.46	40.79	46.12	48.92	55.12	43.67	58.44	59.32	48.37
Value of imports (in billions of U.S. dollars)	0.29	0.26	0.29	0.37	0.40	0.49	0.62	0.71	0.63	0.55	0.56	0.61
(In millions of Malawi kwacha)	492.90	478.00	643.30	948.82	1,117.58	1,338.85	1,725.38	2,567.19	2,787.41	4,847.21	8,514.28	9,350.46
(As percentage of GDP)	24.52	20.49	21.50	25.92	24.52	25.08	27.59	35.38	28.89	34.95	34.41	26.78
Value of exports (in billions of U.S. dollars)	0.25	0.25	0.28	0.29	0.27	0.41	0.48	0.40	0.32	0.37	0.40	0.49
(In millions of Malawi kwacha)	429.65	462.21	615.07	751.71	741.71	1,123.15	1,333.14	1,431.87	1,425.63	3,256.71	6,163.91	7,537.33
(As percentage of GDP)	21.37	19.82	20.56	20.54	16.27	21.04	21.32	19.74	14.78	23.48	24.91	21.59
Tax revenue (in millions of Malawi kwacha)	373.40	391.10	450.20	653.60	844.70	888.10	1,021.70	1,126.70	1,407.60	2,031.50	3,854.40	5,651.20As
(As percentage of GDP)	18.58	16.77	15.05	17.86	18.53	16.64	16.34	15.53	14.59	14.65	15.58	16.19
International trade taxes (In millions of Malawi kwacha)	92.60	80.20	86.60	113.80	152.20	162.80	211.50	256.40	269.90	458.60	1,121.40	1,358.70
(As percentage of GDP)	4.61	3.44	2.89	3.11	3.34	3.05	3.38	3.53	2.80	3.31	4.53	3.89
(As percentage of tax revenue)	24.80	20.51	19.24	17.41	18.02	18.33	20.70	22.76	19.17	22.57	29.09	24.04

Import duties (in millions of Malawi kwacha)	74.30	75.80	86.40	117.10	152.20	162.80	210.00	255.50	267.90	457.00	746.40	1,018.20
(As percentage of GDP)	3.70	3.25	2.89	3.20	3.34	3.05	3.36	3.52	2.78	3.30	3.02	2.92
Collected international trade tariff = international trade taxes/value of trade	10.04	8.53	6.88	6.69	8.19	6.61	6.92	6.41	6.41	5.66	7.64	8.05
Collected import tariff = import duties/value of imports	15.07	15.86	13.43	12.34	13.62	12.16	12.17	9.95	9.61	9.43	8.77	10.89
Domestic taxes on goods and services (in millions of Malawi kwacha)	129.30	146.20	189.70	258.40	336.30	347.20	391.00	423.00	619.40	816.60	1,439.90	1,965.00
(As percentage of GDP)	6.43	6.27	6.34	7.06	7.38	6.50	6.25	5.83	6.42	5.89	5.82	5.63
(As percentage of tax revenue)	34.63	37.38	42.14	39.53	39.81	39.09	38.27	37.54	44.00	40.20	37.36	34.77
Budget deficit excluding grants (in millions of Malawi kwacha)	–201.50	–304.10	–273.10	–266.80	–301.40	–359.00	–395.00	–1,048.00	–799.00	–3,891.60	–3,427.30	–2,793.70
(As percentage of GDP)	–10.02	–13.04	–9.13	–7.29	–6.61	–6.72	–6.32	–14.44	–8.28	–28.06	–13.85	–8.00
Budget deficit including grants (in millions of Malawi kwacha)	–156.70	–224.50	–197.00	–57.70	–91.50	–246.30	–187.00	–874.00	–515.00	–2,376.30	–1,441.10	–1,086.00
(As percentage of GDP)	–7.80	–9.62	–6.58	–1.58	–2.01	–4.61	–2.99	–12.05	–5.34	–17.14	–5.82	–3.11
Current account balance (in billions of U.S. dollars)	–0.07	–0.04	–0.03	–0.02	–0.14	–0.06	–0.15	–0.22	–0.22	–0.15	–0.11	–0.11
(As percentage of GDP)												
Excluding official transfer	–8.55	–5.98	–5.19	–8.23	–13.97	–8.02	–9.77	–19.99	–16.96	–17.93	–15.95	–8.49
Including official transfer	–6.38	–3.54	–2.60	–1.36	–9.07	–3.52	–7.05	–12.08	–11.00	–11.42	–7.84	–5.19

Sources: Ministry of Finance; IMF staff estimates; IMF, *World Economic Outlook* (May 1997).

Table 15. Central Government Revenue in Malawi
(As percentage of GDP)

Component	1980/81	1981/82	1982/83	1983/84	1984/85	1985/86	1986/87
Total revenue	19.36	19.40	18.94	19.09	20.41	21.99	21.13
Tax revenue	16.22	15.72	16.10	15.94	17.11	18.58	16.77
Taxes on income, profits, and capital gains	6.31	5.43	6.16	6.26	6.77	7.43	6.96
Individual	2.48	2.43	2.66	2.70	2.60	2.34	2.51
Corporate	3.83	3.00	3.50	3.56	4.17	5.09	4.45
Other taxes on income, profits, and capital gains	. . .	. . .	. . .	. . .	. . .	. . .	. . .
Taxes on property	0.01	0.01	0.01	0.02	0.01	0.02	0.02
Taxes on payroll	. . .	. . .	. . .	. . .	. . .	. . .	. . .
Social security contributions	. . .	. . .	. . .	. . .	. . .	. . .	. . .
Domestic taxes on goods and services	5.75	5.81	5.73	5.74	6.39	6.43	6.27
Taxes on general sales, turnover or VAT	4.72	4.74	4.52	4.53	5.32	5.16	5.08
Excises	0.76	0.79	0.90	0.87	0.72	0.68	0.59
Other taxes on domestic goods and services	0.27	0.27	0.31	0.35	0.35	0.60	0.60
Taxes on international trade	4.09	4.41	4.07	3.91	3.85	4.61	3.44
Imports	4.09	4.41	4.07	3.91	3.85	3.70	3.25
Exports	. . .	. . .	. . .	. . .	. . .	0.91	0.19
Other taxes on international trade	. . .	. . .	. . .	. . .	. . .	. . .	. . .
Other taxes[1]	0.06	0.07	0.14	0.02	0.09	0.08	0.09
Tax refunds	—	—	—	—	—	—	—
Nontax revenue	3.14	3.68	2.84	3.15	3.30	3.41	4.36

Sources: Country authorities; and IMF staff estimates.
Note: Fiscal year beginning April 1.
[1]Includes stamp duties and drought levy.

ternational commitments) and declining administrative effectiveness in this period.

In the most recent phase of reform, tax revenues have begun to strengthen, rising to 16.2 percent of GDP in 1996/97. In part, this increase reflects the stabilization of the economy and rapid growth in recent years, the cessation of reductions in marginal tax rates in the domestic tax system, some improvements in tax administration, and the effect of the temporary export levy. International trade taxes were 24.0 percent of tax revenues in 1996/97, after peaking at 29.1 percent the previous year. This increase appears to reflect a combination of both the temporary export levy and an increase in the collected im-

1987/88	1988/89	1989/90	1990/91	1991/92	1992/93	1993/94	1994/95	1995/96	1996/97
19.50	21.26	21.81	19.54	18.90	18.36	16.88	16.09	17.93	17.02
15.05	17.86	18.53	16.64	16.34	15.53	14.59	14.65	15.58	16.19
5.73	7.60	7.67	6.96	6.60	5.86	5.28	5.39	5.68	7.05
2.50	2.99	3.15	2.78	2.74	3.00	2.67	2.95	2.89	3.17
3.24	4.61	4.52	4.17	3.86	2.85	2.61	2.44	2.79	3.88
. . .	. . .	. . .	. . .	. . .	. . .	. . .	. . .	. . .	. . .
0.01	0.01	0.03	0.01	0.01	0.01	0.01	—	—	—
. . .	. . .	. . .	. . .	. . .	. . .	. . .	. . .	. . .	. . .
. . .	. . .	. . .	. . .	. . .	. . .	. . .	. . .	. . .	. . .
6.34	7.06	7.38	6.50	6.25	5.83	6.42	5.89	5.82	5.63
5.33	6.13	6.44	5.65	5.48	5.13	5.68	5.05	5.01	4.74
0.44	0.57	0.63	0.57	0.52	0.53	0.62	0.76	0.75	0.83
0.57	0.36	0.30	0.28	0.24	0.17	0.12	0.08	0.06	0.05
2.89	3.11	3.34	3.05	3.38	3.53	2.80	3.31	4.53	3.89
2.89	3.20	3.34	3.05	3.36	3.52	2.78	3.30	3.02	2.92
0.01	–0.09	—	—	—	—	—	—	1.43	0.95
. . .	. . .	. . .	. . .	0.02	0.01	0.02	0.01	0.08	0.02
0.07	0.08	0.12	0.12	0.10	0.30	0.09	0.06	0.04	0.05
—	—	—	—	—	—	—	—	–0.49	–0.43
4.45	3.41	3.28	2.91	2.56	2.83	2.29	1.44	2.36	0.84

port tariff rate. This latter increase is surprising given the reductions in tariff rates. It probably reflects a combination of both improvements in administrative effectiveness and perhaps some compositional changes in imports toward finished goods, which face higher tariffs. Domestic indirect taxes have not shown the same improvements, in part because of delays in implementing a fully fledged VAT.

Conclusions

In the past decade, Malawi has liberalized its trade regime by eliminating virtually all quantitative and foreign exchange restrictions, lib-

Figure 3. Malawi: Summary Measures of Economic Performance and Revenue Trends, Percentage of GDP

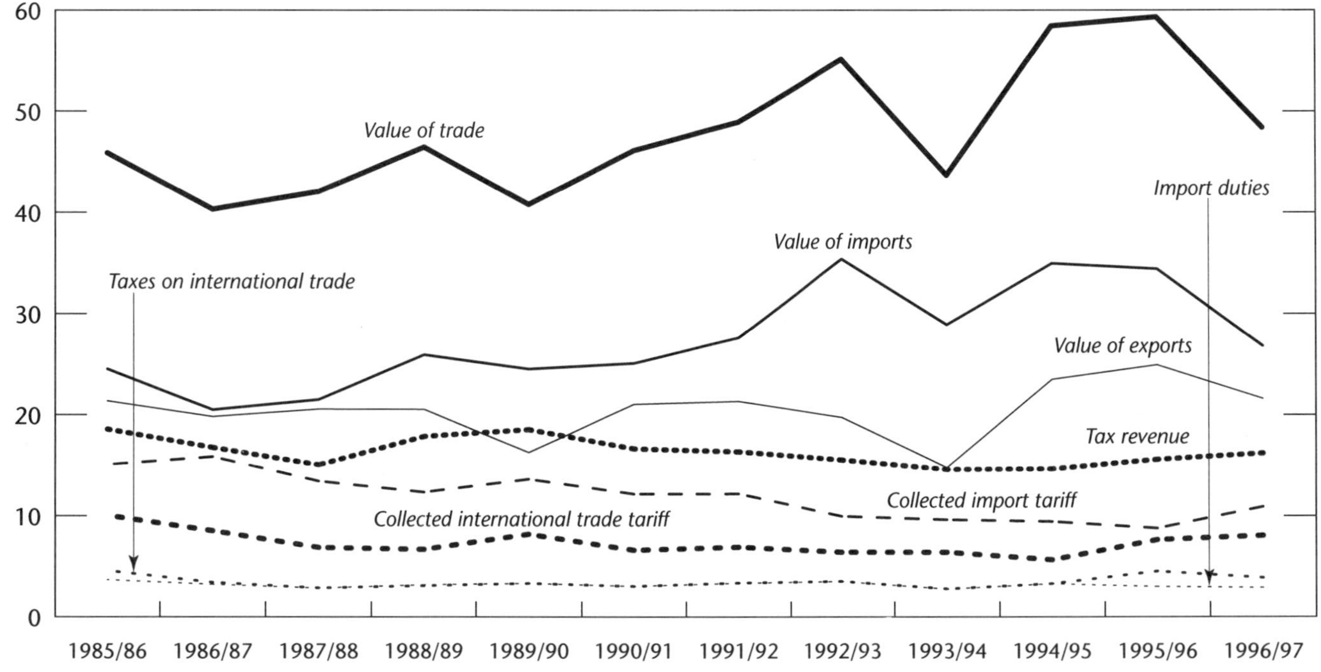

Sources: Ministry of Finance; IMF staff calculations; IMF, *World Economic Outlook* (May 1997).

Figure 4. Malawi: Central Government Revenue, Percentage of GDP

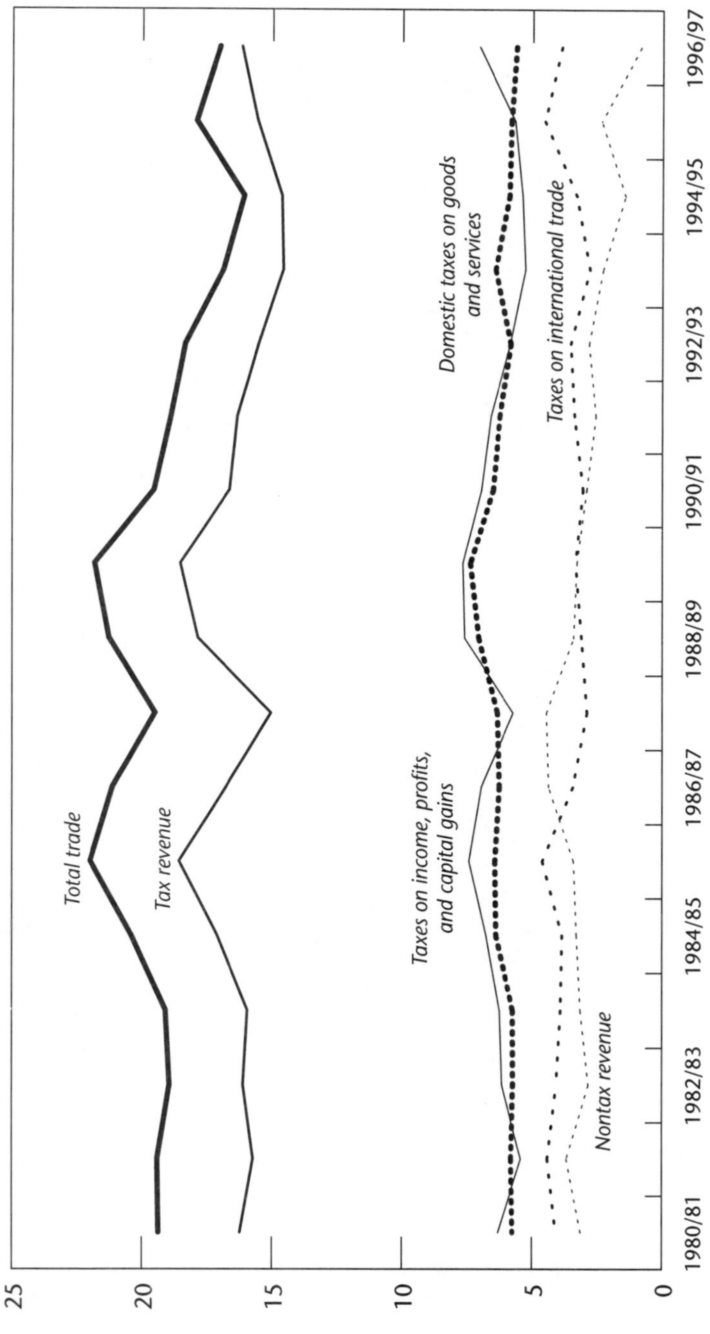

Sources: Data provided by the country authorities; IMF staff estimates.

eralizing and improving the operation of foreign exchange markets, simplifying and consolidating the tariff schedule, and reducing tariff rates. In recent years, there has been some reduction in the collected import tariff rate, reflecting tariff cuts. The introduction of a temporary export levy for revenue reasons in 1995 has been the only backsliding on trade liberalization. Despite this impressive record of trade liberalization, Malawi continues to depend heavily on trade tax revenues. Continuous and significant reform of the domestic tax system has eliminated elements of protectionism and has dramatically improved its structure. Nevertheless, Malawi has yet to implement a fully fledged VAT, and tax and customs administration reform has lagged seriously—though, with the aid of technical assistance, it is now under way. Malawi's experience with trade liberalization leads to several conclusions:

- Strengthening the domestic tax system and removing elements that contribute to protection for domestic industries are essential components of successful reform; however, reforms that reduce marginal tax rates may entail revenue losses if they are not accompanied by measures to improve tax administration and if they proceed too rapidly.
- Strengthening customs administration is an equally important component of successful reform. Preshipment inspection is no substitute for adequate reforms.
- Rationalizing and simplifying tariffs and liberalizing foreign exchange markets are also essential components of successful reform and should be undertaken early in the process.

Morocco

Morocco is an example of a country that has achieved substantial liberalization of its economy. The country implemented comprehensive trade and other structural reforms in the context of IMF- and World Bank–supported adjustment programs during the period 1980–92. Subsequently, Morocco has further liberalized its trade and exchange system, launched a privatization program, and undertaken a comprehensive overhaul of the financial sector.

Trade and Tax Reforms

Initial Conditions

Until the early 1980s, Morocco's trade policy attempted to promote industrialization through protectionism and to use trade restrictions to raise revenues and contain external imbalances. There was extensive resort to both quantitative restrictions and high tariffs, resulting in high effective protection and discrimination against labor-intensive activities. Specifically, imports were regulated by a program, which categorized goods between those that could be freely imported, those for which quantitative restrictions applied, and those whose importation was prohibited. Quantitative restrictions were enforced through import licensing and state trading. Supplementing these restrictions were foreign exchange controls on, inter alia, the repatriation of profits and capital, foreign ownership of local enterprises, and foreign borrowing by local firms. Exporters were required to surrender foreign exchange earnings. In addition, ad valorem taxes applied to exports of agricultural products and their derivatives (1 percent) and mineral products (5 percent). Phosphate exports were subject to a specific tax.

Trade Policy Actions

During the 1980s, the trade and foreign investment regimes were reformed in a shift toward outward-oriented development. Focusing on the trade liberalization strategy adopted in 1983, which was intended to reduce gradually the level and dispersion of tariffs, important reforms included:

- Quantitative restrictions on imports were gradually eliminated, although licensing requirements remained.
- The maximum tariff rate was cut from 400 percent in 1982 to 60 percent in 1984 (except for a few agricultural goods), and the special import tax rate was cut from 15 percent in 1983 to 5 percent in 1987. Import taxes other than tariffs were simplified in 1988 by replacing the special import taxes and stamp duties on imports with a single flat import levy of 12.5 percent applied to virtually all imports. This rate was raised to 15 percent in 1993 for most products. The number of tariff bands was reduced from 47 in 1980 to 26 in 1988 to 9 in 1992 and to 6 in 1996.
- As regards exchange restrictions, import deposit requirements were abolished in 1984, and the requirement of approval from the Moroccan Exchange Office for payments for imports on goods subject to quantitative restrictions was eliminated in 1990.

Additional important reforms were implemented during the 1990s:

- The ad valorem taxes levied on exports were abolished in 1995, leaving only raw phosphate exports subject to a specific tax. Export licensing requirements were virtually abolished by 1994.
- There were measures to improve tax administration in the areas of procedures for tax assessment, collection, and auditing, though

important deficiencies remain. Since late 1996, a complete overhaul of the customs administration has been undertaken.[14] These reforms emphasize value controls, improved electronic data processing, staff training, and codification of customs legislation.

- Morocco accepted Article VIII status in January 1993. Moreover, by the end of 1993, Morocco had achieved virtually full capital account convertibility for foreign investors. Additional steps were taken to liberalize capital mobility for domestic residents as well, through the elimination of surrender requirements and foreign borrowing restrictions.

Although most quantitative restrictions were replaced with tariffs, the collected import tariff rate fell from 26.3 percent in 1980 to 19.3 percent in 1993 and to 14.9 percent in 1995 (see Tables 16 and 17 and Figures 5 and 6). However, numerous commodities remain subject to reference prices, thus rendering collected tariff rates on some of them as high as 300 percent. Moreover, tariffs are still widely dispersed, with higher rates on locally produced goods and lower rates on inputs, equipment goods, and nonlocally produced goods. Although quantitative restrictions applied in 1994 to only a few goods, and although over time there has been a reduction in licensing requirements, many imports are still subject to licensing, particularly in the food, beverages, tobacco, and fuel and lubricants areas.

Complementary Policy Actions

Reform of the domestic tax system has taken place along with trade reform. Morocco reformed its import and manufacturing-stage turnover tax that was associated with cascading and multiple rate excises with a VAT in April 1986 on goods and services. The VAT initially had five rates, ranging from 7 to 30 percent with the basic rate fixed at 19 percent, but the number of rates was subsequently reduced to three in 1993 (7, 14, and 19 percent). The VAT has, to a large extent, achieved simplification and neutrality by unifying the two sales taxes, extending the tax base to the distribution sector, reducing the number of rates, and generalizing the tax credit mechanism to eliminate the cascading effects of the tax on services. The introduction of the VAT also spurred increased use of computerization. A corporate tax was intro-

[14]Customs administration has been in sore need of reform. Obsolete procedures imply that the average period of stay of goods in port can be 16 days (as compared with 1–3 days in most industrial countries). Moreover, there are numerous exemptions, leading to loss of revenue and creating opportunities for evasion and fraud.

duced in 1988 at a rate of 40 percent, which was reduced to 36 percent in 1994. The personal income tax was introduced in 1990. The maximum rate of 52 percent had been reduced to 46 percent by 1994.

International Commitments

In addition to commitments under the WTO-GATT agreement, Morocco signed an Association Agreement with the European Union in February 1996 which calls, inter alia, for a gradual removal of all tariffs on industrial goods imports from the EU during 12 years. Tariff removal will be fastest for imported inputs and investment goods and slowest for imports competing with domestically produced consumer goods. While agricultural trade is not liberalized under the agreement, preferential access for certain Moroccan exports is increased, and the regime for agricultural trade will be reviewed in 2000 with a view to moving to a more liberal regime.

Morocco is also a member of the Arab Maghreb Union (AMU), which includes Algeria, Libya, Mauritania, and Tunisia. Two conventions have been signed within the framework of the Union. The first, dating from 1991, has yet to be ratified. It exempts a number of goods from nontariff barriers and provides for the application of a compensatory tax of 17.5 percent on goods benefiting from a special customs regime. The second convention, dating from 1990, deals with trade in agricultural products. The AMU intends to establish a free trade area.

The authorities are committed to further trade liberalization and tariff reforms under WTO-GATT and AAEU. During a period of 12 years, Morocco will dismantle its import duties on imports from the EU according to a timetable depending on the nature of the good—capital goods not manufactured in Morocco will be duty free as from the implementation of the agreement, whereas the reduction on duties on most items manufactured in Morocco will be reduced by 10 percentage points each year during the 12 years following the date of implementation. Quantitative restrictions on imports from the EU were abolished in 1997.

Revenue Implications of Reform

Despite extensive trade reform, Morocco maintained a relatively stable tax revenue share in GDP during the 1980s. The ratio remained in the range of 18 to 21 percent, only rising substantially toward the end of the decade, reflecting the influence of the introduction of the VAT in 1986. This overall trend contrasts with that for international trade taxes, mainly import duties, which declined steadily from 1982 to

Table 16. Summary Measures of Economic Performance

Measure	1980	1981	1982	1983	1984	1985
GDP (at current market prices, in millions of Moroccan dirhams)	74,090.0	79,034.0	92,898.0	99,143.0	112,345.0	129,507.0
Exchange rates						
(In national currency per U.S. dollar)	3.9	5.2	6.0	7.1	8.8	10.1
Value of trade = value of imports + exports						
(In billions of U.S. dollars)	6.2	6.2	5.9	5.4	5.7	5.7
(In millions of Moroccan dirhams)	24,490.0	31,867.0	35,456.0	38,239.0	50,578.0	57,121.0
(As percentage of GDP)	33.1	40.3	38.2	38.6	45.0	44.1
Value of imports						
(In billions of U.S. dollars)	3.8	3.8	3.8	3.3	3.6	3.5
(In millions of Moroccan dirhams)	14,845.0	19,864.0	22,986.0	23,482.0	31,460.0	35,370.0
(As percentage of GDP)	20.0	25.1	24.7	23.7	28.0	27.3
Value of exports						
(In billions of U.S. dollars)	2.5	2.3	2.1	2.1	2.2	2.2
(In millions of Moroccan dirhams)	9,645.0	12,003.0	12,470.0	14,757.0	19,118.0	21,751.0
(As percentage of GDP)	13.0	15.2	13.4	14.9	17.0	16.8
Tax revenue						
(In millions of Moroccan dirhams)	13,888.0	15,321.0	18,141.0	19,093.0	21,173.0	23,695.0
(As percentage of GDP)	18.7	19.4	19.5	19.3	18.8	18.3
International trade taxes						
(In millions of Moroccan dirhams)	4,121.0	4,892.0	5,792.0	5,262.0	5,627.0	5,771.0
(As percentage of GDP)	5.6	6.2	6.2	5.3	5.0	4.5
(As percentage of tax revenue)	29.7	31.9	31.9	27.6	26.6	24.4
Import duties						
(In millions of Moroccan dirhams)	3,907.0	4,635.0	5,546.0	5,039.0	5,331.0	5,438.0
(As percentage of GDP)	5.3	5.9	6.0	5.1	4.7	4.2
Collected international trade tariff = international trade taxes/value of trade	16.8	15.4	16.3	13.8	11.1	10.1
Collected import tariff = import duties/value of imports	26.3	23.3	24.1	21.5	16.9	15.4
Domestic taxes on goods and services						
(In millions of Moroccan dirhams)	5,806.0	6,040.0	7,813.0	8,693.0	9,561.0	10,847.0
(As percentage of GDP)	7.8	7.6	8.4	8.8	8.5	8.4
(As percentage of tax revenue)	41.8	39.4	43.1	45.5	45.2	45.8
Overall balance (payment – order basis						
(In millions of Moroccan dirhams)	–7,510.0	–11,098.0	–11,522.0	–11,985.0	–12,575.0	–12,457.0
(As percentage of GDP)	–10.1	–14.0	–12.4	–12.1	–11.2	–9.6
Overall balance						
(Cash basis, in millions of Moroccan dirhams)	–7,246.0	–11,229.0	–8,561.0	–11,413.0	–9,061.0	–11,104.0
(As percentage of GDP)	–9.8	–14.2	–9.2	–11.5	–8.1	–8.6
Current account balance						
(In billions of U.S. dollars)	–1.5	–1.6	–1.9	–1.0	–1.4	–0.7
(As percentage of GDP)						
Excluding official transfer						
Including official transfer	–7.76	–10.75	–12.29	–7.32	–10.95	–5.79

Sources: Moroccan authorities; IMF staff estimates; and IMF, *World Economic Outlook* (May 1997).

and Revenue Trends for Morocco

1986	1987	1988	1989	1990	1991	1992	1993	1994	1995
154,725.0	156,690.0	182,230.0	193,931.0	212,820.0	242,360.0	242,910.0	249,223.0	279,295.0	276,878.0
9.1	8.4	8.2	8.5	8.2	8.7	8.5	9.3	9.2	8.5
5.9	6.6	8.0	8.3	10.5	10.5	10.7	11.9	13.2	16.1
53,797.0	55,435.0	65,544.7	70,670.0	86,625.5	91,729.0	91,074.9	110,807.0	121,166.0	137,829.0
34.8	35.4	36.0	36.4	40.7	37.8	37.5	44.5	43.4	49.8
3.5	3.9	4.4	5.0	6.3	6.3	6.7	7.0	7.6	9.3
31,691.0	32,184.0	35,789.2	42,400.0	51,767.5	54,445.0	57,114.9	64,911.0	70,201.0	79,149.0
20.5	20.5	19.6	21.9	24.3	22.5	23.5	26.0	25.1	28.6
2.4	2.8	3.6	3.3	4.2	4.3	4.0	4.9	5.5	6.9
22,106.0	23,251.0	29,755.4	28,270.0	34,858.0	37,284.0	33,960.0	45,896.0	50,965.0	58,680.0
14.3	14.8	16.3	14.6	16.4	15.4	14.0	18.4	18.2	21.2
27,835.0	30,702.0	37,577.0	40,458.0	46,462.0	50,452.0	57,952.0	57,868.0	59,386.0	60,885.0
18.0	19.6	20.6	20.9	21.8	20.8	23.9	23.2	21.3	22.0
5,600.0	5,639.0	7,345.0	8,512.0	10,038.0	11,466.0	12,286.0	12,556.0	12,990.0	11,843.0
3.6	3.6	4.0	4.4	4.7	4.7	5.1	5.0	4.7	4.3
20.1	18.4	19.5	21.0	21.6	22.7	21.2	21.7	21.9	19.5
5,376.0	5,456.0	7,176.0	8,335.0	9,875.0	11,346.0	12,258.0	12,547.0	12,978.0	11,811.0
3.5	3.5	3.9	4.3	4.6	4.7	5.0	5.0	4.6	4.3
10.4	10.2	11.2	12.0	11.6	12.5	13.5	11.3	10.7	8.6
17.0	17.0	20.1	19.7	19.1	20.8	21.5	19.3	18.5	14.9
14,710.0	16,530.0	19,923.0	20,469.0	20,926.0	23,042.0	26,380.0	27,528.0	28,629.0	30,299.0
9.5	10.5	10.9	10.6	9.8	9.5	10.9	11.0	10.3	10.9
52.8	53.8	53.0	50.6	45.0	45.7	45.5	47.6	48.2	49.8
–8,290.0	–9,270.0	–8,397.0	–11,589.0	–7,526.0	–7,515.0	–5,338.0	–7,521.0	–8,854.0	–1,4553.0
–5.4	–5.9	–4.6	–6.0	–3.5	–3.1	–2.2	–3.0	–3.2	–5.3
–8,834.0	–9,938.0	–10,482.0	–9,389.0	–9,830.0	–7,518.0	–4,997.0	–8,932.0	–9,143.0	–9,430.0
–5.7	–6.3	–5.8	–4.8	–4.6	–3.1	–2.1	–3.6	–3.3	–3.4
–0.7	–0.2	0.2	–1.1	0.1	–0.1	–0.6	–0.5	–0.7	–1.5
		0.68	–4.81	–2.71	–2.11	–2.37	–2.08	–2.53	–4.91
–3.88	–1.07	1.08	–4.65	0.36	–0.22	–2.03	–1.97	–2.35	–4.69

Table 17. Central Government Operations in Morocco

(As percentage of GDP)

Component	1980	1981	1982	1983	1984	1985	1986	1987	1988	1989	1990	1991	1992	1993	1994	1995
Total revenue[1]	22.09	22.57	22.05	21.27	20.89	20.65	18.84	20.90	22.53	22.60	23.95	22.92	26.21	26.04	24.19	23.92
Tax revenue	18.74	19.39	19.53	19.26	18.85	18.30	17.99	19.59	20.62	20.86	21.83	20.82	23.86	23.22	21.26	21.99
Taxes on income, profits, and capital gains	4.51	4.77	4.12	4.38	4.44	4.58	4.03	4.52	4.76	5.02	5.28	5.49	6.84	6.11	5.37	5.75
Individual	1.47	1.65	1.68	1.86	1.80	1.87	1.74	1.90	1.86	2.04	2.01	2.18	2.73	2.80	2.60	2.78
Corporate	2.32	2.28	1.68	1.80	1.91	1.92	1.63	1.80	2.04	2.07	2.56	2.32	2.97	2.16	1.85	1.86
Other taxes on income, profits, and capital gains	0.72	0.83	0.76	0.72	0.73	0.80	0.66	0.82	0.86	0.91	0.72	0.99	1.15	1.16	0.92	1.11
Taxes on property	0.38	0.34	0.33	0.35	0.35	0.36	0.34	0.40	0.39	0.36	0.38	...	...	...	...	...
Taxes on payroll	...	...	...	...	...	...	...	...	...	...	...	...	...	...	...	...
Social security contributions	...	...	...	...	...	...	...	...	...	...	...	...	...	...	...	...
Domestic taxes on goods and services	7.84	7.64	8.41	8.77	8.51	8.38	9.51	10.55	10.93	10.55	9.83	9.51	10.86	11.05	10.25	10.94
Taxes on general sales, turnover or VAT	4.95	5.11	5.85	6.06	5.84	5.98	5.07	5.23	5.23	5.45	5.63	5.54	6.12	5.86	5.37	5.71
Excises	2.46	2.21	2.09	2.31	2.23	1.99	1.71	2.02	1.94	1.99	2.09	3.91	4.61	5.13	4.80	5.14
Other taxes on domestic goods and services	0.43	0.32	0.47	0.41	0.45	0.41	2.73	3.30	3.76	3.12	2.12	0.06	0.12	0.06	0.08	0.08
Taxes on international trade	5.56	6.19	6.23	5.31	5.01	4.46	3.62	3.60	4.03	4.39	4.72	4.73	5.06	5.04	4.65	4.28
Imports	5.27	5.86	5.97	5.08	4.75	4.20	3.47	3.48	3.94	4.30	4.64	4.68	5.05	5.03	4.65	4.27
Exports	0.29	0.33	0.26	0.22	0.26	0.26	0.14	0.12	0.09	0.09	0.08	0.05	0.01	0.00	0.00	0.01
Other taxes on international trade	...	...	...	...	...	...	...	...	...	...	...	...	...	...	...	...
Other taxes	0.46	0.44	0.43	0.45	0.54	0.52	0.50	0.52	0.50	0.53	1.62	1.09	1.10	1.02	0.99	1.02
Nontax revenue	1.76	3.18	2.52	2.01	2.04	2.36	0.85	1.31	1.91	1.74	2.12	2.10	2.35	2.82	2.93	1.93

Sources: Country authorities; and IMF staff estimates.

[1]Includes extrabudgetary revenue in 1980. Excludes receipts from privatization.

Figure 5. Morocco: Summary Measures of Economic Performance and Revenue Trends, Percentage of GDP

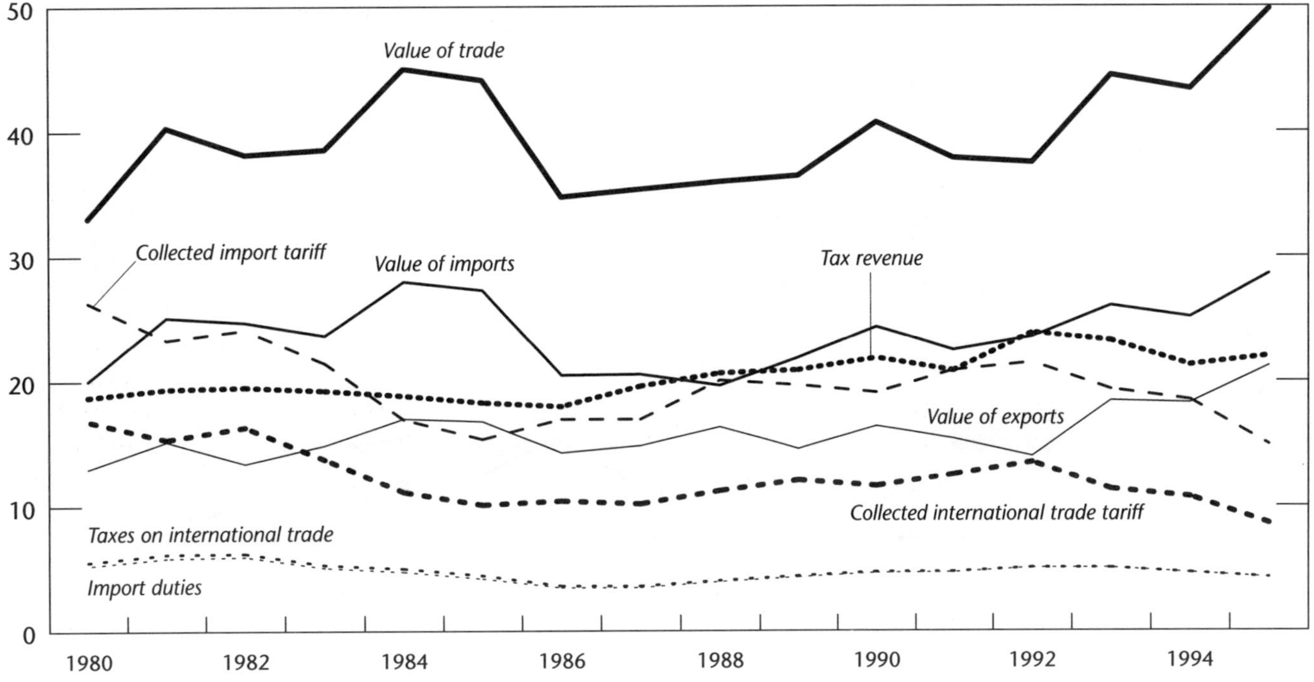

Sources: Data provided by the Moroccan authorities; IMF staff estimates; IMF, *World Economic Outlook* (May 1997).

Figure 6. Morocco: Central Government Operations, Percentage of GDP

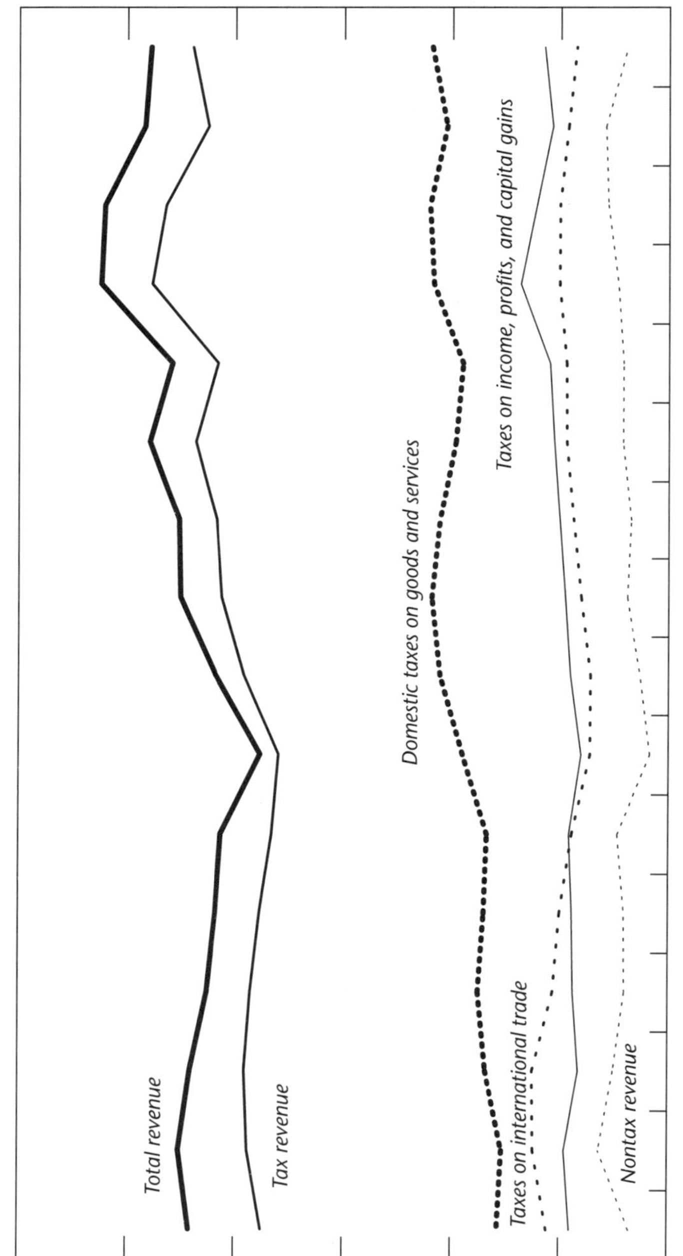

Sources: Data provided by the authorities; IMF staff estimates.

1987, during the initial period of reform. The collected import tariff rate dropped sharply between 1983 and 1984 (from 21.5 to 16.9 percent) in response to the initial round of trade reforms. The value of imports, in contrast, did not rise during this period but remained relatively stable. Toward the end of the decade, imports, the collected import tariff rate, tax revenues, and international trade taxes reversed their trend and rose. The increase in the collected import tariff may have reflected the beneficial effect of consolidation and simplification of the import levies (and therefore an effective increase), or a shift in the composition of imports. Exports, in contrast, fluctuated in this period. In the 1990s, tax revenues continued to strengthen, reaching 22 percent of GDP by 1995. A large increase in imports was accompanied by a sharp decline in the collected import tariff rate (reaching 14.9 percent of GDP in 1995), leading to a decline in international trade taxes as well (falling to 4.3 percent of GDP in 1995).

The implementation of the AAEU in the next few years is expected to result in a gradual loss of tariff revenue from EU imports, estimated by the Moroccan Customs Office to reach cumulatively up to 3.2 percent of 1995 GDP after 12 years; the loss of tariff revenue will ultimately depend on the extent to which imports from non-EU countries will be replaced by imports from the EU.

Conclusions

As the above discussion makes clear, Morocco has succeeded in achieving a substantial liberalization of its economy without to this point experiencing a sharp deterioration in revenue performance. Several features in the reform process should be highlighted:

- The revenue from international trade taxation has held up, despite the many tariff rate reductions reflecting, inter alia, the positive impact on revenues of (1) the elimination and reduction of quantitative restrictions on trade, (2) the relaxation of foreign exchange controls, and (3) the lowering of tariff rates that were effectively prohibitive.
- More generally, the combination of trade liberalization and improved stabilization policies has resulted in a significant increase in the openness of the economy, resulting in a strengthened revenue performance.
- The broadening of the tax base, notably by the introduction of the VAT, has supported the process of reform by helping to insulate budgetary revenues from the direct impact of trade liberalization.

However, with the next stage of trade reform arising from Morocco's closer association with the EU likely to have a significant impact on revenues, Morocco faces the challenge of having to further broaden the tax base.

The Philippines

Since the debt crisis of late 1983, the Philippine authorities have been working to place the economy onto a path of sustained growth. The first growth spurt, in 1988/89, proved to be short, however, because the economic structure that had precipitated the 1983 default remained unchanged and because the economy was subjected to a number of shocks. On the former, sheltered by protectionist barriers, the industrial sector was oriented toward the domestic market. Consequently, the higher demand arising from growth quickly spilled over into an import surge and a large overall balance of payments deficit. On the latter, the shocks included an attempted coup, a sharp rise in world oil prices, and several natural disasters. The result was a large fiscal deficit and significant debt accumulation. The authorities responded by encouraging export-oriented growth and pursuing sound financial policies, in particular fiscal consolidation. To open up the economy, quantitative restrictions were eliminated and replaced by tariffs. The foreign exchange system was liberalized and fiscal policy was tightened. The consolidated public sector deficit was reduced to near budget balance in recent years.

Trade and Tax Reforms

Initial Conditions

As noted above, the trade regime in the Philippines has been characterized by a high degree of protectionism to encourage import substitution. In addition to tariffs, the trade regime has also relied on quantitative and foreign exchange restrictions.

Trade Policy Actions

Trade tax reform in the Philippines took place in three phases. The first two phases covered 1980–85 and 1986–90 and achieved the following:

- Between 1980 and 1985, the average statutory tariff was reduced from 41 to 28 percent. The import ban on 921 consumer goods was lifted, although their importation continued to require government approval. Domestic indirect taxes were reformed to remove the anti-import bias, including the elimination of differential excise taxes and sales taxes on imported and domestically produced goods.[15]

- Between 1986 and 1990, when the focus was on the tariffication of quantitative import restrictions, import quotas were liberalized for 1,477 items, representing about 17 percent of total imports in 1987. Generally, quotas were replaced by tariffs, which in some cases reached 100 percent.

As regards the impact of the liberalization, in value terms, imports of liberalized goods increased by a multiple of 2.5, whereas imports in general doubled; this small difference implies that either a number of import quotas were nonbinding, or that quotas were replaced with equivalent tariffs. The developments, however, are strikingly different across product groups. Whereas import growth of liberalized capital goods was not significantly different from that of other capital goods, the share of the liberalized imports of consumer goods in total imports of consumer goods increased from 19 percent in 1987 to 47 percent in 1992. This could imply that the quantitative restrictions had been binding, that the tariff imposed was not equivalent, that import patterns changed during the period, or a combination of all three factors.

The more recent third phase of reform is distinguished by the following:

- There were further significant reductions in quantitative restrictions when the number of items subject to quantitative import restrictions was reduced from 447 in 1990 to 126 in 1992. In March 1996, quantitative restrictions were lifted on all agricultural goods except rice and were replaced with the maximum tariffs allowed under the Uruguay Round (40–100). Apart from rice, the only remaining quantitative restrictions were imposed for health, safety, and environmental reasons.
- Reacting to fiscal exigencies, a 9 percent import surcharge was levied on non-oil imports in 1990, which was to be eliminated in mid-1992, but extended at a lower rate (5 percent) through 1993.
- There was some additional progress with tariff reform. In 1994/95, the maximum standard tariff was reduced from 50 to 30 percent.
- All foreign exchange restrictions were eliminated as of September 1, 1992.[16] In addition, in 1992, all foreign exchange surrender requirements were eliminated.

[15]Only a higher excise on imported cigarettes was left in place.

[16]The peso had been allowed to float since 1985, albeit with significant central bank intervention.

As regards the impact of these measures, reflecting the modest impact of the reforms, the average statutory tariff fell only minimally from 28 percent in 1990 to 25 percent in 1995, and the collected tariff rate fell only slightly between 1985 and 1995 (Tables 18 and 19 and Figures 7 and 8). Tariffication of quantitative restrictions led to modest changes in average tariffs and tariff dispersion. Moreover, the higher excise for imported cigarettes remained, duty exemptions remained a problem, and the valuation of imports continued to be based on home consumption value (rather than transaction value in accordance with WTO rules).

Complementary Policy Actions

As a cornerstone of their overall reform efforts, the government initiated a wide-ranging tax reform in 1986. The tax reform package included (1) a shift from a schedular to a global income tax (reversed in 1992); (2) a shift from the family to the individual as the unit of taxation; (3) an increase in withholding tax rates on interest income and royalties, combined with a reduction in the withholding tax rate on dividends; (4) a shift from a two-rate corporate income tax to one rate of 35 percent; (5) the introduction of a 10 percent VAT and the concurrent elimination of a number of nuisance taxes in 1988 (fixed taxes on businesses, the compensatory tax, the miller's tax, the contractor's tax, and the broker's tax); and (6) a shift from specific to ad valorem excise taxes.

Reform in tax administration did not keep up with the pace of tax reform. The main weaknesses in the Philippine tax administration remain the extreme centralization of the collection system, the lack of cooperation among agencies relating to tax collection, lack of resources, especially reflected in lack of computerization, and poor personnel management. Manasan (1994) estimates that in 1992 the collection rate for income taxes was only about a third of the potential revenue and for the VAT less then 40 percent. She also estimates that only about 23 percent of all potential taxpayers actually pay taxes.

The Revenue Implications of Reform

The revenue trend in the Philippines in recent years has been positive. Total revenue increased from 13.1 percent of GNP in 1980 to 19 percent of GNP in 1995. The 6 percentage point increase was to a large extent owing to an increase in tax revenue, which increased from 11.5 percent of GNP in 1980 to just under 16 percent in 1995.[17] Focusing on

[17]Nontax revenues also increased significantly, due to receipts stemming from the privatization process.

Table 18. Summary Measures of Economic Performance and Revenue Trends for the Philippines

Measure	1985	1986	1987	1988	1989	1990	1991	1992	1993	1994	1995
GNP (at current market prices)	595.10	619.80	673.10	795.20	913.80	1,078.00	1,255.00	1,375.00	1,500.00	1,737.00	1,968.00
Exchange rates											
(In national currency per U.S. dollar)	18.61	20.39	20.57	21.09	21.70	24.30	27.50	25.50	27.12	26.42	25.71
Value of trade = value of imports + exports											
(In billions of U.S. dollars)	9.77	9.89	12.46	15.23	18.24	20.39	20.89	24.34	28.97	34.82	43.84
(In billions of pesos)	181.72	201.53	256.21	321.34	395.81	495.53	574.50	620.75	785.72	919.84	1,127.07
(As percentage of GNP)	30.54	32.52	38.06	40.41	43.31	45.97	45.78	45.15	52.38	52.96	57.27
Value of imports											
(In billions of U.S. dollars)	5.14	5.04	6.74	8.16	10.42	12.21	12.05	14.52	17.60	21.33	26.38
(In billions of pesos)	95.59	102.83	138.56	172.11	226.09	296.63	331.40	370.24	477.23	563.60	678.20
(As percentage of GNP)	16.06	16.59	20.59	21.64	24.74	27.52	26.41	26.93	31.82	32.45	34.46
Value of exports											
(In billions of U.S. dollars)	4.63	4.84	5.72	7.07	7.82	8.18	8.84	9.82	11.38	13.48	17.46
(In billions of pesos)	86.13	98.71	117.65	149.22	169.72	198.89	243.11	250.51	308.49	356.24	448.87
(As percentage of GNP)	14.47	15.93	17.48	18.77	18.57	18.45	19.37	18.22	20.57	20.51	22.81
Tax revenue											
(In billions of pesos)	61.19	65.40	85.50	90.40	122.50	151.70	182.30	208.70	230.30	271.40	310.60
(As percentage of GNP)	10.28	10.55	12.70	11.37	13.41	14.07	14.53	15.18	15.35	15.62	15.78
International trade taxes											
(In billions of pesos)	18.17	17.80	26.00	25.60	38.90	46.50	65.00	73.60	82.70	82.30	97.90
(As percentage of GNP)	3.05	2.87	3.86	3.22	4.26	4.31	5.18	5.35	5.51	4.74	4.97
(AAs percentage of tax revenue)	29.70	27.22	30.41	28.32	31.76	30.65	35.66	35.27	35.91	30.32	31.52
Import duties											
(In billions of pesos)	15.97	16.80	25.70	25.00	38.40	45.90	64.40	72.90	82.00	81.60	97.60
(as percentage of GNP)	2.68	2.71	3.82	3.14	4.20	4.26	5.13	5.30	5.47	4.70	4.96

Table 18 (*concluded*)

Measure	1985	1986	1987	1988	1989	1990	1991	1992	1993	1994	1995
Collected international trade tariff =											
international trade taxes/ value of trade	10.00	8.83	10.15	7.97	9.83	9.38	11.31	11.86	10.53	8.95	8.69
Collected import tariff =											
import duties/value of imports	16.70	16.34	18.55	14.53	16.98	15.47	19.43	19.69	17.18	14.48	14.39
Domestic taxes on goods and services											
(In billions of pesos)	22.93	26.70	35.90	33.00	42.00	49.20	49.60	55.40	63.80	76.10	84.40
(As percentage of GNP)	3.85	4.31	5.33	4.15	4.60	4.56	3.95	4.03	4.25	4.38	4.29
(As percentage of tax revenue)	37.48	40.83	41.99	36.50	34.29	32.43	27.21	26.55	27.70	28.04	27.17
Overall deficit excluding grants											
(In percent of GNP)	–1.88	–5.05	–2.99	–2.92	–2.14	–3.45	–2.10	–1.16	–1.46	0.00	–0.19
Excluding central bank restructuring	. . .	. . .	. . .	. . .	. . .	. . .	. . .	. . .	. . .	0.94	0.57
Current account balance											
(In billions of U.S. dollars)	0.52	1.21	0.20	0.32	–1.46	–2.70	–1.03	–0.86	–3.02	–2.95	–3.26
(As percentage of GDP)											
Excluding official transfer						–6.92	–3.05	–2.27	–6.10	–5.34	–5.01
Including official transfer	1.70	4.04	0.60	0.84	–3.41	–6.11	–2.27	–1.62	–5.55	–4.60	–4.40

Sources: Philippine authorities; and IMF staff estimates; and IMF, *World Economic Outlook* (May 1997).

Table 19. National Government Revenue in the Philippines

(As percentage of GNP)

Component	1980	1981	1982	1983	1984	1985	1986	1987	1988	1989	1990	1991	1992	1993	1994	1995
Total revenue	13.11	11.84	11.39	12.05	10.80	11.59	12.78	14.38	14.00	16.01	16.37	17.21	17.37	17.23	20.05	18.99
Tax revenue	11.52	10.35	10.07	10.44	9.50	10.28	10.55	12.70	11.37	13.41	14.07	14.53	15.18	15.35	15.62	15.78
Taxes on income, profits, and capital gains	2.74	2.56	2.47	2.33	2.34	3.09	3.08	3.21	3.51	4.11	4.58	4.87	5.10	4.99	5.29	5.56
Individual	. . .	. . .	. . .	. . .	. . .	. . .	. . .	. . .	. . .	. . .	. . .	. . .	. . .	. . .	. . .	. . .
Corporate	. . .	. . .	. . .	. . .	. . .	. . .	. . .	. . .	. . .	. . .	. . .	. . .	. . .	. . .	. . .	. . .
Other taxes on income, profits, and capital gains	. . .	. . .	. . .	. . .	. . .	. . .	. . .	. . .	. . .	. . .	. . .	. . .	. . .	. . .	. . .	. . .
Taxes on property	. . .	. . .	. . .	. . .	. . .	. . .	. . .	. . .	. . .	. . .	. . .	. . .	. . .	. . .	. . .	. . .
Taxes on payroll	. . .	. . .	. . .	. . .	. . .	. . .	. . .	. . .	. . .	. . .	. . .	. . .	. . .	. . .	. . .	. . .
Social security contributions	. . .	. . .	. . .	. . .	. . .	. . .	. . .	. . .	. . .	. . .	. . .	. . .	. . .	. . .	. . .	. . .
Domestic taxes on goods and services	4.13	3.81	3.65	3.46	3.57	3.85	4.31	5.33	4.15	4.60	4.56	3.95	4.03	4.25	4.38	4.29
Taxes on general sales, turnover or VAT	1.88	1.76	1.68	1.49	1.40	1.45	1.66	1.98	1.61	1.87	1.88	1.93	2.02	2.23	2.10	2.20
Excises[1]	2.24	2.06	1.97	1.96	2.17	2.40	2.65	3.36	2.54	2.72	2.68	2.02	2.01	2.02	2.28	2.09
Other taxes on domestic goods and services	. . .	. . .	. . .	. . .	. . .	. . .	. . .	. . .	. . .	. . .	. . .	. . .	. . .	. . .	. . .	. . .
Taxes on international trade	4.39	3.68	3.65	4.34	3.39	3.05	2.87	3.86	3.22	4.26	4.31	5.18	5.35	5.51	4.74	4.97
Imports	4.23	3.58	3.56	4.27	3.00	2.68	2.71	3.82	3.14	4.20	4.26	5.13	5.30	5.47	4.70	4.96
Exports	0.16	0.10	0.09	0.07	0.33	0.17	0.10	0.00	0.00	0.00	0.00	0.00	0.00	0.00	0.00	0.00
Other taxes on international trade[2]	. . .	. . .	. . .	. . .	0.07	0.20	0.06	0.04	0.08	0.05	0.06	0.05	0.05	0.05	0.04	0.02
Other taxes[3]	0.26	0.30	0.30	0.30	0.20	0.28	0.29	0.30	0.49	0.44	0.61	0.53	0.70	0.60	1.21	0.96
Nontax revenue[4]	1.58	1.49	1.32	1.61	1.30	1.31	2.23	2.35	2.83	3.27	2.71	3.07	2.47	2.01	4.47	3.26

Sources: Country authorities; and IMF staff estimates.

[1]Data on the components of excise duties are based on Bureau of Internal Revenue collections, which differ slightly from the records of the treasury from 1981 to 1985.

[2]Includes travel tax and foreign exchange tax from 1981 to 1985.

[3]Property taxes, travel tax, and others from 1981 to 1985.

[4]Includes grants and Economic Support Fund.

Figure 7. The Philippines: Summary Measures of Economic Performance and Revenue Trends, Percentage of GDP

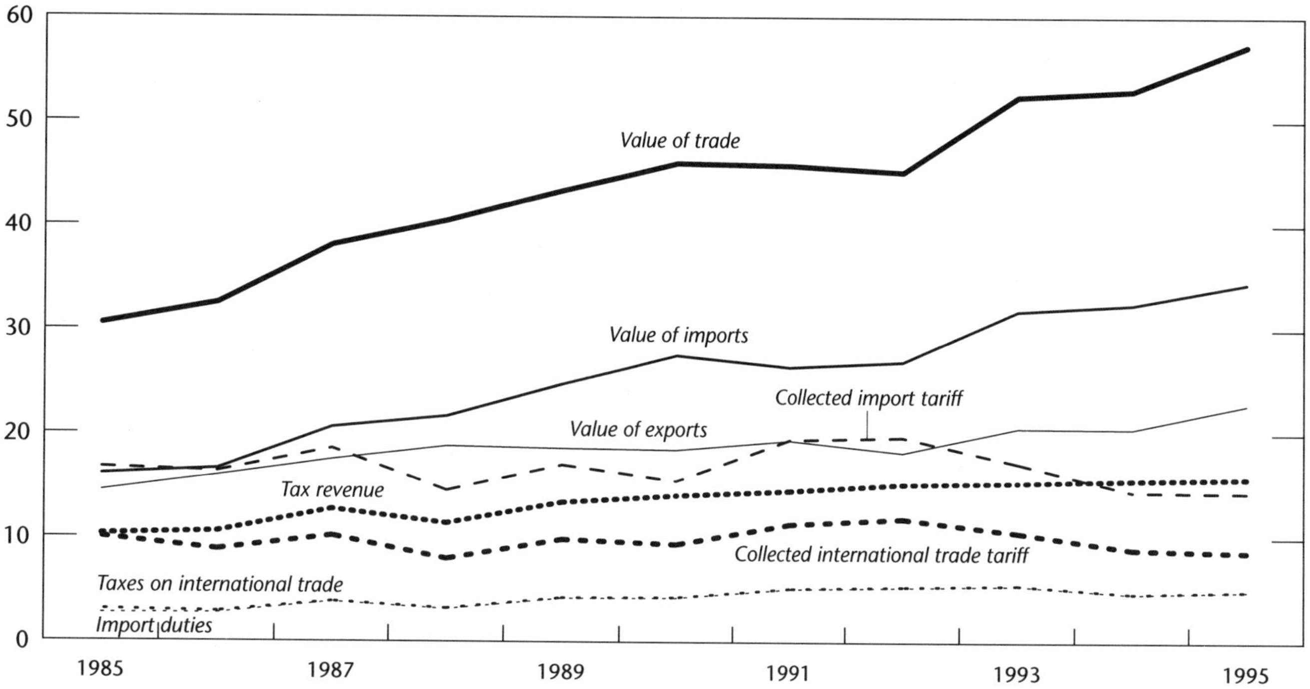

Sources: Data provided by the Philippine authorities; IMF staff estimates; IMF, *World Economic Outlook* (May 1997).

Figure 8. The Philippines: National Government Revenue, Percentage of GDP

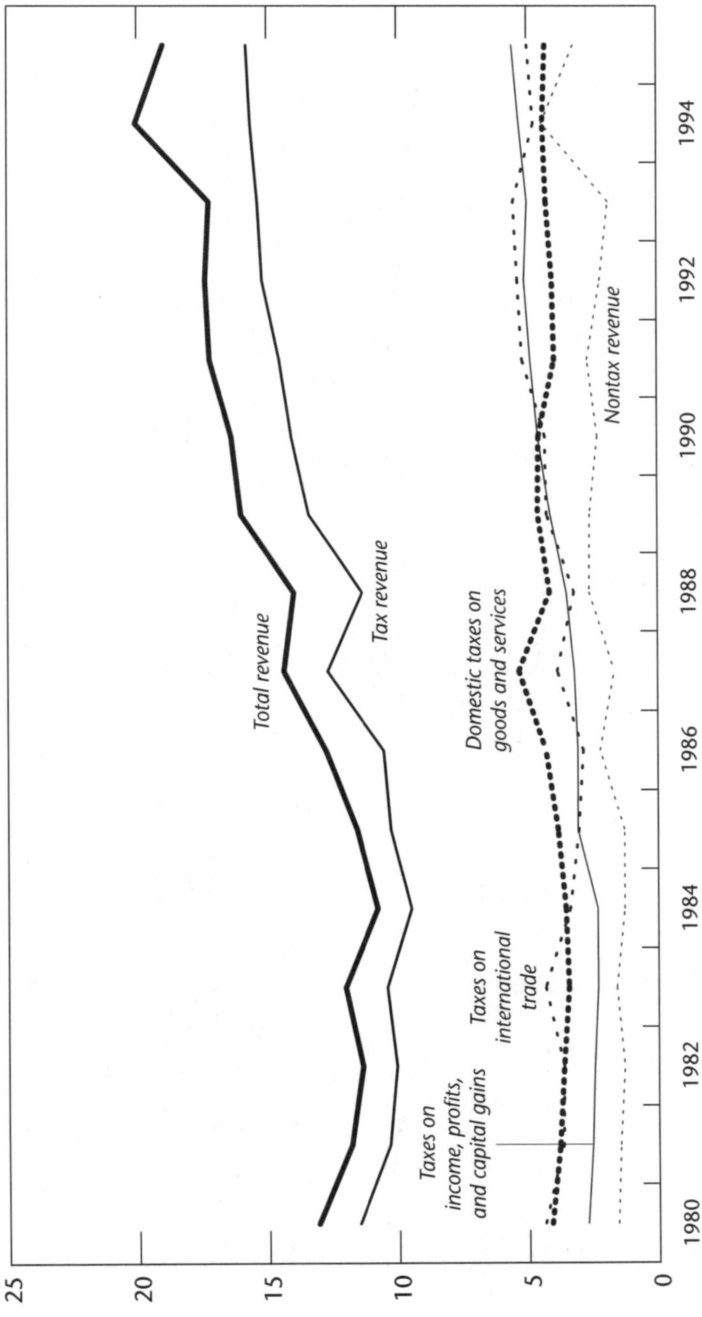

Sources: Data provided by the Philippine authorities; IMF staff estimates.

the entire 15-year period would overlook, however, the two distinct phases in the revenue development in the Philippines. Phase one, which lasted from 1980 to 1986, saw a continuous erosion in revenues and coincides with the persistent high-inflation, low-growth period. The fundamental tax reform outlined above, which was initiated in 1986, and marks the beginning of the second phase, is reflected in a significant and rapid improvement in the tax revenue to GNP ratio; from the trough in 1984 to 1987 revenue as a percentage of GNP increased by more than 3 percentage points, with an increase of an additional 3 percentage points during the late 1980s and early 1990s. At the same time, the composition of tax revenue also changed. Whereas taxes on goods and services, despite the introduction of a VAT, stayed constant as a percentage of GNP, both income taxes and taxes on international trade increased substantially. The 1986 tax reform package immediately reflected upon higher income tax receipts, but it was only able to stem the erosion of taxes on goods and services.

Trade reform in the Philippines has been revenue enhancing. Revenue-enhancing components of trade reform were pursued with greater vigor than revenue-reducing measures, such as a substantial reduction in tariffs and a corresponding reduction in tariff dispersion. The introduction of the temporary surcharge of 9 percent and the replacement of import quotas with high (temporary) tariffs is evidence that revenue preserving or even enhancing objectives were paramount in the minds of the authorities. This goal was accomplished. Trade tax revenues increased from a trough just before the reform of less than 3 percent of GNP in 1986 to around 5 percent of GNP in the early 1990s. In part, this increase is attributable to the surcharge of 9 percent on all non-oil imports that was imposed in 1990 and then maintained at 5 percent until 1993.

Comparing trade tax revenue data for the period 1994–96 with data for the years during which the surcharge was in effect, a rough estimate can be made of the revenue effect of the surcharge. Of the total increase in trade tax revenue of 2.4 percentage points, just under 1 percentage point can be attributed to the surcharge; the remainder is owing to increased imports and to the revenue from tariffs levied upon goods previously subject to quantitative restrictions.

Conclusions

Trade tax reform in the Philippines resulted only in a small reduction in the average statutory tariff and no reduction in the collected tariff rate. Nevertheless, almost all quantitative restrictions were eliminated or converted into tariffs, improving the transparency of the trade system. In total, the reform was revenue enhancing, but this is in part due to the surcharge of 9 percent imposed in the early 1990s. In summary, the following conclusions can be drawn from the Philippine experience:

- The Philippines implemented the revenue-enhancing aspect of trade reform at the outset, possibly necessitated by the weak revenue performance and substantial fiscal imbalances. As a result, trade tax reform was called upon to contribute significantly to improvements in the fiscal balance.
- The Philippine experience shows that the elimination of quantitative restrictions and their replacement with equivalent tariffs can lead to significant increases in revenue, while improving the transparency and fairness of the trade system.
- The accompanying tax reforms appear to put the Philippines in a position where revenue losses that might arise from reductions in tariffs could be relatively easily compensated for by domestic taxes.
- The most urgent problem to be solved before more significant reduction in tariffs can take place would be the problem of lack of administrative capacity, both in customs and in tax administration.

Senegal

As a member of the CFA franc zone, Senegal's currency is pegged to the French franc. Accordingly, the marked appreciation of the French franc after 1985 had a significant influence on the country's competitiveness. Nonetheless, since 1985, Senegal has experienced two distinct trade liberalization episodes. The first, in 1986, was unsuccessful since many of the reforms were reversed in the face of tax revenue and budgetary constraints. The second, which is ongoing, followed the 50 percent devaluation of the CFA franc in 1994.

Trade and Tax Reforms

Initial Conditions

In the early 1980s, trade policy in Senegal, in common with other countries in the CFA franc zone, was very restrictive, characterized by high tariff protection and widespread use of quantitative restrictions (except on imports from countries in the franc zone and on imports from the six original countries in the European Union), and selective trade and tax preferences. Unlike non-CFA counterparts, however, there was no widespread reliance on foreign exchange restrictions. Taxes on international trade were a principal source of government revenue.

First Reform Period: Trade Policy Actions

The first major trade reform program began in 1986, the major elements of which were:

- Quantitative restrictions were reduced, initially on goods not produced locally, followed by a more general and gradual lifting of restrictions, though with some exceptions.
- Tariff reform entailed progressive reduction and narrowing of the bands of harmonized tariffs in stages over the 1986/87–1988/89 period to achieve a lower and more uniform level of effective protection. In the first stage, inter alia, the basic customs duty was fixed at a single rate of 15 percent for most-favored countries. Supplemental/special duties were also reduced. The second round of reductions in July 1988 cut the basic tariff by 5 percentage points and the maximum fiscal duty rate (applying to goods competing with finished goods produced locally) to 50 percent.
- Reference prices on some goods were also abolished.

First Reform Period: Complementary Policy Actions

Following the 1986 trade liberalization, the domestic tax system was reformed to bolster fiscal revenues. A new tax code implemented in 1987 simplified the tax schedule, improved the structure of the tax system, and modernized a number of administrative procedures, which included improving the computerization of the tax and customs administrations.

Background to Second Reform Period

Reflecting the economic difficulties that afflicted the CFA franc region in general, Senegal experienced significant revenue shortfalls, which by 1989 had led to an almost full reversal of the 1986 trade liberalization. Despite the trade reform reversals, the government continued to improve the domestic tax system. In 1990/91, a corporate profits tax of 35 percent and a single personal income tax were introduced. The taxation of petroleum products was reformed in favor of a simpler and more transparent system. These measures were accompanied by improvements in the tax and customs administrations during the 1988–92 period.

By 1992, Senegal's economic difficulties had worsened. Further tariff rate increases followed. As a result, by 1993, tariff rates ranged from 0 to 65 percent, the customs stamp rate ranged from 6 to 12 percent, and there were five different VAT rates ranging from 7 to 34 percent. This led to cumulative tax rates on imports—excluding excise duties—ranging from 12 to 127 percent. These rates were supplemented by quantitative restrictions, mostly in the form of import licenses (mainly on agricultural commodities). In addition, monopoly import rights were granted through special agreements (*conventions spéciales*) with large domestic firms and a system of prior authorization for the import or export of numerous products.

Second Reform Period: Trade Policy Actions

The second major phase of trade reform began in 1994 as part of a major adjustment effort in connection with the 50 percent devaluation of the CFA franc. Elements to be highlighted include:

- Tariff reductions and simplification, the latter by reducing the number of tariff categories from seven to five. The customs duty rate was reduced from 15 percent to 10 percent and the maximum fiscal duty rate was reduced tp 50 percent. The customs stamp rate was also reduced 5 percent and was extended to all imports with only a few exceptions. In addition, surtaxes of 10 or 20 percent were applied to a limited number of agricultural producers.
- Most import and export licenses were eliminated. For some products that had been previously covered by import licenses, temporary tariff surcharges over the customs and fiscal duty were introduced to provide local producers time to adjust to foreign competition. In March 1995, rice imports and prices were completely liberalized.

Reflecting these reforms, by September 1995, there were five different customs tariffs ranging from 0 to 60 percent and a 5 percent customs stamp. Including the impact of the VAT, this implied that total taxation of imports ranged from 5 to 98 percent, excluding surtaxes.

Second Reform Period: Complementary Policy Actions

Again with a view to bolstering revenues while making the tax system as a whole more efficient, the domestic tax system was reformed to broaden the tax base, reinforce tax collections, and reduce fiscal fraud. Initially, the number of VAT rates was reduced from five to three (0, 10, and 20 percent), with the base also being enlarged and some goods being taxed at the standard rate rather than at preferential rates. More recently (1996), the VAT base was expanded by including all importers and manufacturers' clients, converting the informal sector's equalization tax into a withholding tax on VAT payments, and incorporating excise taxes into the VAT base.

International Commitments

As a member of the West African Economic and Monetary Union (WAEMU)[18]—established immediately after the devaluation in January 1994—Senegal is committed to further liberalize its international trade with other member countries and is preparing for the implementation by January 2000 of the common external tariff, announced in November 1997. In that context, Senegal introduced in April 1998 a new tariff structure with four rates (0, 5, 10, and 25 percent) and the 5 percent customs stamp. In addition, Senegal participates in two other regional agreements, namely: (i) the Economic Community of West African States (ECOWAS),[19] which in 1990 introduced a liberalization scheme to phase out a number of tariffs on industrial goods produced by enterprises granted ECOWAS community status—this is prospective since the basic customs documentation remains to be agreed upon; and (ii) the Organization of African Unity (OAU), which in 1991 agreed to create an African Economic Community by the year 2000.

Revenue Implications of Reform

For the better part of the past 15 years, Senegal's tax effort has been declining. The relatively poor revenue performance can be explained by the narrow tax base, weak customs and tax administrations, persistent fiscal fraud, and a growing informal sector not captured in the tax net. From 1982/83 to 1988/89, tax revenue as a percent of GDP declined from 18.5 to 13.3 percent of GDP (Tables 20 and 21 and Figures 9 and 10). Import duties fell from 5.9 to 3.7 percent of GDP during the same period. Since the collected import tariff rate rose during the period, this decline mainly reflected import compression. The decline in domestic taxes on goods and services may also have reflected the decline in import volumes, since domestic indirect taxes on imports are substantial. Initial trade liberalization efforts in 1986 appear not to have resulted in increased trade volumes, likely reflecting the steady appreciation of the CFA franc over this period.

[18]WAEMU membership includes Benin, Burkina Faso, Côte d'Ivoire, Mali, Niger, Senegal, and Togo.

[19]ECOWAS was founded in 1975 and comprises 16 countries.

Table 20. Summary Measures of Economic Performance and Revenue Trends for Senegal

Measure	1985/86	1986/87	1987/88	1988/89	1989/90	1990/91	1991/92	1992	1993	1994	1995	1996[1]
GDP (at current market prices)	1,244.30	1,342.60	1,432.80	1,479.90	1,514.60	1,551.20	1,581.40	1,612.80	1,586.60	2,155.10	2,429.80	2,637.50
Exchange rates (in national currency per U.S. dollar)	449.26	346.30	300.54	297.85	319.01	272.26	282.11	264.69	283.16	555.20	499.10	511.60
Value of trade = value imports + exports												
(In billions of U.S. dollars)	1.31	1.54	1.63	1.63	1.77	2.06	1.92	2.02	1.79	1.81	2.19	2.25
(In billions of CFA francs)	588.62	533.42	488.83	486.80	564.09	560.40	540.78	534.59	507.95	1,006.57	1,090.88	1,152.86
(As percentage of GDP)	47.31	39.73	34.12	32.89	37.24	36.13	34.20	33.15	32.02	46.71	44.90	43.71
Value of imports												
(In billions of U.S. dollars)	0.80	0.88	0.96	0.96	1.00	1.16	1.11	1.19	1.09	1.02	1.22	1.27
(In billions of CFA francs)	357.47	305.93	287.23	284.66	320.32	317.04	314.33	315.49	307.67	567.45	607.46	648.40
(As percentage of GDP)	28.73	22.79	20.05	19.24	21.15	20.44	19.88	19.56	19.39	26.33	25.00	24.58
Value of exports												
(In billions of U.S. dollars)	0.51	0.66	0.67	0.68	0.76	0.89	0.80	0.83	0.71	0.79	0.97	0.99
(In billions of CFA francs)	231.15	227.49	201.60	202.14	243.77	243.36	226.46	219.10	200.28	439.13	483.42	504.47
(As percentage of GDP)	18.58	16.94	14.07	13.66	16.09	15.69	14.32	13.59	12.62	20.38	19.90	19.13
Tax revenue												
(In billions of CFA francs)	185.10	196.00	205.50	196.20	219.00	241.40	264.10	247.10	222.20	267.90	330.30	369.30
(As percentage of GDP)	14.88	14.60	14.34	13.26	14.46	15.56	16.70	15.32	13.88	12.43	13.59	14.00
International trade taxes												
(In billions of CFA francs)	55.35	60.15	62.73	55.90	68.33	78.08	86.70	83.55	71.63	93.00	116.78	133.73
(As percentage of GDP)	4.45	4.48	4.38	3.78	4.51	5.03	5.48	5.18	4.51	4.32	4.81	5.07
(As percentage of tax revenue)	29.90	30.69	30.52	28.49	31.20	32.34	32.83	33.81	32.53	34.71	35.35	36.21
Import duties												
(In billions of CFA francs)[2]	55.05	59.55	62.03	55.20	68.33	78.08	86.70	83.55	71.63	93.00	116.78	133.73
(As percentage of GDP)[2]	4.42	4.44	4.33	3.73	4.51	5.03	5.48	5.18	4.51	4.32	4.81	5.07

Table 20 (*concluded*)

Measure	1985/86	1986/87	1987/88	1988/89	1989/90	1990/91	1991/92	1992	1993	1994	1995	1996[1]
Collected international trade tariff = international trade taxes/value of trade	9.40	11.28	12.83	11.48	12.11	13.93	16.03	15.63	14.10	9.24	10.70	11.60
Collected import tariff = import duties/value of imports	15.40	19.47	21.59	19.39	21.33	24.63	27.58	26.48	23.28	16.39	19.22	20.62
Domestic taxes on goods and services												
(In billions of CFA francs)	76.35	80.25	79.98	76.60	83.08	88.93	86.30	85.35	79.58	100.00	122.63	139.18
(As percentage of GDP)	6.14	5.98	5.58	5.18	5.48	5.73	5.46	5.29	5.02	4.64	5.5	5.28
(As percentage of tax revenue)	41.25	40.94	38.92	39.04	37.93	36.84	32.68	34.54	36.14	37.33	37.13	37.69
Overall fiscal balance (deficit –) commitment basis												
(As percentage of GDP)												
Including grants	–2.30	–1.50	–1.20	–2.10	–3.10	2.00	0.20	–2.50	–3.00	–1.80	–0.20	–0.20
Excluding grants	–3.80	–2.60	–2.60	–4.00	–4.40	0.30	–1.00	–3.80	–4.00	–5.70	–3.20	–2.00
Overall fiscal balance (deficit –) (Cash basis, as percentage of GDP)	–3.30	–3.40	–3.80	–2.40	–1.90	. . .	0.40	0.50	–0.20	–9.30	–2.70	–0.20
Current account balance												
(As percentage of GDP)	–0.27	–0.27	–0.31	–0.41	–0.38	–0.44	–0.45	–0.48	–0.50	–0.19	–0.24	–0.27
Excluding official transfer	–16.82	–12.09	–11.61	–10.63	–10.22	–8.92	–9.39	–9.09	–9.99	–8.92	–7.56	–6.87
Including official transfer	–10.54	–7.11	–6.65	–8.32	–8.23	–7.79	–8.20	–7.84	–8.90	–4.94	–4.84	–5.32

Sources: Country authorities; IMF staff estimates; and IMF, *World Economic Outlook* (May 1997).

[1]Preliminary estimate.

[2]Data for 1989/90–1990/91 are IMF staff estimates. For some years, the authorities did not distinguish between VAT in imports and custom duties; for those years we estimated the VAT on imports and reclassified under VAT.

Figure 9. Senegal: Summary Measures of Economic Performance and Revenue Trends, Percentage of GDP

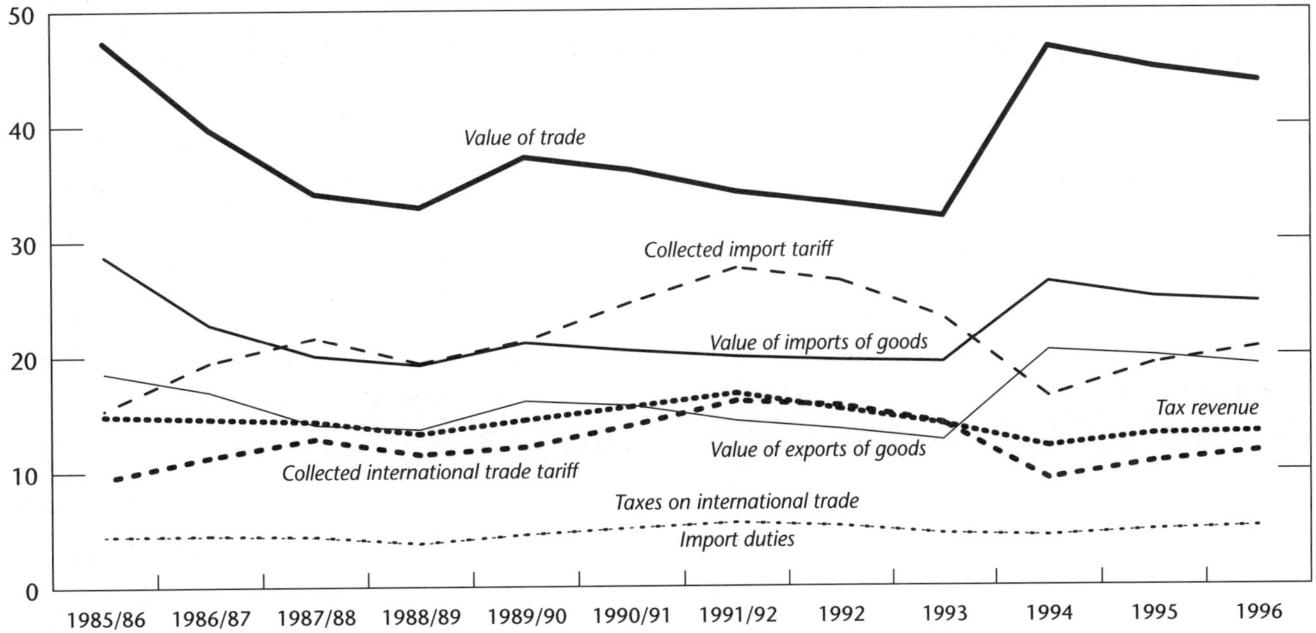

Sources: Data provided by the Senegalese authorities; IMF staff estimates; IMF, *World Economic Outlook* (May 1997).

Note: Data for 1989/90–1990/91 are IMF staff estimates. For some years, the authorities did not distinguish between VAT on imports and custom duties; for those years, we estimated the VAT on imports and reclassified it under VAT. Fiscal year ended June 30, through 1991/92; calendar year data starting in 1992.

Table 21. Budgetary Revenue in Senegal
(As percentage of GDP)

Component	1980/81[1]	1981/82	1982/83	1983/84	1984/85	1985/86	1986/87
Total revenue	19.35	20.07	19.70	19.38	18.83	17.58	18.70
Tax revenue	18.22	18.46	18.45	18.15	17.55	14.88	14.60
Taxes on income, profits, and capital gains	4.53	4.23	4.12	4.10	4.05	3.54	3.38
Individual[3]	1.29	1.66	1.33	1.26	1.20	1.11	1.08
Corporate	1.59	1.18	1.10	1.08	1.22	0.97	0.95
Other taxes on income, profits, and capital gains	1.65	1.39	1.68	1.76	1.63	1.45	1.35
Taxes on property	0.60	0.45	0.31	0.29	0.26	0.27	0.25
Taxes on payroll	0.32	0.21	0.43	0.44	0.42	0.38	0.38
Social security contributions	...	...	...	...	...	...	...
Domestic taxes on goods and services	7.30	7.38	7.44	7.42	7.19	6.14	5.98
Taxes on general sales, turnover or VAT[4]	6.05	6.32	6.35	6.34	6.24	5.38	5.22
Excises[5]	0.92	0.79	0.81	0.84	0.66	0.53	0.52
Other taxes on domestic goods and services	0.32	0.26	0.28	0.25	0.28	0.23	0.23
Taxes on international trade	5.21	6.05	6.02	5.71	5.48	4.45	4.48
Imports[6]	4.98	5.88	5.90	5.64	5.44	4.42	4.44
Exports	0.23	0.17	0.12	0.07	0.05	0.02	0.04
Other taxes on international trade	...	...	...	...	...	...	...
Other taxes	0.25	0.15	0.13	0.18	0.16	0.11	0.13
Nontax revenue	1.13	1.61	1.26	1.23	1.27	2.70	4.10

Sources: Country authorities; and IMF staff estimates.

[1]Fiscal year ending June 30, through 1991/92; calendar year data starting in 1992.

[2]Preliminary estimate.

[3]Includes tax on wages and salaries.

[4]For some years the authorities did not distinguish between VAT in imports and custom duties; for those years, we estimated the VAT on imports and reclassified under VAT.

[5]Includes taxes on alcohol and cement.

[6]Data for 1989/90–1990/91 are IMF staff estimates.

1987/88	1988/89	1989/90	1990/91	1991/92	1992	1993	1994	1995	1996[2]
17.55	16.60	17.16	19.40	19.43	18.19	16.13	13.99	15.07	14.95
14.34	13.26	14.46	15.56	16.70	15.32	13.88	12.43	13.59	14.00
3.57	3.45	3.65	3.95	3.81	3.71	3.49	2.74	3.09	3.00
1.24	1.22	1.49	2.23	2.28	2.18	2.06	1.60	1.81	1.72
0.95	0.89	0.99	1.04	1.09	1.04	0.72	0.68	0.85	0.86
1.38	1.34	1.18	0.68	0.44	0.50	0.71	0.47	0.43	0.41
0.24	0.28	0.25	0.23	1.23	0.42	0.27	0.29	0.24	0.23
0.33	0.32	0.32	0.29	0.28	0.27	0.26	0.19	0.19	0.21
...	...	...	...	...	...	...	...	...	...
5.58	5.18	5.48	5.73	5.46	5.29	5.02	4.64	5.05	5.28
4.81	4.50	4.90	5.09	4.84	4.73	4.45	4.23	4.64	4.91
0.54	0.47	0.40	0.47	0.46	0.41	0.40	0.30	0.28	0.25
0.23	0.21	0.18	0.17	0.16	0.15	0.16	0.11	0.14	0.12
4.38	3.78	4.51	5.03	5.48	5.18	4.51	4.32	4.81	5.07
4.33	3.73	4.51	5.03	5.48	5.18	4.51	4.32	4.81	5.07
0.05	0.05	0.00	0.00	0.00	0.00	0.00	0.00	0.00	0.00
...	...	...	...	...	...	...	...	...	...
0.24	0.26	0.24	0.33	0.43	0.45	0.33	0.25	0.21	0.22
3.21	3.34	2.70	3.84	2.73	2.87	2.25	1.56	1.48	0.95

Figure 10. Senegal: Budgetary Revenue, Percentage of GDP

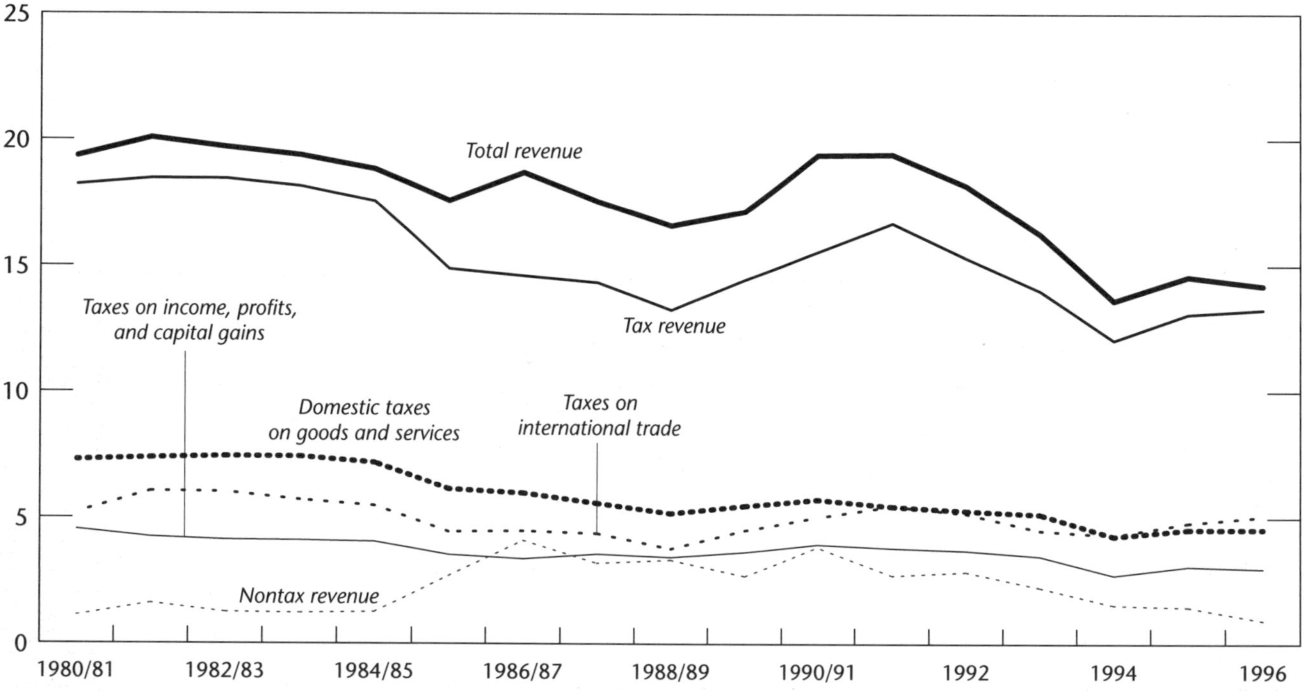

Sources: Data provided by the authorities; IMF staff estimates.
Note: Fiscal year ended June 30, through 1991/92; calendar year data starting in 1992.

There was a temporary reversal in these adverse trends in the period FY1988/89–1991/92, reflecting both the overhaul of the tax code and improved efficiency in the tax and customs administrations. Taxes on international trade rose during the period, as did the collected import tariff rate. By 1991/92, the collected import tariff rate was a record 27.6 percent. However, the adverse trends re-emerged, with tax revenues falling to a new low of 12.4 percent of GDP in 1994,[20] this time reflecting a decline in all major taxes.

Since 1995, however, there has been a clear improvement in tax revenues, reflecting reforms in the trade and domestic tax systems and the recovery of economic activity that followed the devaluation. By 1996, tax revenues had increased to 14 percent of GDP. The most noticeable recovery was in customs tax collection, which increased between 1994 and 1996 by almost 1 percent of GDP to 5.1 percent. Senegal's tax system remains heavily dependent on trade taxes, reflecting the high proportion of imports in GDP and the aggregation of tariff receipts with revenues from the VAT on imported goods.

Conclusions

The contrast between the effectiveness of Senegal's two reform efforts is instructive. In particular, the more recent successful reform drive demonstrates that a precondition for successful reform is sound macroeconomic policies. In the Senegal context, the CFA franc devaluation in 1994 alleviated many of the pressures that had been building up in the economy, with the result that tax revenues have since increased somewhat, reflecting mainly an increase in taxes on international trade. This increase in tax revenues has been based on an increase in the volume of trade in reaction to the successful stabilization and trade liberalization and demonstrates that trade liberalization is not inconsistent with a subsequent enhanced revenue performance.

References

Abed, George T., 1997, "Trade Liberalization and Tax Reform in the Southern Mediterranean Region" (unpublished; Washington: International Monetary Fund).

Abed, George, and a staff team, 1998, *Fiscal Reforms in Low-Income Countries: Experience Under Fund-Supported Programs,* IMF Occasional Paper No. 160 (Washington: International Monetary Fund).

[20]In 1992, Senegal reverted to a system where fiscal years coincide with annual years.

Asher, Mukul, 1997, "Recent Tax Reforms in Southeast Asia: Lessons and Challenges" (unpublished; Singapore: National University of Singapore).

Bhattacharya, Amarendra, and Johannes F. Linn, 1988, "Trade and Industrial Policies in the Developing Countries of East Asia," World Bank Discussion Paper No. 27 (Washington: World Bank).

Blejer, Mario, and Adrienne Cheasty, 1990, "Fiscal Implications of Trade Liberalization," in *Fiscal Policy in Open Developing Economies,* ed. by Vito Tanzi (Washington: International Monetary Fund).

Clément, Jean, A.P., S. Cossé, and J. Le Dem, 1995, *Aftermath of the CFA Franc Devaluation,* IMF Occasional Paper No. 138 (Washington: International Monetary Fund).

Datta-Mitra, Jayati, 1997, *Fiscal Management in Adjustment Lending* (Washington: World Bank).

Dean, Judith M., Seema Desai, and James Riedel, 1994, "Trade Policy Reform in Developing Countries Since 1985: A Review of the Evidence," World Bank Discussion Papers, No. 267 (Washington: World Bank).

Dixit, Avinash, 1985, "Tax Policy in Open Economies," in *Handbook of Public Economics,* Vol. 1, ed. by Alan J. Auerbach and Martin Feldstein (Amsterdam: North Holland).

———, and Victor Norman, 1980, *Theory of International Trade* (Cambridge: Cambridge University Press).

Escolano, Julio, 1995, "International Trade Taxes," in *Tax Policy Handbook,* ed. by Parthasarathi Shome (Washington: International Monetary Fund).

Farhadian-Lorie, Ziba, and Menachem Katz, 1988, "Fiscal Dimensions of Trade Policy," IMF Working Paper 88/44 (Washington: International Monetary Fund).

Foroutan, Faezeh, 1993, "Regional Integration in Sub-Saharan Africa: Past Experience and Future Prospects," in *New Dimensions in Regional Integration,* ed. by Jaime de Melo and Arvind Panagariya (Cambridge: Cambridge University Press).

Greenaway, David, and Chris Milner, 1991, "Fiscal Dependence on Trade Taxes and Trade Policy Reform," *Journal of Development Studies,* Vol. 27, No. 3, pp. 95–132.

Hadjimichael, M., M. Nowak, R. Sharer, and A. Tahari, 1996, *Adjustment for Growth, the African Experience,* IMF Occasional Paper No. 143 (Washington: International Monetary Fund).

Harmsen, Richard, and Michael Leidy, 1994, "Regional Trading Arrangements," in *International Trade Policies: The Uruguay Round and Beyond,* Vol. II, Background Papers (Washington: International Monetary Fund).

IMF (International Monetary Fund), 1982, *Issues and Developments in International Trade Policy,* prepared by a staff team led by Margaret Kelly and Anne Kenny McGuirk (Washington: International Monetary Fund).

———, 1994, *International Trade Policies: The Uruguay Round and Beyond,* Vol. 1, "Principal Issues," prepared by a staff team led by Naheed Kirmani (Washington: International Monetary Fund).

———, 1997, *Trade Liberalization in Fund-Supported Programs,* prepared by the Policy Development and Review Department (Washington: International Monetary Fund).

Krueger, Anne O., 1995, *Trade Policies and Developing Nations* (Washington: Brookings Institution).

Leidy, Michael, 1994, "Antidumping: Solution or Problem in the 1990s," in *International Trade Policies: The Uruguay Round and Beyond,* Vol. II, Background Papers (Washington: International Monetary Fund), pp. 53–67.

Manasan, R., 1994, "Reforming the Fiscal System" (unpublished; Manila: Philippine Institute for Development Studies).

Mitra, Pradeep, 1992, "The Coordinated Reform of Tariffs and Indirect Taxes," *World Bank Research Observer,* Vol. 7, pp. 195–218.

Nsouli, Saleh M., Sena Eken, Klaus Enders, Van-Can Thai, Jorg Decressin, and Filippo Cartiglia, with Janet Bungay, 1995, *Resilience and Growth Through Sustained Adjustment,* IMF Occasional Paper No. 117 (Washington: International Monetary Fund).

Papageorgiou, Demetrios, Armeane M. Choksi, and Michael Michaely, 1990, *Liberalizing Foreign Trade in Developing Countries: The Lessons of Experience* (Washington: World Bank).

Pritchett, Lant, and Geeta Sethi, 1994, "Tariff Rates, Tariff Revenue, and Tariff Reform: Some New Facts," *World Bank Economic Review,* Vol. 8, No. 1, pp. 1–16.

Rajaram, Anand, 1994, "Tariff and Tax Reforms—Do World Bank Recommendations Integrate Revenue and Protection Objectives?" *Economic Studies Quarterly,* Vol. 45, No. 4, pp. 321–38.

Ram, Rati, 1994, "Level of Economic Development and Share of Trade Taxes in Government Revenue: Some Evidence from Individual-Country Time-Series Data," *Public Finance,* Vol. 49, No. 3, pp. 409–26.

Stotsky, Janet G., and Asegedech WoldeMariam, 1997, "Tax Effort in Sub-Saharan Africa," IMF Working Paper 97/107 (Washington: International Monetary Fund).

Subramanian, Arvind, Ali Ibrahim, and Luis A. Torres-Castro, 1993, "Optimal Tariffs: Theory and Practice," IMF Working Paper 93/50 (Washington: International Monetary Fund).

Takacs, Wendy E., 1990, "Options for Dismantling Trade Restrictions in Developing Countries," *World Bank Research Observer,* Vol. 5, No. 1, pp. 25–46.

Tanzi, Vito, 1987, "Quantitative Characteristics of the Tax Systems of Developing Countries," in *The Theory of Taxation for Developing Countries,* ed. by David Newbery and Nicholas Stern (New York: Oxford University Press).

———, 1991, "The Impact of Macroeconomic Policies on the Level of Taxation (and on the Fiscal Balance) in Developing Countries," in *Public Finance in Developing Countries* (Aldershot, England: Edward Elgar).

———, 1994, "Customs Administration and the Economy—Keeping Pace with Development" (unpublished; Washington: International Monetary Fund).

———, 1995, *Taxation in an Integrating World* (Washington: Brookings Institution).

———, and Parthasarathi Shome, 1993, "A Primer on Tax Evasion," *Staff Papers,* International Monetery Fund, Vol. 40, pp. 807–28.

Thomas, Vinod, John Nash, and associates, 1991, *Best Practices in Trade Policy Reform* (New York: Oxford University Press).

Globalization: Implications for Africa 6

Paul Collier

Africa has long been strongly integrated into the global economy. In respect of product markets, the typical African country trades a high share of its GDP, its economy being small and specialized in primary exports. In respect of capital markets, Africa was arguably the first continent to become highly integrated: a higher proportion of African wealth is held internationally than on other continents. Thus, in one sense "globalization" is not new to Africa, but it has meant primary exports and capital flight. However, when economists now talk of globalization they mean something rather different. Specifically, they mean falling trade barriers, integrating financial markets, and transnational corporations. In this chapter, I argue that these changes can potentially integrate Africa into the world economy in a new way, but that whether these opportunities are taken up depends upon African economic policy.

Trade barriers have come down around the world, in particular with the phased elimination of QRs. Although restrictions on textiles and garments will not be fully lifted for a further 7 years, the fact that there is a timetable and a commitment has revolutionary implications for the newly industrializing developing countries. Given Africa's present pattern of exports, this international trade liberalization is of little consequence since Africa does not face important barriers for its present exports. The reduction in trade barriers is only of significance if Africa changes its comparative advantage. I argue that its present comparative advantage is determined mainly by its policy environment rather than by its factor and natural resource endowments.

Financial capital markets are becoming much more internationally integrated. Financial capital is increasingly flowing to developing countries as pension funds realize the advantages of international diversification. At present, Africa is not attracting significant portfolio capital inflows and so is not benefiting from this globalization of portfolios. I argue that again this reflects its policy environment rather than its endowments.

Further, manufacturing firms are internationalizing their production, shifting investment to lower cost environments. At present, Africa is not attracting footloose manufacturing, except for production for its highly protected domestic markets, and so is not in a position to benefit from this globalization of production. I argue that again this reflects policy rather than endowments.

Thus, on present policies, Africa has little to gain from globalization. At the same time, it has little to lose. This is in sharp contrast to the integrated economies of Europe and East Asia. There, the domestic policy environments are now subject to a new discipline. If governments impose high taxes on manufacturing profits or embark upon reckless fiscal policies, there is a capital outflow. No one is in control of these market forces: even the largest speculators are tiny relative to the size of the market. International capitalism does not mean that "capitalists" have power, but that no one has power. Globalization thus constitutes a much larger loss of power for the governments of Europe and East Asia than for the governments of Africa.

In the next section, I consider the potential of reduced trade barriers for African exports. In particular, I speculate on Africa's comparative advantage. Two distinguished economists have recently advanced propositions that taken at face value are quite disturbing. Rodrik (1997) argues that Africa already has a level of trade to GDP that is normal given its level of income, and that trade liberalization cannot be an engine for African growth. Wood and Berge (1997) and Wood and Owens (1997) argue that Africa's natural resource and human capital endowments imply that its comparative advantage is inevitably in unprocessed primary commodities. They argue that Africa will not be able to export manufactures even if it liberalizes its trade policy. An implication that can easily be drawn from these papers is that it is endowments rather than policies that have determined Africa's present trading pattern, so that there is little that governments can do. I challenge this proposition.

In the third section, I consider the potential of financial market integration. I argue that there is scope both for large capital inflows and for risk bearing. In particular, I suggest that Africa is in the anomalous position of facing the highest underlying level of risk in the world, while having the lowest supply of risk-bearing instruments. As a result, it has the highest price of risk.

African Trade in a Globalizing Economy

Since 1970, world trade has risen much more rapidly than world GDP. By contrast, Africa's GDP (despite growing more slowly than that of other regions) has risen more rapidly than its trade. Further, Africa's exports have remained overwhelmingly concentrated in the same narrow range of primary commodities; indeed, on some measures, export concentration has actually increased. Even within this narrow range of export products, it has drastically lost market share. Evidently, something has been seriously amiss with Africa's trade performance.

Rodrik (1997) shows that Africa does not trade less than predicted by its low level of GDP relative to Asia or Latin America: Asia "overtrades," while Latin America "undertrades." However, this is quite a misleading statistic. Being on the regression line has no normative significance; it simply shows that on this measure African policies were less anti-trade-oriented than Latin American ones. It does not contradict the proposition that Africa has lost heavily from its anti-trade-oriented policies, which have caused its declining share of trade to GDP.

In this section, I investigate how globalization of goods and capital markets will affect Africa's trade. In particular, I focus on whether Africa has a future as an exporter of manufactures. I use a suite of (informally presented) simple models. Which of these best depicts reality turns out to be critical for analytic prediction of Africa's response to globalization, both in terms of what will happen to its exports and what should happen to its policies.

Africa's Comparative Advantage: What Moves Where in a Globalizing Economy?

Reflecting its poverty, the returns to labor are very low in Africa. In a simple two-factor, common-technology world, there are three mechanisms, each of which enables globalization to raise the returns to labor and so reduce African poverty. These three mechanisms are labor emigration, an influx of capital, and the export of labor-intensive goods. If a previously autarkic, poor economy were suddenly opened to the global economy, all three of these mechanisms would operate simultaneously and each would be poverty-reducing. In effect, Africa has three degrees of freedom before globalization becomes ineffective as a poverty-reduction mechanism.

In parts of Africa, the two-factor, common-technology model is an adequate characterization, albeit obviously a radical simplification. An interesting question, then, is which of the three mechanisms is more and which less important. There are some obvious differences within Africa that make each mechanism more or less important for each country. For example, labor migration is probably more sensitive to distance than is trade in products. Hence, Northern Africa is best located to benefit from emigration to Europe. Capital inflows are, as I discuss below, sensitive to perceptions of investor risk. Risk ratings differ greatly among African countries. South Africa and Mauritius, with *Investor International* ratings in the 40s (on a scale where 0 = maximum risk and 100 = minimum risk), are better placed to attract capital than Nigeria, with a rating below 20.

In the two-factor, common-technology model, the circumstances that give rise to a labor exodus would necessarily give rise to both a capital influx and a comparative advantage in labor-intensive exports. However, once we turn to a more sophisticated model, this need not follow. Two modifications to the model are particularly pertinent for Africa. The first is to introduce additional factor endowments, which unlike labor and capital cannot be traded. Two obvious such endowments are natural resources and public infrastructure. If natural resources are introduced, there is a further modeling choice. A simple approach is to treat natural resources as equally complementary, with both labor and capital in all production activities. A more complex approach is to distinguish between activities that intensively use natural resources and those that do not.

Immobile Natural Resources as a Generalized Productivity Shift

In the first approach, a natural-resource-abundant economy would have higher returns to both labor and capital than one that was resource poor. A resource-poor economy opened from autarky might then experience an exodus of both labor and capital.

In some African countries, the natural resource endowment, broadly interpreted, is indeed so poor that factor exodus will be the main way in which globalization will help to reduce poverty. Since such economies start, in autarky, with abundant labor but little capital, the most important exodus will be their labor. Several African economies are currently at this stage. For example, Eritrea, Burkina Faso, Cape Verde, Malawi, and Lesotho all have huge expatriate communities making remittances. Typically, these economies have a large endowment of labor relative to capital, but also, and more important, have some deep-seated disadvantage (which might be thought of as a natural resource disadvantage) that makes production of an export good very difficult. Eritrea experienced 30 years of war and so has very poor infrastructure, including negative infrastructure in the form of landmines, and is also arid. Burkina Faso is landlocked and arid. Cape Verde is small and arid. Malawi is landlocked, and its international transport lifelines have been partially destroyed by neighboring wars.

In such countries, policy can promote remittances, and there is some evidence that governments could do more. For example, Ethiopia and Egypt have virtually identical populations and similar locations. Earning opportunities within Egypt are better than in Ethiopia, with per capita purchasing power parity income around eight times higher. Yet workers' remittances are 20 times higher in Egypt than in Ethiopia. One reason for this massive difference is that the earning power of Egyptians abroad is much higher than Ethiopians, reflecting past differences in educational policies. As of 1980, 61 percent of Egyptian males were enrolled in secondary schooling, as opposed to only 11 percent of Ethiopians. A second reason is the exchange rate and financial regimes. Egypt has a convertible currency, and workers abroad can deposit in Egyptian banks at competitive interest rates (Shafik, 1998). By contrast, Ethiopia has an overvalued and inconvertible currency, with a financially repressed banking system. Thus, even when Ethiopian workers have earnings abroad, they have little incentive to repatriate their savings.

Immobile Natural Resources as an Alteration in Comparative Advantage

A more complicated model with natural resource endowments distinguishes between products that are differentially intensive in them. Thus, primary products are more intensive in natural resources than are manufactures. Adrian Wood has used variants of such a model to predict the composition of Africa's exports. In a series of papers, Wood argues that Africa cannot industrialize because of its factor endowments: large amounts of natural resources and little human capital. Here I focus on the natural resource argument, since the human capital argument can be subsumed into it.

Wood establishes two important facts. First, he shows econometrically on a global sample that countries that are well endowed with natural resources tend not to export manufactures. He interprets this as showing that countries that are abundant in natural resources do not have a comparative advantage in manufactures, so the capital needed to produce them goes elsewhere. Second, he shows that Africa has an atypically large endowment of natural resources and does not export manufactures. His explanation for the lack of African manufactured exports follows: Africa is simply an instance of the general phenomenon.

The Wood thesis is theoretically entirely correct within its own terms. In the simple common-technology, mobile-capital, immobile-natural-resources model, countries well endowed with natural resources will not export manufactures. However, it is important to understand the mechanism whereby, in the natural-resource-augmented model, abundant natural resources would indeed crowd out manufactured exports.

Were the only difference between Africa and Asia in the endowment of natural resources, then Africa would be uncompetitive in manufactures *because its labor would be more expensive than that of Asia.* In effect, Africa would experience Dutch disease. The high natural resource endowment would raise the productivity of African labor and thereby crowd out manufactures. However, this would not be a problem because, after all, Africa would have higher wage levels than Asia, so that its labor force would earn more. Below, I will argue that Wood's apparently easy passage from a statement about factor endowments to the inference that Africa cannot export manufactures via an inference from its comparative advantage is too hasty. However, I first continue my taxonomic review of the globalization models. One of these becomes my alternative explanation for Wood's results.

Immobile Public Infrastructure

I now introduce the other type of immobile factor, namely public infrastructure. Findlay (1996) sets out a simple political economy model of the effects of globalization in a model with infrastructure. Private capital is complementary with publicly provided infrastructure. In this sense, infrastructure is like natural resources in the first of the two models discussed above: it makes the whole environment better for other factors. However, the interest of the Findlay model is that, whereas natural resources are exogenous, the amount of infrastructure is a choice variable of the government. In the model, the government has a choice between using its revenue to provide infrastructure and using it to redistribute income to its supporters.

Clearly, in an autarkic world the government can choose to spend its revenue on redistribution without dire consequences for the private capital stock. However, in a globalized world in which capital is mobile, if it persists with this choice, then private capital will relocate to countries in which the government makes the opposite choice. If the redistributive expenditures favor labor, then the exodus is confined to capital: unlike the previous model, the lack of the immobile factor does not produce a generalized factor exodus (which in poor countries would be predominantly labor).

If, as a result of globalization, the government changes its policy, then globalization hurts the social group that was previously benefiting from redistributive expenditures. More generally, the model would predict that as a result of globalization governments around the world

Table 1. Infrastructure versus Redistributive Government Spending
(Percentage points of GDP)

Category	Sub-Saharan Africa	South Asia	East Asia
Economic services	5.7	7.2	6.1
General public services	6.9	6.2	6.3
Ratio	0.83	1.16	0.97

Source: Collier and Gunning (1997), Table 11.
Note: the proxy for infrastructure is "economic services" and for redistributive expenditure "general public services" (taking the main redistribution mechanism as being the public sector payroll).

would switch their expenditures toward infrastructure and away from redistribution.

Governments that wished to maintain redistributive expenditures would attempt to prevent their economies from globalizing by retaining restrictions on capital outflows. An example of this might be Zimbabwe.

The Findlay model may have some applicability to Africa. In Africa, the composition of public expenditure is, on one measure, more skewed toward redistributive expenditures and away from infrastructure expenditures than in Asia (Table 1).

However, the differences shown in Table 1 are hardly dramatic. Further, there are grounds for doubting whether infrastructure expenditures are more productive than redistributive expenditures. Devarajan and others (1996) found that in developing countries as a whole government recurrent expenditure was conducive to growth whereas government capital expenditures actually reduced growth (an interpretation being that capital expenditures were more associated with rent seeking).

Policy Technology as a Generalized Productivity Shift

I now introduce the second modification to the simple-mobile-factor, common-technology model, relaxing the assumption of common technology. Technology here needs to be understood in its proper technical sense as defined by the model rather than by reference to popular imagery about machinery. Of course, it is true that producers in Africa often tend to use different machinery from that used in industrial countries. This is, however, endogenous; that is, it is the result of other differences rather than itself being the problem. For Africa to have a technological disadvantage would mean that the same bundles of inputs, machines, and labor, when used in Africa, produce less than when used elsewhere. I have already considered differences in the endowments of immobile factors as a possible explanation for such differences in the productivity of mobile factors. Here I want to abstract from this explanation and focus instead on the policy environment. As with natural resources, there is a modeling choice. Differences in policy technology can have a generalized productivity effect across the economy, or they can affect activities differentially. I first consider the former.

Assume that countries differ in their policy environments as well as in their labor forces and private capital stocks. Initially, assume that both of these are immobile. Africa has a worse policy environment than the rest of the world, and as a result the returns on both labor and private capital are reduced. Imagine, first, that goods cannot be traded internationally. Real wages will differ between countries, reflecting differences in policy and in capital: Africa will have low wages both because it has little capital and because it has poor policies. Now open economies up to trade in goods. Trade will raise average incomes but redistribute from the scarce to the abundant factor. In Africa, labor will gain and capital will lose, with labor gaining more than capital loses.

Now open up private capital to international mobility. Suppose that the African policy environment is so much worse than those of other regions that the return on capital is lower than elsewhere despite the low ratio of capital to labor. Capital will leave those countries in which it has a low return and move to where it has a high return. This will be globally Pareto-efficient: the gainers could compensate losers. The gainers are owners of private capital in initially low-return-on-capital countries, and wage earners in initially high-return-on-capital countries. The losers are owners of capital in initially high-return-on-capital countries. When U.S. financial capital shifted to the Republic of Korea because returns were higher, the beneficiaries were U.S. pensioners and Korean workers, and the losers were Korean owners of capital and U.S. workers. When Nigerian financial capital moved to the United States, the gainers were Nigerian owners of capital and U.S. workers and the losers were Nigerian owners of labor.

Even in a poor policy environment, globalization of the capital market is Pareto-efficient: the gainers (owners of African capital) could compensate the losers (owners of African labor) and still be better off. However, the mechanisms for such compensation are obviously liable to be weak. Hence, there may appear to be a presumption that unless African governments improve their policy environments, the new globalization of world capital markets will make most Africans worse off. This is wrong for a simple reason: African-owned wealth globalized many years ago. I return to this below.

Policy Technology as an Alteration in Comparative Advantage

If factors are differentially mobile, then a common reduction in factor productivity across both factors and all sectors will still change the composition of activity. If, for example, capital is mobile but labor is immobile, then capital will leave poor policy environments while labor is locked in.[1] In turn, the alteration in the factor endowment will change comparative advantage. If Africa loses capital (and human capital), then it becomes more heavily concentrated in labor-intensive activities.

However, policy differences are not neutral across activities. The core point of this chapter is to argue that Africa has turned its comparative advantage away from manufacturing because its poor policy environment has been particularly hostile to manufacturing activity. The normal focus of discussion on the African policy environment vis-à-vis manufacturing is on trade policy. This is not my focus. Rather, I will discuss a constellation of policies, all of which have the affect of raising the cost of transactions.

Manufacturing is a transactions-intensive activity, much more so than natural resources and agriculture. Manufacturing involves the purchase of a wide variety of inputs from multiple sources, their storage, and the storage and sale of the output to a variety of customers in multiple destinations. While the image of manufacturing is to classify it as a "productive" activity like agriculture, it is in fact much more akin to shopkeeping. As in shopkeeping, there is a high ratio of purchased nonfactor inputs to value added. By contrast, natural resource extraction, like agriculture, has a much lower ratio of inputs to value added, and a much narrower range of suppliers and customers. Storage of inputs and outputs is much less central to the operation.

Transactions costs are high in Africa for several distinct reasons. First, transport costs are high (Amjadi and Yeats, 1995). In some countries, this is because of poor location: a higher proportion of the African population lives in countries that are landlocked than do the Asian and Latin American populations. Landlocked countries and those with poor port facilities tend to grow more slowly (Sachs and Warner, 1997). However, perhaps a more important reason is that the transport sector is insufficiently competitive. This is most obvious for

[1]Were the analysis to be extended to human capital, it might be regarded as being of intermediate mobility, less mobile than capital but more mobile than unskilled labor. Hence, Africa's shortage of human capital might be seen as partly endogenous to its poor policy environment. There are, for example, reputedly more Malawian doctors in Manchester than in Malawi.

air transport. The privileges given to national airlines have raised prices and reduced reliability. For example, the landlocked francophone economies have handicapped themselves by maintaining Air Afrique as a high-cost operator. In Zimbabwe, the diversion of planes of the national airline to presidential use delayed the delivery of roses in Europe for Christmas Eve, when the price was high, to the dead period between Christmas and New Year's, when they were much less valuable. Private airlines take advantage of this situation to overprice their African routes (Okeahalam, 1996). In sea transport, preferences for nationally registered shipping have reinforced shipping cartels, raising freight rates (Amjadi and Yeats, 1995). Internally, railways are sometimes given legal monopolies over certain categories of traffic. For example, in Uganda until the early 1990s the main export, coffee, could only legally be transported by rail. The small scale of road transport also lends itself to cartels. For example, once Uganda legalized the transport of coffee by road an unexpected benefit was that the expansion of road transport broke the cartel so that road freight changes approximately halved.

Transport is not only expensive; it is unreliable. As a result, firms must keep higher levels of inventories. Efficient East Asian producers using just-in-time production methods are able to reduce inventories of inputs to only 20 minutes of production. By contrast, African firms are commonly holding 2 or 3 months worth of inputs. This is all the more striking because it is much more costly to hold inputs in Africa than in Asia, because interest rates are usually much higher, reflecting Africa's cartelized banking system and lack of financial integration into the global economy. The unreliability of supply "ripples through the system" (Fafchamps, 1996). Let down by one supplier, a firm in turn lets down its own customers. The level of inventories necessary fully to protect a firm from unreliable supplies would be prohibitively expensive.

A second reason why transactions costs are high is that contract enforcement is difficult. Paradoxically, this is more of a problem in the modern sector than in the traditional economy, which has evolved institutions such as the kin group. Modern sector firms are usually not able to use kin groups because too few members of the group are modern sector entrepreneurs. The exception is the ethnic minority communities whose kin groups are heavily specialized. For example, in Kenya African-owned and Asian-owned firms use different means of assessing whether a potential new business customer is creditworthy (Biggs, Raturi, and Srivastava, 1996). The Asian firms largely rely upon information from their kin-based social network. The African firms, lacking such a business-oriented network, rely predominantly upon the visual inspection of the premises of the potential customer. Lacking informal enforcement mechanisms, firms need reliable courts, yet the courts function badly (Widner, 1997). In much of Africa, firms are very reluctant to resolve disputes through the courts. Where the courts are perceived as more reliable, as in Zimbabwe, around three times the proportion of disputes are settled in them as in the rest of Africa.

A third reason why transactions costs are high is because of the high cost of information. Partly, this is because of the small scale of the African business community. For example, in most countries the market for a financial press is too small to sustain the fixed costs of information gathering. A further reason is the high cost, unreliability, and low density of telecommunications. The high cost and unreliability reflect the restriction of telephone services to public monopolies.[2] Telephone charges, especially for international calls, are the highest in the world, and Africa has three times the rate of faults per line as in other developing regions. Being on the telephone conveys externalities; for example, if nobody else is on the telephone, there is no point in being on oneself. Hence, the high cost and unreliability, which directly discourage use, have an additional indirect discouraging effect as a result of the reduction in telephone density. Africa has the lowest telephone density in the world. The poor phone system is an obvious direct impediment to manufacturing exports. However, it also feeds back onto the formation of social capital. Social capital is formed by the interaction of business managers. A bad phone network raises the cost of such interaction and so reduces it. Social networks are important mechanisms for the gathering of information about manufacturing techniques as well as reducing problems of contract enforcement. For example, Barr (1996) in a study of Ghanaian manufacturing firms finds that the social network of the firm substantially and significantly affects its productivity: the larger the network, the more productive the workforce. She further shows that foreign-owned firms in Ghana are significantly more productive than Ghanaian-owned firms only because they have larger networks of foreign contacts. The years of anti-trade-biased policies in Ghana reduced the opportunities for businesses to make foreign contacts, so that foreign ownership provided an important social advantage. In a more outward-oriented policy environment, firms would have been able to make foreign contacts through trade, so ownership would probably have been less important.

[2]Even when these are privatized, the monopoly is sometimes retained, as recently in Côte d'Ivoire.

A final reason why transactions costs are high is because of the poor quality of ancillary public services. For example, one of Africa's exports with considerable scope for growth is fish. However, fish exports require health inspection and certification; otherwise, they are not allowed into the importing country. Fish inspectors are public officials. In Uganda, fish exporters complain that they may have to wait several days before an inspector visits, the resultant delay making the fish unexportable. Since modern retailing in European markets itself depends upon the complete reliability of supply, such interruptions may make the product completely unexportable. A second example is the working of certification of truck transportation. While load certification can have some value, its actual operation is a source of competitive corruption (Schleifer and Vishny, 1993). If many enforcement agencies and officers each take the opportunity to exact a rent, the total level of charges can be transaction-prohibiting. In the Côte d'Ivoire in 1997, the syndicate of transport operators went on strike against the predation of the police force. In response, the government confined the police to barracks; it is reported that transport costs fell. In this instance, a public service that should be reducing transactions costs was in fact significantly increasing them. A final example is the failure of duty-drawback schemes to work properly. This is important because tariff levels on inputs for potential manufactured exports are often high. Duty-drawback schemes in Africa, unlike in parts of Asia, do not make use of shortcut procedures such as standardized input coefficients. Instead, every particular drawback has to be established by documentation. This is a recipe for delay, and in the context of high inflation, delay substantially reduces the value of any eventual duty refund.

With high transactions costs, a transactions-intensive activity such as manufacturing is disadvantaged both absolutely and relative to the transactions-extensive exports of agriculture and natural resources. Recall that Wood and Berge (1997) find a negative econometric relationship between the natural resource endowment and manufactured exports. However, this may be due to an entirely different mechanism from that which he assumes. It is now established that there is a relationship from the natural resource endowment to the policy environment: abundant natural resources appear to induce a poor policy environment (Sachs and Warner, 1995). Hence, the empirical result may have arisen not primarily because of the Dutch disease mechanism, but because of the greater sensitivity of manufactures to the poor policy environment that natural resources induce. Thus, Africa has had both poor policies and large natural resources. Natural-resource exports can survive poor policies better than manufactures. For example, once tree crops are planted, it is costly to uproot them, and they stay productive for around 50 years; harvesting, and hence exports, will persist even during severe deteriorations in the policy environment. The economics of mineral extraction is analogous. Africa has thus experienced increased concentration in natural resource exports, and in some instances absolute contraction in manufactured exports. However, this outcome reflects the policy environment rather than the resource endowment. Although Wood controls for trade policy, this is only one aspect of the policy environment affecting the productivity of manufacturing. To summarize, on this thesis, Africa's problem is not that its endowments make it intrinsically unsuited to manufacturing, but that its current policy environment makes it unsuited by raising transactions costs.

Distinguishing Between Endowment and Transactions-Cost Theses

Both Wood's natural-resource-endowment thesis and the above transactions-cost thesis predict that Africa would have low levels of manufactured exports relative to natural-resource exports. However, they are by no means identical in their implications or predictions. In their implications, they are clearly radically different. On Wood's thesis, Africa can forget about manufactures; there is nothing to be done. On the transactions-cost thesis, there is everything to be done. Policymakers can, by reducing transactions costs to world levels, make Africa into the most competitive region in the world for labor-intensive manufactures because of Africa's low and relatively declining real incomes.

Since the implications are so drastically different, it is important to see how the theses can be distinguished. Wood's thesis and the transactions-cost thesis have two testably different predictions. The first testable corollary of the Wood explanation for Africa's failure to export manufactures is that the returns to labor would be higher in natural-resource-abundant environments, such as Africa, than in Asia. Clearly, there are instances in which the Dutch disease mechanism is sufficiently powerful to yield this result. Thus, Saudi Arabia does not export manufactures because its wage levels are too high for it to be competitive, and in Africa the same is likely to be the case for Botswana. Globally, the Dutch disease effects of natural-resource abundance will partially account for the econometric relationship that Wood establishes. However, in Africa it is evidently not the predominant explanation for the failure to export manufactures: income levels are now lower than in Asia, and the gap is widening rapidly. Africa's greater quantity of natural resources evidently has not mapped into a higher price of labor.[3] China already has a purchasing power parity per capita income higher than all sub-Saharan African countries except Botswana, Namibia, and South Africa. During the period 1990–94, it was growing 12 percent annually more rapidly than the average for sub-Saharan Africa. At such growth rates, every 6 years per capita income in China will double relative to that in Africa. By around 2006, even the higher-income African countries, such as Côte d'Ivoire, Kenya, and Zimbabwe, would have per capita incomes less than one-fifth those of China. This evidence must be qualified because there is no necessary mapping from differences in real incomes in the economy as a whole to differences in real product wages in manufacturing. First, the real exchange rate might be higher in Africa than in Asia, so that real incomes (which reflect mainly the price of nontradables) could be higher in Asia, while real product wages could be higher in Africa. However, this itself may be an outcome of policies that keep the exchange rate appreciated. Second, the wage in African manufacturing may be higher relative to the returns to labor in the economy as a whole than in Asia. This might reflect labor market policies, such as minimum wages, or the greater power of African labor to extract rent-sharing wage levels. Again, such wage premiums might be amenable to policy.

While both real exchange rate differences and labor market differences probably considerably reduce the differential in real manufacturing product wages relative to that in incomes, as the income differential widens and as policies change, Africa should become competitive. Africa's favorable endowment of natural resources alone does not make it intrinsically uncompetitive relative to Asia's. On the contrary, Africa will look increasingly competitive, as long as it can offer an environment in which factors can be as productive as in China.

The second testable corollary of Wood's thesis concerns the flow of capital. Natural-resource-based activities may not need as much capital as manufacturing (although some of them clearly need more), so that Africa would not attract a large capital inflow. However, it seems hard to believe that it would, on account of having natural resource abundance, experience a capital outflow. Yet this is what has happened. Table 2 shows that by 1990 Africa had had far more capital flight than any other region relative to its total wealth, despite having a far lower stock of capital per worker.

[3]Similarly, even though the quantity of human capital in Africa is less than in Asia, it does not necessarily follow that its price is higher than in Asia, because the demand for human capital might be lower than in Asia if transactions-intensive activities are also intensive in human capital.

Table 2. Capital Flight and Factor Proportions

Region	Ratio of Capital Flight to Private Wealth	Private Capital per Worker (in U.S. dollars)
Sub-Saharan Africa	0.39	1,069
Middle East	0.39	3,678
Latin America	0.10	17,424
South Asia	0.03	2,425
East Asia	0.06	9,711

Source: Collier, Hoeffler, and Pattillo (1998), Table 1.

The remarkable exodus of capital demonstrates two things. First, it shows that African governments have never really had captive capital. During the 1970s and 1980s, when they behaved as though they had such power, they faced a massive capital exodus. Between 1970 and 1990, 39 percent of African private wealth came to be held outside the continent. Africa was thus the first continent to experience the globalization of its capital market. It was better integrated into world capital markets than other continents because its economies were small and heavily internationalized as a result of the investment pattern under colonialism. A corollary of this is that Africa has little further capital to lose from globalization. Rather, it has enormous potential benefits should globalization develop into a two-way instead of a one-way street.

The second thing that the exodus of capital demonstrates is that the African policy environment has been much worse than elsewhere. Such an exodus cannot be explained in terms of an abundance of natural resources.

Where does this leave Wood's thesis? Evidently, in its initial form it is not sufficient to explain observed phenomena; however, it can be rehabilitated by a modification.[4] The modification combines the assumptions of the Wood model with those of the generalized policy technology model: across all sectors uniformly, Africa is less productive than Asia. This produces a capital exodus and lowers African incomes, but it does not, by assumption, differentially disadvantage manufacturing. Manufacturing then gets hit again by Dutch disease from natural resources, and it is this that determines Africa's comparative advantage.

[4]Wood has proposed this modification to me in discussion, though I do not wish to imply by this that he necessarily accepts that such a modification is necessary.

Wood "Mark II" is consistent with the observed stylized facts of trade, wages, and capital flows, and it carries the same policy punchline as Mark I. Although in Mark II African governments can do a lot to improve the policy environment, this will not bring about manufactured exports; rather, it will lead to more productive natural-resource-based exports. However, Wood Mark II still faces problems with the *detailed* facts of the African policy environment. As discussed above, this environment is peculiarly hostile to transactions. This is why, in the more extreme cases of poor policy, such as Uganda during 1971–86, the structure of the economy shifted heavily out of transactions-intensive activities and back into subsistence agriculture (Collier, 1997). Manufacturing is transactions-intensive. If this is accepted, then Wood Mark II simply falls to Occam's razor: it is unnecessary as an explanation because the phenomenon has already been explained.

What Will Move Where in Africa?

I now return to the notion that, in a globalizing economy, Africa potentially has three degrees of freedom: labor emigration, capital mobility (in each direction), and trade. Different African countries are best suited to different ways of integrating into the global economy.

I have already suggested that one group of economies, which might be thought of as the Burkina Faso–type economies, are most likely to integrate through labor exodus. The policy issue is then to ensure that, instead of whole families leaving the country permanently, workers leave it temporarily and then repatriate their savings.

A second group of economies might be termed the Wood economies. These are the economies in which natural resource endowments are so large that Dutch disease will preclude manufacturing. I think that this applies to Angola, Botswana, and Namibia.

A third group of countries are the Findlay economies. The composition of public expenditure is hostile to capital, so there will be a capital exodus. Zimbabwe and South Africa are the potential candidates for this category. The recent decision of President Mugabe to make large unbudgeted public expenditures on war veterans is a classic instance of such behavior and of the genuine dilemmas that give rise to it.

A fourth group of countries are the high-transactions-cost economies. I would categorize this as applying to most African economies. For these economies, whether globalization achieves anything will depend upon the radical reduction in transactions costs. In the countries that succeed in doing this, there will be a capital inflow, manufacturing exports, rapid growth, and falling poverty.

Trade Policy

So far I have said nothing about trade policy and globalization, either Africa's trade policy or that of the rest of the world. Implicit in what I have said is that trade policy is no longer the central policy aspect of Africa's trade performance, and in this I agree with Rodrik (1997). However, it is evidently of some importance.

Much the most important aspect of trade policy is that African governments should continue to reduce trade barriers. Despite Rodrik's evidence to the contrary,[5] the balance of evidence remains heavily that trade restrictions reduce growth and that they have done so more catastrophically in Africa than any other region (Sachs and Warner, 1997; Collier and Gunning, 1997). Africa continues to have higher trade barriers than other regions (Dollar, 1992), and it participated least in the negotiated reductions in barriers during the Uruguay Round. Fortunately, as Wang and Winters (1997) show, Africa does not face very significant trade barriers in its major markets, so in one sense the lack of participation in the WTO has had little cost. However, highly informed observers such as Richard Blackhurst (the former chief economist of the WTO), think that Africa would have been able to achieve reductions in the barriers that it faces were it to have offered something during the round. Since the reductions in African trade barriers would directly benefit Africa, any further benefit in terms of reduced barriers facing Africa would be an additional bonus rather than the rationale for trade liberalization. I argue below that participation in the WTO is potentially important for African countries, but not primarily because of their opportunities for improved market access.

Probably the most important Uruguay Round change that will affect Africa is the phasing out of QRs, and in particular the demise of the MFA during the next 8 years. This is both a threat and an opportunity. It is a threat because it removes the value of Africa's current MFA quotas. Hence, if by 2005 Africa still needs protection against Asia to be able to sell its garments and textiles, then it will lose its markets. This is very likely in parts of Africa. Conversely, in those parts of Africa that become internationally competitive by 2005, the end of the MFA is a huge opportunity. The world market in garments and textiles is so large relative to Africa's current level of manufacture that being competitive would permit explosive growth even faster than that seen during the 1990s in Bangladesh.

[5]This relies only upon an African sample, and since intra-African variation in trade policy is much more limited than global variation, it is to be expected that trade policy would appear to be less significant as a determinant of growth.

What, if any, role has trade policy had in making African manufacturing more competitive? I have argued above that the core of this process concerns public policy toward reducing transactions costs. I now briefly consider whether there is a case for "industrial policy." There is, in fact, an important role for policy toward industry. That is to confront firms with as much competition as possible, by reducing trade protection, by prosecuting cartels and removing backdoor protection through government procurement privileges. There is some evidence that trade liberalization can raise productivity both by a learning-through-exporting effect, and through increased competition. Current research by Bernard Gauthier on a panel sample of manufacturing firms in five African countries establishes that those firms that were exporting in the first round of the survey experienced significantly faster growth in productivity in the subsequent two years. This is consistent with a learning process from exporting analogous to Barr's result on the efficacy of foreign networks discussed above.[6] Hay (1997) shows that the sharp increase in competition resulting from trade liberalization in Brazil raised total factor productivity by 40 percent. In Africa, the most protected industrial sector was that of Zimbabwe, which had enjoyed blanket QRs from 1965–91. A survey of 1992 found that only 7 percent of manufacturing firms regarded competition as a significant problem. Two years later, after liberalization had started to have an effect, the proportion had risen to 37 percent (Ncube and others, 1997). This strategy of raising productivity through competition is the opposite of "selective protection" to build "capabilities," which has been advocated by some policy commentators.

African Integration into World Financial Markets

The feature of globalization on which I now focus is the increasing integration of the world's financial markets, both for capital and for risk. I consider them in turn.

The Attraction of Capital to Africa

Before 1914, the capital surplus countries, notably the United Kingdom, were running capital outflows of around 9 percent of GDP, and the economies with new investment opportunities and low domestic savings capacity, such as Canada, were receiving capital on a similar

[6]It is, however, not conclusive. Firms with better managements could both be better at exporting and have more rapid efficiency growth.

scale. The various catastrophes of the twentieth century interrupted this process. However, the world financial system now has far better information than it did before 1914, and proportionately much higher levels of securitized assets under professional management. It also faces much lower risks of major warfare, because the precarious balance of power guarantee of peace that prevailed before 1914 has given way to the pax Americana. Hence, it should be possible to reach levels of capital flows to capital-scarce economies that proportionately exceed these earlier levels. Capital flows to developing countries are still proportionately much lower than pre-1914, but they are growing rapidly.

However, flows to Africa other than South Africa are negligible (Bhattacharya, Montiel, and Sharma, 1997). It might appear that Africa has yet to integrate into the world capital market. More properly, Africa has become detached from private capital inflows: 20 years ago, it accounted for around 9 percent of the total private capital flows to developing countries, whereas by the first half of the 1990s its market share had fallen to only 1.6 percent. Even this was an improvement upon the late 1980s; during the period 1989–94, net investment from the OECD economies was $8 billion, a fourfold increase over the period 1983–88.

The investment of the 1990s has been inward looking and confined to a small section of the world's companies that happen to have an informational advantage about Africa. Evidence on the inward-looking nature of foreign investment to Africa comes from a survey conducted of foreign investors to five East African countries conducted in 1994. It found that virtually none had considered a location outside East Africa for their project. Presented the other way round, this shows that East Africa is not on the shortlist for internationally footloose investment projects; it was considered only for those projects that could not be located elsewhere, presumably either because of natural resources or because the investment was intended to serve the local market. While this inward orientation continues, foreign investment will be growth-dependent, rather than growth-generating. Evidence on the informational segmentation of corporate investment in Africa comes from its geographic composition. More than 60 percent of OECD investment in Africa during 1989–94 came from just two medium-sized OECD economies, France and the United Kingdom. That investment to Africa was so skewed toward the two former main colonial powers suggests that other potential investors were deterred by a lack of knowledge. Investment in Africa appears to have been only for the cogniscenti: those firms that had long-established links with Africa, were overwhelmingly British or French, and were in a position to detect the improved investment climate and respond to it. Other foreign firms did not invest because of a lack of knowledge. In these two senses, Africa has yet to globalize. It is not attracting investment from a global pool of investors, and it is not attracting investment that is globally, rather than domestically, oriented.

Until recently, the explanation for this was that, in terms of the rate of return on capital, Africa was not capital-scarce: the poor policy environment had lowered returns below world levels. Collier and Gunning (1997) estimate that during the period 1960–90 the return on capital in Africa has been around one-third less than the world average. However, with the policy reforms of the 1990s this is changing: during 1990–94 the rate of return on FDI was around 60 percent higher in Africa than in other developing regions (Bhattacharya, Montiel, and Sharma, 1997). The phenomenon to be explained is that Africa is not attracting capital despite these reforms.

Africa has failed to attract private capital during the 1990s because it is perceived as a high-risk environment. One measure of this is the *Institutional Investor* risk ratings, which estimate country risk on a scale from 0 (high risk) to 100 (safe). On this scale, Africa deteriorated on average from 30 in 1980 to 21 in 1995, by when it was the most risky region in the world. Jasperson and others (1998) establish that there is a significant econometric relationship globally between the risk ratings and investment. Presumably, the risk ratings are proxying concerns that genuinely deter investment. We can learn more about these concerns from investor surveys. Surveys of investor intentions find that the single main deterrent to investment in Africa is the perceived high risk (Blakey, 1992; World Bank, 1994). Among risks, the most important is the fear of policy reversal: African policy environments are seen as unpredictable. Hence, the task of integrating into world capital markets, on the receiving end of capital instead of in the past as suppliers of capital, is primarily that of African governments building reputations for policy reliability.

Clearly, the most important means by which a government can build reputation is through its performance. However, elsewhere, governments have used commitment arrangements to accelerate the building of reputation beyond that which would occur purely through good performance. In the limiting case, a government that is resolved to maintain good performance simply uses commitment mechanisms as a signaling device. That is, the commitment mechanism merely signals to private agents that the government has resolve, rather than in any way changing government behavior. If the signal is effective, the commitment mechanism may be useful in accelerating the building of reputation and hence in raising investment. However, a government might wish to use a commitment mechanism not only as a signal but also as a discipline that changes its own behavior. For example, a government might resolve to avoid large budget deficits, but nevertheless find that the promulgation of a cash budget procedure provides a commitment mechanism without which it is unable to implement its resolve. In general, commitment mechanisms have both these features: they are signals to private agents about government intentions, and they are also specific procedures for converting good intentions into realized policies. In turn, a mechanism that converts intentions into realized policies will enhance credibility. The cash budget not only signals to private agents that the government is resolved to avoid large fiscal deficits; it also reassures them that a viable means has been put in place for achieving this resolve.

I refer to commitment mechanisms as "agencies of restraint." I classify such agencies according to their domicile and the source of their power. Their domicile can be purely domestic, purely external, or a hybrid. For example, a national central bank is a purely domestic agency, donor conditionality is purely external, and regional agreements are partly domestic and partly external. Agencies of restraint can derive their power through being based on penalties, through the devolution of authority, or through some combination. For example, by establishing an independent central bank, a government is able to restrain itself from interfering with the setting of interest rates. It achieves this through shedding authority. However, an independent central bank thereby also acquires a role as a restraint over the fiscal policy of the government. If the government chooses to run a large fiscal deficit, the central bank can raise interest rates. In turn, this inflicts political costs on the government since electors dislike the increase in interest rates. Hence, an independent central bank is both a restraint upon monetary policy, based upon shedding authority, and a restraint upon fiscal policy, based upon penalties. I now consider various agencies of restraint that African governments can use to reassure investors. I first consider the use of commitment mechanisms to allay investor fears of macroeconomic instability. I start with two purely domestic agencies of restraint, an independent central bank and a cash budget, then introduce two external agencies, capital account convertibility and donor conditionality, and finally the hybrid of regional convergence criteria.

Independent Central Bank

Granting independence to the central bank is the classic way in which the government can restrain itself. The perceived effectiveness of the Bundesbank, the Federal Reserve, and the Reserve Bank of New Zealand has induced a widespread move toward the institution. In 1997, the British government gave the Bank of England independence over monetary policy, and the planned European Central Bank will extend independence to most of Europe. Many African governments have adopted legislation that devolves power onto central banks and protects the governor from dismissal. However, the evidence on the effectiveness of central bank independence in developing countries is not encouraging. Cukierman, Webb, and Negapti (1992) found no relationship between their degree of legal independence and the rate of inflation. Rather, it was the tenure of the governor that was important, suggesting that power relationships remained personalized rather than being embedded in the legal framework. The recent shift to democracy in Africa is likely to change this, making central bank independence a reality rather than a legal fiction. However, it will take time for legally independent central banks to establish their own credibility with private agents. In the short term, central banks face the same credibility problem as the government and so are not an important means for credibility enhancement.

Cash Budget

To date, the most effective domestic agency of restraint upon governments has been the cash budget. The power of this rule derives from its simplicity and its conversion of what is intrinsically a continuum into a specific quantitative target, namely a zero deficit. The principle that spending should not exceed income is readily defensible in cabinet, even though as an economic proposition it is not in fact correct. The economically correct proposition, that a deficit should not over the course of a business cycle exceed the level consistent with sustainable debt accumulation, does not produce a precise target. As a result, it does not provide a defense in cabinet against incremental spending requests.

While cash budgets have proved effective in the short term, given their lack of economic rationale it seems unlikely that they can persist as long-term restraints. They therefore gradually need to be replaced by more sustainable restraints, conceivably by independent central banks.

Capital Account Convertibility

Capital account convertibility provides a restraint upon the government because unsustainable policies are punished by capital flight.

The experiences of the United Kingdom in 1992, of Mexico in 1994, and of East Asia in 1997 demonstrate the power of this mechanism to inflict punishment. However, the very fact of these currency crises also demonstrates that governments have sometimes failed to take the threat sufficiently seriously. A few African governments have recently adopted full convertibility. Since capital controls have been ineffective, the adoption of convertibility is usually unlikely to produce transitional capital flight, although this occurred in Zambia, where the adoption of convertibility preceded fiscal stabilization. Rather, the expectation would be that convertibility would lead to an initial increased inflow of capital. The potential withdrawal of this capital would then constitute the penalty-based restraint mechanism. In several economies, private capital inflows have become bunched into euphoric surges that have appreciated the exchange rate and financed consumption booms. There is clearly a need for macroeconomic management to prevent such unsustainable behavior. One possibility is for the taxation of short-term capital flows. However, this carries a high cost. It signals to potential investors that the government reserves the right to tax them, and reduces the liquidity of their investment, thereby confirming investors in their fears about African governments. Further, it is likely to be highly ineffective in practice because investors can find many illegal routes for removing capital.

Donor Conditionality

Donor conditionality has been used extensively as a macroeconomic policy restraint mechanism. Governments reach agreement with the IMF on monetary targets, which are then monitored. Breaches of the targets in principle attract aid penalties both directly through IMF ESAF financing and indirectly through cross-conditionality between IMF programs and the aid programs of other donors. In practice, donor conditionality has been quite ineffective as a means of enhancing credibility. One measure of this is that, despite being the major recipient of such conditionality, Africa is rated as the riskiest continent for investment. One reason for this is that fully three-quarters of IMF ESAF programs have missed their targets sufficiently badly for the program to be canceled or interrupted. As a result of this history, donor conditionality now faces its own credibility problem as a restraint.

Regional Stability Pacts

A hybrid agency of restraint that has yet to be used in Africa is regional agreements on a "stability pact." Such criteria, encapsulated in the "convergence criteria," have recently proved highly effective in Europe. European governments agreed on targets for fiscal deficits (3 percent of GDP) and for government debt (60 percent of GDP). As with cash budgets, there is no particular economic rationale for these precise numbers. However, their promulgation has a powerful political effect for two reasons. First, the quantitative target converts something that is intrinsically a continuum into something precise. This changes the politics of incremental public expenditure. While ever the cost of deficits is viewed as a continuum (which is correct in terms of economics), no single proposal for additional spending can be vetoed on the grounds of the clear and unacceptable cost of an increased deficit. By contrast, once there is a quantitative target, the political costs of incremental expenditure cease to rise as a continuum but become discrete: any proposal that would push the deficit over the target incurs high political costs and so can be rejected. Second, the power of the convergence criteria rests on the fact that governments that are accepted as peers have reached agreement on them and that many of these governments will meet them. Failure to achieve the target thus signals to the domestic electorate that its government has failed on its own terms. The European agreement on convergence criteria will eventually include fiscal penalties. However, these are probably incidental to effectiveness. To date there have been no fiscal penalties, yet the criteria have already radically changed fiscal behavior as governments make painful fiscal decisions to achieve the targets. This demonstrates that it is the existing political penalties rather than the prospective fiscal penalties that give the institution its power.

There is scope for African governments to use their regional groupings, and indeed their continental groupings (ECA, ADB, OAU) to forge stability pacts. The fiscal and debt targets need not be the same as the European criteria, nor indeed need the coverage of an agreement include or be confined to fiscal deficits and debt. However, the principle should be that African governments would themselves agree on what constituted unacceptably bad economic policies. By delineating such policies and agreeing to avoid them, governments would build political penalties against their adoption that would reduce the perceived risk facing investors. This process has dramatically reduced interest rates across Europe in the past year, and it can have a similar effect on investor confidence in Africa.

I now move from general fears about the macroeconomy to specific fears about investor rights. I consider three agencies of restraint: public insurance arrangements, credit syndication, and investment charters.

Public Insurance Agencies

The most direct way to cope with risks is to insure against them. However, the political and policy risks that concern investors in Africa are only to a very limited extent covered by commercial insurers. Instead, several OECD governments have created public insurance schemes for investment in and exports from their countries, notably the Overseas Private Investment Corporation (OPIC) in the United States and the Export Credit Guarantee Department in the United Kingdom. More recently, the World Bank has created its own insurance arm, the Multilateral Investment Guarantee Agency (MIGA). Although ostensibly insurance arrangements, these agencies are in fact better thought of as commitment mechanisms that can be used by the host government. That is, they are agencies of restraint.

The public insurance schemes act as agencies of restraint because the government of the country receiving the investment is a party to a legal agreement that commits it to compensate the insurance company for any payouts. For example, OPIC recovers 80 percent of the money it pays out to firms on claims from host governments. OPIC thus acts as an intermediary more than an insurer. Its function as an intermediary is nevertheless valuable. Firms gain comfort from the fact that their claim will be assessed impartially and payment will not be delayed. Thus, however suspect is the legal system in the host country, or however impecunious the government, if the firm has a legitimate case it will receive swift compensation. The shifting of the task of recovering compensation from the firm to the insurance agency also increases the chances that the government will indeed pay the compensation. This works in two ways: investor coordination and cross-conditionalities.

Whereas a single firm is likely only to be in dispute once with a host government that (say) arbitrarily confiscates its assets, the insurer and the government are in a long-term relationship. If the government fails to adhere to its agreement with the insurer, the insurer can refuse further business in the country. This acts as a substitute for direct coordination among future private investors. Clearly, such coordination would be impossible because most firms that will become future investors do not know that they will do so. Private firms cannot, therefore, make credible threats of investment strikes in response to government behavior. The threat of withdrawal of insurance for future investors thus acts as an indirect coordination mechanism. Were the risks instead covered by a private competitive insurance market, the insurance companies would not be able to achieve the same degree of investor coordination unless they themselves acted collectively. However, collective action among competitors encounters problems of free riding. With political risk insurance effectively supplied only by MIGA and a few national agencies such as OPIC and ECGD, the scope for collusion is much greater.

Although this coordination of investors weakens the power of the host government, the government can find it valuable. The government faces a problem brought about by the lack of credibility of its own assurances to individual investors, since ex post of investor commitment, the government is in such a strong position. The main consequence of this is not that the government is able to benefit from exploiting naive foreign investors, but that it forfeits the potential benefits of investment as streetwise investors go elsewhere. Investor coordination can thus be in the interests of the host government. An analogy is how the French government of the eighteenth century rebuilt its reputation with potential creditors after a history of bond defaults. The government itself initiated bondholder coordination by creating an officially recognized association with which it dealt. With bondholder collective action facilitated (and thereby bondholder power increased vis-à-vis the government), French government bonds became less risky, and so the government was able to raise more finance.

While the public insurance agencies work in part by indirect investor coordination, their main power probably comes from cross-conditionality. Behind OPIC stands the U.S. government with its multiple powers of enforcement, including both the financial flows from the U.S. Agency for International Development and diplomatic channels. Behind MIGA stands the World Bank. Cross-conditionality between insurance claims and these other relationships does not have to be explicit for it to be effective.

The combined effect of investor coordination and cross-conditionality is that the public insurance agencies function as effective agencies of restraint. Because they recover around 80 percent of claims, their premiums are correspondingly much lower than the underlying nature of the risks involved and so much lower than would be charged by a competitive private insurance market.

However, the public insurance agencies have three disadvantages from an African perspective. First, they do not provide cover for domestic firms. Second, they are highly selective in the business they accept. Third, partly because of highly conservative capital requirements for its guarantees, MIGA is reaching the limits of its capital.

The restriction of coverage to foreign firms clearly places domestic firms at a disadvantage. In the limit, this would give rise to a situation in which African wealth was held in the OECD economies, while the African capital stock was owned by OECD-based firms. Nevertheless,

African firms are able to benefit indirectly from the public insurance agencies in two ways. First, they commonly seek joint enterprises with foreign firms. Association with a foreign firm increases the security of the domestic firm vis-à-vis its own government. Second, the presence of foreign firms that have protection from government abuse of power provides some defense for domestic firms. The standards that the government must adopt toward foreign firms may spill over toward its treatment of domestic firms. More interestingly, foreign firms may regard the way in which the government treats its domestic firms as a signal of its true intentions toward the business sector as a whole, and thus as a guide to their own long-term security. As a result, the government may feel constrained in its behavior toward its captive domestic firms by the response of noncaptive foreign investment. Despite these indirect benefits, if public insurance were the main agency of restraint in Africa, it would clearly disadvantage domestic firms. Although this pro-foreign bias is not Africa-specific, since risk is much more important for investors in Africa than in other continents, its effect in Africa will be disproportionately great.

The public insurance agencies have been accused of cherry picking, in effect restricting their cover to the lowest risk propositions. One reason for this may be that their capital base does not permit them to expand their business very rapidly. The present practice is for an investment guarantee to require capital backing to the full extent of the guarantee. This highly conservative practice has led to MIGA rapidly reaching the limit of its capital base.

The combination of restriction to foreign companies and selectivity among them leaves much potential African investment uncovered by political risk insurance. Hence, it remains important to reduce the risks facing investors through the use of other agencies of restraint.

Credit Syndication

Credit syndication provides a further opportunity for a restraint mechanism. It relies for its effectiveness upon the same two processes used by the public insurance agencies: investor coordination and cross-conditionality. For example, when large mining houses make investments in high-risk locations, they typically build syndicates of as many as 60 banks from different countries. The rationale for this is not that the mining companies need the finance, since they are often among the largest financial entities in the world. Rather, by involving the banks of many OECD countries in their investment, they seek to maximize the international damage that would be done to the host government in the event of default. First, the large network of banks provides a degree of indirect coordination among the unknown population of prospective investors. Second, there is an element of cross-conditionality, both because the banks that are party to the default are less likely to lend to the government, and because they are liable to lobby their own host governments for redress. Syndication functions to orchestrate the response to a default, thereby increasing the penalties and so reducing the underlying risk. Thus, while ostensibly a risk-*sharing* mechanism, it is better regarded as a risk-*reducing* mechanism.

Investment Charters

Recently, African governments have started to promulgate investment codes. Warner (1998) proposes the essential elements that any such charter should contain: basic obligations, specific obligations, and a dispute resolution mechanism. The basic obligations are of transparency, the right of establishment, and the right to equal treatment. The specific obligations are of the adoption of international standards with respect to compensation for expropriation; the avoidance of double taxation; prohibitions on corrupt practices; and a commitment to principles of competition, including the prohibition of cartels. There should be a binding settlement mechanism for disputes between investors and states, a model being that set out in the NAFTA treaty. At present, African investment charters do not usually meet these requirements. Several national charters have recently been issued by investment authorities. However, they tend not to have independent dispute resolution mechanisms, leaving the power of interpretation with either the government itself or with national courts. There have been some investment charters at the regional level. For example, both ECOWAS and the PTA include investment codes. However, these are very general, and the basis for their enforcement is unclear. An alternative advocated by Warner is for African governments to sign up to multilateral investment charters. There have been schemes for an Asia-Pacific Investment Code and an OECD-sponsored Multilateral Agreement on Investment (MAI) that might be lodged with the WTO. Warner suggests that African governments would gain more credibility by signing one of these charters than from producing one that was Africa-specific.

Currently, the proposed MAI is making significant progress and could well become adopted as a part of the architecture of global economic relations. Properly designed, this would most benefit those countries with the most severe credibility problems. Ironically, at present the group of low-income developing countries is seeking to oppose the MAI on the grounds that they do not want to be locked in to good treatment of foreign investors. This is a failure to recognize the time inconsistency problem. A refusal to build lock-in mechanisms does not lead to successful national predation of foreign investors but rather to a low level of foreign investment. Finally, I consider two measures for locking in to liberalized trade policy.

North-South Reciprocity

The model for North-South reciprocity as a lock-in mechanism for trade policy is NAFTA. In principle, the penalty of loss of access to export markets that enforces adherence could be achieved within an African regional grouping. However, the potential intra-African trade (other than that involving South Africa) is still quite limited, so such regional groups as yet cannot impose sufficiently severe penalties. Although there is currently a proposal within the United States for a NAFTA equivalent with Africa, since United States–Africa trade is quite small, the obvious equivalent for Africa is not an arrangement with the United States but with Europe. The revision of Lomé would provide a negotiating context for such reciprocity.

World Trade Organization

The WTO is an external, participatory agency of restraint; a member country binds itself by accepting the GATT-WTO provisions. The most useful provision is the ability to bind tariff rates. Bound tariffs are more credible and so reduce investor risk. To date, African governments have made little use of this opportunity; few tariffs are bound, and even where they are bound they are at levels so far above actual (applied) tariffs that the binding is more likely to signal an intention subsequently to raise tariffs than to maintain a liberalized regime. For example, the government of Zimbabwe undertook to bind its tariffs at the levels in force on the day it signed the Uruguay Round. On that day, it momentarily raised all its tariffs to 100 percent. Not only are African governments failing to make use of the credibility-enhancing opportunities of the WTO, but in an important respect the WTO rules are too weak for Africa's needs. WTO rules do not restrain trade policy in the area that in the past African trade restrictions has been most prominent: foreign exchange rationing.

Summary

Africa currently faces a credibility problem, which is deterring a capital inflow. This is particularly severe with respect to macroeconomic policy, investor rights, and trade policies. If an African government maintains good policies in these three areas, it will eventually overcome the credibility problem. I have reviewed a variety of agencies of restraint that may enable Africa to accelerate this process of reputation-building. There is particular scope for hybrid agencies that involve cooperation between African governments, sometimes in conjunction with OECD governments. There is also scope for the gradual evolution of purely domestic agencies from the present heavy reliance upon cash budgets to reliance upon independent central banks. There is also scope for greater use of instant restraints, notably capital account convertibility.

Integration into Global Risk-Bearing Markets

I now turn to potentially the most important aspect of globalization for Africa: the market in risk. It is important for Africa in two senses. First, Africa is more marginalized in the market for risk than in the markets for products and capital. Second, in many dimensions it is the riskiest continent, and yet it probably has the least (and arguably diminishing) domestic risk-bearing institutions and organizations.

I have noted above that, on the international risk ratings, Africa is the riskiest continent. However, this reflects only a small part of why economic agents in Africa face atypically high risks. In agriculture, Africa is unusually risky, both because of its semi-arid climate and lack of irrigation and because of the high prevalence of pests and disease. In business, risks are high because of the problems associated with the high transactions costs discussed above.

If information is sufficiently abundant and transactions costs are sufficiently low, then risks can be almost entirely pooled and diversified. In OECD economies, the modern corporation need not display risk averse behavior: it can hedge many of its risks at virtually no cost, and residual risks can be borne because its equity is held in portfolios that are highly diversified. As portfolios globalize, the scope for the pooling of incompletely correlated risks is increasingly being utilized.

Since traditional African economies were characterized by high risks with few liquid assets, there was a very high premium upon developing insurance mechanisms. Hence, institutions such as the extended family developed to provide a low-cost solution to the standard moral hazard and adverse selection problems of insurance. In some respects, these traditional institutions are now being undermined by the modern economy; it may now be advantageous for better-off households to opt out of their traditional obligations despite the penalities of exit. That is, there is an increasing problem of adverse selection. Perhaps more important, the modern sector itself, while facing much higher risks than its counterparts on other continents, has been unable to develop either informal insurance arrangements akin to those in the traditional economy or well-functioning formal insurance. The limited nature of formal insurance reflects the high transactions costs that have been a theme of the chapter; insurance is one of the most transactions-intensive activities. As a result, the typical household in Africa, and more especially the typical firm, must behave in a risk-averse fashion in its production and investment decisions, even if these are very costly in terms of loss of income. Thus, in Africa there is much more risk than elsewhere, and it is more expensively priced.

Yet the risks that Africa faces would be almost entirely poolable or diversifiable if the transactions costs were lower. For example, African stock markets are almost completely uncorrelated with each other, let alone with OECD stock markets. OECD pension funds could add Africa to their portfolios without any addition in overall risk despite the high riskiness of individual African stocks and markets. At present, few African stock markets even have unit trust funds that permit probably the single largest reduction in the risk of equity holdings. This makes participation in the local market prohibitively risky for the African small investor. Such investors are far safer purchasing unit trusts of OECD stocks. Again, the main reason for this is that unit trusts become inefficient as transactions costs increase.

A second set of risks that is capable of being borne by modern derivatives markets is that of commodity price fluctuations. A third is that of exchange rate fluctuations. Africa is atypically dependent upon commodities, and it has more currencies relative to GDP than any other region. Yet very little use is made of derivative markets in commodities, and no African country has a fully operating forward exchange market with associated derivatives. Virtually all African trade is at spot prices. This dependence upon spot prices is made more problematic by the atypically poor transport connections facing African businesses. There are inevitably long delays between the sale of an output by one firm and its receipt by another firm. Normally, in OECD economies, these delays would be far shorter, yet they would be covered by a range of derivatives markets; neither firm would itself take the risk that market prices would change during the delivery interval. (Risk reduction gives a further reason for the just-in-time production system.) In Africa, where producing firms are financially much weaker, they are faced with either bearing these risks or off-loading them onto traders. In the event, manufacturing firms in Africa operate to a remarkable extent upon cash-spot transactions. In effect, they buy and sell to traders rather than to each other. The trading sector thus performs an insurance function in addition to its more normal functions of transportation and information. Yet the trading sector is itself ill-equipped to perform this role, and it may help to account for the widespread perception in Africa that traders operate on wide margins.

Globalization of risk-bearing financial markets offers Africa the gains of risk-pooling. In principle, nearly all these gains would accrue to Africa, because the price of risk in Africa would fall to the world price of risk rather than the two prices meeting midway.

However, the obstacles to these gains from globalization are far greater than those to reaping the further gains from trade or the gains from capital market integration. Consider, for example, the obstacles to the creation of derivatives in African currencies. First, there are very few professional players in African currency markets. The scale of the market is too small to justify the high fixed costs of information needed to support professional speculation. Second, there is a scale threshold for the enforcement of proper conduct on the part of market participants. For example, banks require a hierarchy of supervision to prevent rogue trading. Third, derivatives contracts depend upon enforceability, which as discussed above is problematic in Africa. It is well understood that transactions in the formal credit market in Africa are limited by the low creditworthiness of potential borrowers; firms are small, they have little collateral, and there is little reliable information about their performance. Like credit, derivatives involve intertemporal contracts, in which one party will have a strong incentive to default. In effect, the constraints upon participation in the global market for risk are similar to those in the global market for manufactures. While transactions costs are high, transactions-intensive activities, whether manufacturing or financial services, will be curtailed.

Conclusion

I have argued that Africa has much to gain from globalization. Potentially, Africa can expand its exports into manufacturing, attract capital inflows that increase its capital stock, and participate in risk-bearing mechanisms that reduce costly risk averse behavior. However, none of these gains will accrue on present African policies. While trade and exchange rate policies have to date been at the center of African policy debates and might appear to have become even more central as a result of globalization, they are often no longer the policies most in need of reform. I have suggested two types of policies that are now important.

First, African firms operate in an environment in which transaction costs are much higher than elsewhere, directly or indirectly because of government policies. These costs differentially handicap those activities that are transactions-intensive. Both manufacturing and financial services are considerably more transactions-intensive than agriculture or natural resource extraction. These have consequences, both for the comparative advantage of Africa in product markets and for its participation in the markets at risk. In product markets, Africa has a comparative advantage in agriculture and resource extraction, and this is becoming more pronounced as transactions costs continue to fall elsewhere in the world. In the risk market, the price of risk is much higher in Africa than elsewhere: African firms face more risks and yet make the least use of risk-management financial instruments.

Second, foreign capital is deterred from Africa by perceived political risks. There are a variety of agencies of restraint that can be used to reduce these risks. Usually, they involve governments choosing to lock themselves in to policy reforms, either by building penalties against themselves or by shedding authority. To date, African governments have tended to rely upon donor conditionality as their restraint. The poor risk ratings of most African governments indicate that they need to build agencies that have greater credibility.

References

Amjadi, A., and A.J. Yeats, 1995, "Have Transport Costs Contributed to the Relative Decline of Sub-Saharan African Exports?" Policy Research Working Paper 1559 (Washington: World Bank).

Barr, A., 1996, "Entrepreneurial Networks and Economic Growth" (Ph.D. thesis, Oxford University, Oxford).

Bhattacharya, A., P.J. Montiel, and S. Sharma, 1997, "Private Capital Flows to Sub-Saharan Africa: An Overview of Trends and Determinants" (unpublished; Washington: International Monetary Fund).

Biggs, T., M. Raturi and P. Srivastava, 1996, "Enforcement of Contracts in an African Credit Market," RPED Discussion Paper (Washington: World Bank).

Blakey, G.G., 1992, "Economic Integration in Sub-Saharan Africa: Implications for Direct Foreign Investment" (Brussels: European Commission).

Collier, P., 1997, "The Economic Consequences of Civil War," Discussion Paper 97–18 (Oxford: Centre for the Study of African Economies).

———, and J.W. Gunning, 1997, "Explaining African Economic Performance," Discussion Paper (Oxford: Centre for the Study of African Economies).

———, A. Hoeffler, and C. Pattillo, 1998, "Capital Flight as a Portfolio Choice" (unpublished; Washington: World Bank).

Cukierman A., S.B. Webb, and B. Negapti, 1992, "Measuring the Independence of Central Banks and Its Effects on Policy Outcomes," *World Bank Economic Review,* Vol. 6, pp. 353–98.

Devarajan, S., V. Swaroop, and H. Zon, 1996, "The Composition of Public Expenditure and Economic Growth," *Journal of Monetary Economics,* Vol. 37, pp. 313–44.

Dollar, D., 1992, "Outward-Oriented Developing Economies Really Do Grow More Rapidly; Evidence from 95 LDCs 1976–86," *Economic Development and Cultural Change,* Vol. 40, pp. 523–44.

Fafchamps, M., 1996, "The Enforcement of Commercial Contracts in Ghana," *World Development,* Vol. 24, pp. 427–48.

Findlay, R., 1996, "Modelling Global Interdependence: Centers, Peripheries and Frontiers," *American Economic Review, Papers and Proceedings,* Vol. 86, pp. 47–51.

Hay, D.A., 1997, "The Post–1990 Brazilian Trade Liberalisation and the Performance of Large Manufacturing Firms: Productivity, Market Share and Profits" (unpublished; Oxford: Institute of Economics and Statistics).

Jasperson, F.Z., A.H. Aylward, and A.D. Knox, 1998, "The Effects of Risk on Private Investment: Africa Compared with Other Developing Regions," in *Investment and Risk in Africa,* ed. by P. Collier and C. Pattillo (London: Macmillan).

Ncube, M., P. Collier, J.W. Gunning, and K. Mlambo, 1997, "Trade Liberalisation and Regional Integration in Zimbabwe," in *Regional Integration and Trade Liberalization in Sub-Saharan Africa, Volume 2: Country Case Studies,* ed. by A. Oyejide, B. Ndulu, and J.W. Gunning (London: Macmillan).

Okeahalam, C.C., 1996, "An Analysis of Costs and Pricing of Airline Services to Africa" (unpublished; Gaborone: University of Botswana).

Rodrik, D., 1997, "Trade Policy and Economic Performance in Sub-Saharan Africa" (unpublished; Cambridge, Massachusetts: John F. Kennedy School of Government, Harvard University).

Sachs, J.D., and A.M. Warner, 1995, "Natural Resources and Economic Growth," Development Discussion Paper No. 517a (Cambridge, Massachusetts: Harvard Institute for International Development).

———, 1997, "Sources of Slow Growth in African Economies," *Journal of African Economies,* Vol. 6, pp. 335–76.

Schleifer A., and R.W. Vishny, 1993, "Corruption," *Quarterly Journal of Economics,* Vol. 108, pp. 599–617.

Shafik N., 1998, "La Dolce Vita and the Open Door," *Trade Shocks in Developing Countries,* ed. by P. Collier and J.W. Gunning (Oxford: Clarendon Press).

Wang, Z.K., and L.A. Winters, 1997, "Africa's Role in Multilateral Trade Negotiations," Policy Research Working Paper No. 1846 (Washington: World Bank).

Warner, M.A.A., 1998, "A Charter for FDI?" in *Investment and Risk in Africa,* ed. by P. Collier and C. Pattillo (London: Macmillan).

Widner, J., 1997, "The Courts as Restraints," *Risk and Agencies of Restraint: Reducing the Risks of African Investment,* ed. by P. Collier and C. Pattillo (London: Macmillan).

Wood, A., and K. Berge, 1997, "Exporting Manufactures: Human Resources, Natural Resources and Trade Policy," *Journal of Development Studies*, Vol. 34, pp. 35–59.

———, and T. Owens, 1997, "Export-Oriented Industrialisation through Primary Processing?" *World Development*, Vol. 25, pp. 1453–70.

World Bank, 1994, "East Africa Survey of Foreign Investors" (unpublished; Washington: World Bank).

7 Why Is Trade Reform So Difficult in Africa?

Dani Rodrik

The year 1996 was a rare good one for Africa. The continent registered its highest rate of economic growth in two decades: 5.0 percent (IMF, 1997). Among the larger economies, the star performers were Uganda, Ghana, Cameroon, and Côte d'Ivoire, along with Morocco and Tunisia (see Table 1). While these are good signs, it will take many years of growth at such levels (or better) to undo the damage that more than two decades of stagnation and decline have inflicted on most countries of the region.

The turbulence experienced in world markets since the mid-1970s has had severe adverse effects on both Latin America and Africa. The upshot in Latin America has been the wholesale adoption by virtually all governments in the region of orthodox recipes—namely, fiscal retrenchment, deregulation, free trade, and privatization. In sub-Saharan Africa, free market religion has found far fewer converts. Despite tremendous pressure from donor governments and multilateral agencies, African policymakers have generally been more skeptical about the value of opening up their economies and reducing the role of government. Consequently, reforms have progressed rather gradually and have been full of interruptions and reversals. For example, a World Bank review of trade policy reforms in Africa concludes (Dean, Desai, and Riedel, 1994, p. 50):

> Reversal of reform has been frequent. In seven of the countries examined, either restrictions which were removed were reinstated, or some existing barriers were strengthened to offset reductions in others. Nigeria, though it eliminated most quantitative restrictions (quotas and licensing) increased dramatically the number of import bans. Ghana, which was the only country to make great strides in cutting formal tariffs, reversed this with the implementation of large special taxes on imports. Côte d'Ivoire raised tariffs significantly, after having reduced QRs. In some cases the motive for reversal appears to be pressure from import-competing industries as they begin to experience competition from abroad (e.g., Côte d'Ivoire, Ghana). In others, resurgence of foreign exchange shortages have slowed the liberalization of tariffs (Madagascar), or reversed the foreign exchange market reform itself (Kenya).

Inadequate implementation of reforms is one of the most common themes running through the literature on African economic policy (see also Metzel and Phillips, 1997, and Gulhati, 1990).

Table 1. Recent Economic Performance of African Countries, in Comparative Perspective
(Annual percent change)

	Real GDP			Consumer Prices		
Country	**1995**	**1996**	**1997[1]**	**1995**	**1996**	**1997[1]**
	2.9	5.0	4.7	32.1	24.8	12.0
Algeria	3.9	4.0	5.0	21.9	15.1	7.0
Cameroon	7.0	5.0	6.0	14.3	6.3	3.0
Côte d'Ivoire	7.0	6.5	6.0	14.3	6.6	3.0
Ghana	4.5	5.0	5.0	59.5	45.6	21.5
Kenya	4.9	4.2	3.8	1.7	9.0	8.0
Morocco	–7.6	10.3	3.0	6.1	3.0	3.5
Nigeria	2.5	2.1	4.7	70.0	29.3	14.1
South Africa	3.4	3.1	2.2	8.6	7.4	10.2
Sudan	4.5	4.0	4.0	57.0	85.0	55.0
Tanzania	3.8	4.5	5.0	34.0	25.7	15.0
Tunisia	2.5	7.5	7.0	6.3	5.0	4.5
Uganda	9.8	7.0	7.0	7.4	5.0	5.0
SAF/ESAF countries[2]	4.9	6.0	5.5	22.0	15.7	7.4
CFA countries	4.6	5.2	5.7	15.3	6.0	3.2
All developing countries (average)	6.0	6.5	6.6	21.3	13.1	9.7
All developing countries (median)	4.1	4.3	4.7	10.0	7.0	5.4

Source: IMF (1997), Table 6.
[1]Estimates.
[2]African countries that had arrangements, as of the end of 1996, under the IMF's SAF or ESAF.

But more than that, it is also the vacillating nature of policymaking that stands out. Collier cites the Nigerian example: "In the past decade, Nigerian trade policy has swung from intense foreign exchange rationing, indicated by a parallel market premium over 300 percent, to a completely free market, back to even more intense rationing and most recently back to a free market" (1995, p. 548). The contrast with Latin America, where governments have stuck with ambitious reforms even under severe macroeconomic difficulties—for example, during the Mexican peso crisis of 1995—is quite striking. As a result, the credibility of African reforms tends to be low, which itself creates a severe problem. The desired supply responses—in investment and exports—are unlikely to materialize when significant uncertainty is attached to the continuation of the reforms.

The very recent evidence notwithstanding, there remains considerable controversy over whether World Bank–IMF-type adjustment programs, of the sort adopted in Latin America, *do* work in Africa. Compare, for example, the World Bank's own positive evaluation (World Bank, 1994) with the critique by Lall and Stewart (1996).[1] Fortunately, for my purposes I do not need to get into the issues involved in this debate. Extremists aside, there is actually a fair bit of consensus on what constitutes a reasonable trade strategy for the countries of Africa. This consensus can be crudely expressed in terms of a number of do's and don't's: demonopolize trade; streamline the import regime, reduce red tape, and implement transparent customs procedures; replace QRs with tariffs; avoid extreme variation in tariff rates and excessively high rates of effective protection; allow exporters duty-free access to imported inputs; refrain from large doses of anti-export bias; do not tax export crops too highly. Not only is there wide agreement on these policies, there is also less dissent than might appear at first sight on what is to be considered "extreme" or "too high."[2] These desiderata still leave considerable room for policymakers to make their own choices over a wide range of trade and industrial-policy options.

Some aggressive reformers like Ghana and Uganda (and Mauritius before them) have implemented most, but not all, of the above agenda. But even in this group, reversals have not been uncommon. Ghana, as mentioned in the quote above, has implemented a special import tax of up to 40 percent on top of its import tariffs and retains a relatively large tax on cocoa exports (GATT, 1992). Other countries have done much less. Tariffs remain high, trade monopolies continue to exist in many sectors, export crops continue to be taxed, and trade procedures continue to be characterized by red tape and corruption (see the discussion in Metzel and Phillips, 1997). The main question, then, is why so little progress has been made with reforms that are endorsed by economists of diverse persuasions.

[1]There is a related debate about the sources of the relative economic decline of Africa during the past three decades, especially as regards its trade performance. Most Western analyses lay the blame on African countries' policies, rather than on the policies of Western nations or on underlying trends in world markets. See Yeats (1997) and Svedberg (1991).

[2]Consider, for example, the well-known paper by Sachs and Warner (1995). In this paper, the authors showed that countries classified as "open" grew at significantly higher rates than countries classified as "closed." Five indicators were used for purposes of classification (tariffs, NTBs, black market premiums, socialist regime, and export marketing boards), with failure to pass any of the thresholds associated with these five indicators resulting in classification as "closed." The threshold for tariffs was set at 40 percent, while the threshold for NTBs was set at 40 percent coverage. What is noteworthy is how permissive these levels are, even by African standards. In fact, only *five* sub-Saharan African countries fail to pass either one of these two tests (according to the Sachs-Warner data): Burkina Faso, Malawi, Nigeria, Rwanda, and Zimbabwe. (The bulk of African countries were classified as "closed" on the basis of the other three criteria.)

As usual, when economists' prescription meets reality, the answer is: politics. Political scientists who study Africa have long argued that it is distributional issues that prevent the adoption of economically sensible policies. Bates (1981), for example, has provided the classic argument for why African governments tax agricultural exporters so exorbitantly: the motive is to transfer wealth from politically unorganized rural groups to vocal urban groups. Bienen (1991) faults the policymakers more directly (1991, pp. 76–77):

> Trade liberalization policies are often extremely hard to formulate and implement in Africa precisely because it is powerful officials (civilian and military) who benefit from the controls that have been established over imports and exports. It is government officials who ration and distribute scarce imports, including foreign exchange. They realize the rents which accrue from the systems they construct and control. Of course, officials have allies—import-substituting manufacturers and urban workers employed by state enterprises who are interested in subsidized urban consumer goods.

Bienen argues that the main constraint is not import-substituting urban producers themselves but self-interested government officials: "A policy that moves away from tariff protection of domestic industries will not face strong *private* sector capitalists or workers in Africa. Such policy shifts face strong *public* opposition in Africa . . ." (1991, p. 82).

To a first degree of approximation, such distributional arguments are indeed powerful, and I will elaborate on them below. But they need to be complemented with other stories. Consider some of the problems.

First, the distributional or interest group perspective is too static and deterministic. The more complete is an explanation of why the prevailing, economically dysfunctional policies are the endogenous outcome of interest group pressures, the harder we make it to understand why governments sometimes *do* reform (or, for that matter, how they *can* reform). After all, the relative powers of interest groups rarely change very quickly. Governments, conversely, sometimes do reform, and occasionally do so quite rapidly. In Latin America, where many of the same distributional arguments were made to explain the prevalence of import-substitution policies, we have observed governments undertaking wholesale reforms in a relatively short period of time. Moreover, some of the leading reformers were drawn from the constituencies most associated with the previous set of policies—for example, the Peronist Menem in Argentina.

Second, distributional arguments often have an element of circularity. Every policy configuration generates winners, and it is all too easy to associate the raison d'être of some particular configuration with the political salience of a set of winners. Often unasked is the question:

couldn't an alternative set of policies benefit these winners even more? This is not a hypothetical question. It is a good bet, for example, that the primary beneficiaries of the reforms in the Republic of Korea and Taiwan Province of China around 1960 were the import-substituting industrialists who were resisting these reforms. A corollary is that interest groups can apparently change their minds, as certainly happened in East Asia once exports took off. In Africa, the great majority of civil servants whose salaries greatly eroded during the 1980s as a consequence of fiscal cutbacks would almost certainly have been better off had they followed fiscally more conservative policies and safeguarded the tax base. More broadly, since reforms are expected to enlarge the economic pie, why can't the losers be compensated through transfers or other policies?

Third, distributional arguments often fall far short of explaining certain typical outcomes. The extreme fiscal distress to which many African countries have succumbed, and the associated macroeconomic instability—inflation, widespread shortages, reduced incomes—do not create any obvious winners. It is hard to identify significant interest groups that benefit from such difficulties. Another manifestation of this same issue is that the extremes of taxation that have often been observed in Africa are actually inconsistent with maximizing the well-being of even the recipients of the revenues thereby generated. For example, export crops have frequently been taxed at rates surpassing the revenue-maximizing level. As McMillan (1997) has recently argued, the conventional story of urban bias (for example, Bates 1981) cannot account for this feature of policy. After all, why would governments, and the urban groups they represent, want to kill the goose that lays the golden eggs? Once again, we need to complement the conventional distributional story with other elements (as McMillan does; see below).

I will focus in this chapter on a succession of models that yield partial insights on each of these puzzles. I will start with the standard distributional story, cast in an appropriately general equilibrium framework. Going beyond the identification of losers and gainers, the discussion here will emphasize the likely *magnitude* of distributional consequences. In particular, I will argue that, in a typical African country, compensating the losers from trade liberalization is impossible for all practical purposes; the amount of redistribution required will more than eat up the efficiency gains generated by the reform. Next, I will turn to a setup where it is the government's inability to discipline itself—rather than distributional imperatives per se—that lies at the root of the problem. I will illustrate the issues using McMillan's (1997) argument about the dynamic inconsistency of export taxation. These ideas turn out to be relevant and powerful in the African context, and they also have important institutional implications. Finally, I will turn to incompleteness of information as a source of resistance to reform. Relying on the argument of Fernandez and Rodrik (1991), I will suggest that uncertainty surrounding the identity of likely gainers is a severe obstacle to garnering political support for reform. Paradoxically, however, it can also be a source of unraveling of support over time. This set of ideas puts a heavy burden on the need to identify gainers from reforms early on.

My objective is to show how such models can help us develop a more sophisticated understanding of the political economy of policy choice. In addition, I hope to demonstrate that they can be used to inform policymaking as well.

Distributional Consequences of Trade Reform

It is well understood that trade reform typically entails a redistribution of income among various sectors of the economy. Less well understood is how large the redistributions are relative to the efficiency benefits of the reform. This creates a political problem of major proportions.

To appreciate the issues, it is helpful to lay out a simple model of an archetype African economy. Consider an economy divided into a rural sector and an urban sector. Assume that exports originate from the rural sector, while the urban sector produces import-competing goods. Each sector has one factor of production specific to it: land in the rural sector and capital in the urban sector. In addition, the two sectors employ labor, which is freely mobile between the two. So far, the model is a standard specific-factors (Ricardo-Viner) model. To make it slightly more realistic, I assume that urban capitalists' profits (rents) are shared with urban workers, so that wages in urban areas exceed rural wages, even though labor is intersectorally mobile. We are interested in the qualitative and quantitative implications of trade liberalization in an economy of this sort.

Formally, let Y and X represent the outputs of the urban and rural sectors, respectively. We assume the two goods are produced by neoclassical production functions of the form:

$$Y = F(L_y, K) \qquad (1)$$

$$X = G(L_x, T) \qquad (2)$$

where K and T stand for the economy's (fixed) endowments of capital and land, respectively, and the economy's labor endowment L is divided between the two sectors:

$$L_x + L_y = L \tag{3}$$

Let the ad valorem equivalent of import restrictions be given by t. The rural or informal sector wage is given by the value marginal product of labor in the two sectors:

$$w_r = (1 + t)F_L(L_y, K) \tag{4}$$
$$w_r = G_L(L_x, T) \tag{5}$$

Note that I have normalized the relative border price of the importable at unity. The domestic relative price of the importable is consequently $1+t$. The urban wage equals this base wage plus a share of urban profits, and is expressed as:

$$w_u = w_r + \gamma \frac{\pi K}{L_y} \tag{6}$$

where π is the return to capital and γ is the rent-sharing coefficient. The way we model the urban wage implies that sharing rents (or profits) is efficient; urban employers equate the value marginal product of labor to its opportunity cost, which is the rural wage. The return to capital is given in turn by the residual income in the urban sector (per unit of capital) after labor is paid its marginal product:

$$\pi = \frac{(1 + t)Y - w_r L_y}{K} \tag{7}$$

On the demand side, we assume preferences are identical and homothetic, so that they can be aggregated. The economywide demand for the importable can be expressed using the Marshallian demand function $D((1+t), I)$, where I is national income at domestic prices:

$$I = (1 + t)Y + X + tm \tag{8}$$

The quantity of imports, m, is given by the difference between demand and supply of the importable:

$$m = D((1 + t), I) - Y \tag{9}$$

The nine equations above determine the nine endogenous variables in this model (X, Y, L_x, L_y, w_r, w_u, π, I, and m) as functions of factor endowments and of trade policy, t.

A social planner who does not care about income distribution would maximize the value of national output at world prices, $X + Y$. This yields the familiar prescription $t = 0$, as trade restrictions are, by assumption, the only market imperfection in this framework.

Consider now the more realistic setting where distributional issue do carry weight. There are five distinct groups in this model whose interests are at stake: (1) farmers (that is, owners of T), (2) informal-sector workers, (3) urban workers, (4) urban employers, and (5) recipients of revenues that derive from trade restrictions. The last group is likely to be a mixture of rentseekers, government officials, and the national treasury. The incomes of each of these groups (in terms of the exportable) are expressed as follows:

Farmers	$X - w_r L_x$
Informal workers	$w_r L_x$
Urban workers	$w_u L_y$
Urban employers	$(1 + t)\, Y - w_u L_y$
Trade rents or government revenues	tm

It is straightforward to lay out the distributional impact of trade liberalization on each of these groups. Farmers are clear winners, as the domestic relative price of their output is inversely proportional to t. Informal, or nonurban, workers are also winners, provided not too much of their budget is spent on the exportable. Urban employers and workers are clear losers. What happens to trade rents and/or government revenue depends on which side of the Laffer curve we initially were on. When reform is large scale (that is, t is brought close to zero), or when QRs are converted into tariffs, recipients of trade rents are necessarily affected adversely.

Hence, trade reform pits rural groups against urban groups, and ultimately against recipients of trade rents as well. Since urban groups tend to be much better organized, and their ability to bring governments down is considerably greater, reformist politicians face a serious dilemma. This is the conventional account of the political economy of trade reform in the African context, as discussed, for example, in the works cited in the previous section.

To quantify these distributional consequences, I have run some numerical simulations using the model above. For these calculations, I take production functions in both sectors to be Cobb-Douglas, with a labor share of 0.40 in each. Preferences are similarly Cobb-Douglas, with the budget share of the importable set at 0.40. The urban profit-sharing parameter γ is fixed at 0.25. Other parameters (that is, endowments and technical coefficients) are selected so as to produce a baseline solution with a trade and production structure bearing some resemblance to a "typical" African country. The first column of Table 2 shows this baseline equilibrium, with t set to 40 percent initially. In the baseline equilibrium, 27 percent of national income accrues to farmers (owners of land), 61 percent to workers (both rural and urban), 8 percent to urban capitalists, and 3 percent to recipients of trade rents and/or tariff revenue. Urban workers earn a premium of about 17 per-

Table 2. Distributional Implications of Trade Reform in an Archetypal African Economy

Measure	Baseline Solution, $t = 40$ percent	Percentage of Income	Percentage Change from Baseline Solution			
			$t = 30$ percent	$t = 20$ percent	$t = 10$ percent	$t = 0$
Real national income	1.574	100	1.08	1.97	2.54	2.80
Real income by group:						
Farmers	0.431	27	6.26	12.76	19.95	27.61
Urban employers	0.133	8	–12.03	–23.31	–34.59	–45.11
Informal-sector workers	0.647	41	6.18	12.67	19.78	27.51
Urban workers	0.309	20	–11.65	–23.30	–34.30	–44.98
Quota rents/ government revenue	0.054	3	5.56	–5.56	–40.74	–100.00
Informal wages	1.043		–1.92	–3.84	–5.47	–6.90
Urban wages	1.217		–1.97	–3.78	–5.51	–6.98
Output of rural sector	1.233		3.08	6.08	8.84	11.52
Output of urban sector	0.361		–7.76	–15.79	–24.10	–32.69
Employment in rural sector	0.709		5.22	10.30	15.23	19.89
Employment in urban sector	0.291		–12.71	–25.09	–37.11	–48.45
Consumption of urban goods	0.514		5.84	12.06	18.68	25.88
Volume of imports	0.153		37.91	77.78	119.61	164.05

cent over other workers. Imports are somewhat less than 10 percent of national income (0.153 ÷ 1.574), and 71 percent of the labor force is employed in the rural sector.

The other columns display the consequences of progressively reducing trade restrictions, expressed as percentage changes from the baseline situation. As tariffs are reduced from 40 percent to 30, 20, 10, and 0 percent, aggregate real income increases by 1.1, 2.0, 2.5, and 2.8 percent, respectively. These magnitudes are in line with findings of most computable general equilibrium models, at least those that do not allow scale economies. If anything, they are perhaps a bit on the high side. Note also that most of the gains are concentrated in the initial reductions of restrictions: going from $t = 0.40$ to $t = 0.20$ yields a real income gain of 2 percent, while going the full way to complete free trade ($t = 0$) yields an additional gain of only 0.8 percent (2.80 – 1.97). This is not an artifact of the specific assumptions made here. It follows from economic theory, which suggests that the welfare cost of distortions rises with the square of the distortion.

From our standpoint, the results on the distribution front are more interesting. As discussed above, there are clear losers and winners from trade reform; urban groups lose and rural groups gain. Even more to the point, the *magnitudes* of the distributional impacts are very large. Consider for example the scenario where trade restrictions are reduced from a tariff equivalent of 40 percent ($t = 0.4$) to a tariff equivalent of 10 percent ($t = 0.1$). In this scenario, urban employers incur a real income loss of 35 percent, while recipients of quota rents suffer a loss of 41 percent! The gain to farmers is 20 percent. The net gain to the economy of 2.5 percent is an order of magnitude smaller than these distributional impacts. Put differently, the efficiency consequences of trade reform pale in comparison to its redistributive effects. (Once again, this conclusion is a general feature of models of this sort, and does not depend on any particular parameterization.)

This is the sense in which price reforms, and trade reforms in particular, tend to have high *political* cost-benefit ratios (Rodrik, 1994). It is not only that such reforms entail redistribution, which is well recognized. More significant is that they entail *so much* redistribution *relative* to their efficiency benefits—a point that is surely not lost on those groups whose incomes are at stake. This makes it easier to understand why trade reforms are so vigorously resisted, and why it has generally proved difficult to convince African policymakers to embark on ambitious reform efforts.

These numbers also make clear why the economist's standard trick of assuming (or advocating) compensation is quite unhelpful to the policymaker. Of course, since there are aggregate gains to the economy—the size of the pie is larger—it is in principle possible to compensate all losers and still leave some groups better off. But what is implicit in this recommendation is the idea that the requisite transfers can be accomplished in a relatively efficient manner—in the limit by employing lumpsum transfers. This is counterfactual, especially in sub-Saharan African countries where tax instruments and administrative capacity are extremely weak.

Suppose, for example, that policymakers wished to neutralize the negative impact on urban employers arising from the above trade liberalization scenario. Since this group constitutes 8 percent of national income and its losses are 35 percent, its loss amounts to roughly 2.8 percent of GNP (0.35x0.08). Hence, the government now needs to raise 2.8 percent of GNP in taxes to finance transfers to this set of urban interests. These taxes will naturally engender their own set of distortions. The magnitude of these distortions can be gauged by considering that in the United States most studies estimate the marginal excess burden (MEB) of taxation to be in the range of 0.30–0.40 (see Hall and Rabushka, 1995). This means that raising $1 of revenue in the United States (so as to transfer it to some other group) costs the rest of the economy $1.30–$1.40. In the African context, the MEB of taxation is unlikely to be anything less than twice this figure, that is, 0.60–0.80. Consequently, the proposed compensatory transfer will entail an efficiency loss of at least 1.7–2.2 percent of GNP (0.028 multiplied by either 0.60 or 0.80). Therefore, compensation in this manner would eat up the bulk of the efficiency benefits that arise from the trade reform in the first place (which stood at 2.5 percent). And this before other losers (urban workers, recipients of trade rents) get their turn at compensation, and without taking into account the distortions that are likely to arise in *subsidizing* the losers.

In practice, there are two ways of getting out of this conundrum. One is to package the trade reform with other reforms that promise to provide substantial all-around gains to significant interest groups in urban and rural groups alike, and thereby dilute the redistributive effects of the former. Such opportunities rarely present themselves, because most reforms do have sharp distributional consequences. An exception is the situation that prevails following a prolonged period of economic decline and macroeconomic instability. There are few identifiable winners in an economy in near-hyperinflation, or where economic institutions and output have completely collapsed. The prospect of stabilization and recovery under such conditions, which would benefit most everyone, can allow trade reforms to be packaged along with the broader macroeconomic reforms. Consider, for example, the situation prevailing in Ghana during the early 1980s (Herbst, 1991):

> Rent seekers who can control import licenses are usually a potent source of opposition to devaluation, but the crisis had become so bad in Ghana that the group benefiting from administrative allocation of foreign exchange was extremely limited. Indeed, by the early 1980s, the economy had deteriorated to such an extent that even senior government officials, who normally benefit from access to imported goods even in times of shortage, reported that they were going hungry and were concerned that they could not find food for their families.

From this perspective, it is no surprise that the most ambitious trade reforms in sub-Saharan Africa have been undertaken in countries like Ghana and Uganda where the previous economic decline was sharpest. Extraordinary times provide a window of opportunity for policymakers to undertake reforms that would be politically explosive in normal times.

The second strategy for dealing with redistributive conflict is to undertake partial, or two-track, reforms that preserve the privileges of the existing beneficiaries. This type of reform has been raised to an art form in China, where it has been systematically used to neutralize opposition from groups whose privileges would otherwise be threatened by market-oriented reforms. Hence, two-track pricing and incentive systems have operated in rural and urban areas of China, and in trade and investment regulations, apparently with considerable success.

In Africa, Mauritius provides a nice illustration of this strategy. This country is an African success story, despite its inauspicious beginnings. During the 1960s, Mauritius was a monocrop economy facing a population explosion. A report prepared by James Meade in 1961 was quite pessimistic about the island's future: "unless resolute measures are taken to solve [the population problem]," the report stated, "Mauritius will be faced with a catastrophic situation" (Meade 1961, 37). To an important extent, the economy's success was based on the creation of an export processing zone (EPZ) operating under free-trade principles, which allowed an export boom in garments to European markets.[3] Yet the island's economy has combined this EPZ with a domestic sector that was highly protected until the mid-1980s. Gulhati (1990,

[3]The full story is of course more complicated than that. There were highly profitable sugar exports, thanks to a generous quota in the European market. The EPZ appears to have been spurred, in its initial stages at least, by local capital and domestic investments. Profits from the sugar trade appear to have been the source of the savings that financed early growth in the EPZ.

Table 2.10) reports an average effective rate of protection in 1982 for manufacturing in Mauritius of 89 percent, with a range of –24 to 824 percent (see also Milner and McKay, 1996, pp. 72–73). Hence, Mauritius is an example of an economy that has followed a two-track strategy.

The circumstances under which the Mauritian EPZ was set up (in 1970) are instructive. Here is how one account describes it (Alter, 1990, p. 4):

> Given the small size of the domestic market and the negative experience elsewhere, import substitution was not regarded as a viable long-term strategy; therefore, as soon as import-substitution opportunities were exhausted, Mauritius switched to an export-oriented development policy, with the EPZ as the main element of its new industrial policy.

Were things so easy! As in other countries, policymakers in Mauritius had to contend with the import-substituting industrialists who had been propped up by the restrictive commercial policies of the 1960s. Under the development certificates (DC) scheme, local industrialists were provided with tax holidays and protection from imports via tariffs and QRs. A range of industries were set up using these incentives. These industrialists were naturally opposed to relaxing the trade regime.

The EPZ scheme provided a neat way around this difficulty. The point is made nicely in this account by Wellisz and Saw (1993, p. 242):

> A completely outward reorientation was politically unfeasible in the 1970s—since protection was the key to the prosperity of the import-substituting industry and DC certificate holders constituted a powerful lobby. But the DC certificate holders were not disturbed by the formation of an export-oriented enclave: on the contrary, they welcomed it as another potential source of profits. Mauritian labor also favored economic segmentation: the high-wage sector—sugar and import-substituting industries—constituted a male enclave. The EPZ industries employed women, whose earnings supplemented family incomes and who did not compete with the men. For the export-oriented industries, too, the enclave solution had obvious advantages in that the quasi-extraterritorial status provided a degree of protection against the government's dirigiste tendencies.

This passage illustrates the political advantages of the two-track strategy. The creation of the EPZ generated new opportunities of trade and of employment (for women), without taking protection away from the import-substituting groups and from privileged male workers. The segmentation of labor markets was particularly crucial, as it prevented the expansion of the EPZ from driving wages up in the rest of the economy, and thereby disadvantaging import-substituting industries.[4] New profit opportunities were created at the margin, while leaving old opportunities undisturbed. There were no identifiable losers.

Time Inconsistency: Government Against Itself

Distributional considerations of the type discussed above explain a lot about the pattern of policymaking in Africa. But there are other pervasive features of African policy that cannot be explained without adding an additional layer of complexity on these distributional issues: Many policy distortions are excessive even from the standpoint of the purported beneficiaries of the distortions.

Trade policies, for example, are often too restrictive in that the rents they generate could be increased by relaxing them somewhat. This possibility is illustrated in one of the scenarios presented above in Table 2. We see that trade rents actually increase as t is reduced from 0.40 to 0.30. In other words, when t is set at 0.40, we are on the wrong side of the Laffer curve for trade revenues. This is not an outlandish possibility. With realistic import demand elasticities, and especially with the ever-present reality of smuggling factored in, the revenue-maximizing level of trade restrictions in much of Africa are unlikely to be above 40–50 percent. When we observe restrictions beyond that level, we must question the argument that these restrictions are in place simply because they enrich the government officials who administer them.[5]

This issue is particularly relevant to the taxation of export crops in many African countries. It is well recognized that export crops have been taxed at extremely high levels in Africa, with the result that export agriculture has often been decimated. According to estimates by Krueger, Schiff, and Valdés (1987), the direct taxation of agriculture—through marketing boards and low producer prices—has averaged 23 percent in Africa, compared with 2.5 percent in Asia and 6.4 percent in Latin America. When the effects of exchange rate overvaluation and import restrictions are added in, total taxation of agriculture more than

[4]This segmentation lasted until the mid-1980s. According to Wellisz and Saw, "As of 1985, the minimum wage for male workers ceased to apply to EPZ enterprises" (1993, p. 248), after which the EPZ began to compete for male workers with the sheltered parts of the economy, and the share of male workers in the EPZ rose rapidly.

[5]One caveat is that such "inefficient" outcomes can arise when policymakers do not coordinate in setting the level of trade restrictions. With each official having decisionmaking authority over part of the trade apparatus, the Nash equilibrium of the game will typically entail too restrictive a trade regime overall and too little revenues for the officialdom in the aggregate.

doubles to 51.6 percent (Krueger, Schiff, and Valdés, 1987). These tax rates are a large part of the explanation for why Africa has consistently lost market share in world trade.

At least since Bates's (1981) seminal work, the conventional explanation for these pricing policies has been the argument that African governments have used such policies to transfer income to politically powerful urban groups. Since import restrictions are functionally equivalent to export taxes, the logic is similar to that coming out of the model laid out in the previous section.

If this were the whole story, rates of direct taxation of agriculture would never exceed their revenue-maximizing levels. Yet the reality is different. According to calculations by McMillan (1997, pp. 2–3):

> Even using the most conservative supply elasticity estimates . . . governments have taxed cocoa at a rate greater than the revenue maximizing tax rate 63% of the time in the 1970s and 25% of the time in the 1980s. Coffee has been overtaxed 35% of the time in the 1970s and 23% of the time in the 1980s and vanilla [has been] always overtaxed in both periods.

If the principal reason for taxing export agriculture is to raise revenues to be used on behalf of urban groups, why would governments impose taxes that exceed what is required to maximize revenue? More broadly, why would governments discriminate against their cash crops so badly that this sector would be devastated over time, depriving the government of revenues in the longer run? In other words, why would anyone want to kill the goose that lays the golden eggs?

McMillan (1997) provides a convincing explanation, which also provides a neat way of conceptualizing the institutional weakness of African states. She starts by distinguishing between planting and harvesting costs. The former are sunk costs. Therefore opportunistic governments have an incentive to cheat farmers out of these sunk costs by paying them the minimum required for them to bring their crops to market; that is, to pay them only their harvesting costs. Anticipating this eventuality, farmers of course will have no incentive to plant in the first place. Therefore, if the government is unable to precommit to an adequate price, the static, one-shot equilibrium in this game is one in which farmers withdraw from production and the government gets no revenue.

Now consider the more realistic case where the government and the farmers interact repeatedly. As McMillan notes, many more outcomes then become possible. She focusses on trigger-strategy equilibriums, under which farmers "punish" the government by not planting for k periods whenever the government deviates from the "first-best" pricing policy by offering a price below the full (planting plus harvesting) costs. McMillan shows that the condition under which the first-best strategy—government's price covers the full cost, and farmers' plant—can be sustained is given by the following expression:

$$\frac{\textit{sunk costs}}{\textit{total costs}} < \textit{discounting term} \times \left(\frac{\textit{future world price}}{\textit{total costs}} - 1\right)$$

The term on the left-hand side of the inequality represents the one-period gain to the government from deviating from the first-best strategy: the higher is the share of sunk costs in total costs, the lower is the price that the government can offer to the farmers and still get the crop to market, *once farmers have already planted*. The right-hand side represents the cost that the government bears when it deviates in this fashion. These costs are increasing in the future profit margin that the government will have to forsake when farmers stop planting for k periods. They also decrease with the government's impatience. Hence, for the first-best strategy to be viable, the ratio of sunk to total costs must not be too high, future world prices must be anticipated to be favorable enough, and the government must not be too impatient.

McMillan confronts these implications with the evidence, using data on costs, prices, and taxes for six crops (cocoa, coffee, cotton, groundnuts, tobacco, and vanilla) drawn from more than 30 sub-Saharan African countries. She classifies her sample of crop-country pairs into subperiods of "high" and "low" taxation, on the basis of whether average (direct) tax rates in each subperiod fall below or above the estimated revenue-maximizing rates. Her results are striking (McMillan, 1997, p. 6):

> Crops for which the ratio of sunk costs to total costs is relatively high, e.g. cocoa, coffee, and vanilla, have been taxed more heavily than crops with relatively lower ratios of sunk costs to total costs, e.g. cotton, groundnuts and tobacco. Using the probability of remaining in power as a proxy for the [political leader's] discount factor . . . leaders with a relatively high probability of remaining in power tend to tax less heavily. And finally, using a twenty-year average of profits as a proxy for expected profitability of a crop . . . crops with [high] expected future profitability tend to be less heavily taxed.

These findings confirm the power of the underlying model of dynamic inconsistency in explaining patterns of policymaking across Africa.

This perspective adds a new dimension to the discussion of the politics of reform. It highlights the significance of credible commitments to policies, and the value of creating institutional settings that provide safeguards against opportunistic behavior on the part of state officials. This point is related to Collier's (1995) discussion of the weakness of the "agencies of restraint" in Africa. As Collier explains, this weakness exhibits itself in all spheres of economic life in Africa: in intra-private transactions, where it shows up as weak contract enforcement and high transactions costs; in intra-public transactions, where it shows up as weakness of central banks and finance ministries relative to spending ministries; and in public-private transactions, as in the export taxation case discussed above.

It is instructive to examine the experience of one country where such problems have apparently not been as severe a problem as in most of Africa. The country in question is Botswana, one of the world's fastest-growing countries. While Botswana has been blessed with diamonds, the presence of a rich natural-resource base must be seen at best as a permissive condition for its superlative economic performance. Too many countries in Africa with rich natural resources have been economic failures to attach much significance to diamonds per se. A lot of Botswana's success has to do with its superior governance. The bureaucracy in Botswana is honest and competent, attaches great value to economic expertise, and has consistently produced sensible macroeconomic policies. There has been no large-scale urban bias and no white elephants (Harvey, 1992, p. 348). The government's philosophy, however, has been far from laissez faire. One indication of this is that government expenditures stood above 50 percent of GDP by the early 1990s, one of the highest levels anywhere in the world. What has distinguished economic interventions in Botswana is its quality, not quantity.

Why this has been so is not altogether clear. The initial conditions, just as in Mauritius's case, were not favorable. When it became independent in 1966, Botswana was one of the poorest countries in the world (Harvey, 1992, p. 338):

> There was not even a capital city before independence; the country was administered from an enclave in Mafeking (now Mafikeng), in the Cape Town Province of South Africa. The education base was negligible. The only tarred roads consisted of a few miles in the towns. There was a railway, built for transit between South Africa and more prosperous colonies to the North, but nevertheless useful to Botswana, an abattoir for the export of beef, and not much else.

Furthermore, Botswana has been virtually surrounded with warfare and violence, as a consequence of wars of independence in Angola, Namibia, and Zimbabwe, and the struggle in South Africa.

One explanation that is often advanced is the rural origin of the political leadership. Harvey (1992, pp. 360–61), for example, emphasizes the

> strong influence of rural exporters on economic policy. A large majority of politicians and senior government officials in Botswana own cattle, and an even higher proportion are related to people who own cattle. The income from cattle comes mostly from exporting.

This, it is argued, explains why policies in Botswana have not been anti-export, and why the economy has never been allowed to succumb to the Dutch disease. On closer look, this explanation is somewhat suspect. The urban origin of political leadership in other African countries can perhaps explain why agriculture was taxed; it cannot explain why it was typically taxed excessively, as discussed above. As McMillan puts it, in dismissing a similar explanation for Côte d'Ivoire's relatively moderate taxation of agriculture (1997, p. 11):

> This explanation is unsatisfactory because even elites who do not own farms may derive a large proportion of their income from the production of export crops in the forms of rent and taxation. Moreover, there are few African elites who do not own land or who could not own land if they wanted to.

The situation is analogous to Mancur Olson's description of the stationary bandit: unlike the roving bandit, the stationary bandit has a stake in maintaining the long-run economic health of his tax base, even if he has no other ties to the society he rules. The social origin of the political elites cannot, in itself, explain why some governments have killed their cash cow while others have nurtured it.

I find an alternative hypothesis more appealing. Along with Lesotho, South Africa, and Swaziland, Botswana has long been a member of the Southern Africa Customs Union (SACU). This means that Botswana has no independent trade policy; goods circulate freely between it and South Africa. In addition, Botswana did not have a national currency and central bank until 1976 (Lewis, 1993, p. 19). The government gets a share of customs revenue collected by South Africa. These customs revenues amount to around 20 percent of the value of Botswana's imports, which is high. What matters, from our perspective, however, is that government officials have no control over this revenue on a day-to-day basis; nor do they have an ability to interfere with the flow of goods from South Africa. Perhaps more to the point, domestic producers in the urban areas *know* that this is so, and therefore realize that lobbying policy makers for favors in the trade arena is a futile exercise. To someone used to reading horror stories arising from tariffs and NTBs in any developing country, opening a lengthy volume on Botswana (such as Harvey and Lewis, 1990) and not finding a long chapter on trade policy is an eye-opening experience. Absence of an independent trade policy is an extreme form of an "agency of restraint" (in Collier's sense of the term).[6]

Could this externally imposed free trade regime be a key reason for Botswana's success on the economic front? Obviously, the government's ability to tax exports, either directly or indirectly, was sharply restricted. But beyond that, the absence of an import-substituting urban lobby—which the free trade regime ensured—could have led to improved governance on other fronts as well. For example, the admirable manner in which the government responded to a large drop in diamond earnings in 1981, by swiftly devaluing the currency and avoiding exchange controls (see Lewis, 1993, p. 19ff), may have been enabled by the absence of entrenched urban interests. Protected behind NTBs, these urban groups would have welcomed such controls and other trade restrictions, and would have made it more difficult for the government to undertake the requisite policy adjustments. That, in any case, was the fate of most countries in Africa (as well as in Latin America), which responded to external shocks by tightening trade restrictions. This is a hypothesis worth examining more closely.

Incomplete Information: The Private Sector against Itself

The frameworks considered up to this point are based on full and complete information. In particular, interest groups are well informed about the precise incidence of gains and losses that would follow from reform. This is a simplification, of course. Relaxing it provides additional insights on the political economy of reform.

The motivation for considering situations of incomplete information is that in reality it is difficult to predict with some certainty who the eventual beneficiaries of reform are going to be. In particular, it is reasonable to expect that while many import-substituting urban groups will be adversely affected, some among them may end up taking advantage of the new opportunities created by the reform. I cited above the examples of Korea and Taiwan Province of China. In both coun-

[6]As a small country in SACU, Botswana was essentially forced to inherit South Africa's relative price structure. Its gains from trade derived from the difference between this relative-price structure and that which would have obtained under autarky in Botswana. The fact that the external tariffs in SACU were fairly high—and that South Africa's relative structure was distorted relative to the rest of the world—is largely irrelevant to the existence of gains from trade for Botswana. To the extent, however, that the external tariffs in SACU pushed South Africa's relative prices in the direction of Botswana's autarky price ratio, these external tariffs reduced Botswana's gains from trade (relative to free trade outside the SACU structure).

Figure 1. Reform and Uncertain Benefits

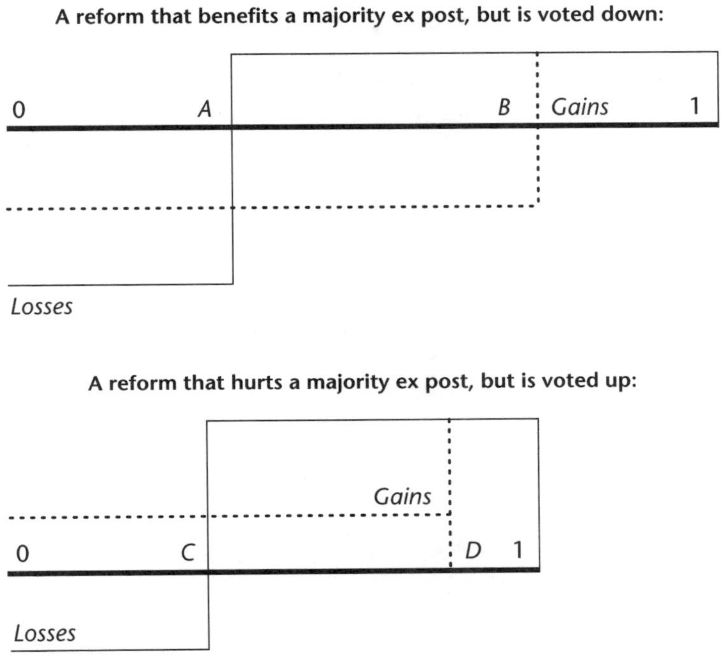

tries, exports were dominated by natural resources before the reforms of the early 1960s. Manufacturers were almost exclusively inward oriented. Yet, many of them discovered during the 1960s and 1970s that they could be successful exporters. Industry as a whole certainly did better under the outward-oriented set of policies than it had under the import-substituting policies of the 1950s. We can expect a similar set of outcomes in many African countries as well. Successful trade reform will spur nontraditional exports. But it is difficult to say ex ante what these exports might be, or who will actually produce them. This unpredictability generates a serious political problem: the politician needs the support of *real* individuals and groups, people one can actually name and collect money from. When beneficiaries exist only in an abstract, statistical sense, the reformer's job is made much harder.

Consider the framework laid out in the paper by Fernandez and Rodrik (1991), and schematically shown in Figure 1. All individuals in the economy are aligned on the horizontal axis between 0 and 1. Look first at the top panel. Before reform, individuals in the interval (0, *B*) are assumed to be in the import-substituting sector, while individuals in the interval (B, 1) are in the exportable sector. After reform, some of the individuals who are in the import-substituting sector—those in the interval (A, B)—will move to exportables; they will be winners as well. Note that subsequent to reform, there will be a majority of gainers: those in the interval (A, 1). Therefore, if the precise distributional incidence of the reform was known in advance, a majority of the individuals would support it.[7]

But consider now the outcome if the aggregate consequences of reform are known, but the individual-specific outcomes are not. More precisely, suppose that individuals in the import-competing sector—those in the interval (0, B)—are ex ante all alike, and they do not know who among them will be able to move to exportables. Suppose further that the prospective gains or losses per individual are represented by the height of the boxes in the figure, and that individuals are risk neutral. The way the figure is drawn, *all* individuals in the import-competing sector are *losers* in expected-value terms. And since a majority of the population is in the import-competing sector initially, there will be only minority support for the reform. Hence the reform is rejected by a majority, even though a majority would benefit from the reform *and* it is common knowledge that it would do so. This is a case where incomplete information blocks a reform from being adopted even though the reform would be politically popular if imposed dictatorially.

This is not the only perverse possibility. The other case is illustrated in the bottom panel of Figure 1. Here, a majority—individuals in the interval (0, C)—would end up losing from reform. But in expected-value terms, the reform is a winner for all individuals in the import-competing sector initially—those in the interval (0, D). Consequently, there is unanimous support for reform ex ante, but there will be a significant backlash against reform once the distributional effects become clear for specific individuals.

One general implication of this line of reasoning is the following: over time, there will be a bias toward the status quo and against reforms that would prove ex post popular. This is illustrated in Figure 2. Consider two stages of voting. In the first, a reform is either adopted (Yes) or not adopted (No). Subsequently, there is a second vote that decides whether to continue with reform, to abort it, or, if the reform had

[7]Although I will use the language of majority voting for the purposes of this discussion, the ideas are more general. One could think of decisions being made by leading interest groups instead, with the support of a plurality or majority of groups needed for the reform to be undertaken.

Figure 2. Status-Quo Bias: Voting on Reforms Over Time

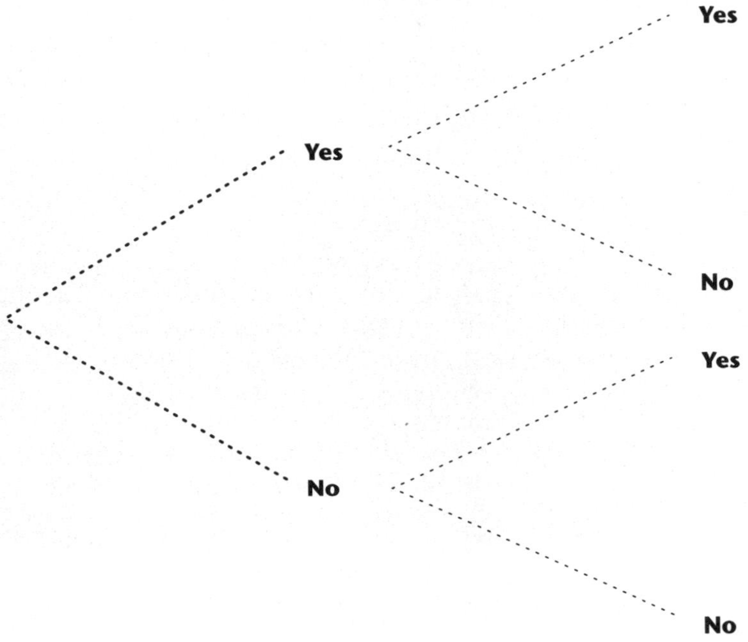

not been adopted in the first vote, to do so now. There are four possible sequences of votes: Yes-Yes, Yes-No, No-Yes, and No-No. Of these, No-Yes is not an equilibrium outcome, since no new information is revealed when reform is not undertaken. If reform is rejected once, it will continue to be rejected in the future. Hence, reforms that are "mistakenly" adopted—mistakenly from a political perspective—will soon be reversed, while reforms that are "mistakenly" rejected will not get a second chance. There will be a systematic bias against reforms.

A second implication is that there are circumstances when the promise of compensating the losers, even when economically feasible, will not be sufficient to eliminate resistance to reform. To see this, return to the case illustrated in the top panel of Figure 1. Remember that in this case, there will be majority support for reform if the reform is ever adapted, even absent compensation. What this implies is that a strategy of compensating losers is not time consistent for the reformers; why compensate the losers if the reform will stick even without their support? Of course, the losers can anticipate this result ex ante, and they will therefore not buy the promise in the first place.

This framework shows the importance of incomplete information and the dynamics of information revelation in shaping the configuration of interests for and against reform. It highlights the importance of identifying winners and reaching out to them. The task is especially difficult in sub-Saharan Africa, where informational incompleteness of the type discussed here is likely to be particularly severe. It is all the more urgent, for the same reason.

Concluding Remarks

The value of thinking analytically and coherently about the political economy of trade reform is not only that this helps us understand the sources of resistance to reform, but that it also helps us think creatively about ways of circumventing the resistance. Hence the difficulties identified in this chapter—the strength of the redistributive effects, the low credibility and commitment inherent in government policies, the uncertainty surrounding the identity of the gainers—are suggestive of broad strategies that can be employed to evade them. I have cited instances of such strategies above, using African and other examples. However, I have only scratched the surface. There is no substitute for creative political leadership in identifying and exploiting the opportunities that difficult times present.

The larger methodological point underlying this chapter is that advocacy of reform has to be complemented with a more sophisticated understanding of what blocks it. Stock phrases like "ownership of reform" or "commitment of the leadership" that one encounters in discussions of failed reform attempts do not begin to do justice to the real political challenges that reformers face. Strengthening the reformers' hand requires not only technical economic advice, but also help with political strategies.

References

Alter, Rolf G., 1990, "Export Processing Zones for Growth and Development: The Mauritian Example," IMF Working Paper 90/122 (Washington: International Monetary Fund, December).

Bates, Robert, 1981, *Markets and States in Topical Africa* (Berkeley: University of California Press).

Bienen, Henry, 1991, "The Politics of Trade Liberalization," in *Trade and Development in Sub-Saharan Africa*, ed. by J.H. Frimpong-Ansah, S.M.R. Kanbur, and P. Svedberg (Manchester: Manchester University Press).

Collier, Paul, 1995, "The Marginalization of Africa," *International Labour Review*, Vol. 134, No. 4–5, pp. 541–57.

Dean, Judith M., Seema Desai, and James Riedel, 1994, "Trade Policy Reform in Developing Countries since 1985: A Review of the Evidence," Discussion Paper 267 (Washington: World Bank).

Fernandez, Raquel, and Dani Rodrik, 1991, "Resistance to Reform: Status Quo Bias in the Presence of Individual-Specific Uncertainty," *American Economic Review*, Vol. 81, No. 5, pp. 1146–55.

GATT (General Agreement on Tariffs and Trade), 1992, *Trade Policy Review: Ghana* (Geneva, General Agreement on Tariffs and Trade).

Gulhati, Ravi, 1990, *The Making of Economic Policy in Africa* (Washington: World Bank).

Hall, Robert E., and Alvin Rabushka, 1995, *The Flat Tax*, 2d ed. (Stanford, California: Hoover Institution Press, Stanford University).

Harvey, Charles, 1992, "Botswana: Is the Miracle Over?" *Journal of African Economies*, Vol. 1, No. 3, pp. 335–68.

———, and Stephen R. Lewis, Jr., 1990, *Policy Choice and Development Performance in Botswana* (London: Macmillan).

Herbst, Jeffrey, 1991, *Exchange Rate Reform in Ghana: Strategy and Tactics* (Washington: World Bank).

IMF (International Monetary Fund), 1997, *World Economic Outlook* (Washington: International Monetary Fund).

Krueger, Anne O., Maurice Schiff, and Alberto Valdés, 1988, "Agricultural Incentives in Developing Countries: Measuring the Effect of Sectoral and Economywide Policies," *World Bank Economic Review*, Vol. 2, No. 3, pp. 255–71.

Lall, Sanjaya, and Frances Stewart, 1996, "Trade and Industrial Policy in Africa," in *Agenda for Africa's Economic Renewal*, ed. by Benno Ndulu and Nicolas van de Walle (New Brunswick, New Jersey: Transaction Publishers).

Lewis, Stephen R., Jr., 1993, "Policymaking and Economic Performance: Botswana in Comparative Perspective," in *Botswana: The Political Economy of Democratic Development*, ed. by Stephen John Stedman (Boulder, Colorado: Lynne Rienner Publishers).

McMillan, Margaret, 1997, "A Dynamic Theory of Primary Export Taxation: Evidence from Sub-Saharan Africa" (unpublished; New York: Columbia University).

Meade, J.E., 1961, *The Economics and Social Structure of Mauritius—Report to the Government of Mauritius* (London: Methuen).

Metzel, Jeffrey, with Lucie Colvin Phillips, 1997, "Bringing Down Barriers to Trade: The Experience of Trade Policy Reform" (Washington: U.S. Agency for International Development).

Milner, Chris, and Andrew McKay, 1996, "Real Exchange Rate Measures of Trade Liberalization: Some Evidence for Mauritius," *Journal of African Economies*, Vol. 5, No. 1, pp. 69–91.

Rodrik, Dani, 1994, "The Rush to Free Trade in the Developing World: Why So Late? Why Now? Will It Last?" in *Voting for Reform: Democracy, Political Liberalization, and Economic Adjustment,* ed. by S. Haggard and S. Webb (New York: Oxford University Press).

Sachs, Jeffrey, and Andrew Warner, 1995, "Economic Reform and the Process of Global Integration," *Brookings Papers on Economic Activity: 1* (Washington: Brookings Institution).

Svedberg, Peter, 1991, "The Export Performance of Sub-Saharan Africa," in *Trade and Development in Sub-Saharan Africa,* ed. by J.H. Frimpong-Ansah, S.M.R. Kanbur, and P. Svedberg (Manchester: Manchester University Press).

Wellisz, Stanislaw, and Philippe Lam Shin Saw, 1993, "Mauritius," in *The Political Economy of Poverty, Equity, and Growth: Five Open Economies,* ed. by Ronald Findlay and Stanislaw Wellisz (New York: Oxford University Press).

World Bank, 1994, *Adjustment in Africa: Reforms, Results, and the Road Ahead* (New York: Oxford University Press).

Yeats, Alexander J., 1997, "Did Domestic Policies Marginalize Africa in International Trade?" (unpublished; Washington: World Bank).

Africa's Role in Multilateral Trade Negotiations: Past and Future 8

Zhen Kun Wang and L. Alan Winters

There is now a very broad consensus that open economies grow faster than closed ones, and nowhere is this message more important than in Africa. While opinions differ about exactly what constitutes openness and integration with the world economy, there is also little disagreement that most African economies need to liberalize their international trade regimes significantly during the next decade. Multilateral trade negotiations cannot lead or force that process of reform, but they can almost certainly assist it. Thus this chapter looks at the role of African countries in the last, Uruguay Round of multilateral trade negotiations and their potential role in the next one. It also argues that, in terms of access to partners' markets, trade preferences are no substitute for bound MFN tariff reductions, and that Africa should focus its negotiating efforts on the latter rather than the former.

The chapter is organized as follows. The second section briefly presents the background to the study. It reviews the arguments and evidence that African economies need to open up to world trade to stimulate their economic growth, drawing and elaborating upon a major program of research in the World Bank—Amjadi and Yeats (1995a, 1995b); Amjadi, Reincke, and Yeats (1996); Ng and Yeats (1996); and Yeats (1997b).[1] The evidence suggests that it is African countries' own trade policies and not those of their partners that must be changed to promote growth.

The third section analyzes the African economies' role in the Uruguay Round. It briefly notes that they undertook rather little liberalization themselves and then quantifies the concessions that they received from their trading partners in the round. It concludes that,

The authors are grateful to Ying Lin, Francis Ng, Ulrich Reincke, and Alexander Yeats for help with some of the calculations, to Audrey Kitson-Walters for first-rate logistical assistance, and to Alan Gelb, Jan Gunning, and Ademola Oyejide for comments on the first draft. The findings, interpretations, and conclusions expressed in this chapter are entirely those of the authors. They do not necessarily represent the views of the World Bank, its Executive Directors, or the countries they represent.

[1]In addition to their printed form, the later papers of this series are available at the World Bank's International Trade Division website (http://www.worldbank.org/html/iecit/archive.html).

while African countries achieved less in the round than did other developing countries (possibly because they offered less), they still emerged from it facing fewer or lower trade barriers than others.

The fourth section asks what role African countries might play in the next round of trade negotiations. Despite their very small size economically, they still have negotiating rights, under GATT-WTO Principal Supplier conventions, on the tariffs levied on between one-third and one-half of their exports to the European Union. By offering suitable reciprocal concessions, they should be able to achieve significant liberalization in these areas. Following the second section, we believe that ideally trade reform should be started—or, rather, accelerated—unilaterally as soon as possible in Africa. Nonetheless, it is still useful to consider the role that multilateral trade negotiations could play, for they can support domestic reform efforts by providing reciprocal concessions from trading partners that help to turn exporters into a more coherent force for import liberalization. Negotiations probably also improve the general atmosphere for liberalization and, of course, generate some direct benefits as well. We consider, therefore, how African countries have, and might in the future, use concessions in periodic rounds of trade negotiations to underpin their own reform efforts.

The fifth section notes that African exports receive tariff preferences in their major markets. It argues that preferences are not a constructive way of pursuing long-run integration with the global economy, and that instead African countries should use their negotiating rights to achieve unfettered access to markets on a bound-MFN basis. The sixth section concludes.

One important caveat is in order. Analysis of the type conducted here is very data intensive and thus depends critically on data availability and quality. It is widely recognized that data on sub-Saharan Africa are weak not only in terms of collection and quality within the countries of the region themselves, but also in terms of reporting to international organizations. Indeed, the failure of many sub-Saharan African countries consistently to report their international trade data to the United Nations—see Yeats (1997a)—and their trade and trade barriers to the WTO and the United Nations Conference on Trade and Development (UNCTAD) is itself one aspect of their weak commitment to integrating with a world in which "information is king."[2] The failure of sub-Saharan African countries to collect and report data un-

[2]We recognize that data collection and reporting entail costs, but these are not huge relative to the benefits of understanding the economy.

dermines efforts to understand the nature of African economic problems and opportunities, and could clearly lead to misperceptions in important areas such as the effectiveness of policy, the sustainability of growth, and the eligibility for debt packages. To pressure governments to give higher priority to data collection and reporting—including seeking relevant technical assistance—would be a feasible and useful contribution that the African research community could make toward African well-being.

Throughout this chapter, we define "Africa" as sub-Saharan Africa, not because North Africa is unimportant, but to keep the topic manageable. We use the World Bank's definition of sub-Saharan Africa.[3]

Background: Open Economies Work Better

Many scholars have analyzed the impact of openness on economic growth, and the majority have concluded that more open or liberal regimes achieve higher rates of economic growth than closed ones. Among the more recent studies are Dollar (1992), Sachs and Warner (1995), and World Bank (1996). These have used different countries, different periods, and different measures of openness, but all have concluded that outward orientation fosters growth. All also argue that one element of openness is the trade regime and that, at some level, having lower and fewer barriers to trade is likely to enhance growth.

Nowhere are growth-enhancing policies more important than in sub-Saharan Africa. On average, the region's GDP per head was about $509 in 1995 ($297 excluding South Africa) and it has hardly changed during the past three decades. Sub-Saharan Africa accounts for approximately 1.1 percent of world GDP (0.6 percent) and 1.4 percent of world exports (0.8 percent)—according to the World Bank (1997). The region's poor growth performance has been reflected not only in static income per head, but also in a rapidly declining share of world commerce. Ng and Yeats (1996) show that the decline in the sub-Saharan African share of world exports between 1962–64 and 1991–93 has reduced the absolute value of its exports by more than $11 billion per

[3]Sub-Saharan Africa is made up of Angola, Benin, Botswana, Burkina Faso, Burundi, Côte d'Ivoire, Cameroon, Cape Verde, Central African Republic, Chad, Comoros, Republic of Congo, Democratic Republic of the Congo (see next paragraph), Djibouti, Equitorial Guinea, Eritrea, Ethiopia, Gabon, The Gambia, Ghana, Guinea, Guinea-Bissau, Kenya, Lesotho, Liberia, Madagascar, Malawi, Mali, Mauritania, Mauritius, Mayotte, Mozambique, Namibia, Niger, Nigeria, Rwanda, São Tomé and Príncipe, Senegal, Seychelles, Sierra Leone, Somalia, South Africa, Sudan, Swaziland, Tanzania, Togo, Uganda, Zambia, and Zimbabwe.

In May 1997, the official name of Zaïre was changed to Democratic Republic of the Congo. Data in this book for years before 1997 will refer to "Zaïre."

year. This result reflects declining shares in nearly all subsectors of world trade, plus a tendency for sub-Saharan African exports to be concentrated in products whose share of world trade is declining. The top 30 3-digit Standard International Trade Classification (R1) commodity groups that accounted for the largest shares of sub-Saharan Africa's exports in 1962–64 had displayed huge losses of market share by 1991–93, with shares of OECD imports falling from 20.8 percent of these commodities to 9.7 percent.[4]

Ng and Yeats's result might be taken as evidence of poor performance, but it could equally well reflect great dynamism in sub-Saharan African export bundles; after all, Hong Kong's current shares in the products it exported in 1962–64—toys, clothing, and so forth—have fallen dramatically. Unfortunately, however, the latter interpretation does not hold up for sub-Saharan Africa. We have examined the region's performance in the 30 commodities that had the largest shares of its exports in 1991–93.[5] These are the region's major exports at the present time, and if dynamism explained the decline in market shares for traditional exports, these newer ones should show spectacular growth rates. (Also, just as any randomness in market shares would tend to reduce the growth rates of the exports that were largest at the start of the period, it would tend to exaggerate those that were largest at the end of the period.) These 30 commodities accounted for 42 percent of sub-Saharan African exports in 1991–93, compared with 72 percent in 1962–64, which evidences considerable export diversification. Unfortunately, however, even in these "newer" commodities, sub-Saharan Africa's shares of OECD imports have fallen more often than not, and its overall share in them has fallen from 9.4 to 6.3 percent.

Thus the loss of sub-Saharan African market share in the OECD stems from a generalized loss of competitiveness, rather than from the emergence of a particular competitor or change in circumstances. This is important in seeking to understand and address the problem. It is also important to recall sub-Saharan Africa's very small size. Together, these two features mean that even major improvements in the region's export performance will be pinpricks to the rest of the world and hence should be easy for it to accommodate. We do not argue that it is up to others to turn sub-Saharan Africa around—indeed, just the op-

[4]Part of sub-Saharan Africa's loss of share to OECD countries in products such as cocoa, coffee, and tea presumably reflects an increased tendency to trade processed varieties between OECD countries rather than the displacement of raw product exports.

[5]We are grateful to Alexander Yeats for making these calculations.

posite—but it is comforting to see that a turnaround will not generally have serious adjustment consequences for other countries and hence stimulate their opposition.

Having stressed the poor economic performance of the sub-Saharan African countries and the general importance of openness in stimulating exports and growth, it is natural to ask whether the two phenomenons are related. The answer is "almost certainly so." It is well known that during the periods for which analysis is available, most sub-Saharan African countries have maintained extremely restrictive trade regimes. Many studies suggest a strong anti-export bias in sub-Saharan African countries' trade policy, which is frequently further compounded by domestic tax regimes and monopoly marketing arrangements, both of which typically impinge disproportionately on agriculture—sub-Saharan Africa's major export sector. Moreover, although since the mid-1980s considerable progress has been made in liberalization—see, for example, World Bank (1994), Nash and Foroutan (forthcoming), and Oyejide, Ndulu, and Gunning (1997)—sub-Saharan African countries are mostly still substantially less open than those of East Asia and the Western Hemisphere. Updating data in Ng and Yeats's appendix suggests that tariffs average 26 percent in sub-Saharan Africa, compared with 17 percent in other developing countries; total charges on imports average 33 percent, compared with 26 percent; and NTB coverage ratios average 34 percent, compared with 18 percent. Also, as Oyejide, Ndulu, and Gunning observe, even the reforms that have been achieved to date are subject to reversal. In some cases, this has already occurred—for example, Nigeria and Côte d'Ivoire—but even where it has not, questions remain about the credibility and sustainability of the reforms.

An understandable and instinctive reaction to the evidence on sub-Saharan Africa's falling trade shares is to believe that OECD markets are, if not actually closed, hostile to sub-Saharan African exports. There is clearly some truth to these claims so far as temperate agricultural exports are concerned, for they face explicit and, frequently, high barriers in most OECD countries—for example, on beef or sugar. There are doubtless also some cases of tight restrictions on manufactured exports—for example, U.S. QRs on Kenyan exports of shirts. However, as a general explanation of the failure to industrialize and supply manufactured exports, the "hostile markets" hypothesis is not adequate. Several pieces of evidence lead to this conclusion.

First, access to OECD markets is fairly uniform across developing countries, especially when one recognizes that many simple manufactures are footloose in the sense of being as well suited to one developing-country location as another. Thus market access cannot, by itself, explain the huge variance in performance across countries.

Second, the tariffs facing developing-country exporters now are far lower than those ruling in the early 1960s when the first "Asian tigers" took off. To be sure, the MFA was not as deep or as broad then, but few sub-Saharan African countries are subject to the MFA today and there are other manufactured goods than clothing. Moreover, in these other goods, it is probably true that OECD countries were more likely then than now to resort to NTBs—for example, in footwear.

Third, most sub-Saharan African countries receive preferential access to OECD markets through the Generalized System of Preferences (GSP) and/or the Lomé Convention. We shall argue below that these schemes are less beneficial than they seem at first blush, but they do nonetheless offer low, and frequently zero, tariffs on many sub-Saharan African exports. Fourth, sub-Saharan African countries appear to fare relatively better than other developing countries in the face of OECD countries' NTBs (Amjadi, Reincke, and Yeats, 1996).

To conclude, there is, in fact, rather little evidence that hostile markets are the primary cause of sub-Saharan African countries' poor export performance. Indeed, much evidence points to the alternative of these countries' policies themselves. However, if it does not detract from the important business of reforming its own policy stance, trade liberalization abroad will generally confer benefits on a trading country. Regardless of its own policies, lower tariffs abroad will generally allow more trade and/or better terms of trade. For this reason, therefore, and because many commentators link sub-Saharan African liberalization with that of its partners, we now turn to the question of what sub-Saharan African countries did achieve, and might in the future achieve, through international trade negotiations.

Africa and the Uruguay Round

One hears regularly that Africa got little or nothing out of the Uruguay Round—see, for example, Weston (1995). Statements like this depend heavily on what elements of the round one considers and how one evaluates their benefits. For example, the Single Undertaking—which means that all members of WTO are now bound by more or less the same set of rules—newly constrains trade and related policies in sub-Saharan Africa. To some commentators, this is a cost, whereas to others (including ourselves), it is a benefit (Blackhurst, Enders, and François, 1996; Finger and Winters, 1998).

Turning to dimensions that can be quantified relatively easily, a major study conducted by the World Bank concluded that sub-Saharan Africa will make a small loss from the round, reflecting its lack of liberalization, the small increases in world prices for some foods, and the higher prices of imported textile and apparel products (Martin and Winters, 1996, p. 13). There is now a wide body of evidence that suggests that open economies prosper more than closed ones (see above), so it is not surprising that the first factor, which essentially denies sub-Saharan African countries the main benefits that others reaped in the round, should be important. The second and third factors—food and clothing prices—are quantitatively less significant; they reflect the fact that sub-Saharan Africa has previously benefited from the costs that other countries imposed on themselves by protecting agriculture and textiles/clothing and thus driving down world prices in those sectors. No one would wish to argue that the rest of the world should not seek to correct these manifestly large distortions, and so while the (small) income losses for sub-Saharan Africa are real enough, they do not really constitute grounds for criticizing the round per se. At most, they are ammunition for arguing that the transfers implicit in the previous policies should be continued by other, more efficient, means. Overall, therefore, while sub-Saharan Africa may have fared poorly in the round, this was not because the process was biased but because sub-Saharan Africa on the whole stood aside from the general liberalization.[6]

The results of the previous paragraph are, of course, predictions, and thus reflect what economists think will happen rather than what has actually happened on the ground. In this section we ask a simpler, and more empirical, question about how sub-Saharan Africa did in the Uruguay Round. We ask whether, on average, there were larger or smaller cuts in the tariffs on the goods that the region exports than in those exported by other developing countries. Drawing on the analysis of Finger, Ingco, and Reincke (1996), we base this analysis on the tariff concessions made by the 40 major markets that reported data on the Uruguay Round to the WTO's Integrated Data Base. These include all the industrial and transition economies that took part in the round plus 26 developing countries: they cover 100 percent of the non-oil imports of North America, Western Europe, and GATT members in Cen-

[6]Harrison, Rutherford, and Tarr (1997) argue that to generate gains sub-Saharan African liberalization would have had to address not only tariffs but also domestic taxes on agriculture. Indeed they suggest that reducing the former but not the latter would have slightly reduced economic welfare.

tral and Eastern Europe, 90 percent of Asia's, 80 percent of Latin America's, and 30 percent of Africa's.[7] The last figure is small because only three African countries, Senegal, Tunisia, and Zimbabwe, reported data, a fact that in itself is indicative of Africa's weak integration with the world economy.

Table 1 reports five measures of liberalization from the round for three groups of countries: sub-Saharan Africa, other low-income countries (OLICs), and other low- and middle-income countries (OLMICs), as defined by the World Bank (1996). The figures are simple averages of the corresponding measures for individual countries. In summarizing information over countries, we prefer simple to weighted averages because we are interested in how the typical sub-Saharan African country fared relative to other countries rather than in how the region as a whole fared relative to other continents or blocs. Thus each country is an observation of equal value for our purposes. The data for each country, however, are averages weighted by the value of trade undertaken in each tariff code heading or tariff line. Finger, Ingco, and Reincke (1996) report the corresponding weighted averages over countries, which for sub-Saharan Africa differ significantly from our figures because they are dominated by South Africa.

The first two columns of Table 1 report the percentage of sub-Saharan Africa (OLICs or OLMICs) exports that entered partners' markets under bound tariff rates before the round and the increase in this percentage as a result of the round. The trade data all come from 1988, the negotiating base year for the round, so the changes in the coverage of bindings reflect only the increases in the numbers of tariff lines that partners bound and the amount of trade in those lines. Since bound MFN tariffs apply to all exporters (the data exclude trade occurring within free trade areas, or FTAs), the differences between exporters reflect only the differences in their export bundles. But if we take the latter as given, we might view the increase in bindings as a prima facie measure of success in—or at least a measure of the returns to—negotiating in the Uruguay Round.[8]

[7]High-income economies: Australia, Austria, Canada, European Union, Finland, Hong Kong, Iceland, Japan, New Zealand, Norway, Singapore, Sweden, Switzerland, United States; Eastern Europe: Czech and Slovak Customs Union, Hungary, Poland, Romania; East Asia: Indonesia, Republic of Korea, Macao, Malaysia, Philippines, Thailand; Latin America: Argentina, Brazil, Chile, Colombia, El Salvador, Jamaica, Mexico, Peru, Uruguay, Venezuela; North Africa: Tunisia; rest of Europe: Turkey; South Asia: India, Sri Lanka; sub-Saharan Africa: Senegal, Zimbabwe.

[8]Let us reiterate that winning concessions in partners' markets is only one way—probably a minor way—in which trade negotiations raise welfare generally. Far more important is the degree of liberalization that a country undertakes itself.

Table 1. Major Importers' Most-Favored-Nation Tariff Reductions on Exports

(Percentage of GATT-bound exports; average levels and changes weighted by countries' exports)

Sector	Total Pre–Uruguay Round	Increase Due to the Round	Percentage of Exports Affected	Tariff Reduction[2]	Post–Uruguay Round Bound Rate	Post–Uruguay Round Applied Rate
(A) From Sub-Saharan Africa						
Agriculture, excluding fish: estimate 1[1]	80.8	19.2	4.1	0.7	18.6	14.9
Agriculture, excluding fish: estimate 2[1]	79.1	20.9	55.3	2.4	10.0	4.8
Fish and fish products	79.0	20.5	51.2	2.5	7.7	6.6
Petroleum oils	50.0	1.0	10.4	0.6	1.9	3.1
Wood, pulp, paper, and furniture	83.8	8.1	30.5	1.4	2.7	2.7
Textiles and clothing	90.4	4.2	73.6	1.6	10.6	9.8
Leather, rubber, footwear	85.6	8.6	47.0	0.8	4.4	4.8
Metals	87.6	6.6	17.4	0.5	2.0	1.7
Chemical and photographic supplies	70.4	16.2	45.4	2.5	7.7	6.0
Transport equipment	94.8	3.0	27.0	0.8	6.4	6.0
Nonelectric machinery	91.3	5.4	69.1	2.4	2.5	1.8
Electric machinery	88.3	4.4	67.7	1.8	5.6	4.4
Mineral products, precious stones, and metals	88.3	4.4	8.9	0.2	1.3	1.1
Manufactured articles	83.7	9.7	18.3	0.6	5.8	2.7
Industrial goods	86.7	8.9	18.5	0.4	3.2	2.2
All merchandise traded	78.4	13.5	29.7	1.4	4.1	2.7

Table 1 (*concluded*)

Sector	Total Pre–Uruguay Round	Increase Due to the Round	Percentage of Exports Affected	Tariff Reduction[2]	Post–Uruguay Round Bound Rate	Post–Uruguay Round Applied Rate
(B) From Other Low-Income Developing Countries						
Agriculture, excluding fish: estimate 1[1]	59.9	39.8	9.9	1.0	28.5	15.9
Agriculture, excluding fish:estimate 2[1]	55.1	44.7	27.7	1.2	19.9	9.0
Fish and fish products	68.2	25.9	51.8	1.7	4.4	3.7
Petroleum oils	38.8	3.8	0.3	0.0	6.7	1.7
Wood, pulp, paper, and furniture	62.0	32.3	42.4	2.1	6.0	3.2
Textiles and clothing	83.8	7.0	72.2	1.6	11.8	10.8
Leather, rubber, footwear	74.4	20.2	51.2	1.0	9.0	5.6
Metals	74.5	13.2	20.3	0.7	7.1	3.4
Chemical and photographic supplies	66.8	24.7	45.7	2.6	12.4	7.8
Transport equipment	60.1	8.4	21.1	0.4	9.2	8.6
Nonelectric machinery	64.8	24.3	48.3	1.5	6.5	3.9
Electric machinery	55.9	21.0	28.8	0.8	8.9	5.2
Mineral products, precious stones, and metals	63.0	14.7	21.9	0.7	3.9	4.3
Manufactured articles	81.2	14.3	38.5	1.5	7.0	2.1
Industrial goods	76.4	14.2	39.5	1.1	7.4	5.9
All merchandise traded	70.5	18.3	36.0	1.1	8.9	5.8

(C) From Other Developing Countries

Agriculture, excluding fish: estimate 1[1]	57.4	42.6	7.3	1.4	30.3	19.7
Agriculture, excluding fish: estimate 2[1]	59.6	40.3	32.7	1.5	19.0	9.5
Fish and fish products	72.2	24.7	39.2	1.5	5.8	4.5
Petroleum oils	52.4	9.1	4.0	0.1	7.3	3.0
Wood, pulp, paper, and furniture	75.7	20.4	39.5	2.1	6.9	3.1
Textiles and clothing	85.5	10.5	73.9	1.9	14.9	13.3
Leather, rubber, footwear	78.5	16.3	47.9	1.2	10.5	9.5
Metals	75.9	17.5	28.6	1.1	6.4	3.0
Chemical and photographic supplies	66.4	27.0	41.3	2.2	11.8	6.7
Transport equipment	74.7	12.3	27.5	0.7	10.5	7.0
Nonelectric machinery	75.6	19.4	55.1	1.7	7.9	4.3
Electric machinery	74.3	17.9	51.9	1.6	9.8	6.2
Mineral products, precious stones, and metals	75.2	15.1	27.1	0.7	5.9	3.6
Manufactured articles	81.6	14.3	38.2	1.7	6.5	2.9
Industrial goods	78.3	15.8	40.2	1.2	8.3	5.8
All merchandise traded	70.6	18.7	31.2	1.0	9.2	5.7

Source: Authors's calculations based on Finger, Ingco, and Reincke (1996).

Note: Unweighted averages across countries.

[1]See Finger, Ingco, and Reincke (1996), p. 5–6, for the explanation of differences between estimate 1 and estimate 2.

[2]Weighted average tariff reduction measured by $dT/(1 + T)$, in percent.

The striking thing about the second column is that sub-Saharan Africa achieved less by way of new bindings on its exports than did either the OLICs or the OLMICs. Indeed, in no cases in our aggregations of goods did sub-Saharan Africa do better, and in the majority of cases it did significantly worse statistically.[9] But the reason for this is perfectly clear in the first column: in every case, sub-Saharan Africa started off from a more favorable position, that is, with a higher percentage of exports already bound, and these differences were also frequently statistically significant. The round more or less brought other developing countries up to parity with sub-Saharan Africa with respect to bindings. If we consider the percentage of exports bound after the round (that is, the sum of the first two columns), there are only five statistically significant differences between sub-Saharan Africa and OLICs (all in sub-Saharan Africa's favor) and one between sub-Saharan Africa and the OLMICs.

The remaining columns of Table 1 give similar statistics for other dimensions of the Uruguay Round outcome; again, they are simple averages across countries. The third column is constructed from country data on the percentage of exports affected by a reduction in a partners' tariff; it pays no heed to the depth of the reduction. The fourth column, conversely, is based on the reduction in tariffs faced by countries' exports, averaged (weighted by exports) across all export headings for which a reduction is made. Unlike in WTO documents, percentage tariff reductions are measured here by their effect on the landed price of imports, $[dT/(1+\bar{T})]*100$, where $\bar{T}$ is the mean of the "before" and "after" tariffs; hence a halving, say, of a tariff of 2 percent is "worth" five times less than halving of one of 10 percent. To illustrate these two columns, the "average sub-Saharan African country" obtained tariff reductions of 51.2 percent on its exports of fish and fish products, and these reductions potentially reduced the landed prices to customers of those products by 2.5 percent. The average reduction in the landed prices of all fish and fish products was the product of these two numbers, namely, 1.3 percent.

In terms of the coverage of tariff reductions at commodity-group level, there is no systematic difference between sub-Saharan Africa, the OLICs, and the OLMICs: sub-Saharan Africa does better in some

[9]This is based on a statistical test of the difference in means between two samples assumed to have equal variances. Since the change in the percentage of exports bound for each country is derived by weighting together export flows (assumed to be stochastic) across many tariff headings (with weight 1 if there is a new binding and zero otherwise), we can assume that the individual country data are normally distributed. Thus the group averages will also be normal, and the test is justified.

classes and worse in others, with about half of the differences being statistically significant. One interesting and statistically significant contrast, however, is for all industrial goods, in which sub-Saharan Africa obtains only about half the coverage of reductions of the other groups (20 percent compared with 40 percent). This reflects sub-Saharan Africa's heavy reliance on product groups with low coverage rates generally, such as wood, metals, minerals, and manufactures. In this sense, sub-Saharan African countries achieved less on average in the round than did other developing countries, because its principal exports received cuts less frequently than did other products.

This story is compounded by a similar one on the depth of the cuts. There are no major differences at the level of commodity groups, and sub-Saharan Africa obtains larger cuts than the other groups as often as not. However, taking industrial goods overall, sub-Saharan Africa's concentration on sectors with weak liberalization leaves it with an average tariff cut of 0.4 percent, compared with 1.1 or 1.2 percent for the other aggregates.[10] Averaging the tariff reductions over all exports of industrial goods leaves sub-Saharan Africa looking even more worse with cuts of 0.07 percent compared with 0.45 percent for the OLICs and 0.48 percent for the OLMICs.

One should not get carried away with these apparent disadvantages, however, for two reasons. First, once we turn to the aggregate of all exports (and, why focus exclusively on industrial goods?), sub-Saharan Africa does not appear to be unduly discriminated against: on the coverage of cuts, compare 29.7 percent for sub-Saharan Africa with 36.0 percent for the OLICs and 31.2 percent for the OLMICs; on depth, compare 1.4 percent with 1.1 percent and 1.0 percent, respectively, and on the average over all exports, 0.42 percent with 0.40 percent and 0.31 percent.

Second, turning to the final two columns of Table 1, we report the levels of tariffs faced by different exporters after the Uruguay Round: the fifth column is constructed from the average of bound rates (weighted by each country's exports), and the sixth column from that of applied rates projected for the end of the transition period. For each trade heading, the latter equals the minimum of the post–Uruguay Round bound and the pre–Uruguay Round (1988) applied rate, which we assume would continue indefinitely into the future if the Uruguay Round binding did not force it down.[11] Here the story is very clear.

[10]These differences are not significant, however.

[11]In fact, since 1988 many importers have further reduced their applied rates, so this column overestimates the average tariffs that exporters face now and at the end of the Uruguay Round phase-in period.

Africa faces lower bound tariffs on average than do other developing countries—that is, its exports are concentrated, on average, on low-tariff products—and the differences are all significant. At the aggregate levels, for industrial goods, compare 3.2 percent for sub-Saharan Africa with 7.4 percent for the OLICs and 8.3 percent for the OLMICs, and for all goods 4.1 percent with 8.9 and 9.2 percent. Similarly for applied rates, the corresponding triples of (significantly different) figures are 2.2, 5.9, and 5.8 percent for industrial goods, and 2.7, 5.8, and 5.7 percent for all goods, although the individual goods aggregates do not display many significant differences.

In a real and quantifiable sense, the countries of sub-Saharan Africa achieved less in the Uruguay Round than did other developing countries. Following Finger (1979) we might speculate that this is because they gave less by way of their own concessions. Conversely, however, we must also recognize that they had less to achieve, because they started the round with "better" treatment than other countries. Moreover, they finished it in the same condition, facing lower MFN tariffs on their exports on average than did other developing countries.

The Next Round

Rather than considering the Uruguay Round, this section looks forward to the next round of trade negotiations and asks whether the sub-Saharan African countries can reasonably expect to achieve anything. It considers whether they are significant enough partners for other countries to make it worth the latter's while negotiating with them at all. Given our comments above about how small sub-Saharan Africa is economically, it would not be surprising to find that there was no significant way in which they could participate. But in fact the answer is not completely negative. Sub-Saharan Africa may well be able to achieve some useful objectives by contributing actively to the next round.

We focus on two measures of the significance of a country to trade negotiations. First, to what extent are sub-Saharan African countries, either singly or jointly, the largest or principal suppliers of particular goods to the major trading powers of the world. Second, to what extent are those powers' own exports oriented toward sub-Saharan Africa? The first statistic reflects sub-Saharan African countries' "rights" to negotiate; the second, their power or leverage in doing so. In discussing both, we adopt the common, but at best very partial, mercantilist yardstick that sees exports as good and imports as necessary evils, and that interprets reducing one's partners' tariffs as a victory, and reducing one's own tariffs as unavoidable collateral damage.

The WTO's predecessor, the GATT, developed two approaches to tariff negotiation. In the Kennedy Round (1963–67) and Tokyo Round (1972–79), as well as in the recent Information Technology Agreement, tariffs on industrial goods were reduced by formula subject to a complex negotiation (usually bilateral) of exceptions, exemptions, and transitional periods. Small countries benefited from the general reduction in tariffs without having to take any specific action, but would of course have little power to prevent or discourage a large power from claiming exceptions on their main exports if other major powers did not object.

The technique used in the earlier GATT rounds, and also in the Uruguay Round for tariffs on industrial goods, was the so-called request and offer system, whereby one country made a specific request of another to reduce a particular tariff in return for a reciprocal concession. From the early days of the GATT, the convention grew up that only the principal supplier of a particular good to a particular country could request the latter's government to reduce the relevant tariff (see Dam, 1970). Thus a vital part of getting tariffs on your exports reduced was being the principal supplier of those goods. This suggests that small countries would have only a minor role in the process, since they would rarely be principal suppliers. Even if a particular good figured very highly in a small country's export bundle to a market, the small country could not initiate negotiations if some other country supplied absolutely more, even if that flow accounted for a minor proportion of the latter's total exports (see Winters, 1987).

Table 2 reports on sub-Saharan African countries' principal supplier status to the European Union.[12] We use 1995 data from the EU's Comext data base which defines products at the 8-digit level of the Harmonized System (HS). The situation varies somewhat from year to year, but the data analyzed here are probably fairly representative. A full listing of the affected trade headings is available from the authors.[13]

In all, 29 sub-Saharan African countries are principal suppliers of at least one product (heading), and together they account for 289 (out of approximately 9,000) headings in the 8-digit HS trade classification. The distribution over countries is much as expected, with half of the headings stemming from South Africa. The bulk of the headings are in food and agriculture, but of course, given that this is where the high-

[12]Europe takes more than half of sub-Saharan Africa's exports, so the EU is clearly the principal partner to concentrate on.

[13]The authors are grateful to Lin Ying for help with these calculations.

Table 2. Sub-Saharan African Countries as Principal Suppliers to the European Union, 1995

Country or Bloc	Number of Headings for which Principal Supplier	Trade Flows in These Headings, (millions of ECUs)	These Headings as Percentage of Total Exports to EU	Average Share of Principal Supplier in EU Imports in These Headings	Average Share of Total Sub-Saharan African Countries in EU Imports in These Headings	EU Average Post–Uruguay Round Bound Tariff in These Headings	Two Major Products (HS-2)[1]
Angola	1	1.0	0.2	32.4	50.9	1.5	Fish
Benin	2	10.6	18.3	76.3	94.4	—	Meats and oil seeds
Burundi	1	51.9	35.9	34.1	42.9	0.5	Gold
Camero	7	160.3	13.8	57.7	99.3	—	Wood
Congo	1	10.7	1.5	62.0	92.7	0.6	Sheets for plywood
Côte d'Ivoire	24	1,129.8	54.6	45.5	75.6	3.7	Cocoa, wood, fish
Gabon	5	162.5	20.3	60.6	78.9	6.3	Manganese ores, wood
Ghana	7	59.5	7.1	22.3	49.0	10.7	Cocoa, oil seeds
Guinea	1	169.8	56.9	58.0	61.7	0	Aluminum ores
Kenya	17	204.5	31.6	34.8	50.0	6.4	Tea, fruits, vegetables
Liberia	1	578.2	90.7	12.4	33.9	0	Diamonds
Madagascar	10	79.8	23.1	47.1	61.1	5.2	Fruits, clothing (handkerchiefs, scarves)
Malawi	1	32.6	23.1	83.3	87.2	—	Unmanufactured tobacco
Mauritania	1	4.9	1.9	8.5	39.7	—	Frozen fish

Mauritius	7	308.3	30.2	28.5	51.6	14.0	Sugar, clothing (shirts and pullovers)
Namibia	7	46.3	12.6	38.4	62.3	15.5	Fish, meat
Niger	1	83.7	69.2	68.4	84.6	—	Radioactive chemicals
Nigeria	11	78.0	2.3	46.6	63.2	2.8	Sheep skin leather, others
Reunion	7	1.7	1.4	34.9	35.0	4.4	Prepared meats, others
South Africa	143	4,289.8	55.7	35.1	38.5	0.8	Gold, fruits, wine, iron and steel
Senegal	5	84.3	22.8	48.9	64.4	7.9	Nut oil, oil-cake and residuals
Somalia	1	0.7	3.6	53.3	80.8	—	Molluscs
Sudan	4	43.2	25.1	38.2	62.2	—	Oil seeds and natural gums
Tanzania	6	3.4	1.7	36.8	47.1	22.3	Dried leguminous vegetables, rope and cables
Togo	1	1.1	1.5	26.8	69.1	—	Other goods
Uganda	2	14.6	4.1	35.4	75.4	4.6	Fish, raw hides and skins
Zaïre	4	505.0	60.0	53.2	54.2	10.6	Diamonds, plants
Zambia	1	51.8	28.5	45.6	51.2	—	Others goods
Zimbabwe	10	18.2	2.9	38.7	56.0	—	Pepper, powders of pig iron

Table 2 *(concluded)*

Country or Bloc	Number of Headings for which Principal Supplier	Trade Flows in These Headings, (millions of ECUs)	These Headings as Percentage of Total Exports to EU	Average Share of Principal Supplier in EU Imports in These Headings	Average Share of Total Sub-Saharan African Countries in EU Imports in These Headings	EU Average Post–Uruguay Round Bound Tariff in These Headings	Two Major Products (HS-2)[1]
CEAO	37	1,434	47.9	45.6	71.5	5.1	
ECOWAS	63	3,218	38.1	37.5	49.7	3.9	
UDEAC	14	427	14.7	71.6	89.1	1.7	
COMESA/PTA	67	1,108	22.2	42.8	52.1	9.2	
SADC	176	5,055	50.1	36.0	38.2	5.5	
CBI	73	1,179	27.9	44.5	52.4	9.1	
All of region	326	13,615	53.5	40.9			

Note: CEAO is West African Economic Community: Benin, Burkina Faso, Côte d'Ivoire, Mali, Mauritania, Niger, and Senegal. Economic Community of West African States (ECOWAS): all seven members of CEAO and Cape Verde, The Gambia, Guinea, Guinea-Bissau, Liberia, Sierra Leone, Nigeria, and Togo. UDEAC is Central Africa Economic and Customs Union: Cameroon, Central African Republic, Chad, Congo, Gabon, and Equatorial Guinea. Common Market for Eastern and Southern Africa (COMESA)/Preferential Trade Area for Eastern and Southern African States (PTA): Angola, Burundi, Comoros, Djibouti, Ethiopia, Kenya, Lesotho, Malawi, Mauritius, Mozambique, Namibia, Rwanda, Somalia, Sudan, Swaziland, Tanzania, Uganda, Zambia, and Zimbabwe. South Africa Development Community (SADC): Angola, Botswana, Lesotho, Malawi, Mozambique, Namibia, South Africa, Swaziland, Tanzania, Zambia, and Zimbabwe. Cross-Border (CBI): Burundi, Comoros, Kenya, Madagascar, Malawi, Mauritius, Namibia, Rwanda, Seychelles, Tanzania, Uganda, Zambia, and Zimbabwe.

[1]"HS" is harmonized system.

est tariffs are to be found, this might be an advantage rather than the contrary.

It is striking in the third column of Table 2 how large a proportion of certain sub-Saharan African countries' total exports to the EU fall into the principal supplier headings. This reflects the commodity concentration of sub-Saharan African exports noted above, but it also indicates the strong interest, at least on the basis of current trade, that countries of the region have in the advantageous treatment of this subset of their exports.

It is also notable (fourth column) that, on the whole, sub-Saharan African principal suppliers account for between one- and two-thirds of EU imports in the relevant headings. These are relatively high numbers (compare with Finger, 1979, Table 5), which is usually viewed as an advantage in trade negotiations, for it maximizes the degree of internalization in any concession that the EU makes. Internalization is the proportion of the total benefits of a concession that accrues to the negotiating partner requesting that concession. The higher it is, the higher the proportion of the concession that is working toward obtaining reciprocation from the requester, and the smaller the spillover to partners who are not required to offer direct reciprocation when the concession is extended to all partners through the MFN clause. Thus negotiators are attracted to highly internalized concessions because they offer greater returns per unit of concession than do diffuse ones. In the GATT's mercantilist tradition, "benefit" is the product of the proportionate tariff cut and the trade it affects. Clearly the distribution of benefit over partners is proportional to their shares of total imports. The conclusion is, therefore, that generally speaking, a fair proportion of the benefit of EU tariff cuts in these products will accrue to the sub-Saharan African principal suppliers; this will set up fairly strong incentives for the latter to reciprocate, which in turn will help to make the EU correspondingly more sympathetic to requests for tariff reductions.

The fifth column explores the spillovers more directly. It calculates the share of EU imports in headings with a sub-Saharan African principal supplier that comes from the region as a whole. The difference between the fifth and fourth columns is the spillover from each sub-Saharan African country's potential negotiation that accrues to other countries in the region. In general, in goods for which one sub-Saharan African country is the principal supplier, the region supplies at least half of EU imports. Thus this is a set of commodities in which sub-Saharan Africa has quite a strong collective interest.

The final column reports the EU's (weighted) average post–Uruguay Round bound tariff in each sub-Saharan African country's principal supplier exports.[14] This column suggests that in several cases there is little left to negotiate, for MFN tariffs are already nearly or actually zero. Conversely, there are also cases where substantial tariffs on substantial trade flows remain to be negotiated downward—for example, for Mauritius, Namibia, and Tanzania. The goods, in these sets on which Africans have more or less exclusive negotiating rights, are the important opportunities for sub-Saharan African negotiators in the next round.

The top rows of Table 2 treat sub-Saharan African countries as single entities negotiating separately, but the bottom rows combine them into blocs based on current regional trading agreements. If the principal regional blocs in the region negotiated as blocs, they would have stronger principal supplier rights in the EU. Whenever one of their member countries was a principal supplier in its own right, and hence included in the country rows of the table, the bloc would automatically be a principal supplier and would have a market share no less, and probably greater, than that of the individual country. In addition, there would be trade headings for which the bloc collectively was a principal supplier without any individual sub-Saharan African country having that status.[15]

The results for the blocs confirm that, by acting in concert, blocs of sub-Saharan African countries would have a few more negotiating rights and a somewhat greater degree of internalization. Two blocs—the West African Economic and Monetary Union (UEMOA) and South African Development Community (SADC)—have about half of their exports in principal supplier categories and thus have, in some sense, significant influence over the treatment of their exports. The degree of internalization for all blocs is relatively high, as is the spillover to the rest of the region in the case of Western Africa. As might be expected from above, the major EU tariff barriers that are "vulnerable" to sub-Saharan African bloc-based principal supplier negotiations are for Eastern and Southern Africa, especially including those on fish.

[14]The tariffs are taken from the WTO's Integrated Data Base and refer to the bound rates at the end of the transition phase of the Uruguay Round—that is, to the base for the next round. Applied tariffs are occasionally lower. Since the tariff data are on a 1988 classification and the trade data on a 1995 classification, there are some principal supplier commodities for which we cannot identify bound tariffs. We ignore these in the averaging.

[15]One way in which the blocs might negotiate jointly is by forming a customs union—the expressed intention of most of them. Another way, however, is for them to coordinate negotiation on particular headings ad hoc. All that the GATT requires for such coordinated negotiation is that *each* member of the bloc offer reciprocation for the concession so obtained (Dam, 1970, p. 62).

One theoretical complication evident in the note to Table 2 is multiple bloc membership. The countries of UEMOA are also members of ECOWAS, while many from the CBI and some from SADC also belong to COMESA. These countries would need to decide with whom to combine. In fact, however, neither ECOWAS nor COMESA looks sufficiently coherent or active to negotiate with the EU, so this problem will probably not arise for some time.

The last row of Table 2 treats sub-Saharan Africa as a single negotiating unit. Again, it is clear that negotiating collectively would give countries of the region somewhat greater negotiating "rights," but again the difference is not huge. Even acting as a single bloc, they would have only 326 principal supplier items accounting for $13.6 billion of exports compared with 289 accounting for $8.2 billion of exports acting individually. Given the complexities of coordinating bloc positions, it is not clear that the bloc approach would be worthwhile.

Negotiations are, almost by definition, about reciprocity. When sub-Saharan African negotiators approach those from the EU to negotiate on the principal supplier headings just identified, the latter will seek reciprocity in headings for which the EU is the relevant sub-Saharan African country's or group's principal supplier. We do not have sub-Saharan African data with which to identify these headings (presumably sub-Saharan African negotiators will have them), but we are confident that many will exist and that they will have tariffs sufficiently high that the EU will have reasonable incentives to negotiate.

Table 3 looks at EU exports to sub-Saharan African countries from a different perspective that is somewhat informative even if it has no formal role in GATT/WTO traditions. It asks in which commodities (again defined at 8-digit level of HS) is a sub-Saharan African country the EU's principal market. That is, in which commodities will the EU be relatively most interested in liberalizing sub-Saharan Africa rather than other markets? Note that we persist with the GATT mercantilist calculus, which values concessions by the volume of existing trade that they affect. Note also that the comparison here is of the relative market sizes for a given export commodity, and not of the relative values of exports of different commodities to a given market, which would be another valid metric.

Table 3 presents information similar to Table 2 on sub-Saharan African imports: the number of "principal market" commodities, the value of trade within them, the percentage of the EU's total exports to the country falling in those headings, the average percentage of total EU exports of these headings going to the principal market, the average percentage of these exports going to sub-Saharan Africa as a whole, and the main commodities. Perhaps the most striking fact

Table 3. Sub-Saharan African Countries as Principal Markets for European Union Exports, 1995

Country	Number of Headings	Trade Flows in These Headings, (millions of ECUs)	These Headings as Percentage of Total EU Exports to the Country	Exports to Principal Market as Percentage of Total EU Exports in These Headings	Exports to Sub-Saharan Africa as Percentage of Total EU Exports in These Headings	Two Major Products (HS–2)[1]
Angola	17	201.6	25.2	62.4	64.6	Starches, etc., ships
Benin	4	30.0	11.1	18.3	48.6	Cotton, pearls
Botswana	1	2.0	2.3	15.3	50.0	Vehicles
Burkina Faso	1	1.3	0.7	18.5	31.3	Machinery
Burundi	2	1.4	1.9	30.2	55.1	Fertilizer, iron/steel
Cameroon	4	27.6	4.9	7.6	46.9	Other textiles, zinc
Comoros	1	—	0.1	66.7	76.2	Fats, vegetables/ fruit preparations
Congo	3	15.1	3.2	11.5	26.1	Vegetables/fruit preparations
Cape Verde	4	1.8	1.2	35.4	39.3	Iron/steel, machinery
Côte d'Ivoire	9	53.8	4.5	35.8	58.2	Fish, iron/steel
Djibouti	1	—	0.0	33.3	66.7	Cereals
Ethiopia	4	3.8	0.8	26.1	34.4	Stone, machinery
Gabon	3	1.1	0.2	7.5	34.3	Explosives, electrical equipment
Gambia, The	1	1.2	2.1	70.8	93.5	Fats
Ghana	9	9.9	1.3	33.8	40.8	Meat, railway equipment
Guinea	1	0.3	0.1	31.9	36.7	Beverages
Kenya	6	7.3	0.9	27.1	32.6	Organic chemicals, machinery

Liberia	3	897.6	72.4	55.0	55.2	Soaps, ships
Madagascar	1	0.7	0.3	36.0	37.0	Silk
Mali	2	0.3	0.1	37.6	40.3	Fish, organic chemicals
Mauritania	2	4.0	1.7	17.2	29.7	Cotton, iron/steel
Mauritius	1	4.0	0.6	25.3	29.2	Cotton
Mozambique	2	12.8	9.0	26.8	40.8	Cereals, aluminum
Nigeria	32	110.9	5.4	23.5	34.8	Fish, inorganic chemicals
Rwanda	1	—	0.1	20.7	41.5	Photo/cinema products
Reunion	26	25.1	1.7	21.7	29.3	Iron/steel, ships
South Africa	69	298.9	3.5	22.0	24.9	Machinery, electrical equipment
Senegal	8	2.8	0.4	20.3	39.9	Fats, misc. chemicals
Sudan	2	0.8	0.3	10.5	13.4	Inorganic chemicals, glass
Tanzania	2	0.5	0.2	7.9	29.8	Vegetables/fruit preparations, machinery
Togo	1	0.1	0.0	30.5	34.7	Meat preparations
Uganda	4	3.1	1.7	13.6	33.1	Essential oils, stone
Zaïre	9	2.4	0.7	29.7	68.3	Meat, other textiles
Zimbabwe	2	3.5	0.9	29.2	42.8	Staple fibers
All of region	491	4,526.6	18.6	22.1	22.1	

[1]"HS" is harmonized system.

about Table 3 is that it has any entries at all: it turns out that, after all, sub-Saharan African matters to the EU in a mercantilist sense in at least some trade headings. Unfortunately, however, these headings are mostly for very small trade flows—even by the standards of EU-sub-Saharan African trade. Frequently less than 1 percent of EU exports to a sub-Saharan African country fall in headings for which the country is the principal market, and very commonly less than 5 percent does. The main exceptions to this are Angola, which in 1995 was dominated by imports of drilling equipment (HS 89052000), and Liberia, which was dominated by imports of passenger ships (HS 89011010).

The next two columns show that individual sub-Saharan African countries accounted for quite large shares of EU exports of the principal market headings and that in some cases the region as a whole accounted for well over half. These include the major exports to Angola and Liberia.

While sub-Saharan African countries are principal markets for some 238 trade headings in EU exports (491 if we take the region as a whole), these are mostly quite insignificant. Nonetheless, exporters of these commodities are natural allies for sub-Saharan African countries in trade negotiation and should be mobilized to seek concessions on EU imports in return for sub-Saharan African liberalizations on these exports. Sub-Saharan African countries should also identify major imports from the EU in absolute terms and consider how liberalization of these may also be used to improve their access to EU markets. Note yet again, however, that the principal benefit from such exchanges of concessions would be from what sub-Saharan African countries "gave" on their own barriers rather than from what they "gained" on EU barriers.

It would be foolish to view the results of this section as showing that sub-Saharan African countries will have significant power in the next round of trade negotiations. It does show, however, that even on the most bilateral of issues (tariff negotiations) and even with the old-fashioned operating rules—which were frequently criticized for excluding developing countries—(e.g., Johnson, 1967)—sub-Saharan Africa has some role. To us, at least, this was a surprise.

Building upon the base of request and offer tariff negotiation, we believe that sub-Saharan African countries have much to gain by understanding and actively representing their broader interests in the next round. Following the Uruguay and Tokyo rounds, we would expect this to be fairly heavily focused on multilateral activities such as formulaic approaches to liberalization and the negotiation of rules, and there are good reasons to believe that these offer more scope to well-informed small players than do bilateral negotiations. It is a challenge to policy economists in Africa and to those elsewhere who care about Africa to provide the necessary information. The Development Economics Vice Presidency of the World Bank is committed to doing so, but the job will be much more effectively achieved locally than from Washington.

Preferences

The previous two sections have argued that sub-Saharan African countries emerged from the Uruguay Round facing lower tariffs than other developing countries and that, according to GATT conventions, the countries of the region might be expected to have at least some negotiating rights over their major partners' tariffs in the next round. But both pieces of analysis considered partners' MFN tariffs rather than the tariffs that sub-Saharan African countries actually face. The latter are currently mostly governed by arrangements under the GSP or, for the EU, the Lomé Convention, and as a result are fairly commonly zero. Thus our analysis of the Uruguay Round might be considered irrelevant and that of the principal supplier relationship actually perverse in the sense that it suggests that sub-Saharan African countries should be pleased to have the opportunity to negotiate down the tariffs that apply to their competitors but not to themselves!

We respond on two levels. First, on preferences in general—or perhaps on the concept of preferences—it should be noted that they generally deliver very little. First, for most goods, and particularly manufactured ones, the margin of tariff preference granted to sub-Saharan African (and other developing) countries is very small. Amjadi, Reincke, and Yeats (1996) show that, at the end of the Uruguay Round transition period, sub-Saharan African countries will have preference margins averaging slightly under 2.5 percentage points. (One should consider preferences in terms of the price advantage they confer—that is, percentage points—rather than, as is quite common, the percentage of the tariffs they remit. To have 100 percent remission of a 1 percent tariff is worth far less—1 percentage point—than a 50 percent remission of a 10 percent tariff—5 percentage points.)

Moreover, even putting aside their low average level, preferences will be eroded by future multilateral liberalization. The Uruguay Round cut the measured average margin of preference for sub-Saharan African countries from 4.3 percentage points to 2.5. We interpret this not as further evidence of the hardship that the round imposed on sub-Saharan Africa, but as evidence that, in the long run, preferences will be squeezed even further. As the evidence that openness promotes economic performance becomes more deeply and widely accepted around the world, no one is going to arrest the removal of MFN trade barriers for the sake of the sub-Saharan African countries' preferences.

Second, there are cases where tariffs are higher and where, as a result, preferences are deeper and potentially more valuable. Among these cases, there are undoubtedly some for which short-term interests dictate against seeking to erode present agreements (see below on long-run aspects of preferences), but these are not as common as they may appear on the surface. Consider, for example, textiles and clothing. This simple and labor-intensive sector is one in which developing countries clearly have some competitive advantage, and which as a result of having some of the highest MFN tariffs potentially offer the greatest margins of preference. Unfortunately, however, the United States does not grant preferences on textiles and clothing, so that sub-Saharan African countries face the full average tariff of 16.75 percent on all their exports. The EU does grant tariff preferences to sub-Saharan African textile and clothing exports under the Lomé Convention, but they are subject to strict rules of origin. The cumbersomely enforced rules of origin under Lomé, for example, which allow duty-free access only if at least 85 percent of a product's value originates from a beneficiary country, have the effect of denying effective preferences even where the latter exist formally on the books.[16] In addition, the complicated procedures of the rules of origin cost poor-country exporters dearly in paperwork.

It is also worth noting that, while the Lomé Convention places sub-Saharan African textile and clothing exports to the EU outside the purview of the MFA, such commitments have not in the past prevented the EU from seeking and receiving "voluntary" restraint agreements on such exports, as it did with the Mediterranean Associated States.

Turning to agriculture, the EU applies tariff quotas to sub-Saharan African agricultural products covered by the Common Agricultural Policy (CAP). Tariff quotas restrict the volume of imports that receive preferential treatment, so that once a country has exhausted its quota the preference it receives on marginal exports is zero. In addition, primary exports face even stricter rules of origin than manufactures under Lomé. For example, 100 percent of origin—all materials for manufacturing must originate from the African, Caribbean, and Pacific

[16]UNCTAD (1994) reports that in the EU only 68 percent of dutiable imports from beneficiary countries qualify for GSP preferences, of which only 33 percent (slightly below half) actually take them up. The corresponding figures for Japan are 35 and 16 percent, and for the United States 36 and 18 percent.

(ACP) countries—applies to fish products and processed fish, a product in which sub-Saharan African countries such as the Seychelles and Cape Verde have comparative advantage. It is true that derogations from these rules of "originating products" are sometimes granted, as for example for the Seychelles, but only at the cost of facing an annual quota limit.[17]

Even if preferences are small on average, some economists argue that they are desirable, or even important. We disagree. First, preferences to sub-Saharan African countries do nothing to enhance the consumption of the goods concerned in a preference-granting market. In almost all cases, the latter continues to import some of the good from nonpreferred sources and so experiences no decline in its internal price. All that the preferences do is (1) transfer tariff revenue to the sub-Saharan African country on the exports that it would have made in the absence of preferences and (2) allow it to displace some exports from other sources as it expands up its supply curve in response to the higher price received for its exports.[18] As the sub-Saharan African country's supply expands, its costs increase, so that the effect of the preference is to induce inefficiency—to transfer to sub-Saharan Africa the production inefficiencies created by protection in the preference-granting market. If there were no difficulty in reversing such inefficiencies or in restructuring economies when the preferences are removed, it might still be advantageous to sub-Saharan Africa to take advantage of preferences while it may. But, in fact, policymakers generally argue that such restructuring is painful—perhaps very painful, for example, moving out of bananas in the Windward Islands—and so it is arguably best to avoid the distortion in the first place.

Second, and closely related to the previous point, preferences are granted unilaterally, usually one year at a time.[19] This makes them very insecure and also opens the recipient countries to considerable pressure to meet various conditions—for example, labor standards—to continue them. Such insecurity encourages short-termism among sub-Saharan African entrepreneurs and governments. Another insecurity derives from the Article 177 of Lomé Convention IV, which allows the EU to take "safeguard measures" if imports from the ACP countries cause "serious disturbances" in a sector of the EU or a sector of one member country, or if they may result in a deterioration in "exter-

[17]For more detail, see Official Journal, L137, 31.12.1994.
[18]The simple analytics of preferences are set out in the appendix to the chapter.
[19]Lomé preferences are more secure than this.

nal financial stability" of a member. These are less restrictive than the conditions for safeguard protection under GATT Article XIX.

Thus overall preferences represent a very poor basis for investment, and thus probably have very little effect on the incentives for industrialization. They create incentives quite foreign to the notion of long-term development—for example, for investment, learning, efficiency—and instead foster behavior designed to seek and perpetuate the rents that they generate. In the past, developing countries, including many in sub-Saharan Africa, have focused disproportionate diplomatic effort on achieving and maintaining preferences at the expense of identifying and pursuing constructive long-term objectives. For example, the internal politics of trade policy and trade negotiation are far easier to handle if they are focused on trying to persuade OECD countries to provide a free lunch for certain exporters with no obvious costs to anyone else.[20] They are much more difficult if the policy involves liberalizing your own trade. Worse, preferences not only distract attention from sub-Saharan Africa's own liberalization, but have sometimes led commentators in the region to oppose other countries' liberalizations as a means to preserving sub-Saharan African preferences.

Third, the various quantitative limits, exclusions, and tight rules of origin that we have noted above not only reduce the average depth of preferences but do so in a quite perverse fashion. They apply mostly to sensitive items such as clothing, leather, and agricultural products, which, being relatively simple and labor-intensive, are the very goods in which one would expect developing countries to have comparative advantage. These are the products that one typically associates with the first steps in industrialization and development, and thus it appears that the system of preferences tilts relative prices, and hence resource allocation, in developing countries away from rather than toward the critical sectors for development. To our knowledge, no estimates exist of the extent of distortions such as these. However, de Melo and Winters (1990, 1993) study the related problem of the effects of VERs on certain developing countries' footwear exports and find that the costs arising from the distortion of the production structure can easily outweigh the benefits of the increased rents that are collected.

To summarize, the preferences granted to sub-Saharan African countries under the GSP and Lomé Convention seem to confer little benefit

[20]We do not say "with no costs," for other industries will suffer as resources are bid away from them into the preferred sectors.

on them.[21] They are not particularly deep quantitatively but to the extent that they are effective, they are probably perverse. To be sure, preferences transfer some tariff revenues from OECD taxpayers and other exporters to sub-Saharan African exporters, but they do so in ways that could subvert long-run development. They divert resources from critical sectors, create inefficiencies, encourage rentseeking rather than productive investment, and undermine incentives for trade liberalization.

This analysis of the difficulties created by preferences throws the previous sections into perspective. Both on positive grounds (because preferences are not particularly deep), and on normative grounds (because they are probably harmful in the long run), the sub-Saharan African countries should turn away from the GSP and Lomé and focus instead on their partners' MFN tariffs and NTBs. They should ask how these barriers affect their development aspirations and whether they are amenable to negotiation. Those are the tasks initiated in the previous two sections.

Conclusions

Our conclusions are very simple:

- Sub-Saharan Africa's small size economically and the generalized nature of its decline in competitiveness mean that attempts to improve its performance should not unduly disturb other members of the world economy.
- Openness and liberal trade policies are associated with higher exports and economic growth. Sub-Saharan African countries are mostly closed, and one of their top priorities should be to open up. With some (important) identifiable exceptions, African exports are not disproportionately restricted in OECD markets.
- Sub-Saharan African countries won fewer concessions in the Uruguay Round than did other developing countries—possibly because they seem to have offered fewer. Nonetheless, they still emerged from the round facing fewer or lower restrictions than other developing countries.
- In the next round of trade negotiations, sub-Saharan African countries have some rights to negotiate (according to GATT-WTO traditions) and a little leverage. They should be active in this

[21]In spite of more than two decades of Lomé preferences, the ACP countries have generally failed to diversify and have even been unable to maintain their share of the EU market, which has fallen from 6.7 percent in 1976 to 3.4 percent in 1994. Meanwhile, some less preferred developing countries have actually gained market share.

Figure 1. The Simple Analytics of Preferences

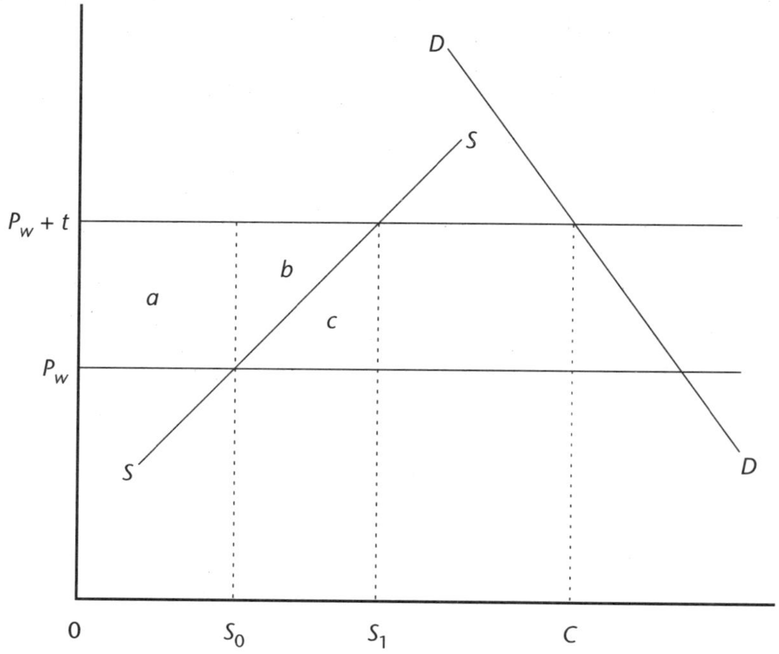

round, both giving and requesting concessions, and economists should help them to prepare the ground.

- Preferences are not the route to integrating with the world economy.

Appendix: The Simple Analytics of Preferences

Consider the market—in, say, the EU—for a single good supplied by imports from two sources (see Figure 1): a sub-Saharan African country with supply curve *SS* and the rest of the world (*RoW*), which is large enough to have a horizontal supply curve at price P_w. If the EU levies a tariff *t* on both suppliers and has demand curve *DD*, consumption *C* is met by imports OS_o from sub-Saharan Africa and $(C - S_o)$ from *RoW*. Now exempt sub-Saharan Africa from the tariff. Since imports from *RoW* continue, the EU's internal price remains $(P_w + t)$, but now the whole of this price accrues to the sub-Saharan African exporters rather than, as previously, just P_w with *t* going to the EU authorities. That is, sub-Saharan African exporters receive a higher price.

On exports OS_0, this is pure rent, amounting to area *a*. In addition, however, sub-Saharan African exporters can now afford to increase their exports to S_1, diverting an equivalent amount of imports from *RoW*. The extra exports drive up sub-Saharan Africa's marginal costs to $P_w + t$, above the efficient level in the absence of preferences. Total cost increases by *c* and producer surplus increases by *b*—both at the expense of EU taxpayers, who would otherwise have received $(b + c)$ in tariff revenue—and the sub-Saharan African export industry has now expanded beyond its sustainable level.

References

Amjadi, A., U. Reincke, and A.J. Yeats, 1996, "Did External Barriers Cause the Marginalization of Sub-Saharan Africa in World Trade?" Discussion Paper No. 348 (Washington: World Bank).

Amjadi, A., and A.J. Yeats, 1995a, "Have Transport Costs Contributed to the Relative Decline of Sub-Saharan African Exports?" Policy Research Working Paper No. 1559 (Washington: World Bank).

———, 1995b, "Nontariff Barriers Africa Faces: What Did the Uruguay Round Accomplish and What Remains to Be Done?" Policy Research Working Paper No. 1439 (Washington: World Bank).

Blackhurst, R., A. Enders, and J. François, 1996, "The Uruguay Round and Market Access: Opportunities and Challenges for Developing Countries," in *The Uruguay Round and Developing Countries,* ed. by W. Martin and L.A. Winters (Cambridge: Cambridge University Press).

Dam, K., 1970, *The GATT: Law and the International Economic Organisation* (Chicago: Univesity of Chicago Press).

de Melo, J., and L.A. Winters, 1990, "Voluntary Export Restraints and Resource Allocation in Exporting Countries," *World Bank Economic Review,* Vol. 4, No. 2, pp. 209–33.

———, 1993, "Do Exporters Gain from Voluntary Export Restraints?" *European Economic Review,* Vol. 37, No. 7, pp. 1331–50.

Dollar, D., 1992, "Outward-Oriented Developing Economies Really Do Grow More Rapidly: Evidence from 95 LDCs, 1976–1985," *Economic Development and Cultural Change,* Vol. 40, pp. 321–44.

Finger, J.M., 1979, "Trade Liberalisation: A Public Choice Perspective," in *Challenges to a Liberal International Economic Order,* ed. by R.C. Amacher, G. Haberler, and T.D. Willett (Washington: American Enterprise Institute).

———, M. Ingco, and U. Reincke, 1996, *The Uruguay Round: Statistics on Tariff Concessions Given and Received* (Washington: World Bank).

———, and L.A. Winters, 1998, "What Can the WTO Do for Developing Countries?" in *The World Trade Organization as an International Institution,* ed. by A.O. Krueger (Chicago: University of Chicago Press).

Harrison, G.W., T.F. Rutherford, and T.F. Tarr, 1997, "Quantifying the Uruguay Round," *Economic Journal*, Vol. 107, No. 444, pp. 1405–30.

Johnson, H.G., 1967, *Economic Policies Towards Less Developed Countries* (London: Allen and Unwin).

Martin, W. and L.A. Winters, eds., 1996, *The Uruguay Round and the Developing Countries* (Cambridge: Cambridge University Press).

Nash, J., and F. Foroutan, forthcoming, *Trade Policy and Exchange Rate Reform in Sub-Saharan Africa* (Canberra: Australian National University Press).

Ng, F., and A.J. Yeats, 1996, "Open Economies Work Better: Did Africa's Protectionist Policies Cause Its Marginalization in World Trade?" Policy Research Working Paper No. 1636 (Washington: World Bank).

Oyejide, T.A., B.J. Ndulu, and J.W. Gunning, 1997, *Country Case Studies of Trade Liberalisation: Introduction and Overview* (London: Macmillan).

Sachs, J., and A. Warner, 1995, "Economic Reform and the Process of Global Integration," *Brookings Papers on Economic Activity*: 1 (Washington: Brookings Institution).

UNCTAD (United Nations Conference on Trade and Development), 1994, *Review of the Implementation, Maintenance, Improvement and Utilization of the Generalized System of Preferences* (Geneva: UNCTAD).

Weston, A., 1995, *The Uruguay Round: Costs and Compensation for Developing Countries* (Geneva: United Nations Conference on Trade and Development).

Winters, L.A., 1987, "Reciprocity," in *The Uruguay Round: A Handbook for the Multilateral Trade Negotiations*, ed. by J.M. Finger and A. Olechowski (Washington: World Bank).

World Bank, 1994, *Adjustment in Africa: Reforms, Results, and the Road Ahead* (New York: Oxford University Press).

———, 1996, *Global Economic Prospects* (Washington: World Bank).

———, 1997, *World Development Indicators 1997* (Washington: World Bank).

Yeats, A.J., 1997a, "Implications of the Quality of African Trade Statistics for the Formulation of Effective Regional Integration and Trade Policies," paper prepared for the Economic Commission for Africa's meeting of African Trade Ministers, Abidjan, May.

———, 1997b, "Multilateral Aspects of Africa's Trade Policies and Performance," paper prepared for Economic Commission for Africa's meeting of African Ministers of Trade, Abidjan, May.

Trade and Growth in Sub-Saharan Africa 9

Benno J. Ndulu and Njuguna S. Ndung'u

The relationship between trade and growth has occupied the development debate for a protracted period. Indeed, the vigor and interest characterizing the debate reflect both its perceived importance and continued elusiveness in settling the main contentious issues on the theoretical and empirical fronts. What appears to be gaining wide acceptance from cross-country evidence is that those developing countries that have been most successful in pursuing growth are also the ones that have taken most advantage of trade opportunities. These countries have experienced high rates of economic growth in the context of rapidly expanding exports and imports. The converse is that countries that have rigidly stuck to import substitution policies and maintained barriers to export have lagged behind. At least this is the long-term association that has been supported by a large range of cross-country studies including Edwards (1993), Tanzi (1995), Sachs and Warner (1995, 1997), and Papageorgiou, Michaely, and Choksi (1991). What is far less clear is the extent to which trade and trade policies have played a causal role, rather than being a facilitator of other more fundamental factors of growth (Rodrik, 1997).

Two significant observations have been made concerning sub-Saharan Africa's trade and growth performance. One is that sub-Saharan Africa is increasingly being marginalized in world trade, as is evident from the decline of its share in world trade from 3 percent during the mid-1950s to the current 1 percent (Yeats and others, 1997). This marginalization in trade is blamed variously on the closedness of trade regimes (Sachs and Warner, 1995, 1997), the fact that the region's economies have become more inward-looking at the same time the rest of the world is integrating into the world economy (Collier, 1995) and persistence of structural and trade policies that militate against international competitiveness (Yeats and others, 1997). A rather important

The authors acknowledge research assistance from Radha Ruparel. They also thank Peter Montiel, Lawrence Harris, and participants in the seminar on which this book is based for useful insights and comments on the earlier draft of this chapter. They, however, remain responsible for any errors and omissions.

finding in this regard is that by Rodrik (1997), which shows that the relatively slow growth of Africa's GDP more than anything else explains the marginalization of the region in world trade. In an analysis that assesses Africa's trade orientation status, vis-à-vis the region's size (population), income per capita, and distance to the world's leading trading nations, he finds that Africa trades as much as is to be expected given its geography and the level of income per capita; that is, it lies on the regression line. East Asia trades more than expected, while Latin America trades less. This is not to downplay the importance of trade policy, which he finds significant in explaining ratios of trade to GDP, but the finding underscores his earlier assertion that the other factors influencing growth augur well for trade performance.

Further information on sub-Saharan Africa's trade performance can be gleaned from Figures 1 through 8. For the period 1970–94, export shares and import shares in GDP for 45 sub-Saharan African countries averaged 22 and 32 percent, respectively, compared with a sample of 99 developing countries as a group. The dispersion of performance among African countries is also very large, ranging from 3 to 60 percent for export shares and 8 to 114 percent for import shares (Figures 1 and 2). What is also revealing is the fact that the regional average trade performance relative to its output did not register as steep a decline over time, in contrast to its share in world trade. In this respect, the decline of export share during 1970–79 and 1990–94 was by approximately 10 percent (Figure 5), import shares remained more or less constant (Figure 6), while that of the share in world trade was much steeper as pointed out earlier. The gap with East Asia's performance is however much more. One obvious conclusion from the above is that even if Africa's shares of trade in GDP had remained constant over time, the fact that its output growth was much lower than that of other developing countries (see Figures 3 and 7) would still have resulted into the region's marginalization in world trade. The reasons behind the much slower export growth relative to other countries or regions should be the focus on the link between openness as more broadly defined and growth rather than the trade shares per se.

The second observation, which has been more forcefully made recently, is that the most significant factor behind the slow growth performance of sub-Saharan Africa is a lack of openness to trade, which constrains the region from exploiting opportunities to trade and stifles efficiency and technological progress associated with engaging in open trade (Sachs and Warner, 1997). This observation borders causality rather than the more modest association which other cross-country

(*Text continues on page 245.*)

Figure 1. Sub-Saharan African Countries' Percentage Shares of Exports in Gross Domestic Product

(Percent)

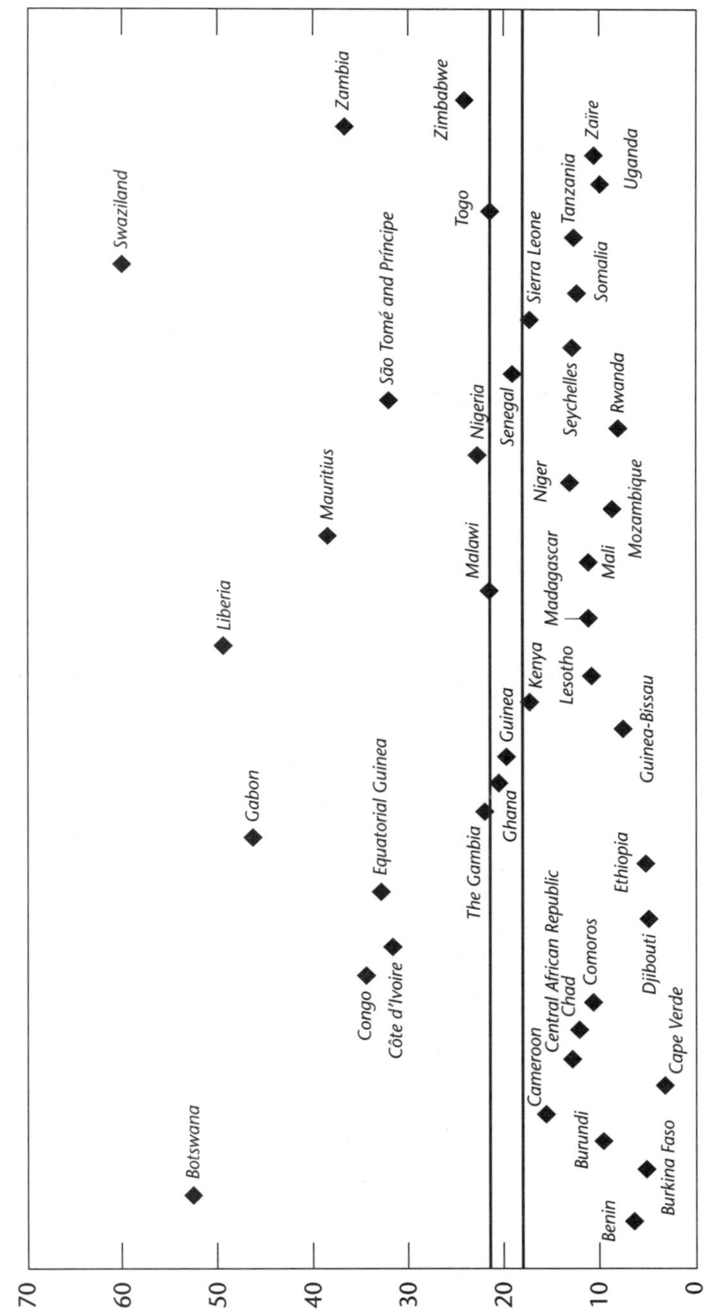

Note: Mean is 22 percent; median is 18 percent. The variable plotted is *XGDP*.

Figure 2. Sub-Saharan African Countries' Percentage Shares of Imports in Gross Domestic Product

(Percent)

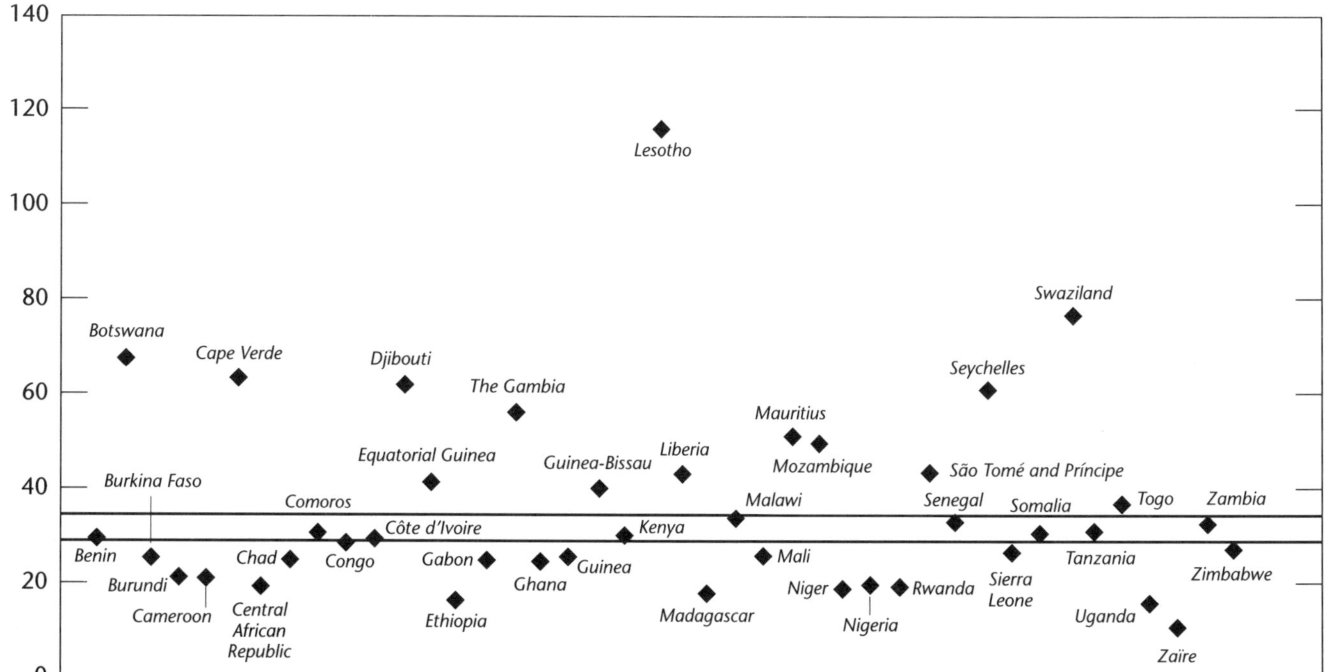

Note: Mean is 32 percent; median is 25 percent. The variable plotted is *MGDP*.

Figure 3. Sub-Saharan African Countries' Percentage Growth of Real Gross Domestic Product

(Percent)

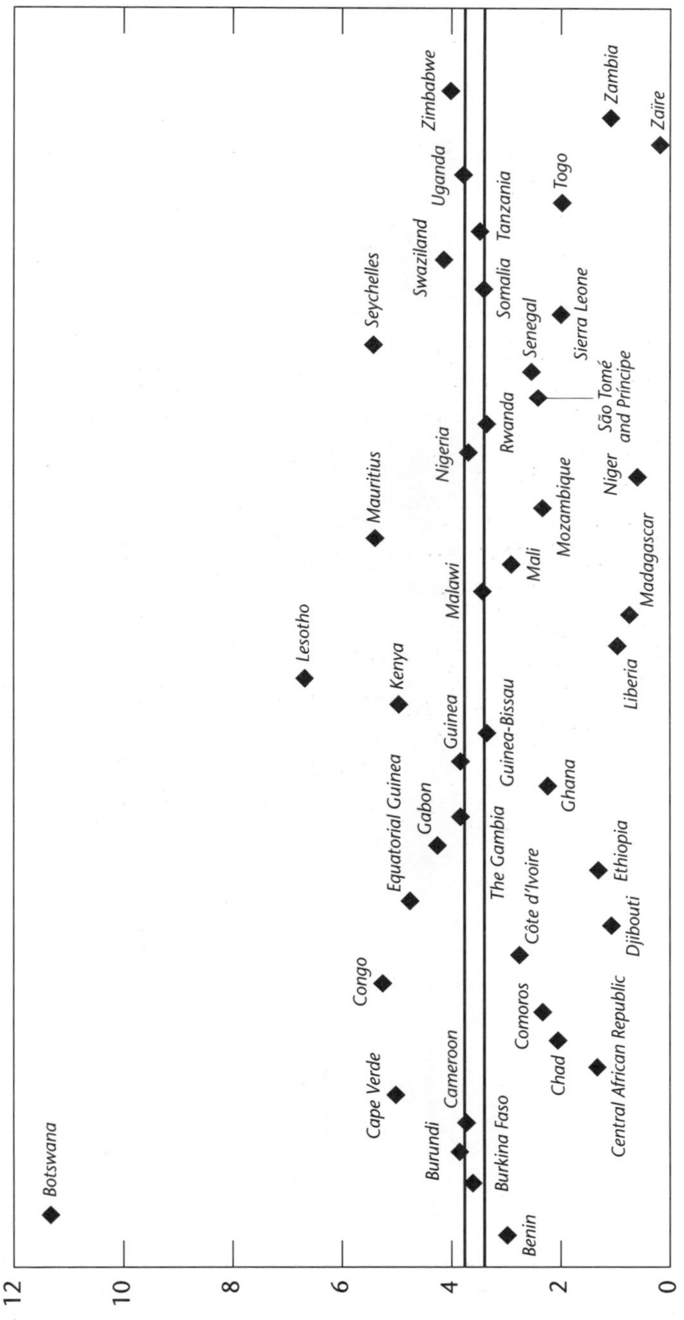

Note: Mean is 3.8 percent; median is 3.6 percent. The variable plotted is *RGDPGR*.

Figure 4. Sub-Saharan African Countries' Percentage Growth of Exports

(Percent)

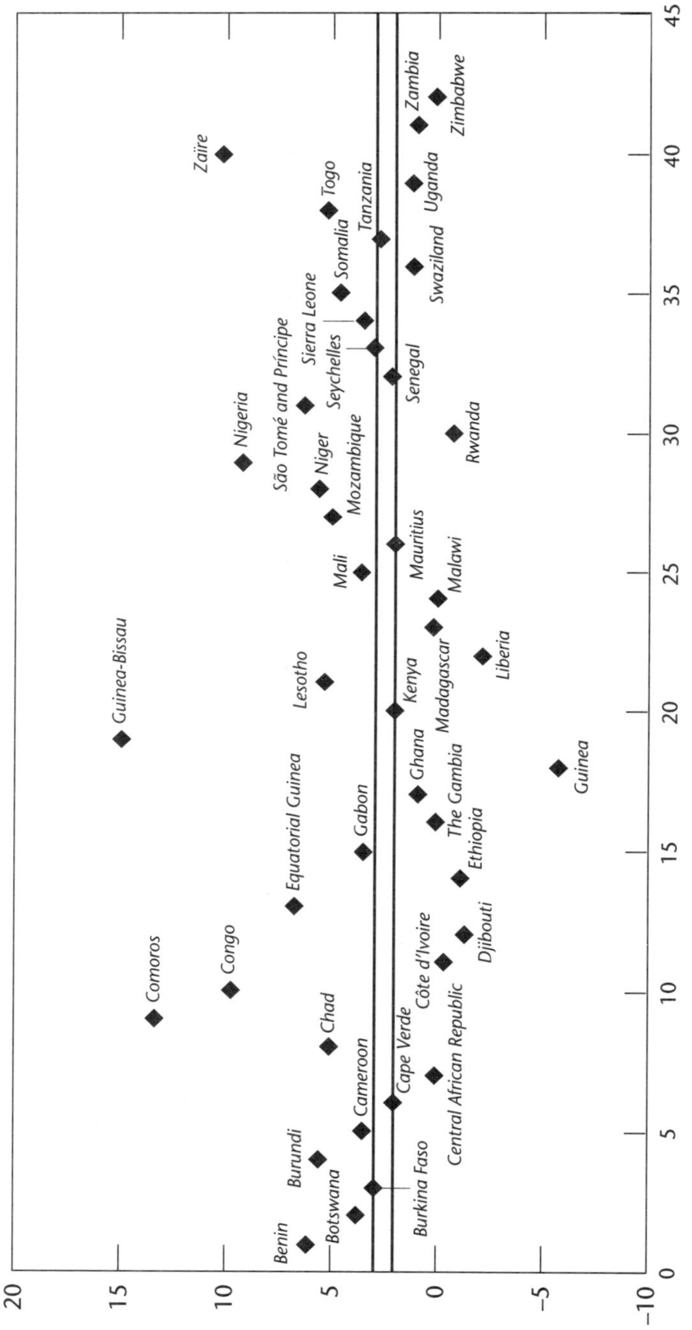

Note: Mean is 3.0 percent; median is 2.7 percent. The variable plotted is *XGDPGR*.

Figure 5. Comparative Percentage Shares of Exports in Gross Domestic Product for Sub-Saharan Africa, Selected Periods

(Percent)

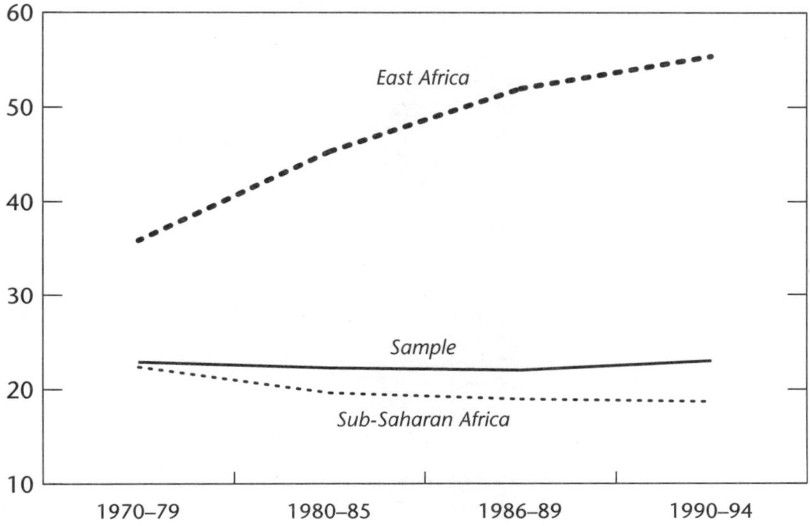

Note: The variable plotted is *XGDP*.

studies pose. In fact, Sachs and Warner conclude from their empirical analysis based on counterfactuals that, if African countries had pursued greater openness (say at East Asia's level) between 1965 and 1995, they would on average have achieved an extra 1.4 percentage points in per capita income growth, which significantly exceeds the actual average of 0.9 percent for the same period. The fundamental policies singled out in this respect are keeping tariffs on imports at less than 40 percent, black market exchange rate premiums at less than 20 percent, average quota and licensing coverage on imports at less than 40 percent and ridding the economies on extreme controls on exports—via trading monopolies. The other study, which took a similar approach to explaining growth performance focusing on trade-influencing factors, is that by Rodrik (1997). Using an Africa-only sample, he finds that trade policies played a much smaller role in long-term growth performance but exert a much more significant influence in the medium term. Wide variations across countries are discerned in sources of growth decomposition for each country, underscoring the caution against generalizations. What is also different in this study is that the

Figure 6. Comparative Percentage Shares of Imports in Gross Domestic Product for Sub-Saharan Africa, Selected Periods

(Percent)

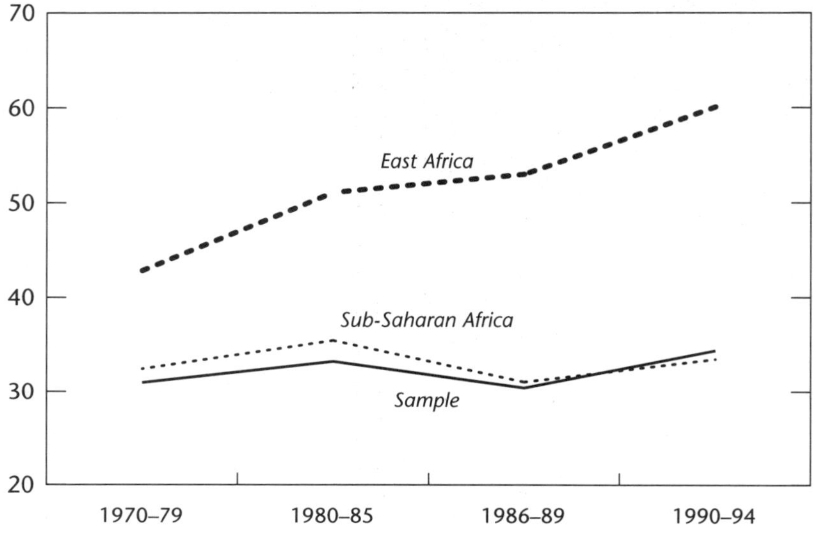

Note: The variable plotted is *MGDP*.

individual components of trade-affecting policies were decomposed, allowing distinct channels of influence on growth to be assessed.

In light of the above observations, this chapter will focus on four dimensions in explaining the relationship between trade and growth in sub-Saharan Africa. The first is to determine what explains trade performance in sub-Saharan African countries. We do this by identifying the key policy and nonpolicy factors that influence trade shares. This is supplemented by a review of recent trade liberalization experience in the region to seek an understanding of motivation behind it, the extent to which it has taken place, and in what forms.

Second is to separate between what we consider to be experiences of trade policy "proper" (for example, trade taxes) and endogenous trade policy measures (for example, quantitative restrictions and policies governing exchange) with the view to establishing the relative impacts of these on growth. The contention here is that endogenous trade policy dominates the out-turn of trade openness and therefore affects growth. This is particularly so when one considers the fact that actual trade taxes applied (revenue from taxes and the tax base) are much lower than statutory levels on account of exemptions offered, particu-

Figure 7. Comparative Percentage Growth Rates of Gross Domestic Product in Sub-Saharan Africa, Selected Periods

(Percent)

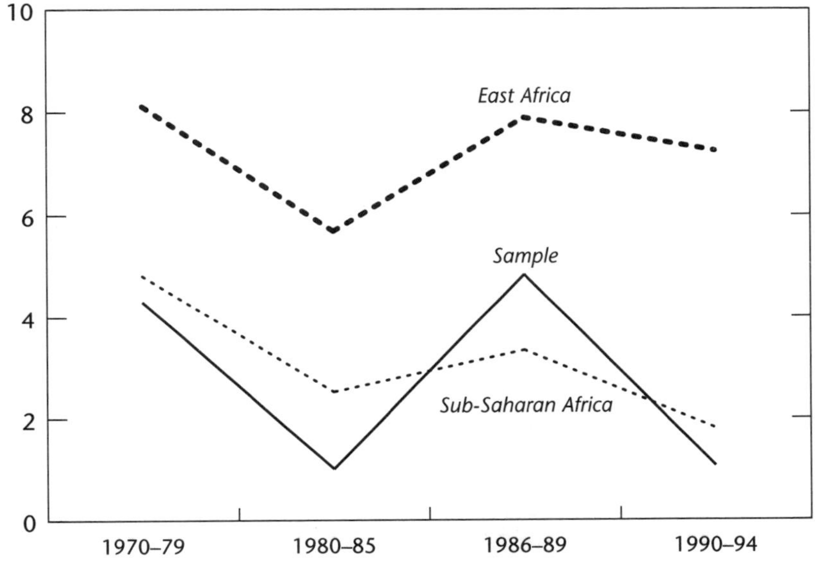

Note: The variable plotted is *RGDPR*.

larly to the dominant importer—the public sector and imports for projects funded by official development assistance and sweeteners provided to investors. The bulk of these exemptions are statutory, and therefore they can be anticipated.

The third area we focus on is the transmission channels from trade openness to growth, by distinguishing to the extent possible the separate effects of import liberalization, export promotion, and the liberalization of exchange regimes. The weights and intensity of application of these vary significantly across countries and over time to enable us to distinguish their impacts. In addition, we consider the technological enhancement impact of openness by incorporating the interaction between trade and FDI as a vehicle for technological diffusion.

The fourth area concerns bringing out the dynamics between trade and trade policies and growth in the medium term, using panel data analysis. We consider this to be the closest approximation of intertemporal country specificity in the context of cross-country studies, and it allows us to obtain some insights on medium-term growth effects to add to the bulk of the literature, which focuses on the long-term growth effects of trade openness. In carrying out this analysis, we exercise caution because

Figure 8. Comparative Percentage Growth Rates of Exports in Sub-Saharan Africa, Selected Countries

(Percent)

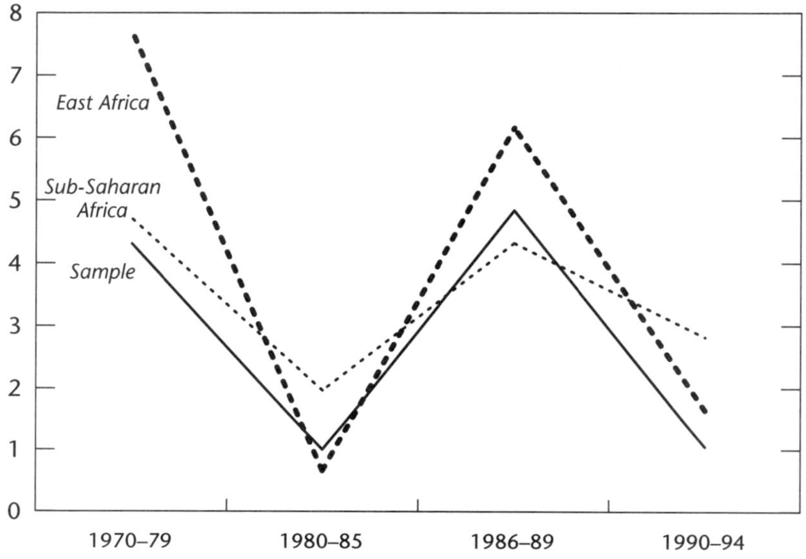

Note: The variable plotted is *XGDPGR*.

trade openness and growth influence each other in both directions and hence require that we check for simultaneity in the relationship.

The second section will review the wisdom from the literature on the influence of openness on growth. In the third section, we review recent experience with trade liberalization in sub-Saharan Africa to establish whether or not it has occurred and in what form, and to highlight the potential channels of influence on growth. In doing so, we are mindful of the fact that a large number of studies on this issue focusing on sub-Saharan Africa have typically not covered the more recent period (post-1990), when more intensive trade liberalization efforts were made and therefore may have missed the fine points of the process of liberalization since the late 1980s. The fourth section presents the conceptual framework and empirical analysis of the relationship between trade and growth in sub-Saharan Africa. It reviews the empirical findings and draws conclusions from them. This includes pursuing (in the empirical analysis) the relative importance of openness to explain Africa's growth, as well as revisiting what we conjectured in the previous sections to draw out policy wisdom in light of the findings. The fifth section briefly concludes.

Linking Trade and Growth: What the Literature Tells Us

Edwards (1993) provides a comprehensive review of the key issues and empirical evidence on the link between trade and growth in developing countries. What is particularly notable from this review is the continuing difficulties in obtaining reliable measures of trade policy and identifying more precisely the channels through which outward orientation facilitates growth. The difficulties also relate to assigning relative importance to trade policy reforms in comparison with consistent macroeconomic policy reforms and investment strategies in explaining growth performance. Furthermore, what complicates matters even more is the fact that some trade policy measures such as quantitative restrictions have been applied for both protective purposes (trade function) and for balance of payments purposes (protecting reserves).

Import substitution strategy was widely embraced by developing countries during the 1960s and 1970s following the influential thoughts of Prebisch and Singer in the 1950s, which propagated protection as a means to industrial development. Its critique rested on the now well accepted assertion that excessive protection of local industry stifled productivity growth, encouraged inefficient industrialization at the expense of agriculture and exports, reduced savings, increased unemployment, and led to very low rates of capacity utilization. The critique began with Little, Scitovsky, and Scott (1970) and was continued by Papageorgiou, Michaely, and Choksi (1991).

The same critics and other more recent studies (e.g., Sachs and Warner, 1997) have instead strongly advocated openness to international trade and finance complemented by consistent macroeconomic policies as the key to successful export-led industrialization and rapid growth. East Asia's phenomenal success in this regard is the centerpiece of evidence based on country experiences, and more recently evidence from cross-country growth regressions identified trade openness to be a critical explanatory factor. We mentioned above that most recent of these cross-country studies as applied to explaining African growth performance to be those by Sachs and Warner (1997) and Collier and Gunning (1997) and Rodrik (1997). The first two studies place trade openness at the top of explaining the slow growth performance of the region. Rodrik finds that a small number of variables—country size, per capita income, geography, and taxation of trade—explains 82 percent of variations in trade shares. Furthermore, Sachs and Warner (1997) find openness to trade to be the single most important influence on long-term growth in Africa, while Rodrik (1997) finds openness to trade as measured by the Sachs and Warner index to be a strong determinant of African growth only in the medium term, using an Africa-only sample (p. 21). In Rodrik's long-term growth equation (again for Africa only), the trade variable that enters with statistical significance is export taxation. Using a sources-of-growth decomposition for the 31 countries included in the regression, Rodrik finds that export taxation did play a more significant role in explaining the growth performance of worst performers.

It is instructive to note that earlier studies focused on searching for evidence by estimating impacts of liberalized trade regimes (with neutrality as the desired state) on export growth, and in turn linked export growth to overall growth of output and employment, thus claiming an indirect causation. This effort proved less successful because empirical evidence linking export and overall growth was rather weak. A few others (for example, Feder, 1983) added the impact of higher productivity of the export sector growth on overall growth via externalities and productivity differential effects with a little more empirical success. Yet others, Esfahami (1991) and Helleiner (1990), sought the link between export-growth and economywide growth through the role of export earnings in alleviating the foreign exchange constraint to imports in the context of import compression, which held back expansion in production and investment, also with some empirical success. The main argument here is that, given the imperfect substitution between imported and home goods, a cut in capital and intermediate goods imports will result in a reduction of real activity and growth (Khan and Knight, 1988; Ndulu, 1986, 1991). Since import capacity has been found to be a relatively more important determinant of imports under a foreign exchange constraint than relative prices (Moran, 1990), overall growth performance, and for that matter export growth, will be stimulated by relaxing this constraint.

We can distinguish three key channels of influence from trade to growth drawing from the foregoing. The first is that of *efficiency-enhancing advantages of a more open trade regime*. These relate, on the one hand, to enhanced competitive environment, and on the other to improved access to better technology. They operate through productivity growth resulting from more efficient allocation of resources, exploitation of comparative advantage and scale economies, and improved technological competence. Foreign competition undermines local monopolies and weeds out inefficient local producers. Transitional costs of de-industrialization may be high, but these are quickly compensated by the growth of new and restructured enterprises, and the expanded market opportunities that a liberalized trade regime offers. A more open trade regime also permits faster technological diffusion through improved access to a larger menu of innovation worldwide. The public nature of such innovation makes it possible to access new technology without typically incurring costs of developing it (Baldwin, 1996).

The second channel is linked to *improved incentives for production of exportables and reduction of the high transactions costs associated with import barriers*. Barriers to imports for protection of local industries are effectively a tax on exports because they raise the domestic resource costs for exports and lead to the appreciation of the real exchange rate, thereby reducing international competitiveness and incentives to export (De Rosa, 1990). Rodrik (1997) further confirms this assertion by empirical results, which show that barriers to imports adversely affect exports in Africa. We show below that import expansion has a residual positive impact on growth, though it is weak.

Improved availability and choice of consumer goods, particularly those considered as incentive goods, which is permitted by import liberalization, plays an important role in enhancing production of the self-employed, the majority of whom are engaged in agriculture. Long periods of frustrated consumer demand were associated with shortages occasioned by quantitative restrictions, which were strongly biased against consumer goods in many African countries. These restrictions were applied in a bid to cope with foreign exchange shortages and were implemented mainly through administrative allocation of the scarce foreign exchange. Import liberalization also reduces enterprise and trade transactions costs associated with measures to circumvent controls, thus incurring additional costs of underground trade, and costs associated with maintaining excessive inventories to avoid production and trade disruptions due to uncertainties linked to trade restrictions. The complexity of the tariff regime introduces opaqueness and uncertainty in business planning and has added to transactions costs associated with rents extorted by authorities through corruption practices.

The third channel relates to *reducing explicit and implicit barriers to export or outward orientation of production*. Explicit barriers here are export taxes, which reduce the profitability of exports and bias the production structure toward nontradables. We did refer above to import barriers being an implicit tax on exports. Other forms of implicit taxation are excessive margins exacted by marketing intermediaries and exchange controls, which for a protracted period forced African exporters to surrender their export proceeds at grossly overvalued exchange rates, thus reducing profit margins when measured in local currency terms. The parallel market exchange rate premium in a sense thus measures the extent of taxation of exports by way of transfer of incomes to the authorities (Pinto, 1989). Dismantling of marketing monopolies and the freeing up of exchange regimes are thus important avenues for raising the profitability of export activities and encouraging outward-orientation of production structures.

There is, however, one important qualification we wish to raise here regarding the effect of import liberalization on growth. A rise in imports is effectively a leakage of aggregate demand and thus (through the Keynesian multiplier) will lead to a short-run reduction in aggregate output. Depending on whether the positive supply-side effects of import liberalization discussed above exceed this negative effect, the net effect of a rise in import share in the short run may thus be ambiguous. This qualification may be particularly important in the case where annual panel data analysis of growth determinants is applied.

A Review of Trade Policy Experience

Preliberalization Trade Policy Stance

For a period of nearly three decades after independence, African countries mounted high trade barriers for three main purposes. The first was to provide protection to infant industries under the widely adopted ISI strategy. High and complex tariff walls, import controls, subsidies via controlled interest rates, and overvalued currencies were among the main instruments applied for the purpose. These were supplemented by trade confinement to public entities covering a wide range of import substitutes and "no objection" certificates for controlling importation of competing goods.

The second purpose was revenue generation. External trade taxes were and continue to be a significant source of government revenue.[1] Import and export duties were raised from year to year to meet budgetary gaps in a scenario of rapidly rising public expenditures. This financing strategy was adopted notwithstanding the fact that there is little if any correlation between high tariff rates and actual revenue collection (Pritchett and Sethi, 1994). As a consequence of frequent annual changes of tariffs to meet revenue shortfalls, large variations in the levels and structure of trade taxes ensued. To a significant extent, this phenomenon was to account partly for frequent reversals of trade liberalization episodes in the future.

[1]Recent research shows that the share of trade taxes in total revenue for African countries ranged from 4 to 52 percent in 1992.

Third, import controls and exchange controls were also used for managing foreign exchange reserves, particularly during periods of balance of payments crises. With exchange rates kept virtually fixed before the period of reforms, this approach to balance of payments management was widely applied. Tightening of import restrictions and exchange controls during crises is widely documented by an AERC study involving 10 country cases (see Oyejide, Ndulu, and Gunning, 1996).

There are two important qualifications to this general scenario of high trade barriers. Large tax exemptions, particularly for public entities and donor-funded projects, significantly lowered effective tariffs. This was done partly to provide further support to import substitution industrialization dominated by public enterprises. As a consequence, a wide gap between scheduled and effective tariffs ensued. Although effective tariff rates in sub-Saharan African countries were higher than in other developing regions, they were not too different from those in Latin America, for example. Table 1 presents a comparison of effective tariff and non-tariff measures applied in a selected number of African countries with a selection of countries from Latin America and East Asia based on data presented in Rodrik (1997). The differences with Latin America particularly since mid-1980 is negligible. There are larger differences, however, in the coverage of nontariff measures of nearly 25 percent for all product categories. This difference is larger for manufactured products pointing to higher trade barriers linked to ISI. One important observation from the table is that of the overall decline in effective import tariff rates from its peak of 32.8 percent during 1980–83 to 22.5 percent associated with the early import liberalization measures in the sample of countries included. We will return to this phenomenon in greater detail later below.

A second qualification relates to partial compensatory measures to correct for anti-export bias resulting from import barriers and exchange controls. These were offered in the forms of cash grants to exporters, export subsidies, foreign exchange retention schemes, and tax rebates or duty drawbacks. The corrective measures reflected the inconsistencies in the ISI strategy. On the one hand, the strategy vastly expanded the demand for intermediate and capital goods imports, while on the other it stifled growth in import capacity through barriers to export. This approach to resolving the inconsistency of the strategy was largely not successful, even though it partially reduced the anti-export bias.

Trade Liberalization Experience

Much of the discussion below draws from the AERC study on trade liberalization experience in sub-Saharan Africa. The study involved in-

Table 1. Tariff and Nontariff Barriers in Selected African Countries

Sub-Saharan Africa	1980–83 13 countries	1984–87 13 countries	1988–90 10 countries
Primary products			
Weighted average tariffs (percent)	24.4	20.1	18.9
NTBs (coverage, in percent)		48.4	47.4
Manufactured products			
Weighted average tariffs (percent)	32.8	23.5	22.5
NTBs (coverage, in percent)		42.7	45.4
All product categories			
Weighted average tariffs (percent)	30.2	22.6	21.3
NTBs (coverage, in percent)		45.5	46.1
Latin America	**4 countries**	**11 countries**	**8 countries**
Primary products			
Weighted average tariffs (percent)	16.8	21.1	17.3
NTBs (coverage, in percent)		42.8	48.6
Manufactured products			
Weighted average tariffs (percent)	23.6	25.1	22.7
NTBs (coverage, in percent)		28.4	20.9
All product categories			
Weighted average tariffs (percent)	21.3	23.9	20.9
NTBs (coverage, in percent)		32.9	30.3
East Asia	**5 countries**	**7 countries**	**7 countries**
Primary products			
Weighted average tariffs (percent)	10.5	10.0	11.1
NTBs (coverage, in percent)		31.1	18.8
Manufactured products			
Weighted average tariffs (percent)	21.6	18.1	18.0
NTBs (coverage, in percent)			
All product categories			
Weighted average tariffs (percent)	18.2	15.8	15.7
NTBs (coverage, in percent)		25.6	11.8

Source: Rodrik (1997), Tables 4 and 5.

depth review of the experiences in 10 countries.[2] A synthesis of the experiences is contained in an overview paper by Oyejide, Ndulu, and Gunning (1996).

[2]These include Côte d'Ivoire, Ghana, Kenya, Mauritius, Nigeria, South Africa, Tanzania, Uganda, Zambia, and Zimbabwe.

Although all of these 10 countries have had episodes of sporadic trade liberalization since the 1970s, the most consistent efforts occurred from the late 1980s. Previous attempts were linked either to commodity price booms, which relaxed foreign exchange constraints, or to attempts at compensating for anti-export barriers through subsidies or export promotional efforts. Most notable, however, was a drastic reduction of export taxes in a few countries during the early 1980s in response to the foreign exchange crunch that set in after the second oil crisis of 1979. These countries included Côte d'Ivoire, Kenya, and Tanzania.

The main stimuli for the more persistent liberalization episodes were twofold. The most important was conditionality imposed for gaining access to external finance under the structural adjustment programs. The policy required changes, and the associated benchmarks were set in the policy framework papers and sector lending programs. They invariably included import and export liberalization, related liberalization of domestic trade environment (particularly dismantling public trade monopolies and decontrol of prices) and liberalization of the payments systems. Import liberalization entailed reduction of tariff levels, compression of the tariff structure, and removal of import licensing. Export liberalization entailed further reduction of export taxes, removal of mandatory surrender requirements for export earnings, and simplification of export procedures. These measures were complemented by macroeconomic adjustment in the negotiated programs. Apart from freeing up the foreign exchange market, reduction of fiscal deficits and containment of monetary expansion were considered as consistent measures for sustaining liberalization. The typical sequence of action across the countries was tariffication of quantitative restrictions, removal of domestic trade barriers, and then reduction in tariff rates.

A second stimulus operating in different countries and at different points in time was "own initiative." Most significant among the cases studied is that of South Africa. Various policy reviews conducted between 1983 and 1993 led to an adoption of a new industrial strategy under a more neutral trade regime with tariffication of QRs and a simpler, more transparent tariff structure. Subsequent binding of lower tariff levels under GATT and negotiated free trade agreements consolidated these changes. Mauritius also pursued own initiatives, successfully focusing mainly on compensatory mechanisms to ameliorate the anti-export bias arising from ISI. Most notable among these measures was the setting up of export processing zones free of trade barriers. In other countries, the own initiatives were largely in the form of Own Funded Import Schemes, which served as launching pads for a more comprehensive subsequent liberalization under the adjustment programs (Kauffman and O'Connell, 1991).

The efforts and consequences of these liberalization measures can be gleaned from Table 2, which is borrowed from Oyejide, Ndulu, and Gunning (1996). It presents the most recent review of status of trade liberalization in sub-Saharan Africa, in a manner which consolidates measures, outcomes and impacts of liberalization. It uses five indicators to measure progress with liberalization: tariffication of QRs, payment liberalization, tariff liberalization, reducing effective rates of protection and export taxes. The link with policy accounts helps to map out attribution of changes in the indicators to policy actions. The impacts are assessed using changes in trade shares, output, employment and industrial efficiency. The table also evaluates the sustainability of liberalization through the number of reversals and whether they were partial or total. This is complemented by a forward-looking assessment of confidence in sustained liberalization by means of responses from a survey of industrial enterprises.

The following broad observations can be made from Table 2. In the 10 countries, quantitative restrictions have been completely or mostly tariffied. Coverage of import licensing is virtually nil in five of the countries for which data were provided. There has been a switch from long positive lists of permitted imports to very short negative lists of prohibited or luxurious items. This has been strengthened by a virtual abolition of exchange controls and complete liberalization of the current account transactions. Four out of five countries for which information was available have signed Article VIII with the IMF to bind this status.

Tariff structures in all the 10 countries have been compressed from the previous high number of more than 60 (for example, Mauritius) to a range of 3–6 categories. Duty rates (scheduled) have been significantly lowered, again virtually across all 10 countries. The reductions are from the maximum, ranging between 150 and 250 percent, down mostly to 30 to 50 percent. A few items remain above these levels. Protection levels (measured by effective rates of protection) likewise have been significantly reduced in 7 out of 10 countries. The individual case studies also present evidence showing significant movements toward more neutral trade regimes. The measurement applied in this regard was the ratio of domestic to world terms of trade, with neutrality implying nonexistence of wedges related to trade policies. This is partly confirmed by the steep decline in black market foreign exchange premiums, which typically reflect the size of the wedges between domestic and border prices of imports and foreign currency.

A critical concern from the review of these experiences pertains to the sustainability of these achievements in light of the fact that they have not

Table 2. Trade Liberalization in Sub-Saharan Africa, Selected Countries

Finding	Kenya	Uganda	Mauritius	Nigeria	Ghana	South Africa	Tanzania	Zambia	Côte d'Ivoire	Zimbabwe
Trade liberalization:										
Did trade liberalization take place?	Yes	Yes	Yes	Yes, very limited	Yes	Yes	Yes	Yes	Yes	Yes (limited)
Tariffication of QRs:	100	100	. . .	. . .	90	. . .	99	97	. . .	. . .
Exchange rate premium decline (percent)										
Imports covered by licensing										
Reduction (percent)	100	64	100	. . .	100	100	100	. . .	22	. . .
Payment liberalization: (reduction of exchange controls)?	Yes	Yes	Yes	Yes	Yes	Yes	Yes	Yes	. . .	. . .
Tariff liberalization?				Yes	Yes					
Reduction in tariffs (percent)	76	. . .	85	. . .	5–10 pts.	38	70	67	36	. . .
Tariff structure compression (percent)	76	. . .	85	. . .	. . .	41	70	50	44	. . .
Effective rates of protection:										
Reduction?	Yes	No	Yes	No	Yes	Yes	Yes	Yes	Yes	Yes
Percent	. . .	. . .	. . .	. . .	60	. . .	50	58	. . .	. . .
Export taxes:										
Reduction?	Yes	Yes	Yes	. . .	No	Yes	Yes	Yes	Yes	. . .
Percent	. . .	. . .	. . .	. . .	. . .	. . .	100	100	100	. . .

Table 2 (*concluded*)

Finding	Kenya	Uganda	Mauritius	Nigeria	Ghana	South Africa	Tanzania	Zambia	Côte d'Ivoire	Zimbabwe
Macroeconomic adjustment:										
Did macroeconomic adjustment accompany liberalization?										
Exchange rate depreciation:										
Depreciation (Nominal local)?	Yes	Yes	Yes	Yes	Yes	Yes	Yes	Yes	Yes	Yes
Foreign (percent)	364	436	45	80	1700	45	530	4800	100	165
Fiscal reform?	Yes	Yes	Yes	No	No	. . .	Yes	Yes	No	No
Reduction of deficit/GDP (percent)	. . .	. . .	. . .	–28	. . .	. . .	44	. . .	1	. . .
Impetus for liberalization:										
What was the impetus for liberalization?										
Positive commodity price shocks?	Yes	No	Yes	No	No	No	Yes	No	No	No
When?	1976/77						1976/77			
Commodity linked to reform?	Yes	Yes	Yes	Yes	Yes	No	Yes	Yes	Yes	Yes
Beginning when?	1980	1987	1979	1986	1983		1986	1983	1984	1990
Membership in a regional scheme?	Yes	Yes	No	No	No	No	Yes	Yes	No	Yes
Own initiative to better performance?	No	No	Yes	Yes	Yes	Yes	Yes	No	No	Yes
Impact of liberalization:										
What impact did liberalization have (+ or -) on:										
Imports (imports/GDP)*	38	123	35	–67	1088	min	*Real –4	*Real –36	–29	mix

Exports (exports/GDP)	62		946	min	723	min	26	–31	–14	+
Output (real GDP growth)	5	6.4	6	min	4	min	4.2	–1.1	. . .	3.4
Employment	+	min	33	min	. . .	min	. . .	. . .	. . .	18
Industrial efficiency	n.s.c.	. . .	. . .	. . .	. . .	. . .	+	. . .	. . .	. . .
Sustainability of liberalization: Was liberalization sustained?										
Number of episodes	7	3	2	4	2	3	4	2	3	4
Any reversals?	Yes	Yes	No	Yes	Yes	No	Yes	Yes	Yes	No
Were reversal partial (P) or total (T)?	P	. . .	. . .	T	P	P	P	P	P	. . .
Did survey results indicate confidence/ support for liberalization?	Yes	. . .	Yes	No	No	Yes	Yes	Yes	No	Yes

Source: Oyejide, Ndulu, and Gunning (1996).

Notes: Where information is not quantified, qualitative indicators are used, if available. This table summarizes the findings of the Regional Integration and Trade Liberalizaton Project. Abbreviations: min: negligible; mix: mixed; pts: percentage points on all imports except luxury goods; n.s.c: no significant correlation; *: nominal unless otherwise stated.

been bound. Although the majority of sub-Saharan African countries are signatories to the GATT, they have bound their tariffs at levels that are significantly above actual. The bound tariffs range from 15 to 280 percent against actual applied average rates ranging from 7 to 47 percent. Furthermore, the frequency of partial reversals noted in Table 2 shows that pressures for reversals abound. Oyejide, Ndulu, and Gunning (1996) make the following assessment of the sustainability of the trade liberalization in the 10 countries in relation to compatibility of macroeconomic policy stances: Exchange rate adjustment appears critical for ameliorating pressures of reversals. The large devaluations that accompanied trade liberalization partly reduced pressures from a potential excessive rise in import demand as liberalization proceeded. Furthermore, the higher revenues from trade taxes, associated with the large change in the valuation of the trade tax base in domestic currency terms, helped to stem potential fiscal problems resulting from the reduction in tariffs and hence pressure for reversal. Replacement of quantitative restrictions likewise helped to reduce potential fiscal pressures. Although in many countries trade reform has been accompanied by high real interest rates resulting from vastly increased government borrowing from the public, as yet there is no evidence that the resultant slowing down of investment, and hence resource reallocation expected from liberalization, has undermined credibility. It is nevertheless a source of concern if benefits from liberalization fail to materialize quickly. Support for it may wane. In 6 out of the 10 country cases, the support for liberalization was quite strong based on surveys of industrialists (see Table 2).

During the relatively short periods of trade liberalization in the case study countries, there has been generally a shift in the allocation of resources toward tradables and away from nontradables and import substitutes. Export orientation has increased, mainly due to a rise in the profitability of exports caused by real depreciation of local currencies and to a much smaller extent on account of trade policy changes. Although de-industrialization occurred as a result of opening up to competition, it appears that the growth of activity from surviving and new firms more than compensated for the collapsed ones.

For the African region as a whole, export growth is rebounding after nearly a decade of decline between mid-1970 and mid-1980. Export earnings grew at an average rate of 3.5 percent between 1986 and 1993 following various reform measures. During 1995 and 1996, a significant acceleration of export growth was achieved. Export earnings grew at an average rate of 8 percent during the 2 years, with half of this expansion attributed to an increased volume of exports (UNCTAD data). This may be the beginning of the more substantial response to the recent intensification of liberalization.

Relationship Between Trade and Growth

Framework of Analysis

This section presents some empirical assessments of the links between international trade and growth. The available literature relates trade regimes to export growth, and in turn export growth to income growth. This shows that there is a direct as well as an indirect link between trade regimes, export performance, and growth, but the direct link has been found to be weak. Part of the problems related to these results is the inherent simultaneity between export performance and growth. Furthermore, data are limited that would empirically help to account for the dynamism between trade performance, export composition, and export growth, on the one hand, and real income growth and the quality of this growth, on the other.

Whereas this section does not claim success in incorporating these shortcomings, it nevertheless starts by explaining the factors behind trade performance. This is accomplished by first estimating cross-country panel regressions for a group of countries that explains trade shares (export and import) in GDP. We estimate two equations for the trade shares, that is, export share and import share. In addition, we show estimates from a growth equation for the same group of countries. Furthermore, to take into account the simultaneity problem alluded to above, these three panel regressions are reestimated simultaneously using the full information maximum likelihood method and the results compared. We use these results to further show the impact effects in an attempt to assess the relative importance of the links between trade and growth.

The main question asked in the empirical analysis is what are the links between trade and growth for the group of countries in the sample for the period 1970–94. Can these links be empirically assessed? The transmission channels recognized in the literature include:

- Openness of the economy. This enhances the efficiency and overall effectiveness of macroeconomic policies and investment.
- Export-led growth, which tends to be more efficient beyond the openness argument. This is because export-based growth will bring in (1) technology transfer, (2) efficient allocation of resources due to international competition, and (3) cost-efficiency and related factors. These effects provide a further impetus to growth beyond what openness can provide, that is, there are dynamic multiplier effects.
- Through the real exchange rate as a policy tool for ensuring competitiveness and minimal price distortions.
- Alleviation of import constraints (foreign exchange supply constraints), which is necessary to ensure supply of intermediate and

capital goods to domestic firms. Import liberalization thus contributes to overall growth through reducing import supply constraints and reduces barriers to entry.

We recognize two further channels that may affect growth:

- Foreign exchange liberalization, where it has occurred, has helped to alleviate foreign exchange constraints. This builds up importing capacity and thus reduces import constraints.
- Quality of growth from export orientation brings with it export externalities, which are partly related to technological advancement, competitiveness, and productivity differential aspects.

To take these factors into account, we introduce in the estimated equations trade-related policies that influence or hamper trade. These include:

- Export taxes: these may be direct taxes levied on export or implicit in the form of real exchange rate misalignment.[3]
- Tariffs and nontariff barriers: exporters have to buy their inputs at higher than world prices but have to sell their goods at world prices. Thus there is a wedge between world and domestic prices of imports, while exports have to be traded at world prices. This is captured by import price index adjusted for domestic duties and real exchange rate misalignment.
- Macroeconomic stability: these are trade-related, in view of the fact that they affect investors (foreign and domestic) and thus technological development. Thus volatilities in macroeconomic variables and the outcome of the macroeconomic stance become crucial in directly and indirectly affecting export performance. For example, macroeconomic instability in general will be reflected by rising inflation domestically, which thus renders exports uncompetitive.
- Uncertainty in the future flow of foreign exchange leads to stockpiling of imports to hedge against future shortfalls. This encompasses wastage in the use of imported raw materials, and there is an element of overpricing. Thus there is a premium due to scarcity of foreign exchange. This leads to the distortionary effects discussed above and thus misalignment of the real exchange rate.

[3]The preferred measure here (if available) is the parallel market exchange rate premiums. This is because exporters download their foreign exchange earnings using the official rate but have to purchase their inputs in the market that includes the parallel market. However, in countries where liberalization has taken place, real exchange rate misalignment is adequate in capturing temporal deviations from the perceived real exchange rate equilibrium. However, data availability may constrain the choice to using a simple proxy of real exchange rate misalignment as a deviation from the average real exchange rate. This is what is used in the chapter.

- Finally, institutional variables are likely to be important in facilitating export and import activities.

These channels are, however, difficult to map out in an empirical exercise. This is because the relationship between export performance, alleviation of import constraints, and overall economic growth may provide direct as well as feedback effects. This may perhaps be captured by simultaneously estimating the three equations and may thus capture the dynamics among them that could otherwise not be possible in a single equation estimation. To take this into account, we first estimate panel regressions for trade shares and growth and then reestimate them simultaneously. The interdependencies between them will thus show up in a reduced number of regressors and the efficiency of the parameters left in the model.

Empirical Results

The results of the panel regression equation that take into account some of these links are shown in Table 3. The table shows the variables used in the first column, the export share equation in the second column, the import share equation in the third column and the real income growth equation in the fourth column. The appendix defines each of these variables.

In the export share equation, $EXPGDP_{t-1}$ is export share lagged one period. This variable captures the past performance of exports and hence constraints related to export bias. If export incentives are appropriate, then past export performance should be positively related to the current export level and should positively stimulate growth. This is because a successful export environment (culture) will simulate further export production, and this stimulates growth with important feedback effects. In the import share equation, the parallel to this is import to GDP lagged ($MGDP_{t-1}$), which stimulates import demand in line with past levels but shows that it is negatively related to growth. There are two competing effects here. One is on the demand side, where imports are seen as a leakage, and thus should be negatively related to growth. The other is on the supply side, where imports constraints are eased with liberalization coupled with efficiency gains. The effect of the latter influence should stimulate growth, and thus be positive. The results show that the leakage effect is stronger, but it is, however, not highly significant in the growth equation.

The second variable in the export share equation is *TOTSHK,* terms of trade shocks. They show that positive shocks have positive effects on exports, imports, and growth, but terms of trade (*TOT*) has a neg-

Table 3. Panel Regression Results (Random Effects Model)

Variable	Export Share Equation	Import Share Equation	Growth Equation
Constant		2.769 (4.536)	1.325 (1.56)
$EXPGDP_{t-1}$	0.0519 (4.031)		0.156 (2.75)
$MGDP_{t-1}$		0.0416 (3.206)	–0.039 (–0.689)
TOT			–0.126 (–7.68)
TOTSHK	0.0689 (5.728)	0.0556 (4.642)	0.387 (24.80)
XPI	0.0425 (7.26)		
MPITX		–0.000013 (–0.126)	
ΔRGDPGR	0.229 (11.778)	0.257 (13.323)	
$RGDPGR_{t-1}$	0.511 (27.242)	0.517 (27.35)	0.265 (18.71)
RER	0.0572 (5.778)	0.0354 (4.629)	–0.047 (–4.57)
RERMIS	–0.049 (–4.11)		
$RERMIS_{t-1}$			–0.016 (–1.96)
FDIOPEN	0.0195 (2.247)		
XPODUTY	–0.0078 (–1.218)		
ICRGE	–0.0318 (–2.850)	–0.030 (–3.068)	
WARSSA	–0.078 (–3.94)	–0.0485 (–2.438)	
ΔDY	0.0431 (3.740)	0.054 (5.338)	–0.0027 (0.161)
GINV			0.620 (32.19)
LSCHOOL			0.017 (2.31)
INFVR			–0.097 (–8.56)
INF			0.171 (12.71)
DSX			–0.066 (–4.27)
GDPRR			–0.020 (–1.99)
R^2	0.820	0.813	0.82

Note: The figures in parentheses are the *t*-values.

ative effect on growth. The export price index (*XPI*) is positively related to export share. This is consistent with a theoretical prediction of a supply function. This is also supported by the results in the table. The next set of variables are lagged growth of real income ($RGDRGR_{t-1}$) and speed of this growth ($\Delta RGDCR$). These two variables are important in both import and export equation, and certainly lagged growth (or past growth performance) explains the observed current growth of incomes. This confirms the observed regularity in the literature that strong growth will stimulate the further growth in future and that a current recession may not stimulate future growth. We come back to this aspect when we look at the impact effects of these variables.

The next set of variables introduces trade-policy-related variables. These include real exchange rate (*RER*) and real exchange rate misalignment (*RERMIS*), as defined above. Real exchange rate depreciation stimulates export supply, while an appreciation stimulates import demand. The results also show that real exchange rate depreciation stimulates growth. In addition, there are tax variables that enter into the trade share equations. The first is computed from taxes on imports, (*MPITX*), which enters into the import demand equation with negative effect (though not statistically significant). The second is a direct tax on exports (*XPODUTY*),which deters exports, and the results corroborate with the expectations (even though they are not highly significant).

The next set of variables looks at the quality of institutions (*ICRGE*) and sudden disruptions due to civil unrest (*WARSSA*), which is an indicator of the number of civil wars crossed with a dummy for sub-Saharan Africa. These two variables are consistently negative for export supply and import demand equations but have no effect on the growth equation. This underscores the importance of institutions and political tensions in supporting or hampering trade.

The final variable that relates to the three panel regressions is the flow of external debt to GDP (ΔDY). This is the first difference of the stock of the ratio of external debt to GDP. This should be positive because it reflects some aspect of financing (that is, official aid flows) and can thus be seen to alleviate foreign exchange constraints. The results support this view, but it is not significant in the growth equation. Even though external debt enters the model, and in first difference is not statistically significant, we have further included the crowding out effect of external debt that would work through investments to reduce growth. This is the debt service ratio (*DSX*), which is negative and highly significant in the growth equation. In addition, the export equation includes a proxy for the technological enhancement impact of openness, as argued in the introduction of this chapter. This is *FDIOPEN,* which is the ratio of foreign direct investment to GDP crossed with openness. This variable is positively related to export supply, which confirms the arguments put forward above. It is, however, not significant in the other equations.

We recognize the fact that growth is affected by other factors besides trade or openness to trade. For this reason, we have included a number of additional variables. They include gross investment (*GINV*), which is a sum of public and private investment rates and which is positively related to growth; human capital, which is proxied by *LSCHOOL,* the number of initial schooling years. This is in line with the recognition of human capital in endogenous growth models, and the regression results support this view.

The outcome of macroeconomic policies effect growth. To take this into account, we include inflation and its variability in the growth equation (*INF* and *INFVR*). Unstable macroeconomic policies are reflected by rising and volatile inflation, which retards growth, while moderate inflation would stimulate growth through revenues from a moderate inflation tax. It appears that the results confirm these links.

Finally, the neighborhood contagion effect is proxied by regional GDP (*GDPRR*), which is negatively related to growth and is significant. Overall, the panel regression results conform to the predictions. But a caution, as argued in the introductory section of the chapter, is that simultaneity may be a problem. To remedy this, we need to re-estimate the panel regressions simultaneously. We do this in full-information, maximum-likelihood estimation (*FIML*), and the results are shown in Table 4.

The variables in the *FIML* estimation were retained in the model as long as they were significant so that the results that emerged were achieved through a process of reduction.

The first thing to note in Table 4 is that the number of regressors is significantly reduced. This is consistent with the time series models where one starts with a large, overparameterized statistical model, and the reduction process ensures efficiency until a parsimonious model is achieved. The second thing to note from this table is that even though the number of regressors have been drastically reduced, the R^2 for these three equations has not significantly declined.

The results show that export success or success of export policy, reflected by lagged export share, is positively related to real income growth. Growth performance, both in terms of lagged performance and its speed, are an important drive to both export and import share equations as well as to the growth equation. Thus, a booming economy also promises growth in the future, so the observed growth level is also a function of past growth performance. The results in this table indicate that 31.4 percent of past growth performance is carried into the current growth record. This is an important stimulus to both trade shares, as well as growth with positive externality effects on all the three variables.

Notably, import share lagged neither affects growth nor its own equation. This is consistent with earlier argument on the net affect from both supply and demand sides. In this case, the import liberalization effect is picked up by growth feedbacks to the import equation.

The next set of variables is the real exchange rate and a dummy for civil war, which have maintained their significance and direction, except that now civil wars do not affect growth directly, but via disruptions of export supply and import demand. Changes in the ratio of external debt to GDP is consistently positive, just like before and is now significant in the growth equation.

From the *FIML* results, we note that trade policies affect imports and exports indirectly. This is because no trade policy variable effects are

Table 4. Regression Results: Trade Shares and Growth

Variable	Export Equation	Import Equation	Growth Equation
Constant	2.38 (1.16)	2.47 (1.26)	2.26 (2.12)
$EXPGDP_{t-1}$			0.0959 (9.79)
TOT			–0.120 (–12.38)
TOTSHK	0.046 (1.68)	0.0447 (1.55)	0.379 (36.59)
$\Delta RGDPGR$	0.268 (6.98)	0.264 (5.97)	
$RGDPGR_{t-1}$	0.495 (15.79)	0.500 (13.938)	0.314 (32.08)
RER	0.029 (1.33)	0.028 (1.14)	–0.057 (–4.35)
WARSSA	–0.071 (–2.302)	–0.0053 (–2.47)	
ΔDY	0.0667 (2.109)	0.067 (2.08)	0.030 (2.36)
GINV			0.470 (48.44)
LSCHOOL			0.021 (2.88)
INFVR			–0.117 (–11.18)
INF			0.166 (14.87)
DSX			–0.067 (–5.60)
R^2	0.795	0.794	0.787

Note: The results are a full-information, maximum-likelihood estimate. The figures in parentheses are *t*-values.

significant in the trade share equations. The results show that trade policy measures are indirect, and we can make three observations in relation to these results. First, trade matters to growth, but macrovariables like the real exchange rate have a strong influence on growth and then work indirectly to affect exports and imports. Second, gross investments, *GINV,* affects growth directly. But investments are usually affected by trade policies. Trade reforms affect investment by improving their profitability. Thus the effect of trade policy on growth is indirect and strong through the channel of investment. Finally, it should be noted that trade liberalization effects occur through capital formation and thus affect growth. These effects do not enter the production functions directly. This perhaps helps to explain why trade shares were not significantly affected by trade policy variables.

We next assess the relative importance of the explanatory variables in explaining sub-Saharan Africa's trade and growth performance by way of contrast with the sample as a whole and with East Asia in particular. The main question asked in these computations is what explains sub-Saharan African countries' trade performance relative to the overall sample of developing countries and the best performers in East Asia. To accomplish this, the sample means of the explanatory variables were computed and used together with the means for the sub-Saharan African and East Asian regions. We then use the regres-

Table 5. Comparative Assessment: Export Share Equation

Variable	Mean: Sample	Mean: Sub-Saharan Africa	Mean: East Asia	Coefficient	Sample Versus Sub-Saharan Africa	East Asia Versus Sub-Saharan Africa
TOTSHK	0.0059	0.0049	0.0338	0.046	0.0046	0.133
ΔRGDPGR	−0.0012	−0.0016	−0.00105	0.268	−0.0107	−0.0147
RGDPGR	0.0391	0.0343	0.0729	0.495	0.238	1.911
RER	0.9755	0.9549	0.9806	0.029	0.0597	0.0745
WARCIV	0.1816	0.1333	0.350	−0.071	−0.3429	−1.5385
DDY	0.0357	0.0498	0.0067	0.0667	−0.0941	−0.287
Overall differential					−0.1454	0.2783

sion coefficients of the respective variables from the *FIML* results to obtain the contribution of each variable in explaining the differential performance effects. In the computations, we subtract the sub-Saharan African mean of the variable from the sample mean (and East Asian means) and multiply by the coefficient from the regression results. The last two columns show the differential contribution effects from the sample and East Asia compared with sub-Saharan Africa, and the last row gives the overall contribution of the included variables to explaining the estimated difference.

These results have thus utilized the interdependence between the equations and the feedback effects. The results are shown in Table 5 for the export share equation, Table 6 for the import share equation, and Table 7 for the growth equation.

These tables show those variables that simultaneously determine trade shares and growth and also the lagged influence of export share on growth. The contributions are arrived at by multiplying the coefficient from the regression results in Table 4 and the difference between the mean of the variable in question, for sub-Saharan Africa and the overall sample of the 99 countries and the mean for East Asia. The results in these two tables are summarized by the respective last rows in Tables 5, 6, and 7.

A positive overall effect shows that sub-Saharan Africa performs worse than the sample average or the average for the East Asian countries. In all cases, when we use the trade shares equations, sub-Saharan Africa performs worse than East Asia and performs slightly better than the average countries in the sample. From these results, it appears that the driving force is real growth, which affects trade shares equally importantly.

Table 6. Comparative Assessment: Import Share Equation

Variable	Mean: Sample	Mean: Sub-Saharan Africa	Mean: East Asia	Coefficient	Sample Versus Sub-Saharan Africa	Asia Versus Sub-Saharan Africa
TOTSHK	0.0059	0.0049	0.0338	0.0447	0.0047	0.129
ΔRGDPGR	–0.0012	–0.0016	–0.00105	0.264	–0.0106	–0.0145
RGDPGR	0.0391	0.0343	0.0729	0.500	0.240	1.93
RER	0.9755	0.9549	0.9806	0.028	0.0577	0.0270
WARCIV	0.1816	0.1333	0.350	–0.0053	–0.0256	–0.1149
DDY	0.0357	0.0498	0.0067	0.067	–0.0945	–0.289
Overall differential					0.172	1.668

Table 7 shows the comparative assessment of growth performance for the two regions with sub-Saharan Africa with similar but this time stronger conclusions. Trade and trade policies affect growth, and growth in turn affects trade performance. This conclusion seems to support the observations made about the marginalization of sub-Saharan Africa in world trade and its poor output growth performance.

Although export shares affect growth, as we saw above, the feedback effects from growth to export are much stronger. The results, which seem to utilize the interdependences of the trade shares and real income growth, seem to point to the fact that output growth performance is key to the successful link between export and growth. The direct effects from trade and trade policies are not as strong as the growth impetus. This result is supported by the overall differential effect shown in Table 7. Sub-Saharan Africa is thus disadvantaged in the growth process, investment, and human capital, and this constrains export performance. This is shown in the differential effect to growth of 6.1 percent favoring the average countries in the sample.

We seem to arrive almost at a similar conclusion as Rodrik (1997), who argues that stimulating economic growth is the key to affecting other aspects that contribute to growth. This is in regard to the important contribution made to trade by successful stimulus from growth. But we qualify our results by utilizing the links we have outlined above and seek evidence from the results we have obtained in these two tables. In addition, we use the growth equation to assess the relative importance of factors contributing to growth and thus assess the role of trade in growth.

Table 7. Differential Effect Assessment: Growth Equation

Variable	Mean: Sample	Mean: Sub-Saharan Africa	Mean: East Asia	Coefficient	Sample Versus Sub-Saharan Africa	East Asia Versus Sub-Saharan Africa
$EXPGDP_{t-1}$	0.227	0.203	0.446	0.0959	0.230	2.100
TOT	0.778	0.775	0.757	–0.120	–0.036	0.252
TOTSHK	0.0059	0.0049	0.0338	0.379	0.0379	1.057
$RGDPGR_{t-1}$	0.0391	0.0343	0.0729	0.314	0.151	1.061
RER	0.9755	0.9549	0.9806	–0.057	–0.117	–0.0291
DDY	0.0357	0.0498	0.0067	0.030	–0.0423	–0.087
GINV	0.208	0.1998	0.279	0.470	0.3854	3.337
LSCHOOL	1.297	0.9297	1.678	0.0212	0.779	0.808
INFVR	0.558	0.696	0.540	–0.117	1.615	0.211
INF	0.494	0.309	0.0838	0.166	3.071	–3.738
DSX	0.155	0.153	0.181	–0.067	–0.0134	–0.174
Overall differential					6.061	4.885

The next stage of analysis looks at the export growth equation. We include most of the variables as before, but in addition we now include lagged export growth and import growth in the equation, and the growth rates of the variables instead of the levels of the variables. In addition, some variables enter in both contemporaneous and lagged values. The results of the export growth equation are shown in Table 8 and Table 9 for the *FIML* estimation.

The real exchange rate enters in its first difference, indicating that it is the real exchange rate movements that are important to export growth. The results show that, to the extent that the real exchange rate changes are favorable to profitability and external competitiveness, they stimulate growth of exports. Real exchange rate misalignment enters with a first lag and is consistent with prediction: it penalizes export performance. In this equation, human capital enters into the growth equation even though it was not significant in the export share equation. The technological-enhancing variable, *FDIOPEN,* also turns out to be significant in the export growth equation. This variable plays the same role as argued previously. Two variables that have now become significant in the export growth equation are the debt service ratio (*DSX*) and inflation (*INF*). *DSX* was significant to the growth equation but not in the export share equation.

To the extent that significant export receipts flow out to service external debt, they are likely to check export growth. The results in Table

Table 8. Export Growth Panel Equation

Variable	Coefficient	*t*-ratio
$EXPOGR_{t-1}$	0.859	52.13
MGDPGR	0.429	32.61
$\Delta RGDPGR$	0.161	11.37
ΔDY	0.260	20.64
TOTSHK	–0.116	–12.14
XPI	0.0189	2.67
XPI_{t-1}	0.0621	8.914
INF	0.0223	2.821
ΔRER	–0.0422	–5.955
$RERMIS_{t-1}$	–0.0135	–1.834
DSX	–0.157	–13.273
LSCHOOL	0.0126	2.434
FDIOPEN	0.0563	9.650
R^2	0.91	0.91

Note: Random effects model.

8 confirm this. For inflation, it shows that it stimulates export production and also growth. This is consistent with the arguments that moderate inflation is likely to stimulate export production through reduced pressure on appreciation of the exchange rate and growth. We added inflation variability (*INFVR*), but this was only significant in the growth equation and not in the export growth equation. The results in Table 8 are reported only for the significant variables. This equation was again reestimated simultaneously with the growth equation. The results are reported in Table 9.

Using the same variables for the export growth equation, we can also assess the feedback effects from growth to export growth. The results in Table 9 show that the speed of growth of real income, lagged export growth, and moderate inflation most significantly explain sub-Saharan African performance relative to the overall sample. Misalignment in the real exchange rate deters both export growth and real income growth. In addition, terms of trade shocks and debt service and import growth make negative contributions to real income growth.

The results of the computed beta coefficients showing the relative importance of the variables in the export growth and output growth equation are shown in Table 10. We have also shown the total contribution of the variables in the model by showing their explained proportion and hence indicating the unexplained proportion. The results give a lot of weight to the export environment, captured by lagged export growth, an inertial effect, which feeds into output growth with

Table 9. Regression Results: Trade and Growth

Variable	Export Growth Equation	Growth Equation
Constant	–5.184 (–5.349)	0.714 (0.983)
$EXPOGR_{t-1}$	0.862 (91.15)	0.0355 (3.835)
$\Delta RGDPGR$	0.161 (19.59)	0.609 (73.02)
XPI	0.021 (3.89)	
XPI_{t-1}	0.054 (11.14)	
ΔDY	0.254 (27.11)	
TOT		–0.157 (–20.67)
TOTSHK	–0.117 (–16.33)	0.345 (49.56)
ΔRER	–0.0429 (–6.320)	–0.0072 (–0.774)
RERMIS	–0.0061 (–0.963)	
$RERMIS_{t-1}$		–0.047 (–6.031)
MGDPGR	0.427 (64.40)	–0.117 (–14.00)
INF	0.0185 (2.74)	0.189 (27.93)
INFVAR		–0.132 (–16.063)
DSX	–0.156 (–18.640)	–0.091 (–11.88)
LSCHOOL	0.0111 (1.84)	
GINV		0.234 (20.96)
R^2	0.91	0.88

Note: Likelihood function = –18,865.1. *NOBS* = 2,475. The results are a full-information, maximum-likelihood estimation. The figures in parentheses are *t*-values.

strong effects. This underscores the importance of incorporating the simultaneity arguments considered above. The other factors behind export growth are external debt flows, import growth, and export prices. On the growth side, lagged effects of growth have the most influence, followed by investment and export growth, while debt service obligations are a strong deterrent to growth.

These results further reinforce the arguments in this chapter that trade performance will be reinforced by output growth as well as growth being sustained by trade performance. Thus export performance contributes to output growth, but more important, output growth explains more of the trade performance in general and has entered significantly in both trade shares and export growth equations.

However, even though a strong conclusion emerges that export growth contributes to overall output growth with strong feedback effects, there are still weaknesses into how much the chapter can contribute toward understanding the transmission mechanisms or channels from export growth to output growth and vice versa. Three issues may be pointed out. First, composition of exports and output may determine the strength of the transmission mechanism and the strength of feedback effects and furthermore the quality of growth. Second, pri-

Table 10. Trade and Growth: Relative Contributions (Estimated Beta Coefficients)

Variable	Export Growth	Growth
$EXPOGR_{t-1}$	26.75	14.44
$\Delta RGDPGR$	4.93	75.77
XPI	6.51	
XPI_{t-1}	6.82	
ΔDY	23.65	
TOT		–2.93
$TOTSHK$	–6.98	0.345
ΔRER	–1.53	–1.04
$RERMIS$	–0.028	
$RERMIS_{t-1}$		–0.874
$MGDPGR$	35.9	–39.99
INF	0.23	9.618
$INFVAR$		–9.054
DSX	–9.01	–21.385
$LSCHOOL$	2.186	
$GINV$		32.323
Explained	85.569	78.6
Unexplained	14.431	21.39
Total	100	100

Note: The beta coefficient helps to assess the relative importance of the variables and factors in the regressions in explaining export growth and trade. The beta coefficients are estimated by using the size of the respective regression coefficient (*x*) multiplied by the ratio of the standard deviation of *x* divided by the standard deviation of the dependent variable. These computations are reproduced in this table.

mary exports will have a different impact on output growth from that of manufactured exports.[4] Finally, we cannot answer the question to what extent trade reforms have affected the composition of exports and thus the transmission channels. Thus, even though we come to a strong conclusion about the relationship between trade and growth, we still need disaggregated export data to map out policy pointers on trade and growth and the strength of the transmission channels. Primary exports will have a differential impact on real income growth and a different transmission mechanism.

Concluding Remarks

There is now increasing evidence that those developing countries that have been most successful in achieving and sustaining high growth

[4]It is quite difficult to assess this proposition due to data requirements. This could be feasible for individual countries rather that the 99 countries used in this study.

rates are also the ones that have taken most advantage of trade opportunities. Openness to trade and international finance has facilitated the effectiveness of investment and macroeconomic conditions that are conducive to growth. In this respect, the recent trend toward opening up the sub-Saharan African economies and reducing barriers to trade and finance augurs well for higher, sustained growth in the future. If we go by the recent encouraging upturn (1995 and 1996) in growth and export performance in the region, there is a good reason to believe that this may be a beginning of a virtuous circle from policy reforms to growth. This particular view is supported by the strong positive inertial influence of past growth and export performance for future improved performance. What is perhaps also a significant finding is the confirmation of the strong influence of overall growth on trade performance. In this regard, Africa's marginalization in world trade will have to find an answer from creating conditions for improved overall growth, which is the base for participation in world trade. That is, poor performance in the past has been due to two factors: Africa did not trade enough, and its trade policy stance is to blame for these outcomes.

The influence of trade-enhancing policies on exports and overall growth has been shown to matter. Explicit trade policies, including trade taxes and nontariff barriers, play an important but less prominent role in this regard than macroeconomic policies that influence trade performance. Most significant among the latter are exchange rate policies, reduction in the exchange controls, price stability, and investment response. These of course operate more effectively in an open trade environment, which permits enterprises to make best and uncumbered use of global opportunities for trade and investment.

A major hindrance to strengthening the virtuous circle as confirmed by the results is that of the debt service burden, which crowds out domestic expenditures needed for supporting expansion of productive capacity and infrastructure for growth. An expeditious solution to this problem arising from the past is key to stemming coordination failures that hamper response of investment and indeed strengthening of the export base. Another structural bottleneck is the underdeveloped state of human capacity, which stifles absorption of technological competence availed through interaction of openness and foreign direct investment. Investment in human capital, particularly education, is thus an important complementary measure for realizing the benefits from opening up African economies.

Finally, the sustainability of the various liberalization measures that have been put in place is fundamental for achieving sustained improved performance in trade and growth. Pressures from fiscal gaps and from interest groups concerned with maintaining the protection of ventures put in place during the ISI era are most worrisome in this regard. Binding achievements toward a more open economy are critical for sustenance. Whether this is done through regional arrangements, WTO provisions, or local constituencies (for example, export lobbies), it is necessary to embark on them before to pressures for reversals mount to critical levels.

Appendix: Variable Definitions

EXPGD	Export share in GDP
MGDP	Import share in GDP
TOT	Terms of trade
TOTSHK	Terms of trade shock *TOTSHK* for year is t is calculated as: $[(Px_t / Px_{base} - 1)^* (X/GDP)_t{-}1] - [Pm_t/PM - 1)^* (M/GDP)_{t-1}]$, where *PX* and *PM* are export and import prices indices respectively deflated by the U.S. GNP deflator; PX_{base} and PM_{base} are the average *PX* and *PM* respectively for the preceding 3 years; *X* and *M* are respectively the exports and imports of goods and nonfactor services.
XPI	Export price index
MPITX	*MPI** [1 + *IMPODUTY* + *RERMIS*], where *MPI* is the import price index and *IMPDUTY* are import duties.
RERMIS	Real exchange rate misalignment, defined as (*RER* – *ERER*)/*ERER*
FDIGDP	Ratio of foreign direct investment to GDP
OPEN	Openness: imports + exports as a ratio of GDP
XPODUTY	Export duties
ICRGE	Measure of quality of institutions
WARSSA	Number of civil wars crossed with the sub-Saharan African dummy
DY	Ratio of external debt to GDP
LSCHOOL	Number of years in school
GINV	Gross investment (sum of ratio of public and private investment to GDP)
INF	Rate of inflation
DSX	Ratio of debt service to exports
GDPRR	Average regional GDP
EXPOGR	Growth of exports
MGDPGR	Growth of imports
RGDPGR	Real income growth
RER	Real exchange rate
INFVAR	Inflation variability

References

Balassa, B., 1978, "Exports and Economic Growth: Further Evidence," *Journal of Development Economics,* Vol. 5, pp. 181–89.

Baldwin, R.E., 1996, "Review of Theoretical Developments in Regional Integration," in *Regional Integration and Trade Liberalization in Sub-Saharan Africa,* Vol. 1, *Framework, Issues and Methodological Perspectives,* ed. by A. Oyejide, I. Elbadawi, and P. Collier (New York: St. Martin's Press).

Collier, Paul, 1995, "The Marginalization of Africa," *International Labour Review,* Vol. 134, No. 4–5, pp. 541–57.

———, and Gunning, 1997, *Explaining African Economic Performance* (Oxford: Centre for the Study of African Economies).

De Rosa, D. A., 1990, "Protection and Export Performance in Sub-Saharan Africa," *Weltwirtsafliches Archiv,* Vol. 128, No. 1, pp. 88–124.

Edwards, S., 1993, "Openness, Trade Liberalization and Growth in Developing Countries," *Journal of Economic Literature,* Vol. 21, pp. 1358–93.

Esfahami, H.S., 1991, "Exports, Imports and Economic Growth in Semi-industrialized Countries," *Journal of Development Economics,* Vol. 35, No. 1, pp. 93–116.

Feder, Gershon, 1983, "On Exports and Economic Growth," *Journal of Development Economics,* Vol. 12, pp. 59–73.

Helleiner, G.K., 1986, "Outward Orientation, Import Instability and African Economic Growth: An Empirical Investigation," in *Theory and Reality in Development: Essays in Honour of Paul Streeten,* ed. by S. Lall and F. Stewart (New York: St. Martin's Press).

———, 1990, "Trade Strategy in the Medium-Term Adjustment," *World Development,* Vol. 18, No. 6, pp. 879–97.

Kauffman, D., and S. O'Connell, 1991, "The Macroeconomics of the Unofficial Foreign Exchange Market in Tanzania," in *Economic Reforms in Sub-Saharan Africa,* ed. by A. Chhibber and S. Fischer (Washington: World Bank).

Khan, M., and M.D. Knight, 1988, "Import Compression and Export Performance in Developing Countries," *Review of Economics and Statistics,* Vol. 70, No. 2.

Little, I.M.D., T. Scitovsky, and M. Scott, 1970, *Industry and Trade in Some Developing Countries* (New York: Oxford University Press).

Moran, C., 1990, "Imports under a Foreign Exchange Constraint," *World Bank Economic Review,* Vol. 3, No. 2, pp. 279–95.

Ndulu, B., 1986, "Investment, Output Growth and Capacity Utilization in an African Economy: The Case of the Manufacturing Sector in Tanzania," *East African Economic Review,* Vol. 2, No. 1.

———, 1991, "Growth and Adjustment in Sub-Saharan Africa," in *Economic Reform in Sub-Saharan Africa,* ed. by A. Chhibber and S. Fischer (Washington: World Bank).

Oyejide, T.A., B.J. Ndulu, and J.W. Gunning, eds., 1996, "Country Case Studies of Trade Liberalization" (unpublished; Nairobi: African Economic Research Consortium).

Papageorgiou, D., M. Michaely, and A. Choksi, 1991, *Liberalising Trade,* 7 vols. (Oxford: Blackwell).

Pinto, B., 1989, "Black Market Premia, Exchange Rate Unification, and Inflation in Sub-Saharan Africa," *World Bank Economic Review,* Vol. 3, No. 3, pp. 321–38.

Pritchett, L., and G. Sethi, 1994, "Tariff Rates, Tariff Revenue and Trade Reform: Some New Facts," *World Bank Economic Review,* Vol. 8, No. 1, pp.1–16.

Rodrik, D., 1992, "Closing the Productivity Gap: Does Trade Liberalization Really Help?" in *Trade Policy, Industrialization, and Development: New Perspectives,"* ed. by G. K. Helleiner (Oxford: Clarendon Press).

———, 1997, "Trade Policy and Economic Performance in Sub-Saharan Africa" (unpublished; Cambridge, Massachusetts: Kennedy School of Government, Harvard University).

Sachs, Jeffrey, and Andrew Warner, 1995, "Economic Reform and the Process of Global Integration," *Brookings Papers on Economic Activity:* 1, pp.1–118.

———, 1997, "Sources of Slow Growth in African Economies" (unpublished; Cambridge, Massachusetts: Harvard Institute for International Development, March).

Tanzi, V., 1995, *"Taxation in an Integrating World,"* Integrating National Economies Series (Washington: Brookings Institution).

Yeats, Alexander J., 1997, with Azita Amjadi, Ulrich Eincke, and Francis Ng, *Did Domestic Policies Marginalize Africa in World Trade?* (Washington: World Bank).

Africa: Industrialization Strategy In the Context of Globalization 10

Charles Chukwuma Soludo

> The crucial challenge facing policy makers in government and the multilateral agencies is that of framing a new industrial strategy for sub-Saharan Africa in the 21st century. Whatever its limited success in other fields, structural adjustment has failed signally not just in reversing the recent trend towards de-industrialization but also in creating an appropriate policy environment for sustained industrial growth. . . . A fresh start—a new approach—is needed. [UNIDO, 1996, p. 122]

It is self-evident that, given the validity of the Prebisch-Singer thesis about the secular decline in primary commodity prices, the limited natural resource endowments, and the teeming population of African countries, future growth and development will hinge critically on the aggressive pursuit of production diversification into industry, technological upgrading, and international competitiveness of manufactures. This realization is not new and has constituted the fulcrum of most development strategies in much of Africa since political independence in the 1960s.

So far, the various models of industrialization—from active industrial policy under import-substituting industrialization (ISI) to "no industrial policy" under structural adjustment programs (SAPs)—have not succeeded in laying the foundations for industrial takeoff in most African countries. While most analysts agree about the distortions and failings of the brand of ISI implemented in much of Africa, evidence now shows that the promises of "incentive neutral" trade policy, and "no policy" framework of industrialization under SAP have not materialized.[1] The extremely low level of industrialization combines with the atypically weak institutions, human capital, and infrastructure to

[1]Africa is the only region whose share of global trade has shrunk from nearly 4 percent in 1950 to about 1 percent in the 1990s; the only region whose production structures have intensified concentration in low technology activities, and the only region whose exports are further concentrated in primary commodities rather than diversification as promised under liberalization. The share in global manufacturing value added (MVA) has shrunk from 0.6 percent in 1970 to 0.3 percent in 1995; growth of MVA deteriorated from 2 percent in the 1970–80 period to 0.1 percent in 1991–95; total export growth per capita deteriorated to –1.6 percent in the 1991–95 period; and manufacturing employment declined from an average

make Africa (with the notable exception of a minority of countries) the world's only region that has intensified its position as a pre-industrial society.

The search for, and effective deployment of, strategies to escape this pre-industrial trap and to lay the foundations for sustainable, competitive industrialization are the fundamental challenges for Africa's development in the years ahead. Recently, the earlier acrimonious debate about the role of the state in industrialization seems to have given way to increasing convergence of views around some strings of "recognitions" for the need for "developmental," "strong," "committed," "effective" state in industrialization. "Without it (the state), sustainable development, both economic and social, is impossible" (World Bank, 1997). Thus, after years of waiting in vain for market forces to unleash industrial development, analysts are beginning to take seriously the political economy, structural, capacity, and institutional issues arising from, associated with, or defining the context for rapid industrialization in Africa. A rediscovery of the state and the potentials of an Asian-style interventionist regime for latecomer industrializers is one thing, while designing appropriate policies in the context of the changed and continually changing global environment is yet another.

Globalization is perhaps the most profound development that not only circumscribes the nature and scope of national policies but more fundamentally defines the context for African industrialization. It defines not just the breakneck technological changes and shrinkage of the global market but more so the take-it-or-leave-it set of neoliberal policies (unfettered market liberalization and competition) that are the fulcrum of international exchange under the WTO. About 40 African countries have signed the WTO rules.[2] In essence, the new framework changes the nature and role of industrial policy, and in particular, severely limits the application of the kinds of the interventions and policies that the more successful Asian industrializers employed.

Africa (together with other regions with developing countries at a similar stage of industrialization) therefore faces atypically Herculean

growth rate of about 5.3 percent in 1970–80 to –1.1 in 1985–90. More fundamentally, the liberalization schemes have been shown to be incompatible with the goals of balance of payments and fiscal viability. Indeed, aside from two or so countries whose trade liberalization has been buoyed up by massive aid inflows, most of the other liberalizations have suffered from some reversals (see Soludo, 1997b).

[2]For Africa, the issue is no longer whether or not to liberalize trade, or whether trade and outward orientation matter for growth. Such debates are now sterile because most countries have signed to binding and enforceable liberalization of trade under the WTO. In the light of the evolving global environment, there is little choice except outward orientation.

challenges. First, the global environment is atypically more competitive than at any other time. Second, Africa would be the only region that would need to transform from a pre-industrial, precapitalist society into competitive market and industrialized society but without the scope for preferential and differential treatments or protective and interventionist regimes available to earlier industrializers. In other words, Africa would, as a toddler, be expected to compete in a game meant for adults. A further problem is that, in some cases, the toddler is even deformed as defined by the initial but deteriorating conditions. For some analysts, it is difficult to see how Africa can make it into competitive industrialization, and they therefore suggest that it should concentrate on primary commodity production and exports. While the need for fuller exploitation of the static comparative advantages in primary commodities cannot be denied, some analysts argue that the goals of industrialization are coterminous with the requirements of long-term development.[3] The issue therefore is not whether Africa should industrialize, but *how* it should *start* and *sustain* the process within the context of a changing global environment. This chapter illuminates some of the issues in the design of such a strategic agenda.

The rest of the chapter is organized as follows. The second section provides an overview of African industrialization policies and performance. In the third section, I examine the causes of Africa's stalled industrialization and the probable lessons from Asia on building systemic competitiveness. The fourth section evaluates the constraints and opportunities offered by the new waves of globalization, while the fifth section articulates a framework for an industrialization strategy and also concludes the chapter.

Africa's Industrialization Efforts and Performance

Africa's quest for industrialization has had a checkered history.[4] The kinds of industrial policies immediately after independence in the 1960s through the 1970s were largely influenced by the reactions to the colonial heritage as well as the dominant development paradigm of the era.

The peculiar colonial legacy in Africa left the continent not only with the most fragile industrial base but also the weakest social infrastruc-

[3]This is more so since most of the advantages of outward orientation accrue to trade in manufactures and services.

[4]See Mkandawire (1988) for a detailed review of the evolution and analysis of determinants of industrialization in sub-Saharan Africa since 1914.

ture that was not conducive to effective industrial takeoff. The colonies were safeguarded as protected markets for imperial export of manufactures, or as monopsonized sources of raw material. Neither production for local markets nor for exports was promoted. The few industrial activities were monopolized by multinational firms, and the emergence of domestic entrepreneurship especially in industry and wholesale trade was stifled through a number of mechanisms. As Mkandawire (1988, p. 18) summarizes:

> We are not referring here to the "poor human resources" constraint rightly brought out in many "manpower" and "human capital studies" of African countries but to the class and state structures that made industrialization, no matter how subjectively willed, so socially "rootless" in Africa. There was not, as in India, an incipient indigenous industrial capitalist class that was to ride on the national wave for its own further accumulation, free of the many colonial shackles that may have impeded its growth. There was no landed aristocracy that, as in Latin America, gradually transformed itself or was forcefully transformed into a capitalist class or, at least, provided the surpluses for industrialization. There was no merchant capital that would have been compelled by post-independence policies to enter into manufacturing.

In addition to the dearth of indigenous capitalist class, the colonial state deliberately prohibited involvement of indigenous people in industrial activities. It was little surprise therefore that the struggle for independence was explicitly linked to the demand for the "right to industrialize." Consequently, the postcolonial state focused on industrialization not only as a means of economic development but also as a strategy to alter some of the vestiges of colonialism and ensure indigenous participation in the otherwise prohibited areas. Foreign companies had a virtual monopoly on manufacturing and other industrial activities, and these were seen as the continuing symbols of imperialism.

Political independence was thought to be hollow without economic independence, and this was seen in the context of exercising "greater control" of their national economies and promoting "self-reliance." Ostensibly contemptuous (in fact, resentful) of the big multinational corporations, the nationalistic mood of the time was much more about ensuring indigenous "participation" in, rather than "efficiency and competitiveness" of, the enterprises. It was therefore little surprise that most African countries enacted and implemented various forms of indigenization laws—which sought to transfer "ownership and control" of certain industrial activities to the "indigenes," as well as prohibit "foreigners" from certain aspects of economic activity. The extreme form of this was the mass expulsion of the Asian community from Uganda in the early 1970s. In other words, the interventions were, unlike the Asian model of the time, not motivated by strategic and selective interventions to acquire technological niches and export competitiveness.[5] Rather, it was nationalistic desires and exercises in bureaucratic experimentation that provided the basis for the industrial efforts. The nascent state, sometimes in collaboration with the multinational corporations through joint ventures or management contracts, or wholly owned parastatals, pioneered Africa's industrialization process.

The major strategy adopted was the ISI strategy. Coincidentally, the early years of independence (1960–70s) saw an era of the intellectual ascendancy of Keynesianism, including development economics as well as the celebration of the benefits of development planning. Keynesianism provided the justification for government intervention to correct market failures, while the experience of the Soviet Union with rapid industrialization under a planned economy (as well as the lessons of "late industrializers," which suggest a prominent role for the state at early stages) acted to promote ISI as the orthodoxy of the era. In addition to nationalization of multinational companies, the other key elements of this strategy in most of Africa consisted, to varying degrees, of protectionist trade regimes which in part were for the infant industry reasons, and a number of incentives to ensure profitability of investing in industries—directed credit; low, differentiated, and administered interest rates; tax incentives; import licensing for procurement of equipment and raw materials; and so forth.

The general thrust (which ironically coincided with the neoclassical preference) was to promote industrialization "generally" without attempts to selectively pick winners and strategically direct policies at them. Given the virtual absence of indigenously owned industries, and the single-minded focus on "controlling" the existing ones, the emphasis was primarily on "increasing local ownership and participation." Any industry at all, provided that it passed the single criterion of high local ownership and participation, was encouraged. On this criterion, it would appear that many industrial policies of the two decades up to the late 1970s were largely successful in many African countries. What suffered however, were the efficiency, productivity, and international competitiveness of such industries. In

[5]This point is very critical, especially in the light of the several casual references to the fact that Africa has implemented the Asian types of interventions and failed. The motivations, circumstances, and in fact the design of such interventions were dramatically different. In reality, only Mauritius could be said to have implemented the kind of "strategic and selective" interventions of the Asian model, and it has succeeded.

fairness however, these objectives were not explicitly pursued in many cases.

For example, there was no explicit emphasis on exports of manufactures, and the firms were not subjected to performance-based criteria for receiving further incentives and protection. The lack of gradual exposure of the firms to international competition contributed partly to the low industrial growth and innovation, as well as its feeble structure. Some analysts argue, however, that unlike the Asian countries with severe resource constraints, African countries (like their Latin American counterparts) earned much of their foreign exchange by exporting primary commodities. Thus, the necessity for exporting was not as urgent and imperative as in the case of the Asians.

The oil price shocks and the bursts in primary commodity exports in the late 1970s and early 1980s exposed this African neglect as unsustainable. With the benefit of hindsight and lessons from Asia, the past policies now appear to have been "mistakes." Unfortunately, it is this policy framework of the 1960s and 1970s that forms the basis for performance evaluations, and these evaluations are predominantly based upon a set of objectives that those industrial policies never set out to achieve.

With the SAPs of the early 1980s came a fundamental change in industrialization strategy that is rooted in neoliberalism. The initial extreme laissez-faire model of just "getting prices right" has, however, evolved in the face of scathing criticisms, to the broader "Washington consensus" as articulated by the World Bank (1991): the "market-friendly" approach. Under this approach, the presence of market failures is acknowledged, but most corrective interventions are rejected as likely to boomerang. In essence, "government failure" dominates market failure. "The appropriate role of government is to ensure adequate investments in people, provide a competitive climate for private enterprise, keep the economy open to international trade, and maintain a stable macroeconomy. Beyond these roles . . . governments are likely to do more harm than good, unless interventions are market friendly" (World Bank, 1993, p. 10). Specifically, according to this model, governments should: "*Intervene reluctantly:* Let markets work unless it is demonstrably better to step in . . . *Apply checks and balances:* Put interventions continually to the discipline of the international and domestic markets . . . *Intervene openly:* Make interventions simple, transparent, and subject to rules rather than official discretion" (World Bank, 1991, p. 5).

This model of little or no industrial policy coheres, under this framework, with the strategy of unilateral, deep, and swift trade policy reforms. The bid to produce a "neutral" trade regime also implies the

Table 1. Regional Percentage Shares of Global Manufacturing Production

Region	1970	1980	1990	1995
Industrial countries	88.0	82.8	84.2	80.3
Developing countries, including China	1.0	17.2	15.8	19.7
Latin America	4.7	6.5	4.6	4.6
Sub-Saharan Africa	0.6	0.5	0.4	0.3
North Africa and West Asia	0.9	1.6	1.8	1.9
South Asia	1.2	1.2	1.3	1.5
East and Southeast Asia, including China	4.2	6.8	7.4	11.1

Source: UNIDO Global Database.

elimination of infant industry protection as a viable strategy of industrialization. This approach to industrialization and growth has been tried since the early 1980s in most African countries.

After nearly forty years of experimentation with various models of industrialization, the results are anything but salutary (see the tables that follow). The share in global manufacturing value added (MVA) has shrunk from 0.6 percent in 1970 to 0.3 percent in 1995; and growth of MVA deteriorated from 2 percent in the 1970–80 period to 0.1 percent in 1991–95 (see Tables 1 through 5). Total export growth per capita deteriorated to –1.6 percent in the 1991–95 period; and manufacturing employment declined from an average growth rate of about 5.3 percent in 1970–80 to –1.1 in 1985–90. For exports, Table 6 points to the rudimentary nature of manufactured exports (accounting for just 18 percent of exports as against 54 percent for other developing regions) while machinery exports account for a mere 2 percent of total exports. Table 7 indicates that Africa is the only region where the concentration of export commodities into primary products has intensified. In Table 8, we observe that aside from a few commodities, Africa has consistently lost market shares in its exports.

Tables 1, 9, and 10 summarize the extent of the de-industrialization that has taken place both in the context of the regional aggregate relative to the rest of the world, and in terms of the individual countries" performance relative to their history. Table 10 particularly compares the manufacturing value added as proportion of GDP in 1980 and 1994, and finds that, for 13 out of 23 countries, there was either stagnation or de-industrialization. Table 1 confirms de-industrialization for the aggregate sub-Saharan Africa. Stewart (1991, p. 429) argues that "indiscriminate import liberalization has been partly responsible for the observed de-industrialization. Some selective protection is necessary for the development of industrial capacity."

Table 2. Structure of Value Added
(Percent)

Region or Country and Sector	1970	1980	1990	1994
World				
Low technology[1]	57.2	54.9	49.7	50.1
Machinery, excluding transport equipment	20.9	22.5	24.2	23.4
Transport equipment	8.3	9.1	10.0	9.9
Chemicals	11.8	12.0	14.7	15.1
Other manufacturing	1.8	1.6	1.4	1.4
North America				
Low technology[1]	52.2	49.7	47.0	45.8
Machinery, excluding transport equipment	23.1	25.8	24.4	25.1
Transport equipment	10.1	10.5	11.7	11.8
Chemicals	13.0	12.5	15.4	15.9
Other manufacturing	1.7	1.6	1.4	1.4
Western Europe				
Low technology[1]	56.3	53.7	49.1	49.6
Machinery, excluding transport equipment	21.5	23.0	24.5	23.8
Transport equipment	8.8	9.9	10.2	10.0
Chemicals	12.4	12.4	15.2	15.7
Other manufacturing	1.0	1.0	0.9	0.9
Japan				
Low technology[1]	50.0	51.7	42.9	44.5
Machinery, excluding transport equipment	25.3	24.7	30.6	28.1
Transport equipment	9.4	9.5	10.7	10.6
Chemicals	13.7	12.6	14.2	15.2
Other manufacturing	1.6	1.5	1.5	1.6
Latin America and the Caribbean				
Low technology[1]	69.3	66.3	64.1	63.2
Machinery, excluding transport equipment	10.2	12.0	11.8	11.7
Transport equipment	6.5	6.6	5.9	6.5
Chemicals	12.6	13.7	17.0	17.4
Other manufacturing	1.3	1.4	1.3	1.2
East Asia and Southeast Asia				
Low technology[1]	68.9	64.3	54.8	54.6
Machinery, excluding transport equipment	9.8	14.2	21.0	22.1
Transport equipment	4.1	5.5	7.9	8.3
Chemicals	14.0	13.2	14.1	13.3
Other manufacturing	3.2	2.9	2.2	1.7
South Asia				
Low technology[1]	66.3	61.8	61.1	57.7
Machinery, excluding transport equipment	11.6	14.6	13.8	14.1
Transport equipment	5.7	7.1	8.0	7.1
Chemicals	15.5	15.8	16.7	20.4
Other manufacturing	0.9	0.6	0.4	0.7

Table 2 (*concluded*)

Region or Country and Sector	1970	1980	1990	1994
China				
Low technology[1]	58.6	59.8	56.3	59.6
Machinery, excluding transport equipment	22.1	19.6	20.3	18.6
Transport equipment	1.8	3.4	4.3	6.5
Chemicals	15.7	15.2	16.8	12.9
Other manufacturing	1.7	2.1	2.3	2.4
Sub-Saharan Africa				
Low technology[1]	83.1	76.3	79.2	80.7
Machinery, excluding transport equipment	3.3	3.5	3.3	2.8
Transport equipment	2.7	7.9	4.8	4.1
Chemicals	9.1	11.1	11.5	11.2
Other manufacturing	1.9	1.2	1.2	1.2

Source: UNIDO Global Database.

[1]Low-technology industries are defined as food, beverages, tobacco, textiles, clothing, footwear, leather products, wood and cork products, furniture, paper and paper products, printing and publishing, petroleum refineries, coal products, pottery, glass and nonmetallic minerals, iron and steel, and nonferrous metals and metal products (excluding machinery).

Table 3. Percentage Share of Manufacturing Value Added in GDP

Region or Country	1960	1970	1980	1990
World	29.0	28.3	25.8	23.0
Industrial market economies	28.7	27.9	25.1	22.7
Developing countries	20.3	20.2	20.9	21.9
North America	27.9	24.8	21.5	18.5
Western Europe	29.8	30.5	27.1	23.9
Eastern Europe and former U.S.S.R.	42.1	41.3	43.9	36.6
Japan	34.6	36.0	29.2	29.1
Latin America	20.9	23.7	24.6	23.1
Tropical Africa	7.0	10.3	10.1	9.5
North Africa and West Asia	10.1	12.5	8.2	13.1
Indian Subcontinent	12.0	12.7	14.3	15.4
East and Southeast Asia (excluding China)	14.4	19.1	22.9	26.6
China	. . .	. . .	38.4	31.5

Source: UNIDO Global Database.

Note: Current prices and dollar exchange rates.

Table 4. World Percentage Growth Rates of Manufacturing Value Added

Region or Country	1970–80	1980–90	1990–95
North America	2.3	2.5	3.1
Western Europe	2.6	1.6	0.5
Japan	5.2	5.8	1.2
Eastern Europe and former U.S.S.R.	7.1	1.6	–9.5
Latin America and the Caribbean	5.5	0.4	2.0
Sub-Saharan Africa	2.0	2.5	0.1
North Africa and Western Asia	7.7	5.5	3.2
South Asia	4.2	6.8	4.5
China	9.4	9.5	15.4
East and Southeast Asia	11.5	8.5	7.4
Developing countries (including China)	6.9	4.7	6.5
World	3.6	2.9	1.9

Source: UNIDO Global Database.
Note: 1990 dollars.

Ndlovu (1996, p. 158) traces the de-industrialization and disinvestment to the SAPs:

> Much of the decline occurred in the 1990s, when economic environments had been altered significantly by the impact of structural adjustment. Bennell found that between 1989 and 1994 over half of British manufacturing firms based in anglophone Africa disinvested on account of shortage of foreign exchange, massive currency devaluations and low profitability. Underlying reasons given for disinvestment were "stalled industrialization in Africa" and, interestingly, the SAPs. The countries most affected are Kenya, Nigeria and Zimbabwe, where 65 percent of equity investment was located. In all, the 14 countries affected account for 54.6 percent of sub-Saharan Africa's population and have been the origin of 58.6 percent of the region's manufacturing value added.

More fundamentally, the trade reforms have been shown to be incompatible with the goals of balance of payments and fiscal viability. Trade reforms have been frequently reversed to the point that, except for the few cases heavily buoyed by aid inflows, almost all the other liberalization schemes can be said to be unsustainable. Evidently, despite the various policies, Africa remains the world's only region still awaiting an industrial revolution.

Table 5. Percentage Growth Rates and Shares of Manufacturing Value Added

Region	1980–95	1995–2000	2000–05
Regional growth rates of MVA			
Industrial market economies	1.5	2.0	2.0
Eastern Europe and C.I.S.	–9.6	1.3	1.9
Developing countries	6.5	6.9	7.8
Latin America	2.0	2.7	2.8
Tropical Africa	0.1	3.3	3.5
North Africa and West Asia	3.2	5.4	5.7
Indian Subcontinent	4.5	4.8	5.0
East and Southeast Asia including, China	10.7	9.2	9.9
World	1.9	3.0	3.4
Shares in global MVA[1]			
Industrial countries	77.5	73.7	68.5
Eastern Europe and C.I.S.	2.8	2.6	2.4
Developing countries	19.7	23.7	29.1
Latin America	4.6	4.6	4.4
Tropical Africa	0.3	0.3	0.3
North Africa and West Asia	1.9	2.2	2.4
Indian Subcontinent	1.5	1.6	1.7
East and Southeast Asia, including China	11.1	14.8	20.0
Shares of MVA in GDP			
Industrial countries	22.5	22.2	21.6
Eastern Europe and C.I.S.	34.0	33.6	33.5
Developing countries	23.6	25.7	28.5
Latin America	22.0	21.8	21.6
Tropical Africa	9.5	10.1	10.8
North Africa and West Asia	14.2	15.7	17.6
Indian Subcontinent	15.5	15.7	15.9
East and Southeast Asia, including China	31.7	34.3	36.9
World	22.9	23.1	23.4

Source: UNIDO Global Database.
Note: "MVA" is manufacturing value added. "C.I.S." is Commonwealth of Independent States.
[1]In the final year of the period.

The Low Level of Industrialization and Lessons on Competitiveness

Industrial Stagnation

It must be stressed at the outset that references to such aggregates as "Africa" or even sub-Saharan Africa can be somewhat misleading. Africa is a highly differentiated aggregate, and care must be taken to underscore the substantial differences across countries and subre-

Table 6. The Structure of Sub-Saharan African Countries' Exports

Exporting Country	Value (millions of U.S. dollars)	By Main Category of Export Products (percentage): Aggregate SITC Groups[1]					Manufactures, of which:			Unallocated Trade
		All foods	Agricultural materials	Fuels	Ores and metals	Manufactures	Chemicals	Other manufactures	Machinery and transport	
Angola	1,296.4	16.4	0.3	82.1	. . .	1.0	. . .	0.5	0.4	0.2
Benin	49.1	61.8	25.0	4.2	1.1	3.4	0.4	1.9	1.1	4.5
Burundi	75.0	65.7	3.6	. . .	2.5	2.0	0.1	1.6	0.3	26.1
Burkina Faso	160.3	27.5	42.0	. . .	0.1	11.0	0.1	8.1	2.8	19.4
Cameroon	1,281.6	35.5	19.0	18.0	11.4	15.2	1.6	8.3	5.2	0.9
Cape Verde	6.5	50.8	3.1	. . .	26.2	12.3	. . .	6.2	6.2	7.7
Central African Republic	139.5	17.3	27.6	. . .	5.2	48.2	0.1	47.6	0.6	1.7
Chad	132.8	44.6	45.9	. . .	0.3	9.0	0.5	3.6	5.1	0.2
Comoros	12.4	71.0	1.6	. . .	0.8	26.6	25.0	1.6	. . .	. . .
Congo	776.9	1.3	9.0	81.4	1.4	6.6	. . .	5.7	0.9	0.4
Côte d'Ivoire	2,940.4	49.9	18.3	14.5	0.3	16.8	3.5	11.3	2.1	0.2
Djibouti	24.9	39.1	4.7	. . .	0.2	7.8	0.2	1.0	6.0	. . .
Ethiopia	294.2	63.3	25.1	6.2	. . .	5.3	2.0	3.2	. . .	0.1
Equatorial Guinea	25.4	57.9	30.0	. . .	7.5	4.0	. . .	2.6	0.6	. . .
Gabon	1,592.8	1.1	10.6	74.2	10.6	4.5	1.7	1.5	0.2	0.2
Gambia, The	40.6	72.9	0.5	. . .	0.2	25.9	. . .	25.1	0.7	0.5
Ghana	1,072.3	41.0	11.1	3.4	21.2	13.4	0.1	13.0	0.3	9.9
Guinea	420.5	3.4	0.3	. . .	95.0	0.5	. . .	. . .	0.2	. . .
Guinea-Bissau	11.7	73.0	2.0	. . .	7.8	4.9	1.6	1.4	1.6	. . .
Kenya	1,054.3	58.5	7.7	14.2	1.4	17.3	3.1	12.6	1.7	0.9
Liberia	404.4	8.8	29.1	0.1	59.7	1.0	0.1	0.4	0.5	1.4
Madagascar	321.9	69.7	4.5	1.0	9.4	15.2	1.5	12.7	1.0	0.2
Malawi	417.6	90.6	3.2	. . .	0.1	4.8	. . .	4.6	0.2	1.4
Mali	270.7	22.6	65.8	0.1	0.1	6.8	0.1	4.4	2.3	4.6
Mauritania	447.1	47.3	0.4	1.9	48.6	0.5	. . .	0.2	0.3	1.1
Mauritius	1,180.5	31.1	0.5	. . .	0.1	68.1	0.3	65.1	2.7	0.2
Mozambique	101.1	65.7	4.0	0.1	12.1	17.5	0.4	15.5	1.6	0.7

Table 6 (*concluded*)

Exporting Country	Value (millions of U.S. dollars)	By Main Category of Export Products (percentage): Aggregate SITC Groups[1]					Manufactures, of which:			
		All foods	Agricultural materials	Fuels	Ores and metals	Manufactures	Chemicals	Other manufactures	Machinery and transport	Unallocated Trade
Niger	579.7	11.4	0.6	1.1	84.7	2.0	. . .	1.5	0.5	0.1
Nigeria	13,649.3	1.8	1.5	93.6	0.7	2.1	0.3	1.6	0.2	0.3
Reunion	185.6	82.4	0.5	0.2	0.4	16.6	2.5	5.8	8.3	. . .
Rwanda	97.6	69.2	9.1	. . .	2.4	4.7	2.8	1.7	0.2	14.7
São Tomé and Príncipe	7.4	91.2	2.2	. . .	0.2	6.3	1.7	1.6	1.6	. . .
Senegal	782.6	53.2	2.7	12.4	9.3	22.5	14.9	5.2	2.4	. . .
Seychelles	34.2	37.1	0.3	55.6	. . .	7.0	. . .	2.0	5.0	. . .
Sierra Leone	142.8	24.6	3.9	3.5	40.9	26.1	. . .	26.0	0.1	1.0
Somalia	81.0	90.4	6.8	0.2	1.1	1.1	. . .	0.5	0.6	0.4
South Africa	18,968.8	13.6	9.2	13.9	26.4	34.4	6.5	24.3	3.6	2.5
Sudan	573.0	38.6	59.5	. . .	0.3	1.0	. . .	0.3	0.7	0.5
Togo	267.9	23.0	21.5	. . .	44.7	9.1	0.4	8.0	0.7	1.8
Uganda	152.1	88.9	10.0	. . .	0.1	1.1	0.1	0.3	0.6	. . .
Tanzania	284.9	49.2	22.4	1.5	14.5	11.8	0.9	8.4	2.5	0.5
Zaïre	999.3	8.7	4.5	12.7	55.2	16.6	0.1	15.7	0.8	2.3
Zambia	1,347.5	3.9	1.4	0.1	83.4	11.2	0.1	10.8	0.3	0.1
Zimbabwe	1,467.6	44.1	7.3	0.7	15.9	30.9	1.7	25.6	3.6	1.1
All sub-Saharan Africa	53,688.4	18.5	8.3	36.3	16.6	18.8	3.0	13.8	2.0	1.5
All developing countries	708,947.0	11.4	3.3	26.0	4.2	53.9	3.8	29.9	17.4	1.2

Source: Data compiled from United Nations COMTRADE record; and UNCTAD, *Handbook of International Trade and Development Statistics, 1992*. In some cases, the total trade values reported in this table may differ from those shown in Table 1. Where this occurs, data on the direction of trade had to be taken from a different year than the above statistics on the composition of trade.

[1]"SITC" is Standard International Trade Classification. In items of the SITC (Revision 1) classification, the product groups shown in this table are defined as follows: all foods and feeds, SITC 0+1+22+4; agricultural raw materials, SITC 2–22–27–28; fuels, SITC 3; ores, minerals, and metals, SITC 27+28+68; manufactures, SITC 5+6+7+8–68; chemicals, SITC 5; other manufactures, SITC 6–68; machinery and transport, SITC 7.

Table 7. Measures of the Concentration of Exports: African Countries Compared with Other Country Groups

Country Group	Share of Three Largest Products in Total Exports (percent)		Product Diversification Index		Product Concentration Index	
	1962–64	1991–93	1962–64	1991–93	1962–64	1991–93
Africa						
North Africa	63.0	68.7	0.74	0.73	0.44	0.43
Sub-Saharan Africa	36.5	62.3	0.71	0.77	0.20	0.49
Low-income countries	39.2	62.9	0.72	0.79	0.22	0.50
Middle-income countries	43.9	74.3	0.76	0.80	0.24	0.60
Low-income Asia	30.4	34.5	0.61	0.53	0.17	0.20
Middle-income Asia	38.5	30.8	0.74	0.44	0.21	0.15
Middle East	92.0	91.0	0.84	0.84	0.82	0.79
High-income non-OECD	41.0	40.8	0.68	0.49	0.25	0.22
Latin America and the Caribbean	38.9	23.8	0.62	0.40	0.22	0.13
OECD	12.8	23.1	0.17	0.14	0.05	0.11

Source: Computed from United Nations Series D Trade Records.
Note: "OECD" is Organization for Economic Cooperation and Development.

gions. For example, in terms of industrial development, we can classify the countries in two categories: countries with fairly developed industrial structure (only five countries are in this group, with manufacturing sectors accounting for more than 20 percent of GDP), and those at the pre-industrial stage of development.[6] Clearly, more than 85 percent of Africa has rudimentary industrial base (of less than 20 percent of GDP). This figure masks the fact of the infinitesimal manufactures

[6](1) Of 35 African countries for which data are available in the *World Development Indicators 1997*, only five countries have a manufacturing share in excess of 20 percent of GDP (Burkina Faso, with an industry share of 27 percent and a manufacturing share of 21 percent; Mauritius, with an industry share of 33 percent and a manufacturing share of 23 percent; South Africa, with 31 percent for industry and 24 percent for manufacturing; Zambia, with 40 percent for industry and 30 percent for manufacturing; and Zimbabwe, with 36 percent for industry and 30 percent for manufacturing). (2) Out of the remaining 30 African countries, another five could be considered as marginal cases with a manufacturing share between 18–20 percent of GDP. Three of these five have a share of 18 percent of GDP for manufacturing (Côte d'Ivoire, Lesotho, and Malawi), while two have a manufacturing share of 19 percent (Morocco and Tunisia). The share of the industrial sector in these countries varies from a high of 56 percent for Lesotho to a low of 20 percent for Côte d'Ivoire. (3) For the remaining 25 countries in the sample, the share of manufacturing varies between a low of only 3 percent of GDP (Angola, Ethiopia, and Rwanda) to a high of 16 percent in Chad (with Egypt's manufacturing share being 15 percent of GDP).

Table 8. Value, Share, and Changes in Sub-Saharan Africa's Major Non-Oil Export Products in OECD Markets

Export Product (Standard International Trade Classification)	Value (millions of U.S. dollars)		Percentage Share of African Exports		Africa's Percentage Share of OECD Imports		Global Export Growth Rates (percent)
	1962–64	1991–93	1962–64	1991–93	1962–64	Change	
Unwrought copper alloys (682.1)	510.8	780.8	14.7	5.16	32.4	–22.5	5.69
Green or roasted coffee (071.1)	447.9	1,053.0	12.91	6.95	22.7	–7.2	4.36
Cocoa beans, raw or roasted (072.1)	337.3	1,338.0	9.72	8.83	80.1	–9.9	5.34
Groundnuts, green (221.1)	185.5	11.1	5.35	0.07	81.6	–79.9	3.68
Nonconifer saw logs (242.3)	176.6	734.2	5.09	4.85	36.1	–16.1	7.20
Raw cotton (263.1)	161.0	379.5	4.64	2.51	11.4	1.8	2.48
Unmanufactured tobacco (121.0)	119.9	589.7	3.46	3.89	13.8	–1.6	6.09
Iron ore (281.3)	115.0	247.3	3.32	1.63	9.5	–6.3	6.65
Raw beet and cane sugar (061.1)	93.0	415.1	2.68	2.74	10.0	5.8	3.64
Palm nuts and kernels (221.3)	84.2	2.6	2.43	0.02	92.3	–69.2	–6.95
Natural rubber and gums (231.1)	77.8	191.1	2.24	1.26	10.3	–2.7	4.22
Fresh bananas (051.3)	61.3	202.8	1.77	1.34	14.2	–9.8	8.52
Palm oil (422.2)	57.5	53.0	1.66	0.35	59.0	–54.1	8.63
Vegetable oil residues (081.3)	54.7	68.7	1.58	0.45	10.1	–8.8	8.06
Agave fibers (265.4)	52.7	15.4	1.52	0.10	33.3	18.5	–5.60
Manganese ore (283.7)	44.8	176.2	1.29	1.16	27.8	4.2	4.33
Groundnut oil (421.4)	39.9	78.2	1.15	0.52	55.3	–19.1	3.85
Shaped lumber (243.3)	38.6	418.1	1.11	2.76	15.5	–6.7	10.69
Tea (074.1)	36.7	246.0	1.06	1.62	8.5	13.7	3.31
Base metals (689.5)	36.4	252.4	1.05	1.67	29.2	–16.0	9.88
Posts and poles (242.9)	32.5	1.4	0.94	0.01	57.5	–56.2	3.40
Fixed vegetable oils (422.9)	31.2	6.5	0.90	0.04	48.4	–46.8	6.41
Nonindustrial diamonds (667.2)	26.4	1,792.7	0.76	11.84	5.2	4.3	13.27
Unwrought tin alloys (687.1)	26.0	2.9	0.75	0.02	8.9	–8.5	3.45
Inorganic bases (513.6)	25.2	35.3	0.73	0.23	12.1	–11.4	11.93

Industrial diamonds (275.1)	23.2	23.0	0.67	0.15	21.0	–16.3	5.31
Unwrought aluminum alloys (684.1)	21.3	272.0	0.61	1.80	4.1	–1.6	11.09
Tin ores (283.6)	20.4	6.9	0.59	0.05	19.1	26.2	–6.49
Crude asbestos (276.4)	19.3	23.3	0.56	0.15	10.1	0.3	0.55
Natural gums and resins (292.2)	18.6	76.7	0.54	0.53	28.4	11.8	3.90
Total	2,975.7	9,495.6	85.79	62.69	20.8	–11.1	7.37

Source: World Bank data.
Note: "OECD" is Organization for Economic Cooperation and Development.

Table 9. Industry in Africa

Country	Manufacturing Value Added			MVA per Person	
	1970[1]	1994[1]	Growth, 1984–94	1970[1]	1994[1]
Angola	2,365	326	–9.2	423	31
Benin	122	180	5.8	45	34
Botswana	25	175	6.5	39	121
Burkina Faso	155	287	2.0	28	29
Burundi	40	167	2.4	11	27
Cameroon	444	1,437	1.0	67	125
Central African Republic	94	166	–4.2	26	27
Congo	112	200	–2.3	89	87
Côte d'Ivoire	677	1,141	–3.0	123	84
Ethiopia	178	385	2.3	6	7
Gabon	286	722	–0.1	566	517
Ghana	644	582	5.4	74	34
Guinea	47	122	7.3	12	18
Kenya	208	976	4.6	18	36
Lesotho	8	95	10.6	8	44
Liberia	50	61	–2.8	36	21
Madagascar	278	268	1.4	41	19
Malawi	89	267	1.2	19	25
Mali	58	227	4.0	11	22
Mauritania	45	160	6.9	36	69
Mauritius	105	667	9.9	127	604
Mozambique	606	477	4.7	65	27
Namibia	109	142	1.4	137	95
Niger	109	184	3.4	26	21
Nigeria	457	1,559	2.7	8	16
Reunion	102	313	4.0	221	486
Rwanda	153	132	–7.0	41	17
Senegal	374	766	2.1	90	95
Sierra Leone	43	85	2.7	16	19
Somalia	27	42	3.4	6	5
South Africa	13,511	22,657	–0.1	602	559
Sudan	408	453	–0.5	30	17
Tanzania	76	107	2.2	6	4
Togo	159	87	–3.3	79	21
Uganda	276	259	9.0	28	13
Zaïre	70	35	–4.3	4	0.8
Zambia	508	856	1.9	121	93
Zimbabwe	644	1,313	2.6	122	119
Total (including others)	23,563	39,106	2.0[2]	39[2]	32[2]

Source: UNIDO Global Database.
Note: "MVA" is manufacturing value added.
[1]Millions of dollars, in 1990 prices.
[2]Excluding South Africa.

Table 10. Changing Percentage Share of Manufacturing Value Added in Gross Domestic Product in Sub-Saharan Africa, Selected Countries

Country	1980	1994	Change, 1980–94
Côte d'Ivoire	15	26	+11
South Africa	23	23	—
Zambia	18	23	+5
Mauritius	15	22	+7
Zimbabwe	25	20	–5
Chad	17	16	–1
Malawi	12	14	+2
Senegal	15	14	–1
Burundi	7	12	+5
Cameroon	8	12	+4
Kenya	13	11	–2
Mali	4	9	+5
Togo	8	9	+1
Tanzania	11	8	–3
Ghana	8	8	—
Niger	5	7	+2
Nigeria	8	7	–1
Guinea-Bissau	21	7	–14
Uganda	4	7	+3
Botswana	4	4	—
Ethiopia	6	3	–3
Rwanda	17	3	–14
Sierra Leone	6	2	–4

Source: World Bank (1996).

exports of the region and the fact that these exports are still in the extremely low technology, mostly semiprocessed, light consumer goods. For more than 85 percent of African countries, therefore, competitive industrialization is a process that is yet to begin. Why is this so?

Explaining Africa's failed industrialization is coterminous with explanations for the observed growth tragedy. We do not rehearse the familiar debate here.[7] The old acrimonious debate has increasingly given

[7]According to the neoliberal framework that underpins SAP, the chief culprit is the poor macroeconomic environment that is hostile to competition and profitable enterprise (macroeconomic instability and inflation; exchange rate overvaluation and volatility; protective trade regimes; and so forth. While this school of thought believes other factors could be important, it lays overarching emphasis on "getting prices right." Once the markets are liberalized under a sound macroeconomic environment, competition would be unleashed and enterprise and industrialization should boom. Conversely, the adherents of "industrial policy" point to the plethora of structural, capacity, and institutional constraints that prevent profitable and competitive industrialization.

way to some convergence of views regarding the importance of the major aspects of both kinds of explanations. Controversies persist, however, about the relative weights to be attached to the factors and, more so, about the sequencing of the necessary reforms. I argue that while the key elements of a stable macroeconomic environment are necessary, they are by no means sufficient. For effective supply response in terms of rapid and competitive industrialization, the other supply side context of the macroeconomic environment is critical. I therefore postulate that the stalled industrialization of most of Africa can be explained by such factors as the initial conditions and, infrastructural, capacity, and institutional constraints, as well as by other factors (domestic and external) that impinge upon the functioning of the various markets, small economies, technological base, export capacity and market access, and so forth.

An example of poor initial conditions is the lack of appropriate sociopolitical environment for the flourishing of private enterprise and growth. Collier and Guillaumont (1996) provide an interesting typology of African countries on the basis of their location within the spectrum of the prerequisites for growth. Focusing on the low-income countries (below $1,000 per capita), they filter the countries through a series of three conditions considered necessary foundations for growth: a minimal degree of social stability, a minimal degree of macroeconomic stability, and a minimal degree of allocative efficiency. The idea is that these form a hierarchy of preconditions for growth: without a minimum of social stability, there is little point worrying about macroeconomic stability. Also, if adequate social order is guaranteed but there is macroeconomic chaos, there is little point in worrying about allocative efficiency. Consequently, low-income Africa is divided into four categories. First are economies without peace. Six countries fell into this category: Angola, Burundi, Liberia, Rwanda, Somalia, and Sudan.[8] National accounts statistics are unreliable or unavailable for most of them. However, these countries account for some 61 million (11 percent) of the population in sub-Saharan Africa. Second are economies without a minimum adequate macroeconomic environment. The following 13 African countries, which satisfied the conditions of minimum social order, failed to meet the minimum macroeconomic stability: Comoros, Democratic Republic of the Congo (formerly Zaïre), Equatorial Guinea, Ghana, Madagascar, Malawi, Mozambique, Niger, Nigeria, São Tomé

[8]This categorization was done in 1996. With the recent election in Liberia, peace is expected to return to the country. However, some other countries have quickly taken its place: Sierra Leone and the Republic of Congo.

and Príncipe, Tanzania, Togo, and Zambia. With 240 million people, this group covers some 46 percent of the sub-Saharan African population. Economic statistics are also unreliable in most of these countries. Third are economies without a minimum adequate resource allocation environment. The following countries satisfied the first two conditions but failed on the allocative efficiency criterion: Cameroon, Chad, Congo, Eritrea, Guinea, Kenya, Lesotho, and Zimbabwe. This group has a combined population of 69 million people, or 12 percent of the sub-Saharan African population. Fourth are the countries whose governments were supplying at least modest levels of social order, macroeconomic order, and resource allocation. They include Benin, Burkina Faso, Cape Verde, Côte d'Ivoire, Ethiopia, the Gambia, Guinea-Bissau, Mali, Mauritania, Senegal, and Uganda. Thus, according to this classification, only about 23 percent of the sub-Saharan African population lives in countries with a minimally adequate environment for growth. The emphasis is on the word "minimally," and some of them could not be said to have basic growth-friendly policies. For example, as the authors observe, "Ethiopia has yet to get in place even elementary property rights: it is not yet possible to purchase land on which to build a factory, and the financial system is rudimentary, until 1995 there being a monopoly state commercial bank. Indeed, none of the countries actually rates high across the board on macroeconomic and resource allocation policies." On the basis of statistics up to 1996, the authors make the following inference about the growth performance of the different groups (Collier and Guillaumont, 1996): for countries with an inadequate social order, with 11 percent of the population, per capita GDP growth was –4.0 percent in 1990–94; for countries with inadequate macro policies, with 46 percent of the population, growth was –1.3 percent in 1992–94; for countries with an inadequate resource allocation, with 12 percent of the population, growth was –2.8 percent in 1992–94; for countries with a minimally adequate environment, with 23 percent of the population, growth was +6.2 percent in 1995; and for countries that were already middle income, with 8 percent of the population, data were not available.

Evidently, only 23 percent of Africa's low-income population lives in countries with a minimally adequate environment for growth, while more than 85 percent of the countries have rudimentary industrial infrastructure. In other words, without a minimally adequate environment, discussions about industrial restructuring and the competitiveness of manufactures become sterile. In such circumstances, it is difficult for private investment to flourish, or for government attempts at creating industrial infrastructure to succeed. Since more than 70 percent of Africa had existed in environments without such minimum conditions, it is little surprise that industrialization has yet to take root.

Another aspect of the initial conditions is the fact that the environment in most of Africa has been atypically hostile to private investment. Industrialization is about investment, and investment is about balancing risks and returns. New investment theories (investment under uncertainties and irreversibility of fixed investment) provide insights into why Africans and foreigners choose not to invest in Africa. On a risk-return analysis, Africa is rated as the worst in the world. From the risk rating index used by institutional investors, Africa is rated as the most risky region in the world, and its position even deteriorated during the 1980s from 31.8 in 1979 to 21.7 in 1995. Risk in this sense is related to a gamut of indexes ranging from political instability, volatile macroeconomic environment, civil strife, and natural disasters, lack of effective mechanisms for enforcement of contracts, and so forth (see Table 11). For foreign investors, risk is the most important impediment to investment. For example, a survey of 225 investors identified fear of political instability as the most important of ten constraints (Blakey, 1994). The World Bank's (1994b) survey of about 150 firms in East Africa found several deterrents to investment, including: political and economic policy uncertainty, the lack of currency convertibility, poor infrastructure and regulation, rudimentary financial and business services, breaches of contract, and high taxation. The risk of policy reversal was ranked as the most important deterrent. Other deterrents cited in the empirical literature include endemic corruption, the uncertain reputation of governments due to a finite possibility of policy reversal, and the illiquidity of firms' fixed assets (which is attributed both to the breakdown of the private audit profession in verifying firms' accounts and to the failure of the civil legal system to establish and enforce legal title). In essence, poor institutions interact with volatile policy and political environments to heighten the riskiness of African environments. It is little wonder, then, that relative to other regions, capital flight is very pervasive, thereby denying the region of the scarce investible resources that could potentially make the difference in its quest for industrial diversification (see Tables 11 and 12 for the incidence of capital flight).

These basic elements of risk interact with the poor provision of public infrastructure, complex regulatory environment, high taxation on capital, corruption, and so forth to make investments in Africa highly unprofitable relative to the rest of the world. Where public infrastructure is scanty, unreliable, and very costly, firms often have to accommodate these through private provisions. For example, more than 80 percent of firms in Nigeria have to provide their own electricity generators, dig their own boreholes for water, buy poles and wires to extend telephones to factory sites, and sometimes have to

Table 11. Aggregate Risk Indicators for Major World Regions

Region	Macrofinancial Volatility Index, 1960–94	Macroeconomic Crisis Index, 1960–94	*Institutional Investor* Risk Rating Index, 1979–94	Capital Flight Stock as Percentage of GDP, 1980–90	Civil Liberty Index, 1960–89
Sub-Saharan Africa	1.05	1.14	1.62	90	5.65
Latin America and Caribbean	1.12	1.69	1.21	30	3.70
East Asia	0.73	0.55	0.56	18	4.90
South Asia	0.73	0.55	0.56	20	4.20
Organization for Economic Cooperation and Development	0.46	0.33	0.32	. . .	1.00
Other (Oceania and Middle East)	. . .	. . .	. . .	110	5.15

Source: Nissanke (1997).

Note: Elbadawi and Schmit-Hebbel's index of macrofinancial policy volatility is an ex post measure defined as the equally weighted sum of the standard deviations of the ratio of public deficit to GDP, the ratio of current account deficit to GDP, the inflation rate, and the real exchange rate. The measure of macroeconomic crisis is proxied by the one-sided deviation of outcomes from sustainable threshold levels of the macroeconomic policy indicators.

Table 12. Capital Flight Stock as a Ratio of Selected Variables

Country	Ratio of Flight Capital Stock to 1991 GDP (Percent)	Estimated Value of Capital Flight Stock for 1991 (Billions of U.S. dollars)	Ratio of External Debt Stock to Capital Flight Stock, 1991 (Percent)
Sudan	290	48.02	31.70
Egypt	250	119.20	27.71
Gabon	230	11.10	38.06
Nigeria	160	50.10	66.95
Uganda	130	10.52	26.40

Source: Computed from data in Claessens and Naude (1993) and World Bank (1997).

Note: Stock of capital flight covered the 1981–91 period only. This grossly underestimates the capital flight from a country such as Nigeria, where the bulk of the flight is estimated to have taken place during the oil boom period of the 1970s.

construct access roads to their factory sites. Investors in most African countries have to go through a hell of complicated procedures and red tape of paperwork to register companies. Endemic corruption, which means that investors have to bribe their way through everything, including installing electric generators, constitutes a high level of taxation on investment. Just the hassles of setting up and running businesses in several African countries are enough to discourage the most ardent investor.

As the new investment theories would predict, private investors have reacted to the hostile and uncertain environment in certain rational ways. First, the option value of waiting increases, and it is little surprise that capital flight is pervasive. Second, agents have structured the composition of their domestic investment to emphasize mostly reversible and safe investments that have self-insurance characters. Agents systematically choose safe and liquid assets over less liquid ones. It is no surprise, therefore, that many African countries have become nations of traders, with the distributive trade sector booming at the expense of the productive (industrial) sector. This environment also has implications for the flow of FDI. When citizens do not have the confidence to invest in their own countries, foreigners have little motivation to be adventurous. This explains why most of the FDI flows to Africa have concentrated in the mining (extractive) sectors.

Tangential to the above is the nature of defective or missing markets and the implication for adjustment costs and supply response. The free trade argument is predicated on efficiently functioning markets, with very little adjustment costs and free mobility of productive resources. Evidently, environments characterized by structural and price rigidities, factor immobility, wage rigidity, defective money and capital markets, and so forth can greatly reduce the speed and nature of supply response.

Interlinked with the poor infrastructural base and defective or missing markets is the atypically poor institutional capacity of the state to manage the economy—including industrialization. This is compounded by the atypically low levels of educational attainment and skills development, as well as the small but nascent entrepreneurial class with requisite capital. Africa is the most illiterate region, and one where the critical technical and managerial skills for the operations of modern industry are in most acute short supply. This is exacerbated by the massive brain drain that is complicated by declining investment in education and soft infrastructure in terms of institutions—capital and money markets, audit and accounting standards and facilities; enforcement of contracts; transparent and efficient bureaucracy that reduces the cost of doing business; institutions for business-government dialogue and understanding; and so forth. In this environment, it is not conceivable how merely "getting prices right" through some trade reforms or just macroeconomic stability can elicit sustainable and competitive industrialization.

In addition, export-oriented industrialization requires the building of export competence. Penetrating and sustaining positions in export markets require a level of productivity and managerial and technical skills that is lacking in most sub-Saharan African countries. It is therefore conceivable that part of the observed sluggish export response can be attributed to the weak technological capability and lack of export competence, as well as the daunting infrastructural costs of exporting. Several African countries are landlocked, and access to cheap sea transport is a tall dream. Even for countries with easy access to the seaports, all studies show that Africa faces the highest transport and telecommunication costs in the world. For example, Yeats and others (1997, p. 17) note that:

> In 1990/91 Sub-Saharan Africa's net freight and insurance payments were about $3.9 billion, or roughly 15 percent of the value of the region's exports, compared with 11 percent in 1970 . . . Individual country statistics, however, show wide variations. Net transport and insurance payments absorbed more than 25 percent of the value of exports for a third of African countries and exceeded 70 percent for Somalia and Uganda. Net payments averaged 42 percentage points for the landlocked African countries—almost 25 percentage points higher than the average for other African countries. The implication is that a large share of Africa's foreign exchange earnings that might otherwise be used for productive capacity-building investments is being used to pay for international transport costs.

Finally, there are a number of other constraints, stemming from both the region's initial conditions and the altered global environment, that obstruct Africa's industrial development (see Box 1).

Box 1 points to the magnitude of the challenges facing African industrialization efforts. We would return to the implications of these for the design of an effective strategy. Before then, we examine the nature of the consensus about the requirements for industrial competitiveness in developing countries.

Systemic Competitiveness and Lessons from Asia

Even though several of the above challenges might be peculiar, Africa's state of underindustrialization is not unique. Several countries have passed through similar phases, and some others in other regions are in an identical situation. There are thus some accumulated experiences on how some countries have managed to leapfrog the process, and achieved miraculous industrial transformation. Some East and Southeast Asian countries provide examples of such bold testimonials. Three key aspects of the emerging lessons within the context of the current global environment are the importance of building market-friendly, systemic competitiveness; the active role of the government in creating dynamic comparative advantages; and the need to acquire technological competence.

"Competitiveness" is a word whose meaning in the context of industrialization is replete with controversy.[9] However, the *World Competitiveness Report* (1994) defines it as "the ability of a country or a company to, proportionally, generate more wealth than its competitors in world markets." Thus, to be globally competitive "is the combination of a country's assets, either inherited (for example, natural resources) or created (for example, infrastructure), and the processes (for example, manufacturing) that transform them into economic results, and which meet with the test of the international market (internationalization)." Achieving national competitiveness requires systemic competitiveness in the sense of a framework for the interaction of the state and societal factors in creating the conditions for successful industrial development and thus national competitiveness.[10] This framework is

[9]Controversies abound, not only about the meaning, measurement, and key characteristics of competitiveness, but also about the extent of application of the term. Some leading economists argue that nations do not compete, because they do not go out of business . . . they have no well-defined bottom line.

[10]See Altenburg, and others (1997), and Kurozumi (1995) for detailed discussions of the elements and ramifications of systemic competitiveness. Much of the discussion here benefits from these.

Box 1. Obstacles to Successful Industrialization in Low-Income Africa

The countries in low-income Africa face several obstacles to successful liberalization.

- Their comparative advantage lies chiefly in low labor costs (sometimes also relatively low raw materials and energy costs). These "lower-order" comparative advantages are increasingly less important in global competition today.
- Their main competitive strengths are in precisely those industries where demand growth is slowest and where international competition, especially from low-cost Asian suppliers, is increasingly intense.
- They are not part of any cluster; there is no Japan, Hong Kong, or Singapore to undertake FDI on the scale witnessed in East or Southeast Asia.
- They are at a serious disadvantage with respect to infrastructural costs, especially transport.
- They are at the bottom of the global league in terms of industrial sophistication and technology.
- The private sector is very weak in Africa, dominated by a relatively small number of major multinationals at one extreme and by a mass of small and microenterprises at the other, the "middle"—made up of medium-sized indigenous firms—is missing.
- The technological terms of trade have moved against late starters. The admission fee for the acquisition of new technology has risen, both in money terms and—more important—in terms of the skills needed by operators, technicians, and managers.
- The increasing importance of labor quality in the attraction of FDI counts against Africa when firms consider offshore investment in manufacturing.
- The region has become excessively and unsustainably dependent on external support, including foreign technology and expatriate skills.

Source: UNIDO (1996), p. 122.

predicated on the assumption that competitive advantages only partially emerge due to the invisible hand of the market, and are to a significant extent being created by deliberate, collective actions.

Lessons of experience show that the sterile debate about state versus markets in industrial development is misplaced. Both have played significant roles in the success stories. The secret of success lies in finding the optimal balance between intervention—formulation and implementation of targeted policies to stimulate and shape industrial development—and market forces. Finding such a balance is not easy and remains the key challenge of industrial development in developing countries. The key elements of the market-state balance involve analysis and actions at four key levels: meta, macro, meso, and micro (see Altenburg and others, 1997, pp. 5–22).

Meta level: This refers to the nature of the control and governance capacity of government and collective problem-solving arrangements. Systemic competitiveness cannot happen without social transformation and social integration. This is more so in the context of the weak markets, weak firms, and weak states that characterize many developing countries. In some countries, this has further deteriorated due to SAP, and failure to establish regulatory and governance capacities (government reform, formation of complex linkages between strategic actors) and the requisite social structures. The governance structure should produce a basic consensus on the necessity of industrial development and integration into the global system.

If fundamental differences exist on these issues, macro and meso policies designed to support industry will be erratic, and firms will develop a defensive posture to be able to react quickly to changes in the rules of the game. Thus some of the major elements of this level include the development-oriented pattern of politico-economic organization, the ability to formulate strategies and policies, learning- and change-friendly value attitudes, and social cohesion.

Macro level: This requires an enabling and well-functioning macroeconomic environment: developed and well functioning factor, goods, and capital markets, as well as a stable and predictable macroeconomic framework. This should include a realistic exchange rate policy and a general trade policy regime that stimulates local industry. Generally, it is almost impossible for firms to become globally competitive when the national macroeconomic environment facing them is not competitive.

Meso level: This refers to specific policies and institutions targeted to shape industries and their environment. In the current world order, it is no longer only individual firms that compete with each other but industrial clusters, groups of firms organized in networks, whose dynamic development depends on the potential of the particular location, in other words continuous and close contact with research and development facilities, technology formation and dissemination institutions, universities, training institutions, finance institutions, export information, and other institutions. There are increasing demands on the local, regional, and national levels to create and support a business-friendly environment, and this applies to demands on business associations and other nongovernmental actors as well as to demands on government at all these levels. The key point here, is that in the highly competitive world trading system, national and regional governments are under pressure to devise institutions to nurture and promote the competitiveness of the industrial clusters and groups of firms.

Thus a major aim of meso policies is to create specific locational advantages. This, among other things, requires actions on the following: (1) technology (contract research, technology extension, consultancy, business associations, universities, selectivity, and networking); (2) education and training (public and private institutions, technical orientation and specialization); (3) finance (investment credit, working capital, equity, insurance, export finance, patience, and risk-friendly disposition); (4) infrastructure (rail, road, water, air transport, harbors, telecommunication, energy, and so forth); (5) exports (foreign market information, design, trade insurance, and trading companies—specialization and close links to private business); and (6) environment (supervision, pressure, support, and so forth).

Furthermore, two key aspects of the mesolevel task with the central government pertain to large-scale technology initiatives and the formulation of an overall long-term strategy. Competitive advantage is increasingly less a function of cost or price and more one of quality, style, design, and timely and after-sales service. For many developing countries, acquiring the necessary competence and sustaining technological upgrading in these areas requires interactions between the various actors.

Micro level: Industrial development requires capable and competitive firms, and networks of firms with strong externalities. To be competitive, firms have to optimize on cost-efficiency, quality, variety, and responsiveness to changes in demand and new opportunities.

The above levels of analysis and requirements for systemic competitiveness can be regarded as a model of industrialization. The four key elements are interrelated, and emphasize the kind of strategic partnership that should exist between business and government. Most advanced industrial countries have passed through such phases, and continue to deepen the interactions. The most recent examples of the payoffs of such strategic process is the East and Southeast Asian experience.

Despite the continuing controversies about the interpretations of some aspects of the experience and the relative weights to be attached to the critical factors, there is a broad consensus that the four elements discussed above played important roles. It is generally agreed that there is no unique Asian model as the detailed strategies differed from country to country. However, certain broad elements characterize much of the experience. The first key element in all the success stories of Asia is the ability to articulate and pursue a strategic long-term vision of industrialization and economic transformation. UNCTAD

(1996, pp. 11–12) summarizes four other major elements of the strategy, as follows:

First, policies and institutions were developed to promote profit-investment nexus, which entailed three activities. (1) A stable political environment and pro-investment macroeconomic policies were fostered to sustain the investors' confidence. (2) Both general and specific investment incentives were provided through measures to create artificially high profits. This was achieved in two ways. First, a range of fiscal instruments was used to supplement corporate profits and to encourage their retention to accelerate capital accumulation; tax exemptions and special depreciation allowances were applied both in general and to targeted industries. Second, a set of trade, financial, and competition policies was used to create "rents" that boosted corporate profits and thus provided investable resources available to corporations. Such policies included a mix of selective trade protection, controls over interest rates and credit allocation, and various strategies to manage competition. (3) Entrepreneurs were disciplined by closing off channels for unproductive investments and capital flight, and restricting luxury consumption. Consumption was restricted directly through curbs on the importing and domestic production of luxury consumption goods, and indirectly through high taxation and restrictions on consumer credits.

Second, an export-investment nexus was promoted by (1) initially promoting traditional exports (primary commodities and labor-intensive industries) to maximize foreign exchange receipts to buy capital goods that embody more advanced technologies; (2) promoting more demanding industries identified on a number of criteria (for example, productivity growth potential, conformity with domestic technological capabilities, demand prospects) through the creation, manipulation, and timely destruction of rents; and (3) upgrading through strategic integration with the international economy, using the disciplinary power of international markets alongside measures of export promotion, and using FDI selectively and strategically to access more advanced technologies abroad.

Third, a strong government-business network was created by (1) promoting an independent economic bureaucracy, including a network of agencies at the sectoral level; and (2) establishing strong links between industrial firms and the financial sector in ways to promote productive investment.

Fourth, the danger of marginalization was addressed by (1) supporting small-scale producers both in the rural and industrial sectors through targeted public investment, subsidized credit, and appropriate advisory services; and (2) supporting upgrading by linking small producers to large firms and public research institutes.

One striking feature of the Asian experience is the successful interaction between the state and the private sector, and more so the ingenuity of the state in creating the institutions (meta and meso level) for industrialization. Both the nature of this strategic partnership between the state and the private sector, as well as the kinds of interventions, raise important questions about the replicability of such an experience in the African context. This concern is ostensibly because of the weak state–weak private sector situation that characterizes most of Africa, and the changed rules of the game under the WTO and deepening globalization. An unresolved question is the nature of industrialization strategy that Africa should adopt in the light of its own initial conditions and the realities of the global setting.

Globalization and Industrialization

"Globalization" is the new buzzword that both describes the breakneck technological changes and rapid market integration, as well as prescribes the set of homogenous (neoliberal) policies toward which all countries are expected to converge. It captures the increasing harmonization of national policies regarding trade, investment, industrialization, and competition, and related issues, especially under the aegis of the multilateral institutions—particularly the WTO. In the light of the extension of issues beyond trade into other areas such as intellectual property, investment and investment measures, agreements on services, communications, information technology, and the environment, the WTO's scope for affecting national policies extend beyond trade. Accession to the WTO has profound implications for the strategy of industrialization as it presents both opportunities and constraints.

In the area of industrialization, two key provisions of the WTO rules with near-term implications are the phasing out of the MFAs on clothing and textiles over 10 years and tariff cuts. Tariffication of NTBs and lowering of tariffs are the hallmarks of the new regime. For developing countries in particular, average tariffs will be cut by about a fifth, and this agreement on tariff binding will mean that developing-country imports of products subject to bound tariffs (that is, that cannot be raised) will increase from 25 percent to 75 percent of their total imports.

Two other aspects of the Uruguay Round–WTO rules that would affect industry are trade-related investment measures (TRIMs) and trade-related intellectual property rights (TRIPS). Under TRIMs, developing countries are required to abolish local content requirements and trade balancing tests within five years (least developed countries have seven years to do so). The TRIPs are designed to protect intellectual property (currently owned mainly by the OECD firms). This eliminates the prospects of copy-technology (reverse engineering), and forces potential users of foreign technology into licensing agreements and royalty payments. This has some adverse consequences for technological upgrading and adaptation.

On the benefits side, market access is expected to improve significantly, and there is an insurance policy against future barriers to the export markets. Beneficiaries of some aspects of the Uruguay Round will be the exporters of leather, rubber, footwear, and travel goods (all of whom will enjoy tariff reductions) and exporters of tanned leather, wood and paper products, and yarns or jute (who gain from the reduction in tariff escalation).

However, even though market access might improve, the generalized system of MFN status and trends in regionalism are likely to reduce the preferences enjoyed by African countries under the Lomé convention and concessions for the least-developed countries under the WTO. As the OECD-based regional blocs extend preferences to one another, any potential preferential and differential treatments granted to the least-developed countries are likely to be eroded. Since the least-developed countries are unlikely to compete on equal footing with the OECD economies, the objective of the WTO in granting them preferential treatments is defeated by regionalism.

In other words, the new global environment and the rules of operation have significantly altered. As UNCTAD (1996, p. 25) observes:

> It is undeniable that the global economy is currently going through significant changes. The new trading regime under the WTO has reduced the scope for using some measures which call for trade-related subsidies, lax enforcement of intellectual property rights, and strategic conditions imposed on foreign investments, which were integral parts of the East Asian development strategy. Certainly, the more generalized protection which provided a backdrop for targeted policies in East Asia is no longer possible, and many of the export promotion policies no longer appear permissible. It may also be true that the changes will reduce the scope for policy maneuver for the developing countries which wish to pursue a strategy involving vigorous infant industry protection and export subsidies.

The situation may not be as hopeless as depicted above (see Soludo, 1997b). Even though the WTO has tried to provide a homogenous set of multilateral obligations, it has also made some "differential and preferential" provisions for the "least-developed countries" as listed in Annex VII to the Agreement on Subsidies and Countervailing Measures. The major threat to the effective deployment of these provisions is the intra-OECD preferential treatments under regionalism as discussed earlier. But there is still some room to maneuver. For example, the infant industry protection can creatively be deployed by developing countries meeting the balance of payments criteria, although the "Understanding" relating to this Article strongly discourages resort to quantitative measures and also provides for stricter multilateral surveillance. To the extent that tariffs remain unbound or bound at ceilings above currently applied rates, countries can creatively deploy the provision for infant industry protection. Furthermore, the Agreement on Subsidies and Countervailing Measures contains some of the most favorable provisions on differential and more favorable treatment, some of which have no precise time limits. The least-developed countries and other 20 countries with per capita GDP of less than $1,000 are exempt from the prohibition of export subsidies as long as they remain in these categories and do not exceed certain thresholds based on shares of world markets for products benefiting from export subsidies. In summary, although the changing international environment could constrain the freedom to conduct East-Asian-style interventionist policies, "There is considerable scope for maneuver, if countries skillfully use various 'permissible' subsidies, balance of payments clauses, non-trade-related policy measures, and are more creative in interpreting the new international trading rules" (UNCTAD, 1996, p. 29).

The major conclusion from the foregoing is that though their scope and pervasiveness have diminished, strategic and selective policies can still be implemented, albeit under different modalities/instruments and changing circumstances. Also, it seems fairly intuitive from the discussions above regarding the plethora of market failures, the disadvantages of late starters, the structure of African industry, and peculiar geographic and structural constraints, that some selective, targeted policies are still necessary (despite globalization). This point is evident also from the discussions on the requirements for systemic competitiveness above. The major challenge pertains to the specific nature of such policies, and whether or how African countries can effectively design and implement them.

Designing an Industrialization Strategy in the New World Order

The Framework

What is evident from our discussions so far is that industrialization strategy in the years ahead cannot be business as usual. Neither the extreme statist model of the orthodox ISI nor the laissez-faire model under SAP will do. An appropriate model, especially for the least-developed countries of Africa, must be of the eclectic, middle-of-the-road kind in which the actors (state and private sectors) strategically cooperate to achieve a well-defined national industrialization vision. Experience teaches that dynamic comparative advantages are not destiny; rather, they are the products of deliberate creations by societal forces. As we noted in the review of the model of systemic competitiveness and also from the latest rediscovery of the state by the World Bank (1997), it is evident that, without an active state working in strategic partnership with the private sector to create and maintain such advantages, they would not happen. A viable blueprint to create and sustain such dynamic comparative advantages and international competitiveness would, among other things, require policies to build and liberalize markets, tackle various facets of market failures, provide critical public goods, and address major capacity and institutional constraints that would not only guarantee property rights and enforcement of contracts but also eliminate the myriad regulatory nightmares that increase the hassle effects of productive investment and enterprise. Details of the policy areas would depend on each country's initial conditions, time horizon, and capacity.

It is easier to agree on the long-term goal of rapid structural transformation, diversification into manufactures, and achieving and sustaining industrial competitiveness. For individual countries, such a goal might be translated into quantitative targets, for example, the alteration of the composition of exports so that manufactures account for, say, 60 percent by the year 2020. The harder job is the design of effective strategy to attain the goal. Effective design of a blueprint must take full cognition of the differentiation in Africa. As indicated above, African countries differ significantly with respect to several key initial conditions that would make a one-shoe-fits-all strategy inappropriate. For example, the first question policymakers face is whether to deepen efforts at fullest exploitation of the static comparative advantages in the primary sector or to become more ambitious in terms of diversification.[11] For some analysts, sub-Saharan Africa should pursue a systematic process of industrial and technological upgrading—initially emphasizing industries that maximize the exploitation of the region's comparative advantages in agriculture and agro-allied industries and over time upgrade to medium-scale and perhaps ulti-

[11]Currently, sub-Saharan Africa's competitive advantage is restricted to resource-based activities, oil, energy, mining, agriculture, and processing industries, with tight primary sector linkages such as food processing and minerals, low-wage labor, and tourism. Should countries risk the deepening of their vulnerability by specializing in natural-resource processing, or should they venture into high-technology, skill-intensive manufacturing? Global competitiveness in manufactures is about skills, and this is where Africa (with the exception of South Africa) is grossly deficient.

mately (long-run) venture into high-technology, capital-intensive manufactures. This is a matter for individual countries to decide upon, depending on their initial conditions. Some countries (Botswana, Côte d'Ivoire, Ghana, Kenya, Mauritius, Nigeria, South Africa, Zimbabwe, and others) can afford to be more adventurous in their bid to develop into best practices, networking, and targeting globally competitive small and medium-sized enterprises. For some others, the key challenge might lie in creating the enabling environment for even the most basic micro and small enterprises to take root. Once the long-term national vision (and perhaps also the sequencing and phasing of the process) is articulated, the next task is that of devising detailed strategies to accomplish it.

Elements of the Strategy

The elements of any country's strategy must be rooted in its initial conditions and circumscribed by the globalizing process. Very broadly, UNIDO (1996) has summarized some of the useful lessons for developing countries (see Box 2).

Box 2 is a useful template, which could be elaborated on or modified to suit individual countries. For the specific case of low-income (pre-industrial) sub-Saharan African countries, we elaborate on several major elements: reorientation to a private-sector-led industrialization strategy and role of the state; appropriate trade policy for industrialization and the role of the international donor community.

Private Sector Investment

A major development experience is that, though the state can do much to create and foster systemic competitiveness, it is ultimately firms that compete in the global arena. Four key ingredients for successful industrialization include competent firms with a strategic vision, a demanding domestic market, highly capable supporting industries, and a well-developed environment of specific supporting institutions (Altenburg, and others, 1997, p. 9). Emphasis is laid on "capable" firms, which arise in an environment that promotes private investment and profitable enterprise.

Rodrik (1995) has shown that the Asian miracle was predicated essentially on governments' ability to "engineer a significant increase in the private return to capital. They did so not only by removing a number of impediments to investment and establishing a sound investment climate, but more importantly by alleviating a coordination failure which had blocked economic take-off." Rodrik observes, however,

Box 2. Elements of the Emerging Consensus on Strategy for Industrialization in the Least-Developed Countries

There is an emerging consensus on the strategy for industrialization that the least-developed countries need to follow. The elements of the growing consensus include the following:

- Because there is no single East Asian model to emulate and no firm consensus on precisely what form of intervention will optimize growth in developing countries, and especially least-developed countries, industrial policy is best viewed as a menu of options. The range of choice open to governments is narrowing as globalization takes hold because although globalization does not eliminate the need for industrial policy, it limits the options.
- The shift in strategy on the part of the East Asian newly industrialized economies themselves, partly in response to the forces of globalization but also reflecting the evolution of industrial policy, suggests that developing countries have more to learn from the recent experience of Southeast Asian economies (Indonesia, Malaysia, and Thailand) than the four original newly industrialized economies.
- One of the most important lessons of East Asian experience is that intervention worked where it was carried out in close coordination with the private sector. Industrial policy responded to the problems and needs of private enterprise rather than seeking to impose elaborate schemes according to the dictates of grandiose national plans.
- Ultimately, competitiveness succeeds or fails at the enterprise rather than the national level. Governments must create an enabling environment for business and investment, but the choices of what to make and sell, and how and where to do it, must be left to entrepreneurs.
- There is broad agreement on the need for some selective, targeted interventions and on the importance of outward-oriented strategies, whereby a country's manufacturing sector is driven by the discipline of market competition.
- Where selective interventions are used, these must be closely coordinated and integrated. Uncoordinated intervention in factor markets without appropriate measures in product markets will be ineffective or even counterproductive.
- Because resources are limited, only a few activities should be supported at any one time. Targeting is crucial.
- Incremental measures and modest technological advances are preferable. Learning is cumulative, and intervention must support activities that have a base in existing skills.

that "for economies at the other end of the spectrum—lacking both skilled labor and capital—the coordination issue is moot because the modern sector is not viable in the first instance." Most sub-Saharan

- The more prosperous the developing country, the greater the range of choice. Least-developed countries in tiny markets, with weak infrastructures and a poor skills and technology base, have little option but to focus on simple, consumer-based industries, initially at least. Given their small markets, their prospects for attracting major FDI inflows (other than into natural resource industries) are poor. For such states the option of shutting out technology and FDI has no advantage, and they may need to concentrate on fostering labor-intensive operations and on developing an export-platform strategy, as in Mauritius.
- Technological upgrading and human capital investment are crucial to competitiveness beyond the year 2000. There is a clear role for the state—and for UNIDO and other international agencies—in both fields.
- Domestic rivalry is a prerequisite for competitiveness.
- Clusters and industrial districts have an important role in the development of globally competitive small and medium-sized enterprises.
- Incentives are more likely to succeed than sanctions. Efforts to constrain FDI or limit technology imports run the risk of deterring investment altogether.
- SAPs should include a specific strategy for manufacturing. The expectation that manufacturing will blossom in the absence of a coherent strategy has not been borne out by African experience.
- Global competitiveness is two-tier in nature, requiring a blend of national (comparative) advantage and enterprise-driven, strategic advantage. Industry-level competitiveness in global markets invariably depends on a combination of the two. Even in globalized industries—and not all industries are global—the home base, and with it national economic policy, is of major importance. Industrial development cannot be imposed from abroad; indigenous industry capability and productive systems are crucial for long-term industrialization. The home base shapes a company's capacity to innovate rapidly in technology and methods and to do so in proper directions. It is the place from which competitive advantage ultimately emanates and from which it must be sustained.

Source: UNIDO (1996).

African countries fall under this second category, and therefore have not reached the threshold required to trigger a profitable investment boom. Evident from discussions of reasons for industrial stagnation is the fact that critical preconditions for industrial takeoff (physical, skill, and institutional mechanisms) are lacking.

Therefore, the first order of business for a majority of countries is to take immediate action to lay the foundations for private investment to thrive and flourish by investing in education and training, especially with respect to science, engineering, and management; provision of basic infrastructure (including the privatization or commercialization of telecommunications and utilities companies); the creation or strengthening of the financial system to finance investment in industry; and promotion of technological learning, acquisition, and adaptation/innovation. "The need for 'critical mass' is paramount—progress must be made on several fronts simultaneously. Policymakers must tackle trade, fiscal policy, law and order, transparency and accountability, infrastructure, human resource development, privatization, agricultural development and industry strategy. Progress on one or two fronts alone is insufficient" (UNIDO, 1996, p. 130).

A strategy to tackle the supply-side constraints might be to resuscitate or create the industrial banks, the import-export banks, and insurance companies. These could be charged with responsibility of financing investment in industrial restructuring, technological upgrading, investments in risky or high-cost projects, extension of credit to industrialists at concessional interest rates (with an incentive system that demands accountability and performance), export subsidies, and/or export promotion measures. The major principle here is that urgent actions are needed to restructure the factor and product markets, and the credit and capital markets are central to any such transformation. More broadly, the financial sector needs to be strengthened to effectively maintain the fine balance between necessary risk-taking and prudent management of shareholders' and depositors' assets. Trade and industrial courts could also be established for dispute arbitration and adjudication over contracts and other industrial matters.

The role of the state should be circumscribed by the requirements to build and strengthen the private sector. To address the issue of the state capability requires honest and serious actions to redress the myriad institutional weaknesses. The World Bank (1997) identifies three conditions that must be present before active state intervention can enhance market operations: "First, and perhaps most important, companies and officials need to be working on a basis of mutual trust . . . Second, initiatives to promote industrial development must be kept honest through competitive market pressures . . . Third, a country's strategy for industrial development has to be guided by its evolving comparative advantage." While the third might be controversial, the first two are not. The first requires ingenuity in creating government-private sector partnerships that involve credible government commitment to involve the private sector in industrial policy design and implementation. Indeed, according to Altenburg and others (1997, pp. 21–22), the two most important "preconditions for a dynamic industrial development process are: first, the key actors in a society (political-administrative system, private sector, trade unions, other parts of civil society) need to share a clear development commitment. Second, there must be a clear consensus about the desirability of an industrial development process (rather than, for instance, a predominant view that the nation's vocation is rather exploitation of natural resources)."

These conditions presuppose the existence of a capable state and a strong private sector. However, aside from a few countries that can be characterized as having both a strong state and a strong private sector, others mostly have one or the other of the three typologies of strong state and weak private sector, weak state and strong private sector, or weak state and weak private sector. Therefore, what makes strategic industrial policies more circumscribed in most of Africa is the unique paradox that, whereas in other regions, the bourgeoisie created the state or collaborated with it, in most of Africa the same poor, and weak states are expected to create and nurture the capitalist class. Evans (1992) has described the kind of institution that propelled the Asian interventionist policies as "embedded autonomy," in which the Weberian bureaucracy interacted actively with private sector (capitalists) to realize the national objectives. Such kinds of interactions requires not only a relatively developed capitalist class but also that they are dominated by "indigenous" capitalists with whom the state can work in pursuit of "national interests." Creating and empowering such a class in much of Africa with diminishing resources, and even more in the context of the WTO and globalization, pose monumental challenges. Furthermore, in some African countries, governments see the emerging capitalist class as potential competitors for power and influence and thus do everything to obstruct them. With the sense of rivalry and mistrust rather than partnership, the private agents have often reacted by keeping the bulk of their wealth abroad or in liquid assets. Such an environment is hardly conducive for effective design and implementation of industrial policy. Creating trust and partnership takes time and effort, and governments must lead the way.

State capacity is not destiny, and ultimately there is no detour around the issue of having a capable and visionary state. While conscious efforts have to be taken to strengthen state capacity to engineer long-term competitiveness, in the short to medium terms, a weak state should recognize its shortcomings and emphasize effectiveness in the delivery of a modest menu of services. Furthermore, some states with some modest capacity should seek to strengthen or create relevant agencies to design and coordinate the implementation of industrial policies. Many countries have ministries of trade and industry, with several other activities that impinge on policy implementation dispersed among a multiplicity of other agencies. A task force on industrial competitiveness could, for example, be created and located within the presidency to coordinate the activities of the numerous agencies and report directly to the president on regular basis. A key goal of the coordination is to ensure transparency, ease of doing business, and effective implementation. Continuing dialogue and exchange between the organized private sector and the agency should be the hallmark of the efforts.

Finally, building market shares and achieving dynamic comparative advantage requires climbing up the technological ladder and shifting from inherited or endowed comparative advantage to dynamic or created advantage. Technological learning and upgrading are critical here. Path dependency in technological learning implies that an enterprise's ability to learn depends on its past learning. Accumulated capabilities therefore significantly influence not just the cost of today's learning but also whether new learning is possible at all. Here, state actions and policies in helping firms break out of the vicious circle of poor initial conditions and thus perpetuation of low-technology equilibrium are critical.

Appropriate Trade Policy Stance

The choice of an appropriate trade policy regime that is consistent with the stage of, and requirements for, industrialization in Africa is a contentious one. Broad consensus exists however about the need for outward-orientation (as opposed to earlier model of ISI). Consequently, there is increasingly a convergence of views about the imperatives of a competitive exchange rate regime, export promotion measures, tariffication of nontariff barriers, and simplification of the tariff structure. Controversy persists about the magnitude, speed, and sequencing of import liberalization. The debate is mostly about whether the nascent industries need any protection, and the consistency of high import tariffs with the requirements for export promotion.

On the need for trade protection, it should be stressed that the infant-industry arguments continue to be valid, and even the special provisions of the Uruguay Round for the least-developed countries recognize these. As some World Bank economists (see Biggs and Srivastava, 1996, p. 25) suggest, "regarding trade policy, there is no a priori reason why Africa should not benefit from some form of infant industry protection to promote learning in domestic firms, as has been evident in the cases of most successful developers in this century." Ndulu and van de Walle (1996, p. 21) corroborate this by noting that "given various disadvantages and constraints facing private investors, states probably need to implement targeted policies to favor key sectors, subsidize the acquisition of needed technologies and skills in the working-age population, or to protect infant industries judiciously and encourage small and medium enterprises." In other words, "there are . . . some problems which might be lessened by proactive, industry-level policies" (Biggs and Srivastava, 1996). For late starters, there is hardly any way to start and become competitive without some form of initial protection.

The emerging consensus on trade reform favors a more graduated approach to liberalization, which usually starts with a tariffication of all trade restrictions, and then followed by the lowering and simplification of tariffs. On the speed of rationalization and lowering of tariffs, it is reasonable to suggest that such speed would depend on each country's initial conditions and the response of its export sector. Industrial and technological restructuring and upgrading are slow and risky, and require some learning and adjustment costs. Thus, the speed of liberalization should be consistent with the learning and adjustment costs that are required. Williamson (1995, pp. 3–4) corroborates this, and in fact, argues that export-orientation and import substitution can or should cohere:

> It would be wrong to see export expansion and import substitution as mutually exclusive, but exports drive the process; that is the essence of what is meant by export-led growth . . . Note that I do not include general import liberalization (as opposed to giving access at world prices to the imported inputs needed for export production) as a prerequisite for export promotion. . . . I favor instead a policy of liberalizing imports gradually as the balance of payments situation provides scope for doing so, but preannouncing one's intentions so as to discourage new investment in import substitution industries that depend upon protection to be profitable.

Thus, there is a sequencing process that runs from export promotion to import liberalization (a reversal of the sequence that the anti-export bias literature proposes). In foreign-exchange-constrained economies, exports provide the critical means with which to purchase increased imports made available through trade liberalization. Therefore, a good export performance (to earn foreign exchange) is critical to sustaining import liberalization. In the light of this, some scholars argue that in countries with clearly defined development strategies and adequate capacity to implement them, appropriate export promotion measures can be used to ensure outward-orientation before a full-scale import liberalization. In other words, the experience of de-industrialization and the payments-incompatibility that have accompanied all the non-aid-driven reforms caution on the need for adequate preparations (in terms of supply-side measures and institutional arrangements to elicit desired export-supply response) to be made before embarking on full liberalization.

Export promotion should also entail selective import liberalization, emphasizing first a tariff structure that allows manufacturers of export goods to have access to inputs at world prices. Second, tariffs on light consumer goods—which form the foundation of initial industrial infrastructure—should be higher (but with a target of its gradual, phased liberalization over time). In other words, the key lesson of economic history that no industrial country attained international competitiveness without some form of protection is still valid. The experiences of Argentina, Brazil, South Africa, Zimbabwe, the East Asian economies, and to some extent Mauritius, bear out this principle. In many of the more successful exporters following liberalization, economic history teaches us that most of the firms and industries that were able to compete and export in the international market matured during the previous ISI phase.

More fundamentally, countries should be wary about appropriate administration, monitoring, and enforcement of the strategic policies. First, governments must design institutional mechanisms to prevent the implementation process from being subject to capture by special interests and ridden with corruption. Second, the principle of ISI should be taken with care, especially for very small economies where the constraints of minimum efficient plant size prevents the exploitation of economies of scale and division of labor. Third, care must be taken to ensure that protection does not lead to infant industries that never attain adulthood. It is therefore necessary to get the incentive structure right, and aggressively promote competition. Complementary policies are needed to build up and strengthen factor, product, and capital markets, and to develop active technology policy. These considerations make the aggressive pursuit of export orientation a desideratum for sustainable industrial takeoff. It is this combination of aggressive export promotion with selective and gradual import liberalization that was the winning strategy of the East Asian tigers. The ISI failed in Africa and most of Latin America because of the lack of compensating pressures to encourage efficiency and international competitiveness.

Regional Integration

Modern industry is large scale and needs a certain minimum scale of operations for maximum efficiency. Clearly, the national markets of most African countries are too narrow to provide adequate incentives for large-scale industries. In this circumstance, industrial productivity is likely to be low in each individual country and, given the implied higher costs of production, such industries are likely to seek and obtain a high level of protection to stay in business. The danger here is to have protected inefficiency within small, self-contained markets. Restrictive economic nationalism is therefore unlikely to provide a lasting, long-term solution to the "small country" problem, and confer benefits of large-scale production and dynamic efficiency.

This limitation of the national markets, and recognition of the constraints of the international trading regime, have encouraged increasing regionalism among developing countries. In Africa, despite the results of empirical research that question the usefulness of regional integration, it is still high on the agenda of African states. A regionally protected market is believed to circumvent the constraints of narrow national markets, and would also make it possible (1) for countries to use existing agricultural and industrial capacities more fully in supplying one another's needs; (2) for new investment to take place in industries that would not be viable if confined to individual national markets; and (3) for both old and new industries to reduce costs through economies of scale and specialization (Dell, 1991, pp. 98–99). Regionalism in this case could serve as an important learning ground where regional firms compete freely and mature, and ultimately become competitive globally. Even within the region, there are still conflicts between nationalistic considerations (to protect home industries and extract government revenues) and the goal of allowing regional firms a free reign of competition to mature. How far individual countries are willing to realize the professed goals of regional integration remains to be seen. But it is difficult to see how significant industrial activities can take place in many countries or even attract FDI without the promise of the regional markets. For countries that resist regionalism on account of the implied short-run costs, the issue is not whether or not it is costly. It is rather a case of integrating now and incurring some costs or integrating later and incurring even more costs. Beside the issue of economies of scale in production, regional integration provides a framework to strengthen the bargaining power of African countries vis-à-vis other regional blocs in North America, Europe, and Asia.

The International Community

Africa, with its dominantly pre-industrial stage of development, faces monumental challenges in its bid to join the rest of the industrialized world. Our analysis so far places the bulk of the adjustments and reforms at the doorsteps of the individual African countries them-

Box 3. Required OECD Actions to Level Global Trading Field for Africa

For the countries of Africa to have a level playing field in global trading, the OECD needs to take the following actions:

- Regional arrangements, like the EU or NAFTA, provide industrial countries trade preferences to each other's markets and discriminate against African and other developing countries. Policy initiatives are needed to, at least, place the latter on an equal basis with OECD members in these arrangements. Some labor intensive products like textiles, clothing, and footwear played a key role in the early stages of the newly industrialized countries' transformation, and have a similar potential for Africa. Where they are now excluded (as in United States) these goods should be incorporated into existing GSP schemes—particularly so since intra-OECD preferences in regional free trade areas may severely disadvantage these exports.
- Since African exports are highly concentrated in primary commodities, there is a strong interest in utilizing natural-resource-based industrialization strategies for their industrialization. Where further processing is suitable for developing countries, OECD preferences should be extended to all stages of a processing chain. Also, an accelerated phase-in of OECD Uruguay Round tariff cuts should be adopted on products of export interest to Africa. This could assist Africa in gaining additional experience in potentially important markets (such as those for textiles and clothing), which will come under increased competitive pressure due to the MFA phaseout.
- Ceilings and quotas should be eliminated from industrial-country preference schemes to be made consistent with unrestricted intra-OECD preferences extended under FTAs. Ceilings considerably reduce the potential worth of the GSP to African countries since, aside from their trade effects, they also introduce further uncertainty regarding the operation of the system (that is, African exporters may not know whether a shipment will qualify for GSP treatment until

selves. However, several constraints emanate from the distorted nature of the global playing field. As part of the leveling of the playing field, the international community, especially under the auspices of UNCTAD, UNIDO, and WTO, should mobilize international support for eliminating the obstacles that impede Africa's integration into the global system. Two key elements should characterize the compact with the international community: trade and the mobilization of donor resources toward infrastructural development.

With regard to trade, Sachs (1996, p. 21) proposes a simple but effective solution: "The biggest source of support from donor nations its arrival in the import market). It is also being alleged that ceilings are sometimes set below minimum efficient plant size. This negates the intended trade and investment increasing incentives of the preferences.

Some OECD policy initiatives are required to alleviate Africa's transport problems:

- Technical assistance: International shipping has undergone a major transformation in which procedures for cargo utilization, port operations, and related logistical functions have evolved into highly complex operations, requiring a considerable degree of technical expertise. Since most African countries have limited access to such expertise, technical assistance programs (such as those provided by UNCTAD and the World Bank) should be expanded and also extended to related activities (such as customs clearance procedures) that impinge on the efficiency of international transport operations.
- Finance and development: Due to insufficient attention and funds, many African countries' fleets, ports, and connecting inland transport infrastructure have deteriorated, or have become technologically outmoded. OECD countries should sponsor a comprehensive survey and report on Sub-Saharan Africa's transport problems along with policy proposals for their alleviation. Given the small size of many African countries, and its influence on cargo volumes and the utilization of efficient transport technologies, further attention should be given to the development of regional ports and required inland infrastructure.
- The situation of landlocked African countries needs special attention given the major problems these countries face in crossing their neighbor's territories. A major effort should attempt to identify the special trade problems of the landlocked African countries and formulate policy suggestions for their reduction.

would also be the cheapest. America, Europe and Japan should launch a 'New Compact for Africa,' guaranteeing open markets for African exports and committing themselves to help reintegrate Africa into the world economy. The commitment would help prove to both sides that the long period of economic marginalization is over, and would energize both African nations and the West to overcome the practical obstacles to a new dawn of rapid growth throughout Africa." Furthermore, Yeats and others (1997) articulate a number of other proposals for actions by the OECD to level the playing field (see Box 3).

The actions on infrastructural development do not necessarily require additional funds. They may need a redirection of existing resource flows. For example, foreign technical assistance costs some $4 billion annually. This amount could go a long way to finance the building and retention of critical skills on the continent, as well as provide some basic infrastructure. A redirection of donor funds from balance of payments purposes to project lending would provide the needed boost for the industrial restructuring.

Conclusions

As the world's last frontier, still awaiting an industrial revolution, Africa faces unique historical challenges. It would be the only region in history that is expected to industrialize and compete but without benefit of much of the preferential and differential treatment that earlier industrializers enjoyed. Clearly, policy options and directions cannot be business as usual. Competition is the only game in town. How countries, as well as groups of countries, brace themselves for this game will largely determine the prospects into the twenty-first century. While the private sector is clearly going to be the flagship of such a new era, much ingenuity in policy design, strategic interactions between state and society, as well as a redefined compact with the international community, would be required. Africa's industrialization is a desideratum and a collective responsibility, but one for which Africans themselves must take the driver's seat and be prepared to think and do things differently and effectively.

References

Altenburg, T., W. Hillebrand, and J. Meyer-Stamer, 1997, "Policies for Building Systemic Competitiveness: Conceptual Framework and Case Studies of Republic of Korea, Brazil, Mexico, and Thailand," paper presented at the UNIDO seminar on New Trends and Challenges in Industrial Policy, Vienna, October.

Amjadi, A., and A. Yeats, 1995, "Have Transport Costs Contributed to the Relative Decline of Sub-Saharan African Exports?: Some Preliminary Empirical Evidence," Policy Research Working Paper No. 1559 (Washington: World Bank).

Auty, R.M., 1997, "Competitive Industrial Policy and Macro Performance: Has South Korea Outperformed Taiwan?" *The Journal of Development Studies*, Vol. 33, No. 4, pp. 445–63.

Biggs, T., and P. Srivastava, 1996, *Structural Aspects of Manufacturing in Sub-Saharan Africa: Findings from a Seven Country Enterprise Survey,* World Bank Discussion Paper No. 348 (Washington: World Bank).

Blakey, G.G., 1994, "Economic Integration in Sub-Saharan Africa: The Implications for Direct Foreign Investment" (Brussels: European Commission).

Chang, H.J., 1996a, "Globalization, Transnational Corporations, and Economic Development: Can the Developing Countries Pursue Strategic Industrial Policy in a Globalizing World Economy?" paper presented at the Economic Policy Institute conference, Washington, June.

———, 1996b, *The Political Economy of Industrial Policy* (London: Macmillan).

Claessens, S., and D. Naude, 1993, "Recent Estimates of Capital Flight," Working Paper No. 1186 (Washington: World Bank).

Collier, P., and P. Guillaumont, 1996, "The Future of Lomé: Europe's Role in African Growth" (unpublished; Oxford: Centre for the Study of African Economies).

Dell, S., 1991, *International Development Policies: Perspectives for Industrial Countries* (Durham, North Carolina: Duke University Press).

Evans, P., 1992, "The State as Problem and Solution: Predation, Embedded Autonomy, and Structural Change," in *The Politics of Economic Adjustment,* ed. by S. Haggard and R.R. Kaufman (Princeton, New Jersey: Princeton University Press).

Haque, N.U., and S. Kim, 1995, "Governance and Growth: Human Capital in Government Management" (unpublished; Washington: International Monetary Fund).

International Finance Corporation, 1995, *Trends in Private Investment in Developing Countries 1990–94,* Discussion Paper No. 28 (Washington: International Finance Corporation).

Khor, M., 1997, "The WTO and the South: Implications and Recent Developments" (unpublished; Penang, Malaysia: Third World Network).

Kim, L., 1997, "Technology Policy and Strategy for Building Industrial Competitiveness," paper presented at the UNIDO seminar on New Trends and Challenges in Industrial Policy, Vienna, October.

Kurozumi, A., 1995, "An Economic Approach to International Competitiveness," Research Report No. 50 (Tokyo: Japan Development Bank).

Mkandawire, T., 1988, "The Road to Crisis, Adjustment and De-Industrialization: The African Case," *Africa Development,* Vol. 13, No. 1.

Ndlovu, L., 1996, "Constraints to Manufacturing Production," in *Africa Now: People, Policies, Institutions,* ed. by S. Ellis (The Hague: Ministry of Foreign Affairs).

Ndulu, B., and N. van de Walle, 1996, *Agenda for Africa's Economic Renewal* (Oxford: Transaction Publishers).

Nissanke, M., 1997, *Africa: Institutions, Policies and Development* (Tokyo: International Development Centre of Japan).

Rodrik, D., 1995, "Getting Interventions Right: How South Korea and Taiwan Grew Rich," *Economic Policy*, No. 20, April, pp. 53–97.

Sachs, J., 1996, "Growth in Africa: It Can Be Done," *The Economist*, June 29, pp. 19–21.

Soludo, C.C., 1997a, "Between Free Trade and Mercantilism: Africa and the Choice of Trade and Industrial Policies" (unpublished; Nsukka: University of Nigeria).

———, 1997b, "Trade Policy Reforms and Supply Responses in Sub-Saharan Africa," paper prepared for the UNCTAD project on East Asia–Africa Comparative Development Project, Geneva.

Stewart, F., 1991, "Are Adjustment Policies in Africa Consistent with Long-Run Development Needs?" *Development Policy Review*, Vol. 9, pp. 420–32.

UNCTAD (United Nations Conference on Trade and Development), 1996, "East Asian Development: Lessons for a New Global Environment," UNCTAD Secretariat Report to the Conference on East Asian Development: Lessons for a New Global Environment, Kuala Lumpur, February.

UNIDO (United Nations Industrial Development Organization), 1996, *The Globalization of Industry: Implications for Developing Countries Beyond 2000* (Vienna: UNIDO).

Williamson, J., 1995, "Exchange Rate Policy and Development Strategy," paper presented at a workshop of the African Economic Research Consortium, Johannesburg, December.

World Bank, 1991, *World Development Report 1991: The Challenge of Development* (New York: Oxford University Press).

———, 1993, *The East Asian Miracle: Economic Growth and Public Policy* (New York: Oxford University Press).

———, 1994a, *Adjustment in Africa: Reforms, Results, and the Road Ahead* (New York: Oxford University Press).

———, 1994b, "East Africa Survey of Foreign Investors" (unpublished; Washington: World Bank).

———, 1997, *World Development Report 1997: The State in a Changing World* (New York: Oxford University Press).

World Competitiveness Report, 1994 (Lausanne: International Institute for Mangement Development).

Yeats, A.J., A. Amjadi, U. Reincke, and F. Ng, 1997, *Did Domestic Policies Marginalize Africa in International Trade?* (Washington: World Bank).

Part II

Regional Integration in Africa

Regional Integration: Lessons from Asia and the Western Hemisphere 11

Gary Hufbauer and Barbara Kotschwar

The 1990s appear to be the decade of the regional trade arrangement. From North to South and from West to East, a large number of regional trade arrangements have blossomed and existing arrangements have revived, some deepening their commitments, others expanding their membership. The European Union has moved to a common market and is on the road toward monetary union. The United States, which has modified its strict multilateralist stance, has entered into a free trade agreement with its two North American neighbors. In Latin America, a "new generation" of regional agreements has abandoned the inward-looking policies that prevailed in the 1960s and 1970s and have adopted more outward-looking principles for regional integration.

The most integrated economic region in the world is Europe, where in 1993 the Maastricht Treaty converted the European Community into the European Union. Since then, the EU has enlarged its membership from 12 to 15 countries and has taken significant steps toward achieving monetary union by 1999. Regionalism has been resurrected in Latin America, as intraregional trade has grown rapidly over the past half-decade. Many existing, but until recently dormant, trade groupings have modernized their goals and structure, and a number of new agreements have surfaced. If bilateral FTAs are included, there are now at least 23 regional trading arrangements in the Western Hemisphere alone, with several new ones being negotiated even now. The Asia-Pacific region includes a number of preferential trade arrangements, both among the Asian countries, such as ASEAN and the Australia–New Zealand Closer Economic Relations Trade Agreement (ANZCERTA), and broader initiatives such as the APEC, which includes four American members. Africa has a long history of preferential regional arrangements, and lately there has been a resurgence of interest in revitalizing these initiatives.

The views expressed in this chapter are those of the authors and are not intended to represent those of their respective organizations.

Various reasons exist for this trend toward regional integration. Popularly cited factors spurring the development of regional initiatives are the impatience with the slow completion of the Uruguay Round, responses in other regions to the European initiative, and the external extension of countries' internal liberalization programs.

For developing countries, regional arrangements can serve as a means to further their economic liberalization programs, and to work toward greater outward orientation, in preparation for their integration into the global economy. If effected in a manner that reduces barriers and liberalizes trade among members, they can also serve as a mechanism to lock in domestically implemented liberalization measures. And, important, regional integration initiatives can help to spur foreign direct investment by providing a more stable and attractive climate for investors. If trade liberalization is a bicycle, then regional arrangements can be seen as one of the many gears furthering the progress of its motion.[1] Thomas and Nash call regional agreements a "halfway house on the path leading to the full benefits of trade liberalization and wider markets" (1991, p. 191).

Economic rationales for expanding trade relations start regionally with the efficiency argument: when producers are able to specialize in the goods that they can produce most cheaply, the economy gains. Second, economies of scale that cannot be achieved in the domestic market can often be reached in a larger regional market. Third, regional integration can provide learning and benefits of competition among generally high-cost producers at a safer level than in the wide open world. The gains from trade creation are assumed to be larger the greater the reduction in tariffs and NTBs among members and the more members differ with respect to resource endowment. The benefits from integrating regionally answer some of the major problems that some developing countries have faced in their efforts to integrate into the world trading system. Generally small commodity exporters, these countries have experienced difficulties gaining access to all inputs necessary to the production process, often for lack of funds and financing, but also due to the costs of transporting the required resources. They have been unable to secure sufficient domestic and international markets for their manufactured goods—and have been unable to take up either heavy or light industrial production, as much equipment is designed for larger-scale production than the domestic market would support.

[1]This analogy was made by Douglas Worth at a European Institute seminar, building on C. Fred Bergsten's bicycle theory.

In step with the growth of new regional arrangements has been a growth in the body of literature addressing the subject. Many articles and books have been penned asking whether regional arrangements are good or bad, trade creating or trade diverting, building blocks or stumbling blocks.[2] This matter has been sufficiently discussed elsewhere, and we will not enter the debate. Rather, we will follow the lead of Paul Krugman and take as our point of departure the fact that regional arrangements exist and are here to stay. They exist among industrial countries, among developing countries, and among countries at differing levels of development. In this chapter, we will set out some simple but important observations derived from the regional experiences in Asia and the Western Hemisphere that may serve as lessons for countries considering the formation of a regional trade arrangement in the current international environment. So, herewith, we offer an 11-step program for countries seeking successful regional integration.

Need for Vision

First, 20/20 vision from the top is important. Leaders must embrace a big vision. To succeed, the commitment to regional integration must come from the top and must be clear. Many regional initiatives have faltered, or have simply not been implemented, due to a lack of political commitment to do so. If the political will is absent, the regional initiative will likely fail. In order to succeed, regional integration should be a firm component of the domestic liberalization agenda of the participating countries. To communicate this commitment, heads of state must convey a grand vision of regional integration, setting forth strong goals and firm deadlines. Unambiguous commitment to the goal of a regional integration arrangement from the highest political level is a must. Heads of state should issue a joint political declaration to this effect, including a clearly worded statement of goals and a deadline for compliance with the goal. This deadline should be within the possible time horizon of participants, not so far into the future that the administrations issuing the declaration are sure to be long gone.

To set the process in motion, negotiators must then focus on the timing and phasing of the implementation, without losing sight of the vision. While these timetables should be flexible enough to adjust in times of stress (e.g., the EU in 1992), negotiators and politicians should make every attempt to keep the process on track. For example, in the case of Mercosur, the political commitment to implementing the com-

[2]Summaries of this literature include Winters (1996) and de Melo and Panagariya (1993).

mon external tariff (CET) on January 1, 1995, forced the countries to harmonize, to a large extent, their tariffs, and to eliminate quotas and supplementary trade taxes before that date. While some exceptions to the CET have been made, this has largely been a result of consultations among the members, rather than through unilateral actions. The CET has survived a number of fiscal crises in the member economies, largely due to the strong political commitments of the member countries.

Two recent initiatives, the Asia Pacific Economic Cooperation forum (APEC) and the Free Trade Area of the Americas (FTAA) have relied on a timetable of high-level meetings to keep the process moving. The APEC Bogor declaration sets out the goals of the initiative: to "complete the achievement of our goal of free and open trade and investment in the Asia-Pacific . . . no later than the year 2010 and developing economies no later than the year 2020" (APEC, 1994). The 2020 vision strains the credibility of many observers, since it is so distant. However, this distant goal is kept aloft by annual meetings of the economic leaders of the member countries: in Seattle in 1993, in Bogor, Indonesia, in 1994, in Osaka in 1995, in Subic Bay, Philippines, in 1996, and in Vancouver in November 1997. Ministers have met to discuss a range of issues, ranging from globalization to the environment to finance to transportation infrastructure. Ten working groups and experts groups were created to foster cooperation within APEC on issues such as trade promotion, trade and investment data, industrial science and technology, telecommunications, and fisheries.

In the Western Hemisphere, the FTAA process was launched at the Miami Summit of the Americas in December 1994. The heads of state and government of 34 countries in the Americas pledged to "begin immediately to construct the Free Trade Area of the Americas, in which barriers to trade and investment will be progressively eliminated." They resolved to "conclude the negotiation of the Free Trade Area of the Americas no later than 2005," with concrete progress toward the attainment of this objective by the year 2000 (Summit of the Americas, 1994). Heads of state and government next met at the Second Summit of the Americas in Santiago de Chile in April 1998 and agreed to launch negotiations. The negotiations are scheduled to conclude at a summit in 2002 or 2003 in Canada.

The first stage of the FTAA has been devoted to preparing for the negotiations. This preparatory process has comprised ministerial and vice ministerial meetings, as well as meetings of 12 working groups, and an intensive information-gathering effort. So far, four annual meetings of ministers of trade have been held—in Denver, in Cartagena, Colombia, in Belo Horizonte, Brazil, and in San José, Costa Rica. The vice ministers of trade have acted as a preparatory committee, coordinating the work of 12 working groups, and serving as a conduit between the working groups and the ministers. The working groups, which have met about seven times each, cover the disciplines that will be discussed in the negotiations. They include market access and traditional disciplines (there are working groups on market access, customs procedures and rules of origin, standards and technical barriers to trade, intellectual property rights, subsidies, antidumping measures and countervailing duties, and sanitary and phytosanitary measures) as well as the newer disciplines of trade policy (services, investment, government procurement, and competition policy). There are also working groups on dispute settlement procedures and on the treatment of smaller economies. The working groups receive their mandates from the ministers and vice ministers and are required to provide regular status reports on their work.

Leadership

Second, the big guy must be on board. If the large country of the region is not sold on the effort, it will not succeed. In fact, leadership from the top is a necessary ingredient. A main reason for entering into a regional trade arrangement is to gain improved access to the market of the largest trading partner. This was the case for Mexico and Canada in NAFTA. Without the United States, NAFTA would not have come about—trade between Canada and Mexico, while now growing, was not highly significant in 1994. This was also the case for Argentina, Paraguay, and Uruguay in Mercosur. The driving force for the Latin American countries in the FTAA initiative is to gain access to the market of the United States. The EU would have enjoyed much less success without the strong political will and active markets of France and Germany. Without the largest market, the gains from integration diminish and may disappear altogether. This proposition may stand to be tested in the FTAA process within the next few months, as the United States—which makes up about 75 percent of the Western Hemisphere's market—grapples with the issue of fast track.

In addition to the market access rationale, the most important trading partner can serve as a moderator and a catalyst. As access to the large market can be a carrot, the threat of losing such access can serve as a stick. Recalcitrant trading partners in a regional arrangement stand to lose preferential access to their main market if they backtrack on their obligations.

The perils of apathy on the part of the largest trading partner are severe. Economic events in one country can spill over into its neighbors. Decisions made in one country regarding economic policy will affect the country's trading partners. If, for example, Brazil sneezes, Argentina, Paraguay, and Uruguay will catch a cold. For Mercosur to remain healthy, thus, Brazil must take care to use a handkerchief—and not to sneeze in the direction of these three countries—to protect its regional trading partners from catching its cold. Easterly and Levine (1995) use regression analysis to find that spillovers from a country's neighbors have an impact on that country's growth and urge the shift from a negative to a positive contagion effect. A regional trade arrangement can allow the opportunity for the large country to foment such positive contagion effects.

Geography

Third, geography and magnitude count. For a regional integration arrangement to be successful, countries should either be adjacent or should have a high volume of trade with each other. The "prize" for entering into a regional trade arrangement is expanded regional trade. Strong trade and investment linkages provide an obvious starting point for negotiations toward a regional integration arrangement. Trade and investment interdependence provide an incentive for countries to expand their access to the known markets of the partner country or countries.[3]

Geography remains an important determinant of trade patterns. Despite great strides in transportation and communications technology, "distance costs" of all kinds sharply limit trade between widely separated countries. Distance between countries is an important natural determinant of the volume of trade between them. In a recently published book, Jeffrey Frankel takes as a point of analysis the existence of what he calls "natural trading blocs"—a unit of countries in which a reduction of trade barriers among them can be economically beneficial (Frankel, 1997, p. 40). Frankel estimates that aggregate transportation costs rise by roughly 1 percent of value for each 1 percent increase in distance (p. 41).

Agreements between widely separated countries, or among countries that do not trade heavily (for example, the United States–Israel FTA or the EU–Israel FTA), are often enacted for political rather than trade reasons and are problematic. Such agreements are not designed to capture the efficiency gains that result from expanded scale, nor do they tap into the gains from lowering barriers and expanding trade

[3]A more elaborate discussion of this can be found in Hufbauer, Schott, and Clark (1994), Chapters 3 and 5.

among countries with relatively low transactions costs. A corollary to this point: *supplement regional commerce initiatives with infrastructure development.*

Potential profits from regional integration may be limited by poor transportation and communication infrastructure among members. Significant gains from trade may be possible for some products—those for which economies of scale are of the essence, and which can be competitively produced regionally and those heavy items that have high transport costs from outside. A special bank, or a facility within an existing institution with funds specified for infrastructure development, can help.

Liberalize First

Fourth, liberalize first. Regional trading initiatives should be seen as an extension of domestic reforms—not as a force to propel such reforms. Before entering into a regional trade arrangement, a country should have its domestic house in order. This means macroeconomic stability and a reasonably competitive domestic economy.

The path to economic liberalization in developing countries has to a large extent been paved with the various components of what John Williamson has termed the *Washington consensus* (Williamson, 1990). These are policy measures that aim to eliminate market distortions, reduce the role of the state in the economy, promote the efficient allocation and use of resources, reduce risk, and establish a framework for economic stability. The Washington consensus includes both microeconomic and macroeconomic policy recommendations.

First in importance is the achievement of fiscal discipline, with caps on public spending. This includes a strong suggestion to eliminate government subsidies. Tax reform is advocated, especially through a broadening of the tax base, while maintaining a low marginal tax rate.

Interest rates should be market-determined and positive, but moderate. Inflation should be low. The exchange rate should be relatively stable and sufficiently competitive to promote a rate of export growth that will allow the economy to grow at the maximum rate permitted by its supply-side potential.

Free trade and investment are fundamental to the Washington consensus recommendations. Import liberalization is a key component of an outward-oriented economic policy. Access to imports of intermediate goods at competitive prices is essential, and import licensing systems, which are vulnerable to corruption, should be eliminated. FDI should be encouraged through open investment regimes. Deregulation and privatization are seen as beneficial, both by increasing competition and by relieving pressure on the government budget.

These policies, summarized by Williamson as "prudent macroeconomic policies, outward orientation and free market capitalism" (1990, p. 18), have been embraced by many developing countries—and by the international organizations that provide advice and finance to these countries—as a means to stimulate sustained economic growth.

Regional integration arrangements can serve as a step in the trade liberalization process. Regional integration, however, is not a substitute for liberalization—and an erratic liberalization program may compromise its success. As Moises Naim points out, "Structural reforms take a long time to mature, they follow highly unpredictable paths, and they have myriad consequences which, in turn, generate other effects that are impossible to foresee" (1993, p. 17). While not all steps of the economic liberalization process need to be in place, governments should at least have brought inflation under control and maintain a relatively stable exchange rate.

Difficulties arise when only part of the Washington consensus is implemented. For example, developing countries that have put in place the recommended macroeconomic policies, but have utilized only half of the suggestions for the microeconomic side, run the risk of exposing the program to corruption. A half-implemented economic program may also leave the financial system vulnerable—a factor that could negatively affect even the most determined of regional trade arrangements—and increase the country's susceptibility to exchange rate or financial crises.[4]

Coordinated Approach

Fifth, a piecemeal approach is inadequate. Proceeding along sectoral lines is difficult. The sectoral approach to preferential trade liberalization was popular in Latin America's regional integration agreements of the 1960s and 1970s. The Latin American Free Trade Area (LAFTA), the Andean Pact, and the Central American Common Market (CACM) all reduced protection on a product-by-product or a sector-by-sector basis, rather than liberalizing across the board. This resulted in long exceptions lists and high tariffs for outside countries.

This approach was part of the larger strategy of ISI, in which countries aimed to protect their manufacturing industries through high barriers to trade. Regional integration was seen as a means to sur-

[4]This section draws upon Hufbauer (1997).

mount the inherent scale limitations of their domestic markets, to allow industries to become competitive on a regional level, and to encourage industrial development within a cooperative framework. Regional markets with high levels of protection vis-à-vis third markets could be used to shift firms from the production of consumer goods toward the development of intermediate and capital goods. Regional trade arrangements aimed to create economies of scale for regional manufacturing industries. In the case of the Andean Group, sectors were allocated among the member countries, through a process of negotiation, with each country focusing its resources on a particular industry. This approach ensured structural rigidities.

Simplicity

Sixth, simplicity is of the essence. The starting point for regional trade integration should be the elimination of tariffs and quotas. While the temptation exists to tackle more complicated issues, it is important to start with basic liberalization. The aim of a free trade initiative should be to eliminate barriers to trade. Auxiliary accords, or "side agreements" can clutter the agenda, diverting policymakers for the goal of free trade. Liberalizing trade under an umbrella agreement that includes multiple objectives is overly complicated. Including trade liberalization as only one objective that shares the agenda with such goals as fiscal and monetary policy harmonization and agricultural and infrastructure development diffuses attention and fails to set out a clear goal.

There are two main hazards to including a wide range of complicated issues on the agenda. First is the danger of negotiating and implementing fatigue. Complicated, wide-ranging trade initiatives are demanding of diplomatic and administrative skills. This is especially so for smaller countries, where a too-large agenda can overburden limited human as well as financial resources. Second, the larger the number of issues on the initial agenda the greater the opportunities for interest groups to enter into the fray, stopping the whole process. If the adjustment costs incurred by taking on too much at a time seem too large, subsequent steps may be stymied and the whole initiative will be in trouble.

From FTA to Customs Union?

Seventh, an FTA is much easier to manage than a customs union. There are various levels of economic integration, ranging from simple bilateral trade facilitation measures (such as agreements on customs procedures and documentation) to the ultimate integration initiative, the formation of a nation-state. The simplest form of commercial integration, beyond bilateral cooperation agreements, is the formation of a free trade area. In the simplest FTA, the participating countries eliminate barriers to trade in goods among each other, while maintaining their individual barriers against the rest of the world. Most modern FTAs also eliminate barriers to trade in services and liberalize investment among the partner countries. The best-known modern FTA is probably NAFTA, which eliminated barriers to trade and investment between Canada, Mexico, and the United States.

The next level of integration is the customs union, which eliminates barriers to trade and investment among the members, and also imposes a CET. This requires member countries to coordinate their tariff policy and agree on common customs rules and procedures. Generally, countries in the process of constructing a customs union proceed through a de facto FTA stage, which allows the progressive harmonization of national tariffs toward the agreed-upon CET. From this stage, countries must move toward a common regional trade policy, coordinating border tariffs, customs procedures, and other policies affecting trade with the rest of the world, such as safeguard measures, antidumping policy, and, possibly harmonization (or mutual recognition) of national standards.

It is evident that the implementation of a customs union is much more complicated than the construction of an FTA. Aside from the obvious administrative resources needed for policy coordination, a customs union can potentially diminish the liberalization possibilities for members—because each is frozen to the policy decisions of the group. This is especially true for the smaller members of the union, which have little influence over the group's decisions. A main impediment in the customs union is its most important feature: the CET. The danger in setting a CET is that the common tariff may, in certain sectors, be significantly higher than national tariffs of some of the members. This would discourage low-tariff members from purchasing goods from more efficient outside suppliers—as they did before the CET. The burdens of a CET have been a factor in several cases. In the 1970s, Chile broke from the Andean Pact for just this reason. Currently, both Bolivia and Peru have refused to implement the Andean Community's common external tariff, preferring their own unilevel or bilevel tariff structures.

Regional arrangements should be viewed by the member countries as a mechanism for their integration into the world economy. Steps toward regional integration should accelerate (or at the very least not impede) members' unilateral liberalization measures (for example, the

CACM policy holds that CACM should not impede members' tariff reduction). Thus, if a customs union is the chosen vehicle for integration, the CET aim should be the tariff level of the least protective member, rather than a regional average.

Simple Rules of Origin

Eighth, keep the rules of origin as simple as possible. Rules of origin—tools used to determine which goods qualify for preferential treatment under a free trade regime—are necessary in free trade agreements, in which each member sets its own external (MFN) tariff to nonmembers. Such rules are used to avoid the transshipment of foreign-produced goods—that is, to prevent third-party producers from selling their goods to the member country with the lowest MFN tariff, for sale in the other, higher-tariff markets. For example, imagine a free trade agreement between three countries, with MFN tariffs of 6, 10, and 14 percent, respectively. Without rules of origin, a third country could ship its goods to the 6 percent tariff country. The goods could then be shipped duty free to the other two countries, avoiding the 10 and 14 percent duties.

There are a number of methods to determine origin. Most commonly used are the value added method, in which a certain percentage of value added must originate within the FTA, and the change in tariff heading method, in which a good imported from a third country must be transformed sufficiently within the FTA to move it to another tariff classification.

Often termed "tools of discrimination," rules of origin can have several negative effects. First, they can be costly to the participants in the FTA. Complex and cumbersome rules of origin add a significant administrative burden to exporters. The time and administrative costs of figuring out the puzzling network of complex and highly detailed rules may even deter regional producers from utilizing the FTA preference system. One estimate of the European Free Trade Association posits that administrative costs relating to rules of origin were in the range of 3 to 5 percent of prices (Wonnacott, 1996, p. 91). Second, they can serve to reduce economic efficiency. Rules of origin can, in fact, penalize member country producers by forcing them to buy their inputs from less efficient local suppliers, thereby increasing the cost of their final goods and lowering their global competitiveness. If, for example, a component from a third-country producer could jeopardize the duty-free shipment of a final good within the free trade area, the manufacturer would implicitly attribute the MFN tariff to the foreign component—thereby rendering the cost of that one part prohibitive, no matter how efficient and cost-effective the part may be. Third, rules of origin can, as has been stated dramatically elsewhere, "become a viper's nest for special interests" (Hufbauer, 1995). As was witnessed in the textiles and automotive sectors of the NAFTA, rules of origin can be tailored to assuage and to guarantee the position of particular sectors and even individual firms, to the detriment of competition.

To avoid these "origin downfalls," the architects of an FTA must take pains to keep rules of origin as simple as possible. The only purpose that rules of origin should serve is to answer the problem of transshipment. One way to do this would be to adopt the proposed "Hufbauer/Wonnacott ROROO (rule on rules of origin)," which says that when tariffs applied to a particular product by the partners in an FTA are within 2 percentage points of each other, and when neither quotas nor other NTBs limit trade with countries outside the FTA, then the imports of that product from a nonmember country shall count as products from the partner country for the purposes of satisfying the FTA rules of origin. This is a feasible proposition; producers are unlikely to incur the extra transactions costs of shipping to another country just to eliminate a 2 percent tariff differential. An example is the case of an FTA between country A and country B in which country A's MFN tariff rate on some component is 6 percent and country B's tariff on that same component is 8 percent. Assuming that neither country has NTBs against this component, if country A buys this component from country C, and uses it as an input for a product that it will sell to country B, the component is considered as originating from country A for purposes of rules of origin determination. This principle would serve to greatly simplify the rules of origin regime.

Political Benefits

Ninth, political benefits may result from trade integration. One important benefit that may accrue from regional integration is closer political ties among members. Using the logic that countries that trade together stay together, strong commercial ties make it more difficult to sever political relations. Argentina and Brazil, countries with a history of border disputes, have forged strong political ties as the result of the 1986 cooperative accords that led to the formation of Mercosur. Recent disputes have been resolved through consultation within the Mercosur framework. Cooperation on trade issues can lead to closer cooperation on initiatives in other areas, such as infrastructure, technology, antiterrorism activities, and so forth.

Another political benefit is the stake that the regional grouping has in the stability of each member country. This was played out in 1995, when Paraguay experienced a near coup. A rallying of forces of the Mercosur countries, along with the United States, convinced the would-be dictator that his actions would be unwise, and democracy was preserved.

Small Economies

Tenth, take care of small economies. Regional arrangements also may have consequences for distribution. These consequences may be more strongly felt in the smaller members. Smaller states tend to exhibit particular characteristics that influence their participation in regional and international trade arrangements. These include a small domestic market, reliance on one or few commodities, high vulnerability to fluctuations in world prices and demand, and limited human and financial capital. Smaller countries entering into regional trade arrangements may need assurances that their vulnerability will not be exacerbated by their participation in the regional trade area.

One of the main incentives to integrate is to attract foreign investment. This is true for smaller, as well as larger, economies. Industries tend to gravitate toward certain countries, logically to those with the best-developed industries and infrastructures. This may, at least in the short run, magnify disparities in levels of development and create friction for those countries that are not yet ready to respond to increased regional trade opportunities. The best way to deal with these problems is to (1) encourage the adoption, especially by the smaller members, of a liberal and transparent investment regime, and (2) create a special bank, or a specific facility within an existing financial institution, to finance investment in the least-developed regions or countries. The European Development Bank is a paramount example.

Private Enterprise

Eleventh, focus on enterprise; the private sector is the protagonist. A trade agreement aims to bring down barriers to trade and investment between countries. The actors within the countries that will be able to take advantage of the new opportunities created by this liberalization are essential to the success of the initiative. The private sector is the constituency for these reforms. Countries make border policies; firms move goods across those borders. To ensure that the regional trade arrangement will ultimately take off, the private sector in each participating country needs to be sold on free trade. Private sector actors must be aware—and convinced—of the benefits that they will receive by opening their economies to their neighbors. They must also be aware of the potential losses as a result of such trade so that these can be built in to the firm's strategic plan.

As such, the private sector should be able to be actively involved in the decision-making process. Firms must have access to information about the trade arrangements and about the member countries. The private sector needs to know the changes that will affect their operation of business.

References

APEC (Asia-Pacific Economic Cooperation), 1994, "APEC Economic Leaders' Declaration of Common Resolve," Bogor, Indonesia, November 15.

de Melo, J., and A. Panagariya, 1993, *New Dimensions in Regional Integration* (Cambridge: Center for Economic Policy Research).

Easterly, W., and R. Levine, 1995, "Africa's Growth Tragedy: A Retrospective," Policy Working Paper No. 1503 (Washington: World Bank).

Frankel, Jeffrey, 1997, *Regional Trading Blocs in the World Economic System* (Washington: Institute for International Economics).

Hufbauer, Gary, 1995, "Comment on Paul Wonnacott, 'Beyond NAFTA: The Design of a Free Trade Ageement of the Americas,'" paper presented at the Conference on Capital Flows and Regionalism, University of Maryland and American Enterprise Institute, Washington, June.

———, 1997, "How Long Will the Washington Consensus Shape Economic Policy?" remarks at the Pacific Council on International Policy, Los Angeles, November.

———, Jeffrey, J. Schott, and Diana Clark, 1994, *Western Hemisphere Economic Integration* (Washington: Institute for International Economics).

Naim, Moises, 1993, *Paper Tigers and Minotaurs: The Politics of Venezuela's Economic Reforms* (Washington: Carnegie Endowment for International Peace).

Summit of the Americas, 1994, Declaration of Principles, Miami, December 11.

Thomas, Vinod, John Nash, and Associates, 1991, *Best Practices in Trade Policy Reform* (Washington: World Bank).

Williamson, John, 1990, *Latin American Adustment: How Much Has Happened?* (Washington: Institute for International Economics).

Winters, Alan, 1996, "Regionalism versus Multilateralism," paper prepared for a Center for Economic Policy Research conference on Regional Integration, La Coraña, Espadín, Brazil, April.

Wonnacott, Paul, 1996, "Beyond NAFTA—The Design of a Free Trade Area of the Americas," in *The Economics of Preferential Trade Agreements*, ed. by Jagdish Bhagwati and Arvind Panagariya (Washington: American Enterprise Institute Press).

Trade Policy and Regional Integration in Sub-Saharan Africa 12

T. Ademola Oyejide

The poor and generally unsatisfactory performance of the economies of the vast majority of sub-Saharan African countries, particularly since the 1970s, has been widely recognized and documented. Various explanations have been offered for this performance record. Of particular interest, from the perspective of this chapter, is the virtually universal focus on trade policy as a (or perhaps the) major factor. Thus, the World Bank (1981) identified what it calls "misguided trade policies" as the main culprit, while the fairly comprehensive review of empirical studies in Collier and Gunning (1997, p. 6) shows that "impediments to openness have been detrimental to African economic performance."

The apparent consensus in the identification of trade policy as the key source of sub-Saharan Africa's inadequate performance had two immediate consequences: policy advice aimed at solving this problem focused strongly on the reform of trade policy, while virtually all structural adjustment policy reform packages gave a prominent position to trade policy reform proposals (Helleiner, 1995; Rodrik, 1988). Although sub-Saharan Africa has a long history of regional integration and contains a large number of regional trade arrangements, neither the trade policy advice offered to specific sub-Saharan African countries nor the trade policy reforms included in country-specific structural adjustment programs paid much attention to the regional dimensions of trade policy.

This chapter concerns itself with two key issues that derive from the discussion above. The first relates to the main features of trade policy for industrialization and development in the context of sub-Saharan Africa. The second explores the scope that exists for sub-Saharan Africa's regional integration schemes to serve as vehicles for more effective trade policy (of the sort articulated under the first issue) in Africa.

Various elements of these issues are taken up in the following sequence. The second section explores the emerging consensus regarding trade policy in sub-Saharan Africa. Then, the third section reviews the extent of trade policy reform in sub-Saharan African countries in recent times. The broad aim of this review is not necessarily to show how far these reforms have moved African trade regimes toward the frontiers of some abstract "best practice" but rather how far they are from the main features suggested by the emerging consensus on this issue. The fourth section sketches a regional approach to African trade policy against the background of contending views regarding the desirability or otherwise of regionalism in sub-Saharan Africa, as well as new insights that might justify dimensions in the region's trade regimes. The fifth section concludes the chapter.

Trade Policy for Industrialization and Development

In general, trade policy measures are targeted at the tradable goods and services sector. More specifically, they influence the overall structure of incentives within this section and thus affect the relative prices between importables and exportables. In the process, trade policy measures exert their impact through changes in the incentives for producing and consuming, as well as exporting and importing various types of tradable goods and services (Helleiner, 1992, 1995). It should be obvious that while trade policy measures aim primarily at influencing the composition and levels of imports and exports, this does not preclude other factors and policies from affecting the levels of exports and imports. Clearly, exogenous changes in levels of income or general economic activity in a country would tend to influence both tradable and nontradable sectors. At the same time, some macroeconomic policies (e.g., exchange rate policy) could alter relative prices between nontradable and tradable goods and hence influence the levels of exports and imports. Disentangling the effects of pure trade policy on the composition and levels of imports and exports from the effects of other policies and exogenous factors remains a difficult challenge for empirical research.

Import Policy

Discussions of trade policy reform, especially in the context of sub-Saharan Africa, are confined almost exclusively to a debate about the pros and cons of import liberalization. How far and how fast should it proceed? What should be its coverage? What measures should be applied and in what sequence?—and so forth. This contextual framework reflects the reality that many sub-Saharan African countries have embraced and have been implementing various forms of trade liberalization measures that have been induced largely by policy advice from various multilateral development institutions.

Within this perspective, trade policy reform is largely conterminous with import liberalization, which in turn refers to policy changes and associated measures that are used to endow the trade regime with a more neutral incentive structure. A neutral trade regime is generally regarded as one whose incentive structure does not discriminate between exportables and importables or between production for the domestic market and for export sales. More specifically, and in the words of Helleiner (1995, p. 30):

> When the incentives for exporting are the same as those for import competing activity, the trade policy is "neutral" in its encouragement of these two kinds of activity. When such neutrality exists or when exporting is favoured in the economy . . . the trade policy is generally said to be "outward-oriented." Otherwise, trade policy is said to reflect anti-export bias and therefore to be "inward-oriented."

The definition and classification of trade policy orientation implied by the above could be sharpened somewhat by eliminating the ambiguity inherent in the interpretation of trade policy neutrality as outward orientation. A three-part classification, that is, outward, neutral, and inward, would clearly be more useful. This would require that trade policy neutrality be distinguished from an outward-oriented policy stance, with the latter concept being used to refer to a trade policy regime that discriminates in favor of exports. Similarly, an inward-oriented trade policy regime would be one that discriminates in favor of import-competing activities. Under this three-part categorization, trade liberalization would imply transforming the trade regime from an inward-oriented stance that discriminates in favor of (and thus protects) import-competing activities into a neutral regime whose incentive structure does not distinguish between exportables and importables—or even into an outward-oriented trade policy regime that discriminates in favor of (and thus actively promotes) exports.

It has been argued that trade liberalization that produces either a neutral or outward-oriented trade regime confers certain productivity-enhancing and growth-promoting features on the liberalized economy (World Bank, 1991). Included among these are improvement in the efficiency with which resources are allocated, increases in competition and product specialization, enhanced ability to attract foreign investment, and the creation of a favorable environment for technology transfer. In the context of a more open trade regime, technology can be transferred in at least three distinct ways: as an integral part of regional investment, through increased trade that allows a country to import capital goods that embody current technology, and through export competition that induces firms to operate at the frontiers of technological development. This perspective thus suggests, first, that a trade regime that enhances import and export competition would induce increased trade and promote more rapid economic growth; and, second, that the key to the productivity increases associated with expanded trade lies predominantly in "exporting [which] strengthens the incentive to adopt new technology by increasing the returns from innovation through expanded market opportunities" (World Bank, 1991, p. 89).

There exists, however, an alternative perspective that associates the growth-promoting effect of expanding trade with productivity-enhancing characteristics of technology embodied in, and the increased capacity utilization permitted by, increased imports of capital and intermediate inputs (Helleiner, 1995). This perspective recognizes three main areas of gain linked to trade expansion. The first derives from the once-and-for-all gain associated with the reallocation of production and consumption generated by trade expansion. A second (also once-and-for-all) gain emanates from increased capacity utilization made possible by the availability of "critically important imports" upon which domestic production in the developing countries is heavily dependent. The third, more dynamic and enduring gain, from trade is technology-based productivity increases. As Helleiner (1995, p. 15) argues:

> It seems more plausible, however, to associate the main externalities associated with trade with imports, particularly those of capital goods and intermediate inputs (when they embody new technology) and technological and other non-factor services, rather than exports. Such imports bring the knowledge upon which long-term growth itself is now seen to be heavily dependent.

This perspective would, in effect, be consistent with a trade regime whose incentive structure discriminates in favor of technology-embodying imports of capital goods and intermediate inputs as a means of capturing the growth-promoting gains derivable from increased capacity utilization and the productivity-enhancing gains emanating from technology transfer. Even in the context of this perspective, however, there is a clear recognition of the important role of exports, not necessarily as the critical vehicle for technology transfer but more significantly as the primary source for financing the indispensable bottleneck-breaking and technology-bearing imports, especially in the absence of adequate capital inflows. Both perspectives suggest that the two (import and export) components of trade policy reform may have important, distinct, and different implications. Hence, their differences deserve to be explicitly taken into account in the design and implementation of trade liberalization programs.

The import component of trade liberalization is of special significance in sub-Saharan African countries for a variety of reasons. The standard instruments of trade policy, such as import tariffs and quantitative import restrictions, are often used to serve multiple objectives in this region, given the country characteristics that limit the availability and effectiveness of alternative policy handles. Hence, trade policy reform, especially as it relates to the import components, needs to be carefully designed to ensure that its full implications for the various objectives are explicitly recognized and taken into account.

The fiscal impact of changes in the form and level of import protection constitutes one of these areas of concern. Compared with other regions of the world, sources of government revenues are much narrower in sub-Saharan African countries. This narrow base translates into an unusually heavy reliance on trade taxes. Receipts from imports tariffs represent a major source of government revenues that cannot be easily dispensed with. This is so not only because of their magnitude (relative to other sources of revenue) but also because mobilizing fiscal resources through other means and in comparable magnitude is costly, if not impossible, especially in the short to medium term. As Lyakurwa (1993, p. 36) observes, "two revenue-related costs of (trade) liberalization, which tend to reduce the budget balance, appear to be unavoidable, even under the most prudent of policy regimes." First, even through trade volumes could increase after liberalization, revenue from trade taxes may fall. As export taxes are virtually eliminated and imports are less heavily taxed, liberalization implies a shift from traded goods in the tax base to traded goods outside the tax base. Second, trade liberalization implies shifting from easy-to-collect trade taxes to more-difficult-to-collect revenue from income and domestic consumption. These tax handles typically require more sophisticated accounting and record-keeping systems than are usually available, and tax revenue losses may be inevitable as some of the income and activities associated with trade liberalization escape the tax net. It should be noted, of course, that to the extent that import liberalization reduces illegal activities, including smuggling, it could expand the tax base and thereby increase total tax revenues derived from lower rates of trade taxes.

Import liberalization may lead to increased trade deficits and thus worsen the usually precarious balance of payment position of the typical sub-Saharan African country. A deep, generalized, and sudden import liberalization program could induce an abnormally high demand for imports, which could place unsustainable pressure on the country's balance of payments, requiring access to substantial aid and capital inflow or a compensating exchange rate policy change. As Collier and Gunning (1992) demonstrate, although import liberalization does not inevitably worsen the balance of payments, it seems likely to do so, particularly in the short or medium term. Increasing trade deficits arising from import liberalization should worry the typical sub-Saharan African country, which lacks flexible access to external financing. To the extent that import liberalization gives rise to fiscal deficits and balance of payments problems, it would worsen the macroeconomic imbalances facing many sub-Saharan African countries and thereby make the process of steady adjustment and recovery of growth more difficult to sustain.

In addition to their use for generating fiscal revenue and confronting balance of payments problems, import protection measures are also used in sub-Saharan Africa as instruments of industrial policy. Many countries in the region are justifiably concerned with the survival and future development of an efficient manufacturing sector as an important component of their development. While it may be expected that the typical sub-Saharan African economy would experience some degree of industrialization as part of its natural process of growth, there are several considerations that provide a basis for suggesting that explicit government policy has an important role in influencing the speed and structure of industrialization. Thus, an initial disadvantage may lead to a sustained low equilibrium level, while an appropriate push can place the same economy on a higher-level equilibrium. The key factors responsible for these results are economies of scale in knowledge, location and transport costs, and overall production. In addition, a basis for an explicit policy in support of industrialization can be found (Rodrik, 1992, p. 310) "in specific market failures and externalities which, in the absence of corrective policies, may leave the industrial sector in command of a socially suboptimal share of the economy's resources." Given that modern manufacturing activities are characterized by learning-by-doing, and that market failures are particularly endemic in sub-Saharan African countries, infant industries may need protection so that they can gain the experience needed to lower costs and become viable in an environment in which more dominant foreign competitors could, otherwise, take advantage of their "infancy" and wipe them out before they can effectively compete.

While a respectable case can be made for trade policy in support of industrialization, drawing both from theoretical considerations and lessons of development experience, the various sources of this case imply a strong caveat: industrial protection has significant negative side effects. Hence, an important challenge of protection-induced industrialization policies is to balance protection, which nurtures domestic industries, with competition, which forces firms to innovate, raise productivity, and reduce costs. This balancing act has at least two key aspects. One is that the level of protection should be moderate, to minimize its negative impact in terms of resource-allocation inefficiencies on the economy. Another is that protection should be temporary or time-bound, so that competition forces the "infant" industry to grow up fairly quickly or die.

In addition to maintaining pressure on domestic firms to improve their productivity by allowing for gradually increasing levels of domestic competition as time-bound protection falls away, the imposition of export performance targets serves as a further inducement for firm-level productivity enhancement. It is not, in fact, unusual in actual development experience to combine export-development policy measures with domestic protection. In the presence of time-bound levels of protection, it would not be realistic to implement immediate and full import liberalization, since this could destroy the original objective of that protection by allowing a surge of import to displace domestic production generated by infant industries that might otherwise have become competitive.

Export Policy

The export component of trade liberalization also deserves scrutiny. This derives from the proposition that good export performance is not just a desirable goal in its own right, but is also a critical means to other important ends, that is, deeper import liberalization and more robust overall economic growth. A successful and sustainable import liberalization program requires successful exports; or, put differently, a country must export to import (Hachette, 1991; Snape, 1991). In the words of Michaely (1991, p. 123):

> The survival of (trade) liberalization attempts tends strongly to be related to a favourable export performance, whereas the collapse of (trade) liberalization is overwhelmingly connected with a dismal export performance.

As it relates to the export sector, trade liberalization would cover policy changes that produce a neutral trade regime that treats exportables and importables similarly as well as an outward-oriented trade regime that favors and actively promotes exports. Establishing a neutral—not to talk of an outward-oriented—trade regime, as defined above, in the presence of some degree of import protection is not straightforward. Those policy measures that endow a trade regime with its import protectiveness, such as tariffs and nontariff barriers, have an anti-export bias. More specially, restrictions on imports translate effectively into a tax on exports; by making import substitutes relatively more profitable, they increase the cost and reduce the availability of imported inputs used in the production of exportables, forcing exporters to use relatively expensive and low-quality locally produced inputs. Import restrictions also subject exporters to a more appreciated exchange rate than they would otherwise have faced. These different elements of the tax on exports imposed by imports restrictions combine to reduce the international competitiveness of the export sector.

To promote exports, the anti-export bias that inherently characterizes a trade regime containing a degree of import protection needs to be eliminated. This can be done through schemes that grant exporters and their suppliers unrestricted access to inputs (imported and locally produced) at internationally competitive prices that are free of import duty and other indirect taxes. Effective systems to provide neutral trade regimes for exporters may be established in the framework of specially created export processing zones. Or this can be done more simply through duty-drawback or exemption schemes as well as bonded warehousing arrangements.

Given the widely recognized role of foreign exchange reserves and export performance in the initiation and sustainability of deep import liberalization, an important question is whether a stage of export promotion aimed at boosting exports should precede that of import liberalization (Shepherd and Langoni, 1991; Nash, 1992). This issue derives an additional relevance from the heavy emphasis of the conventional mode of trade liberalization on opening the domestic economy to competition from imports (Coes, 1991).

Based broadly on the notion that in foreign-exchange-constrained economies, exports can be regarded as a means of acquiring the foreign exchange with which to purchase increased imports made available through trade liberalization, it is suggested (Nash, 1992, p. 63) that "introducing other export policy reform shortly before or at least at the same time as import reforms permits an earlier export supply response and allows unification of the tariff structure to proceed without burdening exporters."

This principle appears to have featured prominently in the trade liberalization experiences of several countries. Thus, Coes (1991, p. 16) reports that "an important feature of the process that opened Brazil to world markets between 1964 and 1974 was the emphasis given to export—not just to the removal of restrictions on imports, as in liberalization of a purely orthodox and conventional kind. . . . Reforms in import policy came later, only after an improvement in Brazil's current account." Similarly, Cavallo (1991, p. 31) points out that, in Argentina, "the program of trade liberalization was a two-stage reform. During the first stage (1976–78), commercial policies relied more heavily on export liberalization and export promotion than on competitive tariff reduction. It was only during the second stage (1979–81) that tariffs were allowed to fall competitively albeit in a gradual and discriminate fashion."

There are, of course, other constraining experiences. For instance, Hachette (1991, p. 51) finds that "the behaviour of exports was crucial in the success of the liberalization episode in Chile; however, it was not the result of a special policy phase designed for that purpose." In his broader review of the trade liberalization experience of several countries, Michaely (1991, p. 123) concludes that "no systematic connection, however, seems to exist between the adoption of export-promotion measures, as a component of the trade liberalization package, and the sustainability of a liberalization policy. Nor does the introduction of an export-promotion policy before import liberalization seem to add materially to the likelihood that trade reform will survive."

Even these contrasting experiences acknowledge the pivotal role of good export performance in sustaining import liberalization. Hence, whenever the required export performance can be more readily induced through specific promotion measures, it would be reasonable to implement them before deeper import liberalization is implemented. In countries with clearly defined development strategies and adequate capacity to implement them, appropriate export promotion measures can be used to achieve trade "neutrality" and thus secure outward-orientation before full-scale import liberalization (Levy, 1993).

The broad features of an appropriate trade policy package for the industrialization and development of sub-Saharan African countries sketched above are summarized by Rodrik (1997, p. 2) as follows:

> Extremists aside, there is actually a fair bit of consensus on what constitutes a reasonable trade strategy for countries of Africa. The consensus can be crudely expressed in terms of a number of do's and don'ts: demonopolize trade; streamline the import regime; reduce red tape and implement transparent customs procedures; replace quantitative restrictions with tariffs; avoid extreme variation in tariff rates and excessively high rates of effective protection; allow exporters duty-free access to imported inputs; refrain from large doses of antiexport bias; do not tax export crops too highly.

African Trade Policy Reform Experience

Between the early 1960s and the early 1980s, many sub-Saharan African countries built up highly interventionist and protectionist trade regimes. These regimes were broadly characterized, on the import side, by restrictive licensing systems' high tariffs, escalated or cascading tariff structures made up of several layers, varying degrees of import prohibitions, and tight foreign exchange controls. On the export side, the trade regimes featured substantial implicit and explicit taxes as well as frequent use of nontariff barriers, such as the prohibition of certain export items. These heavily protectionist trade regimes were motivated, apparently, by several different concerns. The multiplicity of objectives, some of which were conflicting, probably accounts for the rather haphazard, incoherent and internally inconsistent nature of the trade regimes that eventually evolved in many African countries.

One of the key problems that trade policy has had to address in many sub-Saharan African countries is the raising of government revenue. Given the heavy reliance of these countries on tariffs for revenue, it is not surprising that fiscal concern has been a major motive for imposing high import and, in some cases, export tariffs. At the same time, many of these countries were highly susceptible to balance of payments pressures, given their strong commitments to the maintenance of often unrealistic fixed exchange rate systems. In this context, trade policy often became a substitute for more appropriate policies needed to maintain macroeconomic discipline (such as exchange rate and fiscal policies). Hence, nontariff import control measures were often applied whenever it became necessary to deal with recurring balance-of-payments crises.

Some aspects of the preliberalization trade regimes could also be traced to the desire to protect domestic industries in the context of the import-substitution industrialization development strategy that was quite popular in Africa during the 1960s and 1970s. Evidence in support of this include extensive exemptions from tariff duties and low tariff rates on imported inputs used by local producers. The generally escalated structure of tariffs, which imposed high rates on finished products and much lower rates on raw materials, provides additional evidence in this regard. It is important to bear in mind, however, that high tariff rates were also applied to so-called luxury goods. These were import items, however, to be consumed largely by the rich, and were in many cases goods for which no local production facility existed to be protected. Thus high tariffs did not always reflect the desire to protect local industry: in certain cases, they were aimed at raising revenue based on the perceived ability of certain categories of consumers to pay.

The preliberalization trade regimes of many African countries exhibited a strong relationship between the use of import restrictions and the appearance of balance of payments problems. These balance-of-payments concerns, taken together with budgetary needs, probably had a much stronger impact on the evolution and structure of preliberalization trade regimes in many sub-Saharan African countries than the desire to protect local manufacturing activities.

Trade liberalization episodes in many sub-Saharan African countries have been brought about by various types of stimuli (Oyejide, Ndulu, and Gunning, 1996). A two-way classification of these stimuli would identify unilateral and multilateral mechanisms. The unilateral liberalization attempts, in turn, consist of several categories. These include trade liberalization associated with structural adjustment programs; those induced by positive external shocks; and those based on "own initiatives" that reflected internal policy dynamics and the design and use of innovative schemes to finance the liberalization process. The multilateral mechanism for trade liberalization attempts refers, essentially, to those liberalization efforts that were designed and implemented in the context of specific regional integration schemes.

Among the four different types of stimuli for trade liberalization identified above, the most prevalent has been the liberalization process embedded in structural programs. These programs have shaped the design, scope, and sequence of trade liberalization processes in many sub-Saharan African countries since the mid-1980s, the single exception being South Africa.

Positive external shocks have served as the stimulus for some trade liberalization episodes in several sub-Saharan African countries. Liberalization episodes associated with this stimulus have typically been temporary and partial; they were usually characterized by temporary and limited relaxation of import restrictions and exchange controls. In the cases of Kenya and Tanzania, this type of liberalization occurred in response to the commodity booms of 1976–77. The episodes were short-lived; the collapse of 1979–80 generated policy reversals and brought in even more severe import restrictions and exchange control than before (Mwega, 1996; Ndulu and Mbelle, 1996). The Nigerian trade liberalization episode of 1970–76 has a similar origin in the positive external shock generated by the oil export shock, and it suffered a similar fate as soon as the external shock was reversed (Ajakaiye and Soyibo, 1995).

An important variety of own initiative stimulus for trade liberalization is based on the Own Funded Import Schemes. Under these schemes, importers were allowed to bring in goods without official foreign exchange allocation to finance such imports and with no questions asked about source of financing. The schemes were aimed essentially at ameliorating generalized shortage of essential goods and controlling inflation. These schemes were used to support some trade liberalization episodes in Zambia as well as in Tanzania during 1984–86 and Ghana in 1967–72 (Adam and Musonda, 1996; Ndulu and Mbelle, 1996; Tutu and Oduro, 1996).

The least significant stimulus for trade liberalization in many sub-Saharan African countries is membership in a regional integration arrangement. The trade liberalization scheme of ECOWAS remains largely unimplemented (Jebuni, Ogunkola, and Soludo, 1996; Ogunkola, 1994). It has, in fact, been virtually ignored as Côte d'lvoire, Ghana, and Nigeria have concentrated policy and implementation attention on the unilateral trade liberalization process contained in their individual structural adjustment programs. These programs have been designed and implemented at national levels. They have uniformly ignored the regional dimensions of unilateral liberalization and paid no attention to the regional integration obligations of particular countries. With regard to the PTA/COMESA, it seems clear that the pursuit of more intense unilateral liberalization by each member country has overshadowed the preferential trade liberalization scheme. In any case, trade liberalization has progressed much faster under the unilateral mechanism.

It is clear from the above that the most dominant among the stimuli for trade liberalization in sub-Saharan African countries is that linked to conditionality under structural adjustment programs. These trade liberalization episodes have been the longest sustained and the most comprehensive among Africa's trade liberalization attempts.

African trade liberalization processes have covered both tariff and nontariff measures and have had several effects (World Bank, 1994; Oyejide, Ndulu, and Gunning, 1996). They have also, typically, been accompanied by exchange rate reforms. As a result of the trade liberalization attempts, African tariff structures have been compressed substantially, as the average number of tariff categories has been sharply reduced. This has had at least three consequences: the rates of protection have become much less varied, the scope for discretion has been considerably reduced, and tariff policy transparency has been enhanced. Dramatic changes have also occurred with respect to quantitative restrictions; these nontariff barriers have been eliminated in several African countries and partly or fully tariffied in many others. The elimination or relaxation of foreign exchange controls in most African countries has facilitated the reduction of quantitative import restrictions. More generally, both trade and exchange rate liberalization processes have reduced the traditional reliance of African countries on trade policy instruments for managing balance-of-payments pressures; this burden is, increasingly, being shifted to and effectively carried by exchange rate changes.

In general, African trade liberalization attempts have suffered from credibility and sustainability problems. A robust indicator for this apparently inherent nature of African trade liberalization processes is the frequency with which various attempts have been reversed. Examples abound. Both Nigeria (in 1994) and Zambia (in 1986) experienced virtually total reversals (Ajakaiye and Soyibo, 1995; Adam and Musonda, 1996). Kenya and Ghana experienced fairly frequent policy reversals since the early 1970s (Mwega, 1996; Tutu and Oduro, 1996). Many of the African trade policy reversals can be traced to balance of payments and fiscal incompatibility, which many African governments have traditionally used standard trade policy instruments to cope with.

The trade policy experiments of many sub-Saharan African countries during the 1960s and 1970s were not entirely consistent with the broad features of an appropriate trade policy for industrialization and developments sketched above. But the more recent policy reform experience of the 1980s and early 1990s does not fully reflect key elements of this framework either. In particular, while virtually all sub-Saharan African countries liberally used various trade policy instruments to offer high protection and widely differentiated rents to selected individual enterprises and groups, import protection was typically not time bound, and the award of rents and subsidies was usually not related to any objective performance standard. Furthermore, although many sub-Saharan African countries espoused the growth of manufactured exports and, indeed, deployed various trade policy measures in pursuit of this objective, the granting of incentives to beneficiaries was usually not explicitly tied to their export performance.

Recent trade policy reforms have focused primary attention on import liberalization. But while the tariff structure in many sub-Saharan African countries has undergone substantial rationalization as a result, the lack of or inadequate "supply response" (due, perhaps, to the lack of similar concern for the promotion of manufactured exports) may have contributed in some way to those trade policy reversals emanating from balance of payments considerations.

Regionalism and African Trade Policy

Up to the early 1980s, most African countries tried to accelerate their economic growth on the basis of an import-substitution industrialization development strategy. From an economic perspective, the small size of the typical African economy and the perceived disadvantages of smallness in the context of this strategy would appear to be a key reason for the establishment of various integration schemes. In particular, a small population combined with low per capita income placed sharp limitation on the development and growth prospects within the limited market of each country by restricting the ability to benefit from lower unit costs arising from the exploitation of economies of scale and curtailing allocative efficiency gains that could have been generated by increased competition.

Against this background, regional integration suggests itself as a logical way to enable the economy to produce at lower unit costs for a larger (regional) market. It could be embraced essentially as a means of widening market size and thus allowing the benefits of greater specialization and economies of scale to be realized. In this sense, import substitution in the context of larger regional markets could generate greater competition within the region and thus induce higher levels of productivity overall than would be possible within the narrow confines of individual national markets. Compared with global liberalization, regional integration could be regarded as a more viable source of the benefits of economies of scale than the (even larger) world market because of the anticipated problems of market access and the presumed higher transactions costs of producing for the world market.

The above notwithstanding, the arguments for regional integration do not lend themselves to unambiguous conclusions. At the static level and in the context of the simplest models, the desirability of an integration scheme depends on the balance of the opposing forces of trade creations and trade diversion. The case for regional integration in the context of export promotion strategy becomes stronger when dynamic factors are taken into consideration. However, in practice, whether this can be realized depends on the extent to which economies of scale and international competitiveness are achieved, and on the feasibility of setting up a suitable compensation scheme, a key issue given the likelihood that effective regional integration could result in geographic concentration of certain economic activities (e.g., production facilities) within the integrated region.

Even under the best circumstance, however, the second-best theory of regional preferential trading schemes suggests that any effects at the regional level from African integration schemes would be very small. This conclusion derives from the following considerations. At the empirical level, gravity model simulations of trade flows between African countries, in the absence of trade restrictions, generally suggest that the scope for intercountry trade within Africa is intrinsically modest. Empirical results generally confirm that intra-African regional integration arrangements have not significantly increased intraregional trade (Oyejide, Elbadawi, and Yeo, 1996). Results from studies based on gravity models suggest that intragroup trade in Africa is not necessarily low because of trade restrictions, but rather that it is naturally low. Analysis based on comparison of trade ratios also shows that in virtually all the integrating regions these ratios have remained stagnant or even declined, especially since the various integration schemes were formally established. In some of the schemes (e.g., CEAO and UDEAC), the chosen instruments of integration were virtually guaranteed to discourage rather than enhance intragroup trade. In a number of other arrangements (e.g., ECOWAS and PTA/COMESA), noncompliance with or delayed implementation of agreed-on trade liberalization schedules could obviously not have done much to promote intragroup trade.

A juxtaposition of the logic of the second-best theory of regional preferential trading arrangements against the stylized facts of African economies would support these results and lead to the conclusion that regional integration in Africa may not be sufficiently potent to generate worthwhile overall welfare gains. Several theoretical perspectives, however, may offer more robust support for regional cooperation. In the first case, evidence from recent studies of regional spillover in growth effects suggests that neighbors matter (Easterly and Levine, 1995). In other words, if neighboring countries grow rapidly, that appears to assist regional growth. This evidence seems to apply to Africa as well. Hence, regional integration built around some rapidly growing member countries that serve as growth-poles for the integration of the region could have significant growth-enhancing effects for the entire region.

In the second case, insights from new economic geography suggest that the interplay of economies of scale and location specific costs could provide a rationale for regional integration schemes in Africa. The basic idea is that location decisions of producers are based on considerations of internal economies of scales and "trade costs." Trade costs consist generally of transport and information costs (the latter include language and cultural barriers to ease of transactions). These costs increase with distance between the producer and the consumer. The inherited colonial pattern of production and trade between the typical African country and its European "mother" country, combined with high trade costs between African countries, has generated a "hub and spoke" trade pattern in which activities that have powerful scale economies, such as manufacturing, are located in the European hub, from which they supply consumers located in numerous African spokes. In this arrangement, no spoke African country has a sufficiently large enough market to warrant the location of manufacturing production facilities in it unless trade costs within Africa can be drastically reduced.

A regional integration scheme that joins up the spokes by reducing intra-African trade costs could radically alter the existing hub and spoke production and trade pattern and justify the location of production within the integrated region. The same location theory suggests, however, that if intraregional trade costs are initially high, small reductions would tend to *increase* regional concentration of production. Clearly, this would generate greater intergovernmental conflict over compensation arrangements. Happily, though, the theory predicts that more sweeping and deeper liberalization measures that bring about large reductions in intraregional trade costs might substantially counter the trend toward concentration of production. Thus, this analytical perspective not only provides a robust justification for regional integration in Africa but also predicts that such a scheme would be more effective and less contentious if impediments to trade within the integrated region are quickly eliminated.

The third source of insights for constructing an economic rationale for regional interaction in Africa is the "agency of restraint" paradigm (Collier and Gunning, 1995; Fine and Yeo, 1995). This starts from the observation that, in Africa, government policies are frequently reversed. These policy reversals create credibility problems: private economic agents are reluctant to make investment and production decisions for fear of potential losses that could result from such policy reversals. Governments, on their part, can reverse policies easily because they are subject to agencies of restraint that are sufficiently powerful to impose penalties that are severe enough to prevent such behavior. In this context, the purpose of regional integration would be to promote investment and thus contribute to the enhancement of economic growth by helping to enforce the policy restraint necessary for macroeconomic stability. What is required here is a participatory, reciprocal, and supranational agency of restraint that locks in key national economic policies in a reciprocal threat-making arrangement. The agency would ensure that all participating countries commit to sound and stable policies and should be in a position to effectively threaten errant members with credible and costly sanctions. Such an organization would have clear advantages over the essentially alien, unidirectional, and unreliable conditionality of donors and international financial institutions.

While assessments based on changes in intragroup trade volume and shares have generally demonstrated the ineffectiveness of sub-Saharan Africa's regional integration schemes, an appeal to these new insights and their applicability in the regional context may provide more interesting results. It seems that the regional integration schemes in the Southern African subregion constitute a good source of some of these. These are the Southern African Customs Union (SACU) and Southern African Development Cooperation (SADC). As presently constituted, both are built around the pivotal economy of South Africa, with SACU being the older, smaller (in terms of number of member countries) but deeper form of regional integration than the SADC, whose trade integration mandate is of more recent origin. In spite of continuing debate regarding the formula for sharing tariff revenue between the member countries of SACU, it seems clear that Botswana, Lesotho, Namibia, and Swaziland have derived significant benefits from their membership in SACU, both in terms of investment flows geared by the opportunities offered by the South African market and the "agency of restraint" function performed by SACU to enhance the creditability of some of their policies. In this context, Rodrik (1997) suggests that Botswana's membership in SACU robs it of an independent trade policy imposed a trade regime that is a key factor behind the country's economic success.

In an interesting twist, South Africa has also been using its regional integration linkages with SACU and SADC as a significant lever in its trade negotiation with the European Union. The EU Trade Mandate presented to South Africa in March 1996 offered a free-trade agreement that excluded roughly 40 percent of South African agricultural exports to the EU from liberalization and called for elimination of duties on about 35 percent of South Africa's import from the EU in addition to the former's Uruguay Round commitments. The implication was that South Africa would have to bear quite severe adjustment costs for the proposed free trade area agreement to be implemented. This result is in line with the typical South-North regional trading arrangements that developing countries are usually encouraged to enter into. As Fernandez (1997, p. 5) argues, "since in reality, it is most often less developed, smaller or economically weaker countries that are making the largest reductions in their protection structures, this redistributional cost (i.e., losses in the form of tariff revenue) is most likely to be borne by them."

In responding to the EU offer, South Africa's bargaining position was strengthened by its treaty obligations to both SACU and SADC. In effect, South Africa had to consult its partners in these two organizations before reaching an agreement with the EU. In addition, such agreement had to take cognizance of Article 19 of the 1969 SACU Agreement, which stipulates that member countries have the right to approve or veto any agreement proposed by one member with a third country or multilateral economic grouping. In other words, more detailed study of the revitalized regional integration schemes in Africa may provide more positive evidence of their contribution in terms of the nontraditional gains from regional trading arrangements.

Conclusion

To the extent that misguided trade policies have been blamed for the poor economic performance of many sub-Saharan African countries in the past, it is logical that part of the solution to the problem is being sought in terms of trade policy reform. However, recent efforts at reforming the region's trade regimes do not appear to reflect all the key features of trade policy that emerging consensus would consider as appropriate for many sub-Saharan African countries. In particular, a two-track strategy that balances import protection with export promotion under free trade principles and associates both with time bounds and a reward-penalty system requires explicit recognition. Because of the clear implications of size, scale effects, and spillovers for this strategy, trade policy in sub-Saharan Africa should feature a regional approach. In any case, regionalism in sub-Saharan Africa can serve several additional purposes, ranging from policy harmonization and credibility to regional security and the coordination of negotiating positions as a means of enhancing bargaining power. Evidence is beginning to accumulate that some revived sub-Saharan African integration schemes may thus have a significant role as trade policy vehicles.

References

Adam, C., and F. Musonda, 1996, "Trade Liberalization in Zambia" (unpublished; Nairobi: African Economic Research Consortium).

Ajakaiye, D.O., and A. Soyibo, 1995, "Trade Liberalization in Nigeria, 1970–93 Episodes, Credibility and Impact" (unpublished; Nairobi: African Economic Research Consortium).

Cavallo, D.F., 1991, "Argentina: Trade Reform, 1976–1982," in *Trade Reform: Lessons from Eight Countries,* ed. by G. Shepherd and C.G. Langoni (San Francisco: International Center for Economic Growth).

Coes, D., 1991, "Brazil: Precedents and Prospects in Foreign Trade," in *Trade Reform: Lessons from Eight Countries,* ed. by G. Shepherd and C.G. Langoni (San Francisco: International Center for Economic Growth).

Collier, P., and J.W. Gunning, 1992, "Aid and Exchange Rate Adjustment in African Trade Liberalizations," *Economic Journal,* Vol. 102, pp. 925–39.

———, 1995, "Trade Policy and Regional Integration: Implications for the Relationship between Europe and Africa," *The World Economy,* Vol. 18, pp. 387–410.

———, 1997, "Explaining African Economic Performance," Working Paper No. S97–2 (Oxford: Centre for the Study of African Economies).

de Melo, J., and A. Panagariya, 1992, *The New Regionalism in Trade Policy* (Washington: World Bank).

Easterly, W., and R. Levine, 1995, "Africa's Growth Tragedy: A Retrospective, 1960–89," Policy Research Working Paper No. 1503 (Washington: World Bank).

Fernandez, R., 1997, "Returns to Regionalism: An Evaluation of Non-Traditional Gains from Regional Trading Arrangements" (unpublished; New York: New York University).

Fine, J., and S. Yeo, 1995, "Regional Integration in Sub-Saharan Africa: Dead End or a Fresh Start?" (unpublished; Nairobi: African Economic Research Consortium).

Hachette, D., 1991, "Chile: Trade Liberalization since 1974," in *Trade Reform: Lessons From Eight Countries,* ed. by G. Shepherd and C.G. Langoni (San Francisco: International Center for Economic Growth).

Helleiner, G.K., ed., 1992, *Trade Policy Industrialization and Development: New Perspectives* (Oxford: Clarendon Press).

———, 1995, *Trade, Trade Policy and Industrialization Reconsidered,* World Development Studies No. 6 (Helsinki: United Nations University).

Jebuni, C.D., E.O. Ogunkola, and C.C. Soludo, 1996, "Review of Regional Integration Experience in Sub-Saharan Africa: Case Study of ECOWAS" (unpublished; Nairobi: African Economic Research Consortium).

Levy, B., 1993, "An Institutional Analysis of the Design and Sequence of Trade and Investment Policy Reform," *World Bank Economic Review,* Vol. 7, No. 2, pp. 247–62.

Lyakurwa, W.M., 1993, *Trade Policy and Promotion in Sub-Saharan Africa,* Special Paper No. 12 (Nairobi: African Economic Research Consortium).

Michaely, M., 1991, "The Lessons of Experience: An Overview," in *Trade Reform: Lessons from Eight Countries,* ed. by G. Shepherd and C.G. Langoni (San Francisco: International Center for Economic Growth).

Mwega, F., 1996, "Trade Liberalization in Kenya" (unpublished; Nairobi: African Economic Research Consortium).

Nash, J., 1992, "An Overview of Trade Policy Reform, with Implications for Sub-Saharan Africa," in *Foreign Trade Reforms and Development Strategy,* ed. by J.M. Fountain (New York: Routledge).

———, 1993, "Trade Policy Reform Implications in Sub-Saharan Africa: How Much Heat and How Much Light?" (unpublished; Washington: World Bank).

Ndulu, B.J., and A.V.Y. Mbelle, 1996, "Trade Liberalization in Tanzania" (unpublished; Nairobi: African Economic Research Consortium).

Ogunkola, E.O., 1994, *An Empirical Evaluation of Trade Potential in the ECOWAS* (Nairobi: African Economic Research Consortium).

Oyejide, T.A., 1996, "Regional Integration and Trade Liberalization in Sub-Saharan Africa" (unpublished; Nairobi: African Economic Research Consortium).

———, I.A. Elbadawi, and S. Yeo, 1996, "Introduction and Overview: Case Studies of Regional Integration" (unpublished; Nairobi: African Economic Research Consortium).

———, B.J. Ndulu, and J.W. Gunning, 1996, "Introduction and Overview: Country Case Studies of Trade Liberalization" (unpublished; Nairobi: African Economic Research Consortium).

Rodrik, D., 1988, "Imperfect Competition, Scale Economies, and Trade Policy in Developing Countries," in *Trade Policy Issues and Empirical Analysis,* ed. by R.E. Baldwin (Chicago: University of Chicago Press).

———, 1992, "Closing the Productivity Gap: Does Trade Liberalization Really Help?" in *Trade Policy, Industrialization, and Development: New Perspectives,* ed. by G.K. Helleiner (Oxford: Clarendon Press).

———, 1997, "Why Is Trade Reform So Difficult in Africa?" (unpublished; Nairobi: African Economic Research Consortium).

Shepherd, G., and C.G. Langoni, eds., 1991, *Trade Reform: Lessons from Eight Countries* (San Francisco: International Center for Economic Growth).

Snape, R.H., 1991, "East Asia: Trade Reform in Korea and Singapore," in *Trade Reform: Lessons From Eight Countries,* ed. by G. Shepherd and C.G. Langoni (San Francisco: International Center for Economic Growth).

Tutu, K., and A. Oduro, 1996, "Trade Liberalization in Ghana" (unpublished; Nairobi: African Economic Research Consortium).

World Bank, 1981, *Accelerated Development in Sub-Saharan Africa: An Agenda for Action* (Washington: World Bank).

———, 1991, *World Development Report: The Challenge of Development* (New York: Oxford University Press).

———, 1992, *Trade Policy Reforms Under Structural Adjustment* (Washington: World Bank).

———, 1994, *Adjustment in Africa: Reforms, Results and the Road Ahead* (New York: Oxford University Press).

Beyond Trade: Regional Arrangements as a Window on Globalization 13

Christian A. François and Arvind Subramanian

This chapter argues that regional arrangements can be an important strategic and practical vehicle to help African countries to integrate themselves into the world economy and to take advantage of globalization of trade and financial markets. However, to achieve these ultimate goals, African governments should implement the right kind of regional integration strategies. These strategies should encompass not only broad trade liberalization but also regional mechanisms for ensuring convergence of macroeconomic stability, structural reforms, common management of resources, and policy credibility. Because chapters above have focused on the trade aspects of regional arrangements, this chapter will limit itself to the other factors contributing to the integration of African economies into the world economy.

It is generally recognized that, in recent years, many countries in sub-Saharan Africa have made considerable progress toward achieving macroeconomic stability and restructuring their economies. However, despite bold reform efforts and clear improvements in performance, the challenges that remain in participating fully in the expansion of world trade and in attracting FDI are daunting. To meet these challenges, Africa needs a reinforced growth-oriented strategy that puts in place the conditions for an appreciable increase in private savings and investment and that has a regional dimension.

To give a measure of the policy challenges facing Africa today, it is worth recalling Professor Tybout's observation about the dramatic fall in Africa's share of world exports during the past 30 years.[1] IMF data show that the share of sub-Saharan Africa, excluding South Africa and Nigeria, went from 3 percent of global exports in the early 1960s to only 0.8 percent in 1990. Since then, fortunately, it has gradually recovered to a little more than 1 percent in 1995–96. If Africa had merely managed to grow at the same rate as the rest of the world, and hence maintained the same share of world exports it had achieved in the 1960s, sub-Saharan Africa's exports in 1996 would have not been

[1]Professor Tybout made this observation during discussion at the seminar on which this volume is based.

$44 billion but $152 billion, a level more than $100 billion higher. For Africa to recover its past market share, its exports would need to grow by 10 percent in real terms during the next 20 years.

It is not the purpose of this chapter to analyze the causes of this substantial erosion in the region's ability to compete in and access international markets, although this analysis has major implications for the kind of strategy and policies that Africa should implement to recover the lost ground.

It is clear that the prime responsibility for pursuing the right growth policies rests with the national authorities. However, regional initiatives can also significantly contribute to the establishment of a secure economic and political environment and the removal of uncertainty about commitment of African government to macroeconomic stability, trade liberalization, and private sector development.

Backdrop to Today's Regionalism

Regional initiatives are not new to Africa. Since independence, African countries have formed more than a dozen regional arrangements among themselves, encouraged by the creation of the European Community in 1958. A number of these arrangements have failed and have ceased to exist, others have been revitalized, and new ones have been recently launched. It is important to draw lessons from the various experiences.

The primary motive behind the first wave of regional arrangements was industrialization through regional import substitution. It was thought that high regional tariffs and strong government intervention would promote local industries and prepare them for world competition. In the event, however, it led to the creation of a large number of public enterprises with underutilized production capacities and inadequate competitiveness. The new regional approach developed in the late 1980s is based on outward-oriented policies and private sector initiative. It combines preferential regional tariff with multilateral trade liberalization. It also emphasizes deeper integration involving goods, services, and capital, as well as a range of domestic policies.

As in the rest of the world, the new regionalism in Africa developed from the late 1980s is taking place against the background of *a more open world economy*. And although there is considerable room for further improvement, substantial progress has been made in achieving greater macroeconomic stability, making trade and exchange policies more open, and progressively disengaging the government from economic activity in which the private sector has a comparative advantage. This progress augurs well for regional efforts at integration, as it creates the conditions under which the recent attempts can succeed and potentially yield greater benefits.

Ironically, while regional preferential initiatives are increasing, globalization is clearly posing a threat to the trade preferences enjoyed by the poorer developing countries—many on the African continent. This is happening, of course, indirectly, but through many channels. First, the reduction in MFN tariffs in industrial countries consequent upon the Uruguay Round is eroding preference margins on African exports in these markets. A second channel is through regional integration within industrial countries and between industrial and other developing countries (for example, NAFTA, the EU–East Europe agreement, and the agreement between the EU and the Middle East and North African countries), which is putting African countries on an equal footing with those developing countries that are party to these agreements. The stark illustration of the threat is the recent WTO ruling questioning the Lomé preferences enjoyed by certain banana-exporting countries.

As mentioned above, regional integration attempts of the 1960s and 1970s were confined to liberalizing trade in goods; however, with globalization proceeding apace, regional agreements themselves have had to catch up and broaden their scope to include liberalization of services and investment, and even the harmonization of regulatory standards, domestic policies, and institutions. The EU is probably the most extreme example of the breadth of the issues that are decided and regulated at the supranational, regional level, but the NAFTA experience suggests that even those regional agreements involving developing countries are likely to be more encompassing in their scope. In sub-Saharan Africa, there are also new and deepened regional initiatives between the West African members of the CFA monetary zone (the WAEMU) and between the Central African States (the CAEMC). In addition, there has been a shift of focus in COMESA, while SADC is adopting a new strategy of market integration.

How Can Regionalism Harness the Forces of Globalization?

When we speak of regionalism, we need to keep in mind the two varieties in which it is coming and will continue to come in Africa. The more natural kind of regional integration—and perhaps the one that we instinctively think of—is horizontal integration, that is, integration between African countries. However, there is another—perhaps more powerful—kind of integration that Africa is likely to witness in the years ahead: vertical integration, between African countries and their industrial country partners. One such—involving South Africa and the

EU—is already under way, and the EU has indicated that the future status of the Lomé Convention could well take the form of reciprocal trade liberalization codified in a free trade agreement.

Regional agreements can help African countries foster economic growth and harness globalization in at least nine ways. First, regional arrangement can serve as a vehicle for transmitting good policies through regional *demonstration effects and peer pressures*. This influence can be powerful. The demonstration effect works by provoking the question, If they can do it, why can't we? It also leads to an examination of the reasons for the regional neighbors' success and, over time, to emulation of their policies. In the case of vertical integration agreements, the demonstration effect works more directly by anchoring and locking in the policies of the smaller country to those of its trading partner. This effect was thought to be an important motivation for Mexico's keenness to work toward adoption of NAFTA. An example closer to home, cited by Dani Rodrik, is that of Botswana, which has benefited from the relative macroeconomic stability conferred by its links with South Africa.[2] Demonstration effects can be enhanced and consolidated through mechanisms for regional macroeconomic surveillance, as in the EU. Recent examples in Africa include the WAEMU and CAEMC countries.

Regional agreement can be an effective instrument for ensuring that hard-fought policy reforms—such as trade policy or exchange reform—are not reversed by weaker future governments, as an international treaty or a regional formal agreement is much harder to repudiate than national legislation.

Second, there is the important issue of *size and credibility*. For reasons that may or may not be justified, African countries suffer from the perception that they are too small to be of interest to international investors. Regional integration offers the prospect of building up a critical mass in terms of size (a regional market) that investors might find credible and attractive. In principle, this integration opens up the opportunity to exploit economies of scale, regional specialization, and learning by doing.

Third, to secure an improvement in enabling economic conditions, there is scope for nurturing domestic and *regional institutions* and fostering institutional linkages. Insofar as the intensification of regional linkages stems from the perception that the process is homegrown, with full ownership by governments and bolstered by the participation of the private sector, there is greater likelihood that institution building and the reforms that it promotes will be sustainable.

[2]As discussed in Chapter 7 of this volume.

Fourth, the need to integrate regionally might also serve to focus attention on the building or rehabilitation of long-neglected *regional infrastructure networks*. It is nowhere more true than in Africa that geographical contiguity is not synonymous with economic proximity because of poor regional transportation and communication links. This barrier to the intensification of regional economic links needs to be overcome.

Fifth, in some cases, regional cooperation might serve to enhance the region's bargaining power in its interactions with the rest of the world. One example could be in the area of international trade negotiations. Other examples also come to mind—aid, debt, labor standards, the environment, and so on. The scope of cooperation, from a dynamic perspective, could be large.

Sixth, regional agreements can become agreements for *liberalization that goes beyond trade policies*—for the liberalization of investment, services, and capital markets. These liberalizations could induce not only static but also dynamic gains that bring about durable increases in productivity levels and facilitate faster growth. In the case of NAFTA, there was substantial liberalization—and on a nonpreferential basis—by Mexico of its investment, financial services, telecommunication services, and transportation services regimes. These objectives are also essential elements in the regional initiatives in West, Central, East, and Southern Africa.

Seventh, regionalism can further broaden trade liberalization by acting as a *trial balloon, a kind of learning-by-doing-slowly* phenomenon. Those with vested interests in perpetuating protection may not pose strong objections to this form of limited opening, as the competition unleashed—from other Africa country suppliers—would be limited. Nevertheless, the liberalization that is secured as a result could weaken the power of these interests in the long run, paving the way for further nonpreferential liberalization.

Eighth, in an environment where vertical integration between African countries and the EU or the United States is going to become prominent, the case for horizontal integration will also be strengthened. Vertical integration without horizontal integration creates the risk of what is known in the literature as a *hub and spoke* phenomenon, whereby the incremental foreign direct investment that services the markets in the spokes (the African countries) is located in the hub (the EU or the United States), rather than in the spokes themselves. With horizontal integration, African countries can seek to apply the "cumulative rule of origin" principle in agreements with industrial country partners to maximize the export opportunities.

Finally, an important element in the calculus of regional integration is that regional interaction is likely to be motivated by and, in turn, to facilitate identification of, and cooperation on, a range of *political, security, and social issues* of concern to the region.

The Pitfalls: What to Avoid

That a well-designed regional arrangement can provide a boost to the right domestic policies and foster growth in its own right does not mean that it necessarily will. *There are good and bad regional integration initiatives,* and countries need to be alert to the pitfalls that can attend the latter type of integration. It is useful to bear in mind that the ultimate goal is nondiscriminatory liberalization and that regional initiatives should be—in Jagdish Bhagwati's terminology—building blocks, not stumbling blocks, to this ultimate goal. The following touches upon some of these pitfalls, drawing particular attention to some special features in the African context.

First, there is a risk of setting overambitious goals. With *limited administrative resources and with competing claims on political capital,* the chances of success are very uncertain and of distraction from nondiscriminatory opening are high. There are some advantages to considering a staged approach, whereby the achievement of a minimum degree of integration will be a first step before embarking on deeper integration.

Second, there is the risk that regional agreements may become *bureaucratized* and spawn top-down institutions that are not necessarily responsive to the needs of the private sector and are determined to protect their turf to the neglect of the larger objective that they are intended to serve. Avoiding this obstacle to regional integration is one of the critical challenges facing Africa.

Third, as *regional integration initiatives mushroom* in Africa, we detect the clear risk of a multiplicity of initiatives that overlap each other, leading to potentially conflicting policies. This is clearly a case in which more can not only be less, but damagingly so. For example, in Southern Africa, there are SADC, COMESA, SACU, the CBI, and a number of bilateral agreements. These agreements have overlapping memberships, different objectives (the CBI promotes internal and external liberalization, while the SADC is focused on internal liberalization), different schedules for liberalization, and differences in the scope of liberalization, as reflected in their attitudes toward exclusions. All the effort that is being put into regional integration can easily get diffused, jeopardizing the chances of success for any one effort or initiative. There is clearly scope for rationalizing all these initiatives and adopting a more focused approach to maximize the chances of success.

Fourth, the original insight offered by academics (for example by Viner) about the risks of *trade diversion* and the attendant possibility that regional agreements might be welfare deteriorating may be particularly relevant for Africa. Why is this so? Africa, notwithstanding the considerable progress made in opening its markets, remains among the most protected regions in the world. And when MFN tariffs are high, the risks of trade diversion are particularly great because of the likelihood that inefficient production in partner countries will replace efficient production in third countries. The low levels of intraregional trade in Africa would tend to suggest that, at least for the moment and given the poor infrastructure links, African countries may not be natural trading partners for each other. As a result, regional agreements in Africa are more likely to lead to inefficient trade diversion. To avoid such adverse outcomes, nondiscriminatory liberalization should accompany regional integration, as envisaged in the CBI. A strong dose of MFN tariff cuts by African countries would help maximize the benefits from regional integration.

Fifth, there is the risk—and this applies especially to horizontal agreements—that countries may be locked into *inadequate regional anchors, for example, if the dominant country in a regional arrangement is more restrictive, imparting a protectionist bias to the whole arrangement.* This is the other side of the coin of positive demonstration effects, a kind of Gresham's law whereby bad economic and trade policies could easily drive out the good ones. There is the related danger that regional integration builds up vested interests—especially suppliers in partner countries—that oppose multilateral liberalization.

Finally, there is the broader *political context* that Africa has to contend with or operate within. In light of the various conflicts, political differences, and civil strifes, it is perhaps not surprising that there has not been a broad commitment to regional goals. After all, this commitment necessarily implies a ceding of sovereignty on economic and financial matters that countries may be unwilling or unprepared to accept. Unless this political will exists, nationalist considerations will prevail over regional aspirations.

Conclusions

Regional initiatives can be an effective additional instrument to accelerate economic growth and facilitate the integration of African economies into the world economy. But to play this role, the regional arrangements must emphasize broad liberalization of domestic policies, promote the transmission of good policies through peer pressures, and nurture efficient domestic and regional institutions. In the

African context, many dangers lurk on this path: overambitious goals, overbureaucratization, multiplicity of overlapping initiatives, and weak political will and vision. These traps and pitfalls need to be avoided so that regional arrangements can be building blocks for—not stumbling blocks to—better, more open, and more efficient economic policies in general.

Regional Integration, Trade, and Foreign Direct Investment in Sub-Saharan Africa 14

Ibrahim A. Elbadawi and Francis M. Mwega

At least in terms of pronouncements and declaration, the political commitment to regional integration in sub-Saharan Africa has been very high, despite changes in ideology and approaches to economic development during the past three decades or so. Indeed, many African countries have, for example, equated increased intra-African trade with self-reliant policies required to break from the economically "dependent" trading patterns established during the colonial period (Berg and Associates, 1988). However, most of the available evidence suggests that the African regional integration experience has been rather disappointing, to say the least (e.g., Foroutan, 1993; Elbadawi, 1997). Some of the problems are related to the design features of the African regional integration schemes, such as the lack of mechanism for compensation in cases where benefits were very skewed (Fine and Yeo, 1994). A further and more fundamental criticism is that African regional integration schemes were conceived under a regime of foreign exchange controls and restrictive unilateral trade policies. This has not only aggravated the problems of highly skewed benefits between countries within the schemes (Foroutan, 1993), but it has also rendered many of the arrangements adopted by these schemes to be incompatible with the post-mid-1980s waves of unilateral foreign trade and foreign exchange liberalization, adopted by many reforming African countries as part of their structural adjustment programs. Another fundamental criticism is that given the too similar set of endowments across African countries, regional integration schemes should not be expected to be better than unilateral trade liberalization in terms of trade creation (Collier and Gunning, 1993).

However, aside from the above Vinerian argument, trade-liberalizing regional integration may in fact eventually dominate unilateral trade liberalization, both in trade creation as well as in attraction of

The views expressed in this chapter do not necessarily represented the official view of the African Economic Research Consortium.

FDI. First, regional integration could provide a better lock-in mechanism (against policy reversals) for trade and other economic reforms than the one provided by multilateral and bilateral aid conditionality. Collier and Gunning (1993) argue that a regional scheme could provide a basis for a group of self-governing African countries to form a free trade area and to offer reciprocal free trade to a major external trading partner (for example, the European Union). The threat of losing, for example, privileged access to European markets, FDI, and transfer of technology, among others, would prevent policy reversals and therefore enhance the credibility of policy reforms. Even though, according to this perspective, the primary aim of regional integration is not to directly promote trade or FDI, it in fact provides a powerful stimulus to do both indirectly through enhanced credibility of economic reforms (Collier and Gunning, 1993).

The second set of arguments for economic integration is based on its role as an engine of growth. For example, Krugman (1991a)[1] emphasizes the importance of economies of scale and economic geography. It is argued that deeper economic integration in a given region could permit expansion of the regional economy to generate the threshold scales necessary to trigger the much needed strategic complementarity, and to attract adequate levels of investment (especially FDI) necessary for the development of modern manufacturing cores and the transfer of technology within the region. Given the relatively small scale (both in terms of output level and population size) of the typical African economy, there seems to be a strong a priori case for regional integration on purely normative economic grounds. The empirical evidence from the endogenous growth literature suggests important implications for country-specific growth of regional spillover effects of investment, both on physical and human capital. In addition, the level of regional instability was shown to have had significant impact on individual country growth performances. In fact, when these regional spillovers are taken into consideration, the "African dummy" ceases to be significant in the usual endogenous-growth cross-country regressions (Chua, 1993a, 1993b; Ades and Chua, 1993; Easterly and Levine, 1994). Also, Fine and Yeo (1994) argue that while there is at best mixed evidence directly linking regional integration to economic growth, the experiences of postwar Europe and more recently of East Asia suggest that regional integration has conferred policy credibility at the national level as well as fostered FDI initially and then higher saving and in-

[1]A review of a range of views on the potential role of regional integration as an engine of growth for sub-Saharan Africa is provided in Elbadawi and Ndulu (1994).

vestment within the region at a later stage. Both policy credibility and broad capital accumulation were credited for the stellar growth performance of East Asia (Young, 1994).

As we indicated above, the African regional integration schemes have been associated with low intra-African trade as well as low FDI. The second section of this chapter provides a brief analysis of the trade and FDI flows during the last two decades of the 1970–90 period. To assess the role, if any, of African regional integration schemes in promoting trade and investment, we must estimate the marginal contribution of these schemes in behavioral models that also control for other determinants. The third section uses estimates of an extended gravity model for trade in sub-Saharan Africa (obtained from Elbadawi, 1997) to analyze the marginal effect of African regional integration schemes on intra- and inter-African trade. The fourth section estimates a panel regression of an FDI model, and uses it to assess the impact of regional integration schemes on FDI in sub-Saharan Africa. The fifth section concludes.

Regional Integration and Economic Performance

A rather varied menu of regional integration schemes spans almost the entire space of sub-Saharan Africa. The stated objectives of these schemes range from cooperation between neighboring states in a limited set of policy areas, for example, the Southern African Development Coordination Conference (SADCC); to complete trade and monetary integration, for example, UDEAC; or to currency union and capital and labor market integration, for example, the SACU.[2] More recent developments aimed at reforming and further deepening these schemes include the accession of South Africa to SADCC to form the SADC; the integration of CEAO with the UMOA in a new bloc, the UEMOA, which as before will be externally anchored by France; and preparation for similar arrangements for francophone Central Africa, through the merger of the BEAC and UDEAC.[3] There are two further

[2]Table 1 below gives the country groupings and key economic indicators for African and other regional integration schemes. For a more detailed account containing additional information of the objectives and record of achievements of various schemes, see Table 8.2 of Foroutan (1993) and Table 1 of Lyakurwa and others (1993).

[3]In terms of membership, the mergers in francophone West Africa are not that consequential: the CEAO and the UMOA are almost identical in terms of member countries, since the former includes in addition to Mauritania all the members of the latter except Togo (Togo and Guinea are observers in the CEAO); and the UDEAC is identical to the BEAC. However, Fine and Yeo (1994) argue that the UEMOA arrangement "is more than cosmetic, and marks a radical departure from the past."

arrangements involving the extension of SACU to include other countries in Southern Africa (at this stage conjectural) and the revival of the defunct East African Community (Fine and Yeo, 1994).

Another major distinguishing characteristic stems from the extent of geographical coverage of the regional integration schemes. For example, ECOWAS and the PTA represent the vision of the ECA, which argues that regional groupings in Africa should be made up of a large number of countries to allow development of sufficiently large internal markets, which are necessary to support the process of Africa's industrialization.[4] Conversely, the rest of the schemes are based on a strategy of promoting regional objectives among smaller and hopefully more homogenous neighboring countries.

Unfortunately, trade and FDI data pertaining to the two decades of the 1970–90 period, which encompasses the life span of most of the existing regional integration schemes in sub-Saharan Africa, reveals that FDI in the region and in the individual schemes as well as intraregional trade and even most intrascheme trade has not only been minuscule but nearly stationary as well (Table 1). As indicated above, the "apparent" failure of regionalism in sub-Saharan Africa as reflected by trade flows can at least in part be attributed to the highly protectionist national trade policies that prevailed for much of the 1970–90 period throughout the region; fiscal revenue constraints; the very skewed nature of costs and benefits of integration across countries in the schemes; and the associated difficulty in devising sustainable compensation schemes from the gainer to the losers (Foroutan, 1993). At a more general level, it is argued that the dominant role of the state in African regional initiatives resulted in the marginalization of an already weak private sector, and hence its potentially critical contribution to the success of regional integration could not be realized (Fine and Yeo, 1994). In the case of FDI, the problem of policy credibility even for those countries that started economic reforms; the lack of strong and stable institutional mechanism for protection of property rights; as well as the relatively poor human capital base in most of the countries in the region are the main factors behind the small flows.

However, some argue that the notable exceptions to the above have been the cases of SADCC, SACU, and to some extent CEAO. All of the three cases have been distinguished either by the availability of substantial external support, as in the case of SADCC, or the participation

[4]According to this view, no more than four such regional groupings should exist in Africa: North, West, Central, and East and South. Thus the PTA, like its West African counterpart, ECOWAS, received the active support of the ECA (e.g., Foroutan, 1993).

Table 1. Selected Economic Indicators and Intrabloc Trade Flows

Bloc[1]	GDP[2] (Millions)		*GDPPC*[2]		*RGDPGR*[2] (Percent)		FDI/GDP[2] (Percent)		Intrabloc Trade (Millions)		Ratio of Intrabloc to Total Trade[3] (Percent)	
	1980–84	1986–90	1980–84	1986–90	1980–84	1986–90	1980–84	1986–90	1980–84	1986–90	1980–84	1986–90
ECOWAS	6,404	7,035	534	484	0.745	3.125	0.433	–0.215	399	152	4.95	2.70
CEAO	4,460	4,711	650	570	0.094	6.560	0.371	–0.273	99	82	1.65	1.25
UDEAC	5,136	5,882	2,222	1,936	9.426	. . .	0.356	. . .	37	52	0.80	1.15
CEPGL	3,807	4,359	219	221	. . .	. . .	. . .	6.759	1.9	2.4	0.15	0.05
PTA	3,396	3,941	368	397	2.875	3.508	0.207	0.606	255	278	2.15	1.75
SADCC	2,501	2,876	284	267	0.722	6.450	0.601	4.344	75	105	1.55	1.40
SSA	3,494	3,885	376	371	2.403	. . .	. . .	. . .	867	671	1.20	1.6
LAFTA	64,536	72,407	1,909	1,860	3.178	1.023	0.716	0.925	4,323	7,190	5.30	6.15
CACM	4,562	4,880	1,153	1,058	2.192	0.096	1.112	1.941	515	552	7.55	6.55
ASEAN	39,397	52,440	910	1,048	2.027	4.050	1.300	1.356	5,725	12,099	8.10	8.85

[1]Trade blocs (* after a name denotes a country that belongs to the trade bloc, but was not in the sample): ECOWAS: Benin, Burkina Faso,* Cape Verde,* Côte d'Ivoire, The Gambia,* Ghana, Guinea,* Guinea-Bissau,* Liberia, Mali,* Mauritania, Niger, Nigeria, Senegal, Togo. CEAO: Benin, Burkina Faso,* Côte d'Ivoire, Mali,* Mauritania,* Niger, Senegal. UDEAC: Cameroon, Central African Republic,* Chad,* Congo, Equatorial Guinea,* Gabon. CEPGL: Burundi, Rwanda,* Zaïre. PTA: Angola, Burundi, Comoros,* Djibouti,* Ethiopia, Kenya, Lesotho,* Malawi, Mauritius, Mozambique, Rwanda,* Swaziland,* Somalia, Sudan, Uganda, Tanzania, Zambia, Zimbabwe. SADCC: Angola, Botswana,* Lesotho,* Malawi, Mozambique, Namibia,* Swaziland,* Tanzania, Zambia, Zimbabwe. LAFTA: Argentina, Bolivia, Brazil, Chile, Colombia,* Ecuador,* Mexico, Paraguay, Peru, Uruguay, Venezuela. CACM: Costa Rica, Guatemala, Honduras, Nicaragua, El Salvador. ASEAN: Indonesia, Malaysia, Philippines, Singapore, Thailand.

[2]Real GDP growth (*RGDPGR*) and real FDI/real GDP ratio (FDI/GDP) are derived from panel data and therefore apply to those cases where data were available. *GDPPC* is GDP per capita.

[3]The ratio of intrabloc trade to total bloc exports.

of a dominant regional or Northern partner, as in the cases of SACU and CEAO.[5]

The above conclusions regarding the limited success, if not the failure of regional integration in sub-Saharan Africa, remain largely indicative, since without conditioning for other determinants of FDI or bilateral trade flows, it will be difficult to ascribe the evolution of intra-scheme trade flows or FDI only to the scheme effect. Estimating the marginal effect of regional integration schemes on trade and FDI will be, respectively, addressed in the next two sections.

The Trade Effects of Regional Integration

The standard empirical model for investigating patterns of bilateral trade is the gravity model. Elbadawi (1997) specifies and estimates an extended gravity model. In addition to the traditional set of variables that influence the absolute trade potential of a country, the model also accounts for three extensions: two channels of exchange rate effects (exchange rate variability and exchange rate misalignment, relative to a notional equilibrium) and a trade diversion effect of regional integration schemes (in addition to the usual within scheme trade effect). The absolute trade potential of a country depends on its total economic size (nominal GDP) and the trade intensity (the ratio of trade to GDP). In turn, the trade intensity is determined by economic factors (such as the level of development, proxied by nominal GDP per capita, GDPPC); geographic characteristics (such as the area size, the distance between the economic centers of gravity in the two countries, whether or not the two countries have a common border, and whether the country is an island); and policy and political inducements (or barriers) to trade such as trade, currency, or regional cooperation schemes; and cultural or historical ties, such as a common language or colonial relationships.

An additional variable frequently included in recent versions of gravity models (e.g., Foroutan and Pritchett, 1993; Havrylyshyn and Pritchett, 1991; Montenegro and Soto, 1994) is designed to test two hypotheses related to the effect of the differences between two countries' levels of per capita income. On the one hand, countries with similar

[5]The "frontline" countries of SADCC received significant external support in their bid to minimize their economies' dependence on predemocratic South Africa. Furthermore, the success of SADCC is also credited to the limited set of objectives set forth for the scheme. In the other two schemes, the willingness of South Africa to provide adequate compensation to other smaller countries in SACU, and of France to guarantee convertibility in CEAO, are among the major factors behind their relative success (Foroutan, 1993).

living standards could realize a higher level of intra-industry trade to the extent that they share a broader range of goods to trade (the so-called Linder Hypothesis). On the other hand, to the extent that differences in GDP per capita are highly correlated with differences in factor endowments, interindustry trade driven by comparative advantage could be smaller between countries with similar levels of income.

The model is formally stated in equation 1 below.

$$\begin{aligned} T_{ij} = {} & \beta_0 + \beta_1 \log(GDP_i \cdot GDP_j) + \beta_2 \log(GDPPC_i \cdot GDPPC_j) \\ & + \beta_3 \log(AREA_i \cdot AREA_j) + \beta_3 \log(ISLAND_i) + \beta_5 \log DISTANCE_{ij} \\ & + \beta_6 BORDER_{ij} + \beta_7 \log | GDPPC_i - GDPPC_j | \\ & + \beta_8 LANGUAGE_{ijl} + \beta_9 RI(1)_{ijk} + \beta_{10} RI(2)_{ijk} + \beta_{11} RERVAR_{ij} \\ & + \beta_{12} REROVER_{ij} \end{aligned} \tag{1}$$

In this equation, $ISLAND_i$ is a dummy if I is an island; $BORDER_{ij}$ is a dummy if i,j share a common border; $LANGUAGE_{ijl}$ is a set of dummy variables if countries i,j share a similar language l; $RI(1)_{ijk}$ is a dummy reflecting trade diversion effect of *RI*[6] scheme k between countries i,j and is equal to one if *only* one country belongs to the scheme. $RI(2)_{ijk}$ is a dummy reflecting trade creation effect of scheme k and is equal to one if *both* countries i,j belong to the scheme k. Finally, *RERVAR* and *REROVER* stand for real exchange rate variability and real exchange rate overvaluation, respectively. *RERVAR* and *REROVER* are defined as follows: *RERVAR* = standard deviation of the change of log RER_{ij}; $REROVER_{ij}$ = log [(average $(RER_i)/RER_i)$*(average $(RER_j)/RER_j)$], where $RER_{ij} = RER_i/RER_j$. *RER* is defined as the relative price of tradables to nontradables, and average (*RER*) is the average for the 1970–72 period.[7]

The multiplicative forms of GDP and GDP per capita in the equation are empirically well established in bilateral trade regressions. The justification for this specification can be provided from the modern theory of trade under imperfect competition, which implies that trade between two equal-sized countries (say, of size 0.5) will be greater than trade between a large country and a small country (say, of size 0.9 and

[6]Various regional integration schemes are listed in Table 1, which includes all trade arrangements as well as currency union arrangements: CEAO, UDEAC, and Rand Monetary Area (which includes all SACU countries except Botswana).

[7]For a review of the concept of real exchange rate overvaluation and its calculation relative to a behavioral empirical model of the equilibrium real exchange rate see Elbadawi (1997). This particular measure is a simple approach based on purchasing power parity, which assumes the actual rate for 1970–72 to be consistent with equilibrium behavior for the entire period.

0.1) (Frankel and Wei, 1993). The property of models based on imperfect competition, such as gravity models that include only multiplicative terms on incomes, does not account for the classical Heckscher-Ohlin theory of comparative advantage, however.[8] Fortunately, this limitation does not apply to the model used in this analysis, since the added terms of the per capita income differences allow estimating a Heckscher-Ohlin type comparative advantage effect.

Our model accounts for both the potential trade creation effects within the trade/currency union scheme and their possible trade diversion influences (vis-à-vis nonmembers). The trade creation effect within the union is rather straightforward. It derives from proactive preferential trade arrangements in the case of trade schemes, while currency unions confer on their members the benefits of currency convertibility (at least within the union) and monetary and exchange rate stability (that is, low levels of bilateral *RERVAR*). However, to the extent that macroeconomic policy is not sufficiently restrained to support the currency peg, substantial real exchange rate appreciation and possibly real exchange rate overvaluation (that is, high *REROVER*) may ensue. Furthermore, attempts to defend the union in the face of this adversity can lead to restrictive trade policy (O'Connell, 1994). Hence, just as with trade integration schemes, currency unions can lead to trade diversion. The model accounts for this possibility as well. Finally, it is interesting to test the incremental trade creation/diversion effects of trade/currency union schemes after controlling for the real exchange rate effects (*RERVAR* and *REROVER*) that reflect the incompatibility of macroeconomic policy for a given trade regime.[9]

Given that trade flows (the dependent variables) are bounded from below by zero, estimation by ordinary least squares (OLS) will produce inconsistent parameter estimates and may generate negative predicted trade flows. Also, as noted by Montenegro and Soto (1994), alternative OLS procedures based on eliminating zeros, or replacing them with arbitrary small values, tend to bias the results. Inclusion of zeros is desirable since these observations may contain information on reasons why low levels of trade are sometimes observed. This could be of particular importance in sub-Saharan Africa, where many countries within and outside Africa do not trade extensively with the region.[10]

[8]See Helpman (1987) and Helpman and Krugman (1985), section 1.5.

[9]While Frankel and Wei (1993) include a measure of real exchange rate variability in their gravity model, ours is perhaps the first application of the model that also adds a measure of real exchange rate overvaluation as well.

[10]Eichengreen and Irwin (1993) noted the relevance of this issue for the case of interwar trade.

The appropriate estimation method here is the Tobit model, which allows consistent estimation of censored dependent variables, as in our case.[11] To minimize the effect of extreme observations on the estimates, we use the double logarithmic specification, which also yields direct elasticity estimates for the quantitative independent variables.[12]

Elbadawi (1997) estimates the above model for a sample of 62 *reporting* countries,[13] of which 28 are in sub-Saharan Africa. The sample of reporting countries was restricted to include only those non-sub-Saharan African countries with per capita GDP less than $3,000[14] (for more details see Appendix Table 1 of Elbadawi, 1997). Furthermore, the above model was estimated for two periods (1980–84 and 1986–90), where trade flows are represented by import flows. The results of the Tobit estimation for the full model are presented in Table 2. In addition, Table 3 reports the marginal contribution of regional integration schemes with and without controlling for exchange rate policy (additional estimation results are reported in Elbadawi, 1997). As expected, the empirical performance of the model is consistent with its reputation in this literature.[15] According to the results in Table 2, almost all the traditional variables of the gravity model are significant and have plausible signs. However, there are some interesting differences across time (Elbadawi, 1997, provides a detailed analysis of these traditional effects).

The derived elasticity estimates of the impact of regional integration schemes on trade flows for both of the first and second halves of the 1980s—controlling for traditional gravity model variables but not for exchange rate policy—are reported in panel (1) of Table 3. Panel (2) of

[11]Another advantage of Tobit specifications is the use of maximum likelihood technique yield parameters, which are extremely reliable even when the sample is rather small (Sen and Matuszewski, 1991). In our case, the relatively large sample of 5,104 observations should enhance the confidence in the estimation results.

[12]The elasticities for the qualitative variables are given as the exponential of the estimated coefficients.

[13]The total of 62 reporting countries and 42 partner countries generated 62 x (62 - 1) + 42 x 62 = 6,386 observations on bilateral trade flows. However, due to data unavailability for some right hand side variables in the extended model (Table 2), only 5,104 observations were available for Table 2's regressions.

[14]We follow Foroutan and Pritchett (1993) to make this restriction to ensure that the set of *reporting* countries includes mostly low-income countries that, it is hoped, share the same economic characteristics.

[15]An imperfect measure of the empirical performance of the model is the degree of fit given by the derived Pseudo R^2, which ranges from 0.133 for the smaller model of Appendix Table 2 of Elbadawi (1997) to 0.154 for the full model of Table 2. This, of course, is not exceptional, but it remains admissible for cross-sectional regressions. However, the key test is the ability to corroborate the predictions of the model in terms of the significance of individual effects, which was met by our empirical results.

Table 2. Average Gravity Model Estimates: Sub-Saharan Africa and Low-Income Countries in Other Regions

Variable[1]	Imports, 1980–84[2] Coefficient	Imports, 1980–84[2] t-statistic	Imports, 1986–90[2] Coefficient	Imports, 1986–90[2] t-statistic
Standard gravity model				
Constant	–6.93	–6.79	–9.08	–9.23
log($DISTANCE_{ij}$)	–1.79	–19.43	–1.72	–19.42
$BORDER_{ij}$	1.02	2.73	0.18	0.49
$ISLAND_i$	0.06	0.26	–0.11	–0.5
log($AREA_i.AREA_j$)	–0.35	–12.29	0.37	17.04
log($GDP_i.GDP_j$)	1.60	39.7	0.26	13.52
log($GDPPC_i.GDPPC_j$)	0.01	0.24	1.26	24.2
LINDER: log|$GDPPC_i - GDPPC_j$|	0.14	2.66	0.51	10.01
$LANGUAGE_{ij}$:				
English	0.35	1.58	0.36	1.72
Spanish	1.70	5.83	1.42	5.13
French	1.95	4.89	1.49	3.81
Arabic	0.49	1.14	–0.26	–0.63
Portuguese	1.89	0.55	0.83	0.25
Swahili	1.79	1.23	2.06	1.43
Regional trade and monetary schemes				
Within $bloc_{ij}$:				
ECOWAS[3]	0.13	0.67	–0.22	–1.2
CEAO	3.56	2.44	1.31	0.93
UDEAC	2.37	0.96	–2.61	–1.09
CEPGL	3.7	1.48	3.73	1.48
PTA	2.29	4.58	0.35	0.74
SADCC	–1.83	–1.2	0.38	0.26
LAFTA	0.73	1.41	0.04	0.08
CACM	–1.69	–1.96	0.81	0.98
ASEAN	–0.36	–0.45	2.03	2.68
Bloc $members_{ij}$:				
ECOWAS[3]	. . .	. . .	. . .	. . .
CEAO	0.36	1.64	–1.44	–6.89
UDEAC	–0.23	–0.89	–2.94	–12.48
CEPGL	–1.98	–7.79	–1.53	–6.38
PTA	–0.00	–0.02	–0.64	–4.12
SADCC	–0.33	–1.4	0.39	1.79
LAFTA	–0.53	–3.32	–1.12	–8.19
CACM	–2.08	–11.74	–0.92	–5.36
ASEAN	0.66	4.31	2.1	14.27
Macroeconomic policy stance				
$RERVAR_{ij}$	–0.36	–4.86	–0.41	–7.61
$REROVER_{ij}$	–0.03	3.96	0.00	0.54
Pseudo R^2	0.1537		0.1495	
Number of observations	5,104		5,104	

[1]$BORDER_{ij}$ = 1, if country i and j share the same border. $ISLAND_i$ = 1, if country i is an island. $LANGUAGE_{ij}$ = 1, if country i and j share the same language. Within $bloc_{ij}$ = 1, if both countries belong to the same bloc. Bloc $member_{ij}$ = 1, if either country i or j (not both) belong to the same bloc.

$$RERVAR_{ij} = Var\left[\Delta\log\left(\frac{RER_i}{RER_j}\right)\right] \text{ and } REROVER_{ij} = \log\left[\frac{avg(RER_j)}{RER_j} \cdot \frac{avg(RER_j)}{RER_j}\right]$$

where $RER = \frac{E \cdot P^*}{P}$ and $avg(RER)$ is for (1970–72).

[2]The dependent variables are estimated in logs (for values > 0).

[3]Because of multicollinearity, the effects due to ECOWAS could not be decomposed into within bloc and bloc members; therefore, the estimated coefficient for ECOWAS reflects the net effect.

Table 3. The Marginal Contribution of Regional Integration Schemes and Exchange Rate Policy in Determining Bilateral Trade Flows

(Derived elasticities)[1]

	1980–84			1986–90		
Regional Integration Scheme	Within scheme	Scheme effect	Total effect	Within scheme	Scheme effect	Total effect
(1) Regional integration only (Appendix Table 3 estimates)[1]						
ECOWAS	1.32	. . .	1.32	–1.95	. . .	–1.95
CEAO	32.07	NS	32.07	NS	–2.59	–2.59
UDEAC	NS	NS	NS	–NS	–13.20	–13.20
CEPGL	NS	–7.61	–7.61	NS	–4.22	–4.22
PTA	3.50	–NS	3.50	–NS	–1.90	–1.90
SADCC	–3.89	–NS	–3.89	–NS	–NS	–NS
LAFTA	NS	–2.08	–2.08	NS	–2.53	–2.53
CACM	–5.96	–7.77	–13.73	–NS	–3.97	–3.97
ASEAN	–NS	2.14	2.14	11.82	12.81	24.63
(2) Regional integration and exchange rate policy (Table 2 estimates)[1]						
ECOWAS	NS	. . .	NS	–NS	. . .	– NS
CEAO	35.16	1.43	36.60	NS	–4.22	–4.22
UDEAC	NS	–NS	NS	–NS	–18.92	–18.92
CEPGL	NS	7.24	–7.24	NS	–4.62	4.62
PTA	9.97	–NS	9.97	NS	–1.84	–1.84
SADCC	–NC	–NC	–NC	NS	–1.48	–1.48
LAFTA	NS	–1.70	–1.70	NS	–3.06	–3.06
CACM	–5.42	–8.00	–13.42	NS	–2.51	–2.51
ASEAN	-NS	1.93	1.93	7.61	8.17	15.78
$RERVAR_{ij}$	. . .	. . .	–0.36	. . .	. . .	–0.41
$REROVER_{ij}$	. . .	. . .	–0.03	. . .	. . .	–NS
Total *RER*	. . .	. . .	–0.39	. . .	. . .	–0.41

"NS" means not significant.

[1]The elasticity estimates of this table for the regional integration effects are derived as exponentials of the estimated coefficient of Table 2 and Appendix Table 3 of Elbadawi (1997).

the table reports the corresponding derived estimates when the effect of exchange rate policy was accounted for as well. The estimates of panel (1) were based on Appendix Table 3 of Elbadawi (1997), while those of panel (2) were based on Table 2. The analysis that follows has these objectives: to establish some evidence on the relative effectiveness of the African regional integration schemes compared with other schemes over time; to compare and contrast performances of some selected regional integration schemes; to assess the independent effect of exchange rate policy over time, and the implied effect through the regional integration schemes; and to assess the incremental effect of currency union within trade blocs, by comparing the performances of ECOWAS to that of CEAO (which is a sub-ECOWAS trade and currency bloc), and the performances of UDEAC (a currency and trade bloc in central Africa) to that of CEPGL (a trade but not a currency bloc within the central Africa region).

First, we describe the derived incremental elasticity estimates of the regional integration schemes, controlling for the traditional gravity determinants but not for the effects of exchange rate policy.

Starting with the 1980–84 period, the estimates of panel (1) of Table 3 suggest that, in general, the African regional integration schemes fared better than LAFTA and CACM. On average, the presence of African schemes enhanced intra-scheme imports by about 31 percent without causing trade diversion effects. This compares with negative trade diversion effects for LAFTA (by more than 100 percent) and CACM (by more than 700 percent), including a further negative effect on intra-scheme trade that in the case of CACM led to a total negative effect on trade of about 1,300 percent![16] The exception was ASEAN, which despite the lack of evidence for enhanced import trade within the bloc, did lead to import trade creation with partners outside the bloc by more than 100 percent. Further, there was also considerable diversity within the African regional schemes, with CEAO increasing import flows within the block by a staggering 32 times without creating trade diversion, compared with CEPGL, which caused significant trade diversion by 7.6 times without enhancing intra-CEPGL import flows, and SADCC, which reduced intra-SADCC imports by about 4 times. In between, ECOWAS (PTA) enhanced total (intrabloc) imports by 32 percent (250 percent), while UDEAC had a completely neutral effect.

During the second half of the 1980s, however, the story changed dramatically. The performance of four African regional blocs worsened considerably, especially the two currency blocs, CEAO and UDEAC, which diverted import trade by 160 percent and 1,200 percent, respectively, without positively enhancing intrabloc trade. Compared with the first period, the performance of ECOWAS and PTA also deteriorated, albeit less dramatically, with the first reducing total ECOWAS imports by 95 percent and the latter diverting import trade by 90 percent without leading to increased intra-PTA imports. The exceptions

[16]These estimates may appear implausible; however, they are consistent with other estimates in the literature (for example, Frankel and Wei, 1993; Foroutan and Pritchett, 1993; Montenegro and Soto, 1994).

were SADCC, which had a neutral effect on import flows, and CEPGL, which reduced its trade diversion effect from 660 to 320 percent between the two periods. Conversely, even though the total effect on import trade of LAFTA and CACM was still negative, it worsened only slightly for the case of LAFTA and improved for the case of CACM. However, the most dramatic improvement happened in the ASEAN bloc, which increased total trade by a staggering 25 times, more than 50 percent of which was due to trade creation with partners outside the bloc.

To the extent that exchange rate policy should influence bilateral trade flows, as we argued above, the results discussed above may overstate the effects of regional schemes. Therefore, we here describe the derived incremental elasticity estimates of exchange rate policy and of the regional integration schemes, controlling for the traditional gravity determinants.

The estimates of panel (2) of Table 3 include the effects of exchange rate policy as well as the regional blocs for imports and exports, respectively. Quantitatively, the direct effects of the two components of exchange rate policy (*RERVAR* and *REROVER*) are rather small. The elasticity estimates for *RERVAR* were –0.36 for 1980–84 and –0.41 for 1986–90; for *REROVER,* they were only significant for the first period and were much smaller at –0.03. These results are consistent with those estimated by Frankel and Wei (1993) for trade flows between major regional trade and currency blocs in Europe, North America, and Asia.[17]

However, as argued by Frankel and Wei (1993), the direct effect of real exchange rate policy on trade flows may not tell the whole story about the potential role of exchange rate policy. Also, as we argued above, the full effect of *RERVAR* or *REROVER* may be confounded by the effects of regional blocs, especially currency unions. For example, intrabloc *RERVAR* and *REROVER* are much smaller in CEAO and UDEAC compared with the sub-Saharan African-wide median average. Indeed, accounting for the exchange rate policy does lead to changes in the order of magnitudes of the regional blocs' effects, and in some cases the changes are quite substantial.

Subscribing to the above discussion, when controlling for exchange rate policy the estimates of the regional scheme effects suggest the following broad observations.

First, if anything, the average performance in the first period of the African regional blocs relative to the others was even more impressive. For example, CEAO slightly improved its performance, UDEAC re-

[17]However, Frankel and Wei (1993) only consider the effect of real exchange rate variability.

mained neutral as before, the bias against trade estimated for CEPGL remained virtually the same, while PTA's effect on intrabloc import flows was much higher (it increased imports by 10 times) and SADCC's effect on trade was in fact neutral rather than negative. The exception was ECOWAS, for which the small but positive effect on total import flows appears to be accounted for by exchange rate policy. Conversely, the effects of the non-African regional blocs did not change much. It is clear from this evidence that once we control for the effect of exchange rate policy, some of the African regional blocs had significant positive influence on intrabloc import flows (PTA) or at least a neutral effect (SADCC). The evidence is consistent with the relatively sizable *RERVAR* found in these two blocs during the 1980–84 period.

Second, during the second half of the 1980s, accounting for exchange rate policy results in some interesting differences from the pattern of changes observed for the first half of the decade. The performance of two African trade blocs (ECOWAS and SADCC) was actually better when we controlled for exchange rate policy effect, while the performances of PTA and CEPGL remained similar to the case when exchange rate policy was not accounted for. Conversely, when controlling for exchange rate policy, the already bad performance of the two African monetary unions deteriorated further in the second period, with CEAO and UDEAC reducing total imports by more than 4 times and by about 19 times, respectively. As for the three non-African blocs, controlling for exchange rate policy led to a slight reduction (increase) in the negative effect of import trade diversion of CACM (LAFTA), while the performance of ASEAN was still remarkable though its total positive effect reduced to about 16 times. The evidence suggests that the effect of exchange rate policy (especially *RERVAR*) was much higher in ECOWAS, SADCC, and CACM than the other blocs. Hence, exchange rate policy had deleterious effects on import flows in these blocs, while in CEAO, UDEAC, and ASEAN some of the credit should go to exchange rate policy, which successfully produced relatively more stable exchange rates.[18]

[18]The fact that the "incremental" trade performance of CEAO and UDEAC as regional blocs was even worse in the second period when we control for the effects of exchange rate policy, could have three—not necessarily mutually exclusive—explanations: (1) that *RERVAR*, which remains low in CEAO and UDEAC, is more important as a bilateral trade determinant than *REROVER*, which was very substantial in both blocs during the second period (see Table 1); (2) that there were factors influencing the observed overall worsening of economic conditions in the two blocs in the second period that are also confounded with the bloc effects; and/or (3) that the purchasing-power-parity-based measure of *REROVER* used in the chapter is not a good measure of the true real exchange rate overvaluation in the two blocs during the 1986–90 period.

Third, the comparison of the estimates of regional block effects across the two periods, when adjusting for exchange rate policy, reveals that the performance of the African blocks generally worsened, especially the performance of CEAO and UDEAC, the exception being SADCC. Conversely, to some extent CACM negative impact on import flows declined, but the most dramatic change was the increase of the total trade creation effect of the ASEAN from about 2 times in 1980–84 to a spectacular 16 times in 1986–90, 50 percent of which was due to trade creation with trading partners outside the ASEAN block.

Regional Integration Schemes and FDI

While there has been some turnaround for those African countries implementing reforms, growth has been too slow for these countries to converge with the other regions or to make a dent on the poverty that is pervasive in the region (World Bank, 1994). It is generally agreed that a key factor accounting for this worrisome fragility of growth recovery in the various countries in the region is the slow response of both domestic investment and FDI to reforms, with Africa receiving only about 2–3 percent of the world's FDI.

Regional integration schemes are widely seen as being one of the key factors to progress and one on whose success foreign direct investment is expected to be boosted (Cockcroft and Riddell, 1991). Many African countries are too small and balkanized to provide substantial economies of scale to encourage investment, with only five countries having a population of more than 30 million (8 countries have a population of less that 1 million, and 14 have 1 to 4 million), while 15 countries are landlocked. It is argued that FDI would increase investment and relieve foreign exchange shortages both directly and indirectly if invested in importables or exportables. FDI would also lead to an expansion in productive and technological capacity, and an increase in skill levels and employment besides the standard multiplier effects on the economy.[19] As discussed above, regional integra-

[19]FDI however may induce a reduction in domestic savings and investment rates by stifling competition through exclusive production agreements with the host government. A dominance of FDI may adversely influence the development of indigenous entrepreneurship. Due to liberal tax concessions, excessive investment allowances, disguised public subsidies, and tariff protection often provided to foreign companies by the host governments, FDI's contribution to public revenue via corporate taxes may be less than optimal. Indeed, the theory of immiserizing growth might well apply. In a distorted market, FDI may produce negative value added at world prices accompanied by repatriation of profits and dividends (Fry, 1993; Ekpo, 1996).

tion schemes may also provide credibility to economic policies pursued by African countries (Collier, 1991).

This section analyzes the extent to which regional integration schemes have been effective in promoting FDI in African countries. We consider five broad factor categories likely to influence FDI as in private domestic investment (Elbadawi and others, 1997). First is basic "fundamentals," which include the profitability of FDI as affected by projected returns in the country or subregion vis-à-vis other areas proxied by the real rate of economic growth (*RGDPGR*). More recently, the list of fundamentals has been extended to include human capital proxied by the average years of schooling (*SCHOOL*); and the size of the market and regional spillover effects proxied by regional GDP (*RRPCGDP*), which affect the productivity of fixed capital and therefore returns. These variables are expected to have a positive impact on FDI.

Second is macroeconomic policy variables, which in essence affect the variability of prices and interest rates and therefore the expected net returns on FDI. Macroeconomic policy in the context of this chapter is proxied by the real exchange rate (*RER*) and the fiscal balance income ratio (*FBY*) as well as their variability (*CVRER* and *CVFBY*, respectively) as measured by their five-year moving average coefficients of variation. A depreciation of the real exchange rate can be expected to encourage FDI inflows and to discourage outflows. Conversely, while a rise in the budget deficit may have a positive impact on FDI through its expansionary effects, it may reduce FDI by raising the real cost of bank credit (if firms borrow domestically) and hence increase the opportunity cost of retained earnings. Another important policy variable is the openness to trade (*OPEN*), which determines the ease of transfers across borders as affected by exchange controls. There is also a widespread perception that open economies encourage more confidence and hence FDI (Singh and Jun, 1995).

Third is public investment income ratio (*IGY*), which to the extent that it raises capacity crowds in FDI. State involvement in commercial activities and budgetary financing of these activities may, however, crowd out FDI. The interest therefore is to determine its net effect.

Fourth is the impact of the external shocks captured by terms of trade (*TOT*) and their variability (*CVTOT*). In addition, external debt is accounted for through three channels: first, current debt to GDP (*DY*), which is expected to be positively associated with FDI since contraction of current debt could help relax budget constraints and hence leverage FDI; second, the debt overhang (proxied by squared lagged *DY*), which reflects past debt accumulation and which is expected to be negatively associated with FDI; and third, the debt service ratio

(*DSX*), which captures the liquidity and solvency constraints imposed by the debt burden.

Fifth is risks associated with the sociopolitical environment as well as the quality of institutions. The quality of institutions (*ICRGE*) encompasses bureaucratic red tape involved in undertaking investment and safeguards for property rights.[20] Removing restrictions and providing a good business operating environment will positively affect FDI flows. Good administration of justice, respect for property rights, freedom from political intrusion in private business, low corruption, transparency, and low red tape will promote FDI. Political risks encompass perceptions regarding the likelihood of civil unrest, instability of government, and violation of civil liberties. The factors included under this category are revolutions in sub-Saharan Africa (*REVOLSSA*), which reflect change of government, and presence of civil wars in Sub-Saharan Africa (*WARSSA*), which can be expected to reduce FDI.[21]

As Elbadawi and others (1997) point out with respect to the determinants of private investment, while the focus is mainly on assessing the effects of the current and prospective changes in the above variables on FDI, there are two dimensions of the problem at hand that need to be highlighted. First is the lingering negative effects of bad reputation on investment related to the previous preponderance of policy malpractice, lack of policy credibility, policy reversals, and political instability. The effects of bad reputation linger on for a long time, which exacerbates the tendency of the investors to wait before committing resources to irreversible investment. Hence there are long lags in the influence on FDI. Second is the spillover effects of bad reputation or instability in a regional or subregional context. In the eyes of investors, bad reputation is shared in a neighborhood, introducing a regional dimension to the problem of risk perception. These temporal and spatial effects are partially captured by macroeconomic policy variability, institutional and political variables as well as the regional GDP.

The basic estimation equations are therefore the following, with the indicated postulated direction of effects. The first equation includes an African dummy to test whether the African results differ significantly

[20]*ICRGE* is an index of ordinal ranking, with scores ranging from 0–10, higher score indicating higher quality of institutions. The components making up the index include rule of law, corruption in government, quality of bureaucracy, repudiation of contacts, and expropriation risk (Elbadawi and others, 1997).

[21]The revolutions and civil war variables were not significant for all the regions. These two were thus constructed for Sub-Saharan Africa.

from those of the other regions. Regional integration schemes are then added in the second equation, where the various schemes are as defined above.

RFDIGDP = f(RRPCGDP, RGDPGR, RER, CVRER, FBY, CVFBY, OPEN, IGY, TOT, CVTOT, DY, DYL^2*, DSX, SCHOOL, ICRGE, REVOLSSA, WARSSA, DAFR)* (2)

RFDIGDP = g(RRPCGDP, RGDPGR, RER, CVRER, FBY, CVFBY, OPEN, IGY, TOT, CVTOT, DY, DYL^2*, DSX, SCHOOL, ICRGE, REVOLSSA, WARSSA, ECOWAS, CEAO, CEPGL, UDEAC, PTA, SADCC, LAFTA, CACM, ASEAN)* (3)

where *RFDIGDP* is the ratio of real FDI to real GDP; *RRPCGDP* is regional GDP (+); *RGDPGR* is the country's real income growth rate (+); *RER* is real exchange rate (+) and *CVRER*(–) its variability; *FBY* is fiscal balance income ratio (+/–) and *CVFBY* (–) its variability; *OPEN* is degree of openness (+); *IGY* is the government investment ratio; *TOT* is terms of trade (+) and *CVTOT* (–) its variability; *DY* is external debt income ratio (+); DYL^2 is lagged *DY* squared (–); *DSX* is debt service ratio (–); *SCHOOL* is average years of schooling (+); *ICRGE* is quality of institutions (+); REVOLSSA is number of revolutions in Africa (–); *WARSSA* is the presence of civil war in Africa (–); and *DAFR* is the Africa dummy (+/–).

These two models were estimated using panel data for 43 countries during the period 1970–94. For at least those countries that receive large flows, there are likely to be significant feedback effects from the FDI ratio to economic growth, *RER*, and *FBY*. The latter were therefore replaced by instrumental variables. The instruments used were lagged values of these endogenous variables as well as the contemporaneous values of the exogenous variables. The model was estimated using a homoscedastic-consistent variance-covariance matrix.

Table 4 gives the random effects (generalized least squares) econometric results. Most of the results conform with prior expectations. While the coefficient of regional GDP is insignificant, that of economic growth rate, which measures a country's market potential, is significantly and positively correlated with the FDI ratio. Both the macroeconomic variables—real exchange rate (*RER*) and the fiscal balance ratio (*FBY*)—are also significantly correlated with the FDI ratio, at least at the 10 percent level, although their variability is not. These results suggest that a depreciation of the *RER* has a positive impact on net FDI flows, while it is the expansionary effects of the fiscal balance that dominate its impact on FDI. The degree of openness (*OPEN*) also has a positive influence on the FDI ratio, an important finding since

Table 4. The FDI Model Estimates

Variable	Coefficient	*t*-statistic	Coefficient	*t*-statistic
RGDPGR	10.3364	2.27674	9.60698	2.10686
RRPCGDP	0.000016	0.391261	0.000022	0.548145
RER	7.05243	2.29929	5.74806	1.85614
CVRER	–0.0000016	–0.736875	–0.0000017	–0.749424
FBY	10.0390	3.98846	7.59035	2.84963
CVFBY	–0.015047	–0.961624	–0.011665	–0.716512
OPEN	1.03105	2.79797	1.02961	2.81372
IGY	–0.217597	–0.107522	–0.481161	–0.205627
TOT	–0.024203	–0.026860	–0.071848	–0.079165
CVTOT	0.527444	0.526195	–0.031921	–0.031109
DY	1.64889	3.79365	1.40071	3.22377
DYL2	–0.100651	–0.814866	–0.098762	–0.787751
DSX	–1.39145	–2.58280	–1.41642	–2.53832
SCHOOL	–0.253168	–0.704668	–0.334199	–0.958972
ICRGE	0.244243	2.27989	0.238586	2.44680
REVOLSSA	–1.57513	–2.12415	–1.4452	–1.49101
WARSSA	1.29246	0.925016	2.15421	1.49797
DAFR	–0.261103	–0.704231		
ECOWAS			–0.009731	–0.020323
CEAO			–0.469592	–0.770184
UDEAC			–0.494984	–0.481639
PTA			–0.799709	–1.46517
SADCC			1.78695	2.65285
LAFTA			0.412630	1.31718
CACM			0.728554	1.81207
ASEAN			0.589055	1.65065
Constant	–0.908920	–0.450433	–0.853910	–0.422492
Adjusted R^2	0.27		0.27	
Observations	440		440	
Standard error	1.25046		1.25905	
SSR	592.6		589.7	

African countries are postulated to be among the least open in the world (Collier and Gunning, 1997). The government investment ratio gives an insignificant effect on the FDI ratio, perhaps because it is highly correlated with economic growth (0.49).

Terms of trade and their variability have highly insignificant coefficients. The external debt income ratio (*DY*) has a positive coefficient, implying that the current debt stock stimulates FDI while its lagged squared counterpart (DYL^2) has an insignificant effect.[22] The debt service ratio (*DSX*) has the expected negative (significant) coefficient.

[22] *DY* and DYL^2 are highly correlated (0.75), making it difficult to separate their effects.

The average years of schooling have an insignificant effect on the FDI ratio. The quality of institutions (*ICRGE*) has a positive significant effect on FDI ratio, so that removing restrictions and providing good business operating conditions encourages FDI. While the number of revolutions in Africa (*REVOLSSA*) has a significant negative effect on the FDI ratio in the basic equation, both the variable and presence of civil war (*WARSSA*) have insignificant effects in the second equation. Given the importance of economic and political risks to investment as indicated by recent theory, this result and that for macroeconomic variability are rather surprising. (The African dummy is insignificant, suggesting that the behavior of the FDI ratio in the region does not differ significantly from that of the other regions after controlling for the various fundamentals.)

Table 4 also shows the results from replacing the African dummy with five African regional integration schemes and including two regional integration schemes in Central and South America as well as *ASEAN*.[23] As expected, the results show that, except for *SADCC*, the African regional integration schemes have not significantly increased the FDI ratio after taking into account the various fundamentals discussed above. The average FDI ratio was only 0.43 percent in *CEAO*, 0.49 percent in *ECOWAS*, 1.38 percent in *UDEAC*, and 0.85 percent in *PTA*, compared with 2.74 percent in *SADCC* in the study period. Overall, the results are consistent with Oyejide and others (1997), who provide a detailed discussion of African integration schemes.

In contrast, the results show that *LAFTA*, *CACM*, and *ASEAN* are associated with a higher FDI ratio (at least at the 20 percent level) over and above what is explained by the various fundamentals. Surprisingly, *SADCC* and *CACM* seem to have done better than *ASEAN*, where FDI has grown at a slower pace than the rest of Asia (Kamfai, 1997). The average FDI ratio was 1.48 percent in *ASEAN* in the study period.

Conclusions

This chapter has attempted to analyze the impacts of African regional integration schemes on trade and FDI. The marginal contribution of the African regional integration schemes was analyzed based on an extended gravity model estimate obtained from previous work (Elbadawi, 1997). The analysis of the impact of African regional integration on FDI is based on panel data regressions of a behavioral

[23]*CEPGL* was omitted from the results because of missing data.

model of FDI that also accounts for the effect of regional integration schemes. Consistent with other evidence in the trade and investment literatures, the estimation results of both models were generally sensible and lend themselves to important policy implications.

A summary of the main results and a discussion of policy implications follows.

Trade and FDI Effects of Regional Integration Schemes

Three fundamental conclusions could be drawn from the preceding analysis of the trade effects of regional integration schemes in sub-Saharan Africa. First, the experience of regional integration in sub-Saharan Africa has by and large been rather disappointing. Regarding trade flows, however, the African experience is by no means unique, and there are parallels to it in other developing regions (namely, Latin America). Conversely, the significance of these findings are that they obtain even after controlling for key policy variables (such as exchange rate variability and exchange rate overvaluation) in addition to the traditional trade flow determinants (economic size, distance, and so forth). It is clear, therefore, that the failures of these African schemes (like CACM and LAFTA in Latin America) can at least be partially explained by their own characteristics and the constraints they face, most notably the development strategy upon which they were created.

Second, ASEAN has significantly enhanced both intraregional and interregional trade, even though it was not explicitly designed to be a deliberate trade creating scheme. According the results of Table 3 (and after controlling for other traditional and policy determinants of bilateral trade flows) the ASEAN regional scheme increased trade with the rest of the world in the 1980–84 period by 93 percent. During the following period (1986–90), its performance turned from fair to spectacular: the presence of the ASEAN increased trade within the bloc by 7.6 times, and with the rest of the world increased by 8 times. Clearly, ASEAN and its development strategy should provide a good model for African regional integration efforts (see below). In particular, it is interesting to contrast the stellar performance of ASEAN to the largely ineffective role of SADCC—which is arguably the closest African regional scheme to the concept of ASEAN. In our view, the relatively modest performance of the latter could be explained by the lack of strong economic growth in SADCC. Inadequate commitment to internal cooperation and (by implication) the inability of the group to develop an effective and coordinated strategy for external economic relations have conspired to prevent SADCC from being the African equivalent of the ASEAN.

Third, on the role of CFA monetary unions of West Africa (both the UEMOA and the prospective successor to BEAC), our analysis suggests that the success of these unions in enhancing bilateral trade within and outside the schemes depends on three prerequisites:

- Respecting static macroeconomic balances (especially fiscal balance) on a sustained basis to ensure a positive outcome in terms of economic performance (including trade performance) of the fundamental policy trade-off facing the zone (i.e, lose the exchange rate as an instrument of national policy in return for monetary stability).
- Reforming the inherently trade-impeding zonewide distributional/allocational arrangements before the potentially positive effects on trade of the zone monetary discipline could be realized.
- Favorable external environments, especially a reversal or moderation of the French franc appreciation vis-à-vis the U.S. dollar and the worsening terms of trade for primary commodities.

However, it is pertinent to note that, given the recent and anticipated appreciation of the French franc vis-à-vis the U.S. dollar, the continued pegging of the CFA franc to it is bound to generate problems for the zone in the not too distant future, despite the huge devaluation of the CFA franc in 1994.

On the FDI effects of regional integration schemes in sub-Saharan Africa, our results show that, except for SADCC, the schemes (ECOWAS, CEAO, UDEAC, and PTA) have not significantly increased FDI after taking into account a wide range of fundamental variables. This is in contrast to the results from the other regions where LAFTA, CACM, and ASEAN are associated with significantly a higher FDI ratio (at least at the 20 percent level of significance).

Implications for the Future

Students of African regional integration, motivated by the legacy of the ineffectiveness of regional integration experiences in promoting trade and investment flows on the subcontinent, have argued against renewed regional integration efforts in sub-Saharan Africa along the traditional lines, where the existing regional schemes are called upon to attempt to directly promote regional trade despite repeated failures (e.g., Collier and Gunning, 1993; Fine and Yeo, 1994). The main argument is that these schemes are inappropriately structured, since they were designed to pursue the now ill-fated and outmoded import-substitution development strategy. Instead, Fine and Yeo, for example, propose a new paradigm for regional integration in sub-Saharan Africa inspired by the experiences of post–World War II Europe and the recent "miracle" experience of East Asia. They suggest that regional integration initiatives in sub-Saharan Africa should be designed to achieve the twin objectives of fostering national policy credibility, and rapid accumulation of physical and human capital—the latter being initially triggered by enhanced FDI and by savings and investment surges within the region in subsequent stages. They provide an exhaustive review of the evidence linking regional integration to these two objectives, which are now being accepted as the two main fundamentals behind East Asia's economic miracle.

The key element of this strategy adopts Collier's (1991) and Collier and Gunning's (1993) proposal of "participatory supranational agencies of restraint," in which national economic policy will be tied in a reciprocal threat-making arrangement to a Northern anchor (the European Union). Fine and Yeo then ask the question as to why might the EU be interested in playing such a role; they argue that, unlike the case of Eastern Europe, enhancement of trade, fears of mass migration, or imminent security concerns could not be major factors. However, they suggest that the precedent of UEMOA, the vast interest of the EU in South Africa, the realization that the ACP Agreement—which is administered by the European Commission—has met with limited success, and the growing EU concerns with political stability as a prerequisite for economic growth may prompt a more active policy toward sub-Saharan Africa. Cobham and Robson (1994) adopt similar arguments for the EU as an external anchor in the context of monetary integration in sub-Saharan Africa).

The experience of the ASEAN, which was not explicitly designed to be a deliberate trade creating scheme, deserves a special consideration. The story behind ASEAN is summed up by Langhammer and Hiemenz (1991), who argue that "ASEAN owes its worldwide reputation not to any progress in internal integration or industrial cooperation, but to other factors. These include its role as a representative of the common interests of its members in foreign affairs and in continuing dialogues with the major OECD countries on market accessibility." It was also noted that "ASEAN has achieved some success in increasing its collective bargaining power in dialogues with OECD members (Langhammer, 1985). In addition, ASEAN members have established strong internal networks for business consultation and software cooperation without surrendering national sovereignty with respect to major economic policies." Taking into consideration as well the stellar performances of the ASEAN countries in the areas of economic growth and economic development in general over the past two and a half decades (see, e.g., World Bank, 1993, for a comprehensive review), three interrelated factors behind the success of the association can be identified: first and foremost, a strong country-specific and regional economic performance regarding economic growth, which in turn was substantially enhanced by collective policy credibility and investment spillovers brought about by regional cooperation; second, measured but effective regional cooperation; and third, policy coordination in the area of external economic relations. It is interesting that Collier and Gunning (1993) identified country-specific multilateral trade liberalization, policy harmonization, and regional cooperation in a limited set of areas (for example, infrastructure, power, and communication), and a strong and coordinated strategy for external relations as the best options for sub-Saharan Africa to foster both growth and regional integration (without actively promoting it), as well to avoid marginalization in the global economy.

References

Ades, A., and Chua, H., 1993, "Regional Instability and Economic Growth: Thy Neighbor's Curse," Discussion Paper No. 704 (New Haven, Connecticut: Economic Growth Center, Yale University).

Baldwin, R., 1993, "Review of Theoretical Developments on Regional Integration," paper presented at an AERC conference on Trade Liberalization and Regional Integration in Sub-Saharan Africa, Nairobi, December.

Berg, E., and Associates, 1988, "Regional and Economic Development in Sub-Saharan Africa" (Alexandria, Virginia: U.S. Agency for International Development).

Chua, H., 1993a, "Regional Public Capital and Economic Growth" (unpublished; New Haven, Connecticut: Economic Growth Center, Yale University).

———, 1993b, "Regional Spillovers and Economic Growth," Discussion Paper No. 700 (New Haven, Connecticut: Economic Growth Center, Yale University).

Cobham, D., and P. Robson, 1994, "Monetary Integration in Africa: A Deliberately European Perspective," *World Development*, Vol. 22, No. 3, pp. 285–99.

Cockcroft L., and Roger C. Riddell, 1991, "Foreign Direct Investment in Sub-Saharan Africa," Working Paper No. 619 (Washington: World Bank).

Collier, P., 1991, "Africa's External Economic Relations: 1960–90," *African Affairs*, Vol. 90, No. 360, pp. 339–56.

———, and J. Gunning, 1993, "Linkages between Trade Policy and Regional Integration," paper presented at an AERC conference on Trade Liberalization and Regional Integration in Sub-Saharan Africa, Nairobi, December.

———, and J. Gunning, 1997, "Explaining African Economic Performance," Working Paper No. 97-2 (Oxford: Centre for the Study of African Economies).

Easterly, and Levine, 1994, "Africa's Growth Tragedy," paper presented at AERC Plenary, Nairobi, May.

Eichengreen B., and D. Irwin, 1993, "Trade Blocs, Currency Blocs and the Disintegration of World Trade in the 1930s," Discussion Paper No. 837 (London: Centre for Economic Policy Research).

Ekpo, A.A., 1996, "Government Policy and Foreign Private Investment in Nigeria, 1990–1994," paper presented at an AERC thematic research workshop, Nairobi, December.

Elbadawi, I., 1997, "The Impact of Regional Integration Trade and Monetary Schemes on Intra-Sub-Saharan Africa Trade," in *Regional Integration and Trade Liberalization in Sub-Saharan Africa,* ed. by A. Oyejide, A. Elbadawi, and P. Collier (London: Macmillan).

———, and B. Ndulu, 1994, "Long-Term Development and Sustainable Growth in SSA," paper presented at the SAREC International Colloquium on New Directions in Development Economics, Stockholm, March.

———, B. Ndulu, and N.S. Ndung'u, 1997, "Risks, Uncertainties and Debt Overhang as Determinants of Private Investment in Sub-Saharan Africa" (unpublished; Nairobi: African Economic Research Consortium).

Fine, J., and S. Yeo, 1994, "Regional Integration in Sub-Saharan Africa: Dead End or a Fresh Start?" paper prepared for an AERC conference on Trade Liberalization and Regional Integration in Sub-Saharan Africa, Nairobi, December.

Foroutan, F., 1993, "Regional Integration in Sub-Saharan Africa: Past Experience and Future Prospects," in *New Dimensions in Regional Integration,* ed. by J. de Melo and A. Panagariya (Cambridge: Cambridge University Press).

———, and L. Pritchett, 1993, "Intra-Sub-Saharan African Trade: Is It Too Little?" *Journal of the African Economies,* Vol. 2, No. 1, pp. 74–104.

Frankel, J., and S. Wei, 1993, "Trade Blocs and Currency Blocks," in *The Monetary Future of Europe* (London: Centre for Economic Policy Research).

Fry, M.J., 1993, "Foreign Direct Investment in a Macroeconomic Framework," Working Paper No. 1141 (Washington: World Bank).

Havrylyshyn, O., and L. Pritchett, 1991, "European Trade Patterns After the Transition," Working Paper No. 748 (Washington: World Bank).

Helpman, E., 1987, "Imperfect Competition and International Trade: Evidence from Fourteen Industrial Countries," *Journal of the Japanese and International Economics,* Vol. 1, pp. 62–81.

———, and P. Krugman, 1985, *Market Structure and Foreign Trade* (Cambridge, Massachusetts: MIT Press).

Krugman, P., 1991a, *Geography and Trade* (Cambridge, Massachusetts: MIT Press).

———, 1991b, "The Move Toward Free Trade Zones," in *Policy Implications of Trade and Currency Zones* (Kansas City: Federal Reserve Bank of Kansas City).

Langhammer, R., 1985, "The Economic Rationale of Trade Policy Cooperation between ASEAN and the EC: Has Cooperation Benefitted ASEAN?" *ASEAN Economic Bulletin*, Vol. 2, pp. 107–17.

———, and U. Hiemenz, 1991, "Regional Integration among Developing Countries: Survey of Past Performance and Agenda for Future Policy Action," Occasional Paper No. 7, UNDP–World Bank Trade Expansion Program (Washington: World Bank).

Lyakurwa, W., A. McKay, N. Ng'eno, and W. Kennes, 1993, "Regional Integration in Sub-Saharan Africa: A Review of Experiences and Issues," paper presented at an AERC conference on Trade Liberalization and Regional Integration in Sub-Saharan Africa, Nairobi, December.

Montenegro, C., and R. Soto, 1994, "How Distorted Is Cuba's Trade? Evidence and Predictions From Gravity Model" (unpublished; Washington: Georgetown University).

O'Connell, S., 1994, "Macroeconomic Harmonization, Trade Reform, and Regional Trade in Sub-Saharan Africa," paper presented at an AERC conference on Trade Liberalization and Regional Integration in Sub-Saharan Africa, Nairobi, December.

Oyejide, A., I. Elbadawi, and P. Collier, eds., 1997, *Regional Integration and Trade Liberalization in Sub-Saharan Africa* (London: Macmillan).

Sen, A., and Z. Matuszewski, 1991, "Properties of Maximum Likelihood Estimates of Gravity Model Parameters," *Journal of Regional Science*, Vol. 31, No. 4, pp. 460–86.

Singh, H., and Kwang W. Jun, 1995, "Some New Evidence on Determinants of Foreign Direct Investment in Developing Countries," Policy Research Working Paper No. 1531 (Washington: World Bank).

World Bank, 1993, *The East Asian Miracle: Economic Growth and Public Policy* (New York: Oxford University Press).

———, 1994, *Adjustment in Africa: Reforms, Results, and the Road Ahead* (New York: Oxford University Press).

Young, A., 1994, "The Tyranny of Numbers: Confronting the Statistical Realities of the East Asian Growth Experience," paper presented at the Centre for Economic Policy Research Workshop on Growth, Les Arcs, January.

Sub-Saharan African Experiences with Regional Integration 15

Ernest Aryeetey

Introduction

Regional integration arrangements[1] have had a long history in sub-Saharan Africa, beginning with the customs union in 1900 between Kenya (then the East African protectorate) and Uganda. Integration has generally been perceived by policymakers to be a highly desirable objective, despite the lack of decisive and concrete actions to achieve positive outcomes. There have indeed been many arguments in support of integration at regional meetings and relatively few against. The consequence is that institutions and protocols for regional integration are available in relative abundance. The integration discussions and efforts have covered such varied areas as trade integration, labor market integration, capital market integration, monetary integration, and so forth. Trade integration has naturally attracted greater attention from policymakers and researchers.

The early interest in regional integration in sub-Saharan Africa was driven by the perception that it was a means to achieve structural transformation of the various economies, that is, the industrialization and modernization of these economies. The small sizes of the economies was recognized as a constraint on an efficient, low-cost industrialization strategy. Early analysts provided a rationale for the formation of customs union arrangements among developing countries based on the industrialization objective. Most African policymakers and decision makers refrained from choosing an export-led strategy to deal with the problems of size because of pessimism concerning market access in the industrialized economies. The alternative was to overcome the size constraint through improved market access at the regional level. In this light, the formation of regional integration

[1]The expression "regional integration" is used throughout this chapter to cover the full range of public sector activities that involve permanent collaborative ventures, including economic policy, regional security, human rights, education, health, research and technology, and natural resource management. Regional integration is generally characterized by the establishment of joint institutional mechanisms and a degree of shared sovereignty.

arrangements was pursued as a developmental objective by many governments. At a higher level, the Organization of African Unity (OAU) declared its commitment to the promotion of economic integration of Africa to facilitate and reinforce social and economic intercourse.

Early regional integration efforts were also premised on the need for greater self-reliance. According to the OAU, the structural transformation of African economies was expected to occur within the context of "self-reliant and self-sustaining development of member states." Regional integration and the cooperation that it implies were also expected to increase the bargaining power of African economies in the international economy.

While the appeal for integration has remained strong for several decades, there are differences in the perception today of how integration should be conceived and pursued. After a lull in the discussions in the 1980s, there has been a resurgence of academic interest in the subject (Lavergne, 1997). The domination of the discussions by trade creation is amply reflected in the types of arguments often advanced. A number of scholars continue to argue that regional groupings in sub-Saharan Africa are unlikely to confer net positive static welfare gains on members because they do not have the required conditions to enable their trade creation effects to outweigh trade diversion effects (Jebuni, 1997). They therefore argue for a more cautious approach of generalizing the removal of tariffs and other barriers to trade. They generally believe that the Asian experience may be relevant; hence, formal integration efforts should be abandoned and policymakers should concentrate on developing an outward-oriented trade policy that encourages trade and eventually may result in greater trade integration (Jebuni, 1997).

The arguments for less formal integration have been supported by the limited success of trade integration efforts (Fine and Yeo, 1997; Langhammer and Hiemenz, 1991). It is argued that most of the integration arrangements have not made any headway in achieving their objectives largely because of a lack of implementation of treaties and protocols. Langhammer and Hiemenz (1991) describe the sequence of African integration efforts as "a dynamic initial phase, in which numerous programs are launched . . . followed by a period of implementation difficulties or failures and ratification problems."

Others, however, still see formal regional integration as imperative for sub-Saharan African economies. In the present world economy, with its large trading blocs, sub-Saharan Africa needs to be able to attract foreign investment and technology necessary for investment. "Regional integration may be the most practicable way to minimise the costs of African market fragmentation. . . . It may thus be a precondition for, rather than an obstacle to integrating sub-Saharan Africa more effectively with the world economy" (Robson, 1993, p. 341). It is sometimes argued that regardless of the fact of low net gains from trade integration and the institutions that pursue them, the regional groupings and their institutions are essential for making sub-Saharan Africa respond to increasing global marginalization (Onitiri, 1997).

The current interest in regional approaches to economic development is partly related to changes at the global level, particularly the creation of the North American Free Trade Area (NAFTA) between Canada, Mexico, and the United States of America. It also partly stems from dissatisfaction with the slow pace of negotiations during the multilateral trade talks (the Uruguay Round). The renewed interest within sub-Saharan Africa in revitalizing and resuscitating regional groupings can be seen as a response to these global developments, that is, the seeming evolution of the world economy into regional trading blocs. There is the fear that Africa's position in the world economy will be weakened further if it does not strengthen its already existing regional groupings. This is because, with the changes in the world economy, regions that are not able to reduce market fragmentation and its attendant costs will find it difficult to attract the foreign investment and technological know-how that is required for growth (Mistry, 1996).

The recent inauguration of the African Economic Community (AEC) in June 1997 is the latest example of the renewed interest in regional cooperation. At the inaugural summit of the AEC, the Nigerian foreign minister reiterated the need for African economies to overcome the size constraint. He stated that Africa's economic integration needed to be speeded up because "the European Union, North American Free Trade Area and the Association of South East Asian Nations are striding ahead. If Africa wishes to be part of a better world, we must also group together or risk becoming simple markets for the fast developing countries. If we continue as we are, our future will be as humiliating as our present is distressing."[2]

Some of the newest arguments for integration are, however, based on recent developments in the world's financial markets. Private capital flows—particularly foreign direct investment (FDI) and portfolio equity—into the developing world grew remarkably after the mid–1980s. Their share in total private flows moved to an average 35 percent and 13.5 percent, respectively, in the period 1990–96, up from

[2]*Africa Recovery*, 1997, Vol. 11, No. 1, p. 5.

12 percent and 1.2 percent a decade earlier. The growth is generally attributed to the growing integration of markets and financial institutions, increased economic liberalization, and rapid innovation in financial instruments and technologies, particularly in the areas of computing and telecommunications. For sub-Saharan Africa, however, most of these growing flows were hardly observed, because they were directed at Asia and Latin America. China alone accounted for 86 percent of total FDI flows in 1995. Even though Nigeria is the second largest recipient of FDI, this is not diversified and mainly restricted to the extractive sector of the economy, as is the case in Ghana and other countries.

Thus, sub-Saharan Africa currently attracts only 4 percent of the emerging markets portfolio, which is itself only a small proportion of global capital flows. Despite this low magnitude, sub-Saharan Africa has a significant chance of becoming a major drawer of capital and investments for a number of reasons. The reasons include the fact that, in the last couple of years, the number of operating capital markets has grown considerably, reaching 16 at the beginning of this year, up from under five a decade ago. Aside from this development, they have in the last few years begun to attract international attention. Thus, more than a dozen investment funds have been established since 1993, trading in Europe and New York. These African funds had a total investment of $1 billion at the beginning of 1997, up from zero in 1992.

On the basis of these achievements of the last few years, sub-Saharan Africa is more and more being regarded as capable of attracting more private capital, if only it will put its house in order. With increasing and more effective financial sector reforms, the way should be paved for larger flows as global investors seek out new frontier markets. Since emerging markets are underrepresented in the global market, it is expected that they will seek to increase their share. With improved infrastructure and policies, sub-Saharan Africa should enhance its ability to be a major player, as international investors seek out the last frontier. The integration of financial markets is considered to be a solution.

The experiences of regional integration in sub-Saharan Africa, in relation to those of other regions, need to be analyzed within a broad framework. For this reason, this chapter restates the major experiences that sub-Saharan Africa has had with regional integration. It places the regional integration efforts in sub-Saharan Africa within an appropriate historical and conceptual perspective, while highlighting the influences that have dominated these experiences. The chapter will also shed some light on current thinking on the African continent with regard to what can and should be achieved with regional integration.

Arguments for Formal Economic Integration

One of the most recent restatements of the need for a pan-African economic union has been by Onitiri (1997). He argues that, if sub-Saharan Africa is to avoid being marginalized following the "revolution" in the international economy, it must enhance productivity, a process that requires more than simple trade integration. He says this requires full economic integration. Onitiri's view of integration is as embodied in the treaty of the AEC, assuming that all the intermediate steps have been taken already in the years of experimenting with one grouping or another. For this, "variable geometry" is at variance with the AEC treaty. The AEC is conceived as the means for providing "an effective response to the prevalence of regional economic blocs" all over the world. Onitiri (1997) observes: "Since the treaty embraces all aspects of African economic and social life, it also provides a convenient framework for re-examining and streamlining the activities of the existing African international government organizations, and mobilizing them more effectively to address the pressing problems of African economic and social development" (p. 417).

The AEC is expected to move beyond trade integration into the integration of production and the harmonization of fiscal and monetary policies, as well as into conflict resolution and the coordination of policies on the environment. It is proposed under the AEC treaty to delegate, in addition to the large number of implementing mechanisms, the task of administering and managing the community to a single OAU-AEC secretariat. The restructuring of the present OAU to play the new role assigned to it suggests that it will have an enlarged bureaucracy, a proposal that seems to frighten many African intellectuals (Oyejide, Elbadawi, and Collier, 1997). It will be running the show in concert with the African Development Bank (ADB) and the Economic Commission for Africa (ECA).

The concept of the AEC supported by Onitiri has been treated differently by Mistry (1995), who with an incremental approach has suggested the adoption of sectoral investment coordination and cooperation, trade integration, and the development of an appropriate institutional framework. A regional policy environment must be created to allow the gradual integration of markets. This approach differs from the practice of current regional agreements, which emphasize trade integration without addressing adequately the infrastructural and institutional framework necessary to facilitate the trade integration process. Rather than dismissing variable geometry, Mistry proposes the adoption of a core group willing to implement a customs union and the existence of "a wider group at the periphery which might constitute itself as a free trade area, and be linked with the former in free trade agreement" (Mistry, 1995, p. 42).

Arguments against the AEC include the fact that many of its expected benefits do not require preferential tariffs to be realized (Oyejide, Elbadawi, and Collier, 1997). It is also suggested that, in the past, the coordination of activities that brought net gains to all participating countries (such as joint infrastructures) was impeded by tying their negotiations to trade policies whose gains were not that transparent and discouraged potential losers.

In this regard, it is obvious that recent discussions on the benefits of regional integration have moved beyond the traditional arguments of trade creation and diversion. The old debates for regional integration rested on the expected static gains. Thus, a regional economic grouping was likely to be beneficial to its members only if trade creation effects outweighed any trade diversion effects. On the basis of the traditional concepts of trade creation and trade diversion, it may be concluded that most African regional arrangements, particularly trade integration, will not register net static welfare benefits because the necessary conditions do not exist anywhere. However, the rationale for African integration from within the continent was not premised on expected static welfare gains but on dynamic gains. Recent assessments of the expected benefits of further integration of European economies find that the dynamic gains rather than the static welfare gains dominate.

Robson (1993) argues that the failure of developing-country integration units to generate net static gains of integration because they are not optimal trading or currency areas does not justify the discouragement of the formation of these unions. He criticizes some recent studies of sub-Saharan African integration that focus only on static benefits and that do not also consider the issues that are addressed in assessing industrial-country integration efforts. Mistry (1996, p. 28) has argued that sustainable real income growth as a result of regional integration is possible, even if empirical evidence from a number of regions is inconclusive. Such dynamic efficiency gains are expected to arise from "economies of scale in trade supporting industries and services which are caused by market enlargement, spill-over effects resulting from wider-knowledge transfers across the region on both an intra-industry and inter-industry basis; increased competition; increased levels of investment; stepped up pace of technological change; and consumption smoothing during business cycles." Additional dynamic gains arise from the benefits of policy and investment coordination.

Arguments for Less Formal Integration

An early researcher recommended a focus on unilateral trade liberalization. Jebuni (1997) takes the case a little further as he comes out strongly in favor of unilateral nonpreferential trade liberalization after questioning "whether inward-looking preferential liberalization can increase intra-African trade." After observing a high level of protection that has been provided to import-substitution industries, he suggests that, so long as protection remains alongside import-substitution strategies, preferential trade liberalization will be meaningless. This is because preferential trade liberalization does not provide any incentive for firms to export when there is high protection for import-substitution firms. Indeed, the high tariffs placed on imports affect exports in a significant way in many countries.

The arguments of Jebuni (1997) rest on the nonrecognition of significant positive outcomes from macroeconomic reform in various countries and the small change in domestic policies, even when pursuing preferential trade liberalization. The argument against regional groupings rests mainly on the diversionary effects of preferential tariffs. But those effects remain high because of the relatively high sub-Saharan African tariffs. "At present, despite considerable reductions in trade barriers over the past decade, most African countries impose fairly high barriers through tariffs and export taxes or through managed exchange rate arrangements" (Oyejide, Elbadawi, and Collier, 1997, p. 16). Jebuni (1997) observes that, given that manufactures presently dominate intra-African exports, the potential for expanded exports of manufactures and other nontraditional exports exists, but these are hurt unnecessarily by national protective measures. Countries will therefore have to unilaterally bring down tariffs in a general manner to establish a basic incentive for the growth of exports. Sub-Saharan African trade integration will then take place as an offshoot of the process of lowering tariffs unilaterally. Jebuni suggests that, since tariffs came down somewhat in the last decade through unilateral nonpreferential arrangements, sub-Saharan Africa's intraregional trade has expanded more rapidly than its other international trade, even if it is still slow.

Others have used the unilateral trade liberalization argument for a multilateral development of regional markets (Robson, 1993). Proponents of multilateralism and unilateral trade liberalization would argue that improvements in income could be achieved by greater integration into the world economy. Biasing trade in favor of the region is not the way to go. Robson argues that "regional integration may be the most practicable way to minimise the costs of African market fragmentation. . . . It may thus be a precondition for, rather than an obstacle to integrating SSA more effectively with the world economy" (Robson, 1993, p. 341). The training ground argument presents regional integration as a means to increase the gains Africa may reap through eventual greater integration into the world economy. The regional market provides an opportunity for firms to develop appropriate approaches to medium-term cost reduction with eyes set on a market beyond the regional boundary.

To benefit from dynamic gains, members of a regional grouping do not need to introduce further discrimination through higher protective barriers. Cooperation in the provision of regional economic infrastructure, harmonization of tax and investment codes, and macroeconomic stability are required. Such cooperation will reduce transactions costs, enhancing market access and facilitating greater trade and investment integration. They will also introduce credibility into policymaking, because national policies must be consistent with achieving regional objectives. The creation of strong regional organizations with sanctioning powers is seen as an indication of commitment to the regional integration arrangement by national governments.

Arguments against unilateral trade liberalization rest on the fact that countries will be pursuing their policy objectives at different speeds, which will inevitably lead to a widening of the disparities in tariff structures and hence discourage intraregional trade as the task of harmonization becomes more difficult. On the surface, the promotion of unilateral nonpreferential trade liberalization would appear to be in conflict with the formation of a regional preferential trade area; for, as Oyejide, Elbadawi, and Collier, (1997) point out, the lower the tariffs, the less opportunity a country has to offer a preferential tariff. Conversely, as suggested by Fine and Yeo (1997), lower tariffs reduce the costs of trade diversion that will be observed in a preferential trade area.

Even though many sub-Saharan African governments have pledged to work toward the reduction of tariffs unilaterally as they pursue reform, the pace continues to be slow, and there does not appear to be much prospect in sight for faster action. A major obstacle is the likely loss of tax revenue in the short run, which makes a unilateral tariff reduction appear tantamount to shooting oneself in the foot.

Regional Integration Arrangements

There are broadly two kinds of regional groupings in sub-Saharan Africa, namely, those sponsored by the ECA and those resulting from other initiatives. The ECA has promoted three subregional arrangements. That for West Africa, the Economic Community of West African States (ECOWAS), was established in 1975. That for Eastern and Southern Africa, the Preferential Trade Area (PTA), was established in 1981, and later became the Common Market for Eastern and Southern Africa (COMESA). That for Central Africa, the ECCAS, is still under negotiation. The above-mentioned AEC has recently been finalized.

The quest for industrialization is what has driven the ECA's involvement in regional integration attempts. It considered trade expansion within the region as a priority to achieve the industrialization objectives. The ECA noted, among the constraints on increased intra-African trade, deficiencies in physical (transport and communications) and institutional (commodity exchanges, clearinghouses, and so forth) infrastructure; tariff and nontariff barriers; lack of adequate information on products; relatively high prices of African manufactures and the need for competitive prices; lack of facilities for trade and export credit; inadequate marketing and distribution channels; instability of supply; and payment difficulties. For the industrial development decade, it considered it important that subregional institutions be able to forecast subregional demand for products using analysis and projection, estimate present and future production in the subregion, calculate quantities required to meet demand with existing capacities, and identify other key industrial projects that utilize these basic products as inputs. It proposed arrangements for the financing of subregional programs through such agencies as the ADB and the Arab Bank for Economic Development in Africa (BADEA). It is now obvious that the approach adopted for industrial development focused more extensively on the creation and strengthening of promotional institutions than on facilitating the operation of the production agents themselves.

The African Economic Community

The treaty establishing the AEC agreed upon in Abuja in 1991 may be seen as the culmination of past declarations of African heads of state and governments and their ministers (e.g., the Kinshasa Declaration of 1976 and the Lagos Plan of Action and the Final Act of Lagos of 1980) regarding their desire to create an Africa-wide economic community. The AEC's objectives are to (1) promote economic, social, and cultural development and integration of African economies to increase self-reliance and promote self-sustained development, (2) develop a continentwide framework for the development and utilization of human and material resources, (3) achieve economic stability and peaceful relations among member states through cooperation, and (4) coordinate and harmonize policies between existing and future economic communities as a means of establishing a continental community. These objectives are to be achieved by strengthening existing regional arrangements and establishing new ones where necessary, regional trade liberalization, joint investment programs, harmonization of national policies, establishing a common external tariff, and the eventual elimination of barriers to the free flow of goods, services, factors of production, and information.

In recognition of the uneven development of countries and therefore uneven distribution of costs and benefits from integration, a Community Solidarity, Development, and Compensation Fund will be established. Due consideration will be given to the least-developed, landlocked, and island countries. The evolution of African economies into an economic community is expected to take place within a 40-year period, in six stages. In the first stage, existing regional organizations will be strengthened and new ones created where required. Regional trade liberalization and harmonization of regional tariff codes and sectoral policies will occur during the second phase. Regional free trade areas will be created during the third phase. In the fourth stage, tariffs and nontariff systems will be harmonized among the various regional units. The fifth stage will involve the establishment of an African Common Market. The final stage will be the completion of integration of goods, factor, and sectoral policies and the creation of an African Economic and Monetary Union. The treaty also envisages the creation of a Pan-African Parliament. The treaty provides safeguard clauses for states that have balance of payments difficulties arising from the implementation of the treaty, suffer from import surges "that cause or are likely to cause serious damage to the economy," and that want to protect an infant industry. In the first two instances, the affected member must be seen to have "taken all appropriate reasonable steps to overcome the difficulties." The treaty allows for the imposition of quantitative or similar restrictions or prohibitions on goods from the exporting country as a response to any of the three possible situations.

The Economic Community of West African States

ECOWAS was intended to eventually become a customs union and then a common market while integrating states in the West African subregion. It is made up of 16 member states, 10 of which have allegiances to other subregional groupings. Thus, the Mano River Union embraces Guinea, Liberia and Sierra Leone; the West African Economic Community (CEAO) pulled together Benin, Burkina Faso, Côte d'Ivoire, Mali, Mauritania, Niger, and Senegal; and the remaining 6

ECOWAS states of Cape Verde, The Gambia, Ghana, Guinea Bissau, Nigeria, and Togo had no other subregional trade grouping until recently, when Togo joined the West African Economic and Monetary Union (UEMOA). The ECOWAS arrangement holds together some 200 million people and is operated through a conference of heads of state, a Council of Ministers, an executive secretariat, a development and cooperation fund, and five specialized commissions. The five commissions are (1) Trade, Customs, Immigration, Monetary, and Payments; (2) Industry, Agriculture, and Natural Resources; (3) Transport, Communications, and Energy; (4) Social and Cultural Affairs; and (5) Administration and Finance.

ECOWAS seeks to promote cooperation and development among member states in the areas of industry, transport, telecommunications and energy, agriculture, natural resources, commerce, monetary and financial matters, and social and cultural affairs. Its legal basis is to be found in the Lagos Treaty, supplemented by a series of 29 protocols and supplementary protocols that guide operations in such areas as trade liberalization, transport, community citizenship, rights of free movement and residence, and technical cooperation.

The ECOWAS Fund for Cooperation, Compensation, and Development was established and located in Lome in 1977 under the Trade Commission. The fund has as its objective the promotion of economic development and integration through the financing of industrial and infrastructure projects of common interest to ECOWAS states. In doing this, it also administers the ECOWAS Trade Liberalization Scheme Compensation Fund, which was set up in 1990 to compensate member states for losses in revenue arising from the introduction of trade liberalization measures.

Trade among member states amounts to only about 6 percent of the official recorded trade, having grown from about 2.1 percent in 1970 to 3.1 percent in 1975, 3.9 percent in 1980, 4.2 percent in 1985, and 5.5 percent in 1987. In the period 1980–89, the annual average growth rate of exports for the community was –7.2 percent; thus, it was a shrinking trend in importance to the world market. Mansoor and Inotai (1991) note: "If one takes account of unrecorded trade, which in some cases surpasses the officially registered figures, it is even harder to find evidence of gains."

Ghana's imports from ECOWAS states, for example, amounted to only 8 percent of total imports, while exports to the subregion amounted to about 4 percent of total exports in 1991. Côte d'Ivoire, Burkina Faso, Mali, and Senegal appear to be the only countries with imports from member states exceeding 10 percent of their total exports. Three of those countries (that is, minus Mali) and Benin were also the only ones with exports to ECOWAS states exceeding 10 percent of total exports. Côte d'Ivoire is by far the most important country in terms of intra-ECOWAS trade. It is interesting that while a great deal of traditionally strong trade links exist among the francophone nations (most of which formed the CEAO), these are usually in livestock and agricultural products. Manufactured exports come mainly from Côte d'Ivoire. Nigeria, another major exporter to the subregion, offers mainly petroleum products.

The Common Market for Eastern and Southern Africa

COMESA, which began as the Preferential Trade Area for Eastern and Southern Africa, was originally intended to grow into a common market by the year 2000. It was subsequently transformed in 1993 into the Common Market for Eastern and Southern Africa. COMESA embraces 22 countries and now has more integration objectives after moving from loose cooperation in a free trade area. The most important objective of the earlier PTA was to promote intraregional trade using trade liberalization measures. This was to be achieved through protocols on reduction and elimination of trade barriers, customs cooperation, the rules of origin, reexport of goods, transit trade and transit facilities, clearing and payments arrangements, transport and communications, simplification and harmonization of trade documents, and procedures on standardization and quality control. Other areas of cooperation were given as industry, agriculture, monetary affairs, and natural resources. The PTA expected to achieve its trade liberalization program of reducing tariffs by September 1992, after having reduced initial tariffs by 10–70 percent and planning to reduce these further by 25 percent every two years.

The new COMESA treaty calls for the establishment of a customs union through the removal of all trade barriers and the establishment of a common external tariff and rules of origin. The new treaty has also introduced cooperation in monetary and financial matters. The treaty anticipates coordination of macroeconomic policies as the countries move toward free movement of services and capital as well as the convertibility of currencies. COMESA stresses a commitment to the redistribution of the benefits of integration, an issue that was previously not addressed by the PTA. It plans to achieve this through special regional programs to promote the development of the least-developed countries in the region to achieve balanced development within the common market.

The PTA was probably best known for its institutional growth. It created specialized institutions to coordinate the development and integration processes of member states, including the setting up of the Trade and Development Bank for Eastern and Southern Africa, the PTA Clearing House, and the PTA Federation of Chambers of Commerce and Industry. The PTA was also known to be active in organizing such activities as trade fairs for member states, organizing four such fairs in 8 years.

Even though it achieved a high profile in the region, the PTA has not been known to have created much trade. Langhammer and Hiemenz (1991) reported that "trade liberalization in the PTA framework has been biased toward trade diversion" (p. 28). By 1982, the PTA's share in world trade was 0.56 percent. This dropped to 0.4 percent in 1993, after a decade of PTA operation. More than 94 percent of PTA trade was with nonmember countries. Intra-PTA exports as a percentage of total PTA exports declined from 7 percent in 1982 to 6.6 percent in 1992. At the same time, imports within the region remained at only 4.7 percent of total regional imports. The PTA is seen to have had a number of shortcomings as countries pursued trade policies that did not encourage intra-PTA trade.

Integration Arrangements Not Sponsored by the ECA

Two other subregional groupings operate with almost similar objectives within the ECOWAS states. These were not sponsored by the ECA. They are the Mano River Union, which is a weak alliance of Guinea, Liberia, and Sierra Leone that seeks to develop the river basin jointly, and the francophone UEMOA, whose members include Benin, Burkina Faso, Côte d'Ivoire, Mali, Niger, Senegal, and Togo, all of which share a common central bank (BCEAO). UEMOA came out of the realignment of francophone West African interests in 1994, which saw the demise of CEAO. A major difference between the UEMOA and ECOWAS is that the latter has a functioning monetary integration component. In Central Africa, the equivalent of UEMOA is currently the Central African Economic and Monetary Union (CEMAC), which embraces Cameroon, the Central African Republic, Chad, Congo, Gabon, and Equatorial Guinea. They all aspire to achieving customs unions. It appears that while various countries would like to operate from smaller groupings held together by a certain common factor (language or a river, in these cases), they would not like to give up membership in the larger ECA-sponsored body. It is simply the adoption of a "wait and see" attitude toward the larger body.

A number of other smaller regional integration arrangements not sponsored by ECA may be found in Southern Africa. The Southern African Development Community (SADC), which replaced the Southern African Development Coordination Conference, is the best known of these. It was previously generally perceived to be an organization whose goal was to reduce its dependence on apartheid South Africa (which was not interested in a customs union). In moving toward trade integration in the last few years, SADC (which embraces 11 of the COMESA states) has adopted measures that involve tariff reductions and the removal of nontariff barriers. It seeks greater coordination of external tariffs and the promotion of free movement of capital and people. It also has an interest in setting up regional infrastructural authorities and a development bank. The existence of both SADC and COMESA is certainly questionable, considering the congruency of their objectives and their individual circumstances, a point we discuss again below in more general terms.

Achievements of Integration Efforts

The success of regional integration schemes is generally measured by the share of intraregional trade in total trade, with the qualification that increasing intraregional trade may also reflect a loss in world market positions. When increases in intraregional trade are accompanied by increasing relative weight of the region in world trade, this is seen as positive for integration (Mansoor and Inotai, 1991). This approach at assessment puts almost all the regional groupings in a bad light, for there has been no significant increase in intraregional trade (see Table 1).[3]

The empirical evidence on the causal link between creation of regional integration units and intraregional trade is ambiguous. Foroutan and Pritchett's (1993) study of intra-African trade finds that trade levels are "actually higher than expected on the basis of the underlying determinants" (p. 96). The study finds that the CEAO does have a statistically significant impact on intraregional trade, while ECOWAS does not. Ogunkola's study of intra-ECOWAS trade, conversely, finds that economic integration has had a positive but small impact on trade within the region (cited in Jebuni, Ogunkola, and Soludo, 1995). Kasekende and Ng'eno (1995) estimated that there was a potential for more intra-PTA trade than already existed. Their conclusion is supported by Lyakurwa (1996) who finds that, in addition to COMESA, there is a significant potential for intraregional trade within SADC and ECOWAS.

[3]A substantial amount of unofficial intraregional trade does occur. Most of this, however, is in response to the failure to harmonize monetary, fiscal, and exchange rate policies.

Table 1. Intraregional Trade as a Percentage of Total Exports of Regional Group

Group	1970	1980	1985	1990	1992
AMU	1.4	0.3	1.0	2.3	3.0
UDEAC	4.9	1.8	1.9	2.4	2.1
ECCAS	2.4	1.6	2.1	2.3	2.1
ECOWAS	2.9	10.1	5.2	8.3	7.8
CEAO	6.6	9.8	8.3	9.9	10.5
Mano River Union	0.2	0.8	0.4	0.3	0.0
Economic Community of the Great Lakes	0.4	0.2	0.8	0.3	0.4
PTA (COMESA)	9.6	12.1	5.6	6.6	6.7
SADC	5.2	5.1	4.8	5.2	4.4

Source: UNCTAD (1993).

Again, very little progress has been made in regional cooperation toward infrastructural development. Robinson (1996) has observed that "despite its 'win-win' characteristics, the level of regional cooperation in infrastructure and natural resources in the past has been disappointingly low." In the area of energy supply, there are very few intraregional supply arrangements, even though the potential for intraregional grid connections exists at nonprohibitive costs (Robinson, 1996). Sarfoh (1993) has indicated that the gross potential hydroelectricity that can be generated by sub-Saharan Africa's large water resources has been estimated at 300 gigawatts, out of which only 4 percent has been exploited. The potential also exists to cooperate in the areas of water and transport, with benefits for all parties involved. The absence of appropriate infrastructure remains one of the biggest obstacles to effective regional cooperation.

The assessment of monetary integration efforts, although mixed, is more favorable than the experience of trade integration. Studies of the Communauté francophone d'Afrique (CFA) franc zone find that the growth performance of its members before 1983 was better than for nonfranc zone countries (for example, Guillaumont, cited in Medhora, 1997). The CFA franc zone countries also experienced less nominal and real exchange rate instability, lower monetary expansion, and lower inflation rates than did the nonfranc zone countries (Medhora, 1997). However, not having the exchange rate as a policy instrument resulted in overvaluation of the CFA franc as inflation crept up in the member countries and the terms of trade began to deteriorate. A devaluation of the CFA franc, that is, a realignment of its rate of exchange with the French franc, occurred in 1994. There was a lot of debate about the size of the exchange rate adjustment, especially because the degree of overvaluation varied among the different countries. The issue of the distribution of gains has also been important in connection with the distribution of seigniorage. Since the late 1980s, seigniorage has been distributed increasingly through subsidized lending, and this has created a bias in favor of the larger members of the union, in particular Côte d'Ivoire (Medhora, 1997).

Characteristics of Integration Arrangements

In general, regional integration arrangements in sub-Saharan Africa have been characterized by a number of peculiar features, not always present in other arrangements elsewhere. These include

- Existence of multiple objectives
- Absence of strong supranational institutions
- Inadequate sanctioning authority
- Nonimplementation of harmonization provisions
- Lack of political commitment
- Unclear perceptions about gains
- Inequalities in the distribution of the gains from integration
- Inadequate compensation mechanisms
- Stringent trade liberalization schemes

Multiple Objectives

The groupings tend to be concerned not only with achieving trade integration, but also harmonization of agricultural, industrial, transportation, energy, fiscal, and monetary policies. Until its transformation, for example, SADC was the only large regional grouping that did not have trade integration as an objective. The multiple objectives are related to the perception that integration would lead to greater self-reliance.

Overlapping Membership

Most countries are members of more than one regional arrangement. Problems arise when the various groupings have conflicting means to achieve sometimes similar objectives. As mentioned above, many of the ECOWAS member states also belong to UEMOA.[4] But UEMOA is

[4]Benin, Burkina Faso, Côte d'Ivoire, Mali, Niger, Senegal, and Togo belong to both UEMOA and ECOWAS.

widely perceived to be a means for countering what was seen by the French to be a growing Nigerian influence in the subregion (McCarthy, 1996). It thus poses a challenge to the cohesion of ECOWAS. In Southern Africa, the membership of the Common Monetary Area (CMA) closely overlaps that of SACU, except for the absence of Botswana from the former. The CMA operates under the Multilateral Monetary Agreement (MMA), which is supported by bilateral arrangements between South Africa and its partners. Thus, within COMESA and SADC, there are forms of integration that are more important to some members.

Poor Private Sector Participation

There is very little involvement of the private sector in the formulation of decisions, protocols, and so forth within most regional groupings. This is the outcome of the statist outlook in many countries and also within the ECA, and it might explain why there is often an unwillingness by the private sector to invest time and resources to participate in trade liberalization programs.

Nonimplementation of Treaty Provisions

A major feature of African integration efforts is that very limited progress has been made in implementing integration policies, in particular harmonizing tariff codes and classifications, and introducing positive integration policies. The harmonization of agricultural, industrial, energy, fiscal, and monetary policies, which has been envisaged in some treaties and the Lagos Plan of Action, has not taken place. For example, the decision by ECOWAS to harmonize agricultural policies and adopt a common position during negotiations of international commodity agreements was disregarded during Word Trade Organization negotiations. This trend can be attributed to the unwillingness of governments to make regional objectives a priority.

Inadequate Compensation Mechanisms

Since most integration arrangements include countries with varying levels of economic development, the emphasis on trade integration means that gains from integration will be unevenly distributed. This requires that equity issues be dealt with effectively at the initial stages of the negotiations. Yet the distribution of the gains is hardly adequately addressed in treaties. The inadequacy of distributive measures arises from a fundamental uncertainty about whether the expected gains from integration will indeed materialize.

Stringent Trade Liberalization Schemes

Attempts to reduce the costs of regional trade liberalization on member countries has resulted in stringent programs of trade liberalization. The rules of origin that limit participation on the basis of value added and ownership of enterprises reduces the potential number of participants in trade liberalization schemes. Even though the domestic manufacturing base is small, the trade liberalization schemes of a number of countries further restrict the proportion of output that can actually be exported to regional markets under the scheme.

Absence of Strong Supranational Institutions

Most operating regional institutions lack the legal backing to implement or enforce treaties and protocols. The ECOWAS secretariat, for example, has few powers to force governments to implement trade liberalization measures. The result is a lack of transparency in the implementation of the treaties. The lack of supranationality allows the progress of the integration process to be captured by vested interests. If private economic agents have a complaint regarding the operation of a protocol or article of agreement, for example, this has to be made to a national government body that probably sanctioned the policy that contravened the treaty.

Inadequate Sanctioning Authority

In the absence of credible supranational institutions, the treaties often do not have effective sanctions against member countries pursuing policies that conflict with the articles of agreement. Even where the penalties are spelled out (as in the case of the revised ECOWAS treaty) the cost of not implementing the treaty may be perceived to be less than the benefits of doing so. This perception by member countries is more likely if most members of the union are not implementing the articles of agreement.

Lack of Political Commitment

Shaw (1990) has observed that "the basic issue confronting regionalism in Africa is . . . compatibility with established political economies and ruling classes. And when these are outward-oriented towards extra-continental integration, intra-continental connections remain undeveloped and unimportant" (p. 133). An example of such a concern is the formation of CEAO at the same time that ECOWAS was being negotiated. Other examples are the evolution of CEAO into UEMOA and the increasing importance of France in the new regional arrangement. Regional leaders will adopt integration approaches that allow them to preserve their national interests completely.

Constraints on Effective Integration

The expected benefits of operating within the protected regional market will not materialize if, despite the formation of the regional integration unit, nontariff barriers to integration remain and the issue of how to distribute the gains and costs of regional integration is not adequately addressed.

Mistry (1996) classifies nontariff barriers into three groups, that is, those that affect trade, production, and investment. Quantitative restriction and inconvertible and separate national currencies are the important nontariff barriers that affect intraregional African trade. Differences in national product and service regulations, protection of domestic labor markets, and the predominance in most domestic markets of parastatals that have purely national objectives constitute the nontariff barriers to production. These barriers affect both member countries and third parties. Exchange controls and underdeveloped financial markets act as a constraint on cross-border investment. Nontransparent forms of discrimination against nonmember countries, such as rules of origin, not only discourage foreign investment but can also adversely influence local firms' decisions concerning the sourcing of inputs.

In general, for most integration arrangements in Africa, the constraints on intraregional trade include inconvertibility of member currencies; lack of adequate and cheap transport and communication links between partner countries; differences in national product or service regulations and standards in transport, health, and safety; difficulties in establishing letters of credit; border controls; and lack of information within partner countries about the existence of potential buyers and sellers in other partner countries. These constraints apply with varying intensity to the different integration units. The members of the UEMOA, for example, are not hampered by problems of currency inconvertibility in their intraregional trade, as is the case for the nonfrancophone members of ECOWAS. The PTA tried to address the issue of currency inconvertibility and the difficulties of undertaking intraregional financial transactions with the establishment of the Trade and Development Bank for Eastern and Southern Africa, the PTA clearing house, and PTA travelers checks.

A study of the variables that determine whether a country will join another in a bilateral arrangement found that political relations, proximity, common borders, openness to trade, and small economic size are all important (Brada and Mendez, 1993). These variables were found to be important in explaining whether agreements will be sustained. Although most African countries conclude regional agreements with their neighbors, they have not always pursued open trade regimes, nor have political relations always been cordial. Countries with good political relations will probably have similar ideals. This makes negotiations and arriving at an agreement easier. There will also be more willingness to cede sovereignty in certain policy areas to a regional body made up of members with which each country has good relations. The political instability in several parts of Africa may be important in explaining the unwillingness to develop strong regional institutions and the lackluster performance of the regional integration units.

Aside from the institutional problems that we have considered at length already, two major issues of concern are the macroeconomic policy variations and the differences in infrastructure development approaches. Mistry (1996) and Robinson (1996) deal comprehensively with these issues.

Economic Reform and Regional Cooperation

Most sub-Saharan African countries involved in regional groupings have suffered from macroeconomic instability in the last two decades and are pursuing some economic reforms. They have undertaken reforms with varying intensities and scope. It is acknowledged that the adoption of the strategies inherent in structural adjustment programs can improve the success chances of current regional cooperation attempts. As mentioned above, unilateral trade liberalization, which forms an important component of the structural adjustment programs, has contributed to improving the incentives for exporting. The growing number of firms with an export potential will increase the domestic lobby for further regional trade liberalization.[5] Second, the unilateral trade liberalization programs have resulted in substan-

[5]In West Africa, the West African Enterprise Network is a coalition of business people within the region who are actively lobbying governments, banks, and multilateral agencies operating in the region. Their objective is to reduce existing barriers and encourage the flow of capital and services in the region. The network is also concerned with providing members with regional market information (it has a bulletin) as well as informing members about changes in national policy that impact on regional flows.

tial tariff reductions so that the adjustment shock accompanying regional trade liberalization may be lower than it otherwise would have been.

Despite this potential, there are a number of reasons why reforms aimed at making African economies more outward-oriented can only achieve this at the expense of regional integration. As seen above, regional communication links tend to be underdeveloped, and the unit costs of shipping and other forms of transportation within Africa tend to be more expensive than links with the industrialized countries. Hence, when tariff rates are reduced and quotas removed as part of reforms, it is nonregional trading partners that are better able to take advantage of the reduced protection barriers than regional partners. Second, regional trade liberalization may not be compatible with the fiscal prudence that SAPs require. Countries may not reduce tariffs on regional imports because of the fear that this may hamper their ability to achieve revenue and budget deficit targets. Mistry (1996) has suggested that the considerable variation in intensity, sequencing, scope, and so forth, of the adjustment programs has a significant negative impact on the outcomes of both the reform process and on the objective of regional cooperation and integration. "It is astonishing, . . . that while SAPs have become a feature in Africa since 1985, and (regional integration arrangements) have been pursued with renewed vigour especially over the last five years, there has been no serious, systematic attempt by any agency or donor to operationalize effectively ways in which integration and adjustment might be interwoven and made mutually reinforcing" (p. 2). Mistry goes on to argue that the possibilities of success of these reform programs will be enhanced if they are implemented within a regional context. It may, however, be difficult to develop regional adjustment programs if there is an ambivalence toward existing regional integration units among member countries.

The lack of coordination of reforms has sometimes led to conflicting outcomes in some areas. In West Africa, Badiane (1997) has observed that trade liberalization yielded far fewer outcomes than expected because macroeconomic policy reforms were not uniformly pursued. One aberration was that while the CFA franc remained overvalued for more than a decade, the 1994 devaluation occurred at the same time that Nigeria was revaluing the naira by a similar margin. Similarly, the Ghanaian cedi was appreciating in real terms as the CFA franc was being devalued. The lack of synergy in these policy developments harms the ability to generate substantial benefits from both trade reforms and macroeconomic reforms. It is argued that well-tuned and synchronized macroeconomic reforms are far more likely to generate net gains than preferential trading arrangements.

Indeed, the way instability in one country may affect conditions in other countries à la Easterly and Levine (1995), is quite well understood in sub-Saharan Africa. Mistry (1996) has documented the way in which SAPs in various countries were affected by unstable situations or destabilizing activities in neighboring countries. He provides clear examples of how Zambia's open capital account is used as a convenient route for illicit transactions with South African entrepreneurs to arrange capital flight from Zambia (as South African–made goods are exchanged for U.S. dollars available on the open market). He also shows that unstable macroeconomic conditions in one country are likely to affect the implementation and performance of SAPs in others, with respect to such aspects of policy as the budget and monetary and fiscal stability, as well as the stability of the external sector. As a consequence, individual countries are unable to expand production in response to reforms and are therefore unable to take advantage of opportunities created by regional integration attempts. The solution would therefore lie in a regionally coordinated reform program that allows small countries to benefit from more stable conditions in larger neighboring economies.

Infrastructure and Integration Arrangements

Despite the obvious cost advantages in sharing resources, many countries, out of nationalistic inclinations, often choose to develop infrastructure for mobilizing resources alone. Robinson (1996) has catalogued many schemes developed by various nations and explains the political and economic rationalizations that lead to the choices that countries have made. He also documents the difficulties that have been experienced in previous attempts to achieve infrastructure development on a cooperative basis in several areas, including the Tazara rail project, Zimbabwean energy project, and River Basin development projects of Central and Western Africa. Obviously, while the political, and sometimes security, rationalizations cannot be discounted, the projects considered show how often they were seen to outweigh all economic advantages that shared facilities are expected to bring in.

Reasons why governments seldom pursue the joint development of infrastructure include the fact that "the benefits of regional cooperation have not always been quantified and have not been fully understood and appreciated by the governments involved" (Robinson, 1996). The framework of analysis, incorporating trade options and implications for future investments, is often beyond the grasp of national governments' institutions. The role of nationalism in subverting cooperation in infrastructure development and resource mobilization is clearly underscored by Robinson (1996). The security situation is also given as an important reason why nations often opt to go it alone. Also to be blamed for the poor occurrence of jointly developed infrastructure projects is the role of donors as they "compete with each other for attention" in African countries. Apart from focusing on individual countries most of the time, and hence encouraging separate developments when they get involved in regional cooperation projects, they are often seen to change the scope of projects beyond the expectation of participating nations and institutions, thus making it difficult for countries to effectively match the resources they put into such projects. Robinson (1996) provides the example of the Niger Basin Authority to support this argument.

Recent Proposals for Integration

A number of countries in East Asia have undergone structural change without being part of formal regional integration arrangements. The adoption of policies that encouraged production in the tradable goods sector was accompanied by an expansion in intraregional trade. Should such a strategy be adopted in Africa? As I have shown, the choice of regional integration rather than global integration was made in sub-Saharan Africa because of the small sizes of the economies and the pessimism about market access in the industrialized countries. In addition, there was the need to develop self-reliant economies and improve the bargaining strength of the African countries. The discussion here suggests that the need for regional integration in Africa still exists and may even be more pressing now as market fragmentation in an increasing part of the world is being eliminated and capital mobility is rising while the problem of market fragmentation in Africa remains. Despite the conclusion of the Uruguay Round of trade talks, concerns about market access still remain because of the persistence of tariff peaks and tariff escalation and the increase in tariff rates in some commodity groups during the tariffication of some nontariff barriers (Ingco, 1996; Safadi and Laird, 1996). Thus even though many African countries have implemented unilateral trade liberalization programs, joint action is required among groups of countries. The pace of growth and development may be too slow without joint action by African countries to meet the aspirations of African people. Given that joint action by way of regionalism is required, what form should it take?

It is not surprising that most of the recent proposals on regional integration emphasize initiatives that seek to deal with particular problems. Thus, proposals for the future direction of African regionalism range from focusing only on project coordination to some broader approaches that require trade and production integration, monetary integration, and the creation of an institutional framework. An important factor in assessing proposals for the future form of regionalism is the extent to which the proposals address the issue of poor implementation that has plagued African regionalism in the past. Future regional arrangements should incorporate measures and mechanisms that adequately deal with the issues of overlapping membership, the unequal distribution of benefits and costs, compensation, and financial and human resource constraints.

While accepting the principle of integration, Foroutan (1993) proposes that the trade integration approach be avoided. Langhammer and Hiemenz (1991) support this view. They do not consider trade and factor integration feasible because of the dissimilarity of African economies and the difficulties of putting in place an effective compensation mechanism (Foroutan, 1993). What is considered to be essential are cooperation, coordination, and harmonization. Like many others, they emphasize the provision of infrastructural facilities, training, and research. The advantage of regional cooperation in infrastructure investment is that all members benefit irrespective of their size and level of economic development, thus avoiding the problem of compensation (Robinson, 1996).

Another proposal for enhanced regional integration in Africa is to enter into a union with the European Union, very much like NAFTA (Fine and Yeo, 1997; Collier and Gunning, 1995). A number of advantages is expected to come from such a union. Collier and Gunning (1995) argue that forming an integration unit with the North would generate all the gains from global liberalization. Also, such a union would enhance the credibility of African trade liberalization and generate the desired investment inflows. This is because integration with the North is perceived to contain effective sanctions against policy and can therefore be seen as an effective "lock-in" arrangement. The possible loss of access to European markets may be an effective means of binding governments to a particular line of action, as the European Union becomes the agency of restraint.

The proposal for North-South integration does not address the issue of distribution of gains. One clearly cannot assume that guaranteed access to EU markets is adequate compensation for the revenue loss accompanying regional trade liberalization. Since the EU is the largest trading partner for most sub-Saharan African countries, duty-free entry of EU goods would definitely have a negative impact on trade revenues, and possible negative implications for total revenues in the short run. This might be remedied with aid to finance compensatory schemes and support regional infrastructural and industrial projects.

Another difficulty with North-South integration at this stage of Africa's development is that it runs counter to the spirit of self-reliance that has influenced considerably the goal of integration. These lie at the bottom of the revised ECOWAS treaty and the Lagos Plan of Action. Evidence of how it will be resisted, particularly by sub-Saharan African regional bureaucrats, is provided by Asante (1996). The problem of self-reliance will not be an intractable one, however, if the formation of such a union increases the ability of sub-Saharan African economies to respond to shocks without external assistance and helps them to diversify their production structures and exports. This is a good reason why a number of regional observers are looking for possible pointers from the UEMOA experience.

Mistry (1996) provides arguments for a broad approach to integration. His proposal is similar in many ways to the design of the AEC, even if less ambitious. He supports the development of regional institutions to support the integration process. He suggests a simultaneous adoption of sectoral investment coordination and cooperation, trade integration, and an appropriate institutional framework. It will be necessary to improve the operation of the public sector bodies responsible for the development and maintenance of infrastructure. Existing regional banks will have to be reoriented to address regional issues if they are not already doing so, and subregional banks may have to be created. A regional policy environment must be created to allow the gradual integration of markets. Rather than have progress on regional integration constrained by the partner least willing to fully implement treaty provisions, Mistry suggests a core group willing to implement a customs union and the existence of "a wider group at the periphery which might constitute itself as a free trade area, and be linked with the former in free trade agreement" (1995, p. 42). This concept of variable geometry has been suggested to address the problem of multiple membership of integration units. Thus, for example, COMESA could coexist with SACU (Maasdorp, cited in McCarthy, 1996). This is quite different from the AEC, which expects that integration for all regional arrangements should occur at the same pace.

Mistry's proposals differ from the practice of current regional agreements, which emphasize trade integration without addressing adequately the infrastructural and institutional framework that is necessary to facilitate the trade integration process. A problem with Mistry's strategy, however, is the constraints on the financial and human capacities of the participating countries. These need not be intractable problems if participating in a regional arrangement can be understood by governments, policymakers, and private agents as a reorientation of the development strategy from a national perspective to a regional one. A regional development strategy may not impose severe constraints on financial resources if it is recognized that a reallocation of budgetary resources is required to avoid replication and therefore waste. Scarce skilled human resources will be more effectively used if they are concentrated in regional institutions rather than in several national ones performing the same function.

Africa's New Priorities for Regional Integration

The latest views on regional integration are derived from what are seen to be today's problems. And, indeed, sub-Saharan Africa's problems are wide-ranging. The continent has suffered from prolonged economic and social crises. In many countries, the state suffers from a loss of credibility, which affects its ability to mobilize resources to counter its mounting problems. Growing debt burdens push governments to support their economies increasingly with aid, in magnitudes that are clearly unsustainable. Indeed, some countries, such as Senegal and Tanzania, have aid levels of more than 20 percent of GDP. It is increasingly becoming evident that the institutions of the small countries will have considerable difficulty dealing with these problems on their own. They need more and more to turn to supranational structures and institutions to provide the state with some credibility and provide additional resources.

Current discussions of regional integration "reflect a general desire to break the confines of the nation-state, and a denial of all that divides the region, including the multiple barriers to the free movement of goods and services, people, and capital among countries, and differences in legal, governmental, and educational structures" (Lavergne, 1997, p. 3). A part of the growing scope of regional integration is derived from the new role of the private sector in various countries after many years of economic reforms and changes in the role of the state. The private sector in all countries wishes to see the removal of all impediments to a greater participation in the economic activities of the entire region, as market sizes continue to shrink within countries. This new initiative calls for stronger or more effective supranational bodies that will share sovereignty with governments to make the latter appear credible in the eyes of the private sector.

While it is obvious that sub-Saharan Africa needs to grow as rapidly as possible, this would require considerable investments from both within the region and outside. Even though enhanced trade is an essential requirement for this growth to occur, making good use of the investments, there are other fundamental economic undertakings that need to be in place for that trade to occur. Granted that all the arguments for economic cooperation hold (for e.g., the smallness of single-country markets), there are good reasons why some form of integration must be in place to harness the resources that individual countries cannot gain access to. The continent's integration needs to go far beyond trade creation. Its immediate task is to attract as much investment as possible and use it efficiently for both production and exchange.

To do this, the regional policy choice for sub-Saharan African countries is not necessarily a choice between one bipolar position and the other; that is, between unilateral, nonpreferential trade liberalization or an all-embracing, pan-African economic union. It is more a question of how competently they can use any institutional framework to attract the required investments and stimulate a rational distribution of these across countries in a credible manner. Their inability to attract investments after trade liberalization and other reforms is partly because the reforms have not been deemed to be credible. Will any kind of lock-in arrangement provide that kind of credibility? Does sub-Saharan Africa need a union with the EU? Can the AEC provide policy credibility? Can individual countries guarantee adequate trade reforms and establish credible industrial development programs? Should the discussion of regional integration move beyond the economic variables? These are all empirical questions requiring more detailed study. It is obvious, however, that while most unilateral trade policy reform attempts continue to lack credibility for the fear of reversals, a pan-African economic union is also sometimes regarded to be far-fetched for some of the reasons given above, and considered unlikely to become the major instrument for attracting the required investments. In the end, the choice will be made not only on rational economic grounds, but influenced considerably by politics and diplomacy.

Noting that sub-Saharan African countries have already expressed a commitment to establishing the AEC, our starting point is that it is unlikely that this attachment to the establishment of a community will diminish any time soon. The most rational thing to do, in that case, is to ensure that the institution does what is necessary to attract the required investments. It is essential that the AEC not be perceived as another regional institution whose existence affects only marginally the economic policies and decisions that various countries and their economic agents make. The priorities I discuss below are issues that must be dealt with immediately.

The immediate tasks that need to be undertaken for sub-Saharan African regional integration to become an effective development strategy include:

- Developing appropriate macroeconomic frameworks to facilitate greater interaction among the resources of countries
- Establishing mechanisms for attracting both private and public capital flows from the rest of the world
- Establishing and publicizing the fact that there are gains to be made from cooperation in investment in infrastructure and market integration, indicating clearly the opportunity costs of not cooperating
- Fashioning an appropriate industrial development policy
- Developing an effective compensatory mechanism to ensure that all countries will receive some of the gains from increased trade
- Developing institutional frameworks for the better management of the region's resources, including human resources
- Rationalizing arrangements to reduce replication of efforts and conflicts; in rationalizing those existing arrangements, it is essential that the rest of the world sees sub-Saharan Africa as speaking with a common voice for a clear purpose to strengthen its position vis-à-vis the other regions.

Macroeconomic Reforms to Facilitate Integration

The discussion of economic reforms earlier suggests that, for such reforms to impact positively on regional trade and other developments, neighboring countries must share similar visions that lead to the introduction of similar or complementary policies, particularly with respect to exchange rates, fiscal policy, and monetary policy. The harmonization of these is probably more crucial than trade reforms in the creation of trade. In the absence of such an approach to reforms, the bad policies of neighboring economies will continue to affect performance in other countries.

There is a growing interest in monetary integration on the continent, even if not very widespread. The literature identifies three types of monetary arrangements that can be chosen (Cobham and Robson, 1997). In the informal exchange rate union, there is current and capital account convertibility among members, separate currencies with fixed parities among members, separate national central banks and intervention in the foreign exchange market, and no reserve pooling. The formal exchange rate arrangements have all the features of the informal arrangements, except that there is reserve pooling and a single agency is responsible for foreign exchange intervention. The full monetary union has a single currency and a single central bank. The CFA franc zone may be described as a full monetary union.

In addition to trade integration, monetary integration will contribute to maximizing intraregional flows because of the common currency. The common currency eliminates the transactions costs that different currencies imply. Monetary integration should also economize on the use of foreign exchange by eliminating the demand for it in intraregional trade. A single currency is expected to promote efficiency and stability. When there are several currencies, the law of one price may not hold, and this will distort resource allocation. Resource allocation in the region will also improve because of the removal of capital controls. Price stability should be encouraged with exchange rate stability. The extent to which this will happen depends on the openness of the economy and the proportion of regional trade in total trade. African economies could benefit from the creation of monetary union. A concern is whether the lack of convergence in macroeconomic indicators in the region may not hinder the ability to create these unions. It may be argued, conversely, that the formation of monetary unions may be necessary for convergence to take place.

There are, however, costs associated with monetary integration. There is the loss of the exchange rate as a policy instrument. Adjustment can only be undertaken using expenditure-reducing measures (and not expenditure-switching measures). This may imply a more severe contraction of economic activities. Some have argued that countries pursuing expansionary policies may not be willing to give up the exchange rate as a policy instrument. The analysis of the effects of devaluations using the monetary approach to the balance of payments suggests, however, that the cost of the loss of the exchange rate as a policy instrument may not be very significant. Second, the effectiveness of the exchange rate in adjustment depends upon how long the real depreciation will last before it is eroded by wage and price increases. The other costs of monetary integration are the loss of the inflation tax and seigniorage and the difficulty in having an autonomous monetary policy. The loss of the inflation tax will impact more on high-inflation countries. The extent to which the costs will outweigh the benefits will depend on the degree of labor mobility in the region.

Integration and Private Capital Flows

Following the observation in the first section above that sub-Saharan Africa remains the last frontier to be conquered in the globalization of financial markets, one analyst has proposed a number of developments that should take place in sub-Saharan African economies for them to be considered as serious players. These include:

- The development of public confidence and informational efficiency
- The promotion of financial market integration through regionalization

- The development of human resources and infrastructure
- The promotion of capital market development through privatization
- The globalization of sub-Saharan African financial markets
- The fostering of financial innovation and the use of informal sector signals
- The design of efficient regulatory systems
- A solution to the negative perceptions on risk in sub-Saharan Africa.

Quite a number of the financial sector reforms that sub-Saharan Africa saw in the last decade were attempts to tackle many of these issues. What still remains untouched by the reforms is the issue of globalization and regionalization of the market and the regulatory issues associated with this. With the 16 stock markets generally considered to be thin, the pooling of resources as well as the harmonization of the securities and investment laws should enhance competition among countries in the region and enhance public confidence in the markets. The likely effect of this will be a considerable growth in cross-listing of securities. There is only very little of that happening now, as in Namibia and Zimbabwe and also in the Ashanti Goldfields of Ghana and Zimbabwe.

The development of a regional stock exchange centered on the exchange in Abidjan is currently under serious consideration by the francophone West African countries. The stock exchange operators of Ghana are also considering ways of cooperating with such a regional exchange. There are also a number of proposals for developing stronger linkages between the Johannesburg exchange and the smaller exchanges of Botswana, Namibia, Swaziland, and Zimbabwe for Southern Africa (Jefferis, Okeahalam, and Matome, 1997). One of the burning issues that must be tackled is how to regulate a regional stock exchange.

In the absence of regional stock exchanges and their regulatory bodies, many financial transactions inevitably have to be handled by central banks and the rest of the banking system. Hence, the integration of financial markets across country borders is seen as the major key to the dilemma (Folkerts-Landau and Van Greuning, 1997). A number of sub-Saharan African countries with more internationally oriented emerging financial markets has become interested in strengthening monetary cooperation and financial market infrastructure. The CFA franc zone allows 13 countries to share a common currency with a common central bank. They are moving steadily toward modernizing bank regulation, liberalizing markets, improving supervision, and using indirect monetary instruments at the regional level. They are continuing to develop regional bond and equity markets, as well as regional pension and insurance regulations.

The argument for integrating financial market infrastructure in sub-Saharan Africa is based on the notion that "prudent cross-border lending and investment can diversify financial institutions' asset risks away from the small number of economic sectors that dominate so many national economies and that are prone to frequent shocks" (Folkerts-Landau and Van Greuning, 1997, p. 1). In Southern Africa, for example, it is argued that the concentration of economic activity in a small number of natural resources (e.g., tobacco in Malawi, cattle and diamonds in Botswana, and copper in Zambia) ensures that banks are often largely exposed to only a few industries and crops. They can diversify their asset portfolios by investing abroad, a step that helps them to reduce their exposure to risk while increasing the volume of inflation-adjusted lending.

A further argument for the regionalization of banking is that the new legislation and regulations from an outside body act as an agency of restraint on national authorities when banking regulations have been harmonized. This allows for coordinated supervision. Further benefits come from the possibility of leveraging country resources to mitigate small country concerns and the possibility of a coordinated response to financial crisis as happened with the problems created by the Meridien Bank failure.[6] Folkerts-Landau and Van Greuning (1997) provide many other reasons why such integration would improve the service delivery and efficiency of financial institutions in sub-Saharan Africa.

The main approach recommended for integration is the institution of a regional supervising authority, which might be either private or public, charged with responsibility for off-site analysis of adherence to prudential rules and regulations on a regional basis. Such off-site supervision, which will entail processing returns and manipulating data, will lead to evaluating and interpreting individual banks' risk management processes as well as their performance. The supervisory authority will need to be well-equipped with appropriate standards and regulations, as well as human capacity to establish its credibility.

[6]Meridien was an international banking group with the umbrella bank based in Luxembourg and its treasury based in the Bahamas. It started operations in a number of African countries in the mid-1980s as countries began reforms. The parent bank in Luxembourg held 75 percent of total shares of the group, while Bahamas often held up to 55 percent of the shares of Meridien in various countries. Meridien became exposed (depositwise) to Bahamas in a significant way. When Bahamas, being the treasury of the group, suffered severe overexposure on its assets, this triggered a chain of financial distress within the group, affecting banks in Ghana, Nigeria, Swaziland, and Zambia.

Cooperation in Infrastructure Development

The potential gains from regional cooperation in infrastructure and natural resource development are reflected in the way they contribute to economic growth. The first channel is the direct cost reductions that can be achieved for both capital and operating costs, via economies of scale. Another channel is the reduced opportunity cost for unserved demand. Robinson (1996) argues that "in situations where, for example, investment is inhibited by lack of access to electricity, water, transport or telecommunications facilities, the opportunity cost associated with unmet demand can be very high" (p. 71). It is also argued that supply can be enhanced through the operation of conjunctive systems. An example of this is the cooperation in the supply of energy between Ghana and Côte d'Ivoire, which allows each country to complement the other's supply in times of shortage. Other gains expected from joint infrastructural development are a positive impact on trade as well as the likely savings when investments are lumpy. Robinson (1996) also expects some dynamic gains to be achieved. "Dynamic gains are also likely to accrue from regional cooperation in infrastructure. In infrastructural systems that operate more efficiently as a result of regional cooperation, technological and managerial skills are acquired by the nationals of the countries involved, and these will spread into other activities in the same sector, or into other sectors, contributing to progressive efficiency gains. Foreign investors participating in regional projects are also more likely to participate in member countries when they have acquired some experience and familiarity with the region" (p. 75). One way in which sub-Saharan Africa can effectively achieve an integrated provision of infrastructure is to negotiate together a change in the composition of aid from the industrial world.

Industrial Development Policy

There is often a tendency, particularly under proposals for general trade liberalization, to let trade policy subsume industrial policy. The response of the industrial sector under any liberalization scheme cannot be taken for granted, since that response is also dependent on other factors aside from trade policy, including macroeconomic conditions. The problems that arise from these must be addressed with an appropriate set of regional industrial policies.

Industrial policy should, however, not be seen as a simple collection of policies for intervening in the functioning of markets, as was the case in the early post-independence period. Industrial policy should be conceived only as a tool for assisting markets to function more efficiently.

This point is made considering the fact that, under reforms, the principles of trade liberalization and "getting prices right" were relied on to ensure that industry and other sectors could produce in an assumedly efficient way, to pave the way for an almost self-operating or automated process of development. Inadequate attention was paid to the second best consideration that trade and market liberalization may not increase efficiency when some markets (such as insurance and credit markets) cannot be made to function perfectly (and in practice this is never possible), either as a consequence of more conventional types of market failure or for reasons related to the cost of transactions and lack of perfect information. Also, little importance was attached to the fact that even if static efficiency gains were realized by moving the economy onto the production possibility frontier, this in no way implied that the frontier would subsequently shift outward in a dynamic way.

Hence, harmonized industrial policies would encompass any set of policies that remove structural and institutional bottlenecks to the development of industry, particularly across national frontiers, without the state's direct involvement. This is when the private sector's role in fashioning integration becomes most desirable.[7] Industrial policies complement the development of suitable infrastructure and ensure that institutions work.

Effective Compensatory Mechanism

As indicated above, a major obstacle to galvanizing the political will to lower import tariffs is the likely loss of revenue. Compensatory schemes that have been established for the purpose of minimizing these problems have had little impact on the issue. McCarthy (1996) has suggested that the issue of compensation and the failure of the compensation mechanism to address those concerns was important in explaining the collapse of the East African Community. For ECOWAS, the Trade Liberalization Scheme Compensation Fund (which was set up in 1990 to compensate member states for losses in revenue arising from the introduction of trade liberalization measures) had little impact in allaying the fears of member states.

But the experience of Ghana, for example, shows that there can be reduced dependence on trade taxes as a source of revenue (without

[7]The absence of active involvement of the private sector in the formulation of decisions, protocols, and so forth on regional integration is largely because most of the regimes at the time the agreements were ratified were statist in outlook. Domestic economic policy did not actively encourage private enterprise at the time.

total revenues declining) within the context of unilateral trade liberalization supported by compensating exchange rate adjustments and tax reform measures that tap the potential tax base more effectively. It may be deduced from this that regional trade liberalization need not result in a decline in total revenues. What is essential, in that case, is to ensure that the overall level of trade protection is reduced so that the revenue losses of countries are minimized following unilateral trade liberalization by members.

Cooperation in International Negotiations

Formation of a regional unit can increase the bargaining strength of the member countries. This requires an ability to adopt a unified regional position on the relevant issues, which is particularly important for negotiating trade and international commodity agreements with third parties. A prerequisite for this, however, is the coordination of national agricultural and industrial policies. It may be possible to obtain more trade concessions en bloc as opposed to individually. In this case, sub-Saharan African countries may be more willing to drop the principle of nonreciprocity in their trade negotiations, since they will be negotiating from a more strengthened position.

A clear test of the willingness of sub-Saharan African countries to jointly negotiate for concessions will be when the Uruguay Round comes up for renegotiation. Sorsa (1997) shows that sub-Saharan Africa did not use the Uruguay Round to support domestic efforts to reform trade policy. They did not seek to place on the table for discussion such pertinent issues as agricultural taxation, whereas the agricultural subsidies of concern to the industrial nations were a major item on the agenda. When the Uruguay Round created opportunities for binding tariffs to newly liberalized rates, most sub-Saharan African countries did not take up the opportunity. The round would have provided them with an opportunity to lock their unilateral trade policy reforms into an international framework, which would have provided the needed credibility for foreign investment by making policy easily predictable and stable. Coordinated negotiation would allow the countries to force on the agenda the issues of relevance to the region.

References

Aryeetey, E., and A.D. Oduro, 1996, "Regional Integration Efforts in Africa: An Overview," in *Regionalism and the Global Economy: The Case of Africa*, ed. by J.J. Teunissen (The Hague: Forum on Debt and Development).

Asante, S.K.B., 1996, "Comment on 'Regional Integration Efforts in Africa: An Overview' by E. Aryeetey and A.D. Oduro," in *Regionalism and the Global Economy: The Case of Africa,* ed. by J.J. Teunissen (The Hague: Forum on Debt and Development).

Badiane, Ousmane, 1997, "National Policies as Impediments to Regional Economic Integration," in *Regional Integration and Cooperation in West Africa: A Multidimensional Perspective,* ed. by Real Lavergne (Asmara: Africa World Press).

Brada, J.C., and J.A. Mendez, 1993, "Political and Economic Factors in Regional Economic Integration," *Kyklos,* Vol. 46, No. 2, pp. 183–201.

Cobham, D., and P. Robson, 1997, "Monetary Integration in the Light of the European Debate," in *Regional Integration and Cooperation in West Africa: A Multidimensional Perspective,* ed. by Real Lavergne (Ottawa: International Development Research Consortium).

Collier, P. and J.W. Gunning, 1995, "Trade Policy and Regional Integration: Implications for the Relations Between Europe and Africa," *The World Economy,* Vol. 18, No. 3, pp. 387–409.

de Melo, J., A. Panagariya, and D. Rodrik, 1992, "The New Regionalism: A Country Perspective," in *New Dimensions in Regional Integration,* ed. by J. de Melo and A. Panagariya (London: Center for Economic Policy Research).

Easterly, W., and R. Levine, 1995, "Africa's Growth Tragedy: A Retrospective," Policy Working Paper 1503 (Washington: World Bank).

Fine, J., and S. Yeo, 1997, "Regional Integration in Sub-Saharan Africa: Dead End or Fresh Start?" in *Regional Integration and Trade Liberalization in Sub-Saharan Africa,* Vol. 1, "Framework, Issues and Methodological Perspectives," ed. by A. Oyejide, I. Elbadawi, and P. Collier (New York: St. Martin's Press).

Folkerts-Landau, Elena, and Hennie Van Greuning, 1997, "The Case for Regional Financial-Market Infrastructure in Africa," Informal Discussion Paper, Africa Region (Washington: World Bank).

Foroutan, F., 1993, "Regional Integration in Sub-Saharan Africa: Past Experience and Future Prospects," in *New Dimensions in Regional Integration,* ed. by J. de Melo and A. Panagariya (London: Center for Economic Policy Research).

———, and L. Pritchett, 1993, "Intra-Sub-Saharan Trade: Is It Too Little?" *Journal of African Economies,* Vol. 2, No. 1, pp. 74–104.

Ingco, M., 1996, "Tariffication in the Uruguay Round: How Much Liberalisation?" *World Economy,* Vol. 19, No. 4, pp. 425–46.

Jebuni, C.D., 1997, "Trade Liberalization and Regional Integration in Africa," in *Regional Integration and Trade Liberalization in Sub-Saharan Africa,* Vol. 1, "Framework, Issues and Methodological Perspectives," ed. by A. Oyejide, I. Elbadawi, and P. Collier (New York: St. Martin's Press).

———, E.O. Ogunkola, and C. Soludo, 1995, "A Review of Regional Integration Experience in Sub-Saharan Africa: A Case Study of the Economic Community of West African States (ECOWAS)," paper presented at the AERC Collaborative Workshop on Regional Integration and Trade Liberalization in Sub-Saharan Africa, Harare, March.

Jefferis, K.R., C.C. Okeahalam, and T.T. Matome, 1997, "International Stock Market Linkages in Southern Africa," paper presented at the AERC Research Workshop, Nairobi, May.

Kasekende, L.A., and N. Ng'eno, 1995, "Regional Integration in Eastern and Southern Africa," paper presented at the AERC Collaborative Workshop on Regional Integration and Trade Liberalization in Sub-Saharan Africa, Harare, March.

Langhammer, R.J., 1992, "The Developing Countries and Regionalism," in *Journal of Common Market Studies*, Vol. 30, No. 2, pp. 211–31.

———, and U. Hiemenz,1991, *Regional Integration among Developing Countries: Survey of Past Performance and Agenda for Future Policy Action*, UNDP–World Bank Trade Expansion Program, Occasional Paper No. 7 (Washington: World Bank).

Lavergne, Real, 1997, *Regional Integration and Cooperation in West Africa: A Multidimensional Perspective* (Asmara: Africa World Press).

Lyakurwa, W.M., 1996, "Trade and Investment Integration in Sub-Saharan Africa," paper prepared for the Seminar on Regional Economic Integration and Global Economic Cooperation: The Case for Africa, organized by Forum on Debt and Development, February, Cape Town.

Mansoor, A., and A. Inotai, 1991, "Integration Efforts in Sub-Saharan Africa: Failures, Results and Prospects: A Suggested Strategy for Achieving Efficient Integration," in *Economic Reform in Sub-Saharan Africa*, ed. by A. Chhibber and S. Fischer (Washington: World Bank).

Markusen, J.R., 1985, "Canadian Gains from Trade in the Presence of Scale Economies and Imperfect Competition," in *Canada–United States Free Trade*, ed. by J. Whalley and R. Hill (Toronto: University of Toronto Press).

McCarthy, C., 1996, "Regional Integration: Part of the Solution or Part of the Problem?" in *Africa Now*, ed. by S. Ellis (London: Heinemann).

Medhora, R., 1997, "Lessons from UMOA," in *Regional Integration and Cooperation in West Africa: A Multidimensional Perspective*, ed. by R. Lavergne (Ottawa: International Development Research Consortium).

Mistry, P.S.,1995, *Regional Integration Arrangements (RIAs) in Economic Development: Panacea or Pitfall?* (The Hague: Forum on Debt and Development).

———, 1996, "Regional Dimensions of Structural Adjustment in Southern Africa," in *Regionalism and the Global Economy: The Case of Africa*, ed. by J.J. Teunissen (The Hague: Forum on Debt and Development).

Onitiri, H.M.A., 1997, "Changing Political and Economic Conditions for Regional Integration in Sub-Saharan Africa," in *Regional Integration and Trade*

Liberalization in Sub-Saharan Africa, Vol. 1, "Framework, Issues and Methodological Perspectives," ed. by A. Oyejide, I. Elbadawi, and P. Collier (New York: St. Martin's Press).

Oyejide, A., I. Elbadawi, and P. Collier, eds., 1997, "Introduction and Overview," in *Regional Integration and Trade Liberalization in Sub-Saharan Africa*, Vol.1, "Framework, Issues and Methodological Perspectives" (New York: St. Martin's Press).

Robinson, P., 1996, "Potential Gains from Infrastructural and Natural Resource Investment Coordination in Africa," in *Regionalism and the Global Economy: The Case of Africa*, ed. by J.J. Teunissen (The Hague: Forum on Debt and Development).

Robson, P., 1993, "The New Regionalism and Developing Countries," *Journal of Common Market Studies*, Vol. 31, No. 3, pp. 29–48.

Safadi, R., and S. Laird, 1996, "The Uruguay Round Agreements: Impact on Developing Countries," *World Development*, Vol. 24, No. 7, pp. 1223–42.

Sarfoh, J.A., 1993, "Energy Production and Use as a Strategy for Regional Integration: The Case for Hydro Substitution in West Africa," in *Protection, Cooperation, Integration and Development*, ed. by A.M. El-Agraa (New York: Macmillan).

Shaw, T., 1990, "Regionalism and the African Crisis: Towards a Political Economy of ECOWAS and SADCC," in *West African Regional Co-operation*, ed. by J.E. Okolo and S. Wright (Boulder, Colorado: Westview Press).

Sorsa, P., 1997, "The Uruguay Round and Sub-Saharan Africa's Trade Policies," in *Regional Integration and Trade Liberalization in Sub-Saharan Africa*, Vol. 1, "Framework, Issues and Methodological Perspectives," ed. by A. Oyejide, I. Elbadawi, and P. Collier (New York: St. Martin's Press).

UNCTAD (United Nations Conference on Trade and Development), 1993, *Handbook of International Trade and Development Statistics* (Geneva: United Nations).

Regional Integration Arrangements in Southern Africa: SADC and SACU 16

Trudi Hartzenberg and Gavin Maasdorp

Regional integration in Southern Africa entered a new phase in the 1990s. Developments in regional integration in the European Union and North America, South Africa's democratization, and the conclusion of the Uruguay Round of trade negotiations have all played a role in injecting new vigor into regional integration efforts in Southern Africa.

As is well documented, diversity of size and level of development could pose constraints to integration efforts in the region. The diversity within the region highlights the complementarities and the tensions between regional integration and national economic growth and development priorities.

The multiplicity of arrangements in the region further poses specific challenges. Coexistence of the Southern African Customs Union and the Common Market for Eastern and Southern Africa States is certainly feasible. A symbiosis between the Southern African Development Community and COMESA may be more problematic, however.

This chapter focuses on two Southern African regional integration arrangements, SADC and SACU. It reviews their track records, recent developments within these configurations and future prospects, highlighting a selection of key considerations for regional integration in Southern Africa. These considerations include a focus on the need for institutional capacity development, the lack of comprehensive private sector involvement in the regional integration initiatives and the question of political and economic commitment. The conclusion is that regional integration is likely to proceed haltingly and with difficulty.

The Southern African Development Community

SADC has responded to a number of challenges during the 1990s, and the result has been an expanded regional grouping, including the powerhouse of the region, South Africa. There is also a new focus on trade integration, which was not substantively on the agenda of its precursor, the Southern African Development Co-Ordinating Conference (SADCC).

From Development Coordinating Conference to Development Community

SADCC emerged as a response to the challenges of independence and the impact of apartheid South Africa in the Southern African region. South Africa had attempted to exert its influence in the region mainly through its efforts to establish a Constellation of Southern African States, and subsequently, during the high years of apartheid, through military operations against targets in neighboring countries and other means of destabilizing the region.

The establishment of SADCC in 1980 was an attempt to specifically reduce the dependence of Southern African countries on South Africa; a dependence that effectively dated back to the early days of colonialism in the region. Nine countries were signatories to the SADCC at its inception: Angola, Botswana, Lesotho, Swaziland (the latter three constituting the so-called BLS countries), Malawi, Mozambique, Tanzania, Zambia, and Zimbabwe. This meant that the BLS countries, which formed part of SACU (see below) now formed part of the attempt to reduce dependence on South Africa—somewhat of an anomaly given the operation of SACU.

The founding documents of SADCC focused primarily on the promotion of sectoral cooperation rather than on intraregional trade promotion. The initial emphasis, in the SADCC Programme of Action (SPA), was on transport and communications, since in this sphere marked dependence on South Africa existed. Food security and energy also became key focus areas. Industry and trade followed later under the banner Let Production Push Trade.

In 1985 the project-based approach was adapted to focus more on the coordination of sectoral plans and programs. The aim of this change was to facilitate the prioritization of programs and projects, and to clarify the criteria for the evaluation of progress. Each member state was allocated responsibility for at least one sector. For each sector, a sector coordinating unit was established under an appropriate ministry, to carry out its coordinating responsibility, using its own resources. The year 1987 saw nominal attempts to bring the private sector on board, with the formation of an SADCC Business Council. It remained, however, outside the formal SADCC structures and was not a committed attempt to bring the private sector into the business of regional integration. One annual general meeting was attended by only three countries!

By 1989, it was clear that the number of sectors and the growth of the SPA had outpaced the capacity of SADC to manage and to mobilize resources for the implementation of the SPA. In addition, no clear set of priorities between and within sectors had been established, leading to superficial impact of programs. A moratorium was therefore declared, by the Council of Ministers, in August 1990 on the creation of new sectors, so as to facilitate consolidation of effort within existing sectors. A thorough review of the SPA was also commissioned. This review highlighted a number of key concerns, including: (1) approximately 90 percent of the SPA funding was targeted for external financing by international cooperating partners, with the remaining 10 percent met by member states, which stood to benefit from each particular regional program; (2) by 1989, the SPA included 500 projects, some of which were of doubtful regional importance or feasibility, due to weaknesses in the capacity to process projects on the part of some SADC institutions; and (3) the size of the SPA was unrelated to the resource availability and national development policies and strategies of member states (Chipeta and others, 1997).

Despite the moratorium on the establishment of sectors, and the findings of the SPA review, the areas of cooperation have continued to expand. By 1995, the number of areas of cooperation had expanded from 14 to 18. The reliance on external funding for the implementation of the SPA continues, and so far the SPA has not taken into account the shift in emphasis from coordination of discrete projects to regional integration.

The early 1990s brought the realization that the demise of apartheid was approaching, and that this would bring a new dimension to regional integration in Southern Africa. For SACU, this meant that operation "at arm's length from South Africa" by the BLNS[1] countries would be replaced by closer, more interactive ties. A Customs Union Task Team (CUTT) was appointed in late 1994 to investigate the operation of SACU and recommend changes to the agreement.

For SADCC, the pending democratization of South Africa necessitated a reorientation of its objectives and focus. The outcome was the Treaty of Windhoek of August 1992, which led to the transformation of SADCC into the Southern African Development Community. SADC more closely resembles the PTA, precursor of the Common Market for Eastern and Southern Africa. At the August meeting, a theme document proposing moves away from project cooperation to close political cooperation to pave the way for equitable trade integration was also considered. SADC was now directly concerned with trade integration.

[1]Botswana, Lesotho, Namibia, and Swaziland. In discussing the situation before 1990, the acronym BLS is used.

The SADC treaty focused on

- The harmonization of political and socioeconomic policies and plans of member states.
- The encouragement of economic, social, and cultural ties across the region.
- The development of policies aimed at the progressive elimination of obstacles to the free movement of capital and labor, of goods and services, and of people generally among member states.
- The development of human resources.
- The promotion of the development and transfer of technology.
- The improvement of economic management and performance through regional cooperation.
- The promotion of harmonization of international relations of member states.
- The promotion of international understanding and cooperation and support, so as to mobilize the inflow of private and public resources into the region.

At its independence in 1990, Namibia became the tenth SADC member. South Africa joined in August 1994 and, in terms of the SADC mission of functional cooperation and division of responsibility for the selected areas of cooperation among the member states, was accorded the responsibility for the finance and investment portfolio. Mauritius became the twelfth SADC member in 1995. September 1997 saw the admission of the Seychelles, Africa's richest country, and the Democratic Republic of the Congo, the third poorest in Africa. The admission of the latter two increases the market size of SADC to account for approximately 60 percent of sub-Saharan Africa's GDP (*Business Africa,* October 1–15, 1997), but lowers its per capita GDP to $990 (still double that for sub-Saharan Africa as a whole, however). This latest expansion of SADC brings opportunities as well as risks, especially with the Congo's admission. President Kabila's initial reluctance to cooperate with the United Nations in its investigations of alleged ethnic cleansing by his troops could cost the country dearly in terms of donor community support, and IMF and World Bank funding. The enormous economic potential of this new member state could therefore be seriously compromised by the associated risks, and these costs could be keenly felt by SADC.

A number of key trends and recent developments have confirmed that the SPA, its policies, and the strategies on which it is based are not adequate or appropriate to address the challenges that now face the region. These include the growing global trend toward the establishment of economic blocs so as to take advantage of economies of scale and integration, the competition for scarce resources from the Eastern European states, and the conclusion of the Uruguay Round of trade negotiations. The transformation of the SPA to more closely fit the SADC vision is therefore urgent. This will involve a shift in funding reliance from the international cooperating partners to member states, placing serious emphasis on employment creation through the SPA, finding clear direction in the prioritization between and within sectors, and attempting to address the imbalances in economic development of the region.

Trade Integration: The SADC Trade Protocol

The SADC Trade Protocol was signed in August 1996 at the Maseru Summit, marking a breakthrough in the process of advancing to a free trade area (FTA). The bickering that preceded the signing of the protocol, concerning in particular access to South Africa's markets, did not bode well for the implementation process. The intention of the protocol is to ensure that firms in all countries within the region can compete on an equal footing to provide for the collective market of 150 million consumers. It is anticipated that regional free trade will increase intra-SADC commercial activity, enhance economic growth prospects, create jobs, and raise the standard of living of SADC citizens (SADC Executive Secretary, Harare Summit on Trade and Investment, 1997). At the same summit, President Mandela of South Africa noted the anticipated benefits of a collective regional power within a "world characterized by fierce competition for limited resources." These optimistic expectations may exceed the realm of possibility of the SADC regional integration configuration, however.

At the time of the signing of the Trade Protocol, which provides for the gradual liberalization of intraregional trade, 10 of its members (excluding only Botswana and South Africa) had already effected 70 percent tariff reductions under the COMESA Trade Liberalization Program. The overlap in membership of the various arrangements in the region could hamper implementation of the SADC Trade Protocol.

Trade integration, as envisaged in terms of the SADC Trade Protocol, has the following objectives (as stated in SADC, 1996, Article 2):

- To liberalize intraregional trade in goods and services on the basis of fair, mutually equitable and beneficial trade arrangements, complemented by protocols in other areas.
- To ensure efficient production within SADC, reflecting the comparative and dynamic advantage of its members.
- To contribute toward the improvement of the climate for domestic cross-border investment.

- To enhance the economic development, diversification, and industrialization of the region.
- To establish an FTA among the SADC member states.

In pursuit of these objectives, the Protocol provides for the elimination of barriers to intra-SADC trade. More specifically, import and export duties are to be eliminated, and NTBs are to be eliminated and no new barriers erected, subject to certain exceptions, which are outlined in Article 9 of the Protocol. These exceptions take account of international agreements, conservation of exhaustible natural resources and the environment, and other factors.

The principles outlined in the Protocol, according to which the phased reduction of trade barriers was to proceed, have been overtaken by a recent brief to Imani Development to prepare a report on tariff reduction schedules and a list of sensitive products. Bargaining over these will begin in 1998, and if the protocol is ratified in 1998, then the FTA could be complete by 2006. The SACU countries are currently preparing a collective position on the tariff reductions.

Since the SADC tariffs will be higher than the COMESA's tariffs until at least 2006, trade between SADC members that are also COMESA members will be conducted under the COMESA arrangement. The SADC Trade Protocol will only effectively cover non-COMESA SADC members, since importers will clearly choose to pay the lower rates of customs duties under the COMESA umbrella.

For products to be accorded SADC preferential treatment, rules of origin have to be complied with. Products will be accepted as of SADC origin, if they satisfy the following: (1) They are consigned directly from a member state to a consignee in another member state. (2) They must meet one of these conditions: are wholly produced goods; are produced in the member states wholly or partially from materials from outside the member states or of undetermined origin by a process of production that reflects a substantial transformation of those material, such that (a) the c.i.f. value of those materials does not exceed 60 percent of the total cost of materials used in its production, or (b) the value added resulting from the production process accounts for at least 35 percent of the ex-factory cost of the goods. (3) There is a change in the tariff heading of the product as a result of the processing from the nonoriginating materials.

Under the Trade Protocol, SADC-member states agree to accord one another MFN treatment, so as to ensure equal preferences. An element of contradiction appears in the inclusion of a provision that allows member states exemption from the obligation to extend preferences of another trading bloc of which they were a member at the time of the signing of the Trade Protocol.

Provisions are included to allow member states not to accord preferential treatment to intra-SADC trade for reasons such as national security, cause of serious injury to a domestic industry that produces similar or directly competitive products, and protection of infant industries (this appears to contradict the elimination of infant industry protection referred to above).

A range of measures complementary to trade liberalization, such as the promotion of cross-border investment, protection of intellectual property rights, competition policy, trade development, and coordination of trade policies, are also embraced in the Protocol. In addition, the implementation of intraregional trade measures, such as trade facilitation, transit trade, standards and technical regulations on trade, and monetary and financial arrangements, are also provided for.

The fact that a limited selection of commodities will be eligible for preferential trade under the Protocol can be expected to limit its impact on intraregional trade expansion. Member states can be expected to offer commodities that do not constitute a significant proportion of their imports or those they know are not produced in the region for preferential treatment under the arrangement.

The removal of NTBs is likely to proceed with difficulty—the calculation of tariff equivalents is much easier in theory than in practice, and negotiations are likely to be complicated. In the SADC case, restrictive import licensing, administrative delays, bureaucratic contortions, stipulations of sources of supply, and prohibitions on importation of certain goods may prove to be serious challenges in this regard. SADC may benefit by taking a leaf from the COMESA arrangement to implement a more practical approach to the reduction of NTBs.

An important consideration is COMESA's intention to erect a common external tariff (CET). The SADC countries that are also COMESA members may not be in a position to extend zero tariff preference to countries that are not COMESA members. Taking account of the fact that one SADC country, South Africa, accounts for the bulk of intra-SADC trade, it can be expected that very little intra-SADC trade will be generated as a result of the Protocol. In addition, the confusion that is likely to ensue from having two parallel arrangements, SADC and COMESA, with significant overlaps in membership, liberalizing intraregional trade may be confounded and confused rather than facilitated. In addition, the Cross-Border Initiative, a fast-track regional integration initiative in the region, that commenced in 1993 and has a membership overlapping with both SADC and COMESA, is forcing member countries to lower tariffs to those of the lowest-tariff members—which under structural adjustment programs have already reached levels as low as 5 percent.

South Africa's decision to join SADC rather than COMESA indicated that COMESA's clear objective of the formation of a common market (effective trade integration), was found less appealing than the less comprehensive objectives of SADC at the time, 1992. South Africa's perspective is that a comprehensive approach to regional development encompassing a regional industrial strategy, including regional infrastructure projects and harmonization of the financial sector and not merely free trade, should be on the SADC agenda. It is important to keep in mind that, while governments contribute to the environment within which business decisions, including location decisions, are made, it does not make those decisions. Undeniably, South Africa as the dominant economy in the region, and given its current privileged international status, is uniquely positioned to make a positive contribution to the international investor image and the competitiveness of the region. A query in this regard is whether it can afford to concentrate on regional issues while domestic challenges to policymakers are growing uncomfortably.

The overlap between SADC and COMESA, and the sensitivities related to South Africa's membership in one and nonmembership in the other, are likely to present problems for integration in the region. Some of these arise from the asymmetric trade patterns in the region. South Africa enjoys a significant trade surplus with the region, and this has been enhanced by democratization—the period 1990–94 recorded a 24 percent increase in the dollar value of South Africa's exports to the region (McCarthy, 1996, p.19).

Prospects for Intraregional Trade Growth in SADC

The nature and patterns of intraregional trade in Southern Africa are quite predictable, presenting a familiar developing-country scenario. The region is heavily dependent on the international market for capital and technology-intensive goods, for which there are, with the minor exception of South Africa, few intraregional substitutes. Primary commodity exports dominate the trade profiles of all countries within SADC, recording an average of 82 percent of total SADC exports. South Africa's exports dwarf the SADC total; for 1993, South Africa accounted for approximately 70 percent of SADC total exports and 62 percent of total imports (SADC Secretariat). Table 1 presents South Africa's trade profile, for 1994, with countries in Southern Africa.

The large trade surplus enjoyed by South Africa with the region can be expected to cause much consternation in the region. Access to South African markets has been the cause of much contention in this con-

Table 1. South Africa's Trade with the Southern African Region, 1994
(Millions of dollars)

Country	Exports from South Africa	Imports to South Africa
Botswana	1,146	157
Lesotho	830	69
Namibia	1,014	425
Swaziland	793	323
Malawi	145	52
Mozambique	396	26
Zambia	326	29
Zimbabwe	693	288

Source: Nedcor Economic Unit, Johannesburg.

nection. More recently, however, South Africa has not been alone in attempting to limit access to its markets. In March 1997, Zambia stopped exports of cement to Zimbabwe after the latter increased the import duty from Z$13 to Z$180 per ton (*SADC Today*, April 1997). These are some of the hitches in the way of free trade in the region.

Despite obstacles, expectations for SADC are running fairly high—its growth in membership being one indicator of this. The admission of South Africa, in particular, to SADC and the signing of the Trade Protocol, in spite of a growing literature to show that small countries have more to gain from multilateral liberalization than from regional integration, raise the need for critical inquiry into the prospects for increasing intraregional trade within SADC.

A key question is whether SADC's attempts to increase intraregional trade will be constrained by the structural characteristics of the region. Recent evidence suggests South Africa may be in a position to benefit disproportionately from regional and specifically trade integration initiatives. Relocation of production activities, for example, South African breweries to Tanzania, clothing and textile producers to Malawi, and the expansion of South African retailers into a range of neighboring countries (including Zambia, Zimbabwe, and Mozambique) are evidence of South Africa's benefits from the process of closer integration within SADC. Evidence of the converse can be found more readily in South Africa's informal sector, in particular retail activities, indicating a clear imbalance in the integration process.

SADC's track record certainly leads to cautious optimism regarding its prospects, especially in terms of generating an increase in intraregional trade. Internal dissent, lack of focus on joint objectives, and lack of institutional capacity to efficiently manage programs and projects, have hampered SADC's achievements, and the achievement of a cohesive strategy on external economic relations. However, it appears that since the transformation from SADCC into SADC, the expectations from countries in the region have improved markedly, as is evidenced by the clamor to join the group.

Integration prospects look bleak when the emerging disputes between South Africa and its neighbors are reflected upon. Perhaps one of the most public was the dispute between Zimbabwe and South Africa that emerged at the September 1997 summit in Malawi. Zimbabwean sources accused President Mandela of being a "bully." The latter had taken over the SADC chair in 1996, and had reportedly attempted to oust President Mugabe as chair of the politics, defense, and security wing. As expected, South Africa denied such allegations. Nevertheless the incident is evidence of a perception that South Africa could become the playground bully. Another dispute concerns the negotiations to modernize and streamline SACU. Its five member states form the "inner-core" of SADC. Negotiations to revise the revenue-sharing formula have been going on for the past three years, and little progress has emerged to date. The four smaller members are demanding a share of the tariff-setting machinery, so as to prevent South Africa's Board of Tariffs and Trade from having too dominant a role (see the discussion below on SACU). The director general of the South African Department of Trade and Industry has indicated that it is unlikely that South Africa would agree to a regional tariff-setting body that could potentially outvote it. He argues that this would only be tenable once the other member countries have tabled "clear industrial policies" (*Business Africa*, October 1–15, 1997, p. 2). Further frustrations over South Africa's behavior are being voiced in connection with "Pretoria sabotaging SACU industry". This is discussed below.

Another important consideration is South Africa's proposed FTA with the EU. Critics claim that South Africa is involved in a number of possibly mutually incompatible sets of trade negotiations, including the SADC Free Trade Protocol, SACU negotiations, providing for accelerated tariff cuts; and bilateral negotiations with members of SADC—the SADC Secretariat has indicated that it would prefer focus on regional rather than bilateral arrangements, such as that between South Africa and Zimbabwe, and South Africa and Zambia.

Given South Africa's dominant position in the region, these disputes are to be expected. South Africa's share of SADC's GDP currently stands at 77 percent (*Business Africa*, October 1–15, 1997). In fact, frustration with South Africa can be expected to escalate as negotiations with the EU gather momentum, and as the 14 SADC states attempt to find common ground as regards the timing and method of regional tariff cuts. Furthermore, the upcoming lack of effective leadership in the region to guide SADC forward, is cause for concern. Slow progress toward free trade, in halting and dispute-ridden negotiations, is a very likely scenario.

The implication, from this and other studies referred to above, is therefore that factors that will encourage development and the growth of the individual economies are more likely to enhance the prospects for intraregional trade growth. Diversification of industrial structures, macroeconomic stability, political stability, and policy credibility may also attract FDI, and to this extent, if SADC can contribute to a more stable political and economic environment, it may lead indirectly to increased intraregional trade flows.

The Southern African Customs Union

This section reviews the performance of the Southern African Customs Union, the oldest in the world, and examines its impact in the region while reflecting on the drawn-out renegotiations of the agreement. Its origins date to 1889; incremental growth thereafter saw a common customs union covering the area of present-day Botswana, Lesotho, Namibia, South Africa, and Swaziland by 1904 and, by 1921. SACU, with the exception of Botswana, is overlaid by the Common Monetary Area (CMA).[2] Since Botswana has a convertible currency closely tied to the rand, and there is a high degree of de facto labor mobility among the countries, SACU and the CMA together provide the Southern African countries with an advanced form of economic integration approaching that of a common market. SADC might be the flavor of the year, but its achievements are still in the future: SACU and the CMA already exist.

[2]There are almost exact parallels in the history of trade and customs integration in the region, although formalization of monetary integration did not occur before 1974 when Lesotho, South Africa, and Swaziland signed the Rand Monetary Area Agreement. Botswana had opted out of the negotiations and instead introduced its own independent currency in 1976. In 1986, the RMA became the CMA, which today is governed by the Multilateral Monetary Agreement of 1992 and separate bilateral agreements between South Africa and each of its partners to vary the precise terms of monetary integration. The three smaller partners each have their own currency, which is at par with the rand, although Namibia and Swaziland are entitled to delink their currencies. Other provisions are that common exchange controls apply; there is free movement of funds between member countries; and Lesotho, Namibia, and Swaziland have access to the South African capital markets.

The 1969 Agreement

The present SACU Agreement was signed in 1969. Before that, the customs union had been governed by an agreement of 1910, which was concerned mainly with the allocation of revenue among the four partners (South Africa and the then High Commission Territories, HCTs, of Basutoland, Bechuanaland, and Swaziland). On the basis of figures for the previous three financial years, the share of customs revenue allocated to the HCTs was fixed at 1.31097 percent and, within this figure, the allocation to each of the territories was also fixed. This arrangement became outdated as the various economies grew at different rates. Thus, from 1965/66, The United Kingdom, as the administering power, changed the allocation among the three territories, with Swaziland gaining at the expense of the others, especially Basutoland.

After the independence of the three territories as Botswana, Lesotho, and Swaziland, a new, more comprehensive agreement was negotiated. It was explicitly aimed at encouraging the development of the BLS group and the diversification of their economies. Moreover, to compensate BLS for what they argued were the disadvantages of being in a customs union with a more-developed country—namely, the trade diversion effects, the polarization of industrial development between core and peripheral areas, and the loss of fiscal sovereignty[3]—Article 14 of the Agreement inserted an enhancement factor into the revenue-sharing formula.

The formula works as follows. All customs, excise, and sales duties (but not general sales tax) as well as import surcharges collected in the five countries are pooled at the South African Reserve Bank. The formula provides the basis for calculating the amount due to each of the BLNS countries. There are three stages in this calculation. First, the basic amount due to each country, let us say Swaziland, in any financial year is given by the equation

$$R = \frac{A + B + C}{D + E + F + G}(H), \tag{1}$$

where R = the amount payable to Swaziland; A = c.i.f. value (including all duties) at border of imports into Swaziland from all sources; B = value of excisable and sales duty goods produced and consumed in Swaziland; C = excise and sales duties paid on B; D = c.i.f. value at bor-

[3]South Africa's Board of Tariffs and Trade sets import tariffs, excise duties, and surcharges, ostensibly in consultation with BLNS but in practice calling the tune.

der of imports into the common customs area from the rest of the world; E = customs and sales duties paid on D; F = value of excisable and sales duty goods produced and consumed in the customs union; G = excise and sales duties paid on F; and H = total revenue pool of customs, excise, and sales duties.

The formula thus seeks to divide the common revenue pool among the partners in proportion to their annual imports and their production and consumption of dutiable goods, but, as mentioned above, an enhancement factor was added, so that the formula may be rewritten as

$$R_c = \frac{A + B + C}{D + E + F + G} (H)\ (1.42), \qquad (2)$$

where 1.42 = enhancement factor.

The enhanced rate of revenue received by Swaziland is then

$$\frac{R_c}{A + B + C},$$

In 1976, the formula was amended to provide BLS with a stabilized rate of revenue of about 20 percent. This may be written as

$$R_s = \frac{R_c}{A + B + C}, \qquad (3)$$

subject to the constraints

$$0.23 \geq \frac{R_c}{A + B + C} \geq 0.17\ .$$

First, the amount due to Swaziland is calculated as in equation (2). Then, if the enhanced rate of revenue

$$\frac{R_c}{A + B + C} \neq 0.20,$$

half of the difference between the enhanced rate and 20 percent is either added to or subtracted from 20 percent subject to the constraints that the stabilized rate may not be less than 17 percent or greater than 23 percent.

The reason for the introduction of the stabilization factor was that, in 1969, BLS had wanted a rate of revenue of 20 percent—the average in African Commonwealth countries. However, the rate was fluctuating widely from year to year, and this made revenue forecasting and economic planning difficult. Thus, they negotiated for an amendment that would guarantee them a rate of revenue of 17–23 percent fluctuating around a mean of 20 percent.

There are five pertinent issues concerning revenue sharing. First, the formula includes BLNS imports from South Africa, but not vice versa. The inclusion of South Africa's imports from BLNS would increase the denominator, albeit by a relatively small amount, and thus reduce the share payable to BLNS. Walters (1989) points out, however, that the cost to South Africa of maintaining customs posts at BLNS borders to record imports might well be more than the revenue it could earn from the inclusion of those imports. Nonetheless, because the great majority of BLNS imports are from South Africa and hence are duty free, they contribute very little to the common revenue pool by way of duties collected.

Second, by including excise duties and sales tax, the formula takes the agreement beyond that of a pure customs union and some way along the path of fiscal harmonization, which is a characteristic of an economic union.

Third, if one accepts 20 percent as a target rate of revenue on the part of BLNS, there is a case for increasing the stabilization factor range given the tendency for the rate to approximate only 17 percent. But, as Walters (1989) points out, if 20 percent is an acceptable target, why then not simply fix R_s at 20 percent rather than retain the constraints in equation (3) above? It is noteworthy that the effect of the stabilization factor is that, in recent years, the nominal multiplier has exceeded 1.42, standing at 1.94 in 1991/92. However, Leith's (1993) calculations show that Botswana could gain slightly, on a static basis only (ignoring transitional and long-term dynamic effects), from having its own independent tariff regime. It may well be that iso-price tariff calculations of what some of the other smaller countries could raise on their own by applying the SACU common external tariff would also show that the effective enhancement was much lower than the nominal figure of 94 percent.

Fourth, the actual payments made to BLNS out of the common pool in any one year do not equal the accrued revenue, that is, the revenue calculated by the stabilization factor. The reason for this is that relevant statistics are not available to enable their accrued revenue to be calculated immediately; instead, there is an elaborate formula for making payments in respect of any particular year during a two-year period in three installments. A common argument in the literature is that, because the cash flow always lags behind the accruals, this may be regarded as an interest-free loan to South Africa, which has the use of the funds in the meantime. Moreover, the shortfall declines in real value because of inflation. Walters (1989), however, argues that because estimation errors are corrected each year, cash flow will only lag behind accruals if estimation errors are increasing. He interprets the payments formula as a forecasting one based on the assumption that the absolute growth in accrued revenue during any two-year period is constant. Cash flow will then lag only if absolute growth of accrued revenue is increasing, causing the equation to forecast too low a value for accruals. Thus, the alleged two-year lag is a misnomer for a poor forecasting method that consistently underestimates future accrued revenue.

Fifth, there has been an overall downward trend in South Africa's share of the common revenue pool (Table 2). The main reason for this is that the BLNS economies are highly open with a high propensity to import and, with average rates of economic growth exceeding that of South Africa, the numerator in the formula has grown more rapidly than the denominator.

Development Objectives

It is important that all member countries share in the benefits of economic growth and development. A review of comparative performances of the economies since the signing of the 1969 Agreement shows that BLS have enjoyed far higher average annual real growth rates than South Africa. It is clearly impossible to disentangle and to quantify the effects of the various forces that were at work, but South Africa's virtual stagnation is attributable very largely to domestic political volatility from 1976 onward and the effect that this had on investment. For BLS, it is clear that SACU membership did not prevent them from achieving satisfactory rates of real economic growth or from transforming the sectoral composition of their GDP, agriculture's share falling significantly and that of industry rising. In terms of per capita income growth, BLS have improved their position relative to South Africa during the past twenty years. World Bank figures (*World Development Report*, annual) show that Botswana's per capita GNP as a proportion of South Africa's increased from 30.6 to 92.1 percent between 1976 and 1994; during the same period, Lesotho's rose from 12.7 to 23.4 percent, and Swaziland's from 35.1 to 36.2 percent.

During the 1969 negotiations, South Africa agreed to infant industry protection (Article 6) and a pioneer industries-type clause (Article 7) for BLS. If by "development" is meant industrial development, however, then economic integration schemes cannot guarantee that all member countries will attract industry. Textbook advocacy of a planned program of industrial development for such schemes fails in practice, because locational decisions are made not by governments but by firms, and firms cannot be coerced into locating in countries to which they do not want to go. The tendency of industries to polarize in the most developed country would mean, in the case of SACU, that

Table 2. Payments from Common Revenue Pool

Fiscal Year	Pool (Millions of Rand)	To BLS		To Namibia[1]		To South Africa (Percent)
		Millions of Rand	Percent	Millions of Rand	Percent	
1969/70	430.7	16.9	3.9	. . .	. . .	96.1
1970/71	463.9	16.0	3.4	. . .	. . .	96.6
1971/72	640.7	22.7	3.5	. . .	. . .	96.5
1972/73	747.3	29.7	4.0	. . .	. . .	96.0
1973/74	859.1	48.9	5.7	19.6	2.3	92.0
1974/75	864.3	66.3	7.7	22.1	2.6	89.7
1975/76	1,010.9	58.1	5.7	30.1	3.0	91.3
1976/77	1,113.6	51.1	4.6	36.0	3.2	92.2
1977/78	1,447.5	104.9	7.2	46.2	3.2	89.6
1978/79	1,723.6	162.6	9.4	47.6	2.8	87.8
1979/80	2,290.3	228.7	10.0	44.5	1.9	88.1
1980/81	2,246.4	260.1	11.6	41.5	1.8	86.6
1981/82	2,122.6	243.8	11.5	257.8	12.1	76.4
1982/83	2,418.8	314.7	13.0	250.0	10.3	76.7
1983/84	3,167.8	390.8	12.3	250.0	7.9	79.8
1984/85	3,299.8	462.5	14.0	250.0	7.6	78.4
1985/86	3,614.6	472.1	13.1	300.0	8.3	78.6
1986/87	4,118.0	496.9	12.1	350.0	8.5	79.4
1987/88	4,706.6	577.3	12.3	350.0	7.4	80.3
1988/89	6,867.5	719.8	10.5	394.2	5.7	83.8
1989/90	7,675.6	918.0	12.0	447.8	5.8	82.2
1990/91	7,922.2	1,353.7	17.1	657.6	8.3	74.6
1991/92	8,017.0	1,814.2	22.6	735.5	9.2	68.2
1992/93	8,917.9	2,248.7	25.2	751.6	8.4	66.4
1993/94	10,136.5	2,307.5	22.8	765.8	7.6	69.7
1994/95	11,222.1	2,346.4	20.9	902.4	8.0	71.1
1995/96	12,257.8	2,734.4	22.3	1,155.7	9.4	68.3

Sources: McCarthy (1986); *Report of the Auditor General for the Financial Year* (annual); Department of Trade and Industry, Pretoria.

[1]Namibia's first receipts as an official member were for 1990/91. Before that, South Africa used the pool for arbitrary transfers to Namibia (South West Africa).

South Africa would attract the great bulk of new industrial investment. This tendency was exacerbated shortly after the signing of the 1969 Agreement by South Africa's industrial decentralization policy, adopted to further the development of the Bantustans, and later by a more sophisticated Regional Industrial Development Programme (RIDP) from 1982 onward. BLS simply did not have the resources to match the incentives available under the South African program (Maasdorp, 1988). McCarthy (1986) correctly pointed out that the industrial polarization problem in a customs union cannot, in principle, be countered by compensatory revenue transfers.

Unfortunately for BLS, neither these articles nor Article 11 (which allows member countries to prohibit the importation of goods for economic, social, cultural, and other reasons) were sufficient to offset the forces of polarization in the 1970s. Furthermore, BLS did not always make the maximum use of these articles, and some differences of interpretation also occurred (Maasdorp, 1982). Cases in which South Africa was accused of attempting to crush new industrial ventures in BLS by acting ultra vires the agreement in fact related to instances in which proposed industries in BLS would have penetrated the South African market by flouting NTBs applicable there (Maasdorp, 1982). Article 11(5) allowed BLS to import goods from outside the SACU without regard to South Africa's import controls, provided they did not reexport those goods to South Africa and thereby obstruct the attainment of the economic objectives of that import-control legislation. The two controversial cases were a proposed fertilizer factory in Swaziland and motor vehicle assembly plant (Honda) in Lesotho: both were designed primarily to serve the South African market, and represented attempts to penetrate that market by avoiding NTBs imposed by South Africa on its own industries. South Africa therefore invoked Article 11(5), but it could also have used Article 17, which states that if one member sells a product to a partner in such increasing quantities as to threaten producers in the partner country, the two governments should consult and cooperate in finding a mutually acceptable solution.

The best prospects for industrialization in BLS in the 1980s seemed to lie in their attracting as much industry as possible while South Africa was being subjected to disinvestment and sanctions campaigns, and to using the articles in the Agreement, especially those relating to infant and pioneer industries, to the maximum. Indeed, membership in the SACU, and the duty free access to the larger South African market that this guarantees, has always been a major promotional point of BLS in attempting to attract foreign investment in manufacturing.

The extent to which SACU membership per se has helped in this process cannot be quantified, but it was certainly a factor. For example, the decision by Conco in 1986 to disinvest from South Africa and relocate its Coca-Cola concentrate plant to Swaziland was based on the continued ability to service the South African market duty free. This is but one example: there is plenty of anecdotal evidence to suggest that this was a factor in the case of other disinvesting companies. However, a number of other factors contributed to speeding up the growth of the manufacturing sector in BLS during the late 1980s. In particular, all three countries revised their incentives for foreign investment in manufacturing, and this attracted firms from the newly industrialized Asian economies; for example, Swaziland's revised incentives of 1985 attracted four textile-related manufacturing plants from Taiwan Province of China the following year, while in Lesotho the annual growth rate in real value added in manufacturing was 10 percent between 1986 and 1991, principally as a result of FDI in textiles and clothing from the Far East.

Mention has been made above of an abortive attempt in the 1970s to establish a motor vehicle assembly plant in Lesotho. This industry has once again become an issue within SACU. In recent years, a French manufacturer (Peugeot) planned to set up a plant in Namibia to serve the South African market, but South Africa objected. Surprisingly, however, a Swedish truck manufacturer (Volvo) and a Korean car manufacturer (Hyundai) went ahead with assembling in Botswana. The difference between the Hyundai venture and those of Honda and Peugeot are: (1) The local content program of the South African government in respect of the motor vehicle industry has progressed significantly since the 1970s, and is no longer regarded as an import control measure as it was at the time the Honda plant in Lesotho was being planned. Thus Article 11(5) was not a valid mechanism for South Africa to use to stop the Botswana project. (2) The Namibian government requested that excise-duty relief be given for the proposed Peugeot plant, but this was not acceptable to South Africa. By contrast, Botswana saw a loophole in the form of imports under rebate of customs duty in respect of semi-knocked-down (SKD) units. In fact, a number of enterprises in South Africa was making use of the same loophole to assemble vehicles that were not being manufactured in South Africa.

The South African motor industry and trade unions were upset at these developments, and requested the South African government to intervene. The Board of Tariffs and Trade agreed to abolish the rebate, and there were also proposals to raise excise duty on imported vehicles and components not conforming to a definition of completely knocked-down (CKD) units that had been revised in 1993. The South African industry wanted Botswana's imported SKD kits reclassified as completely built-up (CBU) units, which would carry a much higher duty. Botswana complained that this would adversely affect its vehicle assembly. The Board of Tariffs and Trade did not implement its new policy pending resolution at the SACU level. The matter was resolved in July 1995 when South Africa and BLNS agreed that the motor industry should be based on CKD units. A new definition of CKD came into effect in April 1995 and allowed SKD assemblers two years to convert their facilities; later, this was extended until 1999. In terms of the GATT offer, the SACU is moving away from excise duties to customs duties, and will allow rebates to manufacturers and assemblers on the basis of their export/import ratios: a favorable ratio will allow an individual manufacturer to import even CBUs.

Intra-SACU Trade

South Africa has tended to underestimate its benefits from the SACU. Together, BLNS are South Africa's major trading partner. For example, in 1994 exports to BLNS were worth R13,788 mn (more than double that to any other country) while total trade with BLNS was R17,131 mn as against R16,678 mn with Germany, South Africa's largest single trading partner. Moreover, South Africa has a favorable balance of trade with the BLNS, running at about 5.9:1, and they take approximately 25 percent by value of its manufactured exports. South Africa traditionally has been by far the major supplier. These statistics refer to goods "from or through" South Africa; that is, they include goods that were imported through South African commercial channels but that might have had their origin elsewhere. In other words, the figures for South Africa reflect the role of South African producers as well as distributors in supplying the BLNS market. Since 1969, Swaziland has imported at least 90 percent of its requirements from South Africa in all but five years. Lesotho obtains more than 90 percent of its imports from South Africa, while for Namibia the figure is about 90 percent and for Botswana 80 percent. In the absence of a customs union, some of South Africa's exports to BLNS would face severe competition and be lost to suppliers from abroad. The proportion is difficult to estimate because many retail and wholesale firms in BLNS are branches of South African companies and are linked into the buying patterns of their head offices. However, there is no doubt that there are trade-diverting effects in South Africa's favor. Moreover, apart from being a market for goods, there is a substantial flow of services from South Africa to BLNS. Clearly, BLNS purchases contribute substantially to South African company profits and employment attributable to the trade-diverting effects of SACU tariffs, which until the advent of the WTO in 1995 had been set in order to protect South African industry. McFarland (1983) estimated that 300,000 jobs in South Africa were attributable to the SACU, but his methodology might be questioned.

Trade liberalization under the WTO will lead to a reduction of SACU tariffs during the period 1995–99. This will open up the SACU market to competition from overseas suppliers, and it is possible that South Africa might lose some of its hold on BLNS markets. The liberalization of tariffs, therefore, might have the effect not only of reducing the degree of trade diversion in the SACU for BLNS but also of leading to a slightly less skewed balance in their trade with South Africa.

Many BLNS industries predominantly serve the South African market, for example, the range of Swaziland's manufactured exports to South Africa has grown rapidly since the mid-1970s when the industrial diversification of the country started to show in the statistics. This continued in the 1980s, the large increase in exports to South Africa in the second half of that decade being accounted for largely by increases in textiles, miscellaneous manufactured goods, and miscellaneous edible products. Soft-drink concentrate and paper were dominant in these new product ranges. The net result of these developments is that South Africa has become far more important as a destination for Swaziland's exports over the years. Whereas in the early 1970s it took only about 16 percent on average of Swaziland's exports, the figure today is approximately 50 percent. In the case of Lesotho, while the absolute volume of exports to South Africa has grown, the proportion has remained at about 40 percent, Lesotho's growing exports of clothing and textiles being aimed mainly at preferential markets abroad. The exports of Botswana and Namibia are dominated by minerals (especially diamonds) and are sold mainly abroad; nevertheless, South Africa takes 25 percent of Namibia's exports and the major share of Botswana's manufactured exports.

The high level of intra-SACU trade is driven by firms. In a survey in 1992 that covered firms engaged in cross-border trade in BLNS, firms were asked whether or not they had found the various regional groupings to be useful in the course of their business. The CMA (85.4 percent) and SACU (73.3 percent) received the highest rates of approval. The survey did not include South Africa, but organized business in South Africa has generally been very positive toward the Customs Union and, indeed, to some vague notion of deeper integration. The positive experience of BLNS firms in SACU revolved around four points, namely, ease of trade, the lowering of prices, the availability of goods and services, and access to markets. Under ease of trade, answers include: a reduction of import problems (borders/customs problems, documentation, bureaucracy, delays), a simplification of business procedures, ease of contact with suppliers, and good information. The main benefits from the CMA related to issues of mobility, the exchange rate, and convertible currency. Many firms benefited from the free flows of capital and currency; the reduction of exchange control problems (because of the ability to pay in local currency); the reduction of bureaucratic and administrative problems; the absence of delays in payment; and the facilitating of intercompany business activities and transfers of funds. Rand parity was regarded as useful, the exchange rate was favorable for exporters, and foreign exchange fluctuations with neighboring countries were eliminated. The rand was a fully convertible currency and accepted worldwide, and any independent currency would not have had sufficient backing to be stable. The CMA was also good for intraregional tourism.

Cross-Border Investment

If the SACU is to promote higher rates of economic growth in all member countries, this will also imply higher rates of investment. South African firms have been major investors in the smaller countries, and the flow of funds to Lesotho, Namibia, and Swaziland has been facilitated by their membership in the CMA. BLNS have not been left out in South Africa's growing cross-border investments since the political changes of 1990. Indeed, South African firms in banking and finance, retailing and wholesaling, and manufacturing have continued to expand in BLNS, although unfortunately no data are available in respect of these flows.

The Renegotiations

By the end of the 1970s, it was clear that neither South Africa nor BLS were entirely satisfied with the 1969 Agreement, albeit for different reasons. In essence, South Africa and BLS differed in the 1980s as to where the emphasis ought to be placed in the customs union, that is, on revenue or development. According to Walters (1989), the SACU "was to be a tool of integration designed to promote economic development and it was explicitly recognized that this could only be achieved if there were discriminatory measures in favor of BLS." One of these measures was the enhancement factor. Since the new Agreement led to an immediate increase (by a factor of 2.8) in the revenue accruing to BLS, it is not surprising that it was this aspect rather than development that they tended to emphasize.

Whereas South Africa wanted to shift the emphasis to ways and means of encouraging economic development in BLS in line with the preamble, BLS raised a number of problems concerning the formula, proposing that the range for the stabilized rate of revenue be increased to 19–25 percent, and that an econometric method be introduced for calculating cash flows and eliminating the time lag in payments. These proposals were favorably considered by a subcommittee of the Customs Union Commission in 1981–82 but were rejected by Pretoria, which stated that it wished to renegotiate the Agreement as a whole. South Africa then commissioned a study (McCarthy, 1986) to investigate the matter. Thereafter, it advised BLS that it would press for a revised, "clean" formula with no enhancement or stabilization factors; a strategy to counter polarization and to provide for an equitable distribution of economic development in the Customs Union; the establishment of a Council of Ministers and a permanent Secretariat; and ways of improving BLS relations with the then Board of Trade and Industries. BLS contested the main conclusions of the McCarthy report, and it was agreed to establish a study group to investigate the agreement.

With no progress being made in the investigation, BLS took the initiative, and negotiations recommenced in 1990. At that stage the newly independent Namibia joined the SACU as a formal member. South Africa's attitude (in 1991) was that the Customs Union was becoming financially unaffordable, and that it wished to have greater freedom in respect of its industrial development policies. It suggested that the agreement in its present form should continue pending further discussions, but that the terms of reference of the study group should be suspended.

In the following two years, South African government spokesmen from time to time made public comments suggesting that Pretoria wished to dissolve the Customs Union. For example, the minister of finance was reported in the press as having been on the verge of withdrawing South Africa from SACU, being dissuaded from doing so by the Department of Foreign Affairs (*Sunday Times Business Times,* February 7, 1993).

South Africa then suddenly changed its views on SACU, the minister of finance informing his BLNS counterparts in 1993 that SACU was indeed viewed as an important instrument for regional integration. Positive views were also expressed by BLNS, and it was agreed to establish a Joint Technical Group, the first task of which was to deal with the GATT offer. However, with general inaction in government in Pretoria in the runup to the April 1994 elections, other SACU matters took a back seat, and it was only in November that a CUTT was established.

The Current Position

The five SACU countries have been renegotiating the existing Agreement since December 1994. The negotiations have been behind closed doors with very little information being made available to the public, but it is well known that the major issues have been the revenue-sharing formula and the institutional structure of the proposed secretariat together with the control of tariff policy. The new agreement was originally scheduled to be concluded in 1995, but it is now clear that this will not occur before 1998.

The CUTT last met in October 1996, and there has been virtually no movement on the major contentious issues since then. One reason is that the negotiations are being conducted by the South African Department of Trade and Industry which simultaneously has been involved in discussions with the European Union on a free trade agreement and with SADC on a trade protocol for the establishment of a free trade area. More recently, too, the SACU countries together have been negotiating a free trade agreement with Zambia. The labor resources of the DTI are severely stretched, and the SACU negotiations have lagged, presumably because they relate merely to renegotiations of an existing agreement rather than to the establishment of something new. In the meantime, however, South Africa and the BLNS governments have worked closely together on the three trade agreements mentioned above. A bilateral free trade agreement between a customs union partner and a third country is incompatible with customs union membership because of the CET. Thus BLNS felt that they should have been included in the South Africa–EU free trade discussions; this was understood by South Africa, which has consulted with BLNS during the negotiations. Although South Africa has renewed a bilateral trade agreement with Zimbabwe, the five countries agreed to approach the SADC free trade and Zambia free trade negotiations as SACU: the main difficulty in reducing tariffs within SADC is in fact between the SACU and non-SACU countries. However, this cooperation should not mask the fact that there are very real differences between South Africa and the BLNS countries.

The revenue-sharing formula is not one of these differences: although the new formula has not been made public, the South African minister of trade and industry has stated that it would ensure that BLNS revenue was not destabilized. The formula will exclude excise duties,[4] surcharges, and the enhancement and stabilization factors, but will compensate BLNS for the price-raising effects of their total imports. The concept of a residual due to South Africa will disappear. Revenue from SACU has been an important source of central government revenue for BLNS: during the period 1990/91–1995/96, for example, receipts from SACU averaged 17.1 percent of central govern-

[4]This appears to be a retrogressive step. The purpose of excise duties is to raise revenue for a government. Excise duties were included in the formula to reduce the administrative costs that had been incurred under the 1910 agreement, involving rebates on intra-union trade under removal-in-bond procedures. McCarthy (1986) conceded, and both the Margo Commission (South Africa, 1987) and the White Paper (South Africa, 1988) accepted, that practical problems of administering such a system, requiring as it would strict border controls, made it essential to retain excise duties in the formula. This underlines the fact that, if it is the intention to eliminate customs frontiers and documentation in a customs union, a uniform excise tariff is necessary. BLNS will gain some fiscal sovereignty from the new arrangement, but the intensity of integration will be lower.

ment recurrent revenue for Botswana, 50.2 percent for Lesotho, 27.6 percent for Namibia, and 44.8 percent for Swaziland (South Africa's figure is about 13 percent). Under the new formula, BLNS would be responsible for setting and collecting their excise duties, but customs duties would continue to be pooled before being distributed. The net effect will be that BLNS will receive about 60 percent of the new customs duty-only pool; nonetheless, this share, together with the excise duties they raise independently, is expected to result in a decline of customs and excise revenue because of tariff liberalization.[5]

The major issues are those surrounding the institutions to govern the revised Agreement. The idea of a secretariat was that it would also be a supranational tariff-setting institution. However, South Africa has now indicated that it is reluctant to cede such vital decision-making powers to a supranational body as long as there is no agreement on industrial policies. South Africa's problems are principally with Namibia and Botswana.

The problems with Namibia are twofold: first, in textiles and clothing Namibia is apparently not implementing the duty credit rebate scheme correctly, while it is also not applying the agreed-on excise duty on beer. The other countries claim that the excise duty must be levied, but Namibia argues that it is there to protect a South African beer monopoly that wants to expand into Namibia. This issue needs to be resolved to divide the revenue pool among the BLNS countries, and there is no room for flouting the agreed-on formula. Namibia has a point when it argues that the South African monopoly will dump on the Namibian market, and unfortunately the SACU agreement is vulnerable on this score. None of the five countries has the capacity to handle the dumping issue, and this is precisely why a secretariat is needed.

Despite the agreement mentioned above relating to motor vehicles, there remain differences of opinion between South Africa and Botswana in this area. The new plant in Botswana is state of the art, and production will be more efficient than in competitors' South African plants. Botswana argues that the South African policy has been worked out in isolation by individuals favoring a protectionist strategy, but it has not made any counterproposals.

[5]The outcome will depend on the elasticity of substitution between SACU products and imports. On balance, however, in the long run this effect in itself is thought unlikely to be positive, although sufficiently significant positive growth effects from trade liberalization on the SACU economies could generate an expanded common revenue pool.

Another point of dispute—between Swaziland and South Africa on sugar—has occurred mainly at the industry rather than the government level. Swaziland has a comparative advantage in sugar-based manufacturing industries, but the South African industry has complained that it is concerned about the loss of domestic sales to industries that have relocated their processing operations to Swaziland. The Swaziland Sugar Association claims that South African proposals for a protocol limiting such trade violate the free trade provisions of SACU. It now appears, however, that the dispute will be resolved by the conclusion of a special protocol on sugar, which will then also be used in negotiations between SACU and the other SADC countries in respect of the SADC trade protocol.

South Africa's stance has been criticized by other customs union countries, particularly Namibia, but it might stem from a realization that, with Pretoria's hand on the tiller, SACU, unlike all other regional organizations in Africa, has functioned effectively. South Africa is unwilling to lose control of vital mechanisms until clear policies have been agreed upon. In the meantime, it has suggested that the BLNS countries should each have a seat on the Board of Tariffs and Trade, but these countries want a supranational body. Clearly, this is an issue that requires resolution.

There are also apparently some voices in Pretoria that still raise the question as to whether SACU is worthwhile. However, it is essential, for the future of economic integration in Africa, that the SACU Agreement be renegotiated successfully. Failure to do so would send a negative message to the rest of Africa, and especially to SADC and COMESA: the same five countries that had failed to reach an agreement would now be involved in other moves toward trade integration, and the same obstacles would again arise. If South Africa and the BLNS countries are unable to improve the SACU agreement, they are hardly likely to work together more harmoniously under any other institution aiming to become an authentic economic integration arrangement.

Key Considerations for Regional Integration

North-South Versus South-South Arrangements

Collier and Gunning (1993) argue that developing countries have more to gain from North-South than from South-South regional integration arrangements, because the former would bring the benefits of global liberalization and play a role in the enhancement of policy credibility of the South partners. In the Southern African case, South

Africa's concentration on the negotiations for an FTA with the European Union are an attempt at North-South integration. From South Africa's perspective, the question as to whether or to what extent it needs the region is certainly a tough question, particularly in view of the fact that it has bilateral trading arrangements (or is in the process of renegotiating these) with its important trading partners in the region. Hence it is legitimate to examine its effective economic commitment to the region. In addition, the renegotiations of the Lomé Convention, starting in October 1998 may be viewed as more significant to some member states than negotiations in the region.

Trade-Transactions Costs

McCarthy (1996) suggests that infrastructural development should precede regional integration efforts. Mistry (1995) goes further to suggest that a much broader approach to integration is required. Sectoral investment cooperation and development of institutional capacity are included in his list of areas of cooperation. For the Southern African case, as applies to SACU and SADC, the lack of infrastructure (for example, in terms of road and communications networks), bureaucratic delays, customs formalities, and industrial standards contribute to trade-transactions costs. Some of these are noted as NTBs, and in terms of the SADC Trade Protocol these are to be eliminated. However, as noted above, this is a daunting task. Decisions to trade are ultimately not made by governments, but by firms, and these transaction cost calculations will determine whether they focus on the regional market or elsewhere.

Lack of Private Involvement

Firms are the decision makers when it comes to location of industry and the search for new markets. Governments contribute to the creation of the environment within which these decisions are made, and can influence or attempt to guide firm decisions. In this regard, the problem of policy credibility in the region is a key consideration. North-South arrangements would arguably offer less risk for firms because there would be effective sanction (such as withdrawal of market access, for example) in the event of policy reversal.

Although a business council was formed in 1987 by SADCC to bring the private sector into the regional integration process, and Annex V of the SADC Trade Protocol makes provision for the involvement of the business community, there are no explicit provisions to include labor, farmers, commerce, and other social partners in the process. This could prove to be problematic in view of, for example, the response of labor in South Africa to the perceived threats of increased labor mobility and a regional labor market. The involvement of these key partners in the process of regional integration is also important from the perspective of institutional capacity development and the building of a support base for regional integration efforts.

South Africa's role as an investor in the region should not be underestimated. South African firms have responded to the opportunities afforded by flexible labor markets in the neighboring countries, and a more favorable wage-productivity nexus than in the South African economy. The development of manufacturing and retailing activities in countries such as Malawi, Mozambique, Tanzania, Zambia, and Zimbabwe, indicate that the private sector is perceptive to regional opportunities, however these should be supported by a credible policy environment with guarantees against reversals. Ensuring that the private sector has a stake in the regional integration effort could make a positive contribution to the process.

Legal and Political Concerns

Issues of peace and security and political stability in the Southern African region need to be considered. The potential for political instability in Angola and in one of SADC's newest members, the Congo, cannot be ignored. Here the potential impact of political commitment to the region cannot be underestimated. South Africa needs to reflect on its interventions in the region: concerns about the bully on the block do not contribute to a politically stable region! The intricate interplay between political and economic factors should enjoy priority on the regional integration agenda in Southern Africa. An example here relates to the attraction of FDI to the region: the private sector responds to perceived political risk and stability of the policy environment. Recent developments in Zimbabwe (December 1997–January 1998) are adequate evidence in this regard.

Given the provisions for implementation of the Uruguay Round, countries wanting to offer preferential arrangement for some trading partner in services were required to notify a list in 1994. SADC did not do this, so its "view to liberalize their services sector within the Community" may not be easy to achieve. Investment regulation is clearly on the international agenda. SADC and SACU should take note and be prepared.

The legal compatibility of the GATT-WTO agreements, the Lomé Convention, SADC, SACU, COMESA, and the various bilateral agreements in the region needs to be carefully examined to ascertain the impact on the process of implementing of the SADC Trade Protocol and the renegotiated SACU Agreement.

Integration and National Economic Challenges

A number of studies referred to above indicated that regional integration arrangements, in sub-Saharan Africa and also in Southern Africa are not significant determinants of intraregional trade flows; that stimulus to intraregional trade is more likely to come from the development and growth of the national economies and from a reduction of trade transactions costs. The complementarities and tensions between the objectives of regional integration as envisioned by SACU and SADC, and those of domestic economic policy need to be explored. What is, for example, the impact of eliminating subsidies or infant industry protection (assuming that these do not fall under permitted exemptions) as required in terms of the SADC Trade Protocol on the domestic economy.

Another factor in this regard concerns the relative importance attached to regional integration initiatives vis-à- vis domestic economic challenges. As has been pointed out, in the case of South Africa, it is reasonable to expect that the challenges at home are more likely to enjoy the attention of policymakers than regional priorities. And the same can probably be said for a number of other countries battling the effects of structural adjustment.

Institutional Capacity Building

The transformation of SADCC into SADC and the track record of the SPA have highlighted the urgent need for institutional capacity building. SADC institutions require the development of capacity to formulate, coordinate, harmonize, manage, and implement policy. Development of effective coordination and management capability of national structural adjustment program so as to make them responsive to the objectives of economic integration should be pursued by member states.

Conclusion

Regional integration in Southern Africa, with the exception of SACU, does not have an impressive track record. Despite this, SADC is growing, and attempts to invigorate regional integration are being pursued, as the signing of the SADC Trade Protocol indicates. Factors contributing to this optimism include the new role of South Africa in the region, which despite misgivings on certain counts is expected to contribute to the development of the region. In addition, the experience of the European Union and North America has persuaded regional policymakers that the benefits from regional integration extend well beyond static welfare gains, to dynamic benefits that affect the development prospects of national economies.

The fundamental objectives of regional integration in Southern Africa need to be clarified. In this connection, it should be recognized that regional integration in Southern Africa could divert trade from cheaper international sources. This clearly does not enhance the welfare of the region.

Regional industrial development (supported by cooperative infrastructure development) and institutional capacity development to manage the process of regional integration both deserve attention. Regional integration should be seen as a component of a regional development strategy, complemented by coherent national policy initiatives. The conclusion is that, given the track record of Southern Africa and current regional and national challenges, the path of regional integration can be expected to proceed haltingly with disputes among members and diversions, as countries focus on national priorities.

References

Aryeety, E., and A.D. Oduro, 1996, "Regional Integration Efforts in Africa: An Overview," in *Regionalism and the Global Economy: The Case of Africa* (The Hague: FONDAD).

Cassim, R., and T. Hartzenberg, 1997, "Trade-Related Aspects of Regional Integration in Southern Africa: The Case of SADC," work in progress, AERC Thematic Research Programme.

Chipeta, C., Council for Scientific and Industrial Research, and Imani Development, 1997, "Review and Rationalisation of the SADC Programme of Action," report prepared for SADC (Gabarone: Council for Scientific and Industrial Research).

Collier, P., and J. Gunning, 1993, "Linkages between Trade Policy and Regional Integration," paper presented at an AERC conference on Trade Liberalization and Regional Integration, Nairobi, December.

Leith, J.C., 1993, "The Static Welfare Effects of a Small Developing Country's Membership in a Customs Union: Botswana in the Southern African Customs Union," *World Development*, Vol. 20, No. 7, pp. 1021–28.

Maasdorp, G., 1982, "The Southern African Customs Union: An Assessment," *Journal of Contemporary African Studies*, Vol. 2, No. 1.

———, 1988, "The Southern African Customs Union," in *South Africa in Southern Africa: Economic Interaction*, ed. by E. Leistner and P. Esterhuysen (Pretoria: Africa Institute).

McCarthy, C.L., 1986, *The Southern African Customs Union* (Pretoria: Central Economic Advisory Services).

———, 1996, "South African Trade and Industrial Policy in a Regional Context," paper presented at the Arne Ryde Symposium, Lund University, Sweden, August.

McFarland, E.L., 1983, "Benefits to the RSA of Her Exports to the BLS Countries," in *Botswana's Economy Since Independence*, ed. by M.A. Oommen, F.K. Inganju, and L.D. Ngcongco (New Delhi: Tata McGraw-Hill).

Mistry, P.S., 1995, "Regional Integration Arrangements (RIAs) in Economic Development: Panacea or Pitfall," revised version of a paper prepared for a FONDAD Symposium on the Future of Regional Economic Integration, The Hague, September 1994.

Page, S., 1997, "Some Implications of the SADC Trade Protocol," TIPS Working Paper No. 2, Johannesburg, June.

SADC (Southern African Development Community), 1996, "Protocol on Trade in the Southern Africa Development Community" (Gaborone: Southern African Development Community).

South Africa, Republic of, 1987, *Report of the Commission of Inquiry into the Tax Structure of the Republic of South Africa*, RP 34/1987 (Pretoria: Government Printer).

———, 1988, *White Paper on the Report of the Commission of Inquiry into the Tax Structure of the Republic of South Africa (The Margo Report)*, WP C–88 (Pretoria: Government Printer).

Walters, A., 1989, "Renegotiating Dependency: The Case of the Southern African Customs Union," *Journal of Common Market Studies*, Vol. 28, No. 1, pp. 29–52.

Regional Trade Arrangements: The COMESA Experience 17

Louis A. Kasekende and Charles A. Abuka

There is a growing consensus that regionalism in Africa has been a dismal failure. In spite of the numerous attempts at regionalism, the actual record of cooperation in the region has not been salutary. Looked at in terms of success in promoting trade, the evidence reveals that trade-creating efforts have been marginal. This is pointed out in Elbadawi (1994), Fine and Yeo (1994), Kasekende and Ng'eno (1995), Lyakurwa (1996), and Aryeetey (1996). It is clear that the apparent failure of regionalism in Africa can at least in part be attributed to several factors: highly protectionist national trade policies; the fact that most countries are too similar in endowments for such collusive policy to lead to substantial trade creation; the failure to design effective arrangements in cases where benefits are skewed in favor of a few among the cooperating partners; limited infrastructural developments linking cooperating partners; and a lack of commitment to agreed-on policies at the regional level.

In spite of the poor record, there are still calls for countries in the region to use integration as a supranational mechanism to foster national policy credibility and convergence. Integration, it is argued, can be used as a means for pooling risks, resolving conflicts, and minimizing political risks. Work by Kiggundu (1990), Adedeji (1989), the ADB (1993), Ng'eno (1994), and Mistry (1995) continues to make a strong case for integration. In particular, regional integration has been championed as a means of overcoming limits on industrialization in narrow domestic markets and thus as an engine for economic growth. It has also been argued that FDI can more easily be attracted through regionalism. Critical impetus to this view has, in particular, been provided by the Easterly and Levine (1994) study of the causes of economic growth in Africa. They found that a country's growth rate is significantly affected by a neighbor's growth rate. Furthermore, economic growth is enhanced when neighboring countries coordinate their economic policies. These arguments make a convincing case for regionalism as a tool to strengthening growth, but the benefits of policy coordination can only be enjoyed if the cooperating partners implement agreed-on policies.

The objective of this chapter is to place the COMESA experience within the perspective of trade reforms and the various attempts at regional integration. The first section reviews what have been the pertinent issues with regard to regionalism in Africa. It also highlights the developments in the PTA, including the measures so far implemented by its institutions. The second section examines the problems that have hindered effective integration in the COMESA states. The third and last section provides some reflections regarding the future of COMESA.

Issues for Regionalism

The guiding principles for the renewed efforts at regional integration are embodied in the Lagos Plan of Action (LPA) and the Final Act of Lagos of 1980. This originally provided a framework for the regional groupings that could evolve into an African Economic Community by the year 2000. The four subregional blocs were the Economic Community of West African States; the Economic Community of Central African States; the Preferential Trade Area for Eastern and Southern African States; and the Arab Maghreb Union in Northern Africa. The Abuja Treaty of 1991, which recognized the difficulty of establishing a continentwide common market by 2000, extended the formation of an African single market to 2025.

Underlying the thinking of the LPA is the need for large markets if Africa is to support its industrialization process. It was believed that, by setting up large trading blocs, sub-Saharan Africa would attain economies of scale necessary to trigger complementarity in industrial production. In addition, the large trading blocs would make Africa more attractive to FDI (Lyakurwa, 1996) and with it, transfer of technology.

Several regional organizations were set up or have been revitalized primarily to promote regional efforts. These include the Southern African Development Coordination Conference, Intergovernmental Authority on Drought and Development, and Kagera Basin Organisation. The SADCC, which concentrated largely on project coordination, has been transformed into the South African Development Community and now incorporates trade integration; the PTA has been transformed into COMESA; and efforts are also under way to revive the former East African Community (EAC). At the moment, the EAC provides for cooperation for an agreed-on set of areas, but pressure is mounting for widening membership to include Rwanda and to cement the relationship into a common market.

In spite of these numerous attempts at regionalism, the actual record of cooperation in the region has not been encouraging. Measured by success at promoting trade, the evidence reveals that trade-creating efforts have been small or nonexistent (Elbadawi, 1994; Kasekende and Ng'eno, 1995; and Lyakurwa, 1996). As pointed out by Elbadawi, the apparent failure of regionalism in sub-Saharan Africa can at least in part be attributed to highly protectionist national trade policies in the region. Other factors accounting for the poor performance of regionalism are articulated in a number of studies.[1] They include the factors given above in the first paragraph. Faced with overwhelming evidence of failure of regionalism in sub-Saharan Africa, one is tempted to ask whether there is still a firm basis for promoting it.

Optimists still maintain that there is a window of opportunity for countries in the region to use integration as a supranational mechanism to foster national policy credibility. It can also be used as a means for pooling risks, resolving conflicts, minimizing political risks, exploiting complementarities, and developing regionally based links within a reciprocal and mutually beneficial arrangement. Moreover, regional integration can permit access to increased investment from outside the region. This can be triggered by the existence of preferential and stable access to a large market,[2] as well as the increased potential for complementarities in resources and growth of productive capacity. In addition, the associated decline in uncertainty on the macroeconomic policies that countries in the regional arrangement follow can provide the desired lock-in effect for policy credibility. This is important because, as shown in Figures 1 and 2, with the exception of Mauritius the rest of the countries are risky investment areas; they score a credit rating of less than 30 on the institutional investor credit score. For Uganda, the scope for improvement is still significantly large.

There is a growing literature pointing to trade barriers, in whatever form, as having growth-reducing effects. In particular, opening the economy to international trade and finance is cited as the single

[1]These include Elbadawi (1994), Fine and Yeo (1994), Kasekende and Ng'eno (1995), and Mistry (1995).

[2]Work by Mistry (1995), Adedeji (1989), the ADB (1993), Ng'eno (1994), Kiggundu (1990), and Easterly and Levine (1994) continues to provide a strong case for integration. In particular, regional integration has been championed as a means of overcoming limits on industrialization in narrow domestic markets and as an engine for economic growth. It is argued to enhance the negotiating ability of members in international forums. More recently, the dimension of attracting FDI has been added as a possible positive effect arising from integration. Easterly and Levine, in particular, argue that a significant explanation of Africa's poor economic performance may be described as the "contagion effect." This implies that a sufficient critical mass of countries may be what is required to provide the demonstration effect to change the negative contagion effect into a positive one with mutually beneficial effects on the growth and development of neighbors.

Figure 1. Credit Ratings of Selected Sub-Saharan African Countries, September 1996

(Risk rating)

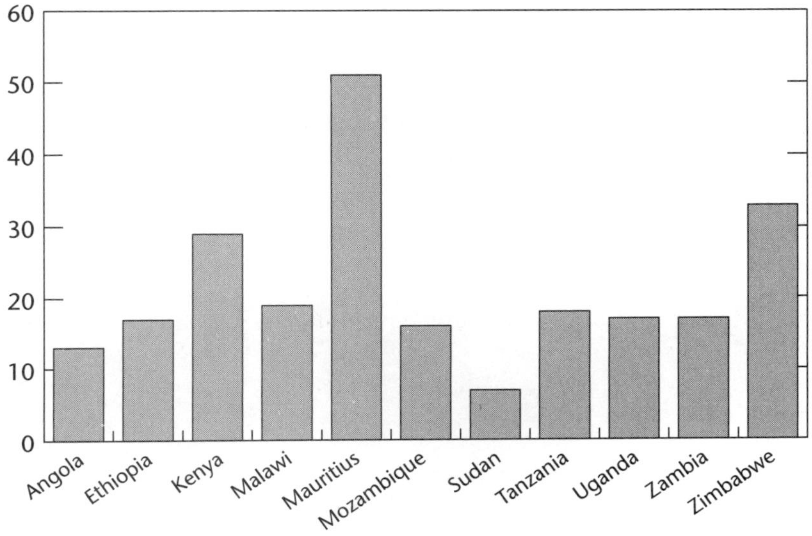

Sources: World Bank (1997); and *Institutional Investor*, various issues.

Note: The rating scale is 1–100, with 1 as the highest risk and 100 as the lowest risk.

biggest spur to growth that a government can provide. It enhances economic efficiency and performance. This view has led governments in sub-Saharan Africa during the past 10 years to change economic policy orientation toward increased openness. As pointed out by Mistry (1995), the pursuit of the twin objective of regionalism and structural adjustment program is neither contradictory nor mutually exclusive. It is, therefore, surprising that efforts to operationalize effective ways in which regionalism and structural adjustment are self-reinforcing are negligible. To the extent that obsession with inward-looking policies at a national level is a constraint on regionalism, liberalization of trade offers a potential opportunity for regionalism. What is required is to design the regional groups to take advantage of the benefits from liberalization.

Of course, the above arguments imply that the new integration initiatives will have to be designed and pursued in an outward-oriented manner, consistent with the achievement of genuine multilateral liberalization. The end result should be to ensure that trade and investment occur easily across national borders. This can allow not only the at-

Figure 2. Uganda's Credit Rating

(Risk rating)

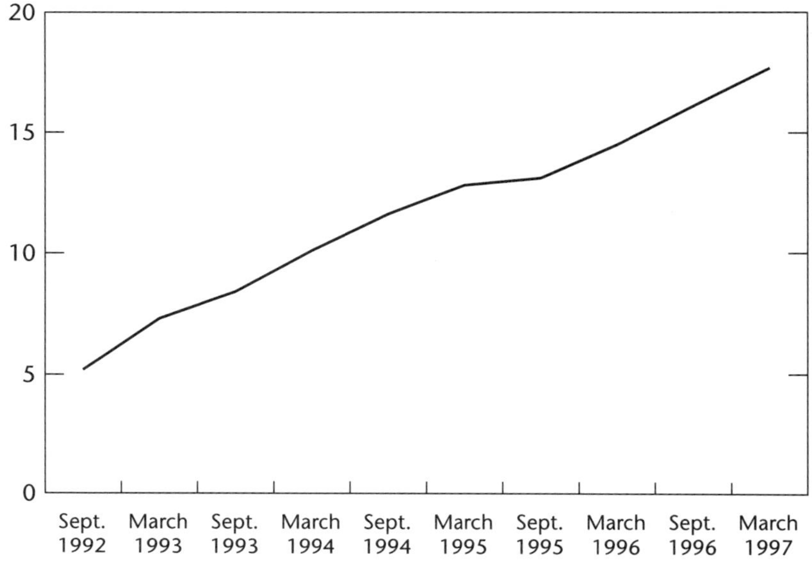

Sources: World Bank (1997); and *Institutional Investor*, various issues.
Note: The rating scale is 1–100, with 1 as the highest risk and 100 as the lowest risk.

tainment of efficiency[3] gains from trade but also reaping economies of scale.[4] What is required is to build up throughout the region the "agencies of restraint." According to Collier and Gunning (1997),[5] these agencies include an independent central bank, the running of cash budgets, effective capital account convertibility, and the design of regional macroeconomic convergence criteria.[6]

[3]Efficiency gains could be captured by enlarging markets and overcoming functional losses in allocative, administrative, and transactions costs associated with small market size, market distortions, and barriers to the movement of productive factors as well as goods and services.

[4]Scale gains would result from large cost savings in major projects realized through regionally coordinated investment in physical, social, and institutional infrastructure.

[5]Collier and Gunning argue further that commitment strategies for investor rights, which include public insurance arrangements, credit syndication arrangements, and liberal investment charters, need to be built up to foster confidence.

[6]The issue of commitment technology is also taken up in Aryeetey and Oduro (1996). Simply put, the building up of credibility through commitment mechanisms is important because investment will only increase if economic agents perceive that the formation of the integration unit will enhance growth prospects regionwide. Investors need to be assured that the macroeconomic environment will remain fairly stable and expropriation of private capital is no longer an issue.

The Preferential Trade Area of Eastern and Southern Africa

In accordance with the LPA, the East and Southern African countries created the Preferential Trade Area in 1982. The objective of the PTA as provided in its treaty is to promote cooperation and development in all fields of economic activity, particularly in trade, industry, transport, communication, agriculture, natural resources, and monetary affairs; with the overall aim of raising the standard of living of its people, of fostering closer relations among its member state; to eventually create a common market that would permit free movement of goods, capital, and labor within the subregion, and contributing to the progress and development of the continent.

The functioning of the PTA was to be reviewed in accordance with the provisions of the treaty with a view to establishing an Economic Community for Eastern and Southern African States. Indeed, in December 1993, a Common Market for Eastern and Southern Africa was formally established as a first step toward this goal. COMESA currently covers most of the countries in Eastern and Southern Africa, with a total population of 258 million people and GDP of $69.8 billion. Its current membership is 23[7] countries: Angola, Burundi, Comoros, Djibouti, Republic of Congo, Ethiopia, Eritrea, Kenya, Lesotho, Madagascar, Malawi, Mauritius, Mozambique, Namibia, Rwanda, Seychelles, Somalia, Sudan, Swaziland, Tanzania, Uganda, Zambia, and Zimbabwe. Three potential members, Botswana, the Democratic Republic of the Congo, and South Africa, are yet to join.

COMESA has immense diversities in terms of economic size, per capita income, level of industrialization, and cultural background (see Tables 1 and 2). Six member countries have a population of less than 2 million while four countries, Ethiopia, Kenya, Sudan, and Tanzania, account for about 60 percent of the population of the region. About 40 percent of the GDP of the region is generated in Ethiopia, Kenya, and Zimbabwe. The income per capita ranges from as low as $100 in Mozambique to as high as $3,380 in Mauritius; only five member states have per capita income over $300. The economies of COMESA remain small relative to most economies in South America. Total GDP of COMESA is less than a quarter of the GDP of Mexico. Figures 3, 4, and 5 show the relative economic size of COMESA, the state of communications infrastructure, and power transmission and distribution losses in selected countries.

In spite of these diversities, emphasis on regional trade expansion continues to be made. The current COMESA economic integration pro-

[7]Some countries have already expressed a desire to pull out of the arrangement.

Table 1. Population and Income Diversity, Preferential Trade Area

Country	Population, 1995 (Millions)	Average Annual Growth Rate of Population, 1980–95	Average Annual Growth Rate of Population, 1992–2010	GDP, 1995 (Millions of dollars)	GNP, 1995 Per Capita (U.S. dollars)
Angola	11	2.9	2.8	3,722	410
Burundi	6	2.8	2.5	1,062	160
Ethiopia	56	2.7	2.8	5,287	100
Kenya	27	3.2	2.2	9,095	280
Lesotho	2	2.5	2.1	1,029	770
Malawi	10	3.1	2.4	1,465	170
Madagascar	14	3.0	2.8	3,198	230
Mauritius	1	1.0	1.0	3,919	3,380
Mozambique	16	1.9	2.4	1,469	1,110
Namibia	2	2.7	2.3	3,033	2,000
Rwanda	6	1.4	3.5	1,128	180
Tanzania	30	3.1	2.6	3,602	120
Uganda	19	2.7	2.6	5,655	240
Zambia	9	3.0	2.1	4,073	400
Zimbabwe	11	3.0	1.6	6,522	540

Source: World Bank (1997a).

Note: Most aggregates for Comoros, Djibouti, Seychelles, Somalia, Sudan, and Swaziland were not reported.

gram places weight on trade liberalization through the removal of tariffs and NTBs as well as the elimination of administrative and institutional barriers to trade flows and transit traffic facilitation.

In spite of the poor indicators shown above, in terms of the resource envelope, Africa, South of the Sahara, produces most of the world's gold, diamonds, platinum, chrome, and manganese. It has 300 billion tons of coal, more than 170 billion cubic meters of natural gas, more than 200 billion metric tons of petroleum, and large quantities of uranium, nickel, copper, and cobalt. The subregion, therefore, has great potential for propelling its economy into sustainable growth.

The Common Market for Eastern and Southern Africa

At its inception, the PTA was planned to be transformed to a common market by the year 2000. In January 1992, the PTA Authority adopted recommendations to transform the PTA into COMESA. The treaty establishing COMESA came into force in December 1994, after it was ratified by the required number of member states.

The COMESA treaty specifies the areas of cooperation as trade liberalization and customs, transport and communication, industry and

Table 2. Economic Indicators, Preferential Trade Area

Country	Average Annual Rate of Change in Consumer Price Index		GDP Growth Rates (Percent)		Gross Domestic Savings as a Percentage of GDP	Merchandise Trade, 1995 (Millions of dollars)	
	1980–90	1990–95	1980–90	1990–95	1993–95	Exports	Imports
Angola	. . .	. . .	3.7	–4.1	35.2	3,508	1,748
Burundi	7.1	10.8	4.4	–2.3	6.7	106	234
Ethiopia	4.0	. . .	2.3	. . .	5.0	423	1,033
Kenya	11.1	27.3	4.2	1.4	5.0	1,878	2,949
Lesotho	13.6	13.0	4.3	7.5	–15.2	143	491
Malawi	16.9	21.9	2.3	0.7	0.3	325	821
Madagascar	16.7	22.0	1.3	0.1	2.7	364	499
Mauritius	6.9	7.3	6.2	4.9	23.4	1,537	1,959
Mozambique	. . .	47.8	–0.2	7.1	4.4	169	784
Namibia	12.6	11.7	1.1	3.8	12.1	1,353	1,196
Rwanda	3.9	13.2	2.3	–12.8	–19.7	45	235
Sudan	37.6	114.3	0.6	6.8	. . .	493	1,275
Tanzania	31.0	27.2	3.8	6.2	–0.2	639	1,619
Uganda	102.4	19.7	3.1	6.6	4.2	461	1,058
Zambia	42.7	112.5	0.8	-0.2	5.0	781	1,258
Zimbabwe	13.8	28.2	3.5	1.0	. . .	1,885	2,241

Source: World Bank (1997a).

energy, monetary policy and finance, agriculture, and economic and social development. The major departure from the PTA treaty is that the countries agreed to adhere to specified fundamental principles, notably those related to recognition, promotion, and protection of human rights; the rule of law; good governance; and economic justice and popular participation in development.

The treaty calls for the establishment of a customs union through the removal of all trade barriers and establishment of a common external tariff and rules of origin. Cooperation in monetary and financial matters, not covered by the PTA treaty, was introduced to allow for macroeconomic policy coordination within COMESA. This is seen as necessary in an environment of free movement of services and capital and a movement toward convertibility of currencies. Cooperation in these areas is also considered as a step toward the establishment of a monetary union. Cooperation in economic and social development is supposed to address the issue of the redistribution of the benefits from integration. This issue was not addressed by the PTA treaty, which stipulated that special programs and projects will be promoted toward the development of the least developed countries in the region.

Figure 3. Relative Sizes of Economies, 1995

(GDP, in millions of dollars)

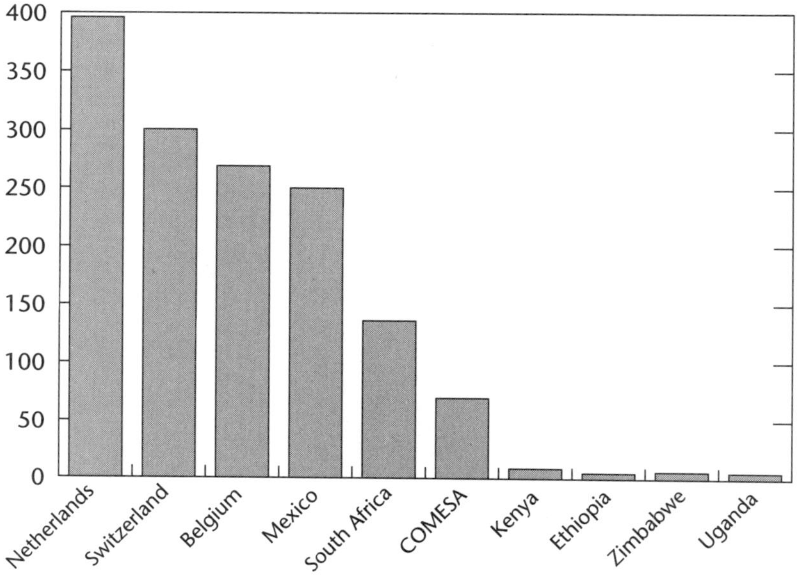

Source: World Bank data.

To facilitate trade, members agreed in January 1993 to the following timetable for tariff elimination: 60 percent by October 1993, 70 percent by October 1994, 80 percent by October 1996, 90 percent by October 1998, and 100 percent by October 2000. This implies that by October 2000 COMESA will have established a free trade area. However, the implementation of the above schedule, as shown in Table 3, has been remarkably slow. To date only 2 of the 20 COMESA member states have reduced tariffs on intra-COMESA trade by the required 80 percent.

The slow implementation of the tariff reduction program has meant that a number of COMESA countries have missed an opportunity to facilitate trade. The loss of this opportunity can be gleaned by examining the standard deviation of tariff rates, which measures the dispersion of rates around their mean value—the argument being that highly dispersed rates are evidence of discriminatory tariffs that may distort production and consumption decisions. Figure 6 shows the dispersion of tariff rates in some COMESA member states between 1990 and 1993.

Figure 4. Efficiency of the Power System, Selected Countries, 1994

(Transmission and distribution losses as percentage of total output)

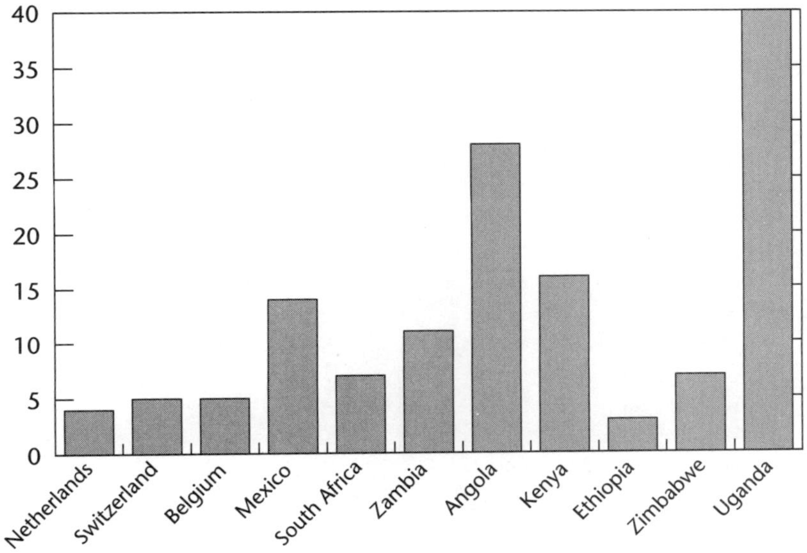

Source: World Bank data.

In parallel with slow movement toward tariff reduction, studies of the potential intra-COMESA trade continue to indicate that, on the basis of the supply and demand patterns, intra-COMESA trade could increase from the current level of \$1.7 billion to about \$4.0 billion annually. Recognizing the slow pace of the COMESA implementation schedule, the COMESA treaty now has two important innovations. The first is the concept of multiple speed or variable geometry, which provides for a group of countries to move faster in regional economic integration process than the slower-moving countries. Second is the imposition of sanctions on those countries that default in implementing agreed-on COMESA programs and settlement of disputes arising from interpretation or in the course of implementation of the treaty (Mwencha, 1997).

Performance of the Institutions

Since its establishment, the PTA has created specialized institutions to help coordinate the development and integration process of its

Figure 5. Coverage of the Telephone System, Selected Countries, 1995

(Telephones per 100 persons)

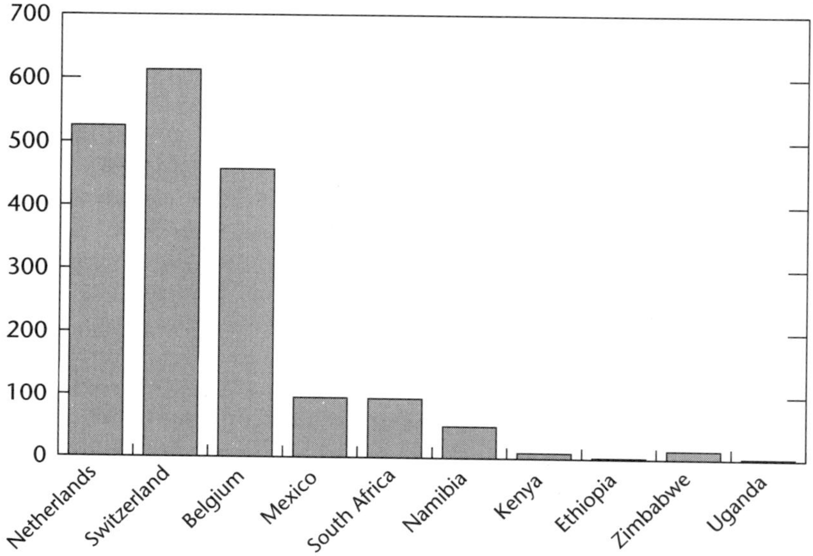

Source: World Bank data.

member states. Its major achievements include the establishment of the Trade and Development Bank for Eastern and Southern Africa (the PTA Bank), the PTA Clearing House, and the PTA Federation of Chambers of Commerce and Industry to enable the private sector to participate effectively in the PTA program for development. To resolve trade disputes, the commercial arbitration center was established in Djibouti, and a PTA tribunal was instituted to settle disputes among member states arising from the interpretation or implementation of the treaty and common decisions.

Success was recorded in the setting up of a well-functioning PTA Clearing House and the PTA Bank. The bank was established in November 1985 as a financial wing of the economic integration arrangement. It is charged with providing financial assistance to promote economic and social development and trade and also to cooperate with other institutions engaged in promoting development of region. To promote intra-PTA trade liberalization and expansion, the member states set up the PTA Clearing House, which began operations in February 1984. The objectives of the Clearing House are, among others: to

Table 3. Tariff Reduction Schedule for Common Market for Eastern and Southern Africa, 1994–97

Country	Implementation Status	Remarks
Comoros and Uganda	Tariffs reduced by 80 percent	
Kenya, Malawi, Mauritius, Zimbabwe, Tanzania, and Eritrea	Tariffs reduced by 70 percent	
Zambia, Burundi, and Rwanda	Tariffs reduced by 60 percent	
Madagascar		In the process of publishing its 80 percent tariff reduction rate
Lesotho, Swaziland, and Namibia	Exempted	These countries have been exempted due to their membership in SACU

promote the use of national currencies in the settlement of all transactions among member states; to establish adequate machinery for the settlement of payments among the member states; to economize on the use of foreign exchange by the member states in their interstate transactions; to encourage the member states to promote and liberalize trade among themselves; and to promote monetary and financial cooperation among the member states and closer relations among banks throughout the PTA subregion.

Other measures introduced to facilitate intra-PTA trade include a road customs transit declaration document, PTA customs bond guarantee scheme, simplification and harmonization of trade documents and procedures, harmonized commodity description and coding system for customs, PTA regional Automated System of Customs Data/EUROTRADE Center, PTA Trade Information Network, and common vehicle insurance through the Yellow Card. Other organs created to facilitate trade were the PTA Federation of Chambers of Commerce, a commercial arbitration center in Djibouti, and the PTA tribunal to settle disputes arising from implementation of obligations.

The method of achieving trade liberalization through the use of the clearing house is the convertibility of all member countries' currencies with one another. This was to be attained through the commitment of the member central banks to discharge their respective foreign currency obligations as notified by the clearing house promptly at the end of the transaction period. Although the clearing house has now been

Figure 6. Tariff Dispersion Rate, 1990–93

(Standard deviation)

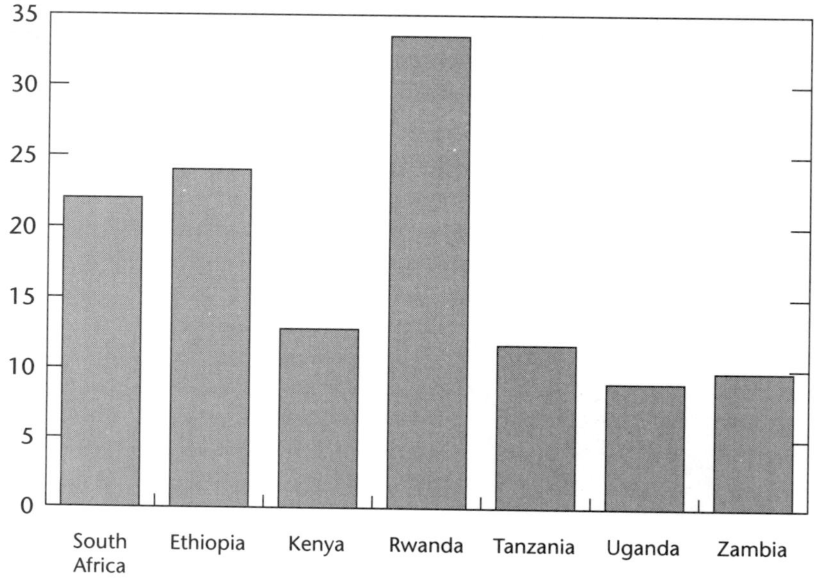

Source: World Bank data.

renamed the COMESA Clearing House, its performance continues to slide. It should be noted that the use of the clearing house witnessed rapid growth up to 1989, when transactions of 441.0 million PTA units of account (UAPTA) were effected. These transactions at the time represented about 56 percent of the total intra-COMESA trade that year. Since then, the use of the clearing house has persistently declined, and only UAPTA 42.90 million was recorded in 1996. The details are shown in Table 4.

Intra-COMESA trade remains sluggish, while COMESA trade[8] with third countries at the moment is estimated to be expanding at an annual rate of 7.2 percent. By and large, the countries in the region are very poor with minimal potential to support large trade flows in differentiated products. The share of intra-PTA trade as a percentage of total PTA trade was about 5.65 percent in 1982, and by 1993 it was 5.51 percent. The problem has been that benefits have tended to be con-

[8]Refer to Mwencha (1997) for a more detailed review.

Table 4. Transactions through the COMESA Clearing House

Year	Value of Transactions (millions of UAPTA[1])	Annual Percentage Change in Volume of Transactions	Percentage Net Settlement Foreign Exchange
1984	74.60		70.00
1985	98.10	31.5	85.70
1986	118.80	21.1	51.70
1987	175.80	48.0	54.80
1988	283.10	61.0	50.10
1989	441.00	55.8	46.90
1990	389.00	–11.8	42.30
1991	348.00	–10.5	33.70
1992	272.40	–21.7	31.10
1993	197.80	–27.4	22.00
1994	136.50	–31.0	24.10
1995	44.90	–67.1	33.00
1996	42.90	–4.4	24.00
1997 (July)	13.60[2]	. . .	. . .
Total	2,636.00		

Source: COMESA Secretariat.

[1]"UAPTA" is the unit of account for PTA transactions.

[2]From May 1997, the unit of account of the Clearing House was changed from UAPTA to the COMESA dollar. The COMESA dollar is equivalent to 1 U.S. dollar.

centrated among countries with developed manufacturing sectors, such as Kenya and Zimbabwe. To promote regional trade, there are currently serious efforts aimed at introducing an export guarantee scheme.

The East African Community

One of the more initially successful (especially during the colonial period) regional groupings in Eastern and Southern Africa was the East African Community (EAC). The three countries making up the EAC, namely Kenya, Tanzania, and Uganda, had achieved significant integration during the colonial period. The treaty for the establishment of the community provided for the removal of all trade barriers, and the community had a common external tariff and excise duty plus common services.

Tensions that had emerged in the preindependence era heightened in the postcolonial period as Kenya opted for a market-oriented approach, while Tanzania and Uganda leaned more toward a socialist system. This was exacerbated by disputes over the distribution of benefits. Kenya, being more industrialized than the other two, derived a higher benefit than Tanzania and Uganda. Efforts to use the East

African Development Bank to promote balanced industrial development failed because the bank focused its financing only on viable projects which largely favored Kenya. The above problems, among others, resulted in Tanzania and Uganda pressing for dissolution. This was followed by the closure of the Kenya-Tanzania border and political tensions between Tanzania and Uganda during the 1970s, which were exacerbated by the internal conflicts in the regional group. The community finally collapsed in 1976. Several lessons emerge from the experience of the regional integration efforts under the EAC, but only a few are mentioned below:[9]

- Disputes over distribution of benefits provide fertile ground for increased preference for economic nationalism and imposition of unilateral import restrictions on intra-regional trade.
- Failure to coordinate policies can be a source of weakness for a regional group.
- Surrender of power to supra-national agencies as was attempted under the EAC can be a source of strength for a regional group if they are effective.
- Political tensions between cooperating partners weaken regional groupings.

More recently, there have been serious efforts toward the revival of East African cooperation. This has come about, in part, with a realization by Kenya that being the bigger of the three economies there are benefits it could derive from a reconstituted and expanded market. In addition, Uganda, which is landlocked, requires the port facilities of both Kenya and Tanzania. As a result, the three countries have now promoted currency convertibility. Furthermore, they have also agreed to joint onsite supervision of banks with branches across borders. At the level of immigration, an East African passport is due to be issued to facilitate travel. With regard to policy coordination, the three countries have agreed to the reading of their budgets on the same day as well as to a coordinated approach to foreign investment. The East African Development Bank is due to be strengthened. However, measures need to be put in place to address issues relating to the distribution of benefits or the design of a special regional assistance vehicle. For future cooperation, Uganda may need to develop its power industry with great market opportunities in the region for distribution in mind, while the exploitation as well as the management of the Lake Victoria environment is an area that appears appealing for regional policy coordination.

[9]Refer to Kasekende and Ng'eno (1995) for a detailed discussion.

Impediments to Economic Cooperation

Lack of Political Commitment

The political rhetoric in support of regionalism has not been matched by political commitment to integration efforts. In January 1992, the authorities adopted recommendations to transform the PTA into COMESA. The treaty only came into force in December 1994, after it had been ratified by the required number of member states. In another but related sequence of events, the OAU council of ministers agreed on the principle of an African Economic Community in 1976 under the Kinshasa declaration. This was reaffirmed by the OAU heads of state in the 1979 Monrovian Strategy for Economic Development. The LPA was passed in 1980, but it took the OAU Secretariat 10 years to complete the draft treaty.

This lack of seriousness is also reflected in the manner in which regional groupings are started. As pointed out above, the PTA authority adopted recommendations to transform the PTA into a common market for Eastern and Southern Africa (COMESA) in 1992. However, at a summit meeting of heads of state of the three countries that had formerly been members of the EAC, it was agreed to reactivate cooperation of the three East African countries. The recommendations of the council of ministers mapping out the form that the cooperation would take was ratified by the heads of state in November 1993. Subsequently, the protocol to establish the secretariat for East African Cooperation was signed in November 1994.

In parallel to these developments, the southern African countries were responding to the changed political environment in the region by transforming SADCC, which had earlier been designed to reduce economic dependence on South Africa, into SADC, with South Africa as a pivotal member. Although the SADC agenda continues to be driven by the sectoral investment coordination and harmonization, trade integration issues are gradually creeping in, and efforts to develop SADC as the primary regional group in Southern Africa are gaining strength. This has put SADC in direct competition with COMESA.

The implementation of agreed-on policy decisions is slow at best. For example, the PTA trade liberalization program started in 1984 was expected to be completed by September 1995. Due to the slow progress toward creating a free trade area, the completion dates were pushed forward. The revised requirement was that, by 1993, all members should have attained tariff reductions of up to 60 percent, but at the time only 6 of the 20 members had published their tariff schedule. One main concern for a number of countries was the fiscal revenue loss in according preferential treatment to members. In a PTA study[10] of the equitable distribution of costs and benefits, it was argued that the potential loss to each country would be minimal due to the low level of intra-PTA trade and that, in any case, countries had the option of imposing other taxes to recoup lost revenue. The recommendation was not adopted.

Recognizing that COMESA's member countries have achieved significant unilateral reduction and rationalization of tariffs under structural adjustment programs, one is tempted to believe a lack of commitment to regionalism. Further, in a number of the countries in the region, coordination of regional efforts is weak. In Uganda, for example, COMESA activities are handled by the Ministry of Trade and Industry, while the Ministry of Foreign Affairs handles activities relating to the EAC. It is not always the case that decisions reached in regional meetings are consistent across regional groups to which a country is associated or the macroeconomic framework.

Fine and Yeo (1994) attribute the high appetite for forming regional groups, despite persistent failure, to the irrelevance of regional integration to most national governments and the lack of political or economic cost in reaffirming solidarity toward ineffective agreements. Kiggundu (1990) expressed disappointment with political leadership: "The question that may correctly be asked is: Are the Africans simply paying lip service to economic cooperation because it is theoretically and politically attractive, or are they really serious? From the resolutions and rhetoric it would appear that continental and sub-regional integration is widely supported. But when it comes to implementation or at moments of crucial decisions, Africa does not seem to be equal to the challenge."

Lack of Necessary Conditions

In the search for constraints on successful regionalism in Africa, authors have pointed out that trade creation is, in part, limited by certain fundamental factors. First, the market size is relatively small to support trade in differentiated products (Kasekende and Ng'eno, 1995). Most countries of Africa are too similar in endowment for collusive trade policy to lead to substantial trade creation.[11] The situation is not helped by the absence of uniformity in regional standards and

[10]This is examined in PTA Secretariat (1989).

[11]See Lyakurwa (1996), for example. It has been pointed out that regionalism is—with the exception of schemes involving South Africa—at best vacuous and at worst trade-diverting.

specifications. Multiple national standards add to production costs, distort production patterns, and discourage cross-border business cooperation.

Second, it has been argued that the regional groups were inappropriately structured because they were designed to pursue an outmoded import-substitution development strategy. As indicated in Lyakurwa (1996), participation in a regional trading arrangement should be compatible with the process of multilateral trade liberalization. This has been further supported by Collier and Gunning (1997). They argue that inward-looking policies damaged prospects for regional integration and restricted growth prospects. Countries in the region were slow to abandon their highly protectionist national policies for regional trade. This was due, in part, to the existence of highly protected, inefficient parastatals, which partly explain the low historical trade flows between countries in the region. The recent shift to increased openness and privatization by countries in the region raises the prospects for improved performance of regional trading arrangements.

Third, trade and investment require a reasonably developed transport infrastructure. The COMESA region covers a very wide area, but it does not have a well-developed transport infrastructure. It is difficult for potential traders and investors to fully exploit the market size.

Fourth, at the inception of the PTA, some of the countries in the region suffered from currency overvaluation. This limited convertibility of the domestic currency on the official market and provided fertile ground for the development of parallel markets. Trade transactions conducted at the official exchange rate had an inherent benefit to the importer and a cost to the exporter.[12] As a result, exports in general contracted due to a loss in competitiveness. Efforts by the PTA and COMESA to design tools to promote trade[13] without addressing the inherent distortions in the exchange rate achieved limited success.

Fifth, the wide differences in level of industrialization and disparities in relative dependence on trade taxes were exploited by some countries for the non- or slow implementation of COMESA decisions. In addition, even the tariff reduction program envisaged in the COMESA area is likely to lead to significant revenue losses for countries heavily dependent on international trade taxes. These include Bu-

[12]See Kasekende and Semogerere (1994) for a detailed discussion.

[13]The clearing house was intended to circumvent the problems of limited foreign exchange reserves and the limited convertibility of currencies.

rundi, Ethiopia, Lesotho, Mauritius, Rwanda, Somalia, and Uganda. Because of the risk of fiscal revenue loss, there have been delays in implementing the tariff reduction program. Additionally, the distribution of benefits from financing of projects by the Eastern and Southern Africa Trade and Development Bank has not yet been managed in a manner that favors countries that are likely to lose most from implementing the tariff reduction programs.

Countries feared that according trade preferences to all members would lead to an asymmetrical distribution of benefits. In particular, the less industrialized countries pointed out that a free trade area would mainly benefit Zimbabwe and Kenya, countries with a stronger industrial base. Efforts by the COMESA Secretariat to convince countries that removal of tariffs represents an income transfer from government to the private sector met with limited success. Matters were not helped by the absence of an effective compensation mechanism.

Lack of Common Interests

A major drawback to regional integration in the COMESA area is that countries with few or no common interests have tried to integrate. Many of the countries have little trade among themselves and indeed have well-established trading links with countries outside the region. For many countries, production structures that were developed during the colonial period have not changed and often do not favor intraregional trade. Regional groups have been established with little regard for the necessary initial conditions for integration, which has not only diverted attention from the wider goal but in many cases has lead to wasteful duplication of activities. The regional group brings together more than 22 countries, ranging from Angola in the south to Eritrea in the north. It groups the relatively more industrialized Kenya, Mauritius, and Zimbabwe (and potentially South Africa) and the least industrialized Djibouti, Ethiopia, Somalia, and Uganda. Moreover, COMESA encompasses about five other regional groups, with some members belonging to the three associations. In addition to the PTA, Tanzania also belongs to SADC and the EAC, and Lesotho, Namibia, and Swaziland are members of SADC and SACU (Lyakurwa and others, 1993). The potential for conflicts of interest exists. It is already evident that arriving at consensus necessary for the implementation of regional integration policies within COMESA is often difficult. Proliferation and duplication of functions give rise, at the regional level, to conflicts over mandates and to divided loyalty among governments. At the governmental level, they impose heavy financial and administrative burdens. The institutions' budgets are invariably too small for the tasks governments assign to them. The contrary view now being raised is that smaller regional bodies are more viable in the short run. It is argued that such smaller but well-functioning units would then form a bigger bloc in the long run. Indeed, some SADC member countries have expressed their desire to break away from COMESA.

The biggest challenge facing regionalism in east and southern Africa is the conflict between COMESA and SADC. A summit of the heads of states held in Lusaka in January 1992 agreed to a merger of COMESA and SADC. The argument was that the merger would make cooperation within the region effective by reducing duplication of activities. The effort was also seen as a means to a faster movement toward an African Economic Community through a single subregional group in eastern and southern Africa. The proposal seemed credible, given that the objectives of the two organizations clearly indicate many cases of duplication.

The proposal for merger has largely met with a cold reception among SADC members. This is in part due to their approach to regionalism. COMESA seems to be heavily preoccupied with the grand plan of promoting the African Economic Community. Conversely, SADC is largely project oriented and tends to attract the involvement of member countries. The benefits of the projects to member states are direct and therefore more noticeable than the more policy oriented programs of the PTA and COMESA. Moreover, the projects are mostly donor funded, and therefore member states do not want to risk funds being diverted. More recently, anchoring by the more powerful and prosperous South Africa has strengthened SADC at the expense of COMESA. As a result, some countries in southern Africa have expressed an interest in pulling out of COMESA, while other potential members have indicated that they will not be taking up membership. The former group includes Lesotho, Mozambique, and Swaziland.

Lack of Regional Dimension in Adjustment

At the time of launching the PTA, countries in the region suffered from numerous distortions in the macroeconomic environment, which were characterized by high inflation rates, wide current account and budget deficits, and tight foreign exchange constraints. It had been hoped, in some circles, that some of these could be adequately addressed through regional integration. For example, the requirement to use foreign exchange in transactions would be eased by setting up the clearing house.

Since the setting up of the PTA, economic thinking has changed; structural adjustment programs are being implemented with renewed vigor in the search for efficiency. Almost all countries in the PTA region are implementing such programs, which among other things require the rationalization and lowering of tariffs by the participating countries (but are not necessarily at a similar speed or uniformly sequenced across countries). The problem facing integration arrangements in Africa is that the present economic reform agenda does not necessarily take into account the regional integration dimension.

The inhibiting factors arise from the failure to coordinate trade liberalization programs across countries. For example, a country may reduce external tariffs faster than its neighbors, and internal pressure (especially by manufacturers producing items subject to competition from imports) causes a policy reversal or slowdown in the process. Another possibility is the use of NTBs by neighbors limiting trade-causing retaliatory restrictions. There is, therefore, a need for enhanced coordination among member countries of a regional group to reinforce commitment to announced trade liberalization policies.

Conflict Between Liberalization and Illiberal Arrangements

There have been conflicts between liberalization of economies and illiberal arrangements in the PTA payments systems. For the majority of PTA member states, currency overvaluation characterized exchange rate management for most of the 1975–85 period, and most practiced administered allocation of foreign exchange with the central banks as the apex institution. The PTA clearing and payments arrangements designed during the 1980s suited an administered system centered on the central banks. The UAPTA checks, for example, were guaranteed by the central banks and could only be converted into local currencies. The intention was to save on the use of foreign currencies in financing trade in the region. Holders of checks could neither use them outside the region nor convert any excess holding of the local currency back into UAPTA checks or into any major currencies. Furthermore, conversion of the checks at highly overvalued official rates implied a tax on the holder, and parallel market operators (who offered better rates) did not trade in the instrument. This made the instrument highly unpopular among the traveling public within the region. The checks also suffered from the lack of wide acceptability within the region. In particular, countries with currencies pegged and/or convertible to hard currencies did not offer full support to the UAPTA checks (for example, members of the rand area).

Similarly, the clearing process was centered on an administrative system running from central banks through commercial banks in financing trade and was also intended to save on the use of foreign exchange in the financing of transactions. It was equivalent to an exporter surrendering export proceeds to the central bank at the official exchange rate and the central bank utilizing the proceeds to finance authorized imports from within the region. Under the administrative allocation of foreign exchange, coupled with the licensing of potential importers, the central bank could conveniently route import documentation through the clearing house to take advantage of the credit arrangements therein.

With the surrender of the responsibility of financing foreign trade and services to commercial banks and bureaus, the guarantee of directing documents through the clearing house was eliminated. Further, the dealers in foreign exchange under liberal systems relied on purchases from the market as opposed to allocations from the central banks. The mechanism for using the clearing house linked to central banks is inconsistent with market-based allocation of foreign exchange. It is therefore no surprise that utilization of the clearing house contracted as member countries liberalized foreign exchange dealing (see Figure 7). The COMESA Secretariat should design new instruments and mechanisms to suit a liberal system of managing foreign exchange markets.

The Future of the Common Market

It is still recognized that regionalism has a future in Africa and that regionalism and liberalization can be jointly implemented. However, as a result of the apparent failure of the existing regional groupings to perform as expected, a number of initiatives as well as ideas have been floated to strengthen regionalism in sub-Saharan Africa. One proposal, put forward by Collier and Gunning (1995), is one for "participatory supranational"[14] agencies of restraint, in which national economic policy will be tied in a reciprocal threat-making arrangement to a northern anchor. Another initiative is the CBI supported by the World Bank, European Union, and African Development Bank, where groups of countries within a regional group progress at different speeds (variable geometry) in implementing decisions. This would provide for flexible institutional frameworks and would be consistent with the Abuja principles. It is also aimed at addressing some of these weak-

[14]The absence of strong supranational regional institutions limits their ability to have the required legal backing to implement or enforce treaties and protocols. More important, the lack of a sanctioning authority implies that treaties do not have effective sanctions against member countries pursuing policies that conflict the articles of agreement.

Figure 7. Clearing House Activity

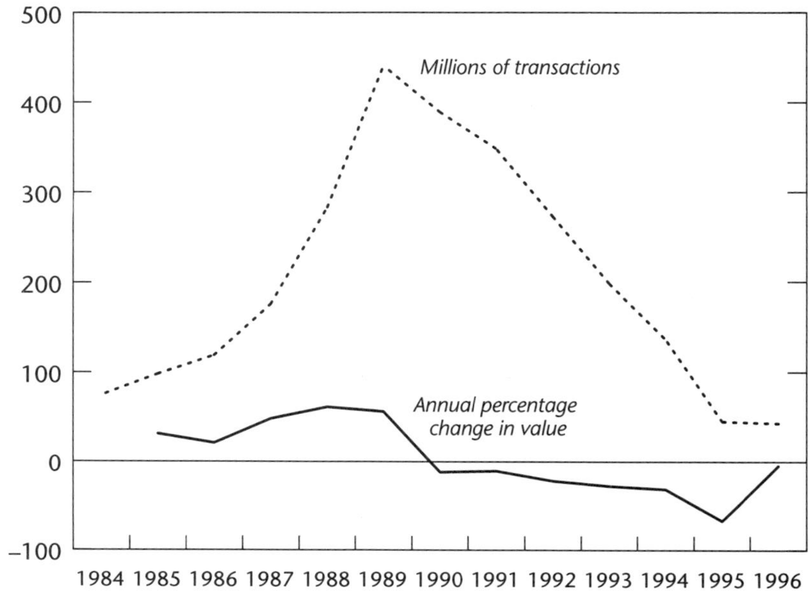

Sources: IMF data; and World Bank data.
Note: Transactions are in UAPTA, the PTA unit of account.

ness in the regional group with a view to strengthening cross-border trade and investment. Under this approach, emphasis is placed on promoting mobility of factors of production, goods, and services across national boundaries in an environment of relatively low tariffs against third countries. Participation of countries in the initiative is voluntary. Each participating country is expected to be implementing policies to promote a sustainable macroeconomic framework, and as much as possible policies should be harmonized. Any policy proposals related to the CBI have to be implemented on schedule by all participating countries, and this is ensured by the cosponsoring agencies. The arrangement is intended to strengthen commitment to the reform process and minimize or eliminate the tendency toward policy reversal. Fine and Yeo (1994) also propose a new paradigm for integration designed to achieve the dual objectives of encouraging national policy credibility and fostering rapid physical and human capital accumulation. These proposals, which enlist both challenges as well as options regarding the future evolution of regionalism, inform the discussion that follows.

The Urgent Need to Return to the Drawing Board

COMESA in its present state has numerous internal weaknesses requiring urgent restructuring if it is to survive. It contains countries with diverse characteristics and economic interests, and the recorded benefits of being a member of such a large regional grouping are minuscule. A possible solution worth considering is to break COMESA up into smaller subgroupings with similar interests. For example, countries near South Africa have common interests in trade, infrastructure, currency, and security, and these could form a strong regional group. The East African states of Kenya, Tanzania, and Uganda also have had experience with regionalism. They also possess a fairly good infrastructure, have common security interests, and share trade. This strengthens the case for the EAC. At the same time, it does not prevent Burundi, the Democratic Republic of the Congo, and Rwanda from joining this grouping. Furthermore, the formation of a subgroup to cover Djibouti, Eritrea, Ethiopia, Somalia, and Sudan may be appropriate. The remaining countries may consider joining any of the three subgroups. The PTA, however, should remain and specialize in areas that cut across all countries in the region. In this regard, the PTA should deal with intraregional trade liberalization and work toward the unification of the subgroupings for a future COMESA. This may help to establish more coherent and cohesive regional groupings.

There are also strong arguments for the need to rethink the concept of regionalism in the COMESA area. For a start, the lack of common interest among COMESA members and the conflict with SADC are not conducive to stable regional cooperation. This may be further complicated by the positive move by Kenya, Tanzania, and Uganda to revive the East African Community. To promote stable economic groupings, countries in the region should belong to the one economic group that fully represents their interests. It is still possible for countries within COMESA to formalize as subregional entities without dual membership. These subgroupings should be responsible for sectoral projects and harmonization of macroeconomic policies in their subregions.

The Positive Role of Political Reform

The changes, both political and economic, have opened up new possibilities for regional cooperation and integration. In particular, the evolution of more open and democratic societies is a pointer in the right direction. The winding down of wars in Angola, Burundi, the Democratic Republic of the Congo, Mozambique, and Rwanda is a welcome development. Developments in the Congo are particularly interesting given its potential for hydroelectricity and mineral resources. These positive movements may rekindle efforts to review and revamp the whole regional integration process. The political question appears to be getting increasingly resolved. The new leadership of Africa is likely to exploit these new developments, and to help strengthen institutions required for integration. Democracy is setting in, with an increasing number of democratically elected governments in the region (Ethiopia, Kenya, Tanzania, Uganda, and Zambia are examples). Efforts have begun to strengthen institutions that act as agencies of restraint, such as independent central banks, capital account convertibility, a strong regional secretariat with established penalties for default, and strong courts and parliaments. They are more likely to devolve power to other agents in view of the strong parliaments and judiciary systems being built up.

Growing Role of Shared Economic Reform

In the medium term, calls for the implementation of SAPs within a regional perspective are likely to gain ground. Already SAPs have helped to eliminate macroeconomic distortions in many of the countries in the region. Studies by Ng'eno (1994), KEDs (1994), and Mistry (1995) show that countries in the region have implemented far-reaching economic reforms in the past few years and are set to continue in the coming years. A number of these countries have market-determined prices, interest rates, and exchange rates. QRs and subsidies have been abolished, and tariffs have been rationalized or are being lowered. Policies to promote the reduction of the anti-export bias and to attract foreign investment have been adopted. Restrictive fiscal and monetary policies are being used to fight inflation, and in some countries, notably Uganda, inflationary tendencies have been checked.

At a more general level, a number of countries are now experiencing a stable economic environment as a result of implementation of SAPs. There are also renewed efforts to strengthen policy coordination by countries in East Africa. The fiscal and monetary authorities in the three countries meet regularly under the auspices of the East African Cooperation arrangement to coordinate policies. A minimum set of convergence criteria[15] has been proposed. This is in addition to efforts in other

[15]On macroeconomic variables, convergency of the following parameters have been recommended in the EAC: (1) achievement of a high and sustainable rate of *growth of real GDP* of at least 6 percent annually by the year 2000; (2) achievement and maintenance of low and stable single-digit *inflation* rates by the year 2000; (3) reduction of the ratio of the *current account deficit* less official grants as a percentage of GDP to sustainable levels; (4) reduction of the fiscal *(budget) deficit* to less than 5 percent by 1998; (5) build up gross *foreign exchange reserves* to a level

areas such as immigration, investment promotion, management of Lake Victoria, and security. In addition, the East African Countries have started dialogue with regard to coordinating developments in capital markets.

Expanding Role of the Private Sector

The expanding role of the private sector may ultimately become the key driving force in regional integration. Already, the private sector is beginning to seek opportunities for greater profit across borders. The need for healthy and sizable economies in which free private enterprise is permitted and the government intervenes intelligently to "govern the market" will be the way forward. This is in line with the concept of "subsidiarity," which involves the broadening of the participation of the private sector and other stakeholders in cooperative decisions and promises to keep the responsibility of dealing with issues of interest as close as possible to the stakeholders. Already, for example, South African private investment is moving northward to the Democratic Republic of the Congo, Kenya, Tanzania, and Uganda in airlines, beer, and wholesaling.

References

ADB (African Development Bank), 1993, *Economic Integration in Southern Africa* (Oxford: Oxprint).

Adedeji, A., 1989, "Financing Economic Development in Africa," The Second Joseph Mubiru Memorial Lecture, Bank of Uganda, Kampala.

Aryeetey, E., and A.D. Oduro, 1996, "Regional Integration Efforts in Africa: An Overview," paper prepared for a FONDAD Conference on Regional Integration in Africa, The Hague.

Collier, P., and J.W. Gunning, 1995, "Trade Policy and Regional Integration : Implication for the Relations between Europe and Africa," *World Economy*, Vol. 18, pp. 387–410.

———, 1997, " Policy Commitment Arrangements for Africa: Implications for Aid, Trade and Investment Flows," paper presented at an AERC Seminar on Africa and the World Trading System, Accra, October.

---

equivalent to 6 months of normal imports in the medium term; (6) raising the national *savings ratio* as a percentage of GDP to at least 20 percent in the medium term; (7) maintain *market-determined exchange rates* through central banks, which may intervene to smooth wide fluctuations in the rates resulting from temporary factors; (8) maintain *market-determined interest rates*, while at the same time addressing policy factors that add up to the costs of commercial banks, such as poor loan recovery and inflationary expectations, in the medium term; and (9) pursue debt-reduction initiatives to reduce domestic and foreign debt, including borrowing limits and stronger debt management.

Easterly, W., and R. Levine, 1994, "Africa's Growth Tragedy," paper presented at an AERC Workshop on Regional Integration, Nairobi, May.

Elbadawi, Ibrahim, 1994, "The Impact of Regional Trade/Monetary Schemes on Intra-Sub-Saharan Africa Trade" (Nairobi: African Economic Research Consortium).

Fine , J., and S. Yeo, 1994, "Regional Integration in Sub-Saharan Africa: Dead End or a Fresh Start?" paper presented to the AERC Workshop on Regional Integration, Nairobi, May.

Kasekende, L., and N. Ng'eno, 1995, "Regional Integration and Economic Liberalisation in Eastern and Southern Africa" (Nairobi: African Economic Research Consortium).

Kasekende, L., and G. Semogerere, 1994, "Exchange Rate Unification and Economic Development: The Case of Uganda, 1987–1992," *World Development*, August, pp. 1183–98.

KEDS (Kenya Export Development Scheme), 1994, "Export Competitiveness Study," report prepared by Kenya Export Development Scheme, Nairobi.

Kiggundu, Suleiman, 1990, "Regional Economic Integration: Africa's Challenge for the 1990's," Joseph Muburu Lecture, Bank of Uganda, Kampala, Uganda.

Lyakurwa W.M., 1996, "Trade and Investment Integration in Sub-Saharan Africa" paper prepared for a FONDAD Conference on Regional Integration in Africa, The Hague.

———, A. McKay, N. Ng'eno, and W. Kennes, 1993, "Regional Integration in Sub-Saharan Africa: A Review of Experiences and Issues," paper presented at an AERC Conference on Regional Integration and Trade Liberalisation in Sub-Saharan Africa, Nairobi, December.

Mistry, P., 1995, "Regional Integration Arrangements (RIAs) in Economic Development: Panacea or Pitfalls," revised version of paper for FONDAD Symposium on the Future of Regional Economic Integration, The Hague, September.

Mwencha, J.E.O., 1997, "COMESA: A Building Block for the African Economic Community," *AEC News Letter*, Vol. 1, No. 3, pp. 17–18.

Ng'eno, N., 1994, "Comparative Analysis of Economic Reform and Structural Adjustment Programs in East Africa: With Emphasis on Trade Policies" (unpublished; Nairobi: U.S. Agency for International Development).

PTA Secretariat, 1989, "PTA Report of the Study Team on the Equitable Distribution of Costs and Benefits in the PTA" (unpublished; Arusha: Preferential Trade Area Secretariat).

World Bank, 1997a, *World Development Indicators* (Washington: World Bank).

World Bank, 1997b, *World Development Report 1997: The Role of the State* (New York: Oxford University Press).

The Role of ECOWAS in Trade Liberalization 18

Charles D. Jebuni

The Economic Community of West African States, which is made up of 16 countries of the West African subregion, was established in 1975 with the ultimate objective of forming an economic community. It was the product of the Pan-Africanism sweeping the African continent at the time, as well as the efforts of the private sector lobby and the encouragement of ECA.

Although, the treaty was signed in May 1975, five protocols critical to the trade liberalization component attached to the treaty were not ratified by the required minimum number of states until November 1976. The Community was, therefore, not operational until early 1977.

The trade liberalization scheme of the Community, which was expected to begin two years after the ratification of the treaty, actually started in 1990. Thus, between 1977 and 1990, the Community was preoccupied with the establishment of institutions deemed important for its success, and the ratification of protocols and conventions to clarify issues relating to the Community. Not much else seems to have been achieved.

Following a number of developments within their domestic economies and in the international environment, the treaty establishing ECOWAS was revised in 1992 as an attempt to revamp the Community. The history of ECOWAS thus falls into two phases: the initial period up to 1991, and the period of the revised treaty starting in 1992. In this chapter, we shall refer to the earlier period as ECOWAS, Part I, and to the period of the revised treaty as ECOWAS, Part II.

It will be argued here that the fundamental problem confronting ECOWAS, Part I, was a domestic policy framework at variance with the ideals of integration or trade liberalization. This was compounded by a weak domestic governance base and a legalistic approach to regional integration.

Since the second half of the 1980s, there has been a wave of political and economic reforms, including unilateral trade liberalization, taking place within individual ECOWAS countries. Economic reforms and their impact on international trade of individual countries can be expected to lead to a certain level of regionalization of trade, in spite of ECOWAS. ECOWAS, it is argued, must renew its commitments and reorient its activities to facilitate the process.

A common feature of Part I and II is that, far from ECOWAS having a dynamic of its own and influencing the policies of member states; if anything, the lines of causality run the other way. The dominant policies of the member states, which are different between the two periods but broadly the same within periods, determined what ECOWAS was to be or not to be.

ECOWAS, Part I: 1975–91

To understand the success or failure of ECOWAS to serve as an effective vehicle for trade liberalization and the approach adopted, it is necessary to examine the prevailing conditions in the region before the establishment of ECOWAS. The interplay of these conditions with world conditions constitutes the fundamental explanation of the difficulties facing the community.

A striking feature of the grouping is the diversity of the member states in terms of their economic size and potential. Twelve of the 16 member countries are classified among the least developed countries. The majority of the member states are, individually, too small in terms of income level and market size to ensure a takeoff to self-sustained economic development. In many of the countries, the smallness of the domestic economy is compounded by poor endowments of natural resources and a very poorly developed human capital base. Table 1 indicates a considerable variation among member countries in terms of GDP and population. GDP ranged from about $79 million in Guinea-Bissau to $11.6 billion for Nigeria in 1970. Only three countries, Nigeria, Ghana, and Côte d'Ivoire, had GDPs of more than $1 billion for both 1970 and 1975. While growth rates were positive, they were generally low. In terms of growth, Nigeria and Côte d'Ivoire dominated, with average growth rates of 8.1 percent per year between 1970 and 1975. Thus individual country markets were small to support viable industries and the total market size for the 16 member countries was less than $50 billion. The diversity and inviability of several states, one would have thought, would encourage the small states to work for the success of ECOWAS. The reality instead pointed to anglophone-francophone rivalry.

Population among member countries ranged from less than 300,000 for Cape Verde to 56.6 million for Nigeria. Population growth rates, however, were high. In terms of linguistic differences, there were only three official languages, English, French and Portuguese. This is a much smaller number than spoken in the European Union, for example. More important, however, in understanding the dilemma ECOWAS was to face, was the domestic economic policy framework of the member states.

Table 1. Economic Indicators for the Economic Community of West African States

Country	GDP, 1970 (Millions of dollars)	Average Annual Growth (Percent)	GDP, 1975 (Millions of dollars)	Average Population, 1970 (Million)	Annual Growth (Percent)	Population, 1975 (Millions)
French-speaking						
Benin	332	1.5	353	2.7	2.38	3.0
Burkina Faso	335	2.6	390	5.6	2.22	6.2
Côte d'Ivoire	1,147	8.1	1,662	5.5	4.15	6.8
Mali	338	3.9	397	5.5	2.35	6.2
Niger	647	−1.2	569	4.2	2.72	4.8
Senegal	865	3.5	972	4.2	2.89	4.8
Guinea	. . .	. . .	. . .	3.9	1.23	4.1
Togo	253	3.4	306	2.0	2.47	2.3
Mauritania	197	1.7	195	1.2	2.32	1.4
English-speaking						
Liberia	. . .	. . .	. . .	1.4	3.00	1.6
Sierra Leone	383	3.9	435	2.7	1.97	2.9
Gambia, The	. . .	. . .	. . .	0.46	3.32	0.55
Ghana	2,214	1.5	2,166	8.6	2.65	9.8
Nigeria	11,594	8.1	15,207	56.6	3.18	66.6
Guinea-Bissau	79	4.1	97	0.53	3.58	0.63
Cape Verde	. . .	. . .	. . .	0.267	0.80	0.278

Source: Calculated from average annual growth (percent) given in World Bank, *World Tables* and *World Population Prospects* (1990).

At the time that West African leaders signed the ECOWAS protocols in 1975, most countries were pursuing import-substitution industrialization strategies behind high protective walls. Each nation state was committed to its own development and to the possibility of becoming the most developed country in Africa. This nationalist sentiment, combined with development theory of the 1950s and 1960s which preached dirigism, led West African states to adopt state-led import substitution development strategies. The resulting import-substitution syndrome (Little, Scitovsky, and Scott, 1970), with accompanying overvalued currencies and controlled regimes, generated rents that developed powerful supportive vested interests. The beneficiaries of this system were usually the politicians, the bureaucrats, the military corps, and the workers, managers, and owners of the dependent industries that relied on the largesse of the state and import licenses. These groups also constituted the ruling coalition and therefore could not be expected to implement policies that would erode their rents.

In West Africa, the fact that almost every country was pursuing these types of domestic economic policies reinforced every other coun-

Table 2. The Structure of Trade of the West African Countries, 1971–95
(In percent)

Standardized International Trade Classification Section	Exports	Imports
0 Food and live animals	17.4	13.4
1 Beverages and tobacco	0.1	1.7
2 Crude materials, excluding fuels	16.4	2.5
3 Mineral fuels	59.2	6.3
4 Animal and vegetable oils, fat	2.3	0.5
5 Chemicals	0.3	9.5
6 Basic manufactures	3.1	24.1
7 Machines and transport equipment	0.5	33.0
8 Miscellaneous manufacturing	0.2	6.6
9 Goods not classified by kind	0.4	1.6

Source: Calculated from Table 6 of ECA, *Foreign Trade Statistics for Africa* (various issues), Summary Table C.

try's commitment to these policies, in spite of the adverse economic consequences. Thus this negative neighborhood effect reinforced and deepened these policies, with no group of countries emerging to champion the cause of ECOWAS.

Table 2 provides the structure of trade of members before ECOWAS. While exports of the group of countries constituting ECOWAS consisted largely of agricultural and mineral products, imports were largely manufactured products. The table indicates that more than 95 percent of exports consisted of agricultural products, raw materials, and mineral products with mineral fuels—crude petroleum—dominating. These products were exported largely to the industrial countries along colonial lines. Only 4.2 percent of exports went to destinations within the region in 1975. More than 75 percent of imports consisted of manufactured products. If one adds processed food, the proportion is even higher (90 percent).

This pattern of exports and imports showed that to increase intra-ECOWAS trade, substantial industrial development was required to compete with imports from industrial countries, or substantial increases in growth and per capita incomes were needed to increase demand and intra-ECOWAS exports.

The Treaty and Trade Liberalization

The treaty establishing ECOWAS, among other things, provided for trade liberalization and the establishment of an economic community among member countries. Specifically, the community would ensure by stages:

- The elimination of customs duties and other charges with respect to trade flows among member countries.
- The abolition of quantitative and administrative restrictions on trade flows among member states.
- The establishment of a common customs tariff and a common commercial policy toward third countries.

The objectives were to be achieved over a 15-year period. The first 2 years were a period of consolidation of customs duties and NTBs. During this period, member states were not bound to reduce or remove import duties.

The second stage was the succeeding 8 years, when member states were to progressively reduce and eliminate import duties. The second phase, which entailed total liberalization of trade, was based on three product types and three groups of countries for its implementation. The three product types included unprocessed goods, which include animal, mineral, and plant products. These products were not eligible for compensation for loss of revenue suffered as a result of their importation from member states. The second group of products was referred to as traditional handicraft products, while the third group of products was classified as industrial products produced within the Community.

While the first two groups of commodities have been enjoying free movement within the Community (i.e., without duties and entry charges), the timetable for the elimination of duties and taxes under the Trade Liberalization Scheme for the third product group was based on a member country's economic state as determined by level of development, the importance of custom receipts in the member state's revenue, and problems deriving from difficulty of access (landlocked members). Thus, the implementation period ranges between 6 and 10 years, with corresponding annual rate of reduction in duties and taxes of between 16.6 and 10 percent, respectively (see Table 3).

The third stage was the next 5 years after the second stage, when member countries were expected to gradually abolish existing differences in their external customs tariffs.

Assessing Performance

In assessing the performance of ECOWAS, a number of methods may be used. One could assess it in terms of the extent to which it was able to achieve its stated objectives. Data difficulties, relating to the levels of tariffs and NTBs among ECOWAS countries, limit the possibility of comparisons in terms of the changes that must have occurred over time. In this section, we first assess the extent to which agree-

Table 3. The ECOWAS Tariff Reduction Schedule

Group of Countries	Implementation Period (Years)	Annual Percentage Reduction Rate of Duties and Taxes
A. Cape Verde, Burkina Faso, The Gambia, Guinea-Bissau, Mali, Mauritania, Niger	10	10.0
B. Benin, Guinea, Liberia, Sierra Leone, Togo	8	12.5
C. Côte d'Ivoire, Ghana, Nigeria, Senegal	6	16.6

Source: ECOWAS Secretariat, Lagos.

ments were implemented and then follow with the extent to which the implementation of the agreement affected intra-ECOWAS trade.

Implementation of Agreements

The provisions of the treaty are meant to be implemented through protocols and conventions. Indeed, five initial protocols, which were annexed to the treaty, provide details of the agreement on the following issues: definition of the concept of products originating from the member states; reexportation within the region of goods imported from third countries; assessment of loss of revenue by member states as a result of implementing the provisions of the treaty; the Fund for Co-operation, Compensation and Development; and contributions by member states to the budget of the Community. These protocols were not signed by the required minimum number of states until 1977. The Trade Liberalization Scheme was therefore expected to start in 1979. The takeoff of the scheme was postponed until 1989, and despite more than eight protocols and conventions, the implementation timetable was later shifted to January 1990.

The revised timetable indicates that NTBs were to be removed gradually over a four-year period (1990–93) in such a way that by January 1, 1994, all NTBs would have been removed. The commencement of the second stage (immediate liberalization of tariffs on unprocessed goods and traditional handicrafts) was also billed to begin by January 1990. The implementation of the third stage, gradual liberalization of tariffs on industrial products originating from member states, took off in 1992.

The implementation of the current timetable was hindered by rules of origin, lists of agreed enterprises and products, and the classification of member states into three economic groups, among other things. The implementation of free movement of persons was met with various obstacles at the final stage. Indeed, the protocol on free movement of persons has not been implemented. To a large extent, the ECOWAS protocols were not implemented under ECOWAS, Part I.

Trade Integration

A second strand in our assessment of ECOWAS, Part I, is to examine the extent to which the existence of ECOWAS led to trade integration. For, as stated by de Melo and Panagariya (1993, p. 12): "Whatever the ultimate goal of a regional arrangement, increased intra-regional trade ranks high among the priorities. It is also the yardstick to measure how deep integration actually is."

Assessing the role of a regional trade arrangement is often complicated by the need to distinguish between regionalism and regionalization. Preferential trade arrangements such as ECOWAS are about regionalism of trade. In the absence of such arrangements, market forces would have led to some level of regionalization of trade.

Two efforts at measuring the impact of ECOWAS on intraregional trade can be identified. First, there are those based on trade ratios (share of intraregional trade in total trade flows). Second, those that are based on the gravity model. The results emanating from these groups of studies conclude that intraregional trade flows remain insignificant and that it has not shown appreciable change over the years. In this section, we shall examine these groups of studies.

Using the trade ratio method, Ariyo and Raheem (1991), Torre and Kelly (1992), Langhammer and Hiemenz (1991), de Melo, Montenegero, and Panagariya (1992), and Foroutan (1992), among others, conclude that the regional efforts have not significantly affected intraregional trade flows. Trade flows are variously defined to include exports, imports, or the summation of exports and imports. Notwithstanding the definition adopted by various researchers, the main finding is that the share of intraregional trade flows of the member states of ECOWAS in total trade is small (in all cases below 10 percent) and at best stagnant. In Table 4, we report intra-ECOWAS trade. From a level of 4.2 percent in 1975, intra-ECOWAS trade as a proportion of ECOWAS exports first declined and then increased steadily, peaking in 1988–89. This increase in intragroup trade is attributed by Foroutan (1992) to the decline in oil prices during the period 1980–90, causing Nigerian and ECOWAS dollar exports to the world to decline by 47 and 35 percent, respectively. It should be noted that the period of the increase also coincides with the adoption of structural adjustment pro-

Table 4. Share of Intra-ECOWAS Exports

Year	Percentage
1970	3.0
1975	4.2
1980	3.5
1985	5.3
1986	6.7
1987	6.4
1988	7.8
1989	7.8
1990	6.0

Source: Torre and Kelly (1992).

grams by West African countries. It is possible that, given the nonimplementation of the trade liberalization component of ECOWAS before 1990, what occurred was a regionalization of trade and not the regionalism that ECOWAS attempted to promote. Whatever the interpretation, Table 4 shows that the level of trade among ECOWAS is low.

A number of studies using gravity models try to estimate the effect of ECOWAS on intra-ECOWAS trade. Foroutan and Prichett (1993) focus primarily on intra-sub-Saharan-African trade. Using trade ratios (measured as share of intra-sub-Saharan exports of sub-Saharan Africa to total exports of the region) the study indicates that intra-sub-Saharan trade flows are small. A gravity model was used to compare actual trade with what a gravity model would predict. The result of the analysis shows that the gravity model predicts very well the low level of intra-sub-Saharan trade. In other words, given the determinants of trade flows, intra-sub-Saharan trade is not low because of factors that work differentially against such trade; rather, it is naturally low. The study concludes that "increasing intra-SSA trade is not just a matter of removing discriminatory distortions or biases in infrastructure. It requires positive action such as providing differential incentives to intra-regional trade."

The estimate of the dummy variable for ECOWAS, which was included in the gravity model, was neither significant nor consistent, as it was positive and negative in import and export equations, respectively. It implies that ECOWAS has not significantly affected intra-ECOWAS trade.

Ogunkola (1994), unlike Foroutan and Pritchett (1993), focused on the regional integration efforts in West Africa, with emphasis on ECOWAS. Similar to Foroutan and Prichett (1993), he used the gravity model to explain the impact of ECOWAS and to measure trade potential in the subregion. Two periods were used: average trade flows for 1970–72, the pre-integration period, and average trade flows for 1978–80, the post-integration period. Comparing the estimates of the dummy for ECOWAS in the two periods, the study concludes that the effect of ECOWAS on intra-ECOWAS trade must have been very small.

Issues and Constraints

In the preceding section, we have demonstrated that most of the ECOWAS protocols were not implemented. Second, in spite of the long-run potential for increased intraregional trade, the existence of ECOWAS did not seem to have increased intraregional trade. This failure could be attributed to a number of factors. In this section, we examine some of these constraints.

Domestic Economic Policies

One of the major factors responsible for both the nonimplementation of the treaty and protocols and ineffectiveness of ECOWAS in increasing intraregional trade was the continuation of the initial domestic policy framework.

As indicated above, all the member states of ECOWAS at the time of signing the treaty were pursuing state-led import-substitution industrialization strategies and continued to do so even after signing. Promoting the ideals of ECOWAS required increasing exports, especially of the nontraditional type, and lowering tariffs. The domestic policy strategy adopted required higher tariffs and discouraged exports. Thus the domestic policy stance of most governments was at variance with the conditions required for the success of ECOWAS.

The initial structure of exports and imports dictated that to increase intraregional trade, manufactured exports had to increase. It is possible that the initial experience with import-substitution industrialization could have provided a basis for the takeoff into exporting through learning-by-doing effects or exports of Linder-type products. This, however, required a change in strategy and domestic policy framework. This change did not occur for reasons discussed above. This hampered the realization of the intent of the ECOWAS treaty and protocols in several ways.

First, the institution of general controls on international trade in terms of tariffs and NTBs tended to adversely affect overall exports and intra-ECOWAS trade. The incidence of these taxes are usually borne to a large extent by the export sector. Estimates of the incidence of these taxes on exports are not available for all ECOWAS countries.

Two examples illustrate the point. For Ghana, it is estimated that approximately 74–85 percent of the import tax was shifted to the export sector (Jebuni and others, 1992). In 1986, an estimate of 55–90 percent was obtained for Nigeria. These negative effects on exporting were reinforced by an inappropriate combination of macroeconomic and exchange rate policies. The result was economies bound to their traditional exports, whose direction of flow and composition were determined largely by their colonial heritage.

Second, the resulting import-substitution syndrome (Little, Scitovsky, and Scott, 1970) with accompanying overvalued currencies and controlled regimes generated rents that developed powerful supporting vested interests of politicians, the bureaucrats, the military corps, and the workers and managers of the dependent industries that relied on the largesse of the state and import licenses. These groups also constituted the ruling coalitions and could not be expected to implement policies that would erode their rents.

With inadequate resources, ECOWAS countries had to rely on external assistance and aid to maintain the tempo of post-independence development. A large part of this aid came in the form of trade credit. This implied that imports had to be made from the donor community. Tying of aid therefore reinforced the colonial pattern of exports and imports.

The private sector, represented by the various national chambers of commerce, was one of the key advocates for the formation of ECOWAS. The Federation of West African Chambers of Commerce, first started by the Sierra Leone National Chamber of Commerce and Lagos Chamber of Commerce and Industry in 1963 and later covering most of West Africa in 1972, had among its objectives the promotion of regional integration. Pursuant to this goal, it set out on a number of campaigns and tours of the countries of the subregion between 1972 and 1974, lobbying heads of state and other government officials on the urgent necessity to formalize the ECOWAS arrangement. The state-led development strategy literally killed the private sector. What was left of the private sector became dependent on the state and the rents from the import-licensing system. Furthermore, the policy and economic environment tended to narrow the horizons of firms to the domestic market.

Dependence on Trade Taxes

The heavy dependence of various governments on taxes on international transactions is another factor that continues to hinder the progress of subregional integration. In fact, this was the focus of Ariyo

Table 5. Tax on Trade as a Percentage of Government Revenue

Country	1975–79	1980–85	1985–89	1991–95
Benin	51.3	. . .	. . .	. . .
Burkina Faso	49.4	38.8	32.1	. . .
Cape Verde	. . .	. . .	. . .	. . .
Côte d'Ivoire	. . .	35.6	33	. . .
Gambia, The	63.5	67.8	66.4	42.4
Ghana	45.8	36.5	39.8	31.2
Guinea	47.5	32.8	15.7	46.1
Guinea-Bissau	. . .	35.2	33.9	. . .
Liberia	32.6	31.1	29.6	. . .
Mali	27.2	19.9	23.3	. . .
Mauritania	26.7	39.4	34.6	. . .
Niger	32.3	. . .	. . .	. . .
Nigeria	16.6	15.5	11.6	. . .
Senegal	44.5	36.2	31.3	. . .
Sierra Leone	46.3	42.3	40.0	37.7
Togo	33.2	30.4	32.1	. . .

Source: For 1975–89, *African Development Indicators,* various issues. For 1990–95, *World Development Report 1997.*

(1992). Some of the countries still depend on taxes on international transactions to the tune of more than 30 percent of government revenue. Table 5 presents the ratio of taxes on international trade and transactions to total government revenue during the period 1975–95.

For the period 1975–79, dependence on trade taxes ranges from 16.6 percent of total government revenues in Nigeria to 63 percent in The Gambia. Fear of loss of revenues had been fully recognized as a major constraint to the success of ECOWAS, and countries were classified into three groups with different speeds for phasing out tariffs.

ECOWAS, Part II: After 1992

In the previous section, we argued that both the economic policy framework and the nature of governance in most member countries did not augur well for trade liberalization under ECOWAS. These circumstances began to change in the late 1980s. These changes provided an opportunity to revamp the ailing ECOWAS. Thus domestic developments, combined with world developments and the poor performance of ECOWAS, led to the revision of the ECOWAS treaty. The revised treaty has moved from mere statement of intention and general prescriptions about integration to defining strategies and even introducing sanctions where appropriate.

The timetable of the Community has been revised, with stages of implementation more clearly defined. The new timetable shows that, within a period of 10 years, effective from January 1, 1990, a customs union among the member states would be established. In other words, by January 1, 2000, a customs union would have been established in the region. Within the five years following the establishment of a customs union, an economic and monetary union would be established. Thus, by the year 2005, an economic and monetary union would be in place in the region. In the rest of the chapter, we examine the new economic circumstances in ECOWAS and how this may impact on the achievement of trade liberalization among ECOWAS countries.

Since the second half of the 1980s, most ECOWAS countries have embarked on some form of structural adjustment. Given the similarity of the initial economic conditions and the central role of the Bretton Woods institutions in the structural adjustment process, the set of policies pursued has also been remarkably similar.

Critical to the issue of trade integration is the pursuit of unilateral trade liberalization, reduction in the extent of overvaluation of currencies, and a greater disposition toward export promotion. Table 6 shows that, between 1985 and 1992, exchange rates of most English-speaking ECOWAS members have depreciated considerably in real terms. Countries with considerable changes include The Gambia, Ghana, Nigeria, and Sierra Leone. The situation in the French-speaking countries changed significantly after the devaluation of the CFA franc in 1994. These changes have tended to create a more conducive atmosphere for export development.

At the same time, as a result of trade liberalization policies included in most SAPs, the levels of both tariffs and NTBs to international trade have been reduced. These policies have had a greater impact on reducing the levels of trade barriers among ECOWAS member countries than the ECOWAS protocols. It might be argued that this unilateral trade liberalization could reduce the margin of advantages that may accrue from preferential trade liberalization. However, this may encourage speedy action by regional groups to remove other impediments to intraregional trade.

Apart from the trade and macroeconomic component, SAPs have also generally aimed at generating competition within the domestic economy, increasing productivity, and simplifying and reducing the administrative, regulatory, and legal impediments to efficient economic activity. If successful, these measures would make transparent the environment for business activity in each ECOWAS member country to the other. The development of transportation and communication networks may be expected to have complementary impact on regional integration.

Table 6. Index of Real Exchange Rates of ECOWAS Countries
(National currency per U.S. dollar)

Country	1985	1986	1987	1988	1989	1990	1991[1]	1992
Benin	. . .	. . .	. . .	. . .	. . .	. . .	. . .	. . .
Burkina Faso	100	85	74	84	85	78	. . .	. . .
Cape Verde	100	78	67	. . .	. . .	. . .	. . .	. . .
Côte d'Ivoire	100	77	65	71	. . .	. . .	. . .	. . .
Gambia, The	100	133	96	92	112	93	103	92
Ghana	100	117	168	174	192	165	. . .	. . .
Liberia	100	93	91	87	83	. . .	. . .	. . .
Mali	100	. . .	. . .	76	77	70	70	. . .
Niger	100	86	78	63	96	89	98	. . .
Nigeria	100	305	351	305	304	345	335	. . .
Senegal	100	78	69	83	83	76	78	. . .
Sierra Leone	100	367	87	116	125	178	20	140
Togo	100	80	68	80	81	73	. . .	. . .

Source: Calculated from IMF, *International Financial Statistics* (Washington, October 1992).

Note: The real exchange rate is defined as *EXR·WPus/CPI*, where *EXR* is the nominal exchange rate expressed in units of domestic currency per U.S. dollar; *CPI* is the consumer price index in the given country, and *WPI* is the U.S. wholesale price index.

[1]Refers to second quarter of 1991.

Furthermore, intraregional trade is much more acceptable and the costs are lower among countries with growing economies in the context of expanding exports. Structural adjustment could provide the instrument for trade integration. The expansion in exports, in combination with unilateral trade liberalization, could increase intra-ECOWAS trade without substantial trade diversion. The resulting economic growth and improvements in fiscal and external balances should reduce the incentive for further trade restrictions and lead to a further improvement in the trade and payments regimes among ECOWAS member countries.

A major consideration in discussions of regional integration in Africa alluded to above is the role of government tax revenues. A large number of African governments depend to a great extent on taxes on international trade. In some cases, revenue considerations have led countries to prefer trade with the outside world to other African countries. Countries take advantage of policy disparities among the countries of the region: trade policy, price policy, monetary policy.

These considerations have also led governments to revenue-compensating arrangements that tend to restrict trade among ECOWAS countries. Given the low levels of intraregional trade, revenue losses to government under preferential trade liberalization should be low, depending on the extent to which member countries can be induced to take advantage of the preferences and the size of the preferences.

At the theoretical level, the effect of trade liberalization under SAPs on tax revenues depends on the direct impact on trade tax revenues and the economy's response to the changes in relative prices. Liberalization may have a positive effect on tax revenue through

- The replacement of quotas and other quantitative restrictions by tariffs.
- Reduction of duties from the prohibitive to a more normal range.
- Putting low tariffs on previously exempted goods (in a situation where exempted goods form a large share of imports perhaps due to import-substitution industrialization policy, this change is potentially very important in terms of revenue yield..
- The likely reduction in smuggling.
- Some positive effects associated with a possible change in the composition of imports in favor of the decreased incentive to bias imports toward raw materials and intermediate products.
- Some positive effects on tradable output, especially over the medium run, associated with the liberalization policy (Tanzi, 1989).

At the practical level, "a serious trade liberalization is likely to increase revenues as it is to reduce them: the elimination of tariff exemption and quantitative restrictions and the ensuing import boom, may more that outweigh the reduction in (statutory) tariffs in practice" (Rodrik, 1993, p. 2). Greenway and Milner (1993), however, find no evident relationship between trade reform and the amount of revenue collected from trade taxes; for a number of ECOWAS countries pursuing liberalization programs, dependence on trade taxes has decreased.

An issue of considerable concern in trade liberalization among ECOWAS countries is the balance of payments effects of such liberalization. It has been argued that, because in the short run at least, trade liberalization may be expected to worsen the trade balance, it may not be a viable policy option for countries with foreign exchange or borrowing constraints. These considerations may lead individual countries to begin to roll back the liberalization effort.

But evidence from both the theoretical and empirical literature indicates that the effect of trade liberalization on the external balance is ambiguous. The current account is identically equal to the difference between national savings and investment. Liberalization can therefore be expected to affect the current account if it induces a differential response of savings and investment flows. Liberalization under the SAPs recognize the likelihood of a deterioration in the short run with the savings rate, even if improving, not enough to finance investment growth required for structural adjustment. Hence the necessity of aid.

Using this savings-investment approach and considering a model that involves reduction of restrictions on imported intermediate inputs, Ostry (1991), for example, concludes, that "if tradables use both capital and intermediate imports intensively relative to the rest of the economy, liberalization leads to an increase in the level of savings and a decline in the level of investment and, hence, unambiguously to an improvement in the external current balance" (1991, p. 476). Of course, the reverse could occur under alternative assumptions.

The use of balance of payments considerations to deny access to products from other ECOWAS countries may be based on short-term trade balance and revenue considerations. Typical of this attitude are the trade relations between Ghana, Nigeria, and Côte d'Ivoire. All three are members of ECOWAS, and all three have embarked on trade liberalization. The manufactured goods to be exported among them and other ECOWAS members are approved and certified by the ECOWAS Secretariat. Yet customs officials deny duty free access of these goods to each other's markets.

Successful adjustment should reduce the dependence of governments on taxation of international trade and make them more willing to grant concessions to other ECOWAS countries. Similarly, the effects of these policies on the external balance of individual countries could reduce the importance of balance of payments considerations in denying markets access to ECOWAS countries.

One of the critical elements of the economic reforms taking place among the domestic economies of member countries is the reduction in the role of government in directly productive activities and the increased importance of the private sector. Under SAPs, both private capital and the private sector are expected to play a leading role in the development of ECOWAS member economies. As indicated above, the private sector was one of the key players in the formation of ECOWAS. However, as the development strategy adopted by these economies reduced the role of the private sector, its involvement and role in ECOWAS diminished. Furthermore, the small private sector left in most of these economies got absorbed into the rentier state system and lost its ambitions beyond national boundaries.

There are no data to indicate the extent to which the new circumstances have led to intra-ECOWAS movement of capital. However, the formation of the West African Enterprise Network is an encouraging sign of the positive role the private sector can play. The network is already leading to joint ventures among private sector individuals and enterprises with some external support.

At the same time that domestic economic policy reform seems to be moving in the right direction in terms of ECOWAS objectives, developments in the international environment in such areas as world technology and the conclusion of the Uruguay Round of GATT are proving to be complementary.

There have been dramatic changes in both production technology and information technology, but much more so in information technology. These developments are reducing the transaction costs of international trade and changing the nature of the basis of comparative advantage. Increasing with improvements in information technology, comparative advantage will no longer be location-specific. It's now possible for firms to source products and services worldwide in a matter of minutes. These developments imply that, unless ECOWAS is able to adapt to the new technology, there will be a tendency for firms within the region to transact business outside the region, as the transactions costs will be lower.

The conclusion of the Uruguay Round of GATT negotiations offered an opportunity for multilateral trade liberalization. Even though African countries' participation in the round was minimal, the round has implications for these economies. The impact of the round on Africa's economies is expected to occur through its effect on the world economy, reduction in tariff escalation and NTBs, loss of preferential market access under the ACP and EU, and Africa's obligations from WTO membership.

Quantitative estimates of the impact range from a 2 percent to a 0.55 percent gain in exports (Harrold, 1995). For West African countries, the significant reduction in tariff escalation for wood and paper products, leather products, and tobacco products should be encouraging. This has to be set against the increasing escalation for cocoa.

What is more important is the extent to which the Uruguay Round will encourage or discourage intra-ECOWAS trade. Unilateral trade liberalization, which is not matched by similar liberalization among ECOWAS members, will tend to increase ECOWAS trade with the rest of the world and probably have adverse effects on intra-ECOWAS trade. Conversely, as has been argued by Harrold (1995), the Uruguay Round offered an opportunity for African countries to "bind their domestic reforms to an international anchor to improve their credibility." The failure of ECOWAS countries to take the opportunity to make a credible commitment to trade liberalization might signal their continuing reluctance to liberalize trade among themselves in spite of the revised treaty.

Conclusion

The Economic Community of West African States was established two decades ago. Its efforts at promoting regional integration have been ineffective. To a large extent, this failure has been due to a domestic policy stance at variance with its ultimate objectives and to misgivings about the effects of the intra-ECOWAS trade liberalization on individual member country's balance of payments and government revenue.

Changing domestic policies occurring under the structural adjustment programs in member countries provided better prospects for intraregional trade than events at the multilateral level. It must be realized that any multilateral arrangements that are not buttressed by a credible commitment to domestic policy reform involving trade liberalization and the development of the private sector are unlikely to succeed.

While the reform process in individual countries could work in favor of the ECOWAS objective, it could also work in the opposite direction. Increased domestic competitiveness could result in exporting to the industrial world. A lot will depend on transaction costs within the subregion. ECOWAS must therefore examine and redefine its role in the new circumstances. While not abandoning its overall objectives, a phased program with one modest objective at a time is perhaps a better procedure.

In the short to medium term, ECOWAS should take advantage of developments in individual countries and concentrate on facilitating trade among ECOWAS countries by measures and investments aimed at reducing transaction costs. This may be achieved through the development of intra-ECOWAS infrastructure and the easing of controls.

References

Ariyo, A., 1992, "Tariff Harmonization, Government Revenue and Economic Integration within the ECOWAS: Some Reflections," *Development Policy Review,* Vol. 10, pp. 155–74.

———, and M.I. Raheem, 1991, "Enhancing Trade Flows Within the ECOWAS Sub-Region: An Appraisal and Some Recommendations," in *Economic Reform in Sub-Saharan Africa,* ed. by A. Chhibber, and S. Fischer (Washington: World Bank).

de Melo, J., C. Montenegro, and A. Panagariya, 1992, "Regional Integration, Old and New," Policy Research Working Paper No. 985 (Washington: World Bank).

———, and A. Panagariya, 1993, *New Dimensions in Regional Integration* (London: Centre for Economic Policy Research).

Foroutan, F., 1992, "Regional Integration in Sub-Saharan Africa: Past Experience and Future Prospects," paper presented at the World Bank and CEPR Conference on New Dimension in Regional Integration, Washington, April, 2–3.

———, and L. Pritchett, 1993, "Intra-Sub-Saharan African Trade: Is It Too Little?" *Journal of African Economies,* Vol. 2, No. 1, pp. 74–105.

Greenway, D., and C. Milner, 1993, "The Fiscal Implications of Trade Policy Reform: Theory and Evidence," Occasional Paper No. 9 (Washington: UNDP and World Bank).

Harrold, P., 1995, "The Impact of the Uruguay Round on Africa: Much Ado About Nothing?" paper presented at a conference on the Uruguay Round and the Developing Economies, World Bank, Washington, January.

Jebuni, C.D., A. Oduro, Y. Asante, and G.K. Tsikata, 1992, *Diversifying Exports: The Supply Response of Non-Traditional Exports to Ghana's Economic Recovery Programme* (London: Overseas Development Institute).

Langhammer, R.J. and U. Hiemenz, 1991, "Regional Integration among Developing Countries: Survey of Past Performance and Agenda for Future Policy Action," Trade Policy Division (Washington: World Bank).

Little, I.M.D., Tibor Scitovsky, and Maurice Scott, 1970, *Industry and Trade in Some Developing Countries* (New York: Oxford University Press).

Ogunkola, E.O., 1994, "An Empirical Evaluation of Trade Potential in the Economic Community of West African States: A Final Report Submitted to the African Economic Research Consortium" (Nairobi: African Economic Research Consortium).

Ostry, J.D., 1991, "Trade Liberalization in Developing Countries: Initial Trade Distortions and Imported Intermediate Inputs," *Staff Papers,* International Monetary Fund, Vol. 38, No. 3, pp. 447–79.

Rodrik, D., 1993, "Trade Liberalization in Disinflation," Discussion Paper No. 832 (London: Centre for Economic Policy Research).

Tanzi, V., 1989, "The Impact of Macroeconomic Policies on the Level of Taxation and the Fiscal Balance in Developing Countries," *Staff Papers,* International Monetary Fund, Vol. 36, No. 3, pp. 633–56.

Torre, A. and M. Kelly, 1992, *Regional Trade Arrangements,* IMF Occasional Paper No. 93 (Washington: International Monetary Fund).

List of Participants

This list includes only authors of papers, speakers, presenters of papers, and discussants at the conference. The titles and affiliations are those that were in effect at the time of the conference (December 1997).

Abuka, Charles A.
External Sector Policies Staff, Research Department, Bank of Uganda

Aryeetey, Ernest
Research Fellow, Department of Economics, University of Ghana

Barber, Edwin
Director, Office of African Nations, U.S. Department of the Treasury

Bayoumi, Tamim
Senior Economist, Asia and Pacific Department, International Monetary Fund

Calamitsis, Evangelos
Director, African Department, International Monetary Fund

Collier, Paul
Director, Centre for the Study of African Economies, University of Oxford

Croce, Enzo
Division Chief, IMF Institute

Dhonte, Pierre
Deputy Director, African Department, International Monetary Fund

Dillon, K. Burke
Director, Administration Department, International Monetary Fund

Ebrill, Liam P.
Assistant Director, Fiscal Affairs Department, International Monetary Fund

Eglin, Richard
Director of Development, World Trade Organization

Elbadawi, Ibrahim A.
Research Coordinator, African Economic Research Consortium

Fischer, Stanley
First Deputy Managing Director, International Monetary Fund

François, Christian A.
Senior Advisor, African Department, International Monetary Fund

Gondwe, G.E.
Deputy Director, African Department, International Monetary Fund

Hartzenberg, Trudi
Academic Coordinator, SAPES Trust, Harare, Zimbabwe

Hernández-Catá, Ernesto
Deputy Director, African Department, International Monetary Fund

Hufbauer, Gary
Director of Studies, Council of Foreign Relations

Iqbal, Zubair
Advisor, IMF Institute

Jebuni, Charles D.
Fellow, Center for Policy Analysis

Kasekende, Louis A.
Executive Director, Research and Policy Department, Bank of Uganda

Kennes, Walter
Principal Administrator, Direction Général du Développement, European Commission

Khan, Mohsin S.
Director, IMF Institute

Kotschwar, Barbara
Trade Specialist, Trade Unit, Organization of American States

Maasdorp, Gavin
Staff Member, SAPES Trust, Harare, Zimbabwe

Montiel, Peter
Professor, Department of Economics, Williams College

Mussa, Michael
Economic Counsellor and Director, Research Department, International Monetary Fund

Mwega, Francis M.
Lecturer, Department of Economics, University of Nairobi

Ndulu, Benno J.
Executive Director, African Economic Research Consortium

Ndung'u, Njuguna S.
Lecturer, Department of Economics, University of Nairobi

Nsouli, Saleh M.
Deputy Director, IMF Institute

O'Connell, Steve
Professor, Department of Economics, Swarthmore College

Ouattara, Alassane
Deputy Managing Director, International Monetary Fund

Oyejide, Ademola
Professor, Department of Economics, University of Ibadan

Rodrik, Dani
Professor, John F. Kennedy School of Government, Harvard University

Russo, Massimo
Special Advisor to the Managing Director, International Monetary Fund

Sharer, Robert
Division Chief, Policy Development and Review Department, International Monetary Fund

Soludo, Charles Chukwuma
Lecturer, Department of Economics, University of Nigeria

Stotsky, Janet G.
Economist, Fiscal Affairs Department, International Monetary Fund

Subramanian, Arvind
Senior Economist, African Department, International Monetary Fund

Tybout, James
Professor, Department of Economics, Georgetown University

Wang, Zhen Kun
Consultant, Economic Development Institute, World Bank

Winters, L. Alan
Division Chief, International Economics Department, World Bank